Foundations of Primary Teaching

Now in its fifth edition, *Foundations of Primary Teaching* will be an essential resource for any trainee or practising primary teacher. Written in a friendly and accessible manner, this book has been updated in line with the new curriculum and provides a comprehensive introduction to all aspects of teaching within the primary school. It blends theory and practice to foster and develop effective pedagogy and, in so doing, to stimulate your thinking, expand your horizons and motivate you to relish one of the most thrilling, frustrating, exhausting, exciting and important jobs in the world.

Written specifically for student teachers on BA, BEd and PGCE courses, as well as students taking Education Studies, this text will encourage you to develop a fuller understanding and appreciation of teaching as professional practice through an emphasis on:

- reflective thinking and action
- relationships and motivation in the classroom
- a full range of tried-and-tested teaching and assessment strategies
- creativity and transferable teaching skills
- personalised learning.

This wholly revised fifth edition incorporates new material on changes and innovations that have taken place in education; childhood; the process of, and context for, learning; and issues teachers face, as well as updated further reading lists. It should be on the bookshelf of all student teachers on initial teacher training courses at the primary level, newly qualified teachers and more experienced teachers wishing to enhance their practice.

Denis Hayes was Professor of Primary Education at the Faculty of Education, University of Plymouth, after spending seventeen years teaching across primary, middle and secondary schools. He is now an education writer and speaker.

Foundations of Primary Teaching

Fifth edition

Denis Hayes

Routledge
Taylor & Francis Group

LONDON AND NEW YORK

First published 1996
by David Fulton Publishers

Second edition published 1999
Third edition published 2004
Fourth edition published 2008

This fifth edition published 2012
by Routledge
2 Park Square, Milton Park, Abingdon, Oxon OX14 4RN

Simultaneously published in the USA and Canada
by Routledge
711 Third Avenue, New York, NY 10017

Routledge is an imprint of the Taylor & Francis Group, an informa business

British Library Cataloguing in Publication Data
A catalogue record for this book is available from the British Library

Library of Congress Cataloging in Publication Data
Hayes, Denis, 1949–
Foundations of primary teaching/by Denis Hayes. – 5th ed.
p. cm.
Includes bibliographical references and index.
1. Education, Elementary–Great Britain. 2. Education, Elementary–Curricula–Great
Britain. 3. Education–Terminology. I. Title.
LB1556.7.G7H388 2012
372.1102–dc23

2011025891

ISBN: 978-0-415-67556-7 (hbk)
ISBN: 978-0-415-67557-4 (pbk)
ISBN: 978-0-203-80941-9 (ebk)

Typeset in Bembo
by Wearset Ltd, Boldon, Tyne and Wear

MIX
Paper from
responsible sources
FSC
www.fsc.org   FSC® C004839

Printed and bound in Great Britain by the MPG Books Group

Contents

Introduction to the Fifth Edition

It was a privilege to be asked by Routledge to write a fifth edition of *Foundations of Primary Teaching*. In creating this book, I have drawn from some of my other David Fulton/ Routledge publications, including *Primary Teaching Today* (2009); *Encyclopaedia of Primary Education* (2010); and *The Guided Reader to Teaching and Learning* (2011).

The fifth edition differs from the last one in four major respects. First, it contains more information for teachers who want to extend their understanding of education issues and the ways in which they influence teaching and learning. Second, there are a number of new chapters that have been added to provide historical background information, to deepen and widen understanding of factors that impinge upon work in school, and to engage with a range of challenges that teachers commonly face. Third, there are a series of cross-references linking aspects of the content to *The Guided Reader* at appropriate places in the text (*Guided Reader Extracts*); it will therefore be worth having a copy of the Reader to hand to gain more information and insights about the themes being addressed. Finally, there are additional extracts, quotations and information sources threaded throughout the book.

Part 1 provides background information about primary education; first, a range of education themes is introduced, which are expanded in later parts of the book; second, an exploration is undertaken of seminal education issues and prevailing political agendas that have dominated debate and influenced practice over recent years. *Part 2* deals with the contribution, concerns and capability of the people that are principally involved in education, namely, the children; the teachers; and other adults, including assistants, outside agencies and parents. *Part 3* forms the practical heart of the book with chapters devoted to the curriculum, learning, planning lessons, the development of teaching skills, organising and managing, assessing pupil progress, and recording and reporting to parents. *Part 4* focuses on every child's needs, including the importance of discipline and the inclusion of each pupil, regardless of academic ability and background. Finally, *Part 5* addresses the induction of newly qualified teachers, some of the challenges they face, and their professional development.

The main theme for each chapter is presented in an introduction and there are a number of 'Activate your thinking!' and 'Good practice' boxes to stimulate a deeper consideration of key issues and their implementation. Every chapter concludes with a case study and suggestions for further reading. Details of individual curriculum subjects form a relatively minor part of *Foundations* but there are summaries of core and non-core subjects and suggestions about their implementation. All names used in the book are pseudonyms and some details in the quoted extracts have been altered to protect identity.

Once again, it is my pleasure to dedicate this fifth edition to aspiring and practising teachers, and all those who, like me, have a passionate desire to help our children learn, grow and prosper: academically, socially, morally and spiritually. I wish you every success and happiness.

Part 1

Background to Primary Education

Education, Teachers and Teaching

Introduction

Most people see a quality education as essential for leading a fulfilled and happy life. Parents make considerable sacrifices to give their children the best opportunities to attend the right schools, gain valuable experiences, benefit from intellectual challenges, learn skills and mix with their peers. People train to become teachers and persevere with the job when qualified because they recognise the significance of their role in helping to provide a good education and becoming a positive influence in the lives of their pupils. This chapter opens up a number of these themes and issues, which are pursued in greater depth throughout the rest of the book.

The teacher's role

Teaching and learning is first and foremost the process by which young lives are influenced in a positive, enriching way, such that children can enjoy happy relationships, find fulfilment and success in their work and play a useful role in the community. The best teachers are systematic but not slavish; they are well informed but also eager to learn; they absorb and implement colleagues' ideas but are also willing to risk creative and innovative practice as a stimulus to liberate and enhance children's learning.

The role of the teacher is complex and demanding – intellectually, physically and emotionally. The challenging enterprise that we refer to by the casual use of the word 'teaching' is associated with confidence, self-assurance, sensitivity and empathy. There are many practical and pragmatic elements with which every teacher needs to be familiar, which are represented by the curriculum, lesson planning, guiding pupils in their learning and assessing their work, but teachers also have a responsibility to carry out these practical elements with a keen awareness of the people involved (pupils and colleagues) and great sensitivity to their personal as well as academic needs.

Care, compassion, understanding, informed tolerance and a deep appreciation of the beauty in the world around us are just as much part of the educative process as the formal curriculum. The barren philosophy of 'anything goes' and 'me first' has been exposed as a dangerous illusion. Sensitivity, creativity and liberation to fulfil our potential and help others to do the same are back on the agenda as the hallmark of a truly educated human being.

Cross-reference: Guided Reader Extract 34

Education that transforms

Children benefit from having opportunities to think and talk about ways in which acts of loving kindness bring joy to the carer as well as the cared for; adults can and should be a role model in demonstrating compassion and consideration in what they say and do. Paley (2000) describes how very young children can transform themselves and one another by memorising, narrating and acting out tales of kindness and other good deeds.

The significance of being caring is given impetus by studies of teacher motivation, which show that a desire to help children and work as part of a supportive team are major professional driving forces and provide a source of considerable personal satisfaction. As children attach great importance to playing with and learning alongside their friends, teachers also have a responsibility to identify and promote harmonious and secure relationships: child-to-child, adult-to-adult and adult-to-child.

Education that transforms is only possible in a school climate where everyone's rights are respected, responsibility for oneself and others is encouraged, and the promotion of positive images of self-worth, potential and belonging are central to the education process. Children are not born with a particular view of themselves and their worth; it is gradually shaped through their experiences at home and their relationships with a wider circle of friends and associates inside and outside school. Some children seem to be naturally anxious and tentative; others express confidence from an early age and develop a higher level of self-esteem than their timid contemporaries. Inexperienced teachers often assume that children with a bright and breezy personality have high self-belief and that quiet, passive children struggle with feelings of self-worth – in fact, there is no simple correlation between personality and confidence. Your job is to bring out the best in every individual. From their study of teachers' and pupils' views of self-worth, Cushman and Cowan (2010) stress the importance of teachers gaining understanding of the inherent uniqueness of their own classrooms and how the dynamics of relationships between themselves and their pupils, and between pupil and pupil, influence self-worth and, thereby, motivation to learn.

Cross-reference: Guided Reader Extract 60

A complete education

Fully educated children are not necessarily the ones who pass examinations and gain top marks, but rather those who develop the skills, knowledge and abilities to foster their physical, social, mental and emotional wellbeing in all aspects of life and help others to do the same. Such pupils have a desire to achieve their full academic potential but also an awareness of their capabilities and limitations. Well-educated children exude a positive attitude not only to themselves and their own learning but also to those around them through (1) building effective relationships, (2) behaving with integrity and (3) demonstrating kindness.

The real world of teaching and learning is far messier and less predictable than a policy or action plan implies. Structure in teaching and learning is preferable to chaos, of course, but account must also be taken of the school context, the personalities of those involved and the need for emotional safeguards, especially for vulnerable children and busy teachers (whose welfare is also important). No amount of strategy or cleverly designed managerial system will be effective if people's emotional wellbeing is neglected. Frightened, insecure or disillusioned children have little hope of achieving their potential, fulfilling their goals or responding enthusiastically to the opportunities presented to them. Whether pupil, teacher, teaching assistant, parent or head teacher, everyone needs encouragement, affirmation and the belief that not only what he or she *does* is valued but also the person that he or she *is*. See White (2011) for a detailed exploration of conflicting perspectives relating to the issue of wellbeing in schools.

In many ways, learning resides as much in the heart as it does in the head. It is not uniform in character but, like the waves of the sea creeping up a beach, it ebbs and flows in unexpected ways with times of calm and moments of unexpected and thrilling progress. And you are now a contributor to this exciting world.

Motivation for teaching

Many teachers of younger children claim that their desire to teach was present from a very early age. The following quotations are typical:

> My mum is a teacher and I would often go into school to help her out whenever I was at home from college. I got on really well with the children. They were so lively and enthusiastic, made me laugh and were a source of joy. I've never felt the kind of exhaustion I felt after coming back from a day spent with 5- to 7-year-olds. It was quite alarming but also felt like a reward for a job well done. Then suddenly the penny dropped that I could be a teacher too if I wanted to be. And I did!
>
> (Shima)

> Initially I worked in advertising and worked my way up to the position of manager by opening up a lot of business with large organisations. However, I wasn't happy in the job and had to make the very hard decision of giving up this very well paid employment to pursue a career that would be more rewarding. At this point I started to think about the possibility of teaching. I decided to do three weeks as a voluntary classroom assistant in two schools with very different catchment areas. Nothing could have reinforced my decision to leave the advertising industry more! I loved my time in the schools and decided that teaching was the only job for me.
>
> (Archie)

Studies of the dominant motivating factors that influence people to select primary teaching as a career point to the importance of altruistic (wanting to do good) and romantic notions of the job ('I've always dreamed of being a teacher') but with a stern realism threaded between. Factors such as salary, holidays, job security and status in society are also attractions, but the principal motivator is the opportunity to exercise a positive influence over children's lives through contributing to their education, including their social and moral development.

In a wide-ranging survey, Spear *et al.* (2000) found that those factors associated with job satisfaction were (in order of priority) the chance to work with children, relating to colleagues, and developing warm personal relationships with pupils. Smethern (2007) and Manuel and Hughes (2006) confirm that altruism and a desire to care for children provide the most powerful incentives for the vast majority of applicants to pursue teaching as a career. The authors conclude that many prospective teachers enter teaching 'with a sense of mission to transform the lives of young people and open opportunities for growth through learning and connecting' (p. 21).

People decide to train as teachers because they are passionate about doing the job (Day 2004). The publicity description offered by the Training and Development Agency (TDA) in England gives the same powerful message:

> Teaching is like no other job. It is as inspiring, challenging and unique as each child you teach. It's a career that genuinely does make a difference.
>
> No two children are the same. No two days are the same. You have the privilege of opening doors to learning, to turning children on to lifelong interests.

In their study of teacher commitment in six primary schools, Troman and Raggl (2008) found that the mission to teach was still strongly evident in these experienced practitioners, together with a desire to nurture expressed as 'love' and 'caring'. These altruistic desires did not mean that the teachers were uninterested in good working conditions, a respectable salary and opportunities for career enhancement, but that nothing could match the satisfaction that comes from making a significant difference to the life of a child.

Cross-reference: Guided Reader Extract 59

Developing as a teacher

Your development as a teacher should start from day one and continue until the end of your career (through continuous professional development, CPD, commonly referred to as in-service training or in-service). See also Chapter 16. The more that you can engage with education issues and think through their practical implications, the more likely that over time they will have a positive impact upon your working practice. The journey will not always be a smooth one. Most trainee teachers find that it is not until they have their own class that they can begin to exercise their preferences and implement their own ideas, and even then the situation is not always straightforward, for school policies and 'the way it is done here' may run counter to their aspirations. Nevertheless, the principle of interacting with teaching and learning issues rather than being a passive recipient of other people's wisdom (however helpful it may be) should characterise your approach. There are five principles for effective development as you train for teaching:

1. To learn from every situation, especially the challenging ones.
2. To clarify and regularly review your beliefs about teaching.
3. To reflect deeply about the things that tutors and colleagues tell you.
4. To consider the implications for practice of the things that you observe happening in the classroom.
5. To monitor your own progress with reference to advice from others and your own evaluations.

When they first go into school, it is a source of amazement for many trainee teachers that experienced teachers seem to cope with classroom life effortlessly, to respond spontaneously to the constant demands upon their time and to always make the best use of learning opportunities with the children. Resources seem to be in the right place at the right time, children do as they are told (usually) and the working atmosphere is purposeful and calm. Inexperienced teachers find it hard to believe that they will eventually become like their experienced colleagues and fear that they face many years of trial and error, setbacks, hardship and emotional strain before they can achieve similar success. It is, however, possible to avoid many of the more stressful experiences by adopting the five principles listed above.

Influencing pupils

As a teacher or teaching assistant, you can make a significant contribution to their education and wellbeing in at least six ways. First, find out what children already know by talking to them, listening to what they say, finding out what is important in their lives and observing how they approach tasks and employ their existing knowledge and understanding. Second, model a positive attitude towards learning by celebrating success, commiserating with failure, being enthusiastic about discovering new facts, specifying alternatives and offering help and guidance. Third, offer close personal attention to children who are struggling, restless or bored, remembering that disaffection is sometimes due to the perceived irrelevance of the work or a fear of failure. Fourth, involve children in learning by sharing the lesson purpose, establishing manageable learning targets and inviting them to comment on the quality of their work and effort. Fifth, acknowledge pupils' points of view and feelings. Finally, emphasise that success is attainable and worth striving to achieve.

Although the route to success requires fortitude and courage, the path to fulfilment in teaching does not have to be tortuous. Whereas mistakes are part of the learning process and your confidence levels may pitch from one extreme to another, it is important to acknowledge that there are proven strategies available to shorten the time needed for you to reach a place of competence and ease in the classroom. While it is true that there is no substitute for hard-earned experience, both trainee and newly qualified teachers can enjoy success in the job by establishing habits and attitudes that ensure optimum progress and personal satisfaction. Read on!

Activate your thinking!

The standards for qualified teacher status (TDA 2011) expect that good teachers will:

- set high expectations which inspire, motivate and challenge pupils;
- promote progress and good outcomes by pupils;
- demonstrate good subject and curriculum knowledge;
- plan and teach well-structured lessons;
- use a range of teaching skills, strategies and resources;
- adapt teaching to respond to the strengths and needs of all pupils;
- make accurate and productive use of assessment;
- manage behaviour effectively to ensure a good and safe learning environment;
- uphold public trust in the profession and maintain high standards of ethics and behaviour;
- contribute to the wider life and wellbeing of the school.

No chance to get bored, then!

TDA (2011) *Standards for Qualified Teachers*, London: Crown Copyright.

Good practice

Base your work as a teacher on the *Five Es*, as originally described by Lickona (1999). Thus:

Example (being a role model)
Exhortation ('It is good to')
Explanation ('I want you to do this because')
Experience (learning from what happens)
Environment that provides stability and love.

Lickona, T. (1999) *Educating for Character*, New York: Bantam Press.

Case study

A primary teacher shared her view of teaching as a vocation:

I get the strong impression that most people see work as a means to an end. They have a job to get enough money to buy food and clothes, pay the bills and – if there's some to spare – enjoy a few of life's little luxuries. Now there's nothing wrong with taking such a pragmatic view of things, but those of us who are called to teach see it as more than just a job. It's a genuine vocation; you could almost say a 'calling'. We are on a sort of mission to make the world a better place by helping children to make the very best use of their talents and intellect, to stimulate their imaginations, give them confidence, light a flame and promote a sincere love for learning. We are also keen to help them develop morally and become young people of true character. So much is expected of me that I sometimes think I've got to be some sort of super-hero with an endless reserve of energy, expertise and talent; in fact, a miracle-worker!

It's difficult to pinpoint why people decide to teach. It certainly isn't the money and it can often be an exhausting, even demoralising job at times. I guess it's a mixture of reasons: a way of expressing our talents, commitment to the betterment of society, love of learning or simply a passion for children. There's no doubt that the greatest rewards are internal; I mean things like the satisfaction that comes from seeing children grasp something for the first time or watching them enthuse over the work or smiling with delight after making a discovery.

I also love to see children happy together: their excited chatter and funny ways are like therapy for me. It's great when a child or parent thanks you sincerely for something special you did with the class or with a group. When we have fun together – perhaps doing drama or practising for an assembly or playing games on the school field or just doing something slightly daft – it brings a thrill that can't be measured or recorded on an assessment sheet. Only people who have experienced this level of happiness can fully understand what I mean.

Further reading for Chapter 1

Acker, S. (1999) *The Realities of Teachers' Work*, London: Cassell.
A book based on research, highly informative and still relevant despite its publication date.
Hayes, D. (ed.) (2007) *Joyful Teaching and Learning in the Primary School*, Exeter: Learning Matters.
This optimistic book consists of chapters contributed by a range of different authors, who write with great enthusiasm about their subject areas.
Koch, J. (2008) *So You Want to Be a Teacher? Teaching and learning in the 21st Century*, Belmont, CA: Wadsworth Publishing.
The text is to help prospective teachers uncover whether they are a good fit for the teaching profession. Part I encourages readers to reflect on why they want to teach and whether 'who they are' matches the qualities needed to be a teacher.
Sedgwick, F. (2008) *So You Want to Be a Teacher?* London: Sage.
A comprehensive and accessible guide for people deciding whether or not to teach and what to expect in the job.
Starkey, L. (2007) *Change Your Career: Teaching as your new profession*, New York: Kaplan Publishing.
A US publication written for people who are considering a career change, providing help in deciding if teaching is the right job for them.

2 Change and Innovation in Primary Education

Introduction

Teachers in every generation have had broadly the same responsibilities and followed a similar routine: arriving at school, teaching children, maintaining discipline, assessing work, liaising with colleagues and parents, writing reports, supervising break times and keeping the classroom in good order. Even so, there have been changes – some subtle, others dramatic – in the way that these familiar duties and functions are carried out and in societal expectations of teachers. Increases in political pressures have made schools a touchstone for measuring government success. Considerable amounts of money have been allocated to schools and colleges to promote higher standards of attainment. Countless numbers of documents, pamphlets, papers and publications have been written to support this or that view on how to achieve the best results. This chapter contains some, but by no means all, of the more significant changes and arguments for change, including two major reports in 2009 by Jim Rose and by Robin Alexander, and examples of recent government thinking. Meanwhile, teachers continue to serve faithfully and do their very best for the children in their care.

Primary reviews 2009

In 2009, two important reviews were published about the condition of primary education in England – the Alexander Review and the Rose Review. Both reviews contained numerous recommendations for future policy and practice but were different in tone and content.

The Alexander Review

The first review was a three-year independent study led by Sir Robin Alexander on behalf of Esmee Fairburn Trust/University of Cambridge, formally known as *The Condition and Future of Primary Education in England* but commonly referred to as 'the Primary Review' (Alexander 2009). The Primary Review identified the purposes that the primary phase of education should serve, the values it should espouse, the curriculum and learning environment it should provide and the conditions necessary to safeguard the future needs of children and society. Alexander's solution to the problems that face primary schooling in England was to extend the Foundation Stage to age 6, prioritise disadvantaged pupils and develop a curriculum based on twelve aims and eight goals. Thus, the review recommended that the primary curriculum be re-conceived under the twelve aims, arranged in three groups:

Group 1: *The needs and capacities of the individual*, with aims relating to: (a) wellbeing; (b) engagement; (c) empowerment; and (d) autonomy.

Group 2: *The individual in relation to others and the wider world*, with aims relating to: (a) encouraging respect and reciprocity; (b) promoting interdependence and sustainability; (c) empowering local, national and global citizenship; and (d) celebrating culture and community.

Group 3: *Learning, knowing and doing*, with aims relating to: (a) knowing, understanding, exploring and making sense; (b) fostering skill; (c) exciting the imagination; and (d) enacting dialogue.

These aims would be achieved through a curriculum consisting of eight domains, as follows:

1. Arts and creativity
2. Citizenship and ethics
3. Faith and belief
4. Language, oracy and literacy
5. Mathematics
6. Physical and emotional health
7. Place and time (geography and history)
8. Science and technology.

The Primary Review also commented on what are perceived to be the damaging effects of national testing on children and recommended a major rethink of assessment policy and practice.

The Rose Review

The second report published in 2009 was the *Primary Curriculum Review* (Rose 2009), a study led and co-ordinated by Sir Jim Rose and sponsored by the United Kingdom government, sometimes referred to as 'The Rose Review'. The review advised on how the primary curriculum should change to ensure that six things were in place: (1) all children would gain a solid grounding in reading, writing, speaking, literacy and numeracy; (2) schools would be offered greater flexibility of choice about content and delivery; (3) time would be allowed for study of a foreign language; (4) there should be more emphasis on personal development; (5) there should be support for a smoother transition from play-based learning to formal learning; and (6) greater levels of creativity should be encouraged. Consequently, the Rose Review proposed six 'areas of learning' as the basis for a revised National Curriculum, as follows:

1. Human, social and environmental understanding
2. Understanding physical health and wellbeing
3. Understanding the arts and design
4. Understanding English, communication and languages
5. Mathematical understanding
6. Scientific and technological understanding.

Each area of learning consisted of further details: (a) a statement about its significance for learning; (b) key ideas to identify understanding; (c) skills and processes to identify what children need to learn to do; (d) progression in learning and curriculum opportunities essential to a child's development. The *Primary Curriculum Review* did not take account of assessment issues in producing its report.

Both the Primary Review (Alexander) and the *Primary Curriculum Review* (Rose) had an impact on education thinking and debate, and much of what was recommended received a broad welcome from members of the teaching profession. Nevertheless, the direct influence of the two reviews on future government policy, curriculum and practice is proving difficult to quantify; it might well be less significant than the authors hoped for and anticipated.

Cross-reference: Guided Reader Extract 52

Faith schools

Government support for 'faith schools' has been consistently strong in recent years. A faith (or 'parochial') school is a primary or secondary school supported by a religious organisation. Approximately one-third of the state schools in England are faith schools, of which about 90 per cent are primary and 10 per cent secondary. In 2007, the UK government agreed to work with faith organisations to remove unnecessary barriers to the creation of new faith schools and to encourage independent schools to enter the maintained sector. Critics of the expansion of faith schools argue that they not only increase segregation of the children who attend them, but also reduce diversity in nearby non-faith schools by attracting away pupils from families with strongly held views about faith. Opponents also express concerns over possible divisiveness, dangers of secretarianism (division of society along faith lines) and indoctrination by sectarian groups. Despite these reservations, it is likely that the number of faith schools will increase in coming years because of their popularity with parents, high standards and pressure from religious groups (see Cairns *et al.* 2005).

Community cohesion

The need for schools to actively contribute towards community cohesion is a requirement enshrined in the Education and Inspections Act 2006. The monitoring body, OFSTED (Office for Standards in Education), has inspected the performance of schools against this community cohesion duty as a part of normal school inspections since September 2008. It uses four criteria about the extent to which: (1) schools are working towards a society in which there is a common vision and sense of belonging by all communities; (2) the diversity of people's backgrounds and circumstances is appreciated and valued; (3) similar life opportunities are available to all; and (4) a society is promoted in which strong and positive relationships exist and continue to be developed in the workplace, in schools and in the wider community. It is plain that although these criteria contain commendable aspirations, they are also highly subjective. In some schools, a named member of staff is given responsibility for overseeing commitment to community cohesion. As with most aspects of primary school life, relationships are at the heart of policy and practice, where people get along through adopting healthy, respectful attitudes. Community cohesion is enhanced by teachers who promote values of social solidarity and mutual responsibility among their pupils in the school as a whole, and during lessons.

Absenteeism

Absence from school has become something of a test bed for evaluating a school's success. The type of absence is broadly categorised as *authorised* (with permission from the school) or *unauthorised* (without reason or permission). Kyriacou (2003) refers to three types of exclusions:

(1) fixed-period – also known as 'suspensions'; (2) permanent – also known as 'expulsions'; (3) hidden – involving an informal arrangement between school, pupil and parent. The main purpose of suspension is supposed to be one of corrective support rather than punishing pupils for misbehaviour. Ideally, suspension allows pupils the time, under the supervision of their parent/guardians, to reflect on their unacceptable behaviour, accept responsibility for the behaviour that led to the suspension and change their future behaviour to meet the expectations of the school. In practice, the process is less systematic than tends to be admitted. Expulsions from primary school are very infrequent.

Regular school attendance is seen to be vital for a number of reasons. First, truants are responsible for a lot of juvenile crime. Second, children that miss a lot of school will inevitably fall behind in their studies and require additional adult support, which is both inconvenient and costly in terms of personnel and resources. Third, school absentees usually underachieve in public examinations and are therefore likely to struggle to find satisfactory and well-remunerated employment.

Issues surrounding school absence are more complex than a simple 'present' or 'not present' might imply. For example, Jonasson (2011) distinguishes between absence *from* class and absence *in* class. She argues that it is quite possible for older pupils in particular to be present in school and attend classes as required but, through their lack of concentration, high level of distraction or poor behaviour, gain little benefit from their education. In effect, children can be physically present but 'absent' mentally and emotionally. The clear message for teachers is to make the work as interesting and relevant as possible as a means of maintaining pupil interest and motivation, though some pupils seem determined to remain detached from school life.

Extended school provision

The concept of extended schools in England, Wales and Northern Ireland is that they provide a range of services and activities to help meet the needs of children, their families and the wider community. In Scotland they are referred to as 'integrated community schools'. Activities such as before-school and after-school clubs are intended to help children develop new interests and skills; enhanced childcare options allow parents to return to work more easily.

There is no single model of what an extended school should be like and each school has to work with the other interested parties (e.g. community groups) to determine what provision is required and to plan how it might best be delivered. Typically, forms of provision include one or more of the following:

- childcare provision on the school site or through other local providers;
- activities such as homework clubs and study support, sport, music tuition, dance and drama, arts and crafts, chess and first aid courses;
- parent support, including information sessions at key transition points (notably when pupils transfer from primary to secondary education);
- parenting programmes run with the support of other children's services;
- family sessions where children and parents learn together;
- referral to a wide range of specialist support services, such as speech therapy, child and adolescent mental health services, family support services and intensive behaviour support;
- community access to adult learning, ICT, sports and arts facilities;
- sexual health services, especially for younger people.

Breakfast clubs have been set up in many schools and are seen as a way to increase the number of children having a meal at the start of the day within a positive social environment. Where possible, the clubs are intended to involve the wider community in the day-to-day running. The clubs also provide a form of childcare and increase the likelihood that children will arrive on time for regular school. *Breakfast Club Plus* is a UK-wide network supported by the Department for Education (DFE) that supports breakfast clubs by providing guidance, information and best practice.

Activate your thinking!

The concept of extended schools is not universally welcomed. Concerns exist about the impact on family life of having both adults in the household working full-time and the sense that state provision is becoming a surrogate for proper parenting.

The Department for Education

Policies and priorities

The Department for Education (DFE) was created on 12 May 2010 as a successor to the Department for Children, Schools and Families (DCSF) and is responsible for education and children's services. With typical vigour after a general election, the Department set out to improve the opportunities and experiences available to children and the education workforce by focusing on six priorities:

1. *To give greater autonomy to schools* in the belief that it is head teachers and teachers, not bureaucrats and politicians, who inspire pupils and drive school improvement. As a result, additions were made to the existing School Academies programme (see below).
2. *To improve parental choice* to make it easier for parents, teachers and charities to set up and run their own schools.
3. *To offer more support for the poorest pupils* by allocating additional money for smaller class sizes, more one-to-one or small-group tuition, longer school days and more extra-curricular activities, especially for children from deprived backgrounds.
4. *To improve the whole education system* by attracting the best people into teaching through expanding 'Teach First' and improving pupil behaviour by insisting that parents accept their responsibilities, teachers are given sufficient power to act and pupils respect adult authority.
5. *To provide quality provision for children* to end child poverty and help the poorest and most vulnerable families through the Sure Start initiative; give greater autonomy to social workers; and improve the systems to safeguard children and young people.
6. *To reform the National Curriculum* so that it reflects the best collective wisdom about how children learn and what they should know.

Academy schools

The establishment of schools with 'academy' status instigated during the year 2000 by the then Labour Government was greatly expanded in England by the incoming Coalition

Government (Academies Act 2010). An academy school is allowed to receive additional support from personal or corporate sponsors, either financial or resources. Parents, teachers and voluntary groups are able to start their own schools, with state funding for each pupil for the first time. Academies are free to set their own curriculum, as long as it is broad and balanced and meeting the standards set in the Education Act 2002. Schools must meet the National Curriculum core subject requirements and are subject to inspection by OFSTED.

National healthy school status

This is a UK government initiative that requires schools to meet criteria in four core themes relating not only to the taught curriculum but also to the emotional, physical and learning environment that the school provides, as follows:

1. Personal, social and health education (PSHE) including sex and relationship education and drug education.
2. Healthy eating.
3. Physical activity.
4. Emotional health and wellbeing (including bullying).

Curriculum changes

A review of the curriculum was conducted during the first part of 2011 with the intention of reducing the overall breadth of the compulsory curriculum but increasing the 'essential knowledge' that all pupils must have by the time they reach the age of 16. English, mathematics, science and physical education (PE) remain National Curriculum subjects at all four Key Stages (i.e. from age 5 to 16). The introduction of the new National Curriculum is phased, with new programmes of study for these four 'core' subjects being taught from September 2013. A further call for evidence was launched in early 2012 in relation to all other subjects – art and design, citizenship, design and technology, geography, history, information and communication technology (ICT), modern foreign languages and music – that will be part of the future National Curriculum, and new programmes of study for those subjects will be taught from September 2014. PSHE and religious education (RE) are not part of the National Curriculum but were considered as part of the curriculum review. In 2011, the government announced its intention to conduct a separate review of PSHE education. No changes to the statutory basis for religious education are planned. Discussions about amending the arbitrary separation between Key Stages 1 and 2 and replacing it with a year-by-year system (as applied in the past) are in progress.

One of the paradoxes in promoting a content-led curriculum was that schools denoted 'academies' and 'free schools' would remain exempt from following the National Curriculum. It was also decided that the DFE itself would be responsible for carrying out the curriculum review, as opposed to the normal practice of appointing an autonomous body. Superficially, the new curriculum places far greater weight on the importance of learning and memorising facts, as opposed to the 'thinking skills' approach popularised during the latter part of the twentieth and early part of the twenty-first century. See also Chapter 9 under 'Thinking and learning'.

The heart of education

Life in school: past and present

Despite the many changes in technology and resources that have taken place in recent times, it is a paradox that, to a large extent, the heart of primary teaching is recognisably the same today as it was a generation ago. That is, a group of pupils spend most of the day together in a room with a teacher and, perhaps, an assistant who strive to pass on knowledge, help children gain understanding, offer opportunities to gain important skills and shape their thinking and behaviour.

Nevertheless, teachers today differ from those a generation or more ago in a number of ways, including the extent to which they are required to pursue ongoing in-service training and the regular scrutiny of their teaching effectiveness. It is also the case that parents are now entitled to receive far more detailed information about their children's progress, as shown through both regular teacher assessment and external testing. Primary teachers collaborate and liaise with one another more systematically than was once the case, partly out of necessity (for planning and joint assessments of children's work) and partly out of conviction (to benefit others).

Cross-reference: Guided Reader Extract 53

Concern for the individual

All children are required to receive an appropriate form of education according to their age and abilities; in the UK this ruling applies from the age of 5 years, though many pupils commence school as 'rising fives', i.e. during the term in which they have their fifth birthday. The vast majority of children in the country attend a school, though there has been an increase in the numbers being educated at home.

Regardless of the quality of the education system, the level of training, the height of test achievements and the accolades that accompany academic success, prosperity in its richest sense ultimately depends upon the way that people relate, respond and use the knowledge they have gained. Individuals matter because education is not principally about helping governments to meet targets or fulfil their political aspirations or even about guaranteeing a job and an income or to satisfy parents and other stakeholders. These goals are worthy ones but pale in comparison with the main aim of education, which is to create a civilised, moral and contented society, at ease with itself.

Activate your thinking!

As a wise person wryly commented: 'A hundred years from now it will not matter what my bank account was, the sort of house I lived in or the kind of car I drove. But the world may be different because I was important in the life of a child' (anonymous).

Good practice

Examples of helpful strategies to encourage and motivate include:

- Praise ... by sincerely saying, 'Well done!'
- Affirmations ... 'You are doing the right thing'
- Positively stated expectations ... 'I want you to do this'
- Language of belonging ... 'We all want you to succeed'
- Language of choice ... 'You take responsibility for your own actions'
- Eye contact ... direct but not intrusive
- Safe physical contact ... appropriate touching
- Appropriate body language ... stance, gestures, facial expression
- Voice tone ... calm but firm.

Moral purpose

Osguthorpe (2008) argues that we need to produce teachers of good disposition and moral character such that their teaching accords with what is good, right and virtuous. Each time a child is admonished by an adult, told how to behave or presented with choices, an ethical position is being reinforced. Whether deliberately or incidentally, teachers have an influence on the development of children's characters and through their role in school are locked into a situation where they exercise moral authority. Thus, Day (2004) claims that: 'Moral purposes are at the heart of every teacher's work. They underpin their sense of commitment to their pupils, which includes but goes beyond the instrumental policy agendas of governments' (p. 24). Eaude (2006) emphasises the role of adult language and gesture in encouraging and caring for children. Thus, 'In comforting a child or sharing a moment of significance, unspoken messages, such as touch or a smile, are just as important as overt ones' (p. 94).

Contrary to scaremongering stories, it is not illegal to touch a pupil. Naturally, you have to be wise about your actions, but there are occasions when physical contact with a pupil is proper and necessary. For example:

- demonstrating exercises or techniques during physical education or sports coaching;
- holding a young child's hand at the front or back of the line when walking in a 'croco-dile' file;
- reassuring a distressed or frightened pupil with a gentle cuddle;
- offering congratulations or commendation to a pupil by a light tap on the back or shake of the hand;
- helping a young child to undo 'hard' buttons or zips;
- demonstrating the correct use of a musical instrument;
- offering first aid (though do not exceed your expertise level).

It is inappropriate, of course, to kiss a child, embrace an older pupil in a way that might be misconstrued, or to use unreasonable force as a control mechanism – for instance, dragging a recalcitrant pupil into the classroom by his collar. The use of 'reasonable force' is a contentious issue but may be used on grounds of health and safety, such as pulling a child away from a potentially dangerous situation or separating two antagonists.

The fact that primary teachers care deeply about the pupils for whom they have responsibility is indicated by the frequent reference they make to 'my children'. Teachers historically see themselves as substitute parents; part of the reason for this 'nurturing' approach might be attributable to the fact that primary teaching has tended to be a female-orientated profession. Despite strenuous efforts by government to encourage a larger number of men to join the profession, it has only been partially successful. The only time that the percentage of males in teaching tends to increase is during a recession when there is a shortage of alternative (better remunerated but less satisfying) employment.

In itself, a teacher's love for a curriculum subject is not normally a sufficiently powerful influence to make pupils want to learn, though enthusiasm and fervour contribute considerably in achieving that aim. Instead, by nurturing what O'Quinn and Garrison (2004) refer to as loving recognition and response, rather than thoughtless habits, and by being brave enough to take risks in learning and allow for their own shortcomings and vulnerabilities, the authors claim that teachers are contributing to the creation and sustaining of a more tolerant, harmonious and caring society.

The care that teachers exercise spills over into every area of life, both inside and outside school. The emotions stirred during regular close encounters with pupils and colleagues every day are wholly absorbing and cannot be left at the school gate but are carried home every evening. Many teachers say that being a teacher is a twenty-four-hour a day job with no remission for good behaviour! Caring about your work is commendable. Caring too much about your work is likely to be damaging to health and general wellbeing. Over a period of time, the emotional demands of caring, coupled with the physical exertion and long working days, can be exhausting and even lead to a breakdown in health, so in your commendable effort to serve your pupils and colleagues, make every effort to take care of yourself, too.

Activate your thinking!

'Your greatness is measured by your kindness; your education and intellect by your modesty; your ignorance is betrayed by your suspicions and prejudices, and your real calibre is measured by the consideration and tolerance you have for others' (William Boetcker, American religious leader and speaker, 1873–1962).

Good practice

It pays to remember that just as every parent is imperfect, so is every teacher. Learn to accept the fact that you can only do what is possible for children, not what is impossible.

Cross-reference: Guided Reader Extract 58

Further reading for Chapter 2

Arthur, J., Davison, J. and Lewis, M. (2005) *Professional Values and Practice: Achieving the Standards for QTS*, Abingdon: RoutledgeFalmer.
The authors use the eight standards from the General Teaching Council as the basis for their book.
Collins, M. (2001) *Because We're Worth It: Enhancing self-esteem in young children*, London: Lucky Duck Publishing/Paul Chapman.

A practical book written in a straightforward style with a host of practical suggestions and their implications for nursery teachers.

Medwell, J. (2007) *Successful Teaching Placement*, Exeter: Learning Matters.

Contains a lot of advice and practical suggestions to assist trainee teachers in preparing for, enjoying and making fullest use of their time in school.

Part 2

People in School

3

The Children

Introduction

This chapter focuses on the issues associated with childhood; the ways in which children view and experience school; and the child–child and adult–child relationships that constitute such an essential part of their lives and learning. The chapter also addresses the realities of school for different children, notably the impact of friendships, behaviour and success or failure on their emotional, social and educational wellbeing. Other key issues include the importance of play, dealing with children's fears and how adults might respond to some of the comments that they make and events that occur from day to day.

Childhood

As a human being remains dependent on his or her parents for many years, Western beliefs about the nature of childhood tend to be based on biological considerations. Left to fend for itself, a baby will die within a short time, and very young children depend entirely on adults for their survival because they cannot feed themselves or look after themselves in any significant way. A variety of laws have been passed to protect children from neglect, abuse and exploitation, though their enforcement is far from easy and the role of social workers in this regard has become increasingly challenging.

A social perspective

The concept of childhood has varied considerably across the generations. For instance, during the industrial revolution of the 1700s and 1800s, the children of poorer families were viewed as a valuable commodity because they were capable of earning money. Childhood as a time to play, develop social skills and become educated was a luxury that few families could afford. By the middle years of the twentieth century, children were no longer seen as economic necessities, as parents provided the main source of income. In today's Western culture, children are generally viewed as a source of pleasure in their own right, though there are fears that childhood is under threat from those with commercial interests and governments that use children's educational attainment as a basis for enhancing their political credibility. Ryan (2008) is among those arguing strongly that an effective education involves much more than passively following government requirements.

Assumptions about children

Smidt (2006) warns against a model of development that views children as incompetent and therefore largely dependent on competent adults to describe, interpret, explain and analyse situations, while the children remain passive and voiceless. Under such conditions, adults are wrongly presumed to possess knowledge and always judge things correctly, whereas children are assumed to be largely ignorant and unable to think for themselves. The author further describes how a Western model of childhood makes certain assumptions about child development that are contestable, especially when seen from the perspective of Developing World countries where different norms often apply. See Music (2010) for an in-depth consideration of children's development from before birth until adolescence, including perspectives from different cultures.

*Cross-reference: **Guided Reader Extract 13***

Spontaneity

From an educational perspective, childhood is characterised by spontaneous enthusiasm for anything that touches hearts and intellects. Children have reservoirs of ideas and interests that wait to be liberated and exploited by skilful teachers. Their heads entertain fantasies, imaginings and extravagant notions about their own and others' lives. They delight to be amazed and yearn to uncloak the mysteries of life. They chatter incessantly about their hobbies, friends and pastimes. They bicker, dispute what is said, grapple with uncertainty and strive to make sense of their place in the world. The teacher's job is to capture this raw energy, harness the cauldron of fervour located in each child, and provide the spark that produces motivation for learning (Hayes 2009a).

Spirituality

It is argued that our innate capacity to sense wonder, beauty and awe is what makes the human soul rise above the rest of the creatures. Erricker *et al.* (2001) maintain that spiritual education needs to be taken seriously because it can radically reshape our educational vision and practice and have a significant effect on religious and moral education. The authors insist that teachers should address spiritual, moral, social, cultural, and emotional and religious education as interwoven and interdependent factors. Lerner (2000) is adamant that awe and wonder should be among the first goals of education that adults help children to experience, whereas Hart (2003) reverses the position by claiming that, in fact, one of the greatest lessons children have to teach adults is the power of awe. Hart goes on to say that wonder and awe do not only describe a spiritual experience but a spiritual attitude (see p. 61). Coles (1990) described children as seekers after truth and young pilgrims. The author asserts that children across cultures and ethnic/ religious boundaries are soulful, spiritual beings who create representations of God to help them make sense of their experiences and the world. In a world of seemingly perpetual motion, saturated with facts and information from countless sources, the cultivation of awe and wonder – and the sheer joy of living – is being increasingly recognised as significant for every child.

Out-of-school influences

Young lives are directly and significantly affected by their experiences outside the school with parents, siblings, relatives and friends. Children who arrive at school in an emotionally or physically distressed condition are unlikely to make the most of their opportunities; they require sensitivity and understanding, even when they are uncooperative or behave inappropriately. Similarly, a child who has a birthday or a special event is bound to be more excitable than usual and may behave out of character. Illness and disappointment can also take their toll, as children struggle to concentrate and apply themselves to their work. Sudden dips in performance might be due to children failing to work hard enough but are often due to extrinsic factors over which they have little control. Perceptive teachers are alert to such circumstances.

Anxiety

Every child has moments of anxiety about events that might appear trivial to adults. Friendship issues, lack of confidence about coping with the work, anxieties about rougher children, fear of humiliation in front of the rest of the class, embarrassment about getting changed for PE, dread of the water in swimming and being labelled as slow can all disturb and worry a child. Older children can become extremely intensive about winning. In particular, juniors become animated and exuberant about competitive team games; they are also anxious not to lose face and desperately want to be included with the majority group, which in part explains the 'gang' culture among children of primary age. Younger children nearly always want someone to play with, though occasionally an aloof child or one on the autistic spectrum will sometimes insist on being left alone and will resist efforts to be included. Eaude (2006) emphasises the role of adult language and gesture in encouraging and caring for children. Thus, 'in comforting a child or sharing a moment of significance, unspoken messages, such as touch or a smile, are just as important as overt ones' (p. 94).

It appears that an increasing number of children are suffering from a variety of stressful conditions. A report by the Children's Society in its *Good Childhood Inquiry* suggested that more than a million children had mental health problems ranging from depression and anxiety to anorexia. The research, conducted between 2006 and 2008 and headed by Stephen Scott, professor of child health and behaviour at the Institute of Psychiatry, King's College London, found that many children felt under pressure to have the latest toys and clothes and were left anxious and depressed if they were unable to keep up with trends. In a subsequent book based on the survey (Layard and Dunn 2009) the authors argue that the greatest threat to children is the present focus on excessive individualism and a belief among adults that individualism is more important than collective responsibility.

Societal pressures

Concerns that young children are being exposed to experiences and ideas that are, in effect, shortening the length of childhood, prompted the United Kingdom government to initiate a review in 2011 of ways to help parents deal with the changing nature of marketing, advertising and other pressures that are aimed at their children. A review of the commercialisation and sexualisation of childhood was intended not only to give parents the tools to combat child exploitation but also to demonstrate how businesses could be encouraged to take their responsibilities seriously. It is important to keep firmly in mind the fact that children have rights, too (Welch and Jones 2010). See also Napoli (2012) for perspectives on ways in which the branding of children's literature affects girls' developing sense of identity and their relationship with consumption.

A child's view of the world

Being in school

Although sensible behaviour and concentration on their work is important, children need to be given the latitude to behave like children and not be expected to conduct themselves as if they were mini-adults. The opportunity to mix with their friends, have a good laugh and feel contented about themselves and their relationships contributes to a purposeful learning environment; such conditions also enhance creativity and generate a sense of enjoyment (Jones and Wyse 2004). Adults working with children have to remember that young lives are directly affected by their experiences outside the school as well as within it.

In a very small number of cases, children may be aware of a conflict between home and school over learning priorities, allocation to a particular ability group, amounts of homework, lost or damaged clothing, personal possessions, and so forth. Children can feel trapped between their loyalty for a parent and a teacher, especially if negative things are attributed to the school by the parent, with which a child is uneasy. As a trainee teacher in the school it is important to refer to the class teacher any adverse comments that a parent might make to you about an aspect of school life but, as far as possible, not to take it personally. Similarly, it is important to pass on to colleagues any commending comments that parents make about them. Being told that their efforts are recognised and appreciated can uplift struggling and weary teachers. See Chapter 5 for an in-depth discussion about issues relating to teacher–parent relationships.

Children's lives are not solely defined by their time in formal education; on the other hand, school offers them a unique opportunity to meet a wide range of other children and adults in a carefully controlled and safe environment where they can learn, socialise and discover their true worth. Naturally, some children find school more palatable than others who struggle to learn, find friendships difficult and resent the obligation of an adult-imposed system. If a child has been used to having considerable freedom prior to entering school, the transition and adjustment can prove very unsettling; some children never seem to fully accept the situation and can be a thorn in the side of staff from the day they begin school to the day they leave. O'Connor (2011) argues that changes at home can have a profoundly negative effect on young children's education; for instance, separation from parents and insecure attachments they experience have a detrimental impact not only on their emotional health but also on their cognitive and intellectual development. Thankfully, the vast majority of children enjoy school and even in the case of those who initially struggled to adjust, it is not unusual for them to be enthusiastic about it eventually.

From a child's point of view, school is real life, not artificial. As such, learning is best viewed as an adventure that is sometimes challenging, sometimes perplexing but always motivating. Although certain parts of the curriculum are less appealing than others, teachers should strive to create a learning environment that offers diverse experiences, excites interest and draws on their enthusiasm. Learning becomes worthwhile and enjoyable for children when the content is interesting and relevant; the lesson is presented imaginatively; the tasks associated with the lesson are manageable; and the learning climate is positive and encouraging. See Katz and Chard (2000) and Chapters 7 and 8.

Children look at the world in their own special and wonderful ways. Each child is a special being with unique ideas, opinions, hopes, dreams and perspectives on life. As adults in school, it is important for us to understand that what works for one child won't necessarily work for another and what makes perfect sense to one will confuse another. Seeing the world from the children's perspective helps us to understand what they really want and how best to go about satisfying (or occasionally, denying) that need. If we are willing to learn, children can teach us a great deal by what they say, the things they do and the way in which they perceive events. And the more carefully we listen, observe and engage with children, the better educators we become.

Adjusting to change

Moving on to another class and particularly changing to another school is a major event for children and as well as being exciting can be extremely disconcerting; children usually become restless and sometimes less well behaved as the transition time approaches. After they move up to a new class at the start of the year, pupils tend to look back wistfully to the time they spent in their previous class and it is not uncommon to hear them complain that they don't like the new teacher as much as the old one. It takes time for the adult–child relationship to stabilise and for the new teacher's methods, preferences and ideas to be communicated to the children.

Every change generates the excitement of new horizons and potential for new friendships, but also strong emotions, not least the heartache that children feel in dealing with disrupted friendships and the fear generated by the unknown. In addition to making friends in a new situation, there are practical considerations for pupils to consider, especially in secondary school, such as adjusting to a new timetable, remembering when to bring in a games kit and making sure homework is completed.

Teachers of the oldest primary children work hard to ensure that the transition from school to school takes place smoothly – in particular, liaison between the 'feeder' primary and 'receiving' secondary school. Primary teachers pass on information about pupils' academic achievements and an indication of their social skills, friendship patterns, behaviour and attendance. Governments are most concerned about the communication of pupils' formally assessed levels of attainment to the receiving schools – principally information about national test scores – but secondary teachers are just as interested in each pupil's character and attitude to learning. It is not uncommon for secondary schools to administer their own internal tests to new pupils as a means of organising ability groups, which causes some primary teachers to complain that their secondary colleagues are failing to utilise sufficiently the pupil data they have passed on to them.

Finding happiness

It is taken for granted that every adult working in school and every parent/carer wants children to find happiness in their lives. Who could possible disagree with such sentiments? Indeed, many teachers speak of the joy that they experience seeing pupils enjoying school, making friends and going home with a spring in their step each evening. Yet there's a range of viewpoints about the significance of happiness as a feature of school life and the extent to which it should be a priority for teachers. Thomas Bray, a seventeenth-century Christian minister advised: 'Never fear spoiling children by making them too happy. Happiness is the atmosphere in which all good affections grow.'

Seldon (2008) suggests that it is possible for a school to 'teach happiness' by ensuring that it is a place children love to be, such that they feel deeply loyal to their school, fellow pupils and teachers. The author argues that teachers should help to develop all aspects of pupils' personalities and aptitudes – not just their intellects; in this way, children learn about their place in the world and how they want to live. The end product is that children learn how to look after themselves and stay healthy, both emotionally and cognitively. Seldon also insists that parents and the wider community should be fully involved in the child's learning; in return, the teachers at the school should be valued and respected, treated with civility and gratitude, through a recognition that teaching is a vitally important job. Other educators argue that happiness cannot be taught; instead, it emerges naturally when life is satisfying and friendships are secure.

Cross-reference: Guided Reader Extracts 15

Creating memories

Looking back

School is an important element of children's lives, and although they may not know or understand everything that happens there, they are aware of a great deal more than some adults give them credit for. Children may not express their views openly to teachers but they do have insights about school life that affect their attitude to work as they interpret and misinterpret situations and circumstances. Teachers who make a habit of inviting children to express their views are often surprised by the perceptiveness and certainty of their comments. One teacher asked the 9- and 10-year-old children in his class to comment on the most significant event that had happened during the past term. Several children referred to the class outings, another to the sports day, but Yvette, a bright girl with a mischievous smile, was happy to share her most vivid memory:

> I remember when you came into the room carrying a pile of books and looking angry. You slammed the books down on the desk, went red in the face and told us that you were ashamed of what another teacher had told you about our behaviour in the playground.

Oh dear! Hopefully there were more positive events that Yvette stored in her memory. Nevertheless, teachers need to be sensitive to the varied experiences of being a pupil in school and the things that they remember with pleasure. There are many aspects of school that children enjoy. They like to have access to friends, to learn interesting things and to feel part of a community. Sadly, a small number of children look back at their school days as a time of struggle and even intimidation. (See Chapter 3 for detailed information about bullying.)

Critical moments

Salo (2002) carried out research into adults' memories of their time in school and discovered that they recalled incidents that probably seemed trivial to the teacher at the time but burned deeply into the child's consciousness. Respondents remembered these critical moments in detail, including the teacher's clothes, the expression on their faces and even the teacher's scent. In particular, moments of humiliation and guilt were powerfully engraved into the mind, as were times of delight and shared pleasures. Teachers bear a heavy responsibility to ensure that pupils are provided with a secure learning climate, and in cases where children have to be disciplined or admonished, that this is done with forbearance and in moderation. Fisher (2005) argues that a positive learning climate evolves out of six conditions: loyalty;

trust; support; dynamism; expectation; and communication. Pupils must be willing to listen attentively to their peers, resist the temptation to put others down, reserve the right to remain silent and respect confidentiality.

Joy and excitement

Children like to enjoy the work they do and have some fun. They love the sense of fulfilment gained from successful task completion, the admiration of friends and adult praise. Children are very happy when they have opportunity to do something practical or go outside to study. All pupils get excited when adults share ideas with them, take an interest in their life beyond the school gate and celebrate their smallest achievements. Children like to get praise from adults they respect (but not from ones they resent) and receive external reward for their efforts (such as certificates and merit cards). Children like teachers who have a sense of humour but are not cynical, and are fascinated when they watch grown-ups behaving in a slightly frivolous way. Nearly all children enjoy games, competitions and puzzles. They love to draw, paint, create things from materials and work with others to produce models and murals. Children are happiest when they feel secure and are clear about what is permissible and what is unacceptable. They respond best when they feel that they are being treated like important individuals and not as 'articles' to be taught, tested and processed through the school system.

Enjoyment

There are two principal forms of enjoyment: enjoyment of learning and enjoyment in learning. Enjoyment of learning involves developing pupils' passion for finding out and discovering new things, whereas enjoyment in learning means that they experience the processes used in finding out as satisfying and meaningful for them. The different forms of enjoyment are two sides of the same coin because children who enjoy learning for its own sake will also find satisfaction in striving to reach their goal; similarly, children who enjoy what they are doing are likely to be motivated to persevere and learn more. Nevertheless, Carr (2003) counsels that while teachers are keen that their pupils should grow in confidence and experience enjoyment and satisfaction in learning, these outcomes are not the intended aim of teaching. Thus, 'parents would have cause to complain about any teacher who had made his or her pupils happy or confident without teaching them anything' (p. 114).

Developing confidence

There are three sets of conditions that assist the promotion of pupil confidence in learning: (1) to feel secure; (2) to know the rules; (3) to be clear about the lesson purpose and how to go about achieving it. The fact that children need to feel secure is particularly important when teachers are asking questions or inviting responses from the class. Timid children are unlikely to risk answering if by doing so they are met by a teacher's exasperated rebuke. Teachers who treat all answers seriously and encourage those who try hard soon have pupils clamouring to participate. The maxim to 'have a go and find out what happens', if promoted and practised within a safe environment, acts as a springboard for progress. Your patience and understanding can transform a nervous child's tentativeness into joyful learning. See Chapter 8 for a discussion about establishing suitable conditions for effective learning.

Things children dislike about school

There are also many things in school that children dislike intensely. They hate to be unfairly accused of something, especially when the adult concerned has jumped to an unwarranted conclusion or refused to give them time to offer their perspective. Children also get irritated if they ask the teacher a question and are scolded for doing so or told that they should have listened in the first place. Teachers who show favouritism are particularly disliked by children, who become resentful if they perceive that one child gets away with something that another child is punished for doing. This perception is difficult to avoid when the adult takes account of a child's past history and temperament when making a decision about appropriate action, and modifies the sanction as a result. Consequently, two children may be treated rather differently for a similar misdemeanour or one child may be given a privilege ahead of the other. If you find yourself in this situation it is important to explain (but not apologise, which should be reserved for when you make a mistake and not for when you make a decision).

Unsurprisingly, children are not impressed by being moaned at by a teacher for working slowly when they are doing their best to be conscientious. Children have little time for teachers who are always serious and those who use an artificial or unnatural voice, especially if it comes across as patronising. While schools do not exist for the sole purpose of keeping their pupils happy (see earlier), it is a long-established principle that children who have a positive view of their situation are more likely to learn effectively than those who have negative ones. Thankfully, studies show that the vast majority of children are contented with their experiences of primary school, though as they get older the percentage begins to drop.

Every Child Matters

The UK government has recognised the significance of these social, physical and emotional factors and introduced the *Every Child Matters* (ECM) agenda into schools, whereby every child should be offered the support that he or she needs to be healthy, stay safe, enjoy life and achieve, make a positive contribution and (rather oddly) achieve economic wellbeing. Issues arising from the ECM 'agenda' are explored more fully in Chapter 13. In practice, this policy promotes the principle that all the child-service organisations should work co-operatively to share information and work together so as to protect children and young people from harm and support their aspirations. Of course, teachers have always tried hard to support children in the way that ECM dictates; however, having a national policy is a means of monitoring implementation and strengthening its impact. Unfortunately, as with every national initiative there is a danger of formal compliance at the expense of a sincere desire to help children.

From a different perspective, a report by the Children's Society (2007) concluded that it was essential that the next generation of children recognised the importance of contributing to the welfare of others rather than always thinking about their own needs, and putting human relationships higher than the accumulation of possessions and acquiring societal status. In a world characterised by self-indulgence and a 'me first' mentality, this aspiration is not easily achieved. Pupil involvement in community projects and actively supporting worthwhile causes (especially involving disadvantaged children) contribute to the creation of a selfless culture in school.

Activate your thinking!

Don't just give the impression of caring by correctly following the ECM guidelines; care deeply and genuinely, because you are passionate about children and their welfare.

Best practice

Find out what children like and dislike by asking them! Don't be afraid to disclose some of the things that you like and dislike, but be aware that children repeat things you say at home, so don't be too candid.

The teacher's responsibilities

Regardless of age, all children want to be valued, respected and treated fairly. Whether you are training to be a teacher or have a class of your own, the same principles apply. Thus:

- to avoid unfairly favouring one group of children over others on the basis of background, ethnicity or home circumstances;
- to help children assimilate and understand school conventions by explaining and reminding, rather than by rebuking and getting exasperated;
- to understand that one measure parents use to judge a school's success is their child's happiness;
- to make allowance for lively, assertive children as much as for passive, compliant ones;
- to reassure parents that the school and the teachers are working in the children's interests;
- to do everything in your power to ensure that children fulfil their academic potential.

Activate your thinking!

Consider the sort of questions that children might be asking when they begin school or change classes:

Where will I sit?
Will the work be hard?
Will I make friends?
Will I be bullied?
Is the teacher strict?
Will I get bored?
What happens if I need the toilet?
Will we do fun things?
Will we go on trips?
Can I bring toys to school?

Giving children a voice

Many schools work hard to include the children in decision-making and give them a 'voice' through the use of school councils and the like. A *school council* is a group of children who are elected by their peers to represent their views with a view to improving the school. The council usually meets with a teacher present to discuss and, if possible, resolve problems that affect a majority of pupils, such as organising playground games during break time, school lunches, unwanted behaviour and bullying, or ideas for fundraising events. Opportunities also exist for adults to ask children what they believe, canvass their opinions and demonstrate an interest in their perspectives. The thinking behind this interactive, transparent approach is that if pupils are invited to contribute to the decision-making process, certain advantages accrue, such as:

- having a sense of ownership about decisions that affect them;
- behaving more responsibly;
- offering a fresh perspective on situations;
- providing suggestions about improving the school that are of genuine value.

Children do not always understand what is happening to them at school or why it is necessary to do or not do something, which to adults is perfectly plain. They will not be pleased or agree with every decision. Their opinions will sometimes be inflexible because of their own prejudices or those of adults at home. Nevertheless, part of the great privilege of being a teacher is to delve into the 'secret world of the child' and discover its hidden treasures. And you are an integral part of this world.

Activate your thinking!

The Education and Skills Act became English law in 2008, an element of which requires that schools will have to listen to pupils on major decisions that affect them. As it is not practical to ask all pupils individually about every issue, an effective council can submit ideas on their behalf. One means of organising the process is the establishment of class councils (i.e. one council per class) to offer each child the opportunity to express a view or to vote for a particular preference from a range of options.

Cross-reference: Guided Reader Extract 55

Assemblies

Assemblies form an important part of school life, though their format has changed considerably over the past generation. Older readers might recall a time when the assembly was conducted formally, with prayers, hymns or Christian songs and, perhaps, a short Bible reading. Today, a relatively small number of schools continue the practice. Although gathering the school together is a statutory requirement, the structure of the assembly varies considerably, depending on the school's location and predominant ethnic groups, the size of accommodation and numbers of pupils. An appropriately calm and relaxed atmosphere is often created through the use of a focal point, such as a colourful display, together with background music to help stimulate a reflective mood.

Primary school assemblies tend to be used to celebrate children's achievements, provide time for contemplation about ethical or moral issues and convey messages – plus occasionally warnings or guidance about behaviour – from the head teacher or assembly leader. Hawkes (2000) notes that regardless of its format and the type of school concerned, there is an assumption that an act of worship experience will be *spiritual* in as much as pupils are given opportunity to explore the 'inner person', associated with feelings, emotions, empathy and a sense of wonder about the world. Today, assemblies are not so much imposed upon the pupils as shared with them and, whether religious in content or not, provide a rare opportunity for children to step outside the daily routine and enjoy a community experience with other children and adults.

Children's different experiences

Effective teachers are professional observers of children (Sharman *et al.* 2000). See Monica, smartly dressed, climbing out of the family car. Her quality clothes and relaxed manner bear testimony to the secure and consistent life that she enjoys. Watch as she runs into school, confident that whatever the day holds for her, there is the safety of home and family awaiting her return. She skips about, calls to her friends, laughs excitedly and, eyes shining, looks expectantly towards the classroom door. Then see Charley as she wanders alone through the school gate shortly before eight o'clock to head for the breakfast club and companionship, still bewildered by the experiences of the previous night: the strange adult behaviour, the responsibility for younger brothers and sisters, the disturbed sleep, the early morning wakening and the temporary lodgings. How will Charley view school life today? As a haven, perhaps, and a chance to escape from the grimness of life she experiences daily in the outside world. Perhaps the harsh words that greeted her from irritable adults when she was scarcely awake will fade from her mind and heart as she now experiences kindness and patience from people like you. In school, Charley will find sensitive and caring adults who will provide security through clearly explained rules, interesting and relevant work and the authority to protect her from the playground bully. Charley can relax now.

Both Monica and Charley enter the school. Both remove their coats, chat to friends, walk towards the classroom door. They notice teachers, assistants, parents, pictures on walls and familiar objects. Their noses tingle at the intoxicating mixed scents from floor polish, humming heaters, damp clothing and toilets. A random set of sounds impinges on their consciousness: chattering voices, clatter and thud of feet, doors creaking and adults talking animatedly. Their eyes light up as they enter the classroom and glimpse the familiar, reassuring sights. They sit down on a carpet or sit at their table, answer to their names, respond to a request or command. They hear the familiar sound of the teacher's voice issuing instructions and mischievous pupils being told to behave; the children are sensitive to the adult's tonal patterns and intonation. They recognise when teachers are cross, sad, bored or pretending, and modify their behaviour accordingly.

The day begins and the bum-numbing effects of registration and, perhaps, class assembly are replaced by work sessions and activities. Playtimes and mealtimes provide relief from their toil. The children disappear into the frantic world of games, chasing, arguments, intensive relationships, erratic behaviours and unpredictable weather. They wonder about the paradoxes of school life: why teachers insist that they wear a coat when it isn't cold or enthuse that going outside is good for them when it is obviously miserable and damp. They see the teachers disappearing into the warmth and security of the staffroom and catch the odd snippet of conversation, wave of laughter, smell of coffee. It all has a magical air.

As each playtime ends, a few children hanker for a turn to knock on the staffroom door, return a teacup and inform the disappointed teachers that Miss Jenkins says that it's in-time (an expression used only in primary schools). The day continues. A hall-time offers chance for some fun ... if teacher allows. Laces are tied, buttons fumbled and feet wriggled into socks. The end-of-afternoon story or sharing draws children and teacher together, and soon home-time heralds the end of another school day. Coats are pulled off pegs or scrambled for on the floor; odd gloves mysteriously disappear and reappear; accusations over property and other disputes reverberate down the corridors. Mothers, fathers and grandparents are there to pick up the children, ask brightly about the day, exchange a word with the teacher, flash a smiling 'thank you' and head for home. Pushchairs and a stream of young mums line up across the front of the building. Parents check lunch boxes, stare at the latest school letter and herd their little flocks towards the exit. Monica skips off happily, keen to tell her mother about her successes and show off her new reading book. Charley edges out of the room, casting a hopeful glance at the teacher, before moving away to pick up her younger brothers and sisters and usher them along the pavements to the local shop to buy a snack for tea. The teacher gives Charley a reassuring smile and wink: 'Take care, Charley. See you tomorrow.' Charley can hardly wait for tomorrow to come: 'Goodbye, Miss.' She sighs inwardly and slopes off into the uncertain world that awaits her.

A few minutes later the welter of bodies has subsided. Children melt into the privacy of their own lives, although a few linger, savouring the last moments of the school atmosphere, swinging their bags around their heads in joyful abandon before racing to the entrance with a whoop and a cry. In the distance, a few others are heard excitedly anticipating the after-school football or netball practice, impatiently waiting for the teacher. A few committed souls find the teacher who is offering them additional support for their work to 'boost' their performance in national tests and settle to work with a will that is not always apparent under normal classroom circumstances. Most of the children leave but the teachers and some assistants remain, engaged in a variety of planning, administrative and organisational tasks that parents and pupils know little about, but which form the engine room of the school. The majority of teachers have already been at school for eight hours, with a lot of work still to be done.

Classrooms are mainly about teaching and learning, but effectiveness depends upon pupils being in the right frame of mind to participate in their education, well motivated and convinced that the effort is worthwhile. Classroom activity can be a mirage. Busy children may or may not be engaged in learning; for no amount of coercion can match a child's genuine desire to succeed. Every adult associated with school has a vital role to play in the process of motivating and encouraging children to engage enthusiastically with the curriculum and, perhaps more importantly, to help them to learn how to learn (so-called 'metalearning'). Schools, therefore, are about people of all shapes and sizes.

Cross-reference: Guided Reader Extract 51

Induction into school life

It is difficult for adults to remember the excitement generated by a special school event, especially if parents are invited, the tingling associated with particular smells or the first cut of a birthday cake. As we grow older, the imaginings of childhood are replaced by more pragmatic considerations and vain efforts to cram too much into too little time. Yet if teachers want to create a purposeful classroom environment, it is worth recalling some of the emotions, ideals and uncertainties which characterise childhood (see earlier in this chapter). Jackson (1987) argues that, to make sense of school, children draw on past experiences and their own understandings. She reminds us that these perceptions 'may not necessarily match the perceptions of the teacher, for learning in school can be a very different thing from learning at home' (p. 86).

The UN Convention on the Rights of the Child states that children should be encouraged to express their views freely and given opportunity to be heard, especially in decisions that relate to life decisions. Yet common experience suggests that a collegial perspective of this kind cannot be taken for granted within each house and home, or even within each classroom. The edict that 'children should be seen and not heard' still has many supporters, notably in the case of very young children, who are not considered capable of offering a considered opinion owing to their alleged inability to distinguish between fact and fantasy. In this regard, Tyrrell (2001) insists that fantasy and the development of the imagination are an integral part of growing up. Put another way, to be deprived of opportunities to explore areas of fantasy means that children are not receiving their entitlement to a full education. While fantasy is normally associated with younger children, it has the capacity to awaken and stimulate the imagination of every child.

Regardless of background, all children are gradually inducted, both by their peers and teachers, into patterns of behaviour and understanding that reflect and maintain school life. It is hard to come to a school for the very first time and have to learn unfamiliar and sometimes baffling procedures, routines and rituals. After all, where else but in school do you need to stick your arm up in the air before being allowed to speak or to sit still on an uncomfortable floor listening to a grown-up reading stories? Only in a classroom do you have to ask for permission to leave the room that you share with around thirty other children, some of whom you would not choose as friends; to have to answer endless questions yet rarely have opportunity to ask any; and to get dressed and undressed with lots of other children before going to clamber over large apparatus in a hall; or to endure the windy and wet conditions of an exposed playground. Contrast the freedom of a park, typified by laughter, yells and screams, with the controlled atmosphere of a gym lesson and the scolding from teachers if the noise level rises. Compare the expectations of school and playgroup, babysitter or home. Little wonder that children who are new to school take time to settle, sometimes become confused, make mistakes, and find the experience unsettling.

Thankfully, over the weeks and months the unfamiliarity fades and is normally replaced by a healthy adjustment to the vagaries of school life (Brooker 2002). Indeed, a reluctance to conform sometimes evolves into a zealous eagerness to defend the status quo. Older infants and younger juniors often vie with one another to see who can most vigorously uphold justice. Everyone that works in a school or pre-school setting will recognise these sorts of comments as typical:

'You're not allowed...'

'Miss says you can't...'

'A-ah, I'm *telling*.'

The above remarks are examples of crossly disputed versions of the truth; gaining the moral high ground from your peers; and the various claims and counter-claims that permeate school life. Being in the right and acknowledged as such by friends and grown-ups is very important for children; experienced adults take the children's concerns seriously but learn to defuse as well as adjudicate situations, while leaving each child with his or her wellbeing intact. In the midst of this network of interaction, forging or relationships and desire for justice, it is hard not to feel sympathy for the plight of the insecure younger child, still unable to place confidence in the teacher, yet shyly longing to hold an adult's hand at playtimes and receive a reassuring look and smile. See the same child in the classroom, holding back when there's a scramble for the best equipment or place in the queue, passively accepting her lowly position in the pecking order and storing up a growing belief that she will never be able to compete with her stronger, more assertive peers. Such children need your attention, care and encouragement if they are ever to fulfil their potential.

Activate your thinking!

In your desire to help the less confident pupils and engage with strong-willed pupils, don't forget the middle-of-the-road children, who never excel and rarely stand out from the crowd, but deserve as much of your time and consideration as the others.

Children's perceptions

As they witness classroom and school encounters, children gain a view of what is important and what is trivial, of adult status and tolerance (Charlton *et al.* 1996; Cullingford 2002). As they become more experienced in school, their intuition and familiarity with school routines and relationships alert them to the teacher's apprehension when certain significant adults (especially if they wear smart suits and carry a clipboard) enter the room. In the playground they are keenly aware of who dominates and who submits; which children are most popular and which are the target of derisive comment; who are the rough and noisy ones and who always get told off. They make a mental note that such-and-such a child can usually be blamed for misdemeanours, regardless of the truth, and occasionally prey upon the fact to divert attention from their own naughty behaviour. Some children discover how to approach a teacher in such a way as to gain sympathy or favour. Some children are expert at handling adults; others don't care enough to try. A few take delight in finding every opportunity to take advantage of grown-ups and luxuriate in the excitement of undetected disobedience.

Children rarely comment at the time but they soon know if different teachers are at odds with one another or if there is tension in the air. Some teachers wonder why the standard of children's behaviour deteriorates when life is most stressful in school. In fact, it is easily explained. Children are extremely sensitive to mood and atmosphere, so as teachers become strained and less able to cope, the children pick up the edginess and respond accordingly. Each adult working in school therefore contributes to the sense of ease or restlessness, to contentment or fractiousness. There are no neutral zones: although pupils might not have a grasp of the reasons for adults' unease or excitement, small deviations in the school and classroom climate will always elicit a reaction.

Hood (2008) set out to discover what a group of young learners might understand by an *identity as learner* under the acronym PPIL, standing for pupils' perceptions of their identities as learners, thereby moving from pupils as sources of data to pupils as agents of change. The 8- and 9-year-old mixed-ability group of children demonstrated that they were

> very capable of talking and writing about their perceptions of a variety of aspects of being a learner, that they respond well to probes which ask for simple opinions or decisions about their lives in the classroom and are willing then to think more deeply in response to supplementary questions which may demand greater reflection.

(p. 149)

Activate your thinking!

Cooper and Hyland (2000) argue that children learn most with trainee teachers who are able to do four things well: (1) convey key concepts; (2) stimulate, challenge and change their thinking; (3) respect them as individuals; and (4) maintain a good classroom ethos.

Cooper, H. and Hyland, R. (2000) *Children's Perceptions of Learning with Trainee Teachers*, Abingdon: Routledge.

School life and culture

Every school has its own culture and traditions that children gradually absorb and accommodate, as they become familiar with them through regular immersion. School life passes through many phases in a year (Brandling 1982; Sedgwick 1989; Smith and Lynch 2005) such as the conker season, marbles, swapping the latest card collections, paper aeroplanes, skipping, dances, songs, hairstyles, humour, plus the quirkiness of the latest electronic gadget and, especially as children grow older, the 'must have' fashions. Playtimes are characterised by waves of chasing games or children clutching the coat tails of a friend to imitate horses, charioteers or railway engines. Junior-age children imitate their favourite pop stars or football hero. Many schools employ a variety of strategies to foster positive play: boxes of dressing-up clothes and toys made freely available; brightly coloured motifs on the walls to stimulate children's imagination; the promotion of traditional co-operative games; and quiet corners for those who simply want to relax and chat to their friends. It has also become popular to implement a policy of ensuring that no child is left out by creating cross-age groupings of children who 'look out' for one another, and the promotion of 'never say no' behaviour whereby it is not permitted to refuse a child entry to an existing playground game if requested. See Smith (2007) for an interesting pupil perspective on life in playgrounds.

Activate your thinking!

Bell (2009) provides advice to teachers about training pupils in school to support their peers during playground problems by using conflict resolution and problem-solving approaches.

Bell, L. (2009) *Peer Support in the Primary Playground*, London: Optimus Education.

Good practice

Results from a study by Lucas and Dyment (2010) suggest that when children are given a choice about where to play, they choose natural areas. As such, green areas of school grounds make an important contribution in providing equitable, inclusive, healthy and inviting play opportunities for children.

Lucas, A.J. and Dyment, J.E. (2010) 'Where do children choose to play on the school ground? The influence of green design', *Education 3–13*, 38 (2), pp. 177–89.

Children as children

Time in school falls into well-defined categories for children, though they can sometimes overlap. The energetic playtime behaviour can be brought into the classroom; the anticipation of going home can result in premature excitement; the tedium of sitting still during a long school assembly can lead to lethargy when work commences. Teachers have to adjust their teaching and temperament to allow for these vagaries without losing the smooth flow of classroom routines or neglecting basic standards or by being unnecessarily strict or grumpy. The best teachers act decisively but refuse to be rattled by spontaneous behaviour that is typical of children the world over. Some inexperienced teachers over-react to these situations and become nervy and edgy, cross and agitated. Wiser ones learn to take it all in their stride, to discriminate between sabotage and exuberance, between insolence and informality, between hostility and high spirits. Children are, after all, children!

A minority of children take a long time to adjust to school life and to a new teacher. Bear this in mind when you take charge of a class. Ironically, the more comfortable and relaxed they feel in the classroom, the more likely the boundaries between home and school will become blurred. The teacher who admonishes a child, 'Don't do that, you're not at home now', might be failing to recognise that such behaviour is often a sign of a positive and relaxed attitude towards school rather than mischievous behaviour. It pays to spend time studying and interpreting the way that children respond and react. You don't have to become a child to understand one.

It should encourage you to know that the vast majority of pupils love being at school. It gives them opportunity to meet their friends, experience challenges, use stimulating equipment, contribute to collaborative ventures and work closely with a range of different adults, all of whom have a concern for them. Little wonder that one little boy commented:

I like school because the teachers care about us and help us to learn good things.

(Wally, aged 6 years)

Enough said!

Cross-reference: Guided Reader Extract 1

Adults helping children

We noted earlier that most children have moments of anxiety about school. Some are concerned with their work and whether they can keep up with their peers; others worry about friendships or how to please the teacher. Even children who seem bold can harbour doubts about their ability to cope. The early days of a new school year can be a particularly troubling time for some children as they try to discover exactly what new teachers expect of them.

Part of a teacher's role is to provide reassurance for children, giving a clear message to them that everything is under control and that adults can be relied upon to be fair, supportive and firm. Occasionally, older children seem to feel that certain adults, particularly those whom they perceive as powerless (notably mealtime assistants, cleaners and even trainee teachers) can be treated casually and mischievous youngsters find great pleasure in pushing their patience to the limit. Happily, the majority of primary-age children are willing to trust adults, enthusiastically enjoy school and do their best. For the adults concerned, this is a privilege and a joy.

Supporting not smothering

It is important for children to know that their teachers and helpers want the best for them and will do all they can to assist them in achieving it. This is different from mollycoddling children or preventing them from gaining independence and the ability to make decisions for themselves. However, some children are only too happy to be told the answer by an adult instead of putting their minds to a problem. A pattern of behaviour emerges whereby the child engages with a task, encounters a difficulty and immediately asks for assistance and advice, which the teacher dutifully provides. Such an immediate response is satisfying for the teacher, and usually elicits a smile from the pupil concerned, but in the long run is unlikely to help children become self-sufficient. The state in which children become over-reliant on adults is often referred to as 'learned helplessness' (LH). Children 'learn' to be helpless and may gradually begin to lose the ability to make their own decisions. Such children are probably already anxious and constantly call for adult help. If you hear a child asking for your approval and advice about every tiny nuance of the work, you can be fairly certain that LH is becoming embedded in the pupil's psyche. It will take time, lots of reassurance and a gradual severing of the reliance link before the child can be delivered from the effects of this condition.

Creating secure relationships

The importance of enjoying a good working relationship with children is rightly stressed as being important for learning, though this should not be confused with over-familiarity. Nias (1997) argues that 'There are dangers in placing too much emphasis upon the help and support which teachers can give to one another or to children' (p. 18). She suggests that although adults in school gain great personal satisfaction in helping children, it is possible to care *too* much and lose sight of the children's academic needs. Nevertheless, MacGrath (2000) reminds us that from a child's perspective it is important to feel special:

> Remembering to make everyone feel special can make a difference. It may be simply a brief word, a warm look, but it can be powerful. It is often paying attention to things, which may seem trivial to an adult but are very big in the life of a child, which help children feel you are on their side, you do notice and care. One of the most important things is to listen.
>
> (p. 74)

Where all teachers actively demonstrate their commitment to children, a framework of mutual support and encouragement helps to build a happy school with contented staff and pupils. Clark (1995), in considering significant factors when studying children, refers to the humbling experience of working with 'flesh-and-blood children in their need and vulnerability, in their optimism and eagerness ... For these children – all children – are subjects, not objects' (p. 21). In similar mode, Killick (2006) reminds us of the sobering fact that 'children who receive persistent criticism will soon learn it is easier not to try than to risk failure' (p. 46). Teachers need to remember that however frustrating or objectionable a pupil may be and without the least bit of sentimentalism, he or she is somebody's precious child.

Against this, every adult has observed the strategies used by a minority of children to gain attention, cause disruption or avoid responsibility. After all, it is easier to fool about and gain the admiration of your peers than to acknowledge that you don't understand, cannot remember instructions or are confused by the teacher's comments. Some of these circumstances are discussed later in the chapter. The teacher's position will be examined more fully in Chapter 4. In your desire to create positive relationships, you have to balance the need for open communication, positive attitude and helpful support against the wiles of a small number of pupils that try to take advantage of your sympathetic nature.

The affective dimension

McNess *et al.* (2003) provide an important reminder that teachers should be deeply committed to the affective ('felt') dimension of teaching and learning. They argue that in the complex and difficult task that teachers undertake, there are many dimensions of their role to consider and negotiate. In the UK there has been increasing emphasis on social and emotional aspects of learning (using the acronym SEAL). The purpose of this school curriculum resource is to develop the underpinning qualities and skills that help promote positive behaviour and effective learning. The materials focus on five social and emotional aspects of learning: self-awareness, managing feelings, motivation, empathy and social skills. The SEAL resources are organised into seven themes:

1. New beginnings
2. Getting on and falling out
3. Say no to bullying
4. Going for goals
5. Good to be me
6. Relationships
7. Changes.

McNess *et al.* (2003) suggest that the emotional factor has great significance for teachers as the affective dimension of teaching 'relied heavily upon joint negotiation and a close personal relationship between the teacher and the learner' (p. 248). In other words, part of the skill of good teaching is not only to possess subject knowledge, or even to be able to put things across systematically and clearly, but also to empathise with the learner and build effective working relationships with each pupil. Richards (2006) is more forthright when he claims that primary teaching is:

> an extremely complex activity ... an amalgam of many elements: interpersonal, intellectual, physical, spiritual, even aesthetic ... It involves notions such as respect, concern, care and intellectual integrity that are impossible to define but which are deeply influential in determining the nature of life in classrooms ... *It is a moral enterprise as well as a practical activity.*
>
> (p. 13, emphasis added)

According to Thornberg (2008), values education is most often reactive and unplanned and embedded in everyday school life, with a focus on pupils' behaviour in school; it is mostly unconsciously rather than deliberately performed. In schools, values reflect the personal concerns and preferences that help to frame relationships between pupils and adults. Rossano (2008) argues that while most children grow up to develop competent moral skills, a small number of them fail to do so and few develop them to a sophisticated level. Consequently, deliberate moral practice is necessary for the acquisition of expertise; religious participation appears to provide one of the basic elements to facilitate it.

In the hurly-burly of daily life in school it is possible to lose sight of the fact that understanding and influencing children is important not only for their sakes but for the welfare of the community and, ultimately, the nation and world as a whole. The 7-year-old with the paint-spattered shirt and flapping shoelaces today is the potential shop assistant, business executive, builder, social worker or dentist of tomorrow. Everyone in society benefits from a good academic, moral and social education. Your job is to assist in providing it.

Good practice

Get into the habit of commending children as much for their kindness, thoughtfulness and the effort that they make to succeed as for the quality of their academic work.

Commitment to pupils

Fairness and trust

All teachers need to demonstrate that they are committed to ensuring pupils are given the opportunity to achieve their potential and meet the high expectations set for them. This priority must also apply to trainee teachers when they enter school on teaching placement. From start to finish you must not only want to benefit children's learning but strongly demonstrate that this is so by your words and actions.

When children meet a new teacher, they want to know whether she or he is going to be fair with them, keep control of the class and provide interesting lessons. Part of your task is to convince them that you will do all of the above, but it will take time to overcome children's understandable reluctance to entrust themselves wholeheartedly to someone before being certain that the person is fully reliable. A small number of trainee teachers have a lot of commitment to the job but little understanding of the way that children react, learn and think. Some trainee teachers have an intellectual grasp of teaching but lack the personality to inspire children in the classroom, while others have understanding and enthusiasm but cannot provide the orderly framework for effective learning and therefore struggle with class discipline.

Clarifying expectations

It is one thing to claim that you are enthusiastic about teaching the children; it is quite another to demonstrate it in the daily encounters with children in what is often a high-pressure classroom environment. Commitment is a professional as well as a moral choice and involves ensuring that your planning is thorough, that you are clear about the teaching approach you intend to adopt (and why) and, in presenting lessons, that you take full account of children's learning needs and preferences. Important elements of the quality assurance process include the following:

- stating clearly to children that you want to help them do well;
- insisting of them that they have a responsibility to do well;
- explaining how they can improve their standard of work by offering them strategies for doing so;
- showing children examples of good quality work and clarifying your expectations;
- offering constructive feedback about their progress and encouraging them to self-evaluate.

Engaging with pupils

In providing this support, remember that enthusing about high standards, improvements, expectations, aiming high or any other superlative will have little impact upon your pupils unless you can succeed in convincing them that these outcomes are worthwhile. Your commitment needs to be transformed into pupil *self-commitment* as they catch your enthusiasm and zest for learning. It is quite common for the same set of children to underachieve with one teacher and excel with another. There is no secret attached to this anomaly. It is simply that the first teacher has engaged with the children and transmitted a 'can do' message, whereas the second teacher has not. The best teachers will always:

- take a keen interest in the standard of a pupil's work and make constructive comments about its quality and, where appropriate, how it can be improved;
- use discipline strategies that avoid humiliation or repression yet maintain consistent control, producing a healthy respect in the children for the teacher as leader;
- answer children's questions helpfully, in which case the child is more likely to venture other questions and see the teacher as an ally, and not as a detached assessor.

Whereas weaker teachers tend to:

- tolerate sloppy standards of work, with the result that the child gains the impression that 'good enough' is all that is expected or required;
- use harsh control methods without taking account of the circumstances thereby, producing fear or resentment in the children;
- ignore or fail to explain and answer questions clearly, in which case the child is likely to feel that it isn't worth making the effort and avoids asking questions in future.

It is also a sad fact of life that some brighter pupils will make minimum effort to reach a satisfactory standard of work when, with greater determination and application, they could achieve far more. The reasons behind this apparent apathy are complex but tend to have their origin in one of three sources: (1) the children do not want to be considered 'swots' or gain a reputation for being too keen on pleasing the teacher; (2) the children find the tasks too easy and can comfortably negotiate them without applying their minds; (3) the children dislike or resent the teacher and use apathy to express the way they feel. If you meet such children – and you will do – don't despair! Read on.

Providing security

Children like teachers who are fair-minded, interested in them as people, transparent in their dealings, clear about their intentions, helpful in their explanations, non-judgemental in their words and unflinching in confronting situations when it is necessary. Fisher (2005) argues that there are occasions when all learners feel vulnerable and need to be reassured. Thus:

> Time spent on building a sense of inclusion and trust is time well spent. Learning is not easy to achieve at times of emotional disturbance or social disruption. If emotional needs are ignored, the energy of the learner is deflected away from his or her capacity to accomplish learning tasks.

(p. 138)

Children are not looking for 'pals' but for approachable, dependable adults who can be relied upon to give and take, provide a relevant learning environment, give credit where it is due, act swiftly to combat unacceptable behaviour and show that they value each child. Furthermore, children are drawn towards teachers who are interesting and interested people. The more that you can use your talents, gifts, experience and knowledge of the wider world in your teaching, the more likely that the children will come to view you as an adult who deserves their loyalty and best effort. It is a mistake to think that maintaining a suitable 'distance' from the class necessitates becoming detached and mechanical; in fact, nothing could be further from the truth.

Activate your thinking!

Use your talents to enhance your teaching and reputation, not to bolster your ego.

Good practice

Stand physically close and face to face with children (though not intimidatingly so) when you are speaking to them or listening to them.

Non-conformist children

Regardless of the care with which teachers handle their day-to-day encounters, there will always be some children who find it difficult to conform or (more seriously) deliberately resist all attempts to help them do so. Some trainees become dispirited when their sincere attempts to support and encourage particular pupils are rebuffed or even scorned. It is important to bear a number of considerations in mind as we examine these important issues. Fuller exploration of these issues is found in Chapter 12.

Misbehaviour

Classroom misbehaviour is many teachers' secret fear. The prospect of indiscipline affects both teachers and children: teachers, because they want to avoid being humiliated; children, because they do not always possess the life skills or strategies to avoid confrontation, steer clear of trouble or helpfully influence the behaviour of their peers. This last point is particularly important, for although a teacher may speak of a class of children as being 'difficult', it is often the case that the problems are confined to a very small number whose influence in the classroom gradually becomes pervasive. While it is true that a minority of children are reluctant to obey, won't listen to adults and prefer to antagonise other children rather than conform to the rhythm of classroom life, the vast majority of children are desperate for the security that comes through effective teacher control. Be careful not to be drawn into constant criticism of a class, even if the regular teacher tends to do so.

We need to be realistic here. Some children are unpredictable and restless; others are born wanderers; some seem unable (perhaps, are unable) to sit and concentrate for long, which might indicate that such pupils are struggling with hyperactivity; a very small number will delight in making life difficult for the teacher, regarding it as a personal challenge to see what they can get away with. It is also true that despite a teacher's best efforts to make lessons relevant and interesting and to create a positive working environment, there may still be children who persist in inappropriate behaviour. For this troublesome minority, there are usually sanctions that can be applied, varying from school to school, but such procedures can be time-consuming and wearisome (though sometimes necessary). In truth, most teachers have no desire to impose a strict regime upon the class if it is possible to avoid it, and would prefer to coax, persuade, encourage and set targets for achievement as a means of keeping children on the straight and narrow. Such action nearly always pays dividends with most children and increases the likelihood that the environment will be relaxed and purposeful, though the rewards are not usually immediate and you will need to persevere.

It is worth reflecting upon the fact that a disruptive child might be used to different codes of behaviour outside school – the degree of strictness employed, use of threats, loudness of verbal exchanges, imposition of sanctions. The accumulation of these emotions, experiences and expectations from home are brought into school and a child may find it genuinely difficult to adjust to different expectations and the need for conformity in school. Such tensions are commonplace and teachers require time and perseverance as they attempt to explain the rules to confused children or to insist upon them with uncooperative ones. This is not to argue for a weak and passive approach to children's misdirected energies but rather to look behind the action and acknowledge the factors contributing to the behaviour before deciding upon appropriate steps.

Despite the temptation to become gloomy about the attitude and behaviour of a minority, it is far better to stress positive aspects of children's actions whenever possible. In particular, it is worth remembering that as well as academic achievements, social successes and responsible behaviour are an important part of a child's full education. As James and Brownsword (1994) rightly remind us, not all children know how to behave; positive reinforcement of the appropriate behaviour of pupils by brief, sincere words of praise can spur other children to adjust and improve their own behaviour. Behaviour management and discipline are dealt with more fully in Chapter 12.

Cross-reference: Guided Reader Extract 50

Success and failure

I like going to school because my teacher tells us to have a go and do our best, then she helps us when we are stuck.

(Clarissa, aged 8 years)

Finding success

Success in learning is the ultimate goal for everyone involved in education, but defining it is difficult. Definitions might include statements such as, 'when things turn out as well or better than expected' or 'achieving what you aim to do' or 'growing, developing, improving and getting better'. Pupils in school often equate success with the pleasant sensation of getting good grades, ticks on a page, commending comments or tangible rewards, such as stickers and house points. Some children find fulfilment in completing a piece of academic work accurately; others in solving practical tasks; yet others in sealing and affirming personal friendships.

Perseverance

Most children are willing to persevere with their work for three principal reasons: (1) to achieve something worthwhile for their own satisfaction; (2) to compete with their class-mates; and (3) to please the teacher. Some children are strongly self-motivated and gain enormous pleasure in achieving something by their own efforts. They show a relentless deter-mination to do well and relish the opportunity to demonstrate their competence publicly. Some children are highly competitive and view every task as a challenge to outperform everyone else. It is not possible to prevent children from being single-minded and it can act as a spur to achievement, but if being ahead of others becomes the dominating factor it can lead to an unhealthy situation in which individuals are vying to complete work quickest or gain the best mark, with scant regard for those around them.

Self-fulfilment

The majority of children want to please their teachers: in most cases because they like them, in a minority of cases because they fear them. While it is obviously desirable for children to want to seek a teacher's approval, it is more important for a child to seek *self-fulfilment* than to hanker after adult approval. You have an important role in encouraging children to feel proud of their achievements, however modest, to allow a degree of competitiveness without tolerat-ing rancour and to acknowledge their successes warmly and wholeheartedly.

Judging success

In its purest form, judging success should lie *within* each child and the degree of satisfaction that she or he feels after completing a task. McNamara (1997) rightly reminds us that if aca-demic attainment is influenced by self-worth, then 'it is possible that a focus on raising self-esteem ... could provide an increase in academic achievement' (p. 73). Consequently, teachers have to exercise fine judgement when offering feedback to children about their work and effort. At one level there is a need to explain to the child how the work can be improved. At another level there is a pressing need, especially with children who have experienced limited academic success in the past, to encourage, praise and celebrate achievement. Katz (1995) suggests that we strengthen and support a healthy sense of self-esteem in children in at least seven ways:

1. Help them to build healthy relationships with peers.
2. Clarify your own values to them and those of others that may differ.
3. Offer them reassurance that your support is unconditional.
4. Appreciate, rather than merely praise, their interests, and avoid flattery.
5. Offer them opportunities to face challenges as well as to have fun.
6. Treat them respectfully, take their views seriously and offer meaningful feedback.
7. Help them to cope with setbacks and use the knowledge they gain to advantage in the future.

Mastery and helpless children

Dweck (2000) points out that children's sense of self-competence and self-efficacy begins to develop from an early age and can have a significant impact on their attitude to learning.

The author suggests that when faced with difficulty or potential failure, children tend to react in one of two ways. The first is when children display a 'mastery-orientated' attitude, characterised by increased effort; the second is when children display a 'helpless pattern' of behaviour. Mastery-orientated children do not blame themselves for not doing well, whereas helpless children feel personally responsible and are reluctant to persist with the task. According to Dweck, mastery-orientated children engage in self-motivating strategies, self-instruction and self-monitoring. They remain confident of success and learn from their failures rather than allowing them to undermine confidence in their own abilities. By contrast, the helpless type of children denigrate their abilities, quickly lose confidence, focus on failures rather than successes, soon lose heart and even abandon successful strategies (see also Robson 2006). It is therefore essential to know your pupils sufficiently well to ensure that your responses and comments are appropriate.

While the categorisation into 'mastery' and 'helpless' does not tell the whole story – such as the way that some children are masterful under one set of circumstances and helpless when faced with another – it alerts us to the different approaches adopted by pupils and helps to explain why some children inexplicably abandon their work and others appear almost arrogantly confident. One important role is for you to get alongside the unhappy child and provide careful advice and feedback, without seeming to 'mollycoddle', and to ensure that the self-confident children are set high standards, so that they don't sacrifice accuracy for the sake of speed.

Background influences

We have already noted that not all children feel equally comfortable in school and this sometimes leads to problems in attention span and conforming to adult expectations. If pupils have come from home backgrounds in which schooling is not considered to be a priority, it is almost certain that their brothers and sisters will exhibit similar nonconformist tendencies and colleagues might even refer to the whole family in terms of being 'a difficult lot'. Many of these unsettled children, though enjoying the companionship and informal opportunities which school provides, fight shy of the formal learning process and question the need to complete tasks that appear to have little relevance for them. Try not to view their negative comments or expressions of dissatisfaction as a personal affront; instead, explain calmly that certain things are necessary even if they don't have immediate appeal. Of course, it helps enormously if you can present learning in such a way that pupils can see its relevance.

Coping with failure

It is important to appreciate what is involved in a child's reaction to *failure*, not least the bearing it has on pupil morale and behaviour. It doesn't take too much imagination to grasp what it is like to be constantly near the bottom of the pile: often coming last, unable to compete with more able classmates, hearing little but criticism from exasperated adults, struggling to make an impression, taken off for 'booster' classes by well-meaning assistants, and over time wondering if their academic struggles are a reflection of their inadequacy as a person. Is it any wonder that a child, after a few years of this type of experience, decides that it simply isn't worth making the effort to conform to the demands any longer? Better, surely, to put his or her efforts into other more interesting and rewarding activities like disrupting the class, spoiling someone else's work or finishing the set task in rapid time with minimum effort in order to move on to an interesting activity. Other children resort to daydreaming or adopt a detached approach to work and may be diagnosed as having an 'attention deficit' (see Chapter 12); yet put the same children with so-called attention deficit disorder in an environment of their choosing and their concentration span is apparently endless.

If adults find failure hard to cope with, it is not surprising if children need help if they are to avoid spiralling into a negative attitude towards schoolwork and adults in school (see, for example, Pye 1987; Varma 1993; Roffey and O'Reirdan 2003; Lloyd 2004). Dalton and Fairchild (2004) offer helpful comment in respect of maintaining a positive climate:

> Some of your best teaching flows spontaneously from your deepest intuition. At its core, teaching is the artistry of creating experiences that lead people into greater awareness. It's an artistry of knowing the moods, needs and expectations of your pupils, while staying fully aware of your own.
>
> (p. viii)

Perceptive and caring teachers, by their attention to the children's individual needs, can play a major role in preventing children from becoming despondent and losing motivation to learn. Houghton and McColgan (1995) suggest that adults can help alleviate children's anxieties by being calm when dealing with their fears, trying to avoid giving the impression that the child is somehow to blame and sensitively encouraging them to 'approach what they fear' (p. 41). Grossman (2003) stresses the need for genuineness of character in teachers, arguing that the pupils soon detect whether they can trust a particular teacher. By ensuring that you are one such trusted teacher, you will be in a strong position to reassure all children that you have their best interests at heart.

Activate your thinking!

Personality is defined by the way you behave in public view. *Character* is defined by the way that you behave out of it.

Good practice

Speak informally over a period of time to a small group of sensible children who are willing to talk naturally about their views of school and other aspects of life. As the conversations unfold, listen carefully to the comments they make that give clues to the insights they possess and the things that matter to them. Reflect upon the impact that such awareness might make on your attitude to the children in your class.

Friendships

From the most immature nursery child to the boldest adolescent, friendships form a significant element of school life. Children rely heavily upon their friends for companionship and, perhaps, for assistance with work. Young children feel more secure when sitting by their best friend; older ones like to be accepted as a member of the group or one of the gang. Although these patterns of relationship are evident in the classroom, it is often during activities that take place outside the classroom that we see the most obvious examples of relationship bonds and failures, such as when children select partners or team members. While some children are sought after and cheered enthusiastically when chosen, others are regularly ignored, chosen last or grudgingly accepted into the team. Competitive children, in particular, can be surprisingly harsh with one of their classmates whom they perceive as being a weak link.

The intensity of friendship patterns and preferences is evident from an early age but intensifies across the primary phase. As alliances and rivalries develop over the years, older children can become entrenched in their views of particular individuals, for good or ill, and sometimes animosity spills over into aggression. Whereas most reception class children will accept their allocated partner, the emergence of prejudice towards children who are 'different' from the majority needs firm, sensitive handling as children move through the school. Negative racial stereotypes are relatively rare during infant days but can become embedded during the upper stages if left unchecked. Most schools have policies to ensure equal opportunities but the teachers' attitudes are an essential factor as they seek to engender a caring and positive environment. Common challenges for teachers of younger pupils include those who:

- become distressed if separated from a classmate on whom they rely;
- physically cling to a friend;
- become upset when someone they want to be their friend chooses not to be;
- do not appear to have a close friend and use the teacher or classroom assistant as a substitute.

Teachers of older children face other challenges with children who:

- opt to work alone and resist collaborating with others;
- will only select the activity preferred by their friends, regardless of their true preference;
- become over-reliant on a friend for academic support;
- struggle with limited success to enter a friendship group;
- behave out of character in order to be accepted by others who exhibit similar behaviour patterns;
- become separated from friends when classes move up at the start of a new academic year.

A friendless child is one of the saddest sights in school. You can help the situation by fostering a climate of 'united we stand', of which friendliness and helping each other becomes an integral element. Children will always have special friends, of course, but a classroom in which everyone is respected helps to create an *inclusive* environment in which no child is excluded or marginalised (see also Chapter 13). Many schools foster a system of *peer mediation*, by which there is a school-wide system of mutual support and pupils trained and designated to act as peacemakers and arbitrators to work alongside adult workers to diffuse conflict and reconcile differences.

Despite your best efforts, there are bound to be times when children fall out with one another, disagree and get upset. Adults have an important role on such occasions to provide a calm and reassuring presence and encourage reconciliation. This process is not always straightforward, especially when children have become over-excited or intensely angry, but there is little point in adding to the conflict by becoming fierce yourself. A composed presence pours oil on troubled waters. As a new teacher you may even find yourself feeling a little intimidated, especially if older pupils speak aggressively and walk away when you are speaking to them or, in rare cases, attack one another in front of you. There are guidelines for action contained in the school's policy but you do not have the luxury of consulting the relevant documentation and must rely on exercising sound judgement on the spot. The key is to deal with the primary behaviour (i.e. the first offence) and protect children from injury, and not worry too much about the secondary behaviour (i.e. subsequent behaviour arising from the first offence), such as foul language, abusive remarks or defiant body language. These issues can be referred to in due course when things are calmer.

Good practice

Encourage a 'count to ten' policy when dealing with irate children. React but don't over-react to the situation. Do not threaten sanctions or give stiff warnings until things are more settled. Make your principal aim one of *resolution* rather than *reprisal*.

Bullying

The word 'bullying' is used to describe a range of circumstances in which the child's welfare is at risk (Sharp *et al.* 2002). Murphy and Lewers (2000) point out that bullying is not confined to mainstream school but can also apply to the pre-school, though in a different form. It is sometimes difficult to discriminate between high spirits and bullying and all children have squabbles that to adult eyes look more serious than they are to the adversaries. Typically, the animosity is forgotten within a short time and the two opponents become the closest of friends. On the other hand, there are situations that can cause long-term distress and unhappiness for children. Rigby (2001) argues that it is important to deal with bullying because it has three potential adverse effects. First, it lowers mental health. Second, it induces social maladjustment. Third, it creates physical illness. Sanders (2004) offers the following observation:

> Most definitions of bullying categorise it as a subset of aggressive behaviour that involves an intention to hurt another person ... [however] ... Not only can it be displayed physically but it can also be subtle and elusive.
>
> (p. 4)

Sanders goes on to warn that 'emotional harassment is much more difficult to identify and prove but should still be included under the definition of bullying' (p. 5). Barton (2006) is more expansive in her definition of bullying to include 'any behaviour that results in physical or emotional injury to a person or animal, or one that leads to property damage or destruction. It can be verbal or physical' (p. 6).

Forms of bullying

Although there are some children who always seem to be in scrapes, it is not always helpful to refer to them as 'bullies' as this can become a label or stigma which hinders them from throwing off their bad reputation and establishing a more positive image. It is better to speak about 'bullying behaviour' with reference to a particular circumstance. Child 1 may bully child 2 who then bullies child 3. In these particular cases, some children are victims, some are bullies and some are both. The situation is made more difficult in that bullying tends to be selective and the pupil who causes grief to one child may be delightful with another.

Regardless of subtle differences in interpretation, bullying is one of the most difficult experiences in a child's life, subordinate only to domestic upheaval (notably, in-fighting and separation). The impact of deliberately hurtful behaviour, repeated over a period of time, where it is difficult for those being bullied to defend themselves, cannot be overestimated. Forms of bullying tend to be described under one or more of three headings: (1) physical bullying, including hitting, kicking and theft; (2) verbal bullying, including name-calling and racially offensive remarks; and (3) indirect bullying, such as spreading rumours. Lawson (1994) suggests that there are three types of bullies: aggressive bullies, anxious bullies and passive bullies.

The *aggressive bully* is potentially the most serious category, as weaker children may be physically injured. Aggressive pupils are often badly behaved in school and require close supervision and monitoring throughout the day. Controlling aggressive bullying must involve the whole staff to ensure that the malefactors are made to adhere to a strictly enforced set of rules governing their behaviour. Parental involvement is also essential in setting targets for improvement. It is fair to add that aggression often lies deep within a child owing to a variety of factors, including brain damage, a dysfunctional family life and abusive situations outside school. It is not easily resolved and requires specialised support.

Anxious bullies see themselves as failures or fear humiliation and vent their frustrations on other children by saying unkind things and undermining their achievements by use of sarcasm or mockery. It is often younger, vulnerable children (unlikely to retaliate) who are subjected to their taunts. It is natural to be repulsed by such behaviour but, as the responsible adult, you need to help this type of bully to gain self-esteem by placing them in a position where they can succeed. Paradoxically, these pupils often relate well to much younger children, who therefore pose no threat to their self-worth, in a structured environment, closely supervised by an adult who can monitor the situation and offer encouragement and direction.

Passive bullies are the 'support' members of bullying groups but not the initiators. The term 'passive bully' is not wholly satisfactory as it implies that such types are less guilty than their leaders. Nevertheless, it is probably true to say that many passive bullies do not particularly relish their role and would prefer to spend their time doing more constructive things. Their fear of losing credibility with the aggressors and perhaps becoming victims themselves if they don't co-operate with the more assertive partner deters them from breaking free. Teachers and assistants need to help passive bullies to develop new friendships by providing them with positive alternatives and ensuring that they have a busy, interesting schedule, especially during break times. It is sometimes appropriate to give them a specific duty that keeps them separate from undesirable influences: for example, tidying library books and sorting equipment. Needless to say, the principal characters in any gang need to be dealt with firmly, but it is important to identify the root causes of the bullying behaviour if long-term solutions are to be found.

Strategies to contain bullying

Thankfully, aggressive bullying is rare in primary schools, but it is important to remember that the types of behaviour which emerge during primary school are likely to be continued once pupils transfer to secondary education and create a climate of fear and uncertainty for the victims (Balding 1996). Parents and adults in school need to be alert to common signs that children are victims of bullying; the symptoms include regular headaches, stomach aches, anxiety and puzzling phases of irritability. Parents who suspect that their children are suffering are encouraged to contact the school immediately. All adults are keen to promote not only a bully-free classroom but also a safe school environment (Varnava 2002; Lee 2004). Teachers can make a considerable difference by modelling behaviour which shows that they value individual children and by actively confronting any unsatisfactory situation using strategies such as:

- listening carefully to explanations, especially from the victim;
- offering opportunities for children who have been bullying others to become involved in positive, supportive activities;
- clarifying expectations about mutual respect and tolerance;
- monitoring the bullied children to ensure that they do not, in turn, bully others.

One of the problems facing teachers in knowing how to deal with aggressive acts (physical or verbal) is that bullying becomes a learned behaviour that eventually acts like a stimulant; in short, bullying becomes enjoyable for the perpetrator. If bullying is not dealt with sooner rather than later, it becomes habit-forming and intervention to stop it being repeated becomes more difficult. Although pernicious bullying and frequent unsatisfactory behaviour which brings distress to others cannot be tolerated, the children concerned must also be shown that there are benefits attached to kindness, consideration and self-sacrifice that cannot be experienced by tormenting someone weaker than themselves. For some bullies this is a hard lesson to learn. Racist bullying is an unpleasant area of school life that has received a great deal of attention in recent years. All schools have to demonstrate that they not only have a policy to combat such behaviour but are active in ensuring that it is implemented and monitored.

Cyberbullying

In recent years, so-called 'cyberbullying' has become a serious issue for teachers and parents. Cyberbullying has been variously defined as the use of an Internet service or mobile technologies, such as email, chat room discussion groups, instant messaging, webpages or SMS (text messaging), with the intention of harming another person, emotionally and psychologically; the use of information and communication technologies to support deliberate and hostile behaviour by an individual or group intended to harm others. High-profile cases of young people being hoodwinked into relationships over the Internet with unscrupulous adults have alerted us to the latent problems that exist for unwary or naive individuals. Additionally, various forms of technology have been employed to send insulting messages or publish unedited photographs and short films about individuals as a means of intimidating and alarming them. Cowie and Colliety (2010) suggest that although there is a case for creating sanctions to discourage inappropriate use of ICT, adults in school also have a critical role to play in preventing and reducing cyberbullying through a process of awareness-raising, the education of the emotions and active participation of children and young people themselves in finding resolutions.

As teachers become aware of the power of friendships and the fears, frustrations and joys of complex child–child relationships, they discover that it is essential to pay attention to their consequences, for better or worse. Children do not attend school solely for developing friendships but attention to the implications arising from the quality of relationships is important in the quest for a good teaching and learning environment (Pollard and Filer 1996; Mosley and Sonnet 2006; Hewitt 2007). Bullied children, whatever the cause, will underachieve and be miserable not only in school but in life generally. They deserve and expect protection from adults.

Activate your thinking!

Which children tend to be marginalised? What practical steps can be taken to help them develop secure friendships?

Good practice

Place heroic and successful characters who are fine examples of decency and self-less behaviour at the heart of your teaching. Promote honour and compassion as essential, not optional, for a happy life.

Cross-reference: Guided Reader Extracts 17 and 18

Citizenship

An important dimension of children's education is developed through citizenship, which in Key Stages 1 and 2 is non-statutory but, in reality, is pursued by all primary schools. The QCA provided a scheme based on twelve individual units, including topics as diverse as 'Choices', 'People who help us' and 'Local democracy for young citizens'. Under the banner of PSHE (personal, social and health education) and citizenship, the National Curriculum non-statutory guidelines provide a framework for Key Stage 1 and for Key Stage 2 under two main headings:

- Knowledge, skills and understanding
- Breadth of study.

The first of these, knowledge, skills and understanding, incorporates four sub-areas:

1. Developing confidence and responsibility and making the most of their abilities
2. Preparing to play an active role as citizens
3. Developing a healthy, safer lifestyle
4. Developing good relationships and respecting the differences between people.

For each sub-area, there are details about what pupils need to be taught. For instance, under 'Developing confidence and responsibility', younger primary children should be encouraged to recognise what they like and dislike, what is fair and unfair, and what is right and wrong. They are also to be taught ways of sharing their opinions, to deal with feelings positively, to recognise what they are good at, and to set themselves simple goals. Older primary children are to be invited to express their opinions and explain their views in writing, identify positive things about themselves, make responsible choices and be responsible about the use of money.

In 'Preparing to play an active role as citizens', younger primary pupils should be taught how to take part in discussions and debates about topical issues, to recognise choices (options/alternatives) and follow group decisions. They also have to be helped to realise their responsibilities to others, to be alert to environmental effects of their actions, to contribute to class and school life, and to understand the place and purpose of money. Older primary children have to be taught how to discuss and debate issues based on research evidence, to understand rulemaking, to realise the consequences of antisocial behaviour and to recognise their responsibilities to the community. They should also be helped to reflect on spiritual, moral, social and cultural issues, to make informed decisions, to understand the meaning of democracy, to recognise the place of voluntary and pressure groups and to appreciate ethnic and religious diversity. Finally, older primary children should have a grasp of economic realities and explore how the media present information. This range of expectations provides a considerable challenge for any teacher and can only be achieved by incorporating several of the elements into a single theme or topic.

Under 'Developing a healthy, safer lifestyle', younger pupils should be taught how to make simple choices that improve health and wellbeing, maintain personal hygiene and to understand how diseases spread and can be controlled. They also have to be alerted to the ageing process, names and parts of the body, harmful household products and rules for keeping safe (including road safety). Older primary pupils should be told about the benefits of exercise and healthy eating, safe routines for minimising the spread of disease, changes to the body as puberty approaches and the availability and effects of common drugs. They also have to be taught about risk assessment, appropriate physical contacts, resisting pressure to do wrong and where to get help (e.g. from teachers, Childline).

Under 'Developing good relationships and respecting differences', younger primary pupils should be taught to recognise how their behaviour impacts upon others, to listen, play and work co-operatively, to identify and respect differences and similarities. They should also be taught about the importance of caring for friends and families, that all forms of bullying are wrong and how to get help to deal with bullying. Older pupils should be alerted to the impact of their actions, to think about the lives of people in other places and times, to be aware of different kinds of relationships and to realise the effect of racism, teasing, bullying and aggressive behaviours. See earlier in this chapter for a fuller discussion. They should also be taught to recognise and challenge stereotypes, understand differences between people groups and know where individuals, families and groups can get help and support.

Finally, for children in Key Stages 1 and 2, there is information about the opportunities that pupils should experience to be taught the knowledge, skills and understanding under the heading 'Breadth of study'. Thus, younger primary pupils should have opportunities to:

- take and share responsibility through, for instance, being given specific classroom tasks as a monitor;
- feel positive about themselves through, for instance, celebrating their own and others' achievements;
- take part in discussions through, for instance, making decisions about class rules;
- make real choices through, for instance, selecting which piece of equipment to use during break time;
- meet and talk with people through, for instance, organising pairing with older children in the school as buddies;
- develop relationships through work and play through, for instance, collaborative investigations and problem solving;
- consider social and moral dilemmas through, for instance, the use of story in which the principal character has a difficult decision to make about an issue;
- ask for help through, notably, adult approachability and a learning climate in which pupil questions are welcomed and encouraged.

Older primary pupils should have opportunities to:

- take responsibility through, for instance, assisting with the management of outdoor equipment or assisting younger pupils;
- feel positive about themselves through, for instance, being provided with the necessary skills to produce a high quality practical product;

- participate through, for instance, giving a short presentation about an area of interest from outside school;
- make real choices and decisions through, for instance, setting their own work targets;
- meet and talk with people through, for instance, inviting guests (e.g. older members of the community, artisans, local celebrities) into lessons;
- develop relationships through work and play through, for instance, team-building exercises;
- consider social and moral dilemmas through, for instance, organising discussions about child-relevant issues;
- find information and advice through, for instance, use of information technology;
- prepare for change, especially in orientating to new situations (e.g. moving class or school).

Assessment of children's progression in citizenship is in terms of what knowledge and understanding most children should have to become informed citizens. Thus, Key Stage 1 children should be able to talk about and consider topics and issues, to begin to show understanding of issues such as fairness and rules, and begin to show understanding of values (notably, concern for others). Children in Key Stage 2 should be able to investigate topical issues and show understanding of rights and responsibilities and values. In respect of demonstrating skills of enquiry and communication, Key Stage 1 children should be able to respond to simple questions and explain their views and to listen to the views of others. Key Stage 2 children should be able to take part in discussions and debates, talk and write about their opinions, ask and respond to questions and understand different viewpoints.

You could be forgiven for thinking that if the non-statutory guidelines were followed thoroughly, there would be little time for anything else to be included in the curriculum. In practice, a number of elements of citizenship are incorporated into assembly times, special projects (such as those dealing with neighbourhood issues; see Hicks 2001) and the warp and weave of daily school life governed, for instance, by behaviour policy and inter-personal relationships. See Alderson (1999) for further insights into issues concerning children's rights.

Teachers helping children

Teaching is not the seamless robe official publications present as being normal and achievable. Owing to the fact that every child is unique, pupil learning is often unpredictable and difficult to assess formally, the teacher's role is a demanding one and every teacher has to be alert to the moment-by-moment needs of each child. Despite the fact that staffroom shelves are groaning with the weight of numerous publications and policies, all claiming to help teachers understand that particular teaching approaches are desirable, the way that children learn best and the implications for classroom practice, the truth is that all teachers rely to a large extent on a cultivated instinctiveness to guide their actions, which are nurtured and honed through months and years of direct experience with children. External forms of advice and knowledge about the work of a teacher ought to be sought and evaluated, but in practice, teachers and assistants know 'their' children and organise things accordingly. This simple truth explains why every class and classroom is subtly different and attempts by external bodies (governments, local authorities, etc.) to enforce particular approaches are counter-productive. Consistency of approach is different from 'sameness'. A casual visitor will be aware that classroom 'atmospheres' differ, but there are important differences between teaching situations that appear, superficially, to be almost identical.

Whatever the nature of the curriculum, the teacher's role is, of course, critical to the process of pupil learning, which results from varied factors (adult knowledge, pupil dispositions, resources, teacher personality, etc.) but is crucially about what motivates and enthrals 'this' child. During a single session, teachers play a variety of different roles, which closely relate to the need for children to learn in particular ways and to deepen their understanding over time. Teachers may act as informer, demonstrator, facilitator or interpreter. Each role carries with it a special emphasis (see Figure 3.1). As these teaching techniques are refined, the children's learning will also be enhanced and enriched (see Figure 3.2).

The stages presented in Figure 3.2 are not in watertight compartments, for during a lesson there will be opportunities for all of them to be woven into the fabric of the learning process. For instance, if the teacher's role is principally that of *informer*, the children's understanding will be limited by what the teacher tells them. However, as a *demonstrator*, the teacher not only tells but also provides evidence to support the claims. In the role of *facilitator*, the teacher establishes the circumstances and provides active support through timely interventions and guidance so that pupils can explore and experiment and investigate processes for themselves. If the role is extended to incorporate *interpreter*, the children's understanding will be deepened as the teacher helps them to make sense of all their learning opportunities and locates it in a wider context. All four roles – informer, demonstrator, facilitator and interpreter – may be evident during a single session, though one will normally predominate (Dean 2008). Judging which teaching role should be adopted with which children requires sensitivity and awareness, and is one of the more important strategy decisions teachers have to make, explored more fully in the next chapter.

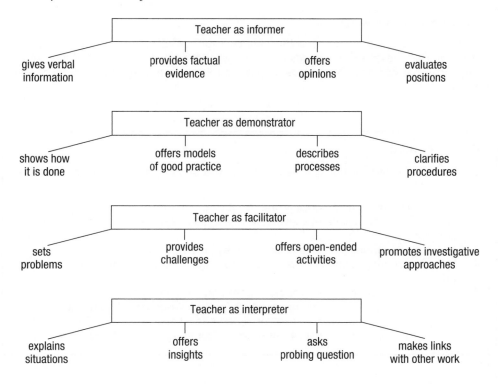

FIGURE 3.1 Teacher roles

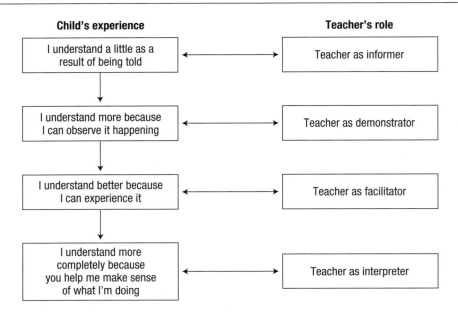

Child's experience / **Teacher's role**

I understand a little as a result of being told ←→ Teacher as informer

I understand more because I can observe it happening ←→ Teacher as demonstrator

I understand better because I can experience it ←→ Teacher as facilitator

I understand more completely because you help me make sense of what I'm doing ←→ Teacher as interpreter

FIGURE 3.2 The relationship between teacher role and child experience

Activate your thinking!

Note how experienced teachers subtly vary their tone of voice, body language, speed of speech and length of explanation according to the child concerned. Watch how they move backwards and forwards across the roles in response to the needs of the moment.

Good practice

To develop effective relational skills that assist you in being a good teacher, practise the following:

1. Learn each child's name quickly and use it respectfully.
2. Get down to the child's eye level and make 'soft' eye contact where practically possible.
3. Listen more carefully; do less talking and less interrupting.
4. Use appropriate vocabulary and a natural tone of voice, especially with older pupils.
5. Be sincere in your manner of speech, behaviour and attitude.

Based on an article by Glen Woods (n.d.), '5 relational tools to make you a better teacher', *Ministry-to-Children.com*, http://ministry-to-children.com/relational-tools-better-teacher/.

Promoting play

All children love to play, such that if a younger child stops doing so, adults become anxious about the situation and wonder if the child has a problem. Playing is an essential element of child development and wherever children are found – in every home, park, pre-school, nursery – play of some sort is evident. Most teachers of young children use play as a vehicle for enquiry-based learning; teachers of juniors tend to encourage play within the confines of a controlled learning environment such as drama.

The significance of play in school has sometimes been a source of disagreement between teachers and parents, and even between teachers. Expressions such as 'She went to school but only played' and 'We didn't do any work, we only played' indicate the way in which play is perceived: that is, as a time-filling activity without educational value that has no place in the school curriculum. The vast majority of teachers, however, view play as an essential part of the educative process and a powerful learning agent.

Directed or spontaneous play

One of the challenges facing teachers of younger children in particular is the extent to which play should be directed or should be spontaneous. Left to themselves, children normally play unprompted and create imaginative situations out of the most ordinary conditions (Duffy 1998). Some teachers argue that play is not play unless it is free of adult contrivance, arguing that even if they try to intervene in a play situation they receive short shrift from assertive infants. For these teachers, manipulating play situations undermines its purpose and produces an artificial learning environment. They argue that children should be liberated to explore and come to terms with ideas without hindrance. In such classrooms, young children are found busily involved in a variety of activities: sand and water play, construction kits and toys, or dressing-up. Noise levels sometimes become high and the teacher, who may be giving an individual pupil close attention or working with a group on basic skills, may choose to ignore the free play activity. Under such conditions, permission for children to spend time in free play is used as a reward for task completion or good behaviour.

Other teachers argue that the extent of the play should be closely controlled and monitored by the teacher. For example, a specific range of games can be provided and activities are deliberately limited by the provision of certain resources and the exclusion of others. Play outcomes are targeted in terms of measurable learning outcomes that relate to social harmony, respect for property, tolerance and so forth. Play is seen as an opportunity for children to work through situations, solve problems, employ their imaginative powers to come to terms with new or exciting situations and exercise authority over confusing circumstances, bewildering paradoxes or worrying uncertainties. For these teachers, children use play to confirm ideas, create solutions and extend their thinking. Teachers use the opportunity to interact with the children, listen to their language and questions, and determine the extent of their understanding. Play thereby becomes a teacher-influenced strategy for learning rather than a completely child-directed one. Macintyre (2011) argues that understanding children in their own context underlies decisions for intervention or non-intervention in their play, which must be carried out sensitively and in a manner that supports and extends their learning. The development of emotional intelligence (see Chapter 4), gender bias and making friends are significant factors in helping children who find play difficult.

Broadhead and Burt (2012) argue that as children become familiar and skilful within open-ended play environments, their co-operative skills gradually develop as they become connected to a particular community of learners. In addition, parents' knowledge and understanding of playful learning helps to build a bridge between home and school.

Activate your thinking!

The 'Reggio Emilia' vision of the child as a competent learner has produced a strong child-directed curriculum model in which teachers follow the children's interests and do not provide focused instruction in reading and writing. Children learn through interaction with parents, staff and peers in friendly settings, where a great attention is given to the look and feel of the classroom in an atmosphere of playfulness. See Thornton and Brunton (2009) for details about applying the approach when working with young children.

Thornton, L. and Brunton, P. (2009) *Understanding the Reggio Approach*, London: David Fulton.

Good practice

Drake (2003) provides advice about implications for the Foundation Stage. She offers suggestions about key areas of learning, resources, preparation, use of vocabulary and activities. Crucially, the author refers to the essential role of adults and follow-up ideas that build on the basic play activity; offers guidance on planning display as part of the curriculum; and suggestions about observing, assessing and recording and reporting. A later publication (Drake 2009) incorporates key points for good practice in each chapter together with direct links to the Early Years Foundation Stage 'Principles into Practice' cards, as well as the professional standards.

Drake, J. (2003) *Organising Play in the Early Years*, London: David Fulton.
Drake, J. (2009) *Planning for Children's Play and Learning*, third edn, London: David Fulton.

Outdoor play

Outdoor education is defined as learning that takes place outside the classroom door. Its benefits include behaviour modification, self-esteem, teamwork development, challenge and self-knowledge. Cramp (2008) describes how the greatest benefit is learners' personal development, as pupils cultivate 'multidimensional views' of teachers, which lead to 'warmer personal relationships, a challenge to labelling and the potential for risk-taking back in the classroom' (p. 180). In her exploration of personal values associated with the outdoors, Waite (2011) refers to freedom and fun; ownership and autonomy; authenticity; love of rich sensory environment and physical challenges. Children begin life as exploratory learners and enjoy the rich experiential qualities of outdoor contexts. Bilton (2002) offers details about design and layout of an outdoor play environment and discusses ways in which personal, social and emotional development, movement and thinking, bikes, fixed equipment and play scenarios can form an integral part of children's learning. See also Featherstone (2001) for suggestions about hundreds of ideas for making the outdoor area into an exciting garden for all children.

Cross-reference: Guided Reader Extract 11

Play in the school day

The place of play in the school day will depend upon the age of the children and the teacher's education philosophy. Very young children enjoy the freedom that comes from playing without restraint and a teacher may decide that this reason is justification in itself, in which case the children are offered the opportunity to use toys and equipment whenever it is practicable and desirable. Younger children, who are familiar with school routines and able to cope with more structure, may be allocated play opportunities on a rota basis or as a reward for working hard, though there is a tendency for children to rush to complete the formal task if they know that extra time to play is an incentive. Sometimes a Foundation Stage teacher needs the space to concentrate on the academic learning needs of a particular group and allows the others to play as a 'holding task', though such a strategy is criticised by purists.

Older children, too, need a chance to play, and although this normally has to be reserved for timetabled break times, the skilful use of improvisation and role play in drama offers them the chance to relax and enjoy the spontaneity while performing an academically purposeful activity. However, Cohen (2006a) warns that we cannot assume that play is necessarily beneficial; thus, 'at what point does larking about start to seem threatening' (p. 139)? Adults need to be alert to occasions when children's natural liveliness and testing of social situations deteriorates into over-assertiveness or even bullying.

Whatever form of organisation pertains, the chance for children to take control over their learning with minimal adult intervention and imposed structure is an essential element of young children's social and intellectual development. This fact is probably truer for play than any other experiential learning.

Cross-reference: Guided Reader Extract 2

Making decisions about, for and with children

Despite a lamentable tendency by some adults outside school to treat children as adults-in-the-making, they are not. It is true that, like adults, children get confused, bewildered, overwhelmed and elated; sometimes they excel; sometimes they struggle with work and their emotions; sometimes the world can seem a confusing, contradictory and rather scary place. However, unlike adults they do not have the life experiences, wisdom and broad perspective to make well-informed decisions, so as the responsible adult, you often have to make decisions on their behalf or direct them to make sensible and wise choices. Children are capable of understanding situations and reaching decisions that sometimes amaze and astound us, so supportive intervention does not mean that children should be denied a voice or that they cannot offer their ideas, insights and suggestions; on the contrary, such contributions should be fostered and encouraged. Your role is one of guardian, guide and guru: as guardian to protect pupils from harm; as guide to point them in the right direction; and as guru to use your superior understanding and knowledge to help shape their thinking.

Active intervention

There are occasions when a pupil will be perplexed by a relational or academic situation and needs your active intervention to resolve the issue or untangle the confusion. If children trust you, they won't be afraid to ask for your advice and check that what they are doing is appropriate. In recent years there has been a trend towards teachers concentrating on the planning, teaching and assessing dimension of the job and assistants taking responsibility for what might be broadly termed the 'pastoral' side. Such distinctions are unhelpful. To a child you are the key person in the classroom and although you will and should delegate tasks to other adults, it is counter-productive to give children the impression that while you are concerned with their achievements, you are unconcerned about their general welfare. This approach is rooted in the fact that a contented child invariably makes better progress academically than a restless or unhappy one. The following list is typical of the experiences and situations that require such interventions, with suggestions about how you might respond:

A child is perplexed because she has lost an envelope containing money

First, make sure that the money really is lost, as apparently lost items are often in the bottom of a bag or a pocket. If possible, check with an older brother or sister or invite an assistant to investigate; ask the school secretary or administrator to contact the parent or try to make contact directly. It is commonly argued that teachers should not deal with such trivial matters; but the matter is not 'trivial' to the child concerned, so must be treated with calm urgency.

A 7-year-old girl complains that a 'funny man' shouted at her outside the school gate

Ask gentle questions about the circumstances; find out without fuss if any other children saw the incident; ask if the man has been there before; if uneasy about the matter, make sure the incident is reported to a senior colleague or to the head teacher immediately; if reassured, log the incident in the book with full facts but without expressing an opinion.

A top junior boy is sulky and refuses to work because he has not been chosen for the school team

Talk the matter through with the boy; ask the games teacher concerned to speak to him; allow him time to get over the disappointment. On a later occasion, speak to him again and monitor any subsequent reaction. If you are in a position to do so, offer some guidance about how he might improve his football skills. Suggest that the best way to be noticed is to be encouraging towards those who are selected and to cheer them on rather than stand sulking. It won't be easy for him. Such matters are of major significance in some children's lives and can adversely affect their work and social relationships if unresolved. Be patient, but if the behaviour persists make achievement in his work a condition of future selection.

A reception-age child continually cries because he wants to go into his older sister's class

This phase usually passes quite quickly. An arrangement can normally be made with the other class teacher to allow occasional access for the purpose of reassurance. Playtime usually offers more opportunities for interaction, so help the child to look forward to this time. A sensitive teaching assistant or playground supervisor will often play a 'surrogate sister' role until the child is calmer. At all costs avoid dismissing the child's concerns as unnecessary; try instead to involve the child in interesting work with other children and foster friendships in the classroom.

A girl who is weak academically produces a wonderful clay model

Celebrate! Contact parents as soon as possible through a congratulatory note, telephone call or face-to-face encounter. Take a photograph of the girl holding the finished model (after checking school policy on photographing children). Ask her to write a large label to accompany the model (if necessary assisted by a more able helpful child). It is important not to miss the opportunity that these critical events afford, so milk them fully, then move on and encourage the child to further achievements for her prestige and self-image.

A boy who was formerly well behaved suddenly begins to behave erratically

The change of behaviour may well have more profound causes. Seek advice from senior colleagues immediately. It is quite likely that the cause lies outside school and contact with the parent is needed; if so, it is wise to do so in liaison with a more experienced teacher. Children sometimes exhibit erratic behaviour if they are victims of bullying, though a more common reaction to suffering is withdrawal and sullenness. If you feel that the child is behaving that way because he is seeking entrance to a gang of 'lads' and wants to 'prove' himself by being unhelpful or rude, make a special effort to praise his sensible behaviour, initiate class discussions about people who were brave enough to say no, and keep a diary of incidents. In the meantime, do not hesitate to rebuke his misdemeanours and impose sanctions for any wilful misbehaviour. Sometimes, a quiet discussion with him conducted away from classmates has the desired effect.

A 4-year-old boy starts to soil himself

Soiling is a humiliating and frightening experience for a child. Provide reassurance and ask an assistant to deal with the matter discretely. Make contact with the parent the same day; ascertain from colleagues whether there have been previous incidents; inform the head teacher if the problem continues. An isolated incident is probably not significant but repeated instances might indicate that there is a more serious issue as the root cause.

A 10-year-old boy with a good voice won't join the school choir

Many older boys lose interest in singing, much preferring sport. The more that singing is a fun element of classroom life, the more likely that boys will retain their enthusiasm for it. Teachers responsible for music and running choirs do well to consider the choir's image and give serious thought to its repertoire and the way it is perceived by all children throughout the school. Mention it to the parents next time you see them if necessary and cheerily encourage him in their presence but without pressure. Further information about singing in school can be found in Chapter 6.

A 9-year-old girl is crying because (she claims) her mother won't let her have a birthday party

Listen carefully to the child; explain that you are sure there is a good reason. If you are on good terms with the parent, quietly mention the matter to her. Generally speaking it is not worth becoming embroiled in domestic matters of this kind unless you have a concern over the child's welfare or conduct. Perhaps you can mark the occasion in class, though be careful not to exceed what would normally be done for other children or it might trigger envy or set a precedent that cannot be maintained.

An 11-year-old boy is heard describing an adult film in graphic detail to his friends

Ask the child directly and unthreateningly whether he saw the film. Ask whether he had permission from a parent to see it. Discuss the issue with the head teacher before taking any further action. The head teacher will know the family and, if relevant, be in a position to gain informal advice from social services. Unless you suspect that there is abuse, it is difficult to do much more than tackle it indirectly through the personal, social and health education curriculum. Quite often an older brother is the source of the problem. Although some efforts have been made in recent years to curb the volume of unsuitable material accessible to children, the reality is that it is difficult to prevent it happening.

Money goes missing and one boy is accused by several classmates

Calm the situation and do not allow pupils to make loud and public accusations. Gently but firmly ask the child if he knows anything about the matter but avoid making accusations; insist that he looks into your eyes when he answers, unless the child is from a culture where direct eye contact is considered impertinent. It is normally better to do this in private, though practically it might prove difficult to do so. Avoid giving the impression that you secretly agree with the accusers. Treat all instances of theft seriously, including those of children's snacks. Persevere with exploring the circumstances with the help of an assistant or colleague until the matter is satisfactorily resolved. Once a child begins to steal it can become an obsession and difficult to prevent it from recurring. Remember to log the incident.

A 10-year-old boy starts to draw weird doodles on scraps of paper

Chat informally to the child about the drawings before deciding whether to seek advice. Images of this kind may be a short-lived phase or can indicate latent psychological problems. If the child has a talent for drawing it might be possible to divert his efforts more constructively and use his creativity in a positive way (e.g. to design a class logo or create 'friendly' cartoons). Some pupils learn best through visual means, so apart from signalling any deeper meaning, drawing images might indicate the child's preferred learning style (see Chapter 9).

An 11-year-old girl, through silliness, breaks an expensive piece of science equipment

It is normally better to console the child rather than condemning her. After the lesson speak to her and explain your disappointment with the silly behaviour. Sensible children who behave out of character will normally confide in their parents about an incident of this kind, so don't be surprised if the parent contacts you afterwards. Although a school can insist that a breakage be paid for, it is often not worth the trouble unless there is a serious matter of principle involved. Again, a senior colleague will offer advice about such matters. Make sure that the girl has opportunity to redeem herself as soon as possible after the incident; she will probably make every effort to do so and your reasonableness will secure her loyalty.

A 6-year-old boy, new to the class, swears when the teacher rebukes him for aggressive behaviour

Firmly explain that such language is not used in school; reinforce this from time to time during the coming days. When younger children use unsuitable language, they have normally acquired it from home in the first place. A child new to school will need time to adjust to the differing expectations. The aggressive behaviour is a more urgent issue and the school's discipline policy will come into play, which may involve the special educational needs co-ordinator (SENCO) if it continues. In the meantime persevere with a 'we are kind to each other in this school' approach. If other children are being hurt or intimidated it is essential to take immediate action and, as so often the case, involve a more experienced colleague and/or assistant. Issues relating to behaviour management are addressed in Chapter 12.

An 8-year-old girl is regularly a few minutes late in the morning

Ask the child why she is arriving late; consult with teachers of her brothers or sisters and with the school administrator/secretary to see if they are also arriving late. If you are a new teacher to the school or a trainee, find out if there is a history of poor timekeeping. In some families, especially where parents leave for work early in the morning, the eldest child has the responsibility for ensuring that the younger ones get to school, sometimes resulting in lateness. If you have concerns about the children's welfare, the head teacher needs to know and will likely pursue the case and may suggest that the family takes advantage of the 'extended school' facilities (e.g. breakfast club or one of the after-school clubs) if available.

A reception child frequently falls asleep during the afternoon story

Speak privately to the parent as soon as possible. Some small children simply get tired and need to sleep. Remember that at one time it was normal for all younger children to 'take a nap' in the afternoon. Even some adults have this problem! Other children stay up too late due, perhaps, to being the youngest in a house full of noisy siblings. Falling asleep may also indicate the presence or imminence of ill health, so it pays to log the occasions and work closely with an assistant where possible to monitor the child's level of activity throughout a day.

Deciding what to do

As a guide to appropriate action, the child's immediate safety is always of prime concern. Once this is secured, the child's longer-term security needs to be considered. From this point onwards, any decisions will depend upon the circumstances of the case, bearing in mind agreed school policy, previous experience of similar incidents and your own judgement. It is usually better to err on the side of caution but avoid being alarmist. The 'funny man' outside the school gate may have been a harmless passer-by with an unusual appearance – or a child molester. The boy describing the contents of an adult film might be unsupervised at home – or have been told the story by his older brother and was showing off to his friends. The reception-aged child falling asleep might be kept awake at night by noisy neighbours – or suffering the effects of a hot and stuffy classroom, and so forth. Naturally, if you have suspicions that a parent might be the cause of the distress or responsible for a child's unsettled behaviour, it would be inappropriate to contact that person directly. Always take advice from an experienced colleague, tutor or the head teacher and monitor the situation informally while advice is sought from the appropriate social service. Trainee teachers do not need to become embroiled in the detail of procedures and processes but have the same responsibility as every other adult to ensure children's physical and emotional wellbeing. You wanted to be a teacher; well, this is part of the job.

Cross-reference: Guided Reader Extract 12

Case study

In many ways Jonny was the ideal pupil and just the sort of 9-year-old that any teacher would want in the class. He related well to his peers and also to adults. He worked hard and used his natural intelligence to maximum effect. Jonny always strove to achieve a high standard, was sensitive to people's feelings and would apply himself to sporting events with great enthusiasm and competitiveness. Jonny was socially aware in that he fitted in well with any group and was popular with his classmates. Jonny was a capable footballer and a member of the cross-country running team. At the end of the year the teacher, Geoff Anscot, was genuinely saddened when Jonny moved on to the next class.

Twenty years later Geoff was walking through an indoor market when he heard a voice call out to him from behind one of the stalls. It was a beaming Jonny, who to Geoff's eyes did not look all that different from the pupil in shorts that he remembered. After they had exchanged pleasantries, Jonny told Geoff proudly that he was now the owner of three small businesses that he ran from different markets. Jonny laughingly described himself as an entrepreneurial market trader. Geoff wondered what Jonny would remember from his days in the class and hoped that he might say something positive. (Even the best teachers need to be reassured sometimes.) Although Geoff recalled the time when Jonny had been in his class as if it were yesterday, for Jonny the same time period composed the majority of his lifetime. It was not long before Jonny's eyes glazed over as the memories flooded back.

'You used to play your guitar in assembly.'

'Yes, that's right, we had some good fun.'

'Mmm. We practised the play for Christmas.'

'Yes, I remember,' the teacher replied.

'And you used to run the football team.'

'Yes, I was a bit slimmer then. You were a good player.' Geoff waited, hoping that Jonny might refer to the excellent learning experiences he had in class, but Jonny's priorities were different. Instead, Jonny's mind was saturated with the fun he had experienced, the personal interactions, the joy of being part of a team, the excitement of public performances in front of the rest of the school, parents and friends. Jonny reminisced about the times that the teacher took them out of school on short trips to explore the lanes and bring small treasures back to examine in class, mount them on displays, create large books with pictures and photographs, and include snippets of writing and photographs. Jonny's memories were full of the things that still served to motivate and inspire him.

What will today's children remember of their schooldays? What will be of value to them in five, ten or thirty years from now? School-based education must be an enabling process that creates a desire in children to discover more about the world and to learn skills and attitudes that will ensure a more productive and harmonious society. Education should excite in children a belief that life has purpose and liberate their imaginations and creativity. Every adult in school is making an important contribution to each child's present and future. As Geoff said goodbye to his former pupil, he felt quietly satisfied that at least some of his aspirations had been fulfilled in Jonny.

Further reading for Chapter 3

Casey, T. (2007) *Environments for Outdoor Play*, London: Sage.
Contains ideas for developing play environments and deals with issues such as inclusion and playground management.

Cheminais, R. (2006) *Every Child Matters: A practical guide for teachers*, London: David Fulton.
The book provides a range of practical resources, including sheets to photocopy and solution-focused advice, which support teachers trying to keep pace with the legislation regarding the *Change for Children* programme.

Cullingford, C. (2008) 'A fleeting history of happiness: children's perspectives', *Education 3–13*, 36 (2), pp. 153–60.
The author argues that teachers who make a habit of inviting children to express their views are often surprised by the perceptiveness and certainty of their comments.

Robson, S. (2006) *Developing Thinking and Understanding in Young Children*, Abingdon: Routledge.
Combines introductions to theories about thinking with observations taken from classroom practice.

Willan, J., Parker-Rees, R. and Savage, J. (eds) (2007) *Early Childhood Studies*, second edn, Exeter: Learning Matters.
Reflects the multi-professional, multi-disciplinary scope of early childhood studies.

4

The Teacher

Introduction

The content of this chapter introduces a range of issues that are expanded in later chapters, but primarily examines aspects that relate to the person of the teacher. A starting point is that the teacher's role is of supreme importance in determining the quality of children's education, so much so that Richards (2009) describes the teacher as 'a frighteningly significant person whose teaching helps to shape attitudes to learning at a most sensitive period in children's development' (p. 20). Whatever else might be claimed about teachers, they are never forgotten by their pupils, as even elderly people will relate incidents from their schooldays that have remained in their minds and hearts throughout life. The positive impact of a good, caring teacher on children's wellbeing cannot be underestimated; unfortunately, the impact of a poor, negative teacher can be equally devastating. The content of this chapter will help to ensure that you are remembered for all the right reasons.

Becoming a teacher

Some people have a sentimental view of the task that teachers face. Visions of children's gentle, eager faces lifting their trusting eyes to gaze expectantly at a much-loved adult, and waiting on her every word, are sometimes far removed from reality. Teachers have to be tough, persevering and determined. The rigours of daily classroom life and the demands of thirty or more children of varying abilities, personalities and enthusiasm can be a daunting business for even the most capable and committed practitioner.

On the other hand, teaching is an important job that offers great reward and satisfaction. There is probably nothing to compare with the thrill of introducing children to new and exciting worlds of learning and to see the glow on their faces when understanding dawns. Teachers might not be admired by all their pupils but most of them are held in high esteem, and the things they say and do are repeated endlessly at home. It might sound rather quaint, but teaching really is a way of life; once you have entered the world of school, things will never be quite the same again. Equally certain is the exciting truth that most children do not forget their teachers. Fifty years and more from now, many children will still speak some of their teachers' names, and refer to their character and the effect they had upon their lives. When much else in life is forgotten, the memory of a teacher lives on. In a quotation from one of his respondents, Cotton (1998) offers an example of the essential characteristics that teachers must put across to the children if they are to earn a special place in pupils' memories:

All have human qualities; they made us feel good about ourselves; they made us see things are possible and they justified our existence as unique human beings, not simply faceless pupils.

(p. 42)

Passion in teaching

Nambiar (2008) argues that good teaching is as much about passion as it is about reason. It is not only about motivating learners but also teaching them *how* to learn, and doing so in a manner that is relevant, meaningful and memorable. Good teaching is not just mastering techniques, utilising resources and having a working knowledge of the curriculum; it also involves keeping abreast with recent developments and being at the leading edge of knowledge as far as possible, eliciting wholehearted responses from pupils and developing highly tuned oral communication skills, especially with less confident children. Even in situations dominated by academic priorities, a good teacher's cheerfulness and optimistic approach can transform a child's attitude and offer much-needed hope and inspiration.

Building a relationship with children takes time and effort. No one can claim the automatic right to be a respected teacher; it has to be earned and, for a trainee teacher in particular, there is little time in which to do so owing to the short-term nature of a school placement (see Hayes 2009a). If there is no mutual adult–child appreciation, then pupils take little account of what a teacher or assistant says, fomenting antagonism and sour relationships. Some inexperienced teachers become despondent when their attempts to establish good relationships with the children are initially rejected. Yet it may be that the class has had some unpleasant experiences with adults and will take quite a lot of convincing that a newcomer is more trustworthy than previous ones. Or perhaps they were very happy when they were with their previous teacher and are less certain about the new teacher's capacity to create such a pleasant atmosphere. Then again, it might be that particular children are shy or fearful and can't respond naturally to a stranger, so they adopt a passive or aloof posture until they feel more secure. In a small number of cases, it can be that certain children are using emotional blackmail – 'I'll give you the satisfaction that comes from seeing me happy and responsive in exchange for staying off my back and not expecting too much from me.' Wright (2006) describes the damaging consequences attached to being a 'passive' teacher:

> The passive teacher is characterised by efforts to be popular that include ingratiating herself. She will have fragile feelings and will take criticism badly. She will plan her lessons in great detail but is not a forward planner in terms of managing the behaviour of her class. She ends up having to react to incidents and usually does it badly because she has not worked out her responses.
>
> (p. 58)

You need to discriminate between children's tentativeness and their wiles. A demonstration of integrity and consistency will convince most children that a good relationship with you is worth the effort, though there may be one or two children who are dismissive of your overtures despite you trying your best to establish a bond with them. If you meet such children it is unwise to dwell unduly on the situation, but rather to persevere to establish a working relationship with them by being relaxed but purposeful, showing flair in your teaching and being clear about where the boundaries of acceptable behaviour lie. Children who are initially reluctant to reciprocate are sometimes the ones with whom you ultimately develop the closest bond, so don't despair. Crucially, don't give the impression that you are trying to win their affections; allow it to happen naturally as the children realise that there is more to be gained from being co-operative than from being awkward.

Procedures and rituals

Every school has its codified and unwritten rules and regulations, which trainee teachers and newly appointed teachers to a school have to make sure that they do not unwittingly contravene. It is worth keeping a record of the procedures and rituals that you observe in the classroom and around the school to avoid too many embarrassing moments when you inadvertently cross the boundaries owing to your ignorance of situations that others take for granted. Most children are ready and willing to offer you information about specific aspects of classroom life, and a friendly member of the support staff will usually alert you to school-wide issues if you ask. It is important not to underestimate the significance of these 'concealed assumptions' in a school, as adherence to them is sometimes unfairly used as an informal measure of a trainee teacher's suitability for teaching. The reason for particular ways of working and attitudes that initially appear strange usually becomes clear after a time. Although every school is inclined to fall into patterns and procedures that would benefit from reconfiguration, it is also true that things happen as they do because it has been found to be the best way to operate.

In particular, knowing about the school policy for discipline and the use of sanctions may avoid problems of inconsistency between you and the class teacher. Children might alert you to the mismatch when they protest by saying something to the effect, 'Miss does not let us do that.' Whoops! If you feel strongly about an issue it is best to tell the children that you will talk about the matter to the teacher and then make a decision, rather than publicly face down the protests on the spot. If you are a newly appointed teacher you might encounter a similar situation but the children will then refer to what their previous teacher allowed. In such a situation you can say that the new conditions pertain because the children are older now, or something similar. On the other hand if (for example) there is an accepted way for children to move around the school (to assembly, say) it is essential that you uphold the required code of behaviour.

Eventually, you must decide upon what you will permit, tolerate and forbid. Reaching such a position involves a degree of trial and error, so don't be dismayed if at first you make a lot of 'error' and it becomes something of a 'trial'. Things will improve if you persevere and learn, rather than agonise over your mistakes.

Activate your thinking!

It has been said that the person who never makes a mistake never makes anything!

Good practice

At first, imitate what colleagues do then very gradually introduce your own ideas. If you are a trainee or new teacher, always discuss strategies with the regular teacher before making significant changes.

Cross-reference: Guided Reader Extract 46

Guiding principles

If anyone suggests to experienced primary teachers that the job is quite straightforward pro-viding they follow procedures as laid down in a document, book or theory, they will prob-ably show that person the door (once they have stopped laughing). In fact, the job of teacher is extremely complex and the act of teaching cannot be reduced to a formula. It requires an array of skills and strategies, thorough and ongoing reflection and no small degree of trial and error. See Chapter 9 for detailed information about teaching skills. Teachers are also learners, and the best teachers show a hunger to find out more about what works best and how they can be even more effective. Once teachers stop thinking about their work, they quickly slip into a dull routine and become tediously predictable. To stay bright and alert you should regularly review the following areas:

- Attitude to learning
- Your reputation
- Commitment and enthusiasm
- Safeguarding children
- Establishing a working relationship
- Attitude to achievement
- Encouragement and praise
- Equal opportunities.

Each of these areas is now considered in turn.

Attitude to learning

Learning does not happen in a vacuum. Teachers need to be clear about the conditions that contribute towards a satisfactory learning environment. Decisions about five key issues are needed: (1) the best conditions for learning; (2) the degree of co-operation and competition; (3) motivation strategies; (4) the criteria used to evaluate success and failure; (5) acceptable behaviour. Thus:

The best conditions for learning

Learning takes place when pupils are well motivated, convinced that the lesson content is worthwhile and clear about what is expected of them by the teacher. If the work is intrins-ically interesting there is less need to explain why the learning is necessary; if the work content does not have immediate appeal you will need to persevere to convince pupils that it is worth trying hard (if only to finish and get on with something more engaging). Pupils make most progress when the challenges they face are manageable and allow them to use their knowledge, skills and understanding to achieve the lesson targets and, ideally, to use their initiatives to delve further into the content area. Children learn best when sessions are fun or, at least, not boring. They like working with their friends where possible and respond to an enthusiastic, committed teacher who introduces ideas in an original way through, for example, use of visual aids, drama, poetry, telling a story, asking a question, and so on. At the risk of being unduly simplistic, it is fair to say that learning happens best when pupils want to learn and happens less when they do not.

The degree of co-operation and competition

Nearly all children want to do well at school. The only exceptions are a small number who are thoroughly miserable or emotionally unsettled. In some classrooms there is a notable co-operative spirit and children are generally courteous and kind to one another; in others, there seems to be an underlying tension and unhealthy rivalry that leads to sullenness and resentment. The ideal situation is one in which pupils are mutually supportive and celebrate other children's success as well as their own. Although competition provides an important element of a pupil's desire to accomplish more and aspire to greater heights of scholastic and sporting achievement, children also need time to relax and have fun. Teachers who achieve this happy state do so through perseverance, modelling an appropriate attitude to their pupils, and valuing children over and above their ability to attain academically.

Motivation strategies

One of Aesop's fables concerns a dispute between the sun and the wind, as to which could make a man walking along the road remove his coat. The wind tries desperately to get the man to oblige by blowing harder and harder; but the man simply wraps the coat more tightly around him. The sun shines brightly and within a short time the man has taken off his coat. Motivation rarely increases as a result of threats or compulsion unless the pupil is intent on being disobedient. The child who is motivated to learn will be more influenced by the warmth of a teacher's personality and encouragement than by icy threats. The greatest motivator should be self-satisfaction, but it sometimes needs a helping hand.

The criteria used to evaluate success and failure

One child works hard and achieves little; another makes minimum effort and achieves a lot. A teacher's attitude to each child will reveal a great deal about the criteria that the teacher is using to evaluate success; praise for the latter and criticism for the former will send a signal that attainment is singularly important as a measure. It is all too easy for teachers unintentionally to make children feel that their worth as a person is directly linked to their success in their schoolwork. Some children like to experiment and do things in a non-conventional way. As a result, they may make more mistakes than their more conventional peers but enjoy a richer learning experience overall. Be careful that you credit children for showing initiative as well as achieving the correct results. Success takes many forms: a task competently performed; a concerted effort to reach a solution; a flow of creative ideas; unusual insights to problem solving; and sheer perseverance to do better.

Acceptable behaviour

It is important for teachers to establish basic classroom rules so that every pupil is clear about what is acceptable and appropriate. This does not mean that there will not be infringements from time to time. Teachers have to decide almost instantly whether a particular behaviour warrants a warning or scolding or raised eyebrow or whether it is best ignored. Inexperienced teachers find it hard to know what actions to overlook and what deserves an immediate response. Though some behaviour is wholly unacceptable at any time and under any circumstances, many forms are merely reflecting a child's immaturity or lack of self-control. Whatever you decide, be adamant that it is children's co-operation you seek, not their indulgence.

Firmness in the early stages may avoid the need for strictness later on. As a rule poor behaviour should never be overlooked other than in exceptional circumstances. It may be that you will decide to speak quietly to the child at the time, or perhaps on a later occasion to avoid spoiling the lesson flow, rather than to utter a public rebuke. A more sophisticated consideration of behaviour factors involved in effective learning is considered more fully in Chapter 12.

Activate your thinking!

Perseverance is an important factor in gaining success and most children are willing to persevere with their work for one or more of four reasons: (1) to achieve something worthwhile for their own satisfaction; (2) to compete with their classmates; (3) to please the teacher; (4) to gain a reward. What motivates your pupils to persevere?

Good practice

Look for things in a child's work and attitude to praise and commend, as much as things to criticise and deplore.

Your reputation

It is said that a reputation is what others think of us and a character is what we are really like, so perhaps the sub-heading for this section ought to be 'character' rather than 'reputation'. Nevertheless, as a new teacher in school you will need to build a reputation quickly: among adults, so that you are treated with respect; among children, so that they grow to like or even love you in the same way they might love a favourite aunt or uncle – but always with a slight sense of awe. It is a mistake to become too much like a 'pal', even if initially it makes you feel good; under such conditions, it is more than likely that you will end up having difficulty with class control and feeling emotionally ragged.

The impression you create

Pupils frequently talk about their teachers. Parents ask their children searching questions about how their day has been and what their teachers are like. Any teacher who wants to play a positive role has to recognise that reputations grow as a result of incidents and responses to situations over a period of time. It is not easy to be a new teacher in school and establish yourself as equal to the existing staff, but it is worth considering the impact that your presence has on the classroom situation. For instance, the way that you dress and conduct yourself, the tone of voice you use, the way that you react to challenges and your attitude to other adults all contribute to the impression that you create. Although you might be more concerned with lesson planning and the mechanics of teaching than you are about how you are perceived by others, the advantages gained through building a good reputation are considerable:

■ Children are proud of you as their teacher and develop a healthy attitude towards learning.

- Children talk positively about you at home, thereby giving encouragement to their parents and constructing a climate of confidence.
- Gossip at the school gate about your competence is passed from parent to parent so that they are eager for their children to be taught by you.
- The host teachers relate to you as a colleague as much as a student.

For a qualified teacher in school, there are additional benefits:

- Parents and children look forward to being in that teacher's class.
- The head teacher is able to speak of the teacher in glowing terms to governors, visitors and prospective parents.

Different perspectives about teachers

A good reputation is not easily established, especially if you are only working in the school for a short period of a teaching experience. Nevertheless, factors such as appropriate relationships with children, adequate preparation for lessons and a positive personality are all relevant factors. The comments and perspectives of five different groups of people on the subject help to illuminate some of the key issues:

From a 4-year-old: 'I like my teacher. She lets us do painting and tells us stories.'

From an 8-year-old: 'My teacher's good. She teaches us to do things and doesn't mind if we talk to her. We do science and make things and we have a laugh sometimes. She's not exactly strict but she doesn't like us to muck about or she can get really cross. She's all right, though, and I like her because she likes us.'

From an 11-year-old: 'My teacher's quite cool. He does sports and stuff with us and tells us really terrible jokes! He's good at helping us with maths and gives you a chance to explain if you're stuck. I don't like it when he gets mad, but it's quite funny sometimes!'

From a parent: 'Lisa's teacher, Mr Andrews, is very nice and friendly. He said at parents' evening that he was really pleased with Lisa's progress and that her maths was improving. He said she was near the top in some subjects and one of the best readers. They went on a trip to the zoo and Lisa really enjoyed it. And when Lisa was unhappy about swimming, he phoned me up and asked to have a chat so we could sort things out and Lisa was fine afterwards. He's strict sometimes but the children think he's great.'

From a teaching colleague: 'Bella's a super teacher. She's got a marvellous way with the kids, somehow, and she really knows her stuff. She's also very creative and seems to have the ability to get children to think deeply and speak confidently. She and the TA did an incredible display for parents' evening, but she still had time to help the newly qualified teacher sort out her reports. The thing about Bella is that she's always got time for you. It doesn't seem to matter how busy she is, you always feel that she's interested in what you've got to say. She's the same with everyone – kids, staff, visitors, cleaners – I don't know how she does it. Even when she's stressed out, she can always raise a laugh! Hope she stays here but I bet she won't.'

From one of the ancillary staff: 'Mr Ryan's lovely. He always speaks to you and smiles. He treats you fairly and remembers to say thank you. He's really appreciative if you do something and doesn't mind a joke every now and then. Mind you, he's a good teacher and keeps order. I was with Mrs Burton last year and it was terrible. She's very nice and friendly but can't control the class at all. I can work with Mr Ryan; you know where you stand with him.'

From the head teacher: 'I appointed Lela four years ago and she settled down well. She got stuck in straight away and wasn't afraid to ask for advice. Even when she was struggling a bit last year with a difficult class, she was very tenacious and kept going when many of us would have been tempted to give up. Parents like her because she's friendly and efficient and says positive things about the children. She's great at fetes and open evenings because she takes an interest in people and always has an encouraging word to say. In fact she's very much a "people person" but doesn't patronise them. As the head teacher, I'm happy because the children learn well with her, she works hard, plans thoroughly, keeps her records up to date and is popular with parents. It's good to have someone so reliable on the staff team who is also willing to learn and take advice. Her comic sketch at the end-of-year concert last term will stay with me forever!'

Reputation and teaching ability

Reputation also has implications for the quality of your class discipline, not least because children, even young ones, quickly decide between themselves which teachers are 'soft' and which teachers have to be obeyed. The most formidable reputations are based on a combination of teaching effectiveness (including an emphasis on interaction with pupils and collaborative activities) and personal qualities. Gill (1998) captures the essence of the issue: 'One of the best ways to eliminate discipline problems is to have a reputation as a good teacher who tries to make learning enjoyable but who will do what she says she is going to do' (p. 42). Sarason (1999) suggests that both teachers and pupils (the audience) should participate in what he calls 'the performance'. Thus:

> Audiences are silent performers. They are silent but not passive; at least they did not come expecting to be inwardly passive. They come expecting to see themselves and a slice of life differently. They do not expect to be bored, unmoved and sorry they came.
>
> (p. 14)

Sarason's description of an audience and performer is easily transposed to the classroom. Pupils have to *believe* in the teacher and be engaged in the proceedings. They are not passively going through the motions of 'being taught' but active learners trying to make sense of concepts, ideas and situations for themselves. In doing so they need to be interested (if not fascinated) by the curriculum, drawn into the lesson through the enthusiasm and authenticity of the teacher and contributing to the proceedings, as invited to do so by the teacher. The use of dialogue in classrooms to explore, test, shape thinking and tease out the unexpected is one such way to ensure that the audience of children is transformed into performers.

Other methods to heighten pupil involvement include free play, experimenting with materials, working co-operatively, collaborating on investigative projects and developing new approaches in solving problems. In developing and extending these approaches, it is important to remember that giving children opportunities to explore and be creative does not guarantee satisfactory outcomes or deep forms of learning (see Kaldi *et al.* 2011). Children can spend hours in aimless (if interesting) pursuits; they can respond to teachers' questions superficially; they can avoid taking risks; they can cloak shallow thinking in a frenzy of activity that yields little in positive learning. Or they can become so enthralled with opportunities to explore and engage with learning that they develop a level of enthusiasm and knowledge that far exceeds anything likely to be achieved under more pedestrian conditions.

Cross-reference: Guided Reader Extract 16

Commitment and enthusiasm

We have noted that it is important for teachers to set a good example to pupils and impress parents and colleagues by the way they present themselves and their general conduct in school. A small number of teachers spend time complaining about poor working conditions, the government, the head teacher and (sometimes) the children. If you encounter such pessimism, it is best to politely avoid being drawn into the conversation, even if you have some sympathy with what is being said. Wise teachers allow themselves the occasional moan but do not let it become a habit or sour the atmosphere. It is surprisingly easy to slide into a negative spiral and depress both yourself and colleagues by constantly complaining, so persevere to make sure that the majority of your comments are positive ones. It takes effort to develop a healthy outlook on life, but the effect can transform the atmosphere and give hope to you and to others. As a trainee teacher you must strike a careful balance between listening sympathetically to colleagues' comments and maintaining a purposeful outlook on life. Do not be fooled into thinking that you will endear yourself to this glum minority by being as miserable as they are sounding. In fact, you will simply gain a reputation as a complainer and may be perceived as a habitual grumbler. By contrast to the despondent practitioner, Fried (1995) promotes the concept of the 'passionate teacher', who is characterised by a positive attitude towards life. Thus:

> To be a passionate teacher is to be someone in love with a field of knowledge, deeply stirred by issues and ideas that challenge our world, drawn to the dilemmas and potentials of the young people who come into class each day – or captivated by all of these. A passionate teacher is a teacher who breaks out of the isolation of a classroom, who refuses to submit to apathy or cynicism.
>
> (Prologue)

Research into the attitudes of host teachers in primary schools who work with trainee teachers indicates that they value a number of characteristics in trainee teachers who are placed in their schools (Hayes 2002), of which the following eight attributes are particularly significant: (1) adopting a forthright attitude; (2) staying focused; (3) showing concern for children; (4) enjoying the work; (5) behaving courteously; (6) monitoring your own learning; (7) extending the professional role; (8) expressing appreciation. Thus:

Adopting a forthright attitude

Trainee teachers should make sure that they get 'stuck in' from the very start, show a genuine interest in what the children are doing, stay calm, poised and vigilant. They should volunteer for jobs where appropriate, including the messy ones. They should not, however, give the impression to the children that they are content to be assistants or helpers. Trainee teachers should let the teacher see that they mean business but avoid becoming so frantically active that they unsettle the classroom atmosphere.

Staying focused

Trainee teachers should offer help, advice and expertise to the children whenever possible and make every effort to concentrate their attention on the work in hand and not be distracted by peripheral matters. If, in the early days of the school placement, while the regular teacher is leading the lesson, children start to show off or behave in a silly fashion, trainees should walk away and help another child. Although a pleasant adult–pupil working relationship assists learning, it should be made abundantly clear that the children are not at liberty to tease trainee teachers, treat them like a favourite cousin or initiate conversations that have nothing to do with the lesson content. Experienced teachers soon discover that the sweet child who asks innocent questions one day can be a source of disruption the next if allowed too much leeway. You need to learn the same lesson fast.

Showing concern for children

Children quickly sense if adults really care about them or if they are putting on an act. Teachers should show that they like the children by establishing bright eye contact and taking an interest in their activities, but avoid being sucked into trivial conversations. When children approach you to ask for guidance, it is right and proper to smile invitingly and offer help willingly, but also to take care that you do not end up doing the work for them. There is a fine line between demonstrating a sincere desire to be helpful and becoming a walking encyclopaedia! Details about the issues attached to intervening in pupils' work can be found in Chapters 9 and 11.

Enjoying the work

Trainee teachers should make it clear to the teacher that they are enjoying their time in school and appreciating the opportunities it presents. Those who speak and act to show that they are keen to be in the school will receive a sympathetic response from the staff. Try to put yourself in the shoes of the host teachers and imagine what temperament and outlook would impress you when you have your own students.

Behaving courteously

As a visitor, trainee teachers are expected to be polite, helpful and well mannered to colleagues and to the children. They should not, of course, be patronising or stuffy, just thoroughly professional in outlook and conduct. Small acts of kindness and courtesy impress staff considerably. Don't always wait to be invited to do something; instead, volunteer to assist others.

Monitoring your own learning

Trainees should regularly ask the teacher how they can improve their teaching and should not be fobbed off by general comments to the effect that they are 'doing fine' but ask instead for specific advice. All unqualified teachers should be encouraged to monitor their professional progress and acknowledge both their weaknesses *and* their achievements. You should maintain a log of key issues that emerge during your time on placement and an indication of what action you took or advice you sought to address the situation. Try not to agonise over things that don't work out so well. Teaching is not for the fainthearted or, when the going gets tough, for the tenderhearted either. You are bound to make errors of judgement; it's simply a case of working hard to minimise the number and seriousness of them and save yourself from unnecessary grief.

Extending the professional role

Teachers spend nearly as much time working outside the classroom as they do inside it, so trainee teachers should be ready to get involved with other duties. However, in your eagerness to participate, it is important that you take care not to become so absorbed in the other duties that you neglect the basic work of planning, teaching and assessing. For instance, it is one thing to offer help with a lunchtime club; it is quite another thing to end up running it and arrive poorly prepared for the afternoon session.

Expressing appreciation

Astute trainee teachers learn to thank the teacher regularly for her or his help and support, and show that they appreciate the effort that has gone into making them welcome and giving them opportunities to gain experience of teaching. Make sure that you give the firm impression that you value and appreciate what the teacher does but without being obsequious. If you appreciate something that a colleague (teacher or assistant or support staff) has done or said on your behalf, say so. Don't assume that the person automatically knows that you are grateful.

There is much for trainee teachers and host teachers to absorb about relating effectively to one another and establishing a partnership for the benefit of the children. Generally, if trainee teachers are willing to learn, respond to advice and make up their minds to be a positive influence in the school, they will receive nothing but support and encouragement. It is obvious that the better that trainee teachers and host teachers work together, understand each other's needs and accept the limitations of their different roles, the more rewarding life in school becomes for all concerned. This ideal state is more likely to happen if teachers and students agree to speak openly and honestly to one another about their feelings and expectations.

Good practice

Each time you respond to a situation, question or comment from a colleague, ask yourself if your response is contributing to your reputation as a decisive, forward-looking person and helping others to be the same.

Cross-reference: Guided Reader Extract 32

Teacher morale

Achieving a work–life balance is now seen as an essential prerequisite for health and welfare, though in reality teachers seem to work as hard as ever. Some schools have developed strategies to stimulate staff and lift spirits. Mosley and Grogan (2002) suggest that high morale is essential if a school community is to prosper, promoted through making school a place of discovery, having fun together, establishing 'cheer-up' and 'words of inspiration' boards and bringing in outside support to provide expertise and inspiration. Mosley and Grogan also suggest that just as children's self-esteem and mutual respect can be enhanced through circle time (see Collins 2001, 2007 for numerous practical suggestions), the same principles apply to adults in school. Thus:

- taking care of oneself as well as taking care of others;
- resisting the urge to bend over backwards to be helpful regardless of the impact on your health;

- recognising that everyone has particular and special needs;
- learning to decline requests without feeling guilty;
- accepting that everyone can only do his or her best;
- expecting to be treated with consideration and courtesy and as someone with intelligence;
- refusing to be dependent on other people's approval;
- recognising that time for relaxation is not wasted time.

It is not always easy to maintain a cheerful outlook, especially if teaching is hard and pupils uncooperative. There are many times when the weight of responsibility can feel overwhelming. One of the best ways to keep your morale high despite unpromising circumstances is to delight in the children – their personalities, energy, enthusiasm, funny ways and even their mischievous antics. The position is well summarised by Suschitzky and Chapman (1998): 'The ways that children view themselves are influenced by the ways others respond to them' (p. 8). And one of the most significant 'others' is you. That is why adopting an affirmative posture is good for you as well as being good for them.

Good practice

Make a deliberate effort to gradually introduce a larger proportion of positive comments into your conversations. Monitor the impact of your changing attitude on pupils and colleagues.

Cross-reference: Guided Reader Extract 33

Safeguarding children

Children who feel safe and secure are more likely to be happy and succeed in their learning. Teachers play a critical role in achieving this objective. In the past, social workers were seen as the principal defenders of vulnerable children but a number of high-profile cases have highlighted the importance of the school's role. Obviously, children cannot concentrate on learning if they are being oppressed in school or in their home environment. Safeguarding children is best viewed as part of the school's equal opportunity policy in as much as pupil anxiety hinders learning – so security, ease of mind and feeling valued not only allays their fears but also provides the best conditions for learning.

Professional responsibilities

All teachers must have a working knowledge and understanding of teachers' professional duties, legal liabilities and responsibilities, so it is essential to be aware of the extent and limits of your duty towards the children. They are protected by the Children Act (first published 1989) that forbids adults to exert unreasonable psychological pressure upon them, such as shouting in their face and hectoring, or physical chastisement and force. There are obvious exceptions to this rule; for instance, screaming out loud may be the only means of preventing a child running in the road, and physical containment may be the only way to prevent one child from injuring another. However, these occurrences are rare and the general principle of treating children with respect and using reason rather than rage is contained within the

Children Act 1989. These sentiments are explored more fully in the *Every Child Matters* agenda (DfES 2005; full details, see Chapter 13). The Children Act 2004 aims to encourage integrated planning, commissioning and delivery of services to children, as well as improve multi-disciplinary working (notably education and social services) and improve the co-ordination of individual and joint inspections in local authorities.

In practice, it may take you a lot of self-discipline to avoid infringing the spirit of the legislation, especially with children who persistently and wilfully take advantage of their freedom and seem determined to push adults to the limits of their patience. Nevertheless, you must learn to remain calm and exercise self-control, regardless of the provocation or personal slights you receive; try hard to ignore the sense of injustice and anger that you feel with a child who is unreasonable and concentrate on a solution. The purpose is resolution, not retribution.

Common Assessment Framework

School inspections examine carefully a school's awareness of its responsibilities in this area and failure to show evidence of compliance is reflected in the report. The Common Assessment Framework (CAF) plays a crucial role in endeavouring to ensure that no child is overlooked in receiving appropriate academic, emotional and social support. It is the process by which schools, social services and other agencies working with children and young people assess and address potential barriers to pupils' achievement and wellbeing. The process is intended to facilitate multi-agency sharing of information and clarifying roles and responsibilities with reference to a particular child or young person. Kyriacou (2009) refers to 'social pedagogy', which is broadly defined as the process of supporting and fostering children's personal development, social education and general welfare.

Hughes (2009) argues that involvement of different professionals helps to improve children's life chances: learning mentors, higher level teaching assistants (HLTAs) and teaching assistants in school; those employed by health/social and other agencies, such as school nurses, educational social workers, study support workers, school attendance workers and educational psychologists. Cheminais (2009) and Knowles (2009) offer suggestions about establishing and maintaining effective multi-agency partnership working in educational settings.

Cross-reference: Guided Reader Extract 24

Exercising self-discipline

While self-control is an essential quality for all teachers, as an inexperienced teacher it is unwise to try and deal with difficult situations without support and advice. If you are uncertain about what constitutes an appropriate response towards children, consult senior colleagues at the earliest opportunity, and keep them informed of subsequent developments. It may feel to you that the child has 'got away with it' because of your hesitation about appropriate action but this is not the case. It is preferable, though not always possible, to get advice privately from the host teacher tutor or mentor and then deal with the matter yourself, based on the advice, than to bring in the other teacher to sort out the matter, while you stand back admiringly. There are two reasons for adopting this approach: first, bringing in another teacher is viewed by many miscreants as something approaching betrayal; second, handling the issue helps you to gain credibility with pupils and boosts your self-assurance. Even so, never hesitate to seek help where needed. Issues about the management of behaviour and discipline issues are addressed at length in Chapter 13.

Gathering together

Children need to feel at ease with one another and also confident about their place in society. The development of personal, social and health education (PSHE) in the curriculum is an important element of effective schooling, as it helps to develop positive attitudes, address issues of significance to children and stimulate an active interest in society and citizenship. There are many occasions when a teacher wishes to develop a more intimate atmosphere by gathering the children together in a smaller, well-defined area in which they can all sit comfortably. The children sit in a circle with the teacher to discuss key issues, share ideas and celebrate events (e.g. Roffey 2006; see also below). This *circle-time* approach, as the name suggests, involves pupils sitting together so that each child is able to see every other child. The strategy is more often used with younger children but can be adapted for all ages. The teacher and assistant will normally be included in the gathering. A successful circle time depends upon everyone agreeing in advance about procedures (such as only one person speaking at a time) and conduct (such as speaking kindly). It is non-threatening (children only contribute when they wish to do so) and is intended to increase co-operation and allow for positive reinforcement, thereby helping to raise the self-image of every child.

On other occasions, the 'carpet time' can be used for sharing books, or the teacher or a capable child reading aloud to the class, or simply a chance to share the enjoyable and interesting things that children have seen and done. For instance, a recent exciting television programme can stimulate great enthusiasm and promote speaking and listening skills. Although some teachers and their classes make fruitful use of carpet time each week, it should be seen only as a component of the overall teaching method. As with any other approach, its value has to be monitored and evaluated to ensure that children gain in knowledge and confidence as a result.

Timing can also influence the circumstances under which you gather together. For instance, it may be unwise to bring the children into close confinement immediately after a long assembly or inactive playtime. Although the end of the day is frequently used for a story and sharing, other times should also be considered, particularly towards the end of a session when children's minds are buzzing. At the end of the day, especially, it is essential to calm the children, relax the atmosphere and send the children from the classroom with a song on their lips and in their hearts, eager to return for more the following day.

Activate your thinking!

Some teachers stand at the door and say a personal goodbye to each child; others have small rituals, such as using a song or chant, or getting children to say something significant before they leave.

Good practice

The physical size of older children can cause problems in fitting them on to a carpet area and can trigger restless behaviour, such as jostling for space and calling out. If you consider that circle time is needed, do not prolong it and only invite children to contribute to discussion if they are sitting still. Many teachers of upper junior pupils prefer to keep the children in their seats, though perhaps with some minor adjustment to the position of the chairs.

Health and safety

It is a seminal principle that pupils' safety must be a priority for every adult working in school. Ensuring secure conditions depends on the nature of the activities, the age of the children and the adult–child ratio. For very young children, basic cleanliness training might be the priority; for older ones, correct use of tools and specialist equipment might be particularly relevant. There are also some common issues such as ensuring that:

- each child is clear about the task and the time constraints involved;
- children have sufficient space to do the task or activity;
- children are aware of others in the vicinity who might be affected by their actions (such as being splattered by paint);
- there is a minimum of hazards on the floor (such as spilled paste) that might be perilous;
- the procedures for movement about the room and the correct place for each piece of equipment have been explained to the children beforehand;
- there is a well-labelled place for every resource.

Prevention rather than cure

Prevention is always better than cure, so it is essential to think ahead about the risk factors associated with specific activities. Sensible health and safety precautions are not for the purpose of limiting what children attempt to do or suppressing their enjoyment of practical activities. On the contrary, good working practices liberate the children to work confidently and assuredly. As the responsible adult, you have to make the final decisions about what is permissible. For instance, in science, warn the children about:

- *The hazards of cuts from split plastic and sharp edges.* Cuts should be treated by holding the damaged area under free-flowing cold water, direct from the tap, into an empty sink.
- *The need to wash hands thoroughly after contact with soil and outdoor activity.* Thoroughly washing hands in warm soapy water is recommended. Of course, children can wear plastic gloves when handling natural objects, though a small number of children find them unpleasant to wear and handle. They are also difficult to put on and take off.
- *The danger of cord or wire being wrapped tightly around a wrist or tangled around the neck.* A pair of wire-cutters should be readily available should instant release be necessary. Children panic easily if they feel trapped.
- *The effect of bright light on eyes and high volume sound on eardrums.* Some flashing lights can trigger epileptic 'fits' in a small minority of children, so a warning should always be given.

In physical activity guard against:

- *Over-exuberant 'warm-up' activities.* These involve children charging around and the potential for nasty collisions. Instead use more 'on the spot' activities and controlled short sprint activities.
- *Body movement that may cause strain without suitable 'warm-up' activities.* Instead, ensure that you have led all the children through the required muscle-loosening exercises. Don't overlook the need for a 'warm-down' time, too.

- *Unstable or damaged equipment.* It is essential to check beforehand or, if this has not been possible, to put to one side any item that is in an unsuitable state. If you find the time spent in carrying out this check to be onerous, console yourself with the thought that it is better than having an injured child and explaining to a parent and the head teacher why you did not check beforehand.

- *Hard equipment, especially wooden or solid plastic bats that might hit a child in the face.* If bats are necessary, you should enforce strict conditions for their use, especially the need to maintain a distance between the batter and the rest of the team. One way to achieve this is to insist that the batter stands at a point that is located at the centre of a concentric circle of outer hoops or a chalk/tape ring. No one else is allowed beyond the perimeter of the hoops until it is their turn to bat.

- *Equipment that allows children to climb beyond the limits of their capability.* Such decisions are not straightforward; while you want to protect children from injury, you also want to encourage them to be adventurous. It's better to err on the side of caution initially until you are more confident about their capability.

- *Long breaks between bouts of physical exertion.* If a lengthy break is necessary, a further warm-up should be used before proceeding. Ideally, it is better to increase the physical demands gradually and equally gradually reduce them.

- *Allowing the noise level to rise too high such that the children cannot hear your commands.* Useful strategies include clear instructions, regular reminders (not nagging) about the need for a sensible noise level and a signal on a whistle or tambourine to indicate the need for quiet.

- *Stopping a lesson abruptly before the children have been led through some 'warm-down' activities.*

Art, design and technology also presents a range of challenges, not least issues relating to resources, grouping and adult supervision of children. Monitoring of activities also makes heavy demands on the teacher. If the whole class is engaged in a variety of targeted activities, you will need to ensure that there are adequate resources available and children have been taught the necessary skills to make the best use of their time. Many TAs are willing and able to assist in the organising of resources and teaching children specific skills. Parent helpers can be tremendous assets but they are unimpressed if they have been invited to participate in something that is poorly organised or asked to carry out duties that are properly the province of trained and salaried staff.

Developing life skills

Concerns have been expressed about the way in which overprotected children are being deprived of life skills experiences. However, safeguarding children does not mean that they should be enclosed in bubble wrap like fragile ornaments. It does mean that teachers have to undertake a risk assessment about the possible consequences of their work with pupils, especially in less familiar situations such as during out-of-school activities and swimming. However, even in regular lessons there may be instances in which special care must be taken. Electrical (mains) equipment should not be used unless it has been checked by a qualified electrician and labelled safe for use. In other words you cannot bring in your own electrical equipment unless a qualified person has certified it to be safe. If children are involved in any process requiring heat or blades they should be properly trained, organised and closely supervised, a point to bear in mind when planning lessons.

Awareness of school procedures

Although accidents are rare in primary classrooms, you should be aware of the correct procedures for dealing with casualties. A course of first aid training, regularly updated, will give you the confidence you need to act promptly in the case of an emergency, though you are not normally permitted to give medicines in school or carry out procedures which require specialist expertise. All schools have a clear written policy on managing medication in school and systems to support individual pupils with medical needs. Dispensing might be supervised by the head teacher (in a smaller school) or senior member of staff, or delegated to a member of the support staff – preferably someone with medical knowledge and first aid training. It is also not unknown for a member of the administrative staff to oversee the procedure. However, schools are not obliged to supervise medication and might refuse to be involved. Should there be an accident in a situation where you are the responsible adult, make sure that it is recorded in the 'accident book' that is often kept in a school's main office or first aid room. If you are unsure about any aspect of safety law, check with the head teacher and refer to the school's documentation.

Listening to children

Health and safety is not only concerned with physical wellbeing, as every adult also has a responsibility to be alert to children's *emotional* condition. This concern should not be confused with the crude notion that taking an interest in children's welfare makes a teacher a social worker. Education involves more than simply teaching facts. It involves helping children to understand their place in the world, the contribution that they can make to society and their responsibilities to one another. Taking time to listen to children, to understand their needs, hopes and desires, should not be seen as a burden for teachers but, rather, as a privilege (see, for example, Corrie 2003).

The act of listening carefully to children is increasingly being recognised as beneficial for children's welfare, and recent developments across children's services in education, health and social welfare have reinforced the value that governments and service providers place on it. Based on a case study of 'looked after children', Leeson (2007) warns about feelings of helplessness, low self-esteem and poor confidence that follow a lack of opportunities made available to young people to talk about and make decisions that directly affect their lives.

Nelson-Jones (2007) stresses the importance of non-verbal signals in establishing a suitable climate for listening, through so-called 'attending behaviour'. A good listener gives the strong impression of being available and not in too much of a hurry to take time or too distracted to concentrate. In the busyness of classroom life, such conditions are not easily achieved but they are essential for effective communication. A listening adult will adopt a relaxed but alert posture and avoid giving out signals that indicate tension or tedium, such as gazing into the distance, wrapping arms around the body, drumming fingers on the table or bringing the conversation to an end.

O'Quinn and Garrison (2004) insist that 'empathy, compassion, commitment, patience, spontaneity and an ability to listen are all closely connected to the trust necessary for creating the conditions for loving relations in the classroom community' (p. 63). See also Clark *et al.* (2005) for further details about how adults listen to young children; the view of the child that different approaches to listening presume; and the risks that listening might entail for young children.

Cross-reference: Guided Reader Extracts 14

Cultivating safe habits

Although it is impossible to guarantee that children will never have an accident or suffer some type of emotional trauma, it is important to take every reasonable precaution without becoming obsessive about it or creating an atmosphere of fear and uncertainty. Casualness about safety issues might result in damage to children and stress for you. For instance, you can be sure that the one time you assume that the equipment is in good order or that all the children are safely away from danger will be the one time that something unforeseen happens. Experienced teachers develop a keen sensitivity to where danger and hazards lie and take steps to minimise risks. If you are new to teaching, however, you cannot rely on such awareness, so it is important to get into the habit of thinking through in advance where things could go wrong and taking preventative action to ensure that children can get on with their learning without undue hindrance. Simple procedures such as ensuring that classroom walkways are free from bags and keeping items within easy reach, rather than children having to stretch for them, make a considerable difference to both the safety of the classroom and its smooth running. Your alertness and thoroughness not only helps children to *feel* secure but also to *be* secure.

> **Activate your thinking!**
>
> The complexity of an activity should never exceed the educational benefit that the children gain from carrying it out.

> **Good practice**
>
> From a health and safety perspective, the rule must always be: *If in doubt, don't!*

Establishing a working relationship with children

Evidence from talking to primary teachers suggests that from among the many roles they undertake, social and emotional considerations are of great significance for them, expressed most keenly in the regular forms of interaction and strength of relationship that develop between adult and pupil. In addition to secure subject knowledge and being able to teach systematically and clearly, an essential part of being a good teacher is to empathise with children and create the type of working conditions that facilitate what is sometimes described as an effective learning climate.

Establishing a working relationship with a class of children requires patient perseverance. In particular, the first few weeks with any new class are always a time of adjustment, identifying established conventions and creating mutual understanding. Children new to school also have to make the transition from the relative security of home, playgroup or nursery to the vagaries of school life. Those who may have received exclusive attention at home from a parent have to learn to accept that they are only one among many other children vying for adults' time and attention. Those who are transferring to a different class in September will have at least a year of routines and procedures behind them which will differ to an extent from those preferred by the new teacher. And in addition to all these changes, you now join the social mix.

Although the process of establishing a working relationship is rarely smooth and unhindered, awareness of the probable course that the process will take allows you to be better prepared and less likely to be perturbed by the circumstances. It is helpful to think of the route to a working relationship in terms of three stages:

1.   Preliminaries
2.   Courtship
3.   Partnership.

Preliminaries

It is rightly claimed that first impressions count for a lot. It is also true that appearances can be deceiving. Nevertheless, early encounters with pupils strongly influence the quality of your future relationships with them. A poor start can jeopardise the remainder of your time in school, so it pays to be diligent from the start. Even qualified teachers who change schools take time to assimilate the culture of their new school, so trainee teachers are bound to struggle in the first days or weeks of a fresh school experience as they grow accustomed to the host teachers' expectations, the class procedures and the 'unwritten laws' of conduct that only become apparent after being immersed in the daily life of the classroom for some days. Preliminary encounters with children are often very demanding owing to the need to strike a balance between establishing a rapport and ensuring that you are not overwhelmed by their demands and questions. Although a degree of sparring is inevitable, new teachers can help themselves by taking account of the following:

Do not allow yourself to be bombarded with questions by pupils

If necessary, a curt refusal to answer all but the most basic questions is needed. Otherwise, a pleasant smile and 'that is mine to know and yours to find out' or similar will usually dissuade all but the most persistent questioner.

Do not court short-term popularity

You might be the most exciting thing that has come into the children's lives for some time, but the novelty will quickly wear off. It is wise to ease into the new situation and gradually to become absorbed into classroom life, rather than to imagine that the initial enthusiastic welcome will be maintained.

Do not attempt too much too soon

Some trainee teachers want to take major responsibility from an early stage, but it is generally more realistic to work alongside the class teacher for a time and gradually increase the breadth and range of your teaching. Some trainees negotiate with the class teacher to take a proportion of the lesson initially and build up expertise in that area, rather than changing from having no responsibility to all of it in one move.

Learn names as quickly as possible

Discipline is much easier if you use children's names when addressing them. It is invariably the case that teachers learn the names of the mischievous and assertive children first, but be careful not to use their names too much and reinforce their 'rogue' status. Quieter children probably hear their names far less often, so may deserve to hear them more. Aim to associate a pupil's name with a commending comment where possible.

Prepare thoroughly

Pupils soon sense any insecurity that exudes from unprepared teachers, so make sure that you have prepared in such a way that you do not need to stare at the lesson plan and, importantly, have thought through the practicalities attached to the session. The more that you are clear about what you are trying to achieve, what the children are trying to learn and how this will all take place, the more likely that they will settle and respond positively.

Promote success for pupils

Nothing facilitates a smooth passage more than when children receive genuine approval for work well done. However, it is worth remembering that children will not automatically celebrate your positive tones until they have learned to trust and respect you. It is better to slightly understate your praise initially than to be unduly exuberant and later retreat from being so positive.

The preliminary stage demands a lot of bridge-building between adult and pupils, who must learn to relax together as trust is slowly gained through regular interaction, resulting in better understanding through the vagaries of classroom life. Teachers have to be willing to persevere and hold their nerve through the difficult days and relish the times when things go well. If you refuse to be unsettled, continue to offer interesting lessons, show a genuine concern in individuals, remain alert and maintain a good balance between listening to children's views and insisting on conformity to agreed behaviour and procedures, you won't go far wrong. However, achieving this state of affairs requires persistence, so don't get discouraged if things take time to fall into place. You can expect some ups and downs; focus on the ups.

Cross-reference: Guided Reader Extract 48

Courtship

When you join a new class, it is obviously not possible to get to know all the pupils straight away. Some children prefer to weigh teachers up and others almost jump into their laps. Some children remain aloof because they are shy or suspicious of teachers or because they are contented with life as it is and do not want to be influenced too much by the presence of another adult. Children's coolness towards new teachers is not an indication that they hold something against them; similarly, effusive children do not necessarily like them. Sometimes you will find that the relationships with children that take longer to establish prove to be the most fruitful in the longer term. You must try to be evenhanded with the children and give them the opportunity to speak when they want to express something and remain silent when they prefer to listen or reflect. Children do not mind a firm teacher, but they despise a gullible, domineering or weak-willed one.

As the courtship continues, boundaries between acceptable and unacceptable behaviour are gradually clarified. Class rules do not define the perimeters of behaviour, though they provide a useful point of reference. Children will test the limits to see how far they stretch. If teachers are too lenient, they quickly discover that the boundary walls they thought were absolutes are made of elastic. On the other hand, rigidity on your part can lead to pupil resentment if perceived as unreasonable or vindictive. It is important for you to explain to your pupils why certain things are permitted and refused, but done so as matters of fact, not as issues for negotiation. Children might not always approve of a teacher's methods but, providing they are seen as fair, adult–pupil relationships will settle and consolidate.

As a guest in the classroom with a limited time in which to make an impression and learn from your experiences, it is sensible to adopt the class teacher's approach as closely as possible until you feel sufficiently confident to adjust your style. Subsequently, you can discuss these variations in approach with the teacher and offer your own perspectives; however, make sure that you do so with humility and in moderation. The last thing a host teacher wants is to be confronted with a supercilious trainee. In the meantime you may have to persevere with implementing the existing policy and make subtle changes in the way that you respond and exercise control.

Partnership

The ideal teaching and learning situation is one in which teachers and pupils are at ease with one another and respond easily and naturally, so that learning is purposeful, children are motivated and discourse is more of a conversation between adult and child, than a monologue dominated by the adult. Exactly how this state is achieved defies easy explanation but it can be recognised instantly by a visitor to the classroom because of the shared trust that exists between teachers and pupils as they work in harmony, celebrate success and handle setbacks resolutely. In such an environment, children have confidence to ask questions and express an opinion without their views being dismissed before they have had a chance to finish speaking. Rules will be adhered to sensibly, though there will be ongoing opportunities to discuss their application as and when they arise. The work will be meaningful and, though there may be spells when the children find the work tedious, they will persevere in the sure knowledge that more exciting experiences are never too far away. The most striking characteristics of the partnership environment will be the mutual respect, good eye contact and natural use of the voice such that both the teacher and the children find fulfilment in their work. Listen to the enthusiasm that oozes from a trainee teacher's comments as she records her experiences:

> Things are going really well. I'm feeling quite happy. I'm really enjoying the school experience, really enjoying the teaching and the teacher has been very, very supportive. I realise that she's been under pressure with the national tests and other things, and she's been worried that she hasn't supported me enough, but it's fine. She's leaving me to my own devices but she's there if I need to ask her any questions and I'm actually enjoying it because it's just as if they are my own class.

There are always going to be ebbs and flows in the struggle to achieve a partnership but the effort is undoubtedly worthwhile. Perseverance, a willingness to evaluate your work as a teacher and a thirst to gain advice from experienced colleagues will help you in your quest for an enduring, positive relationship with the children and the enhancement in learning that accompanies it.

Sad to say, some teachers never get beyond the courtship stage. In exceptional cases the sparring phase will continue for so long that the classroom climate deteriorates and the teacher resorts to harsh tactics and coercion as a means of maintaining control rather than persuade the children to conform. Such circumstances are, of course, very disappointing and frustrating for adult and child alike. Instead of being relaxed and encouraging, the teacher's relationship with the class is tense and unsatisfactory, with the result that learning is ponderous rather than joyful. The teacher feels little satisfaction with the job and goes home feeling jaded and discouraged. Aspire for partnership but don't hesitate to be uncompromisingly firm if children seek to take advantage of your reasonableness.

Activate your thinking!

Consider your responses in the following situations:

1. A 10-year-old girl keeps asking you about your favourite singer.
2. A 5-year-old boy wants you to help him all the time and jealously pushes away other children who seek your assistance.
3. An 8-year-old girl sulkily tells you that you are not her 'real' teacher.
4. An 11-year-old boy angrily accuses you of being unfair when you insist that he stays in to complete a piece of work because, he claims, you did not keep in other pupils who had been naughty.
5. A 10-year-old girl spends ages producing work that is inferior in quality to that from other children in the class, yet you know that she is capable of doing better.
6. A 5-year-old boy produces a colourful painting in half the time allotted and begins to take his apron off to signal that he's finished.
7. An anxious 8-year-old girl constantly seeks your approval and commendation for her work.
8. An 11-year-old boy proudly brings a page of very neat work to you that he has openly copied from a page on the Internet.

Good practice

Stand upright; let a quiet smile play across your lips. When you need to reinforce a point, lower the pitch of your voice and speak more slowly (but not in an affected way). Walk towards a child if he or she is saying something inappropriate. Only jest with a child when you are completely secure in your management of behaviour. Do not allow children to see that you are rattled, even if you are! Remember, you cannot force a child to behave but you can *enforce* discipline.

Cross-reference: Guided Reader Extracts 22 and 28

Responding to children

Here are some suggestions about an appropriate way to respond to the scenarios described in the 'Activate your thinking!' box above. You might like to discuss the suggestions below with your mentor or a colleague:

1. Answer the question and immediately change the subject.
2. Explain patiently to the child that he must take turns. It is likely that the boy is insecure and hankers for exclusive attention. It might be appropriate for an assistant to spend more time with him for a period of (say) one week and monitor progress. If the behaviour persists, mention it to the parent.

3. Do not take offence. Some children are highly protective of their teachers. Smile and say that it is true that you are not the teacher but you are *one* of her teachers. You might want to add that you are working hard to see if you can become as good as the class teacher one day.

4. The boy may be genuinely cross or trying to undermine your confidence. Do not get into an argument with him; instead, repeat that he will not go out until he has completed the work and walk away. If he mutters threats about not doing the work or telling his parents, simply write down (or pretend to) the time and date and read aloud as you write: 'Billy stayed in to finish his work today', then add (as if he had never made any threats) 'Hurry up, Billy, your friends are waiting for you.' When he completes the work, thank him and usher him out for the break. You might want to consider whether keeping children in at break time is an appropriate sanction, especially if Billy is an active or hyperactive type.

5. There are many reasons for poor quality work: (a) weak motivation; (b) uncertainty about what has to be done; (c) fear of failure; (d) illness; (e) friendship problems; and (f) laziness. It is worth finding an opportunity to speak one-to-one with her and explain that you are puzzled about the low standard of work. Ask if she has any ideas. If she refuses to respond or shrugs her shoulders, you may want to write down the six options mentioned above (a–f) in 'child-speak' and ask the girl to comment. Conclude positively by reminding her that you are here to assist her and want her to feel free to ask questions, however minor. Quite often, this intimate, non-threatening conversation is sufficient to trigger improvement and a higher degree of trust.

6. Younger children will often rush to conclude an activity if they think there is something better to follow it. A lot depends on the purpose of the activity; if it is to employ specific skills that the children have learned, you can be gently insistent. If you gave pupils free reign to paint in any way they chose, there is little to be done, as the child was simply following your instructions. Perhaps you needed to be more specific about what you required from the children in the first place and/or have a related back-up activity.

7. The classroom can be a scary place for trainee teachers, but also for some children, who are daunted by the constant need to interpret adults' requirements and accomplish what the teacher wants. Government publications are replete with statements about 'driving up standards' and phrases such as: 'Our children deserve the best', forgetting, perhaps, the pressure that this can create for pupils as well as teachers. Be sympathetic and clear when she is anxious about procedural matters but also offer the girl choices whenever possible, so that she gradually gains confidence in her ability to make decisions.

8. It is important to clarify for pupils the difference between information and knowledge. It is easy to access information; it is more difficult to transform it into enduring knowledge. Commend the boy for his hard work and ask him to make up a quiz for a friend to use, consisting of (say) five questions based on the information he has recorded, two of which are factual, two of which ask for an opinion and one of which asks for an alternative or option. In this way he is forced to think about the facts and their significance. Avoid scolding him but point out the limited usefulness of copying someone else's thoughts.

Attitude to achievement

It would be a strange teacher who did not want pupils to do their very best, be successful in their work and gain good grades in tests. Yet from the sort of political utterances that are sometimes issued, you could be forgiven for thinking that teachers are among the least trustworthy professionals in society. In truth, while people external to the school are primarily concerned with pupil success in examinations, the teachers and assistants who work in the school are concerned both with academic achievement *and* children's happiness. In determining your own attitude to achievement it is important to take account of the child's view as well as the adult's.

Children's attitude to achievement

Picture the scene. Twins Ben and Angie come out of school clutching their recently acquired swimming certificates. Ben thrusts the creased card under his mother's nose and explodes in mock glee about the 10 metres award he has recently achieved. Angie saunters up a few moments later, quietly confident about her coveted 50 metres success. How will the mother respond? Ben knows that his sister is a better swimmer but had secretly hoped that he might match her accomplishments. He had never in his seven years of life shown more determination than in his frantic efforts as he struggled through the final moments of that seemingly eternal swim. The teacher had congratulated him but Ben had shrugged it off, all too aware of his sister's sparkling success a short time before. In his mind he pictured the scene when they met their mother – Angie receiving fulsome praise for her achievements. For himself, the sincere but consoling, 'You've done well, too, Ben.'

Achievement is an important aspect of life and some people obviously achieve more than others do. Children need goals as much as anyone else. It is sometimes difficult for grown-ups to remember the thrill and excitement of scoring a goal in a games lesson, winning a prize for a special painting, enjoying a glass of orange after helping the teacher with a job or having a star placed on the chart for finishing another reading book. These are the moments when children's achievements are openly and publicly acknowledged and savoured. A more difficult challenge for adults is to know how to respond to children whose achievements are limited, where success has only ever been partial and exhilaration has depended upon a surrogate basking in the reflected glow from others.

Central to this matter is the importance of the teacher's concern not solely for children's performance but for children themselves. Liston and Garrison (2004) regret recent trends in education that place more emphasis on meeting the mandates of the state than to satiate children's hunger for learning. They go on to insist that:

> Teaching and learning are activities that work best when we work through our hearts as well as our heads. Teachers have known that [fact] for a long time. It is time for the academy to allow, even invite, the emotions, and more specifically, love, into our understanding and practice of teaching.
>
> (p. 2)

Achievements are notoriously fickle. Children who depend upon tangible evidence of their own worth can become equally unhappy when achievements remain elusive. The hero of the hour is quickly forgotten. Certificates fade and crinkle. Sparkling reports become an archive. It is the children themselves who are the only consistent factor; their wellbeing and contentment must outlive the pleasure of achievement. To base the worth of individuals on these certificated or measurable successes while ignoring the other qualities that characterise their lives is to burden children with the need to gain ever further achievements as a means of recognition and approval. That route can be a recipe for heartache and ultimate low self-esteem as the success and the approval that accompanies it diminish.

Good practice

1. Do not underestimate the importance to children of receiving rewards but avoid them becoming the principal motivator.
2. In allocating rewards, be careful not to restrict recognition to pupils that make a special effort at the expense of children who are constantly good and hard working.

Adult attitudes

Attitude to achievement

Achievement is important. It is good to do well. Some children work extremely hard and persevere to attain their goals. They rightly receive recognition and our congratulations. The achievement itself is not at fault but, rather, our attitude to it as adults if we give children the impression that their personal worth depends upon coming out at the top of the pack. Success should not be measured solely through identifiable and visible outcomes but also in how the outcomes affect the child's character, ability to cope with life, confidence and attitude to others. The child that trails in last at the end of the race, red-faced and sweating but determined to finish, deserves every bit as much recognition as the county long-distance champion who happens to be in the same school. Both children, in their different ways, deserve praise: the winner because of her victory, the loser because of her willingness to try. Both deserve encouragement: the winner to compete for coveted prizes, the loser to take pride in her sporting attitude and gallant endeavours. And we must not forget those between the extremes. It is easy to overlook the also-ran, the average child and the steady-but-unspectacular pupil. Teachers must ensure that the genuine efforts of every child are recognised and acclaimed.

Snippets of conversation reveal a great deal about a teacher's attitude and the adult–child relationship based on whether:

- the adult took a personal interest in each child or was merely going through the motions;
- the adult's comments were positive and truthful, while still affirming genuine effort;
- the child was willing to confide in the adult in the first place (a strong clue about previous adult–child encounters).

Adult negativity

Imagine the impact of adult negative responses to children's unhappy comments:

CHILD 1: I'm rubbish at this.
TEACHER: Stop moaning and get changed.
CHILD 2: Sir, John only beat me 'cause he cheated.
TEACHER: I don't want to hear about it.
CHILD 3: Miss, I was almost last, that's the worst I've ever run.
TEACHER: You'll just have try a bit harder next time then, won't you, so stop moaning.

The teacher in the above set of conversations was unable to discern the feelings and emotions that underpinned the children's comments. Child 1 wanted to be reassured that her poor performance mattered less than genuine effort. Child 2 was upset over the unexpected reverse of fortune and needed a calm adult response to give him space to come to terms with the disappointment. Child 3 was finding failure difficult to handle and looked for confirmation that a single setback was not setting a precedent for all time. Wise teachers look beyond the immediate comment to the child's real needs and respond in a sympathetic yet constructive manner, which assists the child to come to terms with the reality of the situation without humiliation and with self-worth intact.

A teacher's attitude to achievement influences the creation of a healthy classroom climate and helps children develop a positive attitude towards learning. Teachers who are intolerant of low-achieving or underachieving children bring about a deterioration in self-concept and, consequently, invite even lower achievement or acute anxiety, so as teachers we have serious responsibilities and need to ensure that we:

- take every opportunity to give praise where it is due;
- encourage children who have tried hard, even if the end product is poor relative to others in the group;
- ensure that our relationship with the children is one of respect and tolerance.

Being realistic but commending

A proper attitude to achievement for all children is an important element of school life and all teachers must think carefully about where they stand on the issue. A child who struggles with academic work ('cannot do' as opposed to 'will not try') may excel in an area of life that is not represented in the curriculum. For instance, Kelly (2007) cites an instance where a pupil diagnosed the problem he had with his car before he had consulted a mechanic. Being positive and encouraging should not, however, be confused with giving children a false sense of their achievements. Pupils who do not or will not try and make minimal effort should be left in no doubt about your feelings on the matter. Some children have limited academic intellect but are still capable of finding success and fulfilment in other areas of learning. With your guidance and their own efforts, they will certainly do so.

You should aim to communicate to all children, regardless of ability and aptitude, that they are precious and special. Of course, some children are lazy and cannot be bothered to make an effort, but they still require encouragement to improve and our commitment to helping them do so, or they will never behave any differently. At the same time, promote the need for perseverance and use the motto: 'Together, we can!' See also below.

Good practice

Looking the child in the eye, regularly use affirming expressions such as:

Well done, Ben. I'm proud of you.
Top of the class, Vernon.
You should feel very pleased with yourself, Tony. I certainly am.
Champion effort, Jenny. Well done.

Encouragement and praise

A small number of people seem unable or unwilling to encourage, but prefer to criticise and look for opportunities to find fault instead. Others want to be encouraging but somehow can't find the right words. But what is encouragement and praise, and what is its place in teaching and learning?

First, encouragement and praise serve different purposes. *Encouragement* can be given to children at any time to help them improve on their present efforts, complete a difficult piece of work or concentrate harder in order to achieve a higher standard. Teachers can use a variety of expressions to cajole, chivvy, motivate and offer support, accompanied by sparkling eye contact, clapping, smiling, open faces and close body positions. *Praise*, on the other hand, is offered for achievement: good quality work, real effort, instances of sensitivity and responsibility. Praise is usually given with gusto, openly announced.

Encouragement recognises that the present situation is acceptable but the prospect of better things awaits the child who is willing to try harder, seek advice and show determination. *Praise* recognises that the very best has been achieved in the circumstances and nothing more could reasonably be expected. Children won't accept encouragement or praise from someone they don't respect but will see it rather as a subtle form of coercion. It is better to bide your time and be gently approving rather than let loose a flood of commendation in your early encounters with the class. You may discover that the efforts and product that you enthused about is below the child's ability level, so it pays to be cautious in making definite judgements before you have a clear view of a child's potential and previous attainment.

At all stages it is important to invite children to comment on their own work and suggest possible improvements, though you should avoid spoiling the joy of the moment by implying that their present best is not in fact good enough after all. Additional advice about assessing achievement can be found in Chapter 11. Despite these caveats, it is certainly the case that both encouragement and praise can help children in at least three ways:

1.   By revealing that you are interested in what they are doing
2.   By helping them to understand your expectations about acceptable standards
3.   By opening a dialogue that will help them to consider their attainment and monitor their own progress.

This third point is important. Children must learn to evaluate the quality of their own work regularly and explicitly and gain a sense of self-satisfaction rather than to rely wholly on adult approval. Do not try to be too sophisticated about the process; a simple 'good in these ways, less good in those ways' will suffice. Although there is great emphasis on pupils establishing and monitoring their own learning targets, you should not imagine that this process circumvents the need for accurate adult assessment and feedback. Children are entitled to express their views but do not have the overarching perspectives that a teacher possesses.

With these issues in mind, teachers need to think carefully about the forms of encouragement they use. For instance, to tell a child in a dignified monotone that he or she can 'do better than that' is unlikely to inspire greater effort or determination and is more likely to engender disaffection in the pupil. The unspoken message from the teacher's utterance is one of dismay and the threat of further criticism if there is no improvement. Of course, an indifferent child with a poor attitude to work needs to be carefully watched and clear, short-term work targets set, but nine times out of ten children (who are often their own worst critics) will admit if challenged that the work is not their best. This sort of admission opens up the way for you to make specific and non-threatening suggestions about improvement while maintaining an effective level of communication with the child. Classrooms are places where structured learning opportunities are provided in purposeful, amicable conditions – not the educational equivalent of 'payment by results'.

When children accept that you are trying to understand them rather than looking for things to criticise, they are more likely to confide their reasons for the lower than hoped for quality of the work. Perhaps they are bored or uncertain about what's expected or finding it too difficult. Perhaps they are unhappy with their partner. A sympathetic but firm approach unlocks doors that remain tightly shut to adults who adopt a rigid approach carrying a hint of disapproval and disdain. Teachers who constantly carp about how disappointed they are with pupils' efforts might benefit from examining their own teaching methods and attitude.

Most children will also spot insincere praise. The unthinking 'That's good' or dismissive 'Yes, fine' (without paying any real attention to what the child has done or said) is likely to lead to a general malaise as children see how little they can get away with and still be congratulated. Praise has to be merited and should not be offered lightly.

Encouragement is most effective when it is used constructively, without rancour and in the context of clearly defined tasks and expectations. Praise, publicly and sincerely given, should be reserved for genuine instances of quality work and effort. For children who trust their teacher, there is no greater source of satisfaction for them and no greater incentive to continue persevering.

Activate your thinking!

Good quality feedback allows pupils to adjust their priorities, correct misunderstandings and advance their knowledge and, as a result, continue learning with confidence. Poor quality feedback leaves pupils uneasy, muddled about the task requirements and hesitant about how to progress. It's as important as that! See also Chapter 11.

Equal opportunities

When planning, teachers should set high expectations and provide opportunities for all pupils to achieve, including boys and girls, pupils with special educational needs, pupils with disabilities, pupils from all social and cultural backgrounds, pupils of different ethnic groups including travellers, refugees and asylum seekers, and those from diverse linguistic backgrounds.

(*The National Curriculum* 2000: 31)

Equal opportunity should not be confused with identical treatment or 'sameness' of approach. The expression means precisely what it says, namely that every child must be given an equal opportunity to engage with learning by whatever means. It does not mean that no allowance should be made for pupil preferences, personality, maturity, experience and behaviour. Equal opportunity has to be weighed against a pupil's personal responsibility and the teacher's professional judgement about what is in a child's best interests.

Discrimination

Discrimination on any basis is not allowed in schools. Deliberate or unintentional bias towards pupils that can be construed as discriminatory leaves teachers open to charges of unprofessional conduct, so it is important to be as impartial as possible at all times when dealing with children (or adult assistants) or offering a viewpoint. From April 2011, new duties on schools and other public bodies came into force as a result of the Equality Act 2010. The Act strengthens and simplifies existing equality legislation by bringing together existing duties not to discriminate on grounds of race, disability and gender, but also extends these requirements to prohibit discrimination on the grounds of age, sexual orientation, religion or belief, and gender re-assignment. It places a requirement on governing bodies and school proprietors to eliminate discrimination, tackle bullying based on prejudice, and promote equal opportunities.

Not only must pupils be granted the same chances, support and encouragement, but it is not appropriate to label children through circumstances beyond their control such as background or physical appearance. A teasing pleasantry about a child's looks or domestic situation may be more hurtful and do greater damage than you imagine at the time. Children tend to be more literal than adults and a remark that you intend to be interpreted as a whimsical aside can be relayed to parents as an insult.

A useful antidote to discriminatory attitudes is to develop a positive attitude towards achievement and to adopt a 'you can do it' working atmosphere in which all children can fulfil their potential and explore knowledge without undue hindrance. Remember, too, that it is part of your responsibility to foster an environment in which children treat each other respectfully. Yours is the model behaviour to which they should aspire.

Fairness

In addition to the statutory and moral requirements, children like teachers who exercise consistent control and are fair in their dealings with everyone in the class, so fair-mindedness also pays dividends in terms of fostering a settled learning environment. By contrast, adults who exhibit favouritism or indifference towards certain groups or individuals are resented and pupils who are so treated cannot be expected to make an effort to progress. Teachers must therefore regularly interrogate the ways in which their own attitudes towards children might affect learning. In particular, ask yourself whether your reaction, voice tone and response changes significantly when dealing with different pupils under similar conditions.

Gender

Societal expectations

At one time, boys were steered towards the skills and subjects that would provide them with a foundation for working life; girls were expected to become homemakers and were taught accordingly. Today, teachers have to be aware that both girls and boys have an important role in the workplace and in the home and it is important to treat each child as an individual, rather than make blanket assumptions about temperament, ability and life chances based solely on gender. Teachers also have a considerable responsibility to use teaching approaches that appeal to lively children as well as to the compliant ones.

Although expectations and role-orientation are woven into the fabric of society and are hard to disentangle, relatively small instances may reveal deeper assumptions about gender roles. For example, grouping all the girls' names beneath the boys' names on a register may simply be a method of organising, or it may reflect a belief that boys are more significant. Similarly, in the choice of team leaders, allocation of the order in which children take a turn and selection for prestige positions (in taking a leading role in a presentation to parents, say, or a coveted position as a 'prefect') it is necessary to make decisions based on competence, ability and academic priorities, not gender or assertiveness. Knowles (2006) warns that one 'lingering stereotype about boys is that they are innately clever but unwilling to work, whereas any success that girls have is frequently put down to hard work and diligence rather than brilliance' (p. 102). Similarly, a sweet smile from a charming girl should not result in a lesser sanction being imposed on her for a misdemeanour compared with that for an untidy boy with a permanent scowl. Knowles argues that it is easy for teachers to fall into the trap of interpreting the same behaviour differently, based on gender. She offers the example of a mis-behaving girl being described as 'a bad influence' or 'spiteful little madam', while the boy is simply described as 'mucking about'. Fair treatment is not based on the false assumption that girls and boys are somehow 'the same' but that the criteria used for making decisions look first at the facts and the suitability of the individuals concerned, and then at the gender – for instance, to maintain gender balance in a group. See also Chapter 12.

Academic performance

Sometimes gender and not ability or potential appears to be the controlling factor in judging academic potential and progress (Brown 1998; Yelland 1998; Francis and Skelton 2005). However, results from national tests indicate that the position is more complex and girls are forging ahead of boys in most areas of work, especially in language and thematic work requir-ing consistent and dedicated study together with a methodical presentation of results. For example, it is the experience of many reception class teachers that although most girls tend to persevere with reading, take their books home faithfully each night and pick up the necessary skills and strategies with relative ease, the picture among boys is considerably less predictable. Some boys are slow, fail to organise themselves as well as the girls and are attracted more by computer games, construction kits, practical activities and competition than by more sed-entary exercises. It is also ironic that despite girls' tendency to socialise more naturally than boys, it is the independent tasks associated with reading that many girls find fulfilling. Para-doxically, the more independent image frequently attached to boys is counteracted by the unease shown by many of them when faced with solitary work tasks. Older boys in particular often prefer the security of collaborative practical work, especially if it involves 'hand-on' (kinaesthetic) activity. It is also the common experience of teachers that boys who display antisocial behaviour in school often struggle with the basic academic skills (see 'spiral of failure' below).

 Although school inspections show that girls outperform boys in almost every area of aca-demic work, some schools and teachers seem better able to help boys achieve their potential, especially in the problem area of writing (see 'Encouraging children to write', below). The issue of schooling boys (Skelton 2001) has assumed a higher profile for teachers in recent years, though 'quick-fix' solutions are unhelpful (Epstein *et al.* 1998). Eaude (2006) suggests that boys find social development especially hard. Thus:

> The reasons are very complicated but because gender identity is, at least in part, socially constructed, both girls and boys experience strong pressure to conform to the gendered expectations of the family, the peer group and society. Put crudely, boys tend to be

encouraged not to express their emotions, to be wary of intimacy and either to interact through emotionally 'safe' activities, such as sport, or to be less dependent on relationships; while girls interact more by developing close relationships.

(p. 46)

By using the expression 'socially constructed', Eaude and other writers mean that girls and boys behave the way that they do because we ('society') expect it, the implication being that they would behave differently if we held different expectations. Note, however, that Eaude qualifies his statement with the phrase 'in part' because recent research suggests that gendered patterns of achievement might be due to natural differences between the sexes as a consequence of hormonal, chromosomal or brain differences. Francis and Skelton (2005) offer interesting perspectives on gender and brain development, in that while the one author (Skelton) is willing to accept that brain structure research 'offers some potential explanation as to why there are more boys who are autistic, have special needs, or even why boys generally are less adept at literacy than girls', the other author (Francis) 'supports the view that gender is completely socially constructed' (p. 76). See also Chapter 12 for further insights into gender issues affecting older primary children.

Spiral of failure

What might be termed a spiral of failure commonly follows a similar pattern, whereby the child – more often than not, a boy who has always struggled in fundamental areas such as reading and other aspects of English – is marginalised from many of the everyday classroom activities that bring commendation and praise from teachers and peers. Because of his difficulties, an adult, usually a teaching assistant, offers him increasing amounts of support in elementary skills, which is sometimes at the expense of involvement in the more attractive practical and creative tasks that he enjoys. This double deprivation (loss of approval for academic success, fewer exciting activities) can lead to frustration and resentment and an increasingly negative attitude towards school. Teachers, despairing of what to do with these recalcitrant youngsters, resort to strong control strategies or conclude that they are beyond the school's available expertise and are in need of external specialist expertise. In fact, the cause of the unrest is often rooted in early failure, loss of motivation and low self-esteem.

Activate your thinking!

Every child is good at something. Part of your job is to find it, nurture it and allow it to flourish. Nothing succeeds like success!

Good practice

Try to find opportunities for children to talk about and show the rest of the class something outside the regular curriculum in which they are especially interested. You might be surprised at the knowledge and expertise that so-called 'hopeless cases' possess.

Encouraging children to write

Challenges and solutions

There are many challenges for teachers in helping children to learn and progress well at school. The most frequently mentioned areas of difficulty are those of reading and of recording ideas and results by the act of writing down. Issues concerned with reading are explored in Chapter 9. The issue of *writing* is especially true of some boys who, though capable of communicating effectively through speech and visual means, find themselves falling behind classmates and out of favour with teachers through their reluctance or inability to commit ideas to paper. Wise teachers try to harness their enthusiasm, while firmly insisting that they apply themselves to recording ideas and results, though in practical subjects the children's reluctance to write things down can become a significant issue, in terms of both the planning process and tabulating findings. Such 'resistant' pupils are often highly motivated to achieve a result, active in organising the team and willing to apply themselves wholeheartedly in completing the task. However, they then find any excuse to avoid writing or do so casually. Perhaps, unwittingly, these children are conveying an important message, namely, that active forms of learning do not *always* have to be accompanied by a literacy task, though see Myhill and Jones (2009) for a discussion about how talking about an issue or subject beforehand (known as 'oral rehearsal') can facilitate the writing process. As the teacher you may decide that occasionally it is better to concentrate on the practical task and allow verbal feedback to dominate or, if you are anxious that the children must have something to show for their efforts, encourage the use of diagrammatic or other representations.

Shared writing

Shared writing is a process by which a teacher and pupils jointly compose a piece of writing, with the teacher acting as scribe by recording ideas on a board or using IT. The technique is employed to teach children how to translate the writing plan they have formulated into a properly written piece of text. The teacher emphasises how written language sounds (phonic awareness) and the way that it is structured (syntactical awareness) in order to: (1) transform speech into sentences; (2) select appropriate vocabulary, notably words and phrases; (3) choose from a range of connectives, such as words like 'but' and 'so' to sequence and structure the text; and (4) use style and 'voice' appropriate to the type of text, its purpose and audience. In practice, the teacher gathers the children and discusses a shared experience, such as a recent event in school or a popular television programme. The teacher asks questions to stimulate children's thinking; pupils respond by sharing their ideas and insights while the teacher records them both aurally and/or (where practical) written form. The teacher thinks the process through aloud, rehearsing the sentence with the children and making changes to its construction or word choice while explaining why one form or word is preferable to another. The phrase or sentence is re-written, read out loud again and altered further if necessary. This process, while somewhat laborious and highly teacher-intensive, allows every pupil to contribute to the group effort and become involved in final decisions about content. Subsequently, children can copy the agreed sentence format and use it as a starting point for developing their written work further. They are usually more enthusiastic about the work because: (1) they gain confidence from being part of a collaborative venture and (2) they don't have to overcome the psychological barrier of a 'blank page'. The technique is particularly useful for inexperienced writers and children who struggle with literacy.

Younger children

Government figures from 2010, based on teachers' observations, suggest that more than half of 5-year-old boys are struggling with reading and writing, and with emotional and social development. Overall, one in six boys could not write their own name by the age of 5, whereas almost every girl could do so. Some 10 per cent of boys could not say the letters of the alphabet, compared with about half the number of girls with a similar problem. Twice as many boys as girls had difficulty with the task of very simple addition.

The gender gap was exacerbated by the fact that pupils from needy home circumstances, especially poor boys, were seen to fall rapidly behind their more affluent classmates in all areas of work. Thus, one in four poor boys could not write their own name, while around half the number of poor girls had similar problems. About one in six boys from poor homes could not say the letters of the alphabet; for poor girls, the figure was only one in ten. Finally, data from reception teachers suggests that twice as many boys as girls are unable to dress themselves at age 5, though the percentage in each case is very small (around 2 per cent and 1 per cent, respectively).

Ephgrave (2011) argues that reception-age children thrive when an educational setting is organised and managed by the adults, but led by the children. All pupils, boys as well as girls, learn and develop if they are in a stimulating environment that is carefully organised and when teacher observations are used to support their 'next steps'. Children will take risks and surpass expectations when they have clear routines and boundaries, combined with a supportive staff and an enabling environment.

Fostering a positive attitude to school

Knowing the children

It is self-evident that in addition to physical appearance, every child differs in many respects. For example, in their attitudes to life's demands, preferences, interests, sense of humour, openness towards others, ability to engage in conversation, ways of learning, motivation level, confidence, empathy, reaction to difficult circumstances, cheerfulness, determination, sensitivity, and numerous other characteristics that make up each individual. As teacher, you have the daunting and exciting task of knowing and understanding every child in the class. It's a challenge but also a privilege.

As far as possible, you need to make impartial decisions when dealing with children, but this fact should not be confused with the need to take account of individual differences. Children respond differently to situations and behaviour varies according to circumstances; adults must be prepared to adjust their responses and actions accordingly. On the one hand it is necessary for teachers to be consistent in their treatment of children. On the other hand it must be acknowledged that consistency does not mean 'sameness'. Teachers are not judges in a court of law handing down sentences regardless of whoever stands before them according to a pre-determined code. In fact, teachers must exercise great wisdom in the way that they approach all interpersonal encounters with children and, for that matter, with colleagues. Nevertheless, the need for discernment is far removed from a blanket stereotyping of children on the basis of gender or any other defining characteristic (such as background, sportiness or physical height). The key is to treat each case on merit and use a large dose of common sense and reasonableness in making decisions. One of the key skills that all beginner teachers have to develop is to evaluate a situation rapidly and make a response that is not only fair but also *seen* to be fair by the children. You will sometimes get it wrong but don't fret when you do so; children have short memories and are normally very forgiving. As in all aspects of teaching, it is essential to learn from your mistakes and move on.

Establishing the right learning climate

In schools where boys as well as girls progress well, there is a culture where intellectual, cultural and aesthetic accomplishment is valued for all children. Achievement is most pronounced where positive incentives, respect and encouragement for boys to pursue their own interests exist; these elements also help to combat the 'laddish' anti-intellectual culture that is prevalent in some schools. Where boys perform well, they are encouraged to read widely and offered choice about the content of their writing, even when the form or genre is prescribed. Motivation is usually greater where the children are encouraged to write to real audiences within or outside the school.

While attempting to maintain these high levels of motivation, it is important to avoid situations in which a compliant group of passive children (frequently, girls) are given repetitive tasks while a few very assertive children (often boys) are kept occupied with the exciting practical activities with which they are most content. Teachers have to learn to strike a balance between accommodating children's natural preferences and pandering to their stubbornness or unwillingness to toe the line by allowing them excessive opportunities to enjoy favoured options. The best teachers are clear about what they expect and how much flexibility and negotiation they are willing to countenance. Heavy-handedness results in resentment; too much flexibility leads to unease from pupils who like to receive specific guidance, and pressure from mischievous pupils who are seeking concessions. You need to be sufficiently clear about your expectations without suppressing children's creativity or stifling their initiative.

Taking account of pupil personality

Although the majority of concerns about equal opportunities have focused on gender issues, there are studies that suggest that stereotyping is sometimes associated with pupil personality. Teachers can develop expectations about achievement (and behaviour) that are related to their perceptions of pupils' apparent willingness to learn rather than a child's true capability. Thus, the child with a bright personality who volunteers to do tasks and errands, and who is comfortable chatting with adults, might or might not be a capable, committed learner. On the other hand, shy, passive children can be perceived as less capable than they really are. This description is, of course, also in danger of becoming stereotypical. Some articulate children with a bright personality are also clever. Some under-confident, diffident types are strugglers (which is part of the explanation for their timidity). It is best to make decisions about pupils based on reliable evidence rather than instinct; the process takes longer but is normally more satisfactory for everyone.

Our awareness of these interwoven factors suggests that it is foolish for teachers to jump to conclusions about pupils' ability and potential. The outgoing child might, despite an apparently carefree approach to life, be concealing a deep unease that leads to underachievement. The shy child may be lacking self-confidence or may be an uncomplicated and contented person who does not feel the need to be assertive. As a newcomer it is sensible to observe carefully and get to know the children before making a judgement. As a rule and without being naïve, it is good to assume the best and not the worst about a child.

Being aware of social factors

Outgoing non-academic children are sometimes skilled in 'losing' themselves in a group of more capable children and benefiting from the reflected glory of their classmates' expertise and talent. By contrast, however, less confident children can lose out in two ways. First, they are unable to articulate their needs, so remain in ignorance; second, they lack the social and communication skills to find suitable collaborators and contribute effectively. Such children often end up being paired with unsuitable individuals who are left after more popular children have been absorbed into the more stable groups or chosen first for teams and collaborative groups. In sorting out working patterns and organising learning, you should take into account these various factors, step back from making spontaneous decisions about pupils' capability and look objectively at the evidence from completed work, comments made during question-and-answer sessions, and engagement with tasks.

As children work together, they experience a range of emotions and challenges which have as much to do with learning to get along with one another as with solving problems or exploring ideas. With this fact in mind, Baines *et al.* (2008) emphasise the importance of creating an inclusive and supportive classroom by developing the social, communicative and group working skills of all pupils. Quiet children might struggle with transmitting their ideas and relating to others but be capable of making a unique and valuable contribution to the endeavour. Noisy children can be annoying but have the potential to be excellent communicators with guidance and coaching.

In every class, therefore, there are children with varied personalities, talents, ideals and potential. Teachers have a responsibility towards all of them and need to employ different teaching strategies to:

- ensure that passive children are given as many interesting tasks as their assertive peers;
- allow children who do not find it easy to learn in traditional ways to have opportunity to experience different forms of learning;
- make allowance for ebullient behaviour born out of enthusiasm for the task in hand;
- use group work and collaboration as socially welding activities.

Making allowances for left-handed children

Teachers should also be aware of how many left-handed children are in the class and how to help them, including the provision of softer-leaded pencils, left-handed scissors, a left-handed ruler, an ergonomic left-handed mouse or a mouse set up for left-handers and a sloping board beneath paper to assist correct writing and drawing. There is no proof that left-handed people differ from right-handers in terms of educational attainment or IQ and various organisations exist to assist children and teachers, including a club for children. You are advised to watch out for children who sit 'side on' as this may indicate that one eye is weaker than the other, or that the child has a particular spatial preference. Left-handed children tend to write 'into' their bodies and may develop an awkward posture.

Activate your thinking!

Your assumptions about children's ability to learn and make progress have a direct influence upon their attitude to school in general, their willingness to co-operate and persevere, and ultimately their achievements.

> ### Good practice
> - Try not to pay undue attention to the more articulate and outgoing children.
> - Do not make unwarranted assumptions about children without reliable evidence.
> - Be wary of adopting a prevailing view of boys as naughty, girls as biddable.

Teaching children with special educational needs

Terminology

There have always been and always will be some children who struggle with certain aspects of schoolwork or suffer from some condition which prevents them from fulfilling their potential. Arthur *et al.* (2006) remind us that 'teaching in a primary school is a self-giving enterprise concerned with the betterment of [all] pupils' (p. 3). When considering how best to teach and support learning it is helpful to distinguish between children with special needs and those with special *educational* needs (SEN). The terminology is quite confusing: sometimes underachievers are referred to as 'slow learners' or pupils with 'special learning needs'. The term 'disability' is most often used to denote that the child suffers from a physical impairment, but it is also used in conjunction with the word 'learning'; thus, learning disability. The term 'handicapped' is now more often employed to indicate that the circumstances are hindering pupils from reaching their potential. Most often the handicap is resource-based and pupils cannot achieve things of which they are capable because equipment is not available or damaged or inappropriate for use. However, the handicap can also be a lack of time, poor working conditions (such as a stuffy room) or poor teaching. Consequently, children may have physical disabilities that do not, with appropriate support, handicap their educational opportunities or advancement, while some children have congenital problems that impact strongly on their capacity to learn. The remainder of this section is concerned with children who are falling behind in their academic work for a variety of different reasons, and who may or may not suffer from a medically diagnosed disability. Issues raised in the following sections about special learning needs are more fully addressed in Chapter 13.

Pupils labelled as 'less able' tend to fall into one of four categories, though more than one of the factors below may be relevant:

1. Children who do not possess the intellectual capacity to keep pace with the majority of children.
2. Children who are of such a high intellect that they find it difficult to fit into the familiar learning structures and may be unsettled in class.
3. Children who are capable of average to high achievement but underachieve owing to their erratic or uncontrolled behaviour. Such children are often referred to as emotionally disturbed or having behavioural difficulties. More recently, the term 'attention deficit and hyperactivity disorder' (ADHD) is employed when referring to children who struggle to concentrate and become disruptive (see Chapter 12 for details).
4. Children who, though intellectually capable, possess physical disabilities that tend to hinder their ability to attain their full potential.

Fostering achievement

Effective teaching should ensure every child succeeds by providing an inclusive education set within a culture of high expectations, building on what learners already know by structuring and pacing teaching so that pupils know what is to be learnt, how it can be done and why it is necessary. Teachers are encouraged to make learning vivid and real by developing pupil understanding through lessons that involve active enquiry, finding creative solutions, e-learning and group problem solving. Learning can be made more enjoyable and challenging if teachers respond a range of preferred learning styles: that is, showing awareness in your teaching techniques and strategies of the fact that some pupils learn more effectively through use of visual stimuli, some by practical 'hands-on/kinaesthetic' means and others through more traditional auditory means; see Chapter 9 for further information about learning styles/modes. You can enhance the richness of the pupils' experience by making links across the curriculum and inviting children to be partners with you in their learning by clarifying the task purpose, inviting their comments, taking their views seriously and providing specific and constructive feedback. Note, however, that Claxton (2004) is among those that alert us to the danger of taking learning styles too seriously as a rigid attitude can be to the pupil's detriment. Thus:

> The idea that we can find out someone's general-purpose 'learning style' is debunked, and the idea that having done so, we then have to treat it as immutable and teach them as if they were always and everywhere a 'visual learner' or had 'a high level of logical-mathematical intelligence' is not only false but pernicious. It locks [pupils] into a view of themselves, rather than encouraging them to grow.

(p. 9)

Employing the Code of Practice

The Code of Practice (DfES 2002) is a document with which every teacher should be familiar. See Chapter 13 for further details. An equivalent Code operates in Wales but not in Scotland, which has different procedures. It contains detailed information about the identification of children with SEN and suggestions for appropriate action. It is designed as a positive way of responding to the individual needs of children by means of a systematic process that draws upon expertise from inside and outside the school, and places great emphasis upon parental involvement (see Figure 4.1). Children with SEN have a strong right to be educated at a mainstream school and the local authority (LA, England) has to arrange for parents of children with SEN to be provided with relevant advice and information, together with a means of resolving disputes. Schools and nursery education providers have to inform parents when they are making special educational provision for their children, and can request a statutory assessment for a child who is causing concern. It is fair to say that even with the new synergy between schools and outside services the assessment procedures are lengthy and cumbersome. Teachers complain that more urgent action is often required for a particular child with SEN, especially if behaviour issues are adversely affecting class discipline.

Every maintained school must have a member of staff who acts as a special educational needs co-ordinator (SENCO) and a responsible person, usually the head teacher or a governor, who acts as a point of reference for the process. A school governing body has a sub-committee to take a particular interest in such educational provision; it is obliged to report to parents about policies for children with SEN and their implementation.

The Code recommends that in order to help match education provision to children's needs, schools and LAs should adopt a graduated approach through the two-stage process of

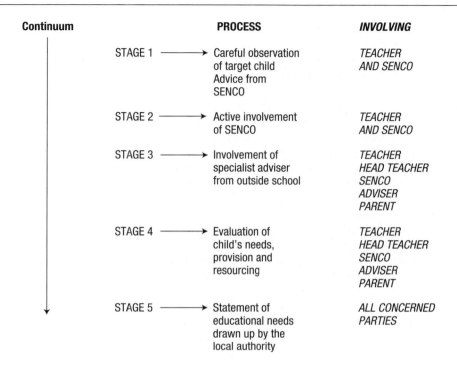

Continuum		PROCESS	INVOLVING
	STAGE 1 ——→	Careful observation of target child Advice from SENCO	*TEACHER AND SENCO*
	STAGE 2 ——→	Active involvement of SENCO	*TEACHER AND SENCO*
	STAGE 3 ——→	Involvement of specialist adviser from outside school	*TEACHER HEAD TEACHER SENCO ADVISER PARENT*
	STAGE 4 ——→	Evaluation of child's needs, provision and resourcing	*TEACHER HEAD TEACHER SENCO ADVISER PARENT*
	STAGE 5 ——→	Statement of educational needs drawn up by the local authority	*ALL CONCERNED PARTIES*

FIGURE 4.1 Special Needs Code of Practice implementation

School Action (when matters are handled internally) and *School Action Plus* (when outside agencies are involved). The same advice pertains to the early years process, namely, *Early Years Action* and *Early Years Action Plus*. The stages of the Code of Practice within *School Action* and *School Action Plus* are not necessarily sequential. A child can enter the process at different points, depending upon his or her circumstances. While all this is going on, class teachers have to do their best to cope with the children in question. The interim period of time can be stressful as events often move more slowly than expected. Long delays prove exasperating for over-stretched teachers as they struggle to help children who may, in certain cases, also suffer from related disorders with the accompanying discipline challenges they bring. All this takes place against a backdrop of government demands for higher standards of achievement in core subjects for every child, including those with SEN. Owing to the length of time involved in the procedures, simplification of the two-stage process by replacing it with a single school-based SEN category is now the preferred option.

Doing your best for children

Relevant provision for children with SEN emphasises *appropriateness* with effective support and monitoring, rather than unsuitable and undifferentiated work, which subsequently necessitates remedial action. Key principles for provision include the following:

- Having high but realistic expectations for all pupils.
- Greater support for parents through information, advice about learning at home and liaison with outside agencies (such as educational psychologists).

- Further inclusion of pupils in mainstream schools by providing appropriate resources, including staffing.
- Close liaison between schools and the support agencies, ensuring that parents are informed at all times except in cases where child abuse may be involved.

You will probably need to make adjustments to the way you explain things, the questions you ask and the tasks you set, such that all pupils can be involved and given opportunities to succeed. For example, use of simpler vocabulary in explanations; questions that invite a whole-group or class response; tasks that are simple to begin with and gradually become more complex; practical activities with equipment; and methods of recording findings that encourage visual as well as written responses. See Chapters 9 and 10 for further details about planning, teaching skills and organising for learning.

All teachers, including trainees, have to work hard to ensure that, regardless of status and previous history, all children are given the opportunity to learn, enjoy school and make best use of their opportunities. The increase in teaching assistants to support children with SEN means that teachers are responsible for more sophisticated patterns of classroom management and organisation, as they take account of the additional adult helpers, as well as a wider ability range of pupils (see, for example, Jacklin *et al.* 2006: 99–103). The greatest challenge for teachers comes from pupils whose educational problems are rooted in their emotional instability and antisocial behaviour. If you find yourself situated with a class of children in which a high proportion of pupils exhibit learning or behavioural challenges, it is essential that you regularly seek advice and support from the regular staff. Don't struggle on nobly in the mistaken belief that you are the only one experiencing these challenges. See Chapter 13 for fuller details about issues relating to inclusion and special educational needs.

Teaching minority ethnic children

In recent years there has been a large influx of immigrants from the EU and Commonwealth countries, together with asylum seekers from many different places in the world. Their arrival has strengthened the diversity of cultures, knowledge and expertise in the country but also created some serious challenges for the communities in which they are located. Particular pressures have fallen upon the education system and social services, as children arrive in school with little understanding of the indigenous norms and, in most cases, with English as an additional language (EAL; sometimes referred to as 'English as an extra language').

Catering for a range of needs

Once in school, children quickly pick up the prevailing language but their parents – notably mothers – might only speak their first language and struggle to master English sufficiently well to engage in a meaningful discussion with a teacher. In practice, there are issues about contacting parents, providing information and other forms of communication that tax teachers' ingenuity and test their resolve (see Chapter 5). There is a considerable amount of advice for school staffs from different groups with an interest in the welfare of immigrants, but it is far from easy to generalise, as each class contains such an exclusive and particular range of pupil needs. For example, Scott (2008) focuses on the particular needs of newly arrived older children (aged 7 to 11 years) and the importance of providing a structured programme for non-expert teachers and teaching assistants to develop knowledge and understanding of early-stage learners of EAL and their language-development needs.

Where possible, an adult who speaks the same tongue and can provide an in-depth evaluation of pupil abilities should be used to assess children for whom English is an additional language. If such a person is not available, the process naturally takes longer and the involvement of a bilingual child might be an alternative. In the absence of adult or child to act as interpreter, parental or family help can be called upon, as it is likely that at least one person has a sufficient grasp of English to explain the new child's needs, strengths and limitations. The process takes time and a school's SENCO is normally well placed to advise and assist.

Sometimes only one child from a particular country of origin will be in the class and receive individual attention; sometimes a number of pupils of similar origin will be in the class but vary in their grasp of English; there might be a large proportion of pupils speaking the same language, allowing for the formation of groups to receive targeted teaching or coaching in speaking, reading and writing. Perhaps the greatest challenge for a new teacher is to co-ordinate the many activities and adults involved in the special educational provision, especially if children are leaving the room at different times for tuition.

A major issue concerns the variation in achievement across ethnic minority groups. Four factors have been identified as significant for helping children to improve their educational attainment:

1. To agree a strategy that applies across the whole school.
2. To strive for effective learning and teaching, including support for bilingual pupils.
3. To create an ethos of respect, with a clear approach to issues relating to racism and behaviour.
4. To encourage parents and the community to undertake a full part in the life and development of the school.

Personal prejudice

The application of an agreed school policy to combat racism and unfair behaviour can only be effective if adults in school examine their own attitudes. Every teacher must be honest in confronting covert beliefs about the breadth of issues embraced by inclusive education and address areas of prejudice. This process is a testing one and sometimes uncomfortable, but unless you are willing to face up to your own disposition, it is difficult for you to make a positive difference to the situation and influence others. As a new teacher you need to be aware of any circumstance in which you may unwittingly show prejudicial attitudes. For example, children may be highly competent in their own language but struggle when expected to use English. It is possible to lower your expectations of the children and assume that they are far less capable than in fact they really are. While it may be tempting to allocate a child with limited English easy tasks to allow for his or her language deficit, it is important to limit the length of time that this happens to avoid tedium and, perhaps, disdain from classmates.

Cross-reference: Guided Reader Extract 56

Variations in achievement

Reasons for underachievement of particular minority groups are partly explained by the social and material deprivation that characterises those groups, as indicated by the incidence of free school meals. For instance, about one-third of Pakistani and Black pupils, and over half of all Bangladeshi and Gypsy/Roma pupils are eligible for free school meals, compared with under 15 per cent for White pupils. However, there isn't a simple relationship between these figures and academic achievement, as the biggest gap in attainment is between White pupils with and White pupils without free school meals. Clearly, there are other factors that need to be taken into account when addressing issues of underperformance. For instance, Gregory (2008) alerts us to the fact that pupils for whom English is not a first language may learn to speak and write but not possess the cultural insights that make learning meaningful for them, resulting in confusion or disaffection.

Strategies to combat underachievement

It is one thing to be aware of the trends noted above, it is quite another to have strategies for improving the situation. Every teacher and trainee should be asking a number of important questions about their teaching approach and attitude towards all pupils. As visitors to the classroom, trainee teachers are in a good position to see the situation with fresh eyes and, perhaps, offer insights that will help the regular teacher. Thus:

1. Are all children achieving their potential and gaining individual benefit from their education?
2. Which in-class factors appear to be contributing to underachievement?
3. Are some children underachieving because of lack of access to curriculum opportunities?
4. What steps can/should be taken to address the unsatisfactory situation, bearing in mind that some pupils may be academically capable but socially immature or unhappy?
5. Would some identifiable groups of children benefit from exclusive attention from an adult or a modified curriculum?

Gardner (2006) summarises ways to improve the quality of learning for all children, including children for whom English is an additional language. Thus, they should

> encounter an element of problem solving if their learning is to be effective. They need to be able to build on prior knowledge, not to be overloaded in terms of the number of objectives for any one lesson, be able to interact with others and be given time to complete tasks.
>
> (p. 78)

Gardner goes on to suggest that using puppets, verbal games involving pairs of children, role play, and rhyme and story, and visual tactile resources are strategies likely to enhance learning and create a language-rich environment.

The strategies you employ to ensure that the child is given appropriate tasks depend upon the extent of the adult language support available and the age of the child. Young children benefit from plenty of play activity, where they can immerse themselves in their imaginations, interact naturally with children their own age and become absorbed into the fabric of class life. Older children may struggle to orientate because they are more acutely aware of their language limitations and may not pick up a second language as easily as their younger brothers and sisters. A variety of approaches are commonly used to promote practice that is rooted in positive and high-expectation practice. Thus:

■ taking account of children's special needs in literacy sessions by implementing individual education plans (IEPs; see also Chapter 13) and utilising opportunities to develop language across the curriculum;

- promoting respect and understanding of diverse cultures, languages, ethnic groups, faith groups, travellers, asylum seekers and refugees in regular interaction with the class and the interest taken in (for example) cultural diversity and special occasions;
- working with parents from different community groups, both informally (e.g. as a classroom helper) and during planned events;
- ensuring that display work reflects the diversity in ethnicity;
- discussing issues relating to prejudice with the children, being careful not to unintentionally excite prejudice as you do so or merely load them with lists of things they should and should not do.

Integrating new children

One of the keys to successfully integrating all new children into the classroom is to assess their academic competence as accurately and swiftly as possible. In her work as a teacher of younger children, Heyda (2002) describes the strategies she employs when dealing with the arrival of new children in the class who speak little or no English:

1. Welcome the child with a big smile and a warm friendly voice.
2. Assign a 'buddy', preferably someone who speaks the language, to accompany the child throughout the day.
3. Take care not to use 'baby talk' that might embarrass the child or speak too loudly as if the child has a hearing impairment.
4. Utilise support staff at an early stage.
5. Be encouraging and positive.
6. Use the child's mistakes as starting points for progress.
7. Use lots of visual aids to get across concepts, such as drawing pictures next to vocabulary and using photographs and diagrams to explain things.
8. Give the child plenty of hands-on experiences.
9. Label the room with key words.

In many respects, Heyda's sound advice applies in many respects to work with children generally. In a multilingual situation in which there are numerous children who speak the same first language, the challenges of incorporating a newcomer into the class are usually less severe than if the child is the only pupil who speaks the language. In such circumstances the school is likely to have additional adult support for EAL, though, as noted above, the proliferation of different languages in the school and the involvement of various language assistants present formidable organisation and management issues.

Good practice

Explore the CRE website with particular reference to the themes of 'curriculum teaching and assessment' and 'pupils'.

Being a child in your class

What is it like to be a child in your classroom: a delight, a bore, an endurance test, a laugh, a puzzle? Much depends upon whether you see the pupils as the enemy to be subdued or a group of inexperienced youngsters with whom you will need to develop a working relationship to ensure that they gain the most benefit from their time with you. To help you decide what it is like for pupils in your class, consider the following questions:

- *Which children do you get to know first?*
  Is this because you are working closely with them or because they are the noisiest or the tallest or the prettiest?
- *Do you tend to ignore some children?*
  Perhaps because they are shy or you feel uncomfortable with them?
- *What kind of behaviour upsets you most?*
  Is this because you don't know how to handle it or because it affronts your dignity?
- *How interested are you in children's opinions?*
  Do you really care or do you go through the motions of appearing interested?
- *How much do you want children to like you?*
  Will you be too soft, try too hard to be nice or perhaps be too fierce and unreasonable?

Cullingford (1997) suggests that successful teachers will be fair and consistent, will praise more than blame, will be clear and patient, will ask questions and listen, rather than shout and present repetitive exercises. Wyse (2001) recommends the acronym REG, where R stands for Respect, E for Empathy and G for Genuineness. Thus: respect can come from your positive attitude to children; empathy is about really trying to understand how the child is feeling and appreciating their point of view; and genuineness is about being honest with the child. In the light of these points, it is worth thinking about the children you know in your class or groups and how you relate to them:

- The children who show the greatest self-confidence
- The children who are ill at ease and in what contexts
- The children who co-operate
- The children who gain most of your approval
- The children who seem to have a bright future in school
- The children who seem to have the odds stacked against them.

And most significantly, what your answers reveal about you as teacher. Remember that children like teachers who are firm but fair, willing to explain things patiently and have a positive attitude to work and people. They are ill at ease with adults who hector, complain, agitate and fulminate. Which of the two descriptions describes you at your best and at your worst?

Making progress as a trainee teacher

Fitting in

Every successful teacher has established routines, procedures and patterns of interaction with pupils that contribute to what may be described as a 'classroom rhythm'; the teacher does not take kindly if this hard-earned efficiency is disrupted by a well-meaning but insensitive trainee. Classroom rhythms are developed by creating a positive learning environment, convincing the children that it is in their best interests to co-operate in maintaining the existing ethos and providing a thirst for knowledge that gains irresistible momentum. While it is true that adult–pupil negotiation forms an ongoing and integral component in defining the social world of the classroom, it is equally the case that teachers need to establish their priorities and boundaries or pupils will attempt to do it for them, leading to disharmony and unnecessary tension as the children vie for influence. Although school policies are useful in broadly establishing the way things happen in a particular classroom, final decisions about day-to-day interactions and routines still belong to the individual teacher.

Trainee teachers are obliged to adopt the supervising teacher's general approach to routine and procedural matters, especially at the commencement of a school placement, regardless of whether they agree with the philosophy underlying them. If you are operating on someone else's 'territory' you will soon discover that it is far from easy to implement someone else's decisions and still remain true to your own beliefs. Nevertheless, that is precisely what you must endeavour to do. In this regard, it is helpful if teachers are able to explain to trainees the rationale for decisions rather than merely expecting unthinking compliance, though you might need to ask for such clarification. Children quickly become alert to any inconsistencies they detect between their regular teacher and the newcomer and may react adversely, usually to the trainee teacher's cost. Sometimes your (apparently) obvious improvement or solution to a problem has already been tried by the resident teacher and found to be unsuitable. You can console yourself with the thought that when you have a class of your own you will be in a position to implement some of the things that were denied to you while in training.

Managing the class

An essential quality for the development of a successful teaching and learning environment is the ability to organise and manage classroom affairs (see Chapter 10). All teachers want to maintain an orderly environment to facilitate progress but order should not be confused with rigidity or passivity for, as Desforges (1995) wittily points out, parade grounds are often associated with firm discipline, clear control and immaculate performances but graveyards are also orderly places. Neither venue, however, is noteworthy for the quality of the learning that takes place there. It is possible to be efficient without being effective.

Arnall (2007) insists that discipline should not be confused with punishment. She suggests that 'you can set limits, provide guidance and correct misbehaviour without the use of punishments' (p. 19). The good practice that adults employ for restless children and those with limited attention spans is relevant in organising learning for *all* children.

At certain times of the year, carefully organised lesson structures are disrupted by events such as a block of the timetable allocated to swimming, play rehearsals, music practices, fire drills and educational visits. Although it is not possible to anticipate every eventuality, an awareness of wider school happenings is essential. Fitting into your new school is smoother when you take account of these and the other issues noted above.

Good practice

In requesting clarification about the regular teacher's way of working and responses to children, be careful not to give your host even the slightest hint of criticism.

Professional learning

All teachers, regardless of whether they are new to the profession or seasoned practitioners, need to think carefully about their practice, seek advice from more experienced colleagues and try to keep abreast of research findings that provide insights into effective teaching and learning. This process is commonly referred to as 'professional learning' and trainee teachers are normally required by their colleges to maintain a written record of their progress across the weeks of school placement as evidence of their development. This type of review should not be confused with providing evidence to show that formal teaching standards have been met. The reviews are intended to be reflective commentaries on school experience to demonstrate your ability to analyse situations constructively as a means of adjusting practice for the benefit of the children you teach and those that you will teach in future classroom situations. The best commentaries combine an awareness of immediate requirements with general principles of practice. One trainee, Helena, wrote at length about the first two weeks of her placement, including the following extracts:

Week One
I found week one fairly challenging because of discipline problems. The class has a number of lower ability children and one child with special educational needs who is on medication to help control his behaviour. My previous experiences in school had not prepared me to deal with anyone like him. However, by observing the strategies used by the class teacher and spending time in a one-to-one situation with the child, I began to feel more confident. I have already begun to change my previous ideas on discipline, as I realise that shouting and constant telling-off is not the best option. Discussion with the class teacher helped me to begin to work out the most effective strategies to use with the class. I am also struggling with managing my time. I have spent every night over the past week preparing literacy and numeracy lessons, leaving me quite jaded. After talking to the teacher and tutor, they convinced me that the pressure would grow easier as I get into the swing of things. I can hardly wait!

Week Two
This week was much busier than the last one. Each lesson flew past and what felt like ten minutes was in fact half an hour and work that I thought would be completed was not. The class teacher assured me that this was a common problem. During Friday's literacy hour I did not check the finishing time and had to rush to assembly. In future I must not make assumptions about times. Each morning I take registration. It made me feel quite insecure with all the eyes looking up at me from the carpet, with the whispering getting louder! During sessions that I taught, the children were less attentive than with the class teacher and I was shocked when some of them back-chatted when I told them what to do. However, I used some of the class teacher's strategies and found that the situation improved slowly. For instance, I separated children if they were noisy together, wrote the names of persistent offenders on the board and made children stay in at break time if they did not respond and concentrate on their work. When I first dismissed the class there was a rush for the door and general pandemonium, so I became much stricter, stood by the door and dismissed them row by row, which improved the situation enormously. I have also come to appreciate the importance of getting resources absolutely ready. I forgot to put spellings examples in order for Thursday's lesson and so produced the difficult words first, which meant that the less able children struggled and became

frustrated. Next time I made sure I started with the easiest ones! I have found that annotating my present lesson plans, thinking positively about failures instead of getting miserable, and modifying my plans so that they took more account of children's needs is starting to have a positive effect on the quality of my teaching.

Helena did not continue to write at such length. However, she started as she meant to go on by taking time to evaluate her progress, gain advice from the class teacher and tutor, and amend her approach on the basis of what she had observed and learned. After the first two weeks Helena began to summarise points, note critical incidents, refer to key decisions and give an indication of the action that she was taking to remedy weaker areas and further strengthen weaker ones. Nonetheless, she was careful not to spend too much time being introspective and certainly did not allow herself to mope. She entered plenty of positive comments, too. See Chapters 14 and 16 for suggestions about professional learning during the induction year and beyond.

Professional practice

Teachers' responsibilities

It used to be said that if teachers weren't exhausted by four o'clock and on their way home by a quarter past, they hadn't been doing their job properly. Today, with the many different demands upon a teacher's time, most teachers consider themselves fortunate to leave before five, having worked throughout the day with little or no break. After-school and lunchtime clubs and activities are now commonplace and almost every teacher has a curriculum or related responsibility. In small schools each teacher may have oversight of more than one curriculum area. Paperwork has increased considerably, and the emphasis on assessment for learning has required that ever more detailed records are becoming the norm. Once home, there is further effort needed to mark pupils' work, prepare resources and make final adjustments to lesson plans. Accountability to parents and the local community has become a key factor as funding increasingly depends upon numbers of children in school and the traditional safety net of the old local education authority has been replaced in many schools by managerial (though less so curriculum) autonomy.

Teachers' emotional security

There is general agreement that children need to feel secure in school but it is possible to overlook the fact that adults, too, need to be relaxed if they are to achieve peak effectiveness in their work. Teaching has always been a demanding and sometimes exhausting job; in the recent whirl of national legislation, however, the demands have increased sharply. Many teachers complain that they have been scrutinised more closely than any other profession and expected to cope with an unreasonable rate of imposed change (Cockburn 1996; Woods 1997). A review of primary teaching chaired by Sir Robin Alexander (Alexander 2009) indicated that, among many other factors, the relentless pursuit of government-initiated targets, constant inspection of teaching quality and a seeming obsession with national test results had placed unreasonable burdens on dedicated teachers, some of whom found that they had lost their enthusiasm for the job. See Chapter 2 for fuller details. While all employment involves stresses and strains, especially those that involve close contact with people, teaching seems to stand alone in its potential for exhaustion and, paradoxically, for rich personal reward.

One of the reasons for this tension between benefits and losses is the extent to which teachers consider themselves to be responsible for children's learning and personal growth. Teachers' self-identity is partly rooted in their classroom competence, so any perceived failures (real or imagined) on their part can leave them feeling demoralised. In addition, the external imposition of targets has done little to relieve the belief in the profession that teachers are losing their autonomy. The whirlwind of initiatives from government has left some teachers feeling breathless and guilty that they are unable to keep abreast of all the changes. Opportunities to 'stop and stare' are few and must be treasured. Even so, without creating these havens of stillness, teachers burn out and lose their sharpness.

Another danger for teachers is that they can grow cynical as they struggle to accommodate the many new requirements into their busy schedules of planning, teaching, assessing, marking, recording and filling reports. The intensity of teaching can easily lead to over-commitment and increased vulnerability (Cox and Heames 1999; Bubb and Earley 2004). In the midst of this, a school's prime resource − reflective and enthusiastic teachers − must be safeguarded and self-management is crucially important in this regard (Thody and Bowden 2004).

Cross-reference: Guided Reader Extract 57

Rite of passage

As noted earlier, trainee teachers have little control over where they are placed to gain experience of teaching and the teacher role, and often enter a school that is largely unknown to them in respect of its ethos, staff membership and patterns of behaviour. Trainees have to cope with the effort required to adjust to the prevailing expectations, establish and maintain relationships with staff, learn procedures and adapt to the school's priorities, some of which may be abstruse and difficult to interpret initially. In addition, as Maynard (2001) describes, trainee teachers have to adopt the class teacher's practices and priorities, which is itself a challenge; even if they quickly orientate, it takes time before they become fully aware of the reasons underpinning the teacher's actions. Thus:

> It was through acting like a teacher, initially through becoming someone else, that students [trainees] began to develop an identity as a teacher. In addition, trainee teachers appropriated their teachers' discourse, even though they did not appear to be aware of doing so, nor initially share the same conceptual understandings as their teachers. The use of this discourse enabled trainee teachers to gain acceptance into the community of practice, the approval of their class teacher, the means by which they could negotiate richer and more appropriate understandings.
>
> (p. 49)

Medwell (2007) suggests that acting like a teacher is part of the contract between a trainee and the placement school. She offers two reasons for children respecting a teacher. Primarily 'because teachers act like teachers, sending out subtle signals that indicate they know what they are doing, have authority and expect children to behave well' (p. 110). Medwell then provides some fifteen strategies to assist the process of 'acting like a teacher', including knowing the children by name as quickly as possible, dressing suitably, moving confidently about the room and sounding confident, having an appropriate signal for gaining pupils' attention and, crucially, knowing the systems and procedures that operate in the particular setting. However, Medwell also alerts us to the sorts of pitfalls awaiting the unwary trainee teacher (indeed, *any* teacher) including inappropriate tasks, poor explanations, dilly-dallying, using inducements to gain popularity and imploring rather than insisting. Notably, the author warns against over-praising, ignoring bad behaviour, using sarcasm, acting inconsistently and failing to employ your personality to full effect (for the complete list, see Medwell 2007: 111–12).

If you want to successfully negotiate this 'rite of passage' and enter fully into the community of practice, you have to make rapid adjustments and learn the unwritten rules that are taken for granted by the regular staff in the school. You may not fully grasp the reasons for teachers' actions and priorities but be assured that understanding will develop as you become absorbed into school life. You will also become aware that subtle differences of approach and emphasis exist within a staff that is apparently wholly united and agreed. Some teachers and assistants might attempt to entice you into adopting a critical perspective on life in school. Resist them!

Cross-reference: Guided Reader Extract 29

Multiple intelligences, teaching and learning

Intelligences

Emotional intelligence (EI) can be measured as an *emotional intelligence quotient* (EQ) and describes an ability, capacity or skill to perceive, assess and manage the emotions of self, of others and of groups. As a relatively new area of psychological research, the definition of EI is constantly changing, but it has been made popular by Goleman (1995, 1999, 2005) who has been instrumental in promoting the central role played by the emotions in decisions and actions. It is fair to add that Goleman's work has not been universally accepted and others in the field regard some of his claims as rather suspect (e.g. Eysenck 2000).

The concept of *emotional intelligence* draws from the work on multiple intelligences by Howard Gardner. The author suggests that the traditional notion of intelligence, based on IQ testing, is far too limiting. Instead, he proposed seven, and later nine different intelligences to account for the range of human potential (see Figure 4.2). Gardner defined the first seven intelligences in his book *Frames of Mind* (1983) and added the last two in *Intelligence Reframed* (1999). He claims that all human beings have multiple intelligences. These multiple intelligences can be nurtured and strengthened, or ignored and weakened.

Disputed forms of intelligence

Gardner argues that while there is a good case to be made for *spiritual* intelligence, he rejects it as a distinctive form of intelligence because people's capacity to grasp transcendent truths ultimately depends on affective ('to do with emotions') characteristics and we have no scientifically reliable way of investigating such traits. Similarly, he rejects *moral* intelligence on the grounds that morality involves value judgements whereas intelligence is by nature value-neutral, though this point of view is an issue of some dispute. As for *naturalist* intelligence – the ability to recognise and classify natural species and understand ecological relationships – Gardner insists that it deserves to be recognised as a genuine intelligence, similar to the seven described in the original theory. He also argues that *existential* intelligence qualifies as 'an intelligence' in its own right, while admitting that there does not appear to be a specific part of the brain dedicated to dealing with such profound questions about deep human issues.

Descriptions of the intelligences vary slightly in the literature but the following is based on the original texts (with a shorthand description in brackets):

Verbal-linguistic intelligence ('word smart'):
well-developed verbal skills and sensitivity to the sounds, meanings and rhythms of words

Mathematical-logical intelligence ('number/reasoning smart'):
an ability to think conceptually and abstractly, and capacity to discern logical or numerical patterns

Musical intelligence ('music smart'):
an ability to produce and appreciate rhythm, pitch and timbre

Visual-spatial intelligence ('picture smart'):
a capacity to think in images and pictures, to visualise accurately and abstractly

Bodily-kinesthetic intelligence ('body smart'):
an ability to control one's body movements and to handle objects skilfully

Interpersonal intelligence ('people smart'):
the capacity to detect and respond appropriately to the moods, motivations and desires of others

Intrapersonal intelligence ('self smart'):
a capacity to be self-aware and in tune with inner feelings, values, beliefs and thinking processes

Naturalist intelligence ('nature smart'):
the ability to recognise and categorise plants, animals and other objects in nature

Existential intelligence ('philosophy smart'):
demonstrating sensitivity and capacity to tackle deep questions about human existence, such as the meaning of life, why we die and how we got here.

FIGURE 4.2 Multiple intelligences theory

Implications for classroom practice

In practice, schools focus most of their attention on linguistic and logical-mathematical learning (see the first and second descriptions in Figure 4.2), sometimes at the expense of other areas; as evidence of this tendency, it is certainly true that we esteem highly the articulate and mathematically inclined people in our culture. However, Gardner argues that we should give equal attention to individuals who tend to learn better by other means: for example, artists, architects, musicians, naturalists, designers, dancers, therapists, entrepreneurs, and others who enrich the world but may not be recognised in school.

Gardner is largely correct when he complains that many children who possess artistic gifts don't necessarily receive much reinforcement for them in school, though in the UK there have been efforts to improve the status of these subjects – for instance, by requiring schools to teach PE regularly and encouraging 'experts' to visit classrooms and share expertise. There is a danger that some children that have a propensity towards the 'Arts' underachieve in literacy and mathematics, which are not aligned to their ways of thinking and learning, and are viewed by teachers as dull or less able. By contrast, the theory of multiple intelligences implies a transformation in the way schools are run. It suggests that teachers be trained to present their lessons in a wide variety of ways by using music, co-operative learning, art activities, role play, multimedia, field trips, inner reflection, and so forth, though it is probably fair to say that good teachers have always employed such diversity of method.

Emotions and the work of the teacher

Regardless of arguments about the validity of emotional intelligence, three general principles should underpin your practice as you focus on recognising that:

Your role is important in helping children feel safe

Without secure and confident teachers and teaching assistants, children are unlikely to gain maximum benefit from their education. You and the other adult staff are undertaking a vital task in helping to educate the nation's children and provide for the future stability of the country and, ultimately, the world. This notion is not a fanciful one. You do not know whether a child sitting in front of you is a prospective genius, leader or entrepreneur. And even if most pupils lead relatively unexceptional lives, they are unique individuals with their own special contribution to make to society. Let that thought motivate you.

It is essential to use every means to encourage and support colleagues

Teachers who spend time praising and helping children to feel positive about themselves and their classmates may need to offer the same level of support to their co-workers. There is a saying that you should not judge a book merely by looking at the cover. In any staffroom there are folk who need reassurance, a word of comfort, a kindly smile and a pat on the back. Even apparently confident and assured characters can be inwardly vulnerable. Schools rely on active collaboration across the whole team, and even if you are a trainee teacher with little direct control over events, a word of appreciation, a short note of thanks or willingness to listen can help to transform someone's day and give that person hope. Such actions not only demonstrate compassion for fellow humans but also provide a foundation for a successful school placement and establish an attitude of mind that you can carry with you throughout the rest of your career.

It is better to focus on your achievements and successes than dwell on failures

Teachers possess and exhibit daily a range of skills and knowledge that are easily taken for granted: organising, planning, summarising information, public exposition, relating to a range of children and adults, using computer technology, curriculum expertise and so on. A bad day often simply means that the call upon these skills has been excessive or you lacked the experience to cope. It is frequently the case that what you consider to have been 'an awful lesson' was, in fact, simply less good than it might have been under ideal circumstances. In evaluating your progress as a teacher and the distance yet to be covered, don't lose sight of how far you have already travelled. Remember that many successful people in other professions would quake at the knees at the thought of being left in charge of a class of children for even five minutes.

Guarding your wellbeing

Teaching is rewarding and occasionally thrilling but as noted earlier in the chapter there are also physical demands (which can lead to exhaustion), psychological factors (rooted in concerns about being good enough to succeed) and emotional stresses and strains to combat. A number of warning signs exist that signal potentially adverse effects on your general health and therefore the ability to carry out tasks efficiently. Five symptoms indicate that difficulties *are* imminent: persistent anxiety; lack of enthusiasm; resentment towards pupils; bad temper and intolerance; reluctance about going to school. Thus:

Persistent anxiety

This unsettling emotion goes deeper than commonplace tinges of worry, and eats into every aspect of life in and outside school. Some people say that they are unable to 'switch off'. They fall asleep straight away at night but find themselves wide awake in the early hours. Sometimes a persistently anxious person takes on more and more responsibilities, well beyond the ability to cope, as a means of combating the rising sense of panic. If this description characterises your experience, it is sensible to seek professional help urgently. Do not imagine that you can somehow 'pull yourself together' or that you will be thought the worse of by asking for assistance.

Lack of enthusiasm for the job

Every teacher entertains feelings of doubt. Every trainee teacher has times when fervour diminishes and he or she may even entertain vocational uncertainty. These emotions are not unusual and can often be attributed to fatigue and poor health. Schools are places where germs are easily transmitted, owing to the close proximity of adults and pupils, so wash your hands thoroughly and often. Minor ill health can have a significant impact on the quality of lessons – or at least that is how it feels to you – which in itself creates additional anxiety. At such times it is essential to remind yourself of two things. First, no teacher is perfect and everyone has off-days. Second, children will learn despite your feebleness. A good night's sleep and a talk with a sympathetic friend will usually remedy loss of appetite for the job. If humanly possible, avoid the work–sleep–work syndrome, where your life revolves around school to the detriment of all else. Although easier said than done when you are immersed in lesson plans, marking and resources, a complete break from the whirlpool of activity is time well spent.

Resentment towards pupils

It is undeniable that some pupils are more troublesome than others. Occasionally, a child gets 'under your skin' and you find that it is hard to resist becoming irritated or convinced that your professional identity is being undermined. See also **Discussion Point 3**, Chapter 15. A small minority of teachers become disillusioned with the job and express their concerns publicly and bitterly after struggling to cope with troublesome individuals over a period of time. Others fall into the trap of compensating for their own shortcomings and difficulties by criticising the children or their upbringing or parental attitudes. While there is often some truth in these allegations, it is all too easy to flounder in a chasm of negativity. However resentful you feel, try hard not to view uncooperative children as your enemies; instead, search for ways to engage them in learning and, while making it absolutely clear that you will brook no nonsense from them, make a concerted effort to convince them that learning is more enjoyable than 'mucking about'.

Bad temper and intolerance

Even the most patient adults sometimes over-react to children's behaviour or adult comments. For the most part the emotion soon passes and is forgotten. However, if you find that you are regularly employing authoritarian tactics to enforce discipline or getting tetchy with adults with whom you work, it is time to take yourself in hand, step back and coolly evaluate the source of your impatience. Sleep deprivation is often the main reason for such an uncharacteristic response, but it can also be due to work overload or feeling threatened. If the situation does not improve, seek help from your tutor or mentor or a trusted friend. It is likely that those who know you will be aware of your irritability and relieved that you are facing up to the problem.

Reluctance about going to school

Even experienced teachers admit that their confidence can sink to a low point prior to going into school, particularly at the start of the week and almost always at the beginning of term. For the vast majority, however, it is also true that they feel completely different once they walk into the classroom. Although as a trainee teacher you are probably not earning a salary (or, at best, just a small remuneration), teachers are paid to teach! Sometimes the pleasure that teaching engenders can cause us to forget that it is a form of employment and, like any other job, requires effort and perseverance and a reasonably consistent standard of performance. On the other hand, if you start panicking at the thought of school, consult medical advice without delay.

Teaching and personal identity

Day *et al.* (2007: 106–7) claim that a teacher's identity consists of competing interactions between professional, situated (socially located) and personal factors. *Professional* identity is 'open to the influence of long-term policy and social trends as to what constitutes a good teacher, classroom practitioner, etc.'. *Situated* or socially located identity within a specified school, department or classroom is 'affected by pupils, support and feedback loops from teachers' immediate working context, connected to long-term identity'. *Personal* identity is 'based on life outside school; it could have various competing elements, such as identity of being a father, son, partner, etc.'. *Feedback* from family and friends often becomes a source of tension as the individual's sense of identity could become out of step. The authors conclude that although pressures are an inevitable part of work and life, nevertheless:

> There are likely to be times when everyday pressures turn into pressures that make teachers more vulnerable which, in turn, can have adverse emotional effects. These can impact on teachers' wellbeing, which can be positively and negatively affected by a number of issues, such as management of the school, the school ethos and culture, staff morale and opportunities for CPD.
>
> (pp. 121–2)

A teacher who works in a school where such feelings and attitudes can be openly expressed and discussed without rancour is fortunate. However, many teachers find that opportunities for such openness are few, either because the school ethos does not espouse it or because life is too busy and colleagues too preoccupied with their own worries to listen. Good team spirit, however, comes from support and encouragement, so making the effort to share constructively pays dividends (see Wilson 2004).

The skills of listening carefully, sympathising and affirming should not be reserved for work with children; adults also need to hear that they are needed, valued and trusted. Publicly expressed statements of gratitude for advice, guidance or example can enliven an ailing colleague. Teachers who are at ease with school life should support those who presently are not, as comradeship and empathy can strengthen and heal. Just as children's experiences and attitudes affect their performance in school, it is similar for adults, though they are usually more skilled in concealing their feelings and often see it as part of their professional responsibilities to remain silent. If, for whatever reason, consolation, sympathy and encouragement are not available within school for you, it is essential to spend time in building an informal network of confidantes outside school as an alternative. In doing so, Lawrence (2006) offers some sensible advice on keeping things in perspective by insisting that while teachers should be careful to take their work seriously they should never take *themselves* so seriously that they lose their sense of humour. Life in school relies on every member functioning efficiently, so effort expended in supporting others benefits everyone, including you.

Whatever the stage of your career, you will be aware that being a teacher is a demanding, exhilarating and emotionally charged experience. There will be good days and not-so-good days, outstanding lessons and mediocre ones. Learn to take it in your stride, reflect upon your practice, keep buoyant and don't allow the job to become such an obsession that it dominates your life.

Activate your thinking!

On your way home every night make a mental list of your many achievements during the day rather than dwelling on the shortcomings.

Good practice

Write down the six things that frustrate you most about being a teacher. List them under three headings: those I can change by myself; those I can change with the help of others; those I cannot change. Begin to work on the items in the first two categories; destroy the third.

Cross-reference: Guided Reader Extracts 25 and 36

Care of the voice

The voice is probably the single most valuable and vulnerable teaching resource that teachers possess, so it pays to take good care of it (Kovacic 2005). For instance, avoid placing undue pressure on the voice by sudden switches from a normal speaking tone to a fierce or artificial one. In particular, pushing the voice so that it becomes a 'bark' will cause serious damage if prolonged. In addition to avoiding smoke and polluted atmospheres, it helps to breathe in carefully through the nose (and out through the mouth); to refrain from eating unsuitable foods (such as very spicy ones); and to use alcohol and dairy products sparingly. General health can be improved through humming quietly before speaking (making the lips vibrate), standing upright (not slouching) and taking regular pauses when addressing the class. Teachers should also keep to a minimum the amount that they clear the throat, which causes the vocal cords to collide with accompanying wear and tear, talk too quickly (which leads to inadequate breathing and increases chest tension) and use an unnatural pitch or forced whisper. Teachers can help themselves by sipping water during the lesson – it is recommended that you drink at least a litre of water each day and avoid excessive drinks that contain caffeine. Make a determined effort not to push your voice when it is tired or hoarse.

It is important to support your voice with deep breaths from the diaphragm, the wall that separates your chest and abdomen, so it pays to persevere in practising good breathing techniques when talking. Once you get into the habit of breathing correctly, it quickly becomes natural, though it is surprisingly easy to lapse into shallow breathing. Singers and public speakers are taught exercises that improve breath control, because it places a great strain on the body if speech is forced from the throat without the help of 'supporting breath' from deeper in the body.

It goes without saying that the ability to relax during teaching assists the health of the voice, too, with the accompanying improvement in speech clarity that results. It is also important to exercise regularly, as this increases stamina and muscle tone, and provides for good posture and breathing, which are necessary for proper speaking. Getting sufficient rest is essential, as studies show that physical fatigue has a negative effect on your voice. Some specialists recommend including a lot of whole grain, fruit and vegetables in your diet, as these foods contain important vitamins A, E and C, which help to keep the mucus membranes that line the throat healthy. Your voice is your powerhouse, so treat it with the utmost respect (Grant–Williams 2002).

Good practice

1. Breathe deeply from the bottom of the lungs
2. Warm up by humming and freeing your jaw, tongue and lips
3. Stand upright when speaking
4. Drink plenty of room-temperature water
5. Take regular breaks from talking
6. Speak naturally.

Case studies

Martha

Martha's classroom seems to flow with paper. Her desk is littered with exercise books, worksheets and half-finished drawings. The walls drip with numerous charts, pictures, unmounted writing and the remains of an earlier display. Tables are pushed together in groups of three and some chairs are touching the wall. There are corners: a play area, large construction, a dressing-up box and a row of CD players strewn about the shelf. Two computers and printers are greatly in demand and children jostle for position. The atmosphere is exuberant, with children moving freely about the room, chattering, laughing and busy. After a few minutes' observation, it becomes clear that much of this activity is rather purposeless. The noise level rises as Martha, immersed in a queue of children, calls out instructions and general warnings that many children appear to ignore or respond to for a short time before resuming their unsatisfactory behaviour.

Martha likes the children to get down to their work quickly. She regularly uses photocopied sheets full of tasks that the children have to work through and hand in when completed. The tasks are varied, some requiring the application of library skills and investigation, the majority desk-bound and requiring a single correct answer.

To cope with the constant flow of queries and questions, Martha and her flustered assistant spend much of their time dealing with children on a one-to-one basis, repeating answers to the same query from different children. Occasionally, she stops the class to remind them of the need to behave or of what they are supposed to be doing.

Although the tasks are not differentiated, the worksheets gradually become more demanding so that although all the children can attempt the first one, less able children find later ones too difficult. As the session continues, some children become restless as they tire of the work and begin to copy from more confident neighbours; others work very slowly, choosing the easiest elements and avoiding anything conceptually difficult; a few hurry through to be ahead of friends. The standard of work is variable. Martha often warns individual children to 'get on with your work'.

At the end of the lesson, she tells the class to clear up and put the completed sheets in a box on her desk and the uncompleted ones in their trays. There is a scramble to do so and some sheets are crumpled. Martha raises her voice and tells the class to 'be more sensible'; one child is strongly rebuked and told to sit down on his own in the corner. Children find their snacks, chatter about card 'swaps' and playground activities as they noisily leave the room; no one remains behind to talk to the teacher about the work. She sends out the last child after saying that she is 'tired of your behaviour'. She walks down to the staffroom and is the first to make a drink before flopping down in an armchair. When the head teacher mentions that it is her turn to have a trainee teacher next term, Martha pulls a face and says that she hopes that this one is 'a bit better than the one I had last year; she was useless; couldn't keep control'. The head teacher smiles to herself but says nothing, secretly hoping that Martha will apply for the vacancy in a nearby school in which she has expressed interest.

A few weeks later, Martha comes across the uncompleted worksheets and throws them away. During the tidying-up prior to a parents' evening, several children ask her what they should do with their completed work from earlier this term found in their trays. The teacher collects them all in and, when the children have gone home, hurriedly ticks the best of them and helps the TA mount them on an empty display board together with some colourful, bold labels and an impressive title.

During parents' evening, Martha speaks loudly to parents, extolling the merits of their children and offering comments about their achievements, edged with inferences about their potential 'if they concentrated better on the work'. She regales the parents with impressive talk about assessment for learning, layered assessments, targets and individualised learning. Parents are quite pleased to hear positive things but feel unaccountably troubled as the teacher's report does not square with their children's diminishing enthusiasm for school.

Diane

Diane's classroom, with its interactive displays, selected examples of children's work, due regard to safety and easy access to equipment is the envy of her colleagues. Children's work is mounted with bold labels that enhance the room's appearance. Most displays consist of children's contributions, though here and there the teacher's artistic touches are evident. Photographs of the children in a variety of formal and informal poses, together with dates of birth and a list of their favourite foods and animals, are arranged on a small board. Well-thumbed documents in carefully labelled folders are in place on a shelf behind Diane's desk. The room is orderly but not clinical; the atmosphere is purposeful yet relaxed.

The class always seems businesslike without being rigid; children work singly and in groups and relate together comfortably. There is little acrimony and many moments of genuine laughter and smiles. On other occasions, there is a serious intent about the children as they concentrate on the task. Peer support is powerfully evident.

Diane has a brisk but friendly manner. She begins a session by reviewing previous work and asking thought-provoking questions, trying to involve as many different children as possible. The children sit up straight in anticipation of what the teacher might say and don't seem afraid to venture an answer even if they are unsure. In turn, Diane treats every response seriously and tries to make a positive comment about its merits; children are encouraged to speculate and offer their own thoughts. She insists that other children respect what is said by others. The overall impression of these whole-class times is one of mutual respect and a healthy learning environment.

Diane introduces the lesson by telling the children what she hopes they will learn and do, explains the activities and gives some specific instruction to each group. It is clear that the children are used to showing initiative as they sort themselves out, gather resources, settle to work and discuss the activities. Different children are engaged in similar tasks but there are subtle differences between the groups: some are using an open-ended worksheet as a starting point for discovering new facts by way of a library search; others are using books pre-selected by the teacher to check some facts; a further group is using a computer databank to extract information. While offering close guidance to one group of children, Diane nevertheless spends some time with each group in turn and tries to give each child some personal attention, even when a TA is supervising them. It is clear who is in charge but Diane relates so easily to people that it doesn't cause any tension. Some pupils wander out of their place to see her but generally the children persevere and appear to have a shared sense of purpose. When a child occasionally becomes over-excited or silly, Diane stands and looks hard at the culprit without saying anything; other children alert the transgressor to the teacher's concerns and normality resumes. Once the situation is calmer, she walks across to the group and quietly enquires if she can assist with anything but does not mention the incident.

From time to time, Diane stops the class to point out an instance of good work or to commend someone who is trying hard; the children listen attentively. Towards the end of the session, she tells the class that in a few minutes there will be opportunity to share with others; one or two children explain anxiously that they have yet to finish and she reassures them that they do not need to rush. About five minutes before the end, the teacher stops the class and invites the children to turn to someone nearby and explain what they have done or discovered; a hum soon fills the room as children share together. After a minute or two, Diane stops the class and asks a few children to tell the rest of the class about their findings. Several children do so with confidence and enthusiasm; others listen carefully, occasionally thrusting their hands in the air to indicate their own willingness to add something. After each contribution, the teacher thanks the person warmly and briefly summarises what has been said. When she tells the children that they have to finish, there is a quiet groan of disappointment and several children ask her whether they are going to continue after the break; several more ask if they can stay in to finish during playtime.

After clearing up thoroughly, the children slowly slide out of the class, some still talking about the work, others engaging the teacher in animated conversation. Diane stops one noisy girl at the door and gently places her finger on her lips. The offending child smiles an apology and saves her exuberance for the playground. Diane is often one of the last into the staffroom and one of the first out; she always asks if anyone else wants her to make them a drink and has time to offer a brief word of encouragement to a trainee teacher who is struggling with his class.

At the open evening, she does as much listening as talking. When she speaks, she impresses parents with her sincerity and knowledge of each child. Diane speaks considerately and positively about the children but does not try to conceal their shortcomings or weaknesses. She has detailed notes about the children, each pupil on a separate page, to which she occasionally refers for fuller information, but she seems more interested in the child than the statistics about the child. When parents make a significant comment, she notes it on her pad and promises to follow it up; parents feel confident that she will.

The head teacher overhears two parents talking as they cross the playground later that evening: 'I wish our Becky had Diane Jones again this year,' sighs one parent wistfully. The other parent nods in agreement.

Further reading for Chapter 4

Alexander, R.J. (ed.) (2009) *Children, Their World, Their Education: Final report and recommendations of the Cambridge Primary Review*, Abingdon: Routledge.
Thorough, research-based perspectives on all aspects of primary education, including assessment.
Cohen, L., Manion, L., Morrison, K. and Wyse, D. (2010) *A Guide to Teaching Practice*, revised fifth edn, Abingdon: Routledge.
Covers important basic skills and issues that student teachers need to consider during their practice, such as planning, classroom organisation, behaviour management and assessment, together with a review of current regulations and guidelines for teachers.
Hawkes, N. (2000) 'The role of the school assembly', *Living Values Education*, on-line at www.livingvalues.net/reference/assembly.html.
Holmes, E. (2004) *Teacher Well-Being*, Abingdon: RoutledgeFalmer.
The author presents strategies for teachers who want to be proactive in dealing with their own welfare.
Sage, R. (2010) *Meeting the Needs of Students with Diverse Backgrounds*, London: Continuum.
A collection of case studies that focus on genuine situations that challenge practitioners, such as issues relating to culture, religion and English as an additional language.
Weatherhead, Y. (2007) *Creative Circle Time for Early Years*, London: Sage.
Suggests music, songs, poetry and practical activities to engage children in circle-time activities.

5

Other Adults

Introduction

Parents are the first educators of their children. Once formal schooling begins, teachers assume some of the responsibility, but the closer the partnership in learning between school and home, the more that children benefit. The first part of the chapter explores the relationship between teachers and parents, including professional boundaries, informal and formal liaison, parent meetings, coping with difficult parents and the role of parents in the classroom. The second part of the chapter considers the increasingly important role of other adults in supporting and enriching children's education.

PARENTS

Home and school

Parental influence

Adults in school spend a great deal of time working with children – so much time, in fact, that it is possible for teachers to believe that they are the only educators of any significance. In truth, parents may not teach their children much of the formal curriculum that they engage with when at school, but they impart other forms of life knowledge. They teach them about living in a community, learning to cope with different sorts of people, discriminating the good from the harmful and spending time wisely. Parents teach their children particular sets of values. They set boundaries for behaviour and the consequences of not obeying the rules. Most parents take children out into the open air to experience nature, observe the changing seasons and marvel at the wonder of creation. They take them into the city to savour the sights and sounds of urban life. They share books, introduce them to games and offer them opportunities to play alone or play and talk with friends. A parent can give close attention to an individual, whereas in school thirty or more pupils have to share one or two adults. In fact, children are being educated at home, both implicitly by absorbing what happens without being consciously aware of it and explicitly by having their consciousness raised and their attention drawn specifically to information and knowledge (Stern 2003). School helps pupils to make explicit the implicit learning they gain every day from experiences in the wider world.

Home and academic performance

Studies show that one of the most important factors in a child's academic performance in school is the quality of parental involvement (see DCSF 2009). Some parents seem to assume that it is sufficient to send their children to school and pop in to see the class teacher once or twice a year to check that all is going well. In fact, a great deal more is necessary if children are to make good progress in learning. A report by Desforges and Abouchaar (2003) about the impact of parental involvement on pupils' education found that what parents do with their children at home is the single most significant factor in determining their progress. The authors quote from Kreider (2000) that the greatest success occurs when parental development is integrated fully into a school's development plan – in other words, when a partnership in learning is created between home and school (see, for example, Hallgarten 2000; McDermott 2008). Although a few parents will be unable or unwilling to help with homework tasks, they all have the potential to contribute to their children's learning in different ways (Burnett and Jarvis 2004). Some schools provide training evenings for parents who are interested in knowing more about how they can help directly. See Filer (2011) for step-by-step guidance about setting up parenting programmes and other initiatives to support parents in early years settings and primary schools. For instance, schools are also obliged to offer parents sessions to inform them about modern methods of teaching mathematics (the Williams Report, P. Williams 2008; see Chapter 6).

All parents want the best for their children, though some do not have a clear understanding of what 'best' means in terms of school-based learning. School reports offer them a limited amount of information about specific aspects of their children's learning, but parents also want to know about their children's behaviour, attitude, friendships and potential. If their children are unhappy in school, parents will be concerned, regardless of academic results. If children are seriously underachieving, then this obviously requires urgent attention, normally commencing through the school's Special Educational Needs Co-ordinator (SENCO), who will ensure that parents are aware of the problem and involved in its solution.

Home–school contacts

Over recent years, legislation has established the rights of parents to be well informed about the curriculum offered by each school and to know about their child's progress through reports and informal access to teachers (see, for example, Vincent 2000; Beveridge 2004; Filer 2011). With each school's budget depending in large measure upon the number of pupils on the roll, there is extra incentive for head teachers and governors to ensure that parents are welcomed and made to feel part of the school community. Inevitably, this new relationship has caused schools to re-evaluate home–school links and to establish procedures for coping with parental concerns. Parent areas have become a common feature in primary schools and almost every school has regular meetings with groups of parents by way of a parent–teacher forum, which often provides the impetus for fund-raising, school events and offering a perspective on policy decisions.

The greatest level of interaction between parents and school staff is commonly found at nursery, reception and Key Stage 1 (see Stacey 1991; Fitzgerald 2004; Crozier and Reay 2005) owing to the fact that parents tend to bring their young children into the classroom and meet them after school. Although every school has its own particular ideas about establishing and maintaining good quality relationships with parents, contact in the foundation years (for children aged 3 to 5 years) and at the start of Key Stage 1 often includes:

- home visits by the reception class teacher close to the start of a child's formal schooling;
- visits to and from nursery schemes and playgroups by teachers from the mainstream school;
- informal meetings between teacher and parents at the start and end of the day when they are leaving or picking up their children;
- involvement of parents in the classroom, both to assist, and in some cases to help ease the transition of their child from home to school.

Many head teachers actively promote home–school liaison through invitations to participate in aspects of school life, ranging from practical and mundane tasks such as mending library books, making tea for special events or tidying classroom cupboards, through to an active contribution to teaching and school effectiveness (Wolfendale and Bastiani 2000; Campbell and Fairbairn 2005).

As children progress through the school, contact with parents tends to become less regular. Older children may travel to school on their own or with friends. Parents, freed from the demands of caring for young children, may find a job or decide that they have 'done their stint' as parent-helper and look elsewhere for fulfilment. Junior-aged children sometimes find their parent's presence in the school an embarrassment and ask them to stay away. So although it may appear that parents lose interest in their child's education over time, in reality parental interest merely changes perspective (Tizard *et al.* 1988). Early on, parents are chiefly interested in basic considerations such as:

- Is my child happy in school?
- Is my child being properly cared for?
- Does my child have friends?
- Is my child getting on well with basic skills such as reading?
- Is my child behaving satisfactorily?

When parents are satisfied that these basic needs are being met, they are more likely to concentrate on specific aspects of teaching and learning:

- How is my child progressing in his or her work relative to others in the class?
- Is my child being offered a full range of educational opportunities?
- Is my child excelling or falling behind in any area?
- Does my child have the ability to achieve success in future education?

Parents of all children are also concerned that their children are not disadvantaged at school, that teachers treat them fairly and that they are encouraged to do their best. It is worth remembering that when adults in school interact with a child, they are not only affecting the child but indirectly influencing the parents, families and friends, too.

Activate your thinking!

All maintained schools in England have to operate a Home–School Agreement (HSA) policy, whereby parents are given details of the school's commitment to the education and welfare of the children and priorities and expectations that are made of parents and pupils.

Parents and homework

Parents are able to assist their children in various ways outside the school day, including support for homework assignments. In advising parents about making the most of their opportunities to influence their children, it is important for teachers to encourage them to communicate by talking about the curriculum, friendships, activities and the demands of the homework. Some parents assume that if the children want to tell them about an aspect of the work, they will do so. In fact, many children wait for an invitation to talk to their parents, and older children in particular are surprisingly coy about sharing openly. Nevertheless, unless parents talk naturally and without pressure to children about the work, they will find difficulty in helping them to set realistic goals, organise their schedule and check progress. Like a good teacher, parents should praise genuine effort but not be gushing about things that would be expected from the child; otherwise, the child's expectations are diminished. A number of parents will feel unskilled in supervising homework, on the basis that the child knows more than them – which may be true. A small percentage of parents take some persuading about becoming what they perceive to be a surrogate teacher and complain that's what they pay you to do, but if you point out that they were the child's first educator (from birth onwards) then monitoring homework can be seen as an extension of this role.

Schools occasionally get parents who are unable or unwilling to participate in a home–school agreement or scheme, but this problem is for senior staff to deal with and trainees don't need to be unduly concerned about it.

It is worth remembering that children from certain backgrounds will be used to the continual presence of family members at home and have had little experience of separation from them until they enter school. Some cultures emphasise the importance of maintaining close family ties and several generations may live in the same household or close to each other. In addition, close chaperoning of children (girls in particular) means that the concept of complete privacy, so cherished by many in the Western world, is largely unknown to some children from different backgrounds. Such factors can explain, for instance, why some children are uneasy about going to the toilet on their own or have reservations about changing in the presence of boys.

In setting homework, bear in mind five points. First, the best homework links directly with class work. Second, you cannot assume that parents can or will assist in the task, so don't disadvantage the pupils who are unable to count on such help. Third, set homework that allows children to deepen their understanding rather than open up fresh avenues of knowledge, other than if the homework is part of an ongoing project. Fourth, make sure that anything that goes home is of appropriate quality. Finally, try to organise for homework to be assessed or marked in class by pupils, rather than taking it away and spending ages doing it yourself.

Activate your thinking!

Sure Start is a programme that aims to achieve better outcomes for children, parents and communities by increasing the availability of childcare for all children and improving the emotional development of young children. The programme also aims to support parents in their aspirations towards employment by the development of helping services in disadvantaged areas, alongside financial help for parents to afford childcare.

New arrivals' experience of adults

It goes without saying that some parents do a better job of bringing up their children than others do. When children arrive in school, they vary in the extent and quality of their experiences; so-called 'baseline' assessment of their capability is a standard procedure for teachers of reception-age children at the end of the Foundation Stage (see below). This initial assessment is not only an evaluation of children's academic ability but of their social skills, and it is often in this area that teachers soon become aware of the widely differing ways in which children have been prepared for life in school. McEwan (1998) claims that 'skilled teachers can often identify several children with problems before the first week of school is over' (p. 42). Nevertheless, Hutchinson and Smith (2003) are among those who stress the importance of remaining positive and inclusive about young children's behavioural disorders. The growth of pre-school education has helped to compensate for the minority of children who have not received adequate parenting and pre-school preparation, but no strategy can wholly redress the handicap placed upon children whose parents are uninvolved in their education.

By the time 'rising 5' Sharmilla joins the reception class, she will already have had four years of experience of adults, most of it helpful, some of it confusing or alarming. A few key adults will have carried out a teacher role – playgroup leaders, nursery assistants – but most have simply been 'the grown-ups' who have, in one way or another, influenced Sharmilla's life. The likelihood is that she has spent most time interacting with a few close family members, notably Mum, Dad, brothers, sisters. Her own behaviour will reflect their attitudes, preferences and personality, and affect her willingness to learn and her satisfaction with school life. Parents, in particular, will remain the most important influence in Sharmilla's world, a world that she carries into school with her every morning (Tizard and Hughes 1984; Hughes *et al.* 1994; Weil 2003; Sclafani 2004: Chapter 5).

The vast majority of parents co-operate fully with teachers to ensure that children receive the best education in the most advantageous way. However, two of the major changes in parental attitudes in recent years have been an increasing awareness of their rights and a willingness to express their views about school individually or through group pressure. Wise teachers are not intimidated by these changes but take account of them in their dealings with parents (see later in this chapter). Part of the formal inspection programme requires that inspectors take account of parental views. Whatever your opinion of parents, you can't ignore them.

Activate your thinking!

Consider what it means for your relationships and professional attitude to see parents as *clients* or *customers* or *partners*. Reflect upon how parents may perceive the relationship.

Educating a child at home

The practice of 'home-educating' or 'home-schooling' has become increasingly popular with parents in the United Kingdom. Ivatts (2006) notes that although the majority of parents come from White British families, a small but significant proportion are from across a wider social and cultural spectrum, who educate their children at home for religious and cultural reasons. In particular, parents that elect home-schooling appear to be anxious about bullying and poor discipline in state schools or consider that the quality of education is inadequate (York Consulting 2007). Others reasons given for choosing to educate at home include: (1) children were required to start formal schooling too young; (2) the education system was overly bureaucratic, inflexible and assessment-driven; (3) children's particular learning needs – such as dyslexia, autism and gifted – were not being adequately catered for. See also McIntyre-Bhatty (2007).

Methods of educating children at home vary considerably. A number of parents use highly structured methods, follow the National Curriculum and hire tutors to teach specialist subjects (e.g. music). Other parents espouse more informal practices by means of thematic and cross-curricular learning; children are encouraged to pursue their interests rather than adhere to a fixed agenda. It appears that in the same way as in the majority of schools, parents use a mixture of formal and informal methods and widen children's knowledge through trips to places of interest.

Enthusiasts for home education claim that it has many advantages over the regular school system in that (1) it leads to higher levels of confidence and self-esteem in children; (2) it creates a close relationship between parent/carer and child; (3) it encourages self-directed or active learning ('discovery learning'; see also Chapter 7); and (4) it facilitates the development of skills that are equivalent, or superior, to those of children of similar age in school. Opponents point to the heavy costs involved, including the fact that one parent is unable to work or restricted in employment choices; the pressure it places on the parents to ensure that their children are not disadvantaged academically and socially; the dangers of isolation and the lack of shared experiences and memories with peers that form the basis for ongoing friendships.

Good practice

If a child comes into your class after being home-educated, it is probable that he or she will take some time to adjust. When finding out how much your new pupil knows and understands, you need to make allowance for the fact that he or she is unlikely to have followed a conventional, systematic curriculum. It is equally likely to be the case that the child is more independent-minded than most of the class and may be unused to working collaboratively. Take these factors into account and be as patient as you can in helping the child to settle.

Professional boundaries

There will be a variety of parents represented in a single class of children, including a few teenagers and the occasional set of grandparents who are the guardians of their own grandchildren. Some parents will have enjoyed their time at school, others will have unhappy memories, and this experience has a strong influence on their attitude and influence on their children. Certain parents are constantly in and out of school; others are never seen. A few parents will be keen to give their time helping the school in whatever way possible. The majority will be too busy earning a living to afford such luxury.

Parents who are struggling with life will occasionally come into school to seek comfort or reassurance from a sympathetic teacher but it pays to be cautious about being drawn into delicate discussions. If a distressed parent approaches you, the general rule is to listen a lot and say little. If there are sensitive issues involved (especially concerning a teacher in the school, another parent or someone else's child) take particular care not to say anything that might be relayed to the person in question or misconstrued as being critical. It requires a disciplined approach to avoid being swept into an ongoing dialogue with anxious or unhappy parents who begin to see you as their ally. On the other hand, a few moments spent listening and showing some interest in their plight is an important humanitarian role. If possible, try to steer the conversation away from personal issues and towards the progress currently being made by the child of the parent in question. Think of something positive and optimistic to say.

If you find that a parent is keeping you from your duties, it is perfectly in order to say something to the effect that you are sorry to have to interrupt them but you will be in trouble if you don't get back to work. A cheery goodbye as you walk away may provide the spark of encouragement that the parent requires. If the parent repeatedly comes to see you, ask for advice from a more experienced colleague. It is important that you never release information about another child or discuss his or her progress to anyone other than the parent or legal guardian (carer). If you feel uncomfortable about an episode, mention it to your tutor/mentor and make a brief record of your conversations with the parent in your private diary. Any interactions that leave you feeling uncomfortable should, of course, be reported to a senior colleague as soon as possible. There is a fine line between liaising with parents and being at their beck and call.

Communicating with parents

Head teachers and governors are always anxious to ensure that parents are kept well informed about aspects of school life that impact upon their children's education. The move towards integrating education and social services has highlighted the importance of establishing and maintaining good relationships. As an important part of the communication network, class teachers are often given the responsibility of ensuring that information reaches home and helping to ensure that parents don't receive conflicting or confusing messages about school life. Information is usually conveyed in one of three ways:

- Printed correspondence, such as a school circular or letter, if the issues affect the whole group or class
- Verbal messages given to an individual child
- Handwritten notes.

Printed correspondence

Printed correspondence in the form of general circulars normally comes from the head teacher; these sometimes unexpectedly arrive on the teacher's desk or are brought in by an assistant or administrator. It is a sensible policy always to check the instructions about sending them out and to follow the head teacher's wishes precisely. A delay (or sometimes premature release) in sending a letter home can cause problems if some parents receive notification and others do not. In the busy end-of-day activity, it is easy to overlook a letter intended for home.

If there is time, and particularly in the case of younger children, each child's name should be written neatly at the top of the sheet: classroom assistants will often help to carry out this task. Many circular letters never reach parents, and, although they usually emerge some weeks later from a child's deep coat pocket, it is useful to be able to tell the parents that the circular really was sent home with a name on it.

It is sensible to maintain a file to hold copies of all circulars; this ensures that they are available for parents who arrive to complain that their children never received the letter. A quick photocopy, pleasant smile and gentle apology can diffuse the situation. Many schools have a special noticeboard for copies of important circulars, such as those from the school governors. If you are especially busy and liable to forget to send the letter home, ask the children or a TA to remind you. One of them is bound to remember.

Written messages sometimes have to be produced in a variety of languages. Although the child may speak good English, parents do not necessarily do so. This situation makes the distribution of letters more time-consuming and you will need to take this into account when organising sessions, so leave a few additional minutes at the end of the session and, where possible, ensure that an assistant is on hand to help with the practicalities.

Verbal messages

There are many occasions when teachers need to communicate verbally with pupils. Adults tend to speak quickly when they get excited or time is pressing, and although a child may nod when asked if the message is understood there remains a good chance that it will not have been heard properly or will not be remembered. This fact is especially true in the case of younger children, so make a deliberate effort to slow your speech.

It is important to be careful when relaying verbal messages. If you hear yourself saying, 'Tell Mummy that...' or 'Ask at home to see if...' then you should not be surprised if the next day a bewildered parent contacts you to ask what the school can possibly want with a pair of Grandpa's old socks or why David has to bring sausages for the school rabbit! Children do not alter a message deliberately; they simply mishear or forget what is said and become confused. It is like the game of Chinese Whispers in which the message becomes distorted out of all recognition by the time it reaches the person for whom it was intended. More significantly, a special effort should be made to communicate effectively with parents for whom English is not their first language. Imagine if you were that parent trying to make sense of it and reluctant to come into school to check owing to embarrassment about your poor grasp of English.

If circumstances oblige you to send a verbal message home that relates to one particular pupil, then the child should be asked to repeat what has been said before leaving. It is sometimes appropriate to use an older sibling to act on the younger child's behalf. Generally, though, it is far better either to write down the information or to contact the parent directly. It can be worrying and irritating for a parent to receive a jumbled verbal message in the evening and have no idea whether it is urgent or important, and no way of finding out.

Handwritten notes

Teachers do not often have the time or inclination to write notes to parents, but if you do it is important to remember that parents expect teachers to maintain high standards, so scruffy handwriting will be viewed badly and any spelling errors jump out of the page and become a topic of conversation. When such errors occur, a teacher's carefully polished image can be damaged. The same is true of everything teachers write that is placed on public view, such as labels for displays or lists of words around the room.

If you feel it necessary to send a personal note home, take great care to be accurate and clear. Many inexperienced teachers have caused themselves considerable anguish by writing to a parent about a child without giving the matter adequate consideration beforehand. It is one thing to drop a note to Meena's mum to ask if she would mind coming in to help in the classroom on Friday instead of Wednesday; it is quite another to send Sam's parents a formal-sounding letter to say that he is banned from recorder club because he hasn't bothered to practise. If in doubt about taking action that has implications for a child's learning or for relationships with parents, it is always worth consulting a tutor or senior member of staff first. While an ill-advised off-the-cuff remark can usually be smoothed over, a letter in the teacher's own handwriting is harder to dismiss and acts as primary evidence if a complaint is made. Always put yourself in the parent's place and consider the likely impact that the letter would have on you, were you to receive it.

If you need to write home to parents, use the opportunity to commend the child who has tried hard or made a special effort in class. Both the parents and the child concerned are delighted to receive that sort of feedback, which is likely to be shown proudly to friends and relatives. Studies suggest that this form of commendation is more important than any number of house points or merit cards (Harrop and Williams 1992; Shreeve 2002).

In any communication sent home, it is essential to be careful about addressing letters. If in doubt, the safest way is to ask the child discreetly what you should write or simply put: 'To the parent (or guardian) of Jody Adamson, class 4E, from Miss Eddis' and seal the envelope. If you are a trainee teacher it is unlikely that you will need to send a note home, but following the commonsense guidance outlines above might save you a lot of trouble if you do. In any case, you need to be aware that attention to detail pays dividends when dealing with parents.

The quality of communication with parents can help or hinder a teacher's attempts to build a good working relationship and may even adversely affect the child's attitude towards school. However, one of the greatest challenges comes when a new teacher meets parents, often for the first time, in the formal circumstances of parent interviews.

Face-to-face with parents

Face-to-face formal encounters with parents take many forms. Some schools operate a rota system, in which a set of appointment times is drawn up for parents to come into the school during the late afternoon or evening. Other head teachers like to foster a less formal approach in which parents are encouraged to wander in and out of classrooms during the teaching day and chat to the teacher. Some schools have experimented by encouraging parents to have their child present during the discussion with the teacher as a means of giving the child some ownership of the process.

A small number of schools allow parents to attend lessons from time to time and see first hand how the teacher fosters learning and how the children respond, though this option is not always successful because the adult presence can impact adversely on the pupils' and the teacher's behaviour; in addition, very young children may understandably want to be near their parents or show them their work, creating logistical problems. Each of these (and other) systems has various advantages and shortcomings, but whatever the form of parent interview adopted, all teachers find their first few formal meetings with parents nerve-racking and a bit stressful. Over time, the experience becomes easier but never easy. Teachers have variously described it as frightening, exhausting and exhilarating – sometimes all three simultaneously – but ultimately very worthwhile. If you are still training, you probably won't have to undertake anything more than a practice event with (say) a teaching assistant playing the part of a parent. However, you should take every opportunity to sit alongside the teacher during a formal event if permitted, both to learn and to experience the strong feelings and sense of responsibility attached to the occasion.

There are ways of reducing the sense of burden and making the meeting with parents positive and beneficial for all concerned. First, the groundwork for the occasion is done well in advance of the first parent entering the room. The teacher's personality, attitude to children in the classroom, pleasantness during informal contacts, willingness to take time finding out something of a child's interests and approach to learning will already have made a mark. Teachers are talked about regularly at home and at the school gate; their reputation goes before them and influences parents' reactions and inclination when they visit the school. The same will be true for you.

Second, some parents are nervous about school and (occasionally) have a negative attitude towards teachers in general, which is often a reflection of their own unsatisfactory schooling when they were pupils. Little wonder that the parent concerned can find it difficult to relax and act naturally, and is either rigid and hesitant or unnecessarily abrupt. It helps to understand that merely entering the school premises requires a considerable mental effort for any disillusioned parents and may not be easy for many others who enjoyed their own schooldays.

Most parents come into school because they are deeply interested in their child's education and want to find out more about their progress, both academically and socially. Teachers have access to this information and therefore something of value to share with them. Very few parents want to 'catch you out' or be intimidating, though some may use the occasion to express frustration about an aspect of their children's learning experiences or wider school issues. It is worth viewing parent interviews as a wonderful opportunity to share knowledge, ideas and concerns, in addition to giving facts and figures about children's academic attainment. Consider it a privilege rather than a chore.

Activate your thinking!

Questions parents might be asking themselves:

Is the teacher taking a personal interest in my child and providing appropriate opportunities for learning?
Is my child happy and doing well?
Can the teacher maintain good order and control?
Does the teacher have an interesting and lively personality?
How well is my child doing compared to others in the class?

Good practice

1. Make your classroom a welcoming place, both in appearance and in the way that you greet visitors.
2. Use informal opportunities for developing positive relationships with parents in the weeks leading up to the meeting.
3. Give advice to parents about helping with their children's education at home, especially ways they can assist with homework.
4. Utilise parental help as partners in education: directly in school or indirectly through (for example) providing items of interest such as family photographs or holiday souvenirs.

Preparing for parents' meetings

Every meeting with parents has the potential to enrich the existing situation and strengthen the home–school partnership in learning. There are a number of practical and organisational points that can facilitate a more successful meeting and increase the likelihood that parents will go away feeling satisfied and that you will also be pleased with the outcome.

Check that the classroom is in good order

Parents are only partly aware of what happens in a classroom from day to day, so it is the teacher's responsibility to offer evidence of the vitality and effectiveness of the learning that takes place. Trays should be tidied, marking completed, wall displays arranged, examples of children's work named clearly and boldly. View the meeting as an opportunity to show off your expertise and express your personality through the classroom. Neatly labelled cards with useful information about the nature of projects focus parents' attention on important elements of learning. As parents enter the room let them be impressed by the marks of industry and creativity. Put yourself in the visitor's place and see what impression you get. If you are a trainee, take the opportunity to wander around the school and chat with other teachers and assistants about the practical and psychological preparation they undertake prior to the visits.

Good practice

Invite a friend into the classroom before the parents' meeting for an objective opinion about its appearance.

Prepare thoroughly

In the hurly-burly of school life, even important events like parents' meetings can arrive with alarming speed and find teachers ill prepared. It is said that great wartime leader Sir Winston Churchill was the best-prepared impromptu speaker the House of Commons has ever known. This paradox (well prepared yet apparently spontaneous) has an easy explanation, as the great man prepared so thoroughly that he could speak with authority without constant reference to his notes. This gave the impression of mastery and spontaneity. Teachers should emulate his example, not least in dealing with parents.

Thus, when a parent comes to talk about her son, Tom, the teacher ought to be clear about Tom's general strengths and weaknesses without the need to fuss about searching for notes and files. It is important to begin the meeting with a clear, positive statement about Tom as an individual that will help to create a bond with the parent. The amount of detailed information needed about Tom's academic, sporting and social achievements will depend upon the purpose of the meeting and Tom's age. Access to notes is usually necessary to look up specific test results and levels of attainment but it is essential that your detailed knowledge about Tom as a *person* as well as a scholar comes across clearly.

At the start of the school year, a parent will probably be satisfied to hear about how Alice has settled down, whether she has made some friends and if she is making good progress overall, especially in reading. Later on, the same parent will look keenly into Alice's exercise book, scan the wall for examples of her work and make rapid comparisons with other children's work. If the teacher needs to disclose or discuss test scores, it is essential to give clear explanations about the circumstances under which the test was carried out, the status of the result and the implications for Alice's future progress. It is important to be honest with parents but not brutally so. If there are serious concerns about a child's work, do not leave it until the formal meeting before revealing them or parents will rightly ask why you waited so long to inform them.

Activate your thinking!

If you display work by one child, it is important to do so for all pupils. If this aim is not achievable on an individual basis, it is best to put out work that has resulted from collaborative ventures or a book containing examples of all the pupils' work, so that every child is represented. It goes without saying that the work must be of high quality.

Know the child

It might seem unlikely, but in the intensity of the moment it is surprisingly easy to confuse the progress of two different children. It is helpful to have a photograph of all the children (or pictures that pupils have drawn of themselves) on a separate page in a folder and write down brief notes for each individual prior to the meeting, as parents are impressed by a teacher who takes a close and personal interest in their child. Having a separate page that you can turn over after each interview also prevents parents reading information about other children. The author once confused the parents of two boys, both called Nicholas, at a parents' evening near the start of the school year. The first boy was tall, blond and sporty; the second was short, suffered from a physical disability and was much less academic than his namesake. Readers can only imagine my horror and desperate backtracking when the truth dawned.

Keeping the event orderly

Assuming that you have completed the background preparation satisfactorily, two guiding principles are important during the meeting: (1) keeping to time by adopting a systematic approach; and (2) keeping the conversation focused on the key issues.

Keeping to time is essential if an appointments system is used. Parents rightly become cross if they have to wait for an unreasonable length of time because a teacher is running late. Sometimes it can take a few minutes before the conversation 'warms up' and the allotted time is used up before the serious business begins. Thinking through in advance about the way the meeting will be handled helps to avoid over-running and keeps the conversation focused on the relevant issues. The following procedure often proves successful:

1. Stand up as the parents approach.
2. Make immediate eye contact, smile, extend your hand, greet them by name (or, if in doubt, say: 'You're Andrea's parents, aren't you?') and invite them to sit down.
3. Tell them that it is good to see them and thank them sincerely for coming.

When you need to refer to the child's performance, make sure that you have already turned to the page on which their child's photograph and details are noted. Don't leave another child's details open in front of a different set of parents.

Begin positively and truthfully: 'I'm really pleased with John's progress this term; he's made a terrific effort' or 'Richard is so persevering. I won't pretend that he has found the work easy but I have tremendous admiration for the way he refuses to give up' or 'Where did Ling learn to play the piano? She was wonderful in the class assembly the other day.'

After this item of conversation has run its course, change direction and state the purpose of the meeting. For instance: 'In the next few minutes I've got to tell you about Stephen's progress in the core subjects' or 'We've got just five minutes to chat about Astra's report and another couple of minutes for you to ask me any questions about the class outing to the Monastery next week.' It is, of course, important to be clear about the purpose of the meeting or you and the parents will either stare at one another blankly or indulge in small talk.

When the time is nearly used up, begin to bring an end to the conversation by saying something like: 'I'm sorry we haven't more time to discuss this. I'm happy to talk again on another occasion if you need to do so. Perhaps you can let me know when you've had chance to think about it but we'll have to draw to a close now.' Stand up and extend your hand.

As you conclude, close with a positive summary comment that gives the parents something to take away with them:

> Mihail's a lively young man and certainly keeps me on my toes. We're doing all we can to help him and there are already signs that things are improving.

> We want Amy to grow more confident in her own abilities because there's no doubt that she can do well.

> Alisya is doing her best and I'm convinced that with a little extra help in maths she'll start to make real progress. We love her sense of humour.

> David's a bit anxious about the trip but we'll keep our eye on him, so don't worry. If you've got any other concerns, don't hesitate to contact us.

As the parents walk away, thank them again for coming. Note the name of the next parent and turn your file to the appropriate page.

Notice how often the above examples include the plural forms 'we' and 'us'. This strategy reinforces the teacher's own comments by emphasising the team effort in what is said and gives parents confidence that the issues are being addressed. Parents expect teachers to act and behave like professionals but also to show compassion and understanding. As the meeting proceeds, make a brief note of any parental concerns, action needed or points of interest. Parents can see that you are taking their child's needs and their comments seriously and are more likely to go away feeling happy and satisfied.

Restawhile Primary has been refurbished and given a cash injection after coming through several years of disruption owing to staff changes. Your class, Year 3, is drawn mainly from a White, working-class population, with a small but growing minority ethnic community and a few middle-class families who want their children to attend the school because it is representative of 'the real world'. The aim of the parents' evening at the end of September is for the teacher to let parents know how their children have started the year and begin to cement a working relationship with them. Detailed information about children's progress is not on the agenda for this fifteen-minute meeting. Consider how you would deal with the following parents:

Parent 1: Miss Small, a shy, retiring person, did not have a successful time at school when she was young. Her daughter, Charlaine, is also timid and underachieving but has shown a growing ability in gymnastics. Miss Small has several younger children and regular contact with social services for support. Charlaine has a small cohort of quiet, compliant friends.

Parent 2: Rupert's parents are among the wealthiest in the school. They are professional people and well aware of their rights, but have agreeable personalities and understand that teaching is a challenging job. They also have high expectations for their son, who is a bright cheery lad but not a high flier. Rupert is passionate about football, sensitive to his parents' aspirations for him and has a growing awareness of his academic limitations. Rupert has a highly intelligent older sister.

Parent 3: Mr and Mrs Singh are very proud of their eldest son, Gulwar, and desperate that he should do well in school. They have considered moving him to another, more academically successful school, but are afraid he will lose his friends and become miserable if they do. Gulwar excels in mathematics but is ambivalent about literacy and restless during formal teaching sessions. He is an enthusiastic, popular boy and prefers to work unaided.

Parent 4: Mr and Mrs Tuffnutt have twins in the class, Marty and Ocean. Marty is a sharp-tongued, irritating child who often succeeds in getting under a teacher's skin. He is adept at being subtly rude (especially to the support staff) yet charming at the same time. He is always on the fringe of trouble. Ocean is a sad-looking child with few friends, who would, given the chance, spend all her time drawing and colouring. She rarely initiates conversations with adults. Mr Tuffnutt is a loud character and can be dismissive of other people's opinions. Mrs Tuffnutt seems to be a little in awe of her husband.

Parent 5: Ms Monroe has five children, allegedly by three different fathers. She has a gushing, breezy manner and teachers consider her to be a genuinely nice person, very willing to help out with school events. Her son, Brixton, is far more intelligent than anyone else in the family but chooses to mask his abilities for fear of being thought of as 'a swot' by his mates. He is very helpful in class and completes his work without fuss.

Guarding your words

It is obvious that a person who wishes to be treated like a teacher must behave like one. This particularly applies when parents are present. Parents do not expect teachers to be casual or indifferent, but rather to be pleasantly professional. Many teachers enjoy chatting with parents and sharing a joke with them, but it is important not to get carried away with the friendliness. Even informal comments from teachers are remembered and taken very seriously by a lot of parents, so careless remarks should be avoided. Teachers in staffrooms sometimes say outrageous things about serious matters but it is unwise to do this publicly. A pleasant smile and a responsive laugh at the right moment are helpful when dealing with parents, but witticisms and subtleties should be saved for when you are mixing with friends outside school.

In a small number of cases, a parent will befriend you in the hope of gaining inside information about the school and staff. Some parents may wish to know about the current state of thinking in the school about issues where a firm decision has yet to be made and probe your knowledge by asking an apparently innocent question. It pays to be cautious and say as little as possible about controversial issues, without giving the impression that there is something to hide. Even if you feel strongly about a particular matter, resist the temptation to vent your feelings in front of parents, as rumours about staff disharmony spread rapidly. Gossip can be fuelled by a throwaway remark from a teacher in an unguarded moment, so be careful that you do not allow yourself to be ensnared in this way. Special care and wisdom is required in discussing matters in front of parents who regularly help in school (as mealtime staff or TAs). It is naïve to think that they operate within the education equivalent of the Official Secrets Act. There is the world of difference between involving support staff in discussions that impinge directly on their work (a commendable thing) and divulging confidential matters that are the sole concern of the teaching staff (a foolhardy thing).

The intensity of parents' meetings and the heavy demands they make on a teacher can easily lead to elementary blunders. These can be avoided with a little forethought and discipline. There are four common mistakes in teacher–parent dialogue to be aware of: (1) saying too much; (2) patronising the parents; (3) promising to do too much; (4) imagining that parents are full of ill intent. Thus:

Saying too much

The most basic and powerful way to connect to another person is to listen. Perhaps the most important thing we ever give each other is our attention. A caring form of silence often has far more power to heal and to connect with others than the most well-intended words. Teachers must learn to listen as well as speak and not become carried away by the sound of their own voices. Nerves can sometimes make a teacher too talkative, but take time out to pause for breath occasionally and allow a parent to clarify a point or ask a question. If you hear yourself 'going on and on', acknowledge the fact by saying something like: 'Sorry, I'm doing too much talking' and change tack.

Patronising the parents

Parents may or may not know much about formal education but they know a lot about their own children. Even if teachers feel that parents are not doing a very good job in bringing up their child, it would be unwise to betray such thoughts in conversation. The key is to listen sympathetically to parents wishing to share their private thoughts but avoid passing judgement. If parents ask your advice, offer a thoughtful response without sounding too assertive, always leaving the final decision with them. The key to teacher–parent relationships is the somewhat over-used word 'respect'; if you give it, you are more likely to receive it. As Beverton (2006: 385) rightly argues:

> So what you are trying to aim at fundamentally is a relationship of balanced and mutual respect. You are not trying to get parents to continue your own teaching into home but rather to develop ways of building trust and understanding between home and school.

Promising to do too much

Parents will sometimes come to a meeting with their own agenda relating to what they want for their children from academic work, extra-curricular activities, sports events or relationships with other children. The frequency with which parents mention these matters reinforces the important truth that they see their own child's needs extending beyond the academic ones. Teachers try to be as accommodating as possible in responding to parental requests, but there is a danger of promising too much. For example, it is unrealistic to offer to establish an individualised teaching programme for a child that cannot be maintained because of the demands of teaching twenty-nine other pupils. Teachers put under pressure to pay special attention to a child who has not been identified as having special learning needs should check with the head teacher or suggest that the parents do so. While it is an admirable thing to 'personalise' the curriculum or even offer one-to-one coaching on occasions, you should recognise the limits of your own abilities and the attention you must give to other priorities. Promises are easy to make to a parent in the intensity of the moment but much more difficult to keep. As a trainee, you can always pass the parent on to the class teacher to deal with; but remember that one day you will be that class teacher, so begin as you mean to continue.

Imagining that parents are full of ill intent

The vast majority of parents are not teacher-consuming monsters. Some are critical and others are not easily satisfied, but most are supportive and as keen for their child to do well as anybody. It would be a mistake to be defensive when meeting parents. Assuming the best, trying to be positive and enthusiastic, and looking upon the parents as allies and partners in teaching and learning provide the basis for happy encounters.

Parents need reason to be optimistic and have confidence in you and it is unusual for them to be negative or abrasive. It is important to give parents hope and the clear message that you can be trusted with their child's education. If you are an inexperienced teacher or do not have children of your own, you may not realise what a transformation a good report from school can make to the atmosphere in the home. Once the parent has left the classroom after the meeting, you immediately forget about what was said; the parent, however, continues to think deeply about the significance of your words and talks to family and friends about them. Never underestimate the power of a teacher's comments and opinions.

Difficult parents and parents with difficulty

From time to time, teachers come into contact with challenging or uncooperative parents; this likelihood is increased with parents of children who are struggling educationally (Greenwood 2004; Jaksec 2005). However, there is a difference between 'difficult parents' and 'parents who have a difficulty with an aspect of school life'. Difficult parents may feel intimidated in the teacher's presence or have bad memories of school or be experienced parents who are hoping unrealistically that their younger child can emulate an older child's success. Sometimes the parents may have had a bad experience with another teacher in the school. Of course, they may just be nasty people. On the other hand, 'parents who have a difficulty' often signal something important about the school or the teacher's own teaching, skills of communication or attitude towards the children.

It is uncomfortable to be confronted by a parent who seems intent on finding fault and hard to detach the issues from the emotions evoked. However, it helps to remember that only teachers have the power to influence the classroom situation directly, whereas parents do not have. Always listen. Never be tempted to belittle parents or, at the other extreme, allow them to intimidate you. Keep the channels of communication open. Maintain a professional attitude at all times but don't tolerate abuse or threats. A more positive way of viewing parents who express dissatisfaction is that they are taking the time and trouble to become involved in their child's education, however clumsily it may be expressed. Nevertheless, when faced with sour or indignant parents, it is important to think through the practicalities.

First, if the confrontation is public, the parents should be asked to accompany the teacher to a more private spot, but not out of sight. If they refuse, ask whether they would like to arrange another meeting in the near future to resolve the problem. Quite often, the parents have already 'had their say', will refuse the offer and march off. In this case, it is essential for tutor, mentor, senior colleague or, if it is serious, the head teacher to be informed as soon as possible. The head will probably want to contact the parent directly and clarify the nature of the grievance. Don't allow matters to remain unresolved in the hope that they will somehow fade from sight. A disgruntled parent will talk to others about the grievance and a small spark can easily become a conflagration.

If the parents agree to sit and talk about their concerns, it is best to maintain 'soft' eye contact and show interest in what is said, resisting the temptation to refute any allegations or become defensive. You might want to summarise the parents' concerns in order to clarify the nature of the grievance to avoid misunderstanding. In most cases, a simple explanation will suffice and the parents will go away satisfied. Thank the parents for taking the trouble to come and encourage them to return should there be any further concerns. If you are a young new teacher (as opposed to a more mature one) you might feel that the parent is scorning your youth and inexperience; however, try to push such thoughts to one side and concentrate on the issues that are being raised. In the unlikely event of parents becoming very agitated or even threatening, you should state that the conversation is terminated, stand up and inform the parents that the matter must be dealt with by the head teacher (or the most senior person available). It is important (though far from easy) to maintain a calm demeanour. Excuse yourself, walk quickly away and find a colleague to assist.

Aggressive behaviour from parents is extremely rare and is normally avoidable by following the advice given in the earlier part of this chapter. It is quite possible that you will never experience such unpleasantness. Most parents are keen to offer their support and will do all in their power to ensure that they maintain a good relationship with their child's teacher. An aggressive parent can leave you feeling vulnerable and shaken, but console yourself with the fact that you have many other satisfied customers.

Parents in the classroom

Over the past twenty years, the number of parents working alongside teachers in the classroom and in other roles around the school (e.g. in the library) has increased significantly. There are many reasons for this trend. First, the publication of numerous reports stressing the importance of closer home–school links. Second, recognition of the useful skills possessed by parents. Third, the need to have more adult support in the classroom, though the expansion in the number of employed teaching assistants has affected the numbers of volunteers.

Most schools have a policy for parental involvement and teachers need to work within these guidelines. Parent helpers are volunteers and could, under other circumstances, be receiving payment for their work. Parents in the classroom can be a bonus or a problem depending on the care with which they are selected and the skill with which they are deployed. When a parent approaches a teacher with an offer of help, it is essential to check first with the head teacher, as some parents are unsuitable for reasons that may not be evident to the teacher. Once a teacher is committed to accepting an offer of help, it is difficult to tell a parent that she or he is no longer needed. Good parent helpers are worth their weight in gold: they are an extra pair of hands and probably possess expertise (including life experience) that is invaluable in promoting learning; poor ones can cause problems by being over-assertive, critical or casual in attendance. Older parents and grandparents can provide stability and a different perspective on matters of concern; they are also a calming influence for careworn teachers.

If you hope to recruit parental help, first make sure that you are aware of the school policy, if such exists. If not, speak to a senior member of staff before initiating proceedings. As a trainee, it is unlikely that you will actively seek parents to assist, other than in the short term to support the development of a specific theme or topic, in which case you will work with the class teacher to organise the arrangements. Assuming that all else is in order, the following procedures might be adopted:

- Make a list of the jobs suitable for parents.
- Find out what prospective parent helpers have to offer.
- Discover specifically what each prospective helper is willing to do.
- Ascertain when the parents are available and how regularly.
- Invite potential parents into school to discuss the implications of assisting.
- Prepare in advance a summary of principles governing adult–pupil relationships (encouragement, listening carefully, eye contact, etc.) to share with the parent.

It is important to understand that a parent who is in and out of the classroom and staffroom picks up a lot of information about individual children and staff, so care about disclosing information which may or may not remain private beyond the school gate is essential. Further discussion about the deployment of teaching assistants may be found later in this chapter.

Bear in mind that a large percentage of a school's budget depends upon the number of children attending the school. The loss of just a few children, especially in a small school, can make a substantial difference to the overall financial position and put pressure on governors and staff to cut resources. Establishing harmonious relations with parents is not simply a matter of good educational practice; it is necessary to ensure that they are sufficiently satisfied to keep their children at the school and recommend it to others. Don't forget that the views of parents (and pupils) are actively sought and reflected in school inspection reports.

COLLEAGUES IN SCHOOL

The following section deals with the different roles of the many other adults other than parents who form part of the school community and contribute to the teaching and learning programme, and to the nurture and care of children.

Working together

Team spirit

Children have their own views on who matters in school and who does not. For instance, mealtime assistants are rarely accorded the same respect as teachers, whereas the school administrator/secretary is seen as being very significant. Nevertheless, in different ways, every adult makes a contribution to school life, so their co-operation, support and encouragement are vitally important in shaping the school ethos and assisting the children's progress (Mills and Mills 1995; Vincett *et al.* 2005). The more successful schools are usually those in which there is a high level of collaboration and a good team spirit (Nias *et al.* 1989; Beaudoin and Taylor 2004), both between members of the same group (such as all the ancillary staff) and across groups (such as the relationship between teachers and assistants). Teachers, in particular, as the most influential people in the children's school education, have a responsibility to consider ways in which they can develop positive links with other staff members, outside agencies and volunteers, for the benefit of children's learning.

Trainee teachers

Trainee teachers are included in the variety of adults who contribute to this complex amalgam of influences. It is not easy to go into a strange school and begin to establish a good working relationship with children and colleagues that trainees have never met. This adjustment is, however, exactly what has to happen in most school placement situations. The skill of trainees in relating to their class teacher and mentor can make the difference between an effective and a disappointing school experience. This fact does not mean that trainee teachers have to like the teacher or fully approve of his or her methods. It does mean that they have to make every effort to show that they appreciate what is being done on their behalf and support the teacher fully in helping pupils to fulfil their potential and behave appropriately. The large majority of host teachers value the presence of trainees in the classroom and want to see them succeed.

Because of the commitment of the host teachers to trainees, under no circumstances should you ever admit to having doubts about your vocation. Teachers are understandably dismayed if they think that they are wasting their time helping trainees to succeed when they have little intention of teaching after they qualify. All members of staff involved with the trainee teacher's placement will give their full backing if they perceive that you are determined to be a positive influence in the classroom, work hard and embrace the realities of being a teacher. They expect you to be willing to listen, learn, respond, acknowledge mistakes and do all that you can to improve your classroom practice. Teachers will judge your commitment by the thoroughness of your preparation, awareness of opportunities to enhance children's learning, positive contribution to classroom decisions and resolute attitude.

Contributing helpfully

Although it is important to demonstrate a willingness to be an active member of the team, it does not mean that you have to passively accept all that is said to you without ever questioning or offering your own opinions. Trainee teachers have to be prepared to reflect, ponder and establish an intelligent dialogue with those who are responsible for their mentoring and training. Always bear in mind, however, that the final responsibility for the children's welfare and achievement lies with the class teacher. You are entitled to your opinion but, unless informed to the contrary, you must always submit graciously to the regular teacher's decisions.

Cross-reference: Guided Reader Extract 31

Developing a supportive attitude

When you are qualified and have responsibility for a group of children, you will understand more fully the concerns that teachers have about allowing a stranger to take charge of the class and make decisions that will have an impact, possibly an adverse one, on pupil progress. Every teacher has some idiosyncratic practices and ideas which others find difficult to accept. However, at the heart of the collaborative endeavour must be a strong inclination on the part of trainee teachers to co-operate with the host teachers for the benefit of the children, even when they don't fully approve of some of the things that are done. For instance, you might not feel that you want to use the same system of rewards and sanctions as the teacher. You might want to do more listening and less speaking than the teacher does. You might wish to give children more freedom or less freedom to make choices, and so on. However, it is important for every trainee teacher to take an unprejudiced view of these sorts of issues, as the more that teachers at all stages of their career can develop an open dialogue with colleagues and mentors about the managing and organising of learning, the more confident they will become in adjusting their approach from the basis of a well-informed and considered perspective. In undertaking such forms of dialogue, it is particularly important to be courteous and non-judgemental because even well-intended comments may be construed by the teacher or assistant as subtle criticism. A school ethos founded upon positive attitudes and affirmative comments towards pupils should also apply to adult–adult relationships, and facilitate open discussions about issues that impact upon teaching and learning and upon staff welfare. Regardless of whether or not you are sympathetic towards a host teacher's priorities and methods, it is essential that you do all you can to be positive and supportive.

Fostering understanding among school staff

As a means of gaining a better understanding of the perspectives of, and demands upon, other adults in school, it is useful to consider some of their roles and examine the ways their work impinges on others. The rest of this chapter provides a synopsis of the work, needs and priorities of key personnel.

The head teacher

Every report about schools stresses the importance of the head teacher ('head') in the success of the school, as together with governors the head teacher is responsible for the running of the school and the wellbeing of staff. The head has overall responsibility for achieving agreed aims, safeguarding children, ensuring curriculum entitlement for pupils, maintaining links with the community, involving parents closely in school life, informing parents about their children's progress and establishing appropriate forms of pupil assessment. All these responsibilities are in addition to oversight for staff welfare, training, development and appraisal, with a view to making decisions about appointments and promotions. In recent years, prospective head teachers have had to undertake a national training course for school leadership before they can take up a headship post.

Head teachers work long hours and this constant pressure can exact a high cost, which is now reflected in their enhanced salaries. A large proportion of the head teacher's day is spent dealing with administrative tasks, meeting people and attending meetings. Unless the school is very small, it is unlikely that the head teacher will have a substantial teaching commitment. While it is true that head teachers are often less informed about the detail of the curriculum than their class teachers, they are certainly interested in what goes on in the classroom. A good head will spend a lot of time encouraging staff to work as members of a team, attending courses to enhance their work and the effectiveness of the school and promoting high standards of pupil attainment and discipline. The numerous education initiatives of recent years, legislation covering the so-called 'work–life balance' and closer links between the education service and social services have made heavy demands of head teachers and their governing bodies.

Whatever head teachers' strengths and weaknesses, they are entitled to every teacher's support and enthusiasm. Some new teachers are in awe of the head but need to remind themselves that the head was once a classroom teacher and only asks that staff work hard, respect their colleagues and help to promote the school's reputation and achievements.

Teachers are most likely to have contact with the head teacher during assembly and at staff meetings, when specific decisions are being made or when their support is needed for policy initiatives. Head teachers also write references for teachers who apply for other jobs, so it is in every teacher's interest to maintain an open, courteous and professional relationship with them. In turn the head teacher expects staff to:

- be trustworthy and hard working;
- prepare lessons thoroughly and teach efficiently;
- show enthusiasm and determination;
- relate well to parents;
- show respect towards colleagues and visitors;
- have a bright and tidy classroom with evidence of good quality children's work on display.

Cross-reference: Guided Reader Extract 45

School governors

Changing role

The role of governors has changed considerably in recent years (see, for instance, Doust and Doust 2001; Adams 2002; see Adamson, 2007 for a summary of key responsibilities). At one time, they were merely figureheads and rarely involved in school life other than for special functions and emergencies. Until the 1980s, governing bodies had few powers and relatively little influence in schools. The head teacher determined most school policies, and teachers largely decided what they taught their children. The Education Acts of the 1980s and 1990s drastically altered the responsibilities and status of governing bodies, all of which must now include representatives from the teaching staff, parents and the local community. The governing body's main role is to help raise standards of pupil achievement. Governing bodies are responsible to parents, funding providers (normally but not always via the local authority) and the local community. The full composition of a governing body commonly includes the following members:

- Local authority governors (unless the school is free from local authority control)
- Teachers elected by their colleagues
- A governor elected by support staff
- Parents elected by other parents at the school

- A governor co-opted by other members of the body
- The head teacher (normally)
- Representatives of churches (in schools with a religious foundation).

Personal motivation

People become governors for a variety of reasons. The majority have a desire to help the school maintain standards and the pupils enjoy happy and safe learning experiences. A small number get elected so as to wield influence on behalf of a particular social, political or religious cause. Governors are normally people of considerable ability and experience, and although they may not have a background in education, they have other skills and attributes that allow them to offer a different perspective on issues affecting the school. Many governors are delighted to offer their help and support in whatever way possible, and although they may not have the time or inclination to give regular classroom support, the best sort of governor will always listen and provide sound advice. Usually, each governor takes responsibility for a different area of the curriculum.

Responsibilities

Governors have become increasingly significant in ensuring that the school operates efficiently. They are accountable to parents and the wider community for the academic performance of the school. They help plan the school's aims and policies and make appointments, including the key role of head teacher, which is probably the most important decision that a governing body ever makes. Governors also make decisions about the school's budget, monitor the curriculum and determine how the school can encourage pupil's spiritual, moral and social development. Governors have a legal responsibility to ensure the school provides for all its pupils, including those with special needs. You should take the opportunity to meet governors, as they have responsibility for every aspect of school life, including the work of trainees, and will value your perspectives and fresh thinking, though you should be careful not to express reservations about the school. Discretion is essential.

Each year, a formal meeting of governors and parents is held at which governors produce a report for parents to discuss the manner in which the school has been and will be conducted, plus any other matters relating to the school that are raised by parents of registered pupils. Commonly, the head and governors use the evening as a celebration of achievement as well as fulfilling the formal requirements; attendance is considerably higher if there is an added social dimension to the evening in addition to the formal element.

Relationship with staff

Governors have the right to enter the school at any time and examine aspects of its life and work, though convention and common courtesy dictate that this should only be done with the permission of the head teacher and, if teaching is to be observed, with the consent of the teachers concerned. Governors are not inspectors or local authority advisers and are generally not equipped to conduct a formal evaluation of teaching quality; this task is within the head teacher's remit. Many head teachers arrange informal gatherings of teachers and governors each term to help cement relationships and celebrate successes. The line between governing bodies offering adequate support to a teaching staff and becoming intrusive is a fine one, but the trend is towards more, rather than less, governor involvement (Dean 2008; Sallis 2007).

These meetings form an important element of professional life. It is also reassuring for the staff to know that at least one colleague will be representing their views by being elected as the 'teacher governor'.

Governor elections

Numbers of governors vary depending on the school's type and size, and appointments last for four years. Parent and teacher governors are also elected. In the case of parent governors, ballet forms are distributed to parents of the children in the school and the candidate with the most votes is elected. If a number of parents wish to stand for the vacancy, they each have a right to circulate their views and win over support; this is sometimes carried out by the simple expediency of allowing each candidate a given number of words in which to set out their position and their manifestos are then copied and sent to all parents. Procedures for appointing the teacher representative are less complex, though equally rigorous. In very small schools with only a handful of staff, there is sometimes a problem in finding a teacher willing to stand.

The head teacher can opt whether or not to be a governor, though nearly all do so. When school inspectors visit, their final report is sent to the chair of governors (not the head teacher); governors are charged with the task of ensuring that the recommendations are followed and perceived shortcomings dealt with. Head teachers often refer to 'my governors', indicating the close relationship which ideally exists between them. A school in which the governors and head teacher have a harmonious relationship is likely to prosper because the head can be confident that when difficulties and problems arise, as they inevitably do, support and encouragement from the governing body can be relied upon.

Teaching assistants

Significance and motivation

Over recent years there has been a considerable expansion in the use of teaching assistants (TAs) in primary schools. Each TA has a job description to which she or he needs to conform, though flexibility is considered to be a great asset. TAs have been employed in larger primary schools over many years for general duties but they are gradually assuming more responsibility for pupils' learning, and the large increase in their numbers is to support the work of class teachers in boosting standards of achievement. However, TAs share with teachers motivation that is driven by a desire to work with children and help them to do well in all aspects of their lives: personal, social, academic and spiritual. Teaching assistants are encouraged to study for NVQ qualifications and there has been a glut of published books to support this endeavour (e.g. Bentham and Hutchins 2008).

The recruitment of tens of thousands of support staff and exploiting their expertise in the classroom is supposed to mirror the situation in hospitals where a senior professional (such as a consultant) is involved only with key decision-making and advanced practice, leaving the subordinates (junior doctors, nurses) to carry out the orders and perform most of the regular work. However, for those assistants wishing to pursue further study there are career routes into teaching.

The strategy of employing more TAs has implications for organising pupil learning, which might involve:

- teachers having to include and direct assistants in planning and managing children's learning;
- teachers sharing and delegating some responsibilities for the teaching and learning process;
- teachers being freed from more routine tasks and concentrating on the more specialised elements of their role, such as planning, preparation and assessment of pupils' learning;
- support staff gaining appropriate skills and knowledge to complement and enhance the work of teachers.

Teaching assistant roles

Teaching assistants might be involved in activities that involve putting up displays, administering money, organising paperwork and pupil records, photocopying, ordering equipment and maintaining essential resources. However, it is clearly a waste of time and money to employ capable assistants and fill their time with menial tasks when they have other talents to offer, so some of the more skilled TAs might be involved in assisting with ICT or acting as counsellor in conjunction with the school's child advocate (who is the named person responsible for dealing with children who wish to share a particular concern or grievance). To use an extreme example, it would be a waste of the TA's time to wash paint brushes when she could be leading a group of able children in mathematical problem solving (see Beam 2009).

A small percentage of teaching assistants (known as learning support assistants or LSAs) are responsible for the needs of a single child. However, assistants are now graded as a TA or as a higher level teaching assistant (HLTA) so labels like LSA tend to be associated with their role rather than their status. HLTAs in particular are likely to work more closely with the teacher with respect to teaching and learning, though all adult assistants can be used in one or more of a variety of ways (see Waters 1996; Burnham 2006).

Although assistants have a job description and hold their own clear views about what they are and are not prepared to do, it is up to you to be specific about your expectations from day to day, and from session to session. The need for clarity is especially relevant in early years classes where additional adult support is often interwoven into the fabric of the teaching day. With older children the TA may be involved in intensive coaching of children who have fallen behind or are struggling; she or he may be allocated to supervise a group of children and guide them in task completion. Whatever the specific responsibility, the principle of working closely with the TA and valuing her expertise is fundamental to a healthy working environment.

Specialised work

The need for developing expertise becomes even more essential when HLTAs take responsibility for teaching a group of children or even the whole class under the general guidance of the teacher (see Rose 2005; Cullingford-Agnew 2006). However, in assuming greater responsibility, part of their essential skills training is to gain more experience in behaviour management (Bentham 2005). The revised National Occupational Standards for teaching assistants offers a basis for every practitioner as a means of effectively supporting individual learning and the wellbeing of children and young people in schools (see Cheminais 2008).

TAs tend to be more common in younger-age classes than in the upper primary range, though the emphasis on providing low achievers with intensive additional support to 'boost' their attainment in Key Stage 2 has required the services of many more trained staff.

Increasingly, all paid assistants possess a qualification and nearly all attend additional in-service courses to develop their expertise (see Watkinson 2003a, 2003b; Cousins *et al.* 2004). Statistically, about 10 per cent of TAs are former teachers who no longer wish to teach but who possess a range of desirable skills. Many assistants are local people who enjoy working in school, have their own children there and have been appointed to support the work of teachers with larger classes. Through funding limitations, assistants may be employed on temporary contracts or work strictly to their hours, making liaison with teachers more difficult.

In many primary schools TAs have been principally used to work alongside children in core subjects rather than in the more creative and aesthetic areas, with the result that some of their traditional responsibilities (such as assisting with basic practical tasks and putting up displays) have assumed secondary importance. However, the situation is dynamic and a new breed of better-trained and remunerated assistants is gradually emerging (see, for instance, Williams 2009).

Co-ordinating the work of assistants

There are specific management skills that teachers must develop, in knowing both how to relate to TAs and how to use them profitably. There are many routine tasks that teachers have carried out in the past but that are now deemed more suitable for classroom support staff. Not all of the items in the list are equally important or relevant to primary schools. The full range of tasks is shown in Figure 5.1.

Although TAs carry out the sorts of tasks listed in Figure 5.1 they still have to be co-ordinated by a teacher. In addition, whereas a simple job such as photocopying does not

1   Collecting money
2   Chasing absences
3   Bulk photocopying
4   Copy typing
5   Producing standard letters
6   Producing class lists
7   Record keeping and filing
8   Classroom display
9   Analysing attendance figures
10   Processing exam results
11   Collating pupil reports
12   Administering work experience
13   Administering examinations
14   Invigilating examinations
15   Administering teacher cover
16   ICT trouble-shooting and minor repairs
17   Commissioning new ICT equipment
18   Ordering supplies and equipment
19   Stocktaking
20   Cataloguing, preparing, issuing and maintaining equipment and materials
21   Minuting meetings
22   Co-ordinating and submitting bids
23   Seeking and giving personnel advice
24   Managing pupil data
25   Inputting pupil data.

FIGURE 5.1 Possible tasks for teaching assistants (based on DfES 2002b)

require specialist expertise, it is not acceptable (for example) for an assistant to carry out minor repairs to technical equipment without full training. Similarly, it is useful if a TA can relieve you of important but time-consuming jobs in the area of health and safety (such as checking the state of games' equipment) providing that legal responsibilities are met. In other words, if a TA says that all is well and the equipment proves to be unsafe, the teacher and not the assistant, takes final responsibility. Again, it saves a teacher a lot of time if an assistant carries out the administration of ordering (say) consumable resources, but the teacher still has to spend time in being familiar with what is needed and liaising with the assistant before the order is sent. In other words, the mere availability of an assistant does not of itself free you to concentrate on the tasks that require more sophisticated professional skills such as planning and preparing, teaching, assessing children's progress, marking and reporting.

It is also the case that an assistant will not always be available when you need support, so there are bound to be times when you have to do the task yourself. Consequently, although you may want to delegate jobs, it is important that you do not lose touch with them entirely or allow yourself to become deskilled. Although an experienced teacher can usually cope with the unexpected absence of a TA, you will find the situation more challenging and have to think on your feet.

One way and another, the involvement of assistants in a variety of activities previously considered the sole province of qualified teachers is likely to become increasingly significant in schools but is not of itself a panacea for reducing teachers' workload. The most important factor is that the benefits that accrue from having an assistant outweigh the additional demands that managing another adult involve for the teacher.

Teacher–TA relationship

Class teachers and their assistants work extremely closely throughout part or all of the day, which necessitates teacher and assistant being careful to avoid any action or attitude that might upset the delicate balance of mutual trust and endeavour that is the mainstay of effective schools. It is essential that the relationship between teacher and assistant is comfortable for both parties and responsive to changing events, such that the TA is prepared and willing to be flexible and respond rapidly to a teacher's requests. Although a lot of lesson planning is done in advance, a great deal of a teacher's day consists of making spontaneous decisions and sometimes adjusting plans on the spot to fit the events of the moment. On the one hand a TA is not a lackey, waiting obediently for the teacher's command; on the other hand a TA must accept that effective teachers modify and adjust priorities and that not everything can be predicted.

Activate your thinking!

Imagine that you have responsibility for managing two TAs, one of whom works with a blind child, the other on general duties, shared half-time with the adjacent class. What factors will you need to consider in managing the situation?

Good practice

Working with reception-age children, one TA's responsibilities included the following:

Hearing children read orally and maintaining records
Assisting with a maths extension group
Assisting during the lesson time, working one-to-one with particular children
Mounting and displaying children's work around the room and corridor
Producing some resources for teaching as requested by the class teacher
Taking children to the library to select books and other general library duties
Assisting the teacher when children were moving around the school and being taken outside the premises
Keeping accident report records and overseeing health and safety requirements
Designing and producing scenery for school plays
The collection and distribution of refreshments, including drinking water
Voluntarily running an after-school craft club.

Cross-reference: Guided Reader Extract 44

Special needs assistants

Special needs assistants are now subsumed under the general title of 'learning support assistant' and undertake a specialist role in working alongside children whose learning needs are sufficiently acute to have been formally identified through a 'statementing' procedure involving the parents, school, educational psychologist and local education authority. The statement is a formal document in which the child's needs and an action plan to support these needs are identified. The local authority, through the school, is legally charged with providing the resources (human and practical) to assist in supporting the child's emotional and academic shortcomings or, quite frequently, addressing a combination of both these problem areas.

Through the policy of placing all children into mainstream schooling, the status of learning support assistants has been enhanced over recent years. Ideally, if there is a child who has been formally identified as having special needs, an assistant will be available for part or all of the day to offer additional learning support or provide an extra adult presence to channel poor behaviour into something more constructive, depending on the nature and severity of the need. However, the concept of one adult clinging like a leech to a single needy child throughout the day is becoming outmoded; rather, the child works intensively with an adult for short periods of time, either inside or outside the main classroom base (see Chapter 13).

Trainee teachers and TAs

It is particularly important for you to maintain good and open relationships with all support staff. If an assistant has been at the school for a long time and has become attached to a particular way of working, she or he will possibly be resistant to change. Under such circumstances, you need diplomacy and patience to introduce new ways of working and make adjustments to the assistant's responsibilities. However, it pays to listen to advice from experienced TAs, as they often possess insights that you lack.

TAs are not assistant teachers, they are assistants *to* the teacher, and this fact must be taken into account when deciding the tasks they are asked to undertake. For instance, if you ask an assistant to hear children read aloud, it is essential that she has sufficient knowledge about how children learn to read so that she can make a positive impact on the pupil's progress. One of the quickest ways to damage a TA's dedication is to make unjustified assumptions about her capability and level of responsibility or to take advantage of her goodwill (Balshaw 1999; Hancock and Collins 2005). On the other hand, take care to assign to their assistants appropriate duties and responsibilities rather than burden them with the mundane tasks that no one else wants to do. Your teaching plan should include details of how TAs will operate during the lesson.

TAs deserve to be treated with appropriate respect and understanding, to be kept informed about the nature of their work and told about any changes to the regular programme of work. A kindly TA can be wonderfully supportive and give you much-needed encouragement during stressful periods of time on the school placement. If the assistant is a parent, your reputation can hinge on the informal conversations that the assistant has with other parents outside school, so be cautious about unguarded comments. Together with every other adult in school, assistants merit and enjoy sincere praise and encouragement, so don't disappoint them.

Good practice

To ensure that your TA contributes effectively to classroom life and gains satisfaction from doing so, it helps to incorporate the following good practice into your weekly schedule:

1. Take time to clarify her duties and your own expectations.
2. Offer her the chance to develop her skills and be involved in those aspects of classroom life she finds enjoyable and fulfilling.
3. In addition to regular communication, set aside a short time each week to discuss matters of mutual concern.
4. Take every opportunity to thank her for her efforts and acknowledge her contribution.

Cross-reference: Guided Reader Extract 43

Caretakers and cleaners

Over the past few years, the demands upon caretakers and cleaning staff have grown considerably. A school that once had three or four staff to secure and clean the premises may now make do with one or two on reduced working hours; some larger schools employ security firms to protect the premises. Such is the world in which we live. There has been a tendency over recent years to employ contracted staff that might or might not have a personal commitment to the school and are probably on low wages.

Caretakers work prescribed hours and are possibly also on call, which means that they have to be available beyond their normal duties. For instance, if a child is sick over the classroom floor, it is normal policy that only the caretaker clears it up, using specific procedures and designated chemicals. Unfortunately, the caretaker may be unavailable or live at a great distance from the school, in which case there will be a school policy about the appropriate procedure. Although such instances may sound trivial, they can be highly disrupting and a health hazard, so make sure that you are informed.

Caretakers are not allowed to perform certain tasks such as climbing ladders above a certain height, lifting heavy weights and carrying out property maintenance. Although many caretakers loosely interpret these rules and bend over backwards to be helpful, it is important to remember that an innocent request for assistance can meet with a reluctant refusal if the request means breaking the agreed contractual terms. The first rule for teachers who hope to develop a good relationship with the caretaker is to discover what duties are specified and which ones are favoured, so make a point of finding out as soon as possible.

One of the caretaker's most demanding tasks in a larger school is to supervise cleaners. Cleaners sometimes work in the early morning before school begins or, more often, for two or three hours after school. In that time they have a lot to do and the caretaker is responsible for ensuring that the work is carried out satisfactorily. In a small school, the same person may be both cleaner and caretaker and will have to do everything from locking and unlocking the school to mopping floors, collecting and depositing rubbish, and controlling stock. Even in a medium-sized primary school, there may be as few as two persons responsible for the whole range of tasks.

You need to be sensitive to the pressures on cleaning staff and bear in mind that their most frequent complaints about the state of classrooms include the mess made by clay and sticky products trodden into carpets, inappropriate use of paper towels, chairs not stacked according to the school's agreed procedure, messy sinks and graffiti on table tops. As cleaners need to come into the room after school, a little consideration to allow them access to your room is both courteous and practical. Making the effort to train the children to clear up and follow sensible rules will avoid irritating cleaners as well as improve your organisational skills.

Caretakers' chief concerns are receiving a visit from their supervisor, cleaner absenteeism and a lack of basic resources to do the job effectively. As in all other aspects of school life, basic courtesy and expressing genuine appreciation helps to make life more pleasant for everyone. Caretakers expect respect and courtesy from teachers, an acknowledgement of the demands of their job and advance notice about forthcoming events. Every time you make an effort to be co-operative and helpful, you will receive double the reward in return.

Activate your thinking!

What does the cleaner say to colleagues about the condition of your room? How does your attitude to the caretaker help in generating a positive working relationship?

Good practice

If your caretaker has an interesting background, extend an invitation to talk to your class about it. Remember that this person is probably not used to addressing children in a formal setting and will need your support and guidance. It is usually better to have two short sessions on different days than a lengthy monologue. The caretaker (or any other adult you invite to speak to the children) might be loquacious with adults but feel constrained when addressing children.

Mealtime assistants

It is sometimes claimed that mealtime assistants (MTAs) have the least enviable job in schools. Playground supervision, in particular, places great demands upon them as they attempt to control large numbers of excitable children, sort out squabbles, tend damaged knees and broken relationships, and direct children to the right place at the right time. Inside the school, there are lunch boxes to open, tables to wipe, slow eaters to encourage and poor manners to correct. Although the majority of MTAs are dedicated and conscientious, their lack of authority can cause them to struggle with uncooperative children, and the sound of strained adult voices is a familiar one in some schools.

Part of the team

An increasing number of head teachers and governors have come to recognise that as MTAs play an important role in the life of the school, it is worth investing time in the provision of training and guidance. As a result, issues such as behaviour management, assertiveness, inter-personal relationships and first aid are addressed through regular training sessions. MTAs need to have a good sense of humour, plenty of stamina and a strong personality. Owing to the low wages, a number of them will have a second job. When MTAs are seen leaving school the moment the dinner break is over, it is tempting to think that this reflects a low level of commitment. In fact, they are likely to have other responsibilities or are understandably declining the opportunity to do unpaid overtime.

Until relatively recently teachers were all expected to undertake a dinner duty, and although in some schools there is still a voluntary rota of teachers who wish to help, very few do so. Larger schools may employ a more highly qualified person to supervise lunchtime arrangements, generate interest in traditional games and activities, and manage the other mealtime staff. Certain MTAs may be allocated to a child with special needs and most of them are encouraged or trained to learn more about the value of play and handling potentially combustible situations. It is noteworthy that Cohen (2006a) claims that there is strong evidence not only that play has a therapeutic function, but also that energetic, spontaneous physical play may facilitate neurological development. Cohen rightly argues that if this is the case, 'stopping children from playing, either by punishing them or medicating them might actually contribute to developmental abnormalities' (p. 162). A large number of schools involve older, responsible pupils to assist through involvement in all-age 'family' groupings, monitoring a 'time out' space or even being trained as counsellors.

With the youngest children, it is quite likely that an MTA will come to the classroom a few minutes before the official end of the morning to take responsibility for the children who stay for lunch. If so, it is important that teachers consider the organisational implications of completing work and tidying up before she arrives. This last point is especially significant if the room is used for children to eat their packed lunches. If it is a wet day, the MTAs will be trying to look after the children all together in the school hall or flitting from classroom to classroom attempting to entertain and subdue the restless children. MTAs are only responsible for children who remain at school to eat their lunch, not for children who go home. Younger children who are going home for lunch have to be supervised by the teacher until an adult collects them. If children return to school too early from lunch, they are not, strictly speaking, the responsibility of MTAs.

Playground duties

When children are together in the playground, it is inevitable that there are disagreements and conflicts from time to time that require adult intervention. Occasionally, MTAs cannot cope unaided and bring a naughty child to the teacher for admonishment. There are a number of principles to consider in evaluating your interaction with MTAs:

- As a teacher, MTAs believe that you are never off-duty.
- MTAs expect teachers, however inexperienced, to be able to deal with instances of pupil misdemeanour.
- It is important to remain detached from the emotions of the moment until explanations are sought and the situation can be properly resolved.
- There is a need to balance the MTA's expectation that she will receive your support with the possibility that the child concerned may also have a genuine grievance.

Lunchtime conflict situations are never easy to deal with but you must expect to meet them from time to time. Frustration on the part of adult or child can lead to over-reaction and a rapid deterioration of the situation; emotionally vulnerable children may become aggressive and require immense patience and calm insistence. A useful guide to the success achieved in deploying and training MTAs in a school is the length of the queue of children outside the head teacher's or deputy's room at the end of the lunch break: the longer the line, the more urgent the problem. Effective MTAs lead to happier children and a more settled start to the afternoon, so it pays to support them in their attempts to do the job well, as you don't want unsettled and resentful children in your class at the start of the afternoon.

Guidelines for managing lunchtime situations

- Do not jump to conclusions. Make sure of your facts first.
- If in doubt about the appropriate course of action, delay in making a decision until you have chance to consult a more senior colleague.
- In the case of serious incidents, always inform the head teacher or deputy as soon as possible. Make a brief note about the details of the incident.
- Never use platitudes to placate an angry adult. Try to find out the facts and remain calm until the position is clearer.
- Be constructive with your comments and search for a resolution or strategies to improve the situation.
- Listen more than talk.
- Always support the MTA where possible but remember that children have rights, too.

What MTAs expect from teachers:

- To be courteous and pleasant
- To acknowledge the demands of their job
- To take direct responsibility for situations when appropriate
- To offer constructive support when necessary but not to undermine their position.

Activate your thinking!

MTAs' chief concerns are individual mischievous children, uncomfortable relationships with colleagues and worries that they have reacted inappropriately or said too much to a particular child.

Good practice

Allocate some time in your schedule to get to know one other adult better each week. Decide how you can demonstrate your gratitude for their contribution to school life and to your own work without appearing patronising.

Adults and educational visits

Children love to go out of school on visits, even quite local ones, and many pupils claim that it is the most exciting part of the school year for them. There are now strict rules governing charges made to parents for school visits and no child may be excluded from an educational visit on the grounds of cost. In other words, visits are for all children, regardless of status or a parent's ability to pay. Teachers have to consult with the head teacher about the procedures for outings before committing themselves or the school to any financial agreement. As a trainee you will not be expected to carry out this preliminary work but you still need to be aware that it happens.

Guidance about trips

School trips, educational visits and other field activities can be great fun and a wonderful opportunity to seal your relationship with the pupils. They can also be times of hazard and potential danger, so a lot of planning is required to ensure that a visit is safe and educationally worthwhile (Smart 1995; Salaman and Tutchell 2005). In addition to checking that the venue is suitable for the age group and is properly managed, trip organisers have to send letters home detailing the itinerary, receive permission slips from parents, order transport, confirm insurance and liaise with colleagues whose lessons may be affected. They also have to ensure that every part of the day has been considered in detail. A 'good practice guide' known as *Health and Safety of Pupils on Educational Visits* (DfEE 1998) was designed to help head teachers, teachers, governors and others to ensure that pupils stay safe and healthy on school visits. It includes chapters on: Responsibilities for Visits; Planning Visits; Supervision; Preparing Pupils; Communicating with Parents; Planning Transport; Insurance; Types of Visit; Visits Abroad and Emergency Procedures. It also includes a number of model forms that can be copied or adapted. The guide is not intended to replace local or other professional guidance or regulations and, for most schools, local education authorities should be the first source of advice to clarify finer points in the guide. A three-part supplement to the good practice guide was produced in 2002, as follows:

Standards for Local Authorities sets out the functions of the educational visits co-ordinator in schools and the levels of risk management that local authorities should take into account in advising schools; and *Standards for Adventure* is aimed at the teacher or youth worker who leads young people on adventure activities.

A Handbook for Group Leaders is aimed at anyone who leads groups of young people on any kind of educational visit. It sets out good practice in supervision, ongoing risk assessment and emergency procedures.

Group Safety at the Margins is aimed at anyone who organises learning activities that take place near or in water, such as a walk along a riverbank or seashore, collecting samples from ponds or streams, or paddling or walking in gentle, shallow water. Comprehensive official guidance containing information and guidelines on all aspects of health and safety that affect schools, including the medical needs of children, emergencies and school security is provided in a document, 'Health and safety: responsibilities and powers', issued to schools in 2001.

Even when all the planning and organising is complete, there is still a lot of work to be done in ensuring that the day runs smoothly. In particular, it is essential to anticipate problems or hazards and the action needed to respond to a situation should something go wrong. It is not only important to have access to a mobile telephone for making immediate contact with emergency services should this prove necessary, but to carry a list of key contacts. Clarifying the role of the different adults involved is vitally important in making the visit a safe and successful one. Colleagues and teaching assistants must be involved in planning and organising but the teacher in overall charge has the formidable task of ensuring that all runs smoothly.

In practice, most schools have a well-ordered programme of visits and new teachers will discover that there are well-trodden paths to museums, landmarks, ancient monuments and adventure courses. Nevertheless, thorough preparation is essential if the trip is to be a success, including the following.

Costs

Some visits are not viable owing to the cost of travel (coach hire is expensive) or entrance fees. Providing the weather is reasonable, however, there are usually numerous outdoor opportunities that offer valuable educational opportunities, as well as having a lot of fun. Waite and Rea (2007) comment that if suitable clothing is worn and sensible precautions are taken, there is no end to the range of opportunities for outdoor learning at minimal cost. Note that access to facilities for hanging wet outdoor clothes might be required.

Timings

Coach travel is slower than travelling by car and an apparently short car journey through country lanes can become a long jaunt as the coach driver is obliged to follow a much longer prescribed main road route. Always leave a few minutes leeway for the journey time at both ends of the trip. Parents are rightly frustrated and anxious if the coach arrives back later than planned. It is important for adults to have a mobile telephone and a list of contact numbers with them at all times. In the intensity of the moment, it is surprisingly easy to overlook the need to telephone ahead and advise that things are running late.

Safety

Coaches must conform to minimum safety standards. Experience has shown that it is better to pay a little more and ensure a high standard of service from a reputable company. Regulations have become much stricter in recent years, but a few rogue companies can still slip through the net. Although it was at one time possible to put three smaller children per double seat, the requirement for coaches to fit safety belts means that this option is no longer available. If private cars are to be used, a list of experienced drivers with current licences should be compiled and confirmed with the head teacher. Check with the head teacher as to whether each parent is required to satisfy a police check requirement beforehand. If the venue involves any activity that carries some risk (such as adventure courses) then basic health and safety regulations must be observed and the activity centre's own safety procedures verified. Educational centres are required to be listed as reputable but it still pays to double-check. Safety first means thinking ahead and following guidelines closely.

Communication with parents

Parents should be notified at least six weeks before the proposed visit. For standard visits, an initial note should first be prepared about the purpose of the visit and the intentions for the day, with information about clothing, lunch arrangements and possible physical demands on the children, plus an invitation for parents to contact the teacher in charge with any queries. A detachable permission slip is normally included as an indication that the parent is willing to permit the child to take part. (Parents can refuse, though they rarely do so.) The form sent home should include space for the child's name, address, contact number and space for the parent to mention any special circumstances (such as the child's need to carry an inhaler, fear of heights or water, etc.). It is better to send two letters: the first, a preliminary note with the basic details requesting parental permission; the second, nearer the time, with more detailed information about the precise nature of the educational visit and journey times (see below).

Itinerary

Each stage of the visit should be allotted a time: setting out, stops and starts, breaks and arrival. Parents and children should be given a copy in advance of the visit. If the visit is likely to continue beyond normal school hours, it is important to stress this fact to parents beforehand. If a number of activities are involved, precise timings are important to ensure that all the children have equal opportunity to engage with them; always leave a margin of error.

Resources

Clipboards, paper, pencils, activity sheets, maps, measuring tapes, cameras and other necessary equipment need to be gathered in advance. Educational visits have a habit of creeping up unawares on busy teachers and it is very stressful to be scurrying about on the morning of the visit in search of an essential item when it should have been ready the previous day. TAs have a significant role to play in the preparation and monitoring of equipment, supervision of children and support for learning – so make sure they are also properly informed and briefed.

Adult–child ratios

Local authorities have guidelines for the amount of adult help required for an educational visit. Younger children obviously require more supervision than older ones and under-5s need a large adult presence. The experience and competence of the adults involved should be taken into account and they should all be fully briefed before the visit. The other adults will vary in competence, so take account of this fact before allocating any vulnerable children to inexperienced helpers. Pupils who are emotionally temperamental should be attached to the more experienced staff. Take advice about how best to involve parents; if one of their relatives is present, younger children will normally want to be with them.

School arrangements

It is essential to check whether mealtime assistants and canteen staff and teachers who normally hold clubs and activities that involve your class have been informed that children will be away during that day. A playground duty may have to be swapped with a colleague. Children bringing dinner money may need to bring money for one day less than usual unless the canteen is providing a packed lunch for them. Children whose parents do not have to pay for meals are entitled to a packed lunch without charge. All these details need to be sorted in advance; leave nothing to chance.

Educational potential

The effort required to plan a successful educational visit demands that in the days and weeks following the visit there is opportunity for children to draw upon their experiences and utilise their newfound skills, understanding and knowledge in a variety of contexts. Many teachers use a visit as a starting point for innovative teaching and learning and the production of stimulating displays and events. The burst of energy from pupils in the days following the visit is often animated, enthusiastic and intense, so be ready to take full advantage of it.

No teacher who has planned an educational visit will underestimate the effort that is required. Trainees and new teachers are advised to collaborate with a more experienced colleague and plan the enterprise jointly. Visits are very hard work but immensely rewarding, and a means of enhancing the pupils' social development and helping adults to gain insights into each child's disposition, interests, strengths and limitations. Pupils also get to know the adults better and trainees do well to note that the adults also learn a lot about you, especially your ability to cope under pressure and keep your mind focused on the job in hand. See Trant (2010).

Activate your thinking!

It can be argued that the expression 'risk management' is an oxymoron. If a risk is managed, it ceases to be a risk!

Good practice

On residential visits, allow children to bring a favourite soft toy but refer to it as a 'mascot'. This approach allows children (usually older boys) who feel embarrassed about admitting their need for the security of a toy to wrap a football scarf (or similar) around the toy and parade it openly.

Case study

Miss Burns is pinning up some children's work on the display board, when the MTA, Mrs Adams, marches in, tugging a reluctant 9-year-old boy by the sleeve.

'Miss Burns, I'm bringing Terry to you because he won't do as he's told. I said to him "Don't throw your trainers up in the air" but he insisted on doing it and now Vicki's got hit on the head and ended up crying. Then him and Shaun set to, and Shaun ends up in tears. And I can't find Mrs Carlevale [the head teacher] or Mr Halpern [the deputy] so I found you instead.' [Sullen looks from Terry.]

'Well, Terry, what have you got to say for yourself?' the teacher ventures. [Shrug of shoulders.]

'He's always the same, Miss Burns; I tell him and tell him but he takes no notice.' [Terry looks at Mrs Adams fiercely but says nothing.] 'Anyway, I'm sick of him.'

'I'm sick of you picking on me,' retorts Terry, provocatively and angrily. The mood is blackening. Mrs Adams and Terry begin to argue in what is clearly a continuation of a longstanding feud. Miss Burns has a few seconds to decide what should be done: shout louder than either of them; walk off to find a senior colleague; deal with it herself. She wisely decides to take firm action.

'Thank you, Mrs Adams; you did the right thing; I'll deal with Terry now. Thank you very much.' Mrs Adams, much relieved to unload the problem, returns to her duties. Miss Burns sensibly stands still for a moment to allow Terry time to regain his composure, then quietly but firmly asks him what happened. Terry is on the verge of tears and clearly frustrated. As Miss Burns listens to his story unfold it becomes clear that the episode with the trainers was a secondary issue and that the real problem has its roots in an argument that took place between Terry and Shaun about team selection. As a result of Shaun's taunts and cutting comments born of superior intellect, the less competent Terry hit back in the only way he knew how. Mrs Adams observed the moment when Terry punched his adversary and, owing to Terry's reputation for fighting, took immediate action. Miss Burns did not blame the MTA, who was only doing her job, but had some sympathy with the boy as he stood in front of her, miserable, resentful and defiant. She told him that she would have to think about what should be done and told him that he must see her straight after the lunch break. She would also ask Mrs Adams whether he had tried hard to behave. After extracting a muttered promise that he would 'do his best to behave' Miss Burns let him go. She immediately started to worry about whether she had done the right thing. After all, the rule was that anyone seen fighting should stand outside the head's door. She did not want to appear to be soft or failing to support the MTA, but she was also aware that the circumstances were not as straightforward as they seemed and wanted to give Terry, who was a child from a very unsettled background, another chance. She is torn between conforming to school policy and using her instincts to guide her actions in the particular circumstances.

Activate your thinking!

Imagine that you are Miss Burns. What next for Terry? Who else will you involve? What will happen tomorrow lunchtime? Terry goes home and tells his mother that Mrs Adams is picking on him at lunchtime. His mother comes in to find out from you what is going on. What will you say?

Good practice

To reduce confrontations, take account of the following:

1. Stay calm, even if your insides are churning.
2. Take charge of the situation by speaking with quiet authority.
3. Insist that one person speak at a time.
4. Listen more than talk.
5. Avoid making judgements about rights and wrongs.
6. Ask the alleged perpetrator to confirm his or her actions.
7. Do not allow any 'yes, but...' comments initially.
8. After the facts have been established, allow the individual an opportunity to explain his or her actions.
9. Ask the main perpetrator what he or she thinks should happen.
10. If no answer to point 9 is forthcoming, offer alternatives.
11. Offer strategies to avoid further problems to those involved.
12. Make it clear what action you now intend to take.

Further reading for Chapter 5

Hughes, M. and Guppy, P. (2010) *Supporting Children's Reading: An INSET course for teaching assistants and volunteers*, London: David Fulton/NASEN.
A practical book, which is of special interest to adults working with children for whom reading is a struggle.
McDermott, D. (2008) *Developing Caring Relationships Among Parents, Children, Schools, and Communities*, London: Sage.
Focuses on parents and teachers as adult learners who should be growing and learning along with the children in their care.
Rose, R. (2005) *Becoming a Primary Higher Level Teaching Assistant*, Exeter: Learning Matters.
A practical guide that provides a combination of theory and practice for TAs on training and assessment routes in achieving HLTA status.
Whalley, M. (2007) *Involving Parents in Their Children's Learning*, London: Sage.
Offers ideas about how early years practitioners can collaborate effectively with parents, including a number of case studies.

Part 3

Teaching and Learning

The Curriculum

Introduction

The word 'curriculum' is used so frequently in schools and in discussions about education, it is tempting to believe that the concept is unproblematic, providing that knowledge is divided neatly into subject areas for teaching purposes; such a systematic approach is, however, far removed from the reality. In this chapter, we explore the various meanings of 'curriculum', the National Curriculum subject areas and some of the strategies and reports that have impinged upon the way that the curriculum is organised and taught.

Definitions

It is far from easy to establish agreement about a definition for 'the curriculum' other than describing the sum total of what pupils need to learn (Ross 2001). The word 'curriculum' might be thought of as a specified course of study (*Collins Dictionary*) but its interpretation and implementation is far more complex. Indeed, there is not even a consistent view about how curriculum translates into practice.

A broad-based definition of 'curriculum' would be everything children do, see, hear or feel in their setting, both planned and unplanned. However, as far back as 1904 we see that educationists were grappling with what the curriculum should entail. The *Suggestions for Teachers Code* stated that the curriculum of the primary school should include the following elements: (1) a training in the English language; (2) handwriting to secure speed as well as legibility; (3) arithmetic, including practical measurements; (4) drawing from objects, memory and brush drawing; (5) geography, history, music, hygiene and physical training; and (6) moral instruction, given both directly and indirectly. Some years later, the 1931 Hadow Consultative Committee suggested that the curriculum should be thought out in terms of activity and experience rather than facts to be stored. By the middle of the 1980s, school inspectors were claiming that a school's curriculum consisted of all those activities designed or encouraged within its organisational framework to promote the intellectual, personal, social and physical development of its pupils. Today, the National Curriculum is the starting point for any curriculum definition (see below).

In addition to statutory requirements concerning content, the present curriculum requires teachers to have due regard for inclusion principles that incorporate setting suitable learning challenges for all pupils such that every child can experience success in the work. The process of providing a relevant curriculum for all pupils involves teachers responding to children's diverse needs, facilitating learning and assessing outcomes. Children with learning difficulties and disabilities, and those for whom English is an additional language, are also entitled to receive a relevant, broad and balanced curriculum. The intention is that children from all social backgrounds, genders and races should receive a high quality education, regardless of their physical, mental or social condition.

Curriculum entitlement

Every child in a maintained school in the UK is entitled to receive an appropriate education as prescribed by the National Curriculum (NC) and associated statutory requirements. The curriculum experienced by the children must reflect the agreed whole-school plans and offer a properly weighted content that reflects the NC and externally imposed requirements, notably in mathematics and literacy. Schools must be able to show that every subject area is receiving an appropriate amount of time and that they are accommodating the needs of each child within the teaching and learning programme, with additional adult support where deemed necessary to reflect the need to provide targeted and individualised coaching (see also Chapter 5).

Although at one level the curriculum can be thought about as everything that a child encounters that might affect learning, the *formal* curriculum for schools presently consists of the Foundation Stage for children aged 3 to 5 years and an NC, separated into Key Stages (1, 2, 3 and 4) for children after the age of 5 years, though discussions about the usefulness of Key Stages is ongoing. Arrangements for statutory assessment at the end of each Key Stage are set out in detail in Qualifications and Curriculum Authority's (QCA) annual booklets about assessment and reporting arrangements. The relevant stages are summarised thus:

Foundation Stage from 3 to 5 years

The reception year is the last year of the Foundation Stage in which the children reach statutory school age (5 years).

National Curriculum

Key Stage 1 from 5 to 7 years (Year 1 and Year 2).
Key Stage 2 from 7 to 11 years (Years 3, 4, 5 and 6).

And in the secondary phase:

Key Stage 3 from 11 to 14 years.
Key Stage 4 from 14 to 16 years.

Subject areas in the NC consist of core and non-core subjects as follows:

Core subjects

English
Mathematics
Science

Non-core subjects

Design and technology
ICT
History
Geography
Art and design
Music
Physical education.

In addition, a programme of religious education (RE) must be provided, which varies from school to school, depending upon its status. Schools with a religious foundation have more flexibility in determining the RE curriculum than secular ones. Citizenship is only statutory in Key Stages 3 and 4 but is receiving considerably more attention in primary schools than hitherto, including the availability of detailed non-statutory guidance. (See also later in this chapter.) Primary schools must also include a modern foreign language (MFL) as part of the curriculum, and all children are required to learn a language from the age of 7 (see Maynard 2011). The NC is broadly organised into three parts: programmes of study, attainment targets and six key skills.

Programmes of study (PoS)

PoS set out what content pupils should be taught in each subject at each Key Stage.
   They also provide the basis for planning schemes of work.

Attainment targets (AT)

ATs set out the knowledge, skills and understanding which pupils of different abilities and maturities are expected to have gained by the end of each Key Stage. They consist of eight level descriptions of increasing difficulty to assess pupils' attainment at the end of a Key Stage (including national tests that are commonly referred to as SATs).

Key skills across the curriculum

- Communication, including speaking, listening, reading and writing
- Application of number
- Developing a range of mental calculation skills and the ability to apply them within a variety of contexts
- Information technology
- Using a range of information sources and ICT tools to find, analyse, interpret, evaluate and present information for a range of purposes
- Working with others
- Contributing to small-group and whole-class discussions
- Improving own learning and performance
- Reflecting on and critically evaluating their work and what they have learned
- Problem solving
- Identifying and understanding a problem, and planning ways to solve it.

The NC also states that pupils should be given opportunities to apply and develop their ICT capability to support their learning in all subjects, with the exception of physical education in

Key Stages 1 and 2. In recent years, ICT (sometimes referred to simply as IT) has assumed greater significance and become, in effect, a fourth core subject.

National Literacy Strategy

Introduction of national numeracy and literacy strategies in the late 1990s had a major impact on the primary curriculum. The framework provided in the National Literacy Strategy (NLS) was intended to cover the statutory requirements for reading and writing, contribute substantially to the development of speaking and listening, and have relevance across the whole of the NC. Consequently, skills in reading and writing non-fiction texts were intended to be relevant to every subject area. In practice, the original concept of a 'literacy hour' gave rise to a self-contained lesson, incorporated into the daily teaching timetable as a distinctive learning episode and rather jealously guarded. The suggested framework for the 'literacy hour' consisted of the following:

About fifteen minutes of shared reading and writing with the whole class.
About fifteen minutes with the whole class on 'word level work' (word recognition, phonics, spelling, vocabulary; also grammar and punctuation in Key Stage 2).
About twenty minutes of group and independent work (including guided reading and writing).
About ten minutes plenary (whole class brought together to share and critically reflect).

However, the rigid composition of the hour, in which attention had to be paid to set extracts from books at a word, sentence and text level, meant that other areas of English received less attention, especially the opportunity for children to experience extended writing opportunities and the development of speaking and listening ('oracy'). Thankfully, the importance of oracy has now received closer attention as an essential element of becoming literate and there has also been a re-emergence of the 'showing and sharing time' (where children bring, and talk about, things of interest to them) that was commonplace in most primary schools in the recent past. Although the framework helped to concentrate teachers' minds on the fundamental skills that children need to be literate, some practitioners found the highly structured and objectives-driven nature of the hour limited opportunities for spontaneity and exploration of unplanned areas of learning, and constrained teachers' attempts to make lessons more relevant. There was also a growing outcry from authors whose books were used for extracts that such 'sampling' practices distorted the quality of their work and did not allow children to become engrossed in the story. Books were increasingly used as a tool to aid reading and comprehension instead of something to be enjoyed in their own right.

In 2006 the government accepted that the NLS was a useful but inadequate way to improve standards in reading, writing and oral communication, and introduced a renewed literacy framework as an electronic version. To simplify the structure of the objectives and to incorporate speaking and listening, twelve strands of learning are now identified to give a broad overview of the curriculum for English in the primary phase. Thus:

1. Speaking
2. Listening and responding
3. Group discussion, interaction
4. Drama
5. Word recognition

6. Word structure and spelling
7. Understand and interpret texts
8. Engage with, respond to texts
9. Creating and shaping texts
10. Text structure and organisation
11. Sentence structure and punctuation
12. Presentation.

There is also a greater focus upon teachers and other practitioners using their assessment to personalise learning for the children: that is, to identify a child's strengths and weakness and provide explanations, information and work tasks to enhance existing knowledge or remedy weak understanding. The teaching of phonics has been highlighted as the principal strategy in word recognition to support reading and spelling (see Chapter 9 for further details about phonics teaching).

Activate your thinking!

For a comprehensive review of oral communication and its history, including recommendations about how best to conduct oral communication assessment, see Morreale *et al.* (2011).

Morreale, S., Backlud, P., Hay, E. and Moore, M. (2011) 'Assessment of oral communication: a major review of the historical development and trends in the movement from 1975 to 2009', *Communication Education*, 60 (2), pp. 255–78.

Writing frames

We noted in Chapter 4 that some children, notably boys, are unenthusiastic about writing things down. The use of writing frames is a method to combat a child's apprehension when faced with having to write something down on a blank piece of paper. Writing frames are formats that were introduced to provide an outline of the overall text structure with additional support provided through headings, phrases and sentences. Each completed writing frame provides experience of the writing process for pupils and is a step towards independent planning and writing of extended pieces. The teacher sometimes 'models' the process by working through the structure with children, offering examples and showing how to organise information. Alternatively, the children can be given the frame and asked to produce a piece of writing, for which the teacher subsequently offers feedback that includes suggestions for modification and improvement. Critics of writing frames are uneasy about the danger that excessive structure might suppress pupil creativity and free expression of ideas. Supporters view frames as a helpful starting point to facilitate writing and engage the interest of less confident children.

National Numeracy Strategy

The National Numeracy Strategy (NNS) was developed in 1998 to be used alongside the National Curriculum, so that their contents would, it was claimed, be broadly compatible. See also Chapter 10. The principles underpinning NC2000 applied to the original NNS and to the new framework (introduced in 2006). Thus: 'Mathematics equips pupils with a uniquely powerful set of tools to understand and change the world. These tools include logical reasoning, problem-solving skills and the ability to think in abstract ways' (DfES 2006a: 60). The NNS framework contained yearly teaching programmes for reception to Year 6 and consisted of five strands, the first three of which linked directly to the NC: number, calculations and solving problems; the last two did not link directly: measures, shape and space, and handling data.

The NNS framework placed a heavy emphasis on the assessment of children's work and their progress and recommended that a typical lesson would consist of about five to ten minutes of oral work and mental calculation (often referred to as the 'mental-oral' phase), about thirty to forty minutes of the main teaching activity and about ten to fifteen minutes of a plenary at the end. Although teachers were given a degree of flexibility in the way they taught, the NNS nevertheless prescribed that each lesson should include direct teaching and interaction with the pupils, and activities or exercises that pupils do.

The renewed framework is, like the literacy framework, an electronic version that allows you to link quickly to a wide range of teaching and learning resources to facilitate planning, teaching and assessment. Another key difference from the previous version is that objectives in the 1999 framework for mathematics have been slimmed down to give a clearer sense of the important aspects of mathematics that need to be taught to children. To simplify the structure of the objectives, seven strands of learning in mathematics are identified to give an overview of the curriculum. The objectives are aligned to the seven strands to demonstrate progression in each strand. The seven strands are as follows:

1. Using and applying mathematics
2. Counting and understanding number
3. Knowing and using number facts
4. Calculating
5. Understanding shape
6. Measuring
7. Handling data.

The early learning goals have all been incorporated within the Foundation Stage objectives. These objectives are all embedded within the area of learning and development structure: problem solving, reasoning and numeracy, all of which form part of the Early Years Foundation Stage framework.

The objectives under Year 6 progression to Year 7 are broadly targeted around level 5 to help to plan appropriately for children working at level 4 or level 5 and to help with transition from Key Stage 2 to Key Stage 3.

Williams Review (2008)

The Review of Mathematics Teaching in Early Years Settings and Primary Schools (P. Williams 2008) was a report produced for the government in June 2008 by a group of experts chaired by Sir Peter Williams. The review called for an urgent shift to reverse the prevailing negative attitudes to maths such that every pupil could leave primary school without a fear of the subject. The report recommended that learning about numbers and shapes should be rooted in play from an early age; children should do more mental maths and problem solving in the classroom (see Pepperell *et al.* 2009). Parents should help their children by means of games, puzzles and activities such as cooking at home. He recommended that there should be a maths specialist in every primary school within ten years. Other findings included:

1. Children's natural interest in numeracy, problem solving, reasoning, shapes and measures should be fostered from the start of schooling.
2. Children should be given opportunities, both indoors and outdoors, to explore, enjoy, learn, practise and talk about their developing mathematical understanding.
3. Children's mathematical experiences must be fun, meaningful and build confidence.
4. Intervention for struggling children should happen before the end of Key Stage 1 (i.e. before the age of 7).

The review claimed that too little attention is paid to building good attitudes to maths, so there must be a culture change inside and outside the classroom. The use and application of maths should be incorporated into the wider curriculum by cutting across subject areas ('cross-curricular') to embed mathematical learning more securely in children's minds. The most able pupils should be provided with more open-ended problem-solving tasks to help them extend their understanding of the subject.

The Williams Report also stressed that parental attitudes to mathematics have a significant impact on their child's numeracy skills, as there is clearly a link between parents with low-level skills and their children's under-attainment in mathematics. Schools therefore need to work with parents to dispel myths about the mystery of mathematics and give both children and parents a good grounding and positive attitude to the subject. Teachers' work with parents should familiarise them with current methods used to teach mathematics. The Williams Report can be accessed on-line at: www.teachernet.gov.uk/teachingandlearning/primary/primarystrategy/mathsreview

Non-core subjects in the NC

In addition to the three 'core' subjects of English (Language), Mathematics and Science, there are seven other subjects that make up the National Curriculum in Key Stages 1 and 2: history, geography; design and technology; ICT; art and design, physical education (PE) and music. In addition, religious education must be taught in all schools, though the syllabus and emphasis varies according to the type of school. At Key Stage 1, citizenship and personal, social and health education (PSHE) have non-statutory programmes of study. At Key Stage 2, a modern foreign language (MFL) is also included.

History

History teaching builds on children's earlier experiences about the world in which they live, in particular, their families and past and present events in their own lives. Teachers often encourage children to bring family photographs to refine their powers of observation and talk about 'time lines' to represent the sequence of events being represented. Experience of history should include listening and responding to stories, songs, nursery rhymes and poems; taking part in role plays; looking closely at similarities, differences, patterns and change; comparing, sorting, matching, ordering and sequencing everyday objects; talking about their observations and asking questions to gain information about why things happen and how things work.

A framework for teaching history includes a separate subject discipline element ('history' per se) and history as part of an interrelated theme or topic incorporating (say) aspects of geography. Through both subject and thematic elements, teachers guide children to under-stand the chronological location and sequences of major events and the place of personalities in influencing events.

Infant children focus on the lives and lifestyles of familiar people in the recent past and about famous people and events in the more distant past, including those from British history. Work with younger primary children is best carried out at a visual and tangible or tactile ('opportunity to see, touch and feel') level, resulting, for example, in children producing a labelled drawing to indicate how well they have identified the defining qualities of the arte-fact being observed. Older primary children focus more directly on people and important events and developments from recent and more distant times in their locality, in Britain and beyond.

Leedham and Murphy (2007) describe the importance of 'getting inside the mind' of his-torical characters and understanding life as they perceived it at the time, rather than imposing a twenty-first-century interpretation on the situation. They point out that the things preoc-cupying people today will seem strange to a historian in fifty years' time.

Activate your thinking!

The Historical Association (www.history.org.uk) is an independent UK national charity that has existed since 1906 and publishes the *Primary History* journal three times each year.

Geography

As part of the geography curriculum, pupils aged 5 to 7 years investigate their local area and a contrasting area in the United Kingdom or abroad; they also find out about the environment in both areas and the people who live there. Teachers have the responsibility to provide an appropriate vocabulary for children as they move from describing what they see, feel and hear to comparing examples from two or more localities (Mackintosh 2007). Children learn about the wider world and conduct geographical enquiries inside and outside the classroom. Pupils are encouraged to ask geographical questions about people, places and environments, and to use geographical skills and resources such as maps and photographs.

The curriculum for junior-aged pupils from 7 to 11 years include an investigation of various people groups, places and environments in the United Kingdom and abroad and make links between different places in the world. Children find out how people affect the environ-ment and how they are affected by it. They also continue the process of conducting geo-graphical enquiries inside and outside the classroom. Importantly, pupils learn to ask geographical questions and use geographical skills and resources such as maps, atlases, aerial photographs and information technology. Teachers are encouraged to adapt ideas from the schemes to meet pupils' needs and the priorities of their school or department (Martin 2006; Catling and Willy 2009).

Outdoor education often contains a geography dimension, frequently using an experiential method of learning ('discovery learning') with the use of all senses that takes place primarily through exposure to the natural environment. Possible locations of outdoor learning for schools include schools' grounds, urban spaces, rural or city farms, parks, gardens, woodlands, coasts, outdoor centres and wilderness areas. The remit of the organisation *Learning Outside the Classroom* (www.lotc.org.uk) in England is that every young person should experience the world beyond the classroom as an essential part of learning and personal development (see Sedgwick 2012). Similarly, the *Institute for Outdoor Learning* (www.outdoor-learning.org) encourages outdoor learning by developing quality, safety and opportunity to experience outdoor activity provision and by supporting and enhancing the good practice of those who work in the outdoors. In recent years there has been an increasing interest in so-called forest schools, which describes a form of education provision set in a wooded area.

Activate your thinking!

Forest schools create a learning vehicle to encourage a range of individuals, community groups and larger organisations to utilise their local open space for interactive play, health, recreation and personal development uses. See, for example, Harriman (2008), Knight (2009), O'Brien (2009).

Harriman, H. (2008) *The Outdoor Classroom: A place to learn*, Swindon: Red Robin Books.

Knight, S. (2009) *Forest Schools and Outdoor Learning in the Early Years*, London: Sage.

O'Brien, L. (2009) 'Learning outdoors: the forest school approach', *Education 3–13*, 37 (1), pp. 45–60.

Best practice

Local Studies is a mapping package that can be used for geographical, historical or environmental mapping projects at Key Stage 2. The programme allows pupils to draw their own background maps, download them from the Internet or use Ordnance Survey maps.

Design and Technology (D&T)

The NC programmes of study for D&T are divided into twenty-four schemes of work, which can be used at a school's discretion and all schools must show that they are teaching a range of knowledge, skills and concepts appropriate for the subject. The subject is also part of the Northern Ireland curriculum; in Scotland the subject is known as 'Craft and design'.

D&T programmes give children opportunities to acquire and apply knowledge and understanding of materials and components, systems, structures and products. They also have the potential to promote pupils' understanding of technological processes by planning and producing products using materials such as card, wood, textiles and natural resources. Pupils are taught specific skills, such as accurate cutting, fixing component parts and interpreting plans; children can also be taught to make predictions and conduct what is popularly referred to as 'fair testing'. Other skills include measuring accurately; drawing and interpreting graphs and bar charts; and handling information through the use of a database or spreadsheet using technology (IT). D&T is an ideal forum for creating meaningful cross-curriculum links.

By the age of about 7 years, most children should be able to use a range of materials to design and make simple products; select materials, tools and techniques and explain their choices; understand simple mechanisms and structures; measure, assemble, join and combine materials in a variety of ways using basic tools safely; and investigate and evaluate simple products. Many activities involve making a product that has a practical use, such as designing a book cover; making a pencil holder; and constructing a simple kite.

By the age of 11, most children can use knowledge and understanding of a range of materials, components and techniques to design and make quality products, evaluate work as it develops and, if necessary, suggest alternatives. They can produce designs and plans that list the stages involved in making a product, and the correct tools and materials to use. Skills include the ability to accurately measure, mark, cut, join and combine a variety of materials, and work safely by recognising potential hazards to themselves and others.

Information and communication technology (ICT)

ICT is an integral part of the modern curriculum and considered to be important to learning across all subjects (with the possible exception of PE and games). The main thrust of learning using electronic means involves finding things out; developing ideas and making things happen; exchanging and sharing information; and reviewing, modifying and evaluating work as it progresses. At one time, ICT was restricted to secondary schools as an element of what was termed 'computer studies'; however, ICT is now taught to children from the reception class (5-year-olds) onwards. For example, Millum (2011) explores ways of inspiring and engaging pupils in reading and writing through a variety of methods that include group and paired discussion, employing a cross-curricular mapping grid to show how the activities can be used across a range of subjects.

As they move through primary school, pupils are taught how to use various computer programs for a particular task and given opportunities to practise their skills. They may, for instance, present findings from an investigation using several forms of information, such as pictures, graphics and text. Extensive use is made of basic software packages with sounds and animation for story-writing, sharing research and presenting information (see Loveless 2009). Teachers and older pupils might work collaboratively on a variety of challenging multimedia projects, such as creating an animated film or using spreadsheets to enter data emerging from a numeracy project. Some schools promote links with pupils from neighbouring schools or further afield and train children to establish their own websites, though with keen awareness of ensuring children's 'cyber safety'. See also Chapter 10 and *Discussion Point 8*, Chapter 15.

Art and design

Art and design in primary schools includes drawing and painting, printing, collage, textiles and sculpture. Nearly all children love to draw and paint, though some sensitive younger children are unwilling to get messy and opt for more sedate activities. Key and Stillman (2009) acknowledge that experiences in art and craft for some children are extremely positive and rewarding, as they enjoy the freedom and spontaneity of exploring materials. Other pupils, however, quickly become frustrated and even anxious about the unpredictability when using paints and the open-endedness of selecting and using materials. These children look for a higher degree of certainty and tend to rely heavily on their classmates for ideas. Teachers have to encourage the less enthusiastic children and reassure them that their ideas are as valid as the next person's, while helping all pupils to hone their skills and be ambitious in what they attempt to do.

At one time it was acceptable to say that every child's work and output was equally valid and that no distinction should be made between them in evaluating quality for fear of suppressing creativity and creating artificial measures of something that is largely subjective in character. More recently, it is recognised that an evaluation based on pupil motivation, willingness to try new things, imagination and concentration can aid learning without damaging a child's self-confidence (see, for example, Eisner 2002). A report by OFSTED (2009) found that in schools in which standards of art and design were high, pupils used sketchbooks regularly, teachers developed pupils' responsibility for making choices, and the whole school used display both to celebrate and evaluate achievement. The use of bringing practising artists into school to stir and enthuse children was also cited as a key factor in success.

Watts (2010) identifies the components of children's competence in observational drawing through a detailed analysis of a drawing made by a 6-year-old child. The author makes connections between the teaching of drawing and the teaching of literacy and concludes that children who are able to make confident representations of the visual world are better placed to express their own ideas, thoughts and experiences.

There are numerous websites dedicated to art and design; for example, teaching ideas across the curriculum can be found at www.teachingideas.co.uk/art/contents.htm and primary school resources for creative arts via www.primaryschool.com.au.

Physical education (PE)

Pupils are entitled to have two hours of PE timetabled per week to develop the six areas of activity as set out in the National Curriculum, namely: dance; games; gymnastics; athletics; outdoor and adventurous activities; and swimming. Children are normally given the opportunity to swim during KS2, though sometimes it is possible to offer tuition earlier, and many schools aim that all pupils leave school being able to swim at least 25 metres. In addition to the six areas, pupils are often given the opportunity to complete the National Cycling Proficiency scheme. As well as athletics, sports commonly include football, tag rugby, netball, basketball, kwik cricket and short tennis. In nearly every school, pupils take part in a range of tournaments and sports festivals both within school between year groups and occasionally in conjunction with, or competing against, other schools.

Teachers emphasise gaining skills rather than simply organising team games, though junior-age children in particular are enthusiastic about competitions. There is also a keener awareness of the need to take account of, and include in lesson planning, children with physical limitations and communication problems ('autism'). To avoid placing undue strain on immature bodies, teachers incorporate 'warm-up' and 'cool-down' activities. Pupils' attainment is generally best where they have opportunity to:

1. use their bodies: for example, in movements such as running, stretching and balancing with increasing control at the early stages, to throwing accurately or varying the rhythm of a dance sequence at the later stages;
2. apply skills: for example, in learning to make a controlled landing from a jump at the early stages, to using skills in orienteering at the later stages;
3. co-operate/share: for example, in taking turns or sharing apparatus at the early stages, to responding to a partner's movements in a game or dance at the later stages.

A report by HM Inspectorate of Education (2001) suggested that very good programmes in physical education occurred when teachers took account of pupils' prior learning and special educational needs, and enhanced children's experiences through visits from a specialist teacher. Programmes focused clearly on teaching the relevant skills, knowledge and understanding and, as far as possible, offered opportunities for choice within the programme or through extra-curricular activities. In the best PE lessons, teachers promoted positive attitudes and showed enthusiasm, used appropriate footwear and clothing for the gym or playing field and gave close attention to discipline and safety. Lessons began with an overview in which teachers shared the purpose of the lesson with pupils and set expectations of what they could achieve. There was often a pattern of 'warm-up' activities followed by targeted teaching and opportunities for pupils to try out and practise skills. There were high levels of sustained physical activity with little time spent in queuing or setting out apparatus. Teachers achieved a good balance between developing particular skills and applying them in contexts such as games, dances or gymnastics routines. Demonstration, evaluation, discussion and brief reviews of progress were important features of the lesson. Teachers identified and paid good attention to differences in pupils' needs and observed the children carefully, praising genuine effort and providing clear and constructive feedback.

Good practice

For a wide range of warming-up and cooling-down activities for use in PE and games, visit *Teaching Ideas* website at www.teachingideas.co.uk/pe/contents.htm.

For ideas about lesson plans and step-by-step content in gymnastics, see two books by Carroll and Hannay (2010, 2011).

Carroll, M. and Hannay, J. (2010) *Developing Physical Health and Well-Being through Gymnastic Activity* (5–7), London: David Fulton.
Carroll, M. and Hannay, J. (2011) *Developing Physical Health and Well-Being through Gymnastic Activity* (7–14), London: David Fulton.

Music

On average, less than one hour per week is devoted to music in primary schools and it has been estimated that only 13 per cent of primary pupils learn to play an instrument. All children in England and Wales should have access to instrumental and vocal tuition but reports about the standard of music education suggest that although the quality of teaching is good in most schools, fewer than half gave pupils any opportunity to practise their musical skills. In 2007, a lot of effort was made nationally to stimulate interest in music and encourage pupils (not least, boys) to become more self-assured and enthusiastic. As part of this initiative, Howard Goodall was appointed as a national singing ambassador for England.

The ability to use the voice effectively through singing is one of the most basic and yet essential music skills. Children need to learn to control the vocal mechanisms to accurately reproduce or manipulate elements of beat, rhythm, pitch, tempo, dynamics, tone and colour. However, J. Smith (2006) suggests that children may need help in singing for a variety of reasons, including a lack of confidence, auditory processing difficulties, hearing impairments and other physical impairments such as a chronically hoarse voice. She claims that all humans sing to express emotions that are beyond mere words, so that even very young children can, and do, express inexpressible feelings in song. Consequently, singing can become a source of joy, comfort and emotional sensation and is the birthright of every child with a normal speaking voice. The Montessori Educational Institute in the UK (www.mariamontessori.org) offers the advice for inculcating a love for singing in children, a modified version of which is listed below:

- Try to have some group singing every day.
- Don't force children to join the group or to sing as some children prefer to listen from a distance for some time before feeling comfortable enough to join in.
- Choose only a few songs and keep the session short (about five minutes).
- Be an enthusiastic teacher, who obviously enjoys the sessions.
- Avoid correcting the children or allowing negative comments.
- Quickly and quietly close the session if the children aren't paying attention or are being unruly.
- Look the children in the eye and talk as little as possible.
- Keep the children busy singing and eliminate pauses.
- Always respond positively to children's suggestions.
- Teach a song step by step and through repetition.
- Sing the songs unaccompanied if possible.
- Always involve the children by asking if anyone remembers a song that was sung the day before or remembers the words.
- Make singing the sole object of the gathering.
- Put recordings of the songs children are learning in a music library for the children.

From the age of 5 to 14 music forms part of the Scottish curriculum called Expressive Arts, which also includes PE, drama and art and design. The curriculum in Wales states that music should enhance pupils' communication, information technology, and creative, personal and social skills. All pupils aged 5–14 have a statutory entitlement to music education in class. The main aim of the music curriculum in Northern Ireland is to develop pupils' musical ability, with children experiencing making and responding to music. Children study music as a compulsory subject from the age of 5 to 14 years.

Although many primary teachers feel ill-equipped and insecure about teaching music, sessions can be enhanced if children are offered opportunities to dance and express themselves physically by stomping, marching, swaying, jumping and shaking. Pupils can also be offered opportunities to hum and sing along with music to enhance their language-development skills. Music can be linked with design technology by allowing children to invent their own instruments from classroom materials or recycled objects and perform for, or with, the rest of the class; and compose music by means of computer technology programs.

Good practice

Highlight a composer each month (say) by providing brief biographical information and playing extracts from his or her work. Some teachers use music as a two-minute stimulus for stretching, moving or dancing, to emphasise its fun side. See Jones and Robson (2008) and Beach *et al.* (2010) who argue that music in the primary school should be based on four principles, namely: integration, creativity, access and inclusion, and collaboration.

Beach, N., Evans, J. and Spruce, G. (2010) *Making Music in the Primary School*, London: David Fulton.
Jones, P. and Robson, C. (2008) *Teaching Music in Primary Schools*, Exeter: Learning Matters.

The place of drama

Drama is located within the English programme in the National Curriculum for England, Wales and for Northern Ireland and is one of the four strands of speaking and listening, by focusing on the processes of *making, performing and appraising*. It is not an NC subject in its own right. Drama is an art form and, as such, gives significance to life and relationships. It allows children to explore and understand order and disorder, harmony and discord, the expected and unexpected, and so forth. Johnson (2004) argues that drama provides a limitless range of contexts, rich with opportunities for developing a deeper understanding of their own creative processes by thinking from within a situation and reflecting on its significance.

As part of their work to enhance speaking and listening ('oracy') and participate in drama activities, pupils at Key Stage 1 (5 to 7 years) are taught to use language and actions to explore and convey situations, characters and emotions; create and sustain roles; and comment constructively on the drama that they see and experience. At Key Stage 2 (7 to 11 years) pupils are taught to create, adapt and sustain different roles; use character action and narrative to convey themes, emotions and ideas in plays they devise and script; use dramatic techniques to explore characters and issues; and evaluate how they and others have contributed to the work in drama.

In Scotland, the *National Guidelines for the Expressive Arts 5–14* set out the aims for drama in primary schools. Implicit in the guidelines is the notion that the four subjects in the expressive arts curriculum are mutually supportive because they share similar principles and engage pupils in similar processes. Aims specific to drama require that pupils should:

- gain understanding of themselves and others through dramatic, imaginative experience;
- communicate ideas and feelings using language, expression and movement in real and imaginary situations;
- develop confidence and self-esteem in their relationships with others and sensitivity towards others;
- develop a range of dramatic skills and techniques.

Activate your thinking!

Doona (2011) claims that engagement with the Shakespearean plays and their language can have a dramatic and beneficial impact on children's literacy and writing.

Doona, J. (2011) *Shakespeare for the Primary School: 50 lesson plans using drama*, Abingdon: Routledge.

Good practice

Become a 'drama teacher' in the fullest sense of the word by making children's learning experiences 'dramatic'. Incorporate an element of mystery and enthusiastic expectation. Propose and communicate ideas expressively, using varied facial expressions and voice tones. Respond to pupil comments and suggestions optimistically. Employ the use of 'just imagine if' and 'suppose that' and 'what would happen if' phrases to stimulate and engage children's interest. Day (2011) outlines thirty-three practical sessions, each one built around developing social skills, which, according to the author, are essential if children are to become effective and positive communicators. See also Clipson-Boyles (2011).

Clipson-Boyles, S. (2011) *Teaching the Primary Curriculum through Drama*, Abingdon: Routledge.

Day, A. (2011) *Drama Sessions for Primary Schools and Drama Clubs*, Abingdon: Routledge.

Further reading for Chapter 6

Dillon, J.T. (2009) 'The questions of curriculum', *Journal of Curriculum Studies*, 41 (3), pp. 343–59.
This academic article reviews and analyses formulations of questions used by curriculum theorists; the various uses of such questions are described.
Kesson, J. and Peacock, G. (2011) *The Really Useful ICT Book*, London: David Fulton.
The authors provide straightforward guidance for practitioners wishing to improve their confidence in using ICT in the classroom.
Jones, P. and Robson, C. (2008) *Teaching Music in Primary Schools*, Exeter: Learning Matters.
The book covers the range of music education from Foundation Stage to the end of KS2 and encourages the use of music both for its own sake, and as a stimulus and support across the curriculum.
Kerry, T. (ed.) (2010) *Cross-Curricular Teaching in the Primary School: Planning and facilitating imaginative lessons*, Abingdon: Routledge.
This book explores how teaching across the curriculum can improve children's learning and suggests ways in which teachers can plan an imaginative and integrated curriculum.
Rowley, C. and Cooper, H. (eds) (2009) *Cross-Curricular Approaches to Teaching and Learning*, London: Sage.
The editors use the humanities as a starting point on which to build case studies and explore the significance of values in the curriculum.
Winston, J. and Tandy, M. (2009) *Beginning Drama 4–11*, third edn, Abingdon: Routledge.
The authors provide lesson ideas for pupils aged 4–11 and also suggest how to successfully incorporate drama into the curriculum.

7

The Process of Learning

Introduction

This chapter concentrates on the ways that children learn and the way in which a teacher's decisions and priorities affect its quality and effectiveness. Throughout the chapter there is a recognition that learning relies on motivation, working relationships and curriculum relevance. By carefully considering these issues, teachers are better equipped to help children achieve their potential. The value of dialogue in learning and the needs of gifted and talented children are also explored.

Learning

The process of learning is complex and unpredictable and no one fully understands what it consists of or how it takes place, though there have been many attempts to do so. Robson (2006) argues that it is difficult to differentiate between learning and thinking, though claims that it is important to try. She offers one example (based on Perkins 1992) that learning is a consequence of thinking. Robson also suggests that it is necessary to take a broad view of learning, 'which includes use of the imagination, a playful disposition, persistence and the ability to learn with and from others' (p. 3). Crucially, success in learning is not solely concerned with things that can be measured (as often promoted by government and its agents). There are occasions when even the least capable children amaze everyone (including themselves) by grasping a difficult concept, mastering a skill or retaining some knowledge when their more illustrious classmates struggle to do so.

When educators speak of an 'able child', they often mean that the pupil is fully literate and numerate. When teachers refer to a pupil as 'very able', it is likely that they mean from an assessment point of view that the child is top of the class in that subject (e.g. high ability in mathematics). Pupils at the other end of the spectrum (i.e. not very able) are often spoken of as being 'slow learners'. With the recent resurgence of interest in exceptionally capable pupils, the terms 'gifted' and 'talented' tend to be used in preference to the general descriptor 'very able' to signal that children are in the top 5 per cent of the school population, as measured in formal tests. See also Chapter 8 for further details about gifted and talented pupils.

Although teachers' enthusiasm and commitment play an important part in bringing about the best conditions for learning, it is essential that they consider things from a child's perspective if effective progress is to be made. Children are not merely recipients of learning but active partners and initiators of it. Three interdependent essential elements of learning are knowledge, understanding and the development of skills.

Knowledge

Knowledge has a safe ring to it but can be slippery and deceptive. There are many different forms of knowledge, including knowledge of facts, of controversies, of situations, of procedures and of people. Thus:

- Knowledge of *facts* involves more than memorising. It needs to take account of new understanding; for instance, we now know that the earth is more or less round, not flat.
- Knowledge of *controversies* requires an awareness of the disputed information; for instance, whether Columbus discovered America.
- Knowledge of *moral dilemmas* demands a wide view of the relevant factors and an ability to make judgements about their significance.
- Knowledge of *procedures* is necessary when a task has to be completed or decisions made about effectiveness.
- Knowledge of *people* is needed to prosper in social situations.

Although at one stage of a child's development it might be sufficient to 'know' something is 'true' it may subsequently be appropriate to point out that things may not be as straightforward as they appear. For example, 7-year-old children can be told that all objects fall towards the ground at the same rate, but 11-year-olds also need to be aware that the principle only holds for objects over a certain density and under normal atmospheric conditions. A 15-year-old may be interested in the variations according to air pressure, the effect of a vacuum, and so forth. Knowledge evolves and deepens with age, experience and a greater facility with language use. The process of returning to a theme over a period of time to deepen knowledge and understanding is sometimes referred to as the 'spiral curriculum'.

Knowledge can be thought of in terms of being *transitory*, such as remembering a telephone number for as long as it takes to dial it but no longer. It can be *accessible*, such as recalling a spelling rule for use when writing but not holding the knowledge at the forefront of thinking for regular use. It can be *immediate*, such as knowing a friend's name or the route to school without needing to think deeply about it. Sometimes, children seem to remain locked in the transitory knowledge zone. They appear to have learned something during the morning lesson but cannot remember it during the afternoon. Sometimes the knowledge is locked into a child's recall system but cannot be accessed, either because it is too deeply stored, or because the child is tired or circumstances (such as stress) create a barrier to remembering.

Knowledge that does not relate to previous learning is no more than mechanical repetition or 'rote learning', a technique that does not necessitate understanding of a subject but instead focuses on memorisation of the content. The principle that underpins rote learning is that children will be able to quickly recall the meaning of the material the more they repeat it. Rote learning is sometimes linked with the derogative expression 'parrot fashion' because, though accurately reproducing the information, children might not have understood what they were saying. For instance, a child could learn a list of Latin names off by heart and get full marks in a test, but have no idea about their meaning or significance.

Finally, children gradually need to gain wisdom about the use of knowledge, its appropriateness, its relevance and its application. Teachers therefore have the challenging task of helping children to locate what they learn in social contexts or at least using case studies to exemplify the principles involved. The notion that knowledge is value-neutral and can be dealt with apart from the moral implications attached to its use deserves close scrutiny.

Many of our teaching techniques rely on children's immediate access to knowledge. A teacher may use a question-and-answer session to draw out what pupils know. One child has her hand flapping in the air every time a question is asked; another remains as still as a statue, eyes lowered, hoping that the teacher does not choose her. You might reasonably conclude that the enthusiastic child has a higher level of knowledge than her timid classmate, but this is not necessarily the case. The second child may have stored the knowledge and, in the intensity of the moment, been unable to draw it out of her memory bank. She may be weighing up other options rather than the obvious response or simply hate answering questions publicly for fear of being wrong. Teachers should be careful to ask both closed questions that test immediate recall, and open questions in which a variety of answers are acceptable.

There are numerous other types of questions, all of which rely on the purpose for asking it. The child who has prompt immediate recall may or may not be able to offer a more considered and thoughtful response. Able children are often the most successful in responding to open questions but all children benefit from being given time to think. The best teachers have fun shooting out closed questions to a class, but also ask speculative types of questions that test a child's ability to reflect and perhaps suggest unlikely possibilities. See Chapter 9 for a detailed examination of question types and their classroom use.

When working with children, it is helpful to think of knowledge from their perspective:

- *Surface knowledge:* I know because I can repeat what you have told me.
- *Descriptive knowledge:* I know because I can tell you about it.
- *Explanatory knowledge:* I know because I can explain why it happened.
- *Applied knowledge:* I know because I can understand the implications for its use.

The most powerful forms of knowledge involve higher levels of understanding that permit its use in a variety of contexts. Knowledge without understanding is merely information. Knowledge that cannot be applied in a practical setting or decision-making is of theoretical interest only.

Good practice

Keep an informal record of the types of questions that you ask. Try to shift the balance away from closed types that rely on memory to ones that require deeper thinking.

Understanding (conceptual development)

A concept is here defined as a perceived regularity in events or objects, or records of events or objects that can be designated by the use of a label. One of the most common questions that teachers ask their pupils is whether they understand something. In the majority of cases, the children chorus 'yes' and the teacher, pleased at her skill in explaining, proceeds to the next stage of the lesson. But do the children really understand? And what does 'being able to understand' mean? These are complex questions. Having asked if the children understood, the teacher might usefully say: 'Well done; now will everyone please whisper to the person next to you what I have said'; and after a suitable time has elapsed: 'Now put up your hand if you think that your partner really understands.' The chances are that a number would be less clear than they imagined they were before having to explain it to a friend.

Understanding is normally gained gradually but owing to the fact that 'the light suddenly comes on' to indicate a grasp of something, it can seem that understanding is instantaneous. Like knowledge, it operates at a variety of conceptual levels and requires considerable reinforcement and testing out in real contexts before a thorough grasp of the issues has been accomplished. Understanding comes initially through *raising awareness*, as many children simply do not properly realise that there is anything to be understood. Raising awareness is followed by *raising interest*. Children are naturally inquisitive, a characteristic which needs to be exploited (by the teacher posing relevant questions or wondering out loud about a situation). The inquisitiveness results in children raising their own questions; this is the point at which the teacher's skill in explaining is important as queries are dealt with and misconceptions/misunderstandings are corrected. Subsequently, children should have opportunity to explore, discover and test propositions, experiment with ideas and raise fresh issues. This cycle of raising awareness and interest, followed by further questions, can be continued until pupils reach the limit of their understanding.

Knowledge and understanding are inextricably entwined. For instance, a young child may understand through observation that seeds grow into plants with roots and a stem. The teacher will probably have to supply the terminology and, as the process takes place, enthuse with the child at the visual growth, raise significant questions about how it happens, and speculate about what might happen next. Older children not only understand the significance of the root system and the influence of different types of soil but can also offer explanations as to *why* it happens, using different vocabulary from their younger counterparts. The 5-year-old who gazed in wonder at the bean plant's speed of growth becomes the 11-year-old who can not only describe what is happening but also use evidence to prove underlying principles. The steady progression from the 5-year-old Karoline who wonders at what she sees happening, to the 11-year-old Karoline who can provide insights about the unseen biological processes at work, is testimony to the levels of understanding that children reach. Examples of this progression can be found in every area of the curriculum. For example:

In moral and social development, children's understanding of ethical issues, social justice and fairness emerge over time as they gain a more complete picture of the prevailing circumstances and conflicting claims of varied viewpoints.

In mathematics, a child may initially understand concepts such as 'smaller and bigger than' but will later apply more varied terms which involve expressions such as 'multiples and factors of'.

In science, the use of a coloured dye in the water used to sustain the plant (such as a piece of celery) results in a gradual discoloration. Young children talk about the colour change; older ones will, with suitable adult guidance, discuss issues relating to capillary action and metabolism.

In art, the 4-year-old's random dabs of paint are gradually replaced by rainbows of colour, which lead to paint mixes and experimentation with other substances. Older primary children draw from their knowledge of techniques and combine these with their own spontaneity and, perhaps, techniques learned from others.

The development of understanding (concepts) therefore involves a combination of intellect, maturity (especially the ability to think abstractly), the opportunity to explore ideas and 'play' with alternatives, facilitated by the teaching skills of teachers who give children appropriate information, strategies and encouragement to speculate, make discoveries, articulate their claims and uncertainties, and eventually reach firm conclusions.

Continuity of learning experiences through concept development is a foundation stone of the National Curriculum (NC) and the different government strategies for literacy and mathematics (formerly referred to, somewhat inappropriately, as numeracy – which, strictly speaking, refers only to the number aspect of mathematics). It is facilitated by lessons that build on previous knowledge and experience, encourage children to explore and question, and allow time for understanding to grow and consolidate by using it in a variety of contexts. Higher levels of understanding come through experimentation and opportunities to explore ideas, discuss findings and investigate possibilities.

Good practice

Merely asking children if they understand something is inadequate. You must be much more specific about discovering what they have grasped and probe the nature and depth of their understanding through appropriate questioning and encouraging them to explain things in their own words.

Skills

The term 'skills' is used to describe a wide range of abilities that children need to function effectively in their lives. Skills may be considered under two broad categories: (1) abilities that children need so that they can find out things for themselves and enhance their existing knowledge and understanding; and (2) abilities and attributes that children will need to acquire if they are to enhance and extend their learning. Skills can also be thought of in terms of those that are principally *cerebral* (mainly to do with active thinking), such as the skill required to express an opinion confidently and clearly, and those that are *manual* (mainly to do with physical co-ordination), such as throwing a ball accurately or kneading a ball of clay. This distinction is not to suggest that manual skills do not require thought and judgement, but that the predominant form of learning is represented by an immediate outcome based on physical action.

Mastery of skills is necessary to support learning. For instance, there is little to be gained from a child being able to open a book and find the index but then being unable to use it effectively. Similarly, it is interesting to study the trajectory and flight of a ball in the air, but this does not ensure that the child will hit the target. Every skill involves judgement, decision-making and evaluation as to the effectiveness of the procedure and the quality of the end result. Skills sometimes need to be exercised in conjunction with discernment or wisdom if they are to be most effective. For instance, skills of persuasion could be used to encourage a classmate to keep trying and succeed, or to share a treasured toy.

National Curriculum skills

The National Curriculum originally used the word 'skills' to denote transferable abilities in areas as diverse as communication, numeracy, problem solving, personal and social relations, and information technology. These skills are intended to be used across the curriculum and apply to every subject area. For example, children should be able to express themselves in speech across the whole curriculum, and use computer software to produce visual representations of findings. The importance of promoting speaking and listening has received closer attention in recent years after being allocated a marginal position in the original literacy strategy of 1999. Concerns that children were unable to express themselves clearly have been given greater urgency by the fact that studies suggest that some parents are talking less to their children because of working long hours and the dominance of television and electronic games. The NC specifies six 'key skills' that are intended to help learners to improve their learning and performance in education, work and life as follows:

Communication, using speaking, listening, reading and writing. Skills required include the ability to take account of different audiences, to understand what others are saying and to participate in group discussions. Pupils should be able to read both fictional and non-fictional texts fluently and with understanding. Although most direct development of communication skills takes place during literacy lessons, consideration should be given to the development of language across the curriculum. The development can be enhanced by promoting a climate whereby children's comments, suggestions and ideas are taken seriously. There are also more formal opportunities to enhance communication skills through drama sessions.

Application of number, including the development of a range of mental calculation skills and their application. The use of mathematical language to process data, solve problems and explain the reasoning behind solutions also forms part of this skill. For example, Fox and Surtees (2010) explain how teachers can use and apply mathematics across the curriculum in every subject, notably through problem-solving activities (see below).

Information technology, developing the ability to use a range of information sources and ICT tools, and to make critical and informed judgements about when it is appropriate to use ICT to access information, solve problems and for creative expression.

Working with others, including the ability to contribute to small-group and whole-class discussion, and to work collaboratively. The interaction requires the development of social skills and an awareness of other people's needs and perspectives (see Cohen 2006b). The importance of identifying and understanding their own and others' emotions has assumed greater urgency in recent years following unwelcome violent trends in society.

Improving own learning and performance, involving pupils in reflection and critical evaluation of different aspects of their work, assessing their own performance and establishing targets for learning. Most schools involve pupils in establishing and monitoring their own progress, both through setting targets and assessing outcomes. It has also become fashionable to encourage peer assessment, whereby pairs of pupils co-operate in assessing the quality of one another's work.

Problem solving, including identifying and understanding problems, planning ways to solve them, monitoring progress and reviewing solutions.

Thinking skills

Thinking skills is a difficult concept to define. Some educationists argue that thought processes cannot accurately be described as skills. Nevertheless, McGuinness (1999) suggests that definitions might include some or all of the following: (1) collecting information; (2) sorting and analysing information; (3) drawing conclusions from the information; (4) 'brainstorming' new ideas; (5) problem solving; (6) determining cause and effect; (7) evaluating options; (8) planning and setting goals; (9) monitoring; (10) decision-making; and (11) reflecting on one's own progress. All these definitions are based upon the assumption that thinking (cognition) goes beyond the acquisition of knowledge and includes the process(es) of knowing and reflecting on thinking – sometimes referred to as 'metacognition'.

Sedgwick (2008) underlines the fact that a teacher will struggle to inculcate thinking and philosophical enquiry without support from a whole-school policy. He argues that treating children as the thinking human beings they are will fail if the teacher in the adjacent class is treating children as 'empty vessels' to be filled or 'clean slates' on which to write the teacher's ideas. The development of thinking skills invites pupils to become partners in learning rather than passive recipients of it.

Five 'thinking skills' are identified in the NC as important in assisting children to know how, as well as knowing what. These skills are: processing information, reasoning, enquiry, creative thinking and evaluation skills. The NC also offers explanations about each of the skills. Thus:

Information-processing skills enable pupils to locate and collect relevant information, to sort, classify, sequence, compare and contrast, and to analyse part/whole relationships. These skills require that pupils are not satisfied with gaining a single piece of information but draw from a variety of sources, including electronic, human and book-based.

Reasoning skills enable pupils to give reasons for opinions and actions, to draw inferences and make deductions, to use precise language to explain what they think, and to make judgements and decisions informed by reasons or evidence. These skills encourage children to express their beliefs and opinions, guided by sensitive adults and an agreed protocol.

Enquiry skills enable pupils to ask questions, to pose and define problems, to plan what to do and how to research the problem, to predict outcomes and anticipate consequences, and to test conclusions and improve ideas. These skills require that children think beyond the immediate circumstances and project into new possibilities and opportunities.

Creative thinking skills enable pupils to generate and extend ideas, to suggest hypotheses, to apply imagination, and to look for alternative, innovative outcomes. The key word in this definition is *imagination*, where the children are actively encouraged and liberated into fresh modes of thought and activity (see, for example, Carter 2002 for ideas for creative writing; Craft 2005 for a more comprehensive review of issues). See later in this chapter for further details about use of the imagination in learning.

Evaluation skills enable pupils to evaluate information, to judge the value of what they read, hear and do, to develop criteria for judging the value of their own and others' work or ideas, and to have confidence in their judgements. These critical thinking skills (Quinn 1997; Haynes 2007; Hooks 2009) are considered to be amongst the most difficult for children to grasp, as they require considerable experience and maturity if they are to be anything more than superficial, spontaneous responses.

Cross-reference: Guided Reader Extract 7

Good practice

Use questions such as the following to stimulate discussion: How would you describe a dinosaur to a visitor from space? If dogs, cats and hamsters could speak, what would they talk about? What would happen to the world if no one ever died?

Cross-reference: Guided Reader Extract 8

Skills, therefore, involve both thinking and dexterity through words and physical means. To be able to think and articulate is important, but without having the necessary skills to complete a practical task children quickly become frustrated. On the other hand, the application of practical skills that involves only a small amount of thinking leads to inertia and passivity, limiting children's capacity to approach their learning more imaginatively. Wenham (1995) graphically expresses the relationship between knowledge, understanding and skills:

'Without understanding, experience is blind; but without experience, knowledge and understanding are empty; and without skill, all of them are dumb' (p. 133).

Forms of learning

Defining learning

'Learning' is a word frequently used in education discussions and documents, and among teachers in school, but it is difficult to define and even harder to explain the processes that combine to produce a learning outcome. Over the past few years a lot of emphasis has been placed on what is sometimes referred to as 'meta-learning', a term coined by John Biggs of the University of Hong Kong in 1985 to show how we can take control of our own learning or, more simply, 'learning how to learn'. One of the key principles is that learning is a skill to be acquired, mastered and improved, not a once-for-all 'hard-wired' trait that pupils (and adults) possess or do not possess. Further, by learning about learning, children find out about themselves: their preferences, desires and the things that enthuse them. If the concept is extended to collaborative settings, it also offers children insights into how others in the group learn.

Although learning comes relatively easily to some children, others find that they have to work hard over a long period of time before things fall into place. Some children seem unable to master quite elementary principles and are adjudged to have special educational needs and require a considerable amount of adult help in remedying the situation. By the time children leave the infant sector (Key Stage 1) and join the big boys and girls in the juniors (Key Stage 2) teachers are normally in a position to predict with some certainty which pupils will succeed academically and which will not. In fact, most playgroup leaders and nursery staffs claim that they can spot danger signs early on: poor vocabulary, difficulty socialising and solitary play. It is not unusual for children who struggle academically to exhibit symptoms such as lack of motivation and general dissatisfaction with life. Some of these children may also have few friends and, occasionally, exhibit erratic behaviour. In addition to academic achievement, therefore, the learning process has implications for children's emotional and social wellbeing.

When asked by the teacher how she understood what was happening when she was working out a problem, Huan, a 5-year-old girl, thought for a moment before replying: 'When I want to understand something I draw a picture of it in my mind.' This small insight into a child's thinking suggests that definitions of learning must be rooted in the effect that the process has upon the learner, rather more than the actions of a teacher (teaching). With this principle in mind, a number of suggestions have been made to describe learning; for instance:

- The process of making sense of information and creating something new from it.
- A process that transforms our current understanding into fresh and more elucidated understanding.
- The process of utilising the knowledge and insights that we have gained from our previous experiences to respond effectively to new ones.
- The process of taking risks and moving away from the security of certain knowledge and exploring less well-considered areas.

None of these definitions offers a complete picture of learning but they share a common thread in emphasising the transformation that takes place in the learner. The teacher's role in the process is to provide the resources, guidance and wisdom that facilitate the learning, which recognises that learning does not consist merely of the linear transfer of an adult's superior intellect to a less knowledgeable pupil but rather children's accommodation of fresh understanding into their existing knowledge. As such, the teacher must be aware of the child's present understanding, not in order to 'tailor make' the teaching programme to fit the needs of all the children (as this would require thirty different approaches and curricula) but to graze contentedly across the pastures of knowledge. The grazing metaphor promotes the idea of 'sampling' from the variety of food available as opposed to being force-fed. The concept of a learning objective, popularised in recent years, is more accurately a learning *intention*, as it is impossible to predict precisely what sort of learning will take place. The fanciful notion that pupils only learn what the teacher intends them to learn is wide of the mark.

Activate your thinking!

Think of a time when each of the four types of learning definitions indicated in the bullet points above has taken place in your *own* experience.

Functional and pervasive learning

Although it is natural to emphasise the importance of making sure that children have 'learned' something after exposure to a planned educational experience, the term has a variety of different meanings, depending upon the context in which it is used. For instance:

- Learned for now but likely to be forgotten very soon
- Learned, never to be forgotten
- Learned within defined limits
- Learned but requiring updating and reinforcement to be secure
- Learned and understood so thoroughly that the learning can be used successfully in different situations.

Thus it is possible for children to learn how to use a piece of computer software early in the school year, but without regular practice they are likely to forget the procedure by the next term. In this case, the learning has been functional and the fourth of the statements given above is relevant. A child may 'learn' how to multiply two numbers by using a certain technique but flounder when given the same problem in a different form. In this case, the third of the statements is relevant. The ideal is for children to have such a grasp of knowledge, skills and understanding that they can use their existing abilities to forge ahead confidently into new areas of learning (the final option in the above list). Furthermore, if learning is only *functional*, it relates solely to the work in hand and has little value outside the immediate context in which it is being used; if it is *pervasive*, it moves outside the boundaries artificially imposed by the task or activity, and has wider applicability.

Learning, then, may be of the restricted type (merely functional) or the transferable type (usable in different contexts). Take, for instance, the earlier example in which children learn to use a software program. Some children will doubtless become adept at using the program and may even be used by the teacher to tutor other children. However, only a proportion of the same group of well-informed children will make connections with the implications for using other, similar programs. The first group, knowing only how to operate the program, will possess a restricted form of knowledge. The second, who can use their knowledge, skills and understanding in less familiar contexts, are of the transferable type. Again, children who learn a set of spellings for a test may get them all correct, yet misspell some of the words in free writing. The aim is, of course, to ensure that children not only master the word list but can also utilise their learning in a variety of active writing situations where spelling is only one of the required skills. To say that something is 'learned' always requires qualifying.

Learning and memory

Some learning is short term; other forms need to become embedded and for all practical purposes permanently etched in the memory (long-term memory). The child who learns lines for a drama sketch in front of the school will memorise them carefully, prompted no doubt by an anxious parent who is keen for the child to do well. This learning may require repetition, frequent reminders and a move from artificial to more natural speech as the words become familiar. A few months after the performance, the words may be largely forgotten, though odd phrases may spring to mind for a while. Contrast this temporary memorising with the ability to interpret words on a page for the purpose of reading, in which the regular use of the words in a variety of contexts (books, worksheets, text on a whiteboard, screen) will ensure that they are never forgotten and can be produced at any time.

A common way in which teachers are alerted to a pupil's weak memory is when the child's written work is characterised by poor sequencing, missing words and inadequate grammar, despite the fact that the child might be capable of articulating his or her ideas. If pupils have problems in absorbing verbal information or are poor listeners they probably need to have directions explained and visually reinforced (e.g. using a diagram). If children have poor visual recall they may forget what they have read or been shown and need to have their learning supported through careful explanation and kinaesthetic/tactile ('hands-on') experiences.

Activate your thinking!

Every teacher is keen for his or her pupils to learn in such a way that they can use their abilities widely and thereby achieve intellectual freedom (or 'conceptual autonomy'), which allows children to free themselves from over-reliance on the teacher. Children will always need teachers, but learning should be an adventure in roaming through the woodlands, not plodding along a narrow path.

Good practice

There are a number of strategies that you can use to build memory in your pupils. For instance:

1. *To offer children opportunities for regular practice.* Typically, by learning sets of numbers or lists of spellings through oral (spoken) means. Such an approach can be made more enthralling by varying the speed of delivery; asking boys and girls to alternate in saying words/giving answers; whispering responses; listing items in reverse order, and so forth.

2. *To utilise spare moments to remind the children about key facts or principles.* A simple activity such as a short quiz or inviting a 'true or false' to an assertion or fact will engage children's interest and reinforce knowledge.

3. *To read well-loved books as a memory tool for pupils.* In particular, being reading aloud to exposes them to language that will be of long-term benefit in resolving problems, discussing decisions and understanding instructions. When younger children ask an adult to read a book again, the repetition assists memory of the story, sequencing of events and the satisfaction that they receive from grasping the plot.

4. *To activate children's memories by stimulating their imaginations.* This creative approach might involve asking them to summarise what has happened so far or retelling the whole story by moving from child to child, each one making a small verbal or mimed contribution. It is also useful to extend the process by asking for suggestions about what happens next.

Enhancing children's learning

Most learning is gained or enhanced by 'experiencing' for which no amount of direct teaching will substitute. For example, pupils' understanding of industrial change is brought to life through a visit to a working museum. Similarly, listening to poets and authors read from their own work, enjoying practical drama, playing with construction materials, touching unusual objects and buying vegetables from a market stall, all help children to understand the world better. Children's learning is also improved through 'investigations' in which the outcome is uncertain. Thus, science experiments, paint mixing, library searches and computer simulations all involve investigations that assist conceptual understanding, skills acquisition and factual knowledge.

Enhanced learning also depends upon the opportunity for children to ask questions and raise issues in the expectation that teachers will respond positively (Wragg and Brown 1993; Morgan and Saxton 1994; D. Hayes 2006). Most children are extremely curious and will, if their interest is aroused, ply adults with queries about how and why. Teachers sometimes need to understand the reason for a child asking a question. An apparently innocent question from a 5-year-old about 'Where did I come from?' may be the first sign of a wish to understand the wonders of human reproduction but is far more likely to relate to the fact that her friend said that she came from Birmingham. Interpreting children's questions is time-consuming but essential if teachers are to help them in finding answers to things that are of real interest to them. Whatever the age of pupils, teachers need to capture their curiosity, encourage an inquisitive attitude, engage with issues that concern young minds and provide enough stimuli to arouse fresh interest.

Deep learning

Most of us will have experienced occasions when we thought that we had mastered a particular skill or absorbed a portion of information, only to find that our grasp of the issue or knowledge was less secure than we had imagined. In particular, on being asked a searching question by someone, having to explain the facts or justify a value position can expose the fact that our understanding of the topic is superficial. *Surface learning* of this kind is often associated with: (1) memorising unrelated fragments of knowledge; (2) an inability to separate principles from specific examples; and (3) completing a task 'instinctively' without fully engaging our minds. In the case of pupils, surface learners often operate defensively through trying to discover and provide what they think will satisfy the teacher – motivated primarily by a fear of failure – rather than being decisive and self-confident.

By contrast, *deep learning* is more likely to happen when the learner makes a conscious effort to do four things. First, to relate previous knowledge to new knowledge and theoretical ideas to everyday experience. Second, to use evidence as the starting point for discussion and decisions. Third, to organise what is already known and new knowledge into a manageable form. Finally, to find a solution by using multiple perspectives, rather than doggedly locking into a single one. Deep learning is closely allied with *deep thinking*, which requires (1) determination to reach a satisfactory outcome; (2) guidance from knowledgeable others; and (3) a willingness to consider a variety of alternatives. Most deep thinkers are careful listeners and good at analysing information. They weigh up evidence, use their imaginations and tend to 'think aloud' (i.e. verbalise their ideas) rather than jump to conclusions. It's an ambitious but worthwhile aim for every teacher and pupil.

All children need to be given the opportunity to transfer what they have learned to new situations, as this is often the acid test for whether or not deep learning has been achieved. Even if all the group or class appear to have grasped the principles and ideas contained within a particular learning objective, some children will retain what they have learned, while others will require regular reminding and refreshing. However, the more that children see the relevance of their learning, the more likely it is that they will engage enthusiastically with the lesson content and retain what they have learned as they apply it to situations.

To help promote deep learning, you must have high quality engagement with learners by taking seriously and exploring points that are raised by the child. The children's understanding and knowledge can be reinforced and developed by asking searching questions, locating the learning in a variety of contexts and analysing points of view constructively, without in any way causing embarrassment to the individual. Naturally, the learning climate must be secure and pupils must feel comfortable in 'taking risks' with what they say, suggest and question.

Good practice

To facilitate deep learning, encourage independence of thought and action, promote a questioning attitude, allow pupils to explore ideas and investigate themes. In addition, where possible, give children the chance to select from a range of alternatives; allow them to justify and make their own decisions; ask them searching questions rather than simplistic ones; and provide materials for play and exploration. Such an adventurous approach to teaching is preferable to that of piling on task after task in a vain hope that some knowledge and understanding will, by dint of repetition, somehow lodge in their minds.

Discovery learning

Discovery learning is an open-ended form of problem solving in which the teacher provides an introductory activity or stimulus on a relevant theme or topic to gain the children's interest, stir their natural curiosity and raise the level of enthusiasm and motivation. Children are then permitted considerable latitude to decide how they will proceed and shape the enquiry. When they have found out as much as they can in the allocated time, the children determine how they will present their findings – orally, formally written or presented diagrammatically.

With younger children, feedback about their discoveries is normally given verbally or presented in the form of a drawing.

Discovery learning is closely related to work by the French psychologist, Jean Piaget and 'constructivist' theory, in which learners draw on their existing knowledge and past experiences to discover facts and relationships and insights. Robson (2006) refers to Penn (2005) and notes that by the 1950s Piaget's ideas had become world-known, especially in the field of early childhood education 'where they were seen as legitimising the idea of learning through "natural" or "free" play [i.e. free from direct adult influence], very much part of the nursery school tradition' (p. 13). In primary schools, discovery learning is normally carried out in pairs or small groups and a report of findings is then made to the rest of the class. Resources are provided by the teacher in advance or created by the children as they proceed with their investigations. The use of information technology (notably through computers) is particularly helpful where the discovery is factual, rather than practical knowledge from hands-on application using materials (kinaesthetic learning).

It has become more difficult to employ discovery methods in recent years with the onset of timetabling, increases in curriculum content with its accompanying time pressures, and formal assessments that are inextricably linked to specified programme content. Supporters argue that discovery learning has many advantages, such as encouraging active pupil engagement; promoting autonomy motivation, responsibility and independence; developing creativity and problem-solving skills and offering an individualised learning experience (see Newton 2012). Critics, on the other hand, have cited possible disadvantages, such as the creation of cognitive overload (i.e. too much to think about at one time); the possibility of pupils developing misconceptions ('wrong ideas') without sufficiently rigorous intervention; and teachers failing to detect and correct mistakes (based on the Learning Theories Knowledgebase website). Either way, there seems to be a consensus among primary educators that discovery learning is most effective when it is guided by a knowledgeable adult and used in conjunction with the more familiar direct instruction method (i.e. teacher-led).

Thematic teaching

Thematic teaching is a method of organising learning around themes or topics, thereby making it possible to integrate knowledge across core areas such as reading, writing, mathematics, history, science and the arts. Because thematic teaching integrates different subject areas, it facilitates long-term memory retaining concepts that apply across the curriculum, rather than specific subject-related facts – for example, concepts such hierarchies, community, cause and effect.

Thematic units are designed to encourage children to delve more thoroughly into topics to develop their awareness and understanding of connections between areas of learning. Thematic instruction integrates basic subjects like reading, mathematics and science with the exploration of a broad subject, such as life cycles, rain forests, the circus, the use of energy, and so on. It is commonly the case that one subject dominates a theme more than others; for instance, a theme based on 'the local community' is likely to emphasise history, map work (geography) and citizenship, whereas the theme of 'minibeasts' is largely science-based.

Thematic teaching is used less commonly in schools today, owing to three factors. First, a focus on core subjects and the crowded curriculum have reduced the time available for pupils to explore and investigate a theme through enquiry methods and following individual pathways that interest them, rather than pre-specified ones. Second, an emphasis on measurable outcomes sits uneasily alongside a form of teaching that offers pupils choice in selecting where they focus their energies; teachers are reluctant to allow children too much flexibility about pursuing their interests if, in doing so, it might adversely affect formal assessment results. Third, thematic work has been tainted by poor practice and superficial learning that sometimes took place under its forerunner, 'project work'.

Creativity and imagination

Defining creativity

'Creativity' is not an easy term to define but basically means the act of bringing something into being, which involves germinating, growing, nurturing, producing and cultivating ideas. Creativity also encompasses dynamic terms such as 'constructing', 'experimenting' and 'devising', together with spiritual terms such as 'inspiration', 'spontaneity' and 'revelation'. Robinson (2001) claims that everyone has the potential to be creative because creativity is possible in any activity in which human intelligence is actively engaged. It releases pupils from the rigid constraints of a formalised scheme of work to explore and investigate ideas by active participation in genuine events and enterprises that interest them.

It is important to be mindful of ways to help pupils to be creative in their work. That is, to encourage diverse thinking, risk-taking and innovative practice (see, for instance, Jeffrey and Woods 2003; Starbuck 2006; Best and Thomas 2007). Fisher (2004) suggests that there are four keys to creativity: motivation, inspiration, gestation and collaboration. *Motivation* relies on feeling that an endeavour is worthwhile. *Inspiration* relies on curiosity and getting involved in finding solutions. *Gestation* allows time for ideas to emerge and to think things through consciously and subconsciously. *Collaboration* involves finding and nurturing partnerships with likeminded people to help them fulfil their potential. Creativity seems to lend itself more naturally to subjects that are not desk-bound owing to the problem-solving and practical activity that characterises work in these areas. Thus, children express their feelings in drama, experiment with models in technology, work out solutions in PE and pour out their inner consciousness through painting.

Creativity in the classroom

The best primary education is rooted in maintaining a balance between mastery of essential skills and promoting activities that allow children to explore and interrogate the unknown or things that are barely understood. However, creativity does not emerge by simply giving children time and space to 'create something', but by generating enthusiasm and offering appropriate adult support within a culture of self-expression where new ideas are actively sought and encouraged. Merely being given opportunity to experiment with ideas without possessing basic skills and devoid of adult intervention has the potential to lead to chaos: too little adult guidance can result in aimlessness; too little opportunity to experiment will almost certainly lead to pupil frustration. However, too much intervention can reduce self-sufficiency, while too much freedom may give children the impression that learning is a random process.

There is a need not only for teaching creatively and teaching for creativity but also for creative learning (Craft and Jeffrey 2008). That is, that children are liberated to engage with learning in such a way that it allows for their proclivities and instincts. It is important that teachers are mindful of ways to help pupils to be creative in their work by encouraging diverse thinking, risk-taking and innovative practice.

Primary children of all ages are stimulated by hearing stories purely for pleasure, without then having to complete a worksheet or a piece of writing. They prosper when they meet poets and authors instead of just seeing photocopied extracts of their work and hearing about them. Theatre attendance, visits to art galleries, museums, exhibitions and concerts all help to stir pupils' enthusiasm, promote purposeful conversation, excite their emotions and extend their horizons. Primary-aged children develop a sense of wonder by spending regular time outdoors to appreciate seasonal change, by tending a garden and by collaborating on projects (Jeffrey and Woods 2009).

Cross-reference: Guided Reader Extracts 9 and 10

Imagination

Stimulating children's imaginations through stories, songs, visual resources and other means taps a rich source of learning in primary-age children and, for younger children, creates a world of fantasy within which they can gradually come to terms with the realities of the world as it exists. Many teachers see stimulating pupils' imaginations as a prerequisite to making an activity of educational value. The root of the word 'imagination' is, of course, 'imagine', which can be thought of as a mental picture or 'seeing in the mind's eye', so that imagination provides pupils with a vehicle to visualise new possibilities.

Authentic imagination, which is said to prompt positive action, is different from *hopeful* imagination that is characterised by a passivity that leaves the active work to others. It is not a means of avoiding problems by fantasising but rather a strategy to *confront* issues and address them innovatively. When applied to real problems, imagination can empower and motivate pupils to act decisively and achieve the desired goal, in spite of setbacks and disappointments. It also has the capacity to assist children in solving problems by helping them perceive and anticipate a variety of potential outcomes to situations, and to cope better with new or challenging circumstances through role play. As children listen to real or made-up stories, their imaginations incorporate a richer vocabulary, which in turn assists them in discussing problems with others and finding solutions to them.

Stories have the potential to create memorable and comprehensible structures with devices such as cause and effect to help the child listener understand a plot, engage with the issues or be drawn into the awe and wonder of how seemingly impossible situations can be resolved. Children usually have firm views about the kinds of stories they like and dislike (Hislam and Lall 2007). They talk with their friends about their favourite characters; they laugh freely at amusing tales; they sit spellbound during tense moments. Although pupils love to see the pictures in a book and will often ask the teacher to show them, some children react more positively to stories being told orally than being read from a book and are capable of repeating the story to friends and people at home with a surprising degree of accuracy. Storytelling assists with transmitting world cultures as children hear about how others live; reinforcing learning experiences as they understand the implications of people's actions and decisions; helping the emerging ego as they grasp the fact that the world does not revolve solely around them; and enjoyment of oral literature for its own sake.

Activate your thinking!

Stories not only fire pupils' imaginations but also offer them models for living, alert them to the danger of foolish decisions and might even inspire them to take action; for example, a story about the plight of deprived children can lead to fund-raising initiatives.

Good practice

For a guide to using creative storytelling in the primary school classroom, including practical ideas, games and oral opportunities, see Parkinson (2010).

Parkinson, R. (2010) *Storytelling and Imagination*, London: David Fulton.

Ownership of learning

Children need to be given some ownership of their learning. That is, they have to feel that the things they learn have relevance, and to find them personally satisfying. After all, it is they who have to use it in their present and future lives. Learning is not, therefore, principally about accumulating sufficient information, knowledge and understanding to gain high scores in national tests and examinations; rather, it is about empowering pupils to live their lives more productively and successfully. Examination success is likely to assist this process of self-fulfilment but there is a danger that anxious teachers may see scores gained during a test as the sole yardstick of achievement. Williams and Ryan (2000) argue that teachers should view the tests as an opportunity to gain information that will help to improve their teaching and raise standards, but a wide range of other eminent educationists disagree. For instance, Kohn (2004) argues from a US context that twenty-first-century children are tested to an unprecedented extent, yet standardised test scores often measure superficial thinking. Ransom (1993) contends that curriculum entitlement and rational planning are inadequate unless pupils are adequately motivated within a community context. He argued that teachers need to develop an 'empowerment curriculum', incorporating the following elements:

- Citizenship in learning
- Active learning through practical reasoning
- Democratic and public organisation
- Partnership.

C. Smith (2006) argues that all pupils, including those with a special need, should be involved in decision-making at two levels. First, and principally, by contributing to decisions about the effectiveness of their own provision. Second, pupils 'can also participate in decision-making at a wider level and thus influence school policy' (p. 146). Although the establishment of pupil 'school councils' and 'focus groups' is an important element of the process, it is more common for children to initially say something to a parent, which is fed back into school via a variety of formal and informal routes. Nevertheless, the principle of the 'pupil voice' is now well established in schools and is a feature that is noted during formal inspections.

Enhancing pupil learning

Pupils' learning can be enhanced in four key ways: (1) valuing pupils' capability; (2) offering an inclusive curriculum; (3) promoting active learning; (4) creating partnerships with parents and the community. Thus:

Valuing pupils' capability

By celebrating the untapped reservoirs of capability in individuals in order to create active rather than passive learners, pupils are endowed with skills to make responsible choices and co-operate with others. Educators often make the point that 'ability' – a fixed quality – should be distinguished from 'capability' – an aptitude that can be developed but is not yet fully formed. Thus, whereas the term 'ability' tends to be used to describe whether an individual has 'got it' or 'not got it' (rather like IQ), *capability* implies that the individual child's present knowledge, skills and understanding can be enhanced by perseverance, good teaching, a wide range of learning opportunities, adult guidance and lots of encouragement. It is also worth remembering that children that struggle in formal curriculum subjects might be 'intelligent' in other ways, such as personal and social skills, sports and drama. See Chapter 8 for information about multiple intelligences.

Offering an inclusive curriculum

Children with learning difficulties and disabilities, and those for whom English is an additional language, are also entitled to quality curriculum provision. Teachers must have due regard for inclusion principles that incorporate setting suitable learning targets and respond positively to diverse needs for all pupils, both individuals and groups, so that they can experience success. Florian *et al.* (2007) argue that high levels of inclusion can be entirely compatible with high levels of achievement and that combining the two is not only possible but also essential if all children are to have the opportunity to participate fully in education. By providing a broad, balanced and, as far as possible, relevant curriculum, all pupils are able to draw upon their experience of living within the community to inform their learning.

Promoting active learning

Learning can be enhanced by involving pupils, engaging their interest, sustaining their motivation to succeed, and encouraging them to take responsibility for their own learning experiences and that of others. Moyles (2007) provides an eight-point approach to promote active learning in (especially) younger children, as follows: (1) an *entering* strategy, consisting of starting points and introduction; (2) an *exploration* mode, where pupils engage with the task supported by adequate resources and directed by adults; (3) consideration of *content* in respect of the subject, processes and skills that the children are intended to learn; (4) clarification about *ownership and responsibility*, especially the presence or absence of adult supervision; (5) *adult intervention*, interaction and level of support for children; (6) *evaluation* and analysis of children's learning; (7) opportunities for *children to reflect* on their learning; (8) *justification* for the work completed and its outcomes.

Creating partnership with parents and the community

By promoting education within the community, notably by involving parents and relatives, children benefit from the wealth of their expertise and knowledge. This aspect of education, once seen as relevant for younger pupils only, has assumed much greater significance for children of all ages, notably supporting reading and homework. See Chapter 5 and Whalley (2007) for fuller details of parental involvement.

Limitations of objectives-led learning

Lessons have to be properly organised, of course, and in the pressure of school life there is a limited amount of time that can be spent exploring and interrogating a given area of work without establishing a clearly defined outcome. Teachers also have to be specific about the things they hope that children will learn (indicated through the learning objectives) and provide a facilitating structure through careful explanations, availability of resources, appropriate tasks and adult support to make it more likely that they will do so. However, learning encompasses more than children satisfying the designated objective, however well designed it may be. Just as children can convince themselves that they must have learned something if they get the right answer by an approved method, so teachers can slip into the same way of thinking and believe that task completion is the primary goal. In fact, finishing a task may or may not involve deep learning. Too many so-called experiential lessons, for instance, consist of little more than mechanically 'predicting' and 'testing' and 'recording' without properly engaging with the principles underpinning the work or employing problem-solving skills. Completing pages of sums might or might not demonstrate that the underlying principles have been mastered.

Praxis and emancipated learning

The word 'praxis' is sometimes used to describe action that is informed by reflection, with the aim to free those involved into more productive forms of learning. Some educators (notably Jurgen Habermas) argue that the teacher's role involves emancipating pupils through the curriculum and developing a liberated and fair world. The curriculum then becomes as much about 'uncovering' fresh truth and insight as it is about 'covering' predetermined content. With regard to classroom teaching, Morrison (2001) refers to the eight principles of pedagogy (the principles and practice of teaching) that Habermas and others propose:

1. The need for co-operation and collaborative work
2. The need for discussion-based work
3. The need for autonomous, experiential and flexible learning
4. The need for negotiated learning
5. The need for community-related learning to explore a range of environments
6. The need for problem-solving activities
7. The need to increase [pupils'] rights to employ talk
8. The need for teachers to act as 'transformative intellectuals'.

This critical form of pedagogy is built upon a belief that 'educators must work with, and on, the lived experiences that [pupils] bring to the pedagogical encounter rather than imposing a curriculum that reproduces social inequality' (Morrison 2001: 219). Setting aside the social equality issues that these educators argue can be addressed in part through the curriculum, the eight principles outlined above provide a useful basis on which to develop a positive teaching and learning environment. Thus, with reference to the eight points noted above:

1. *Pupil collaboration* facilitates a 'fusion' of minds as children grapple with problems and combine their intellects.
2. *Discussions* allow issues and contradictions to surface and demonstrate that nearly every situation has a multiplicity of perspectives.
3. *Experiential learning* allows children to touch, sample, feel, manipulate and handle substances, equipment and circumstances directly.
4. *Negotiated learning* encourages children to advance their own ideas, priorities and suggestions about what is important.
5. *Community-related learning* promotes the value of involvement in the local environment and draws on the expertise of those who live there.
6. *Problem solving* helps children to see that the skills and knowledge they acquire in school have a practical outworking.
7. *Children's rights* to venture their own opinions and ideas encourage self-confidence and a willingness to be innovative, when coupled with an appropriate sense of responsibility.
8. *Change-agent teachers* approach their work with children with a greater sense of purpose than those who rely on systematically structured teaching and learning with predictable outcomes.

Learning and classroom practice

It is one thing to have beliefs and ideals about children's engagement with learning; it is quite another to implement strategies that facilitate them. The implications for classroom practice can be summarised as follows:

1. Pupils need the opportunity to discuss what they are doing and understand where it fits into their existing knowledge. The teacher needs to spend time explaining the context and the links with previous learning. The use of familiar examples and experiences will help children to grasp the concepts more easily.

> ### Good practice
> When discussing the lesson with the children, use phrases such as 'You remember that last time...' and 'It is the same as when you...' (linking with familiar experiences).

2. Pupils will often complete tasks and engage in activities solely because they are set before them by a teacher. Meta-learning encourages children to talk about what they are doing and express how they feel about learning, both verbally and through different media (such as drawings, diagrams and scattergrams).

> ### Good practice
>
> Spend small amounts of time regularly talking to the children about ways in which they can approach their work, probing alternatives and encouraging them to speculate about the challenges and opportunities. These conversations should be underpinned by a positive 'can do' attitude and an acknowledgement that trying different approaches and searching for creative solutions sometimes results in temporary failure/setbacks. Warmly commend pupils who 'have a go'.

3. Pupils should be encouraged to satisfy their own aspirations rather than those of the teacher and be self-motivating rather than relying only the teacher for inspiration.

> ### Good practice
>
> Make a habit of asking children what particularly pleases them about the work that they are undertaking. Encourage them to think about their achievements and share their excitement with others. Use phrases such as, 'You must feel pleased with what you've done.'

4. Some pupils worry about getting things wrong and being in trouble as a result. Other pupils are unwilling to persevere when faced with challenges or try to avoid making more than a nominal effort to achieve a satisfactory outcome. As these negative responses are often the result of emotional insecurity, teachers' reactions need to focus on finding solutions to the root cause rather than merely treating the symptoms. In other words, it is important to make a priority of strengthening children's emotional security while being alert to the sobering fact that some pupils simply cannot be bothered to make the necessary effort.

> ### Good practice
>
> Make it clear that children can use an adult or another child as a source of advice, confirmation or guidance, but that as far as possible they should persevere with work and not be afraid of making genuine errors. At the same time, use mistakes positively by expressing an interest in how the child has gone about the work, explaining the alternatives and using the opportunity formatively to assist understanding. Where significant mistakes are evident, try to determine whether they are due to misunderstanding of the requirements or a lack of skills to address the task or basic misconceptions.

5. Teachers should put themselves in the child's place. Is the classroom environment stimulating or depressing? How does the attitude of adults (teacher, assistants) serve to

motivate or discourage? How do patterns of social interaction, such as friendship patterns, grouping of children and peer support, impinge upon children's appetite to engage with tasks?

Good practice

Observe a child unobtrusively throughout a full day and try to evaluate his or her experience with regard to classroom environment, adult attitudes and social interaction. What does it 'feel' like to be that child? How does s/he perceive the learning experience? Pay particular attention to times when the child glances nervously towards a classmate to gain reassurance or to copy; pairing children to work co-operatively can often mitigate the concerns of less confident children.

It is preferable for children to have an 'adventurous' attitude to learning, where they are eager to try things out, experiment and find solutions to problems, than adopt a 'play safe' approach. Challenges are then viewed as opportunities to use their ingenuity and determination to break through the uncertainty rather than as obstacles to hinder achievement. Children with an adventurous spirit towards learning are not fazed by setbacks. They are persistent and willing to approach the problem from a variety of positions. They are reluctant to take 'no' for an answer and will seek ways to improve their abilities.

Good practice

Think–pair–share is an approach that introduces a 'wait and think' time into co-operative learning. The process begins when you pose a problem or ask pupils an open-ended question. The children are given opportunity to think independently (i.e. without conferring) about the issues involved before turning to face their partners, after which they share ideas, discuss, clarify and challenge each other's thinking. After an appropriate amount of time, each pair joins with another pair to exchange and interrogate their views and conclusions. After a given time, each of the combined pairs feed back to the rest of the class, synthesising points of agreement and disagreement.

Case study

Ten-year-old Alistair was a capable boy who simply did not like doing schoolwork. He would always find some reason to avoid settling down in class and making a proper effort to complete the task or activity. Worse still, his lacklustre approach to life, tendency to annoy adults and somewhat aloof manner did not endear him to other pupils, who were for the most part diligent and sensible. In short, Alistair was the odd one out in the group and a classic underachiever. Reminders and threats of sanctions if he failed to apply himself to the work mereiy elicited a sigh of resignation from him and a short-lived effort to conform, after which he gradually reverted to his 'normal' apathetic state.

Alistair's parents were at a loss to know what could be done to motivate him and, as he was making some progress in his learning (howbeit slowly) and wasn't so badly behaved that it was appropriate to instigate special measures, he did not qualify to receive formally targeted intervention. He therefore drifted along and continued to irritate the normally upbeat teacher, Mrs Goodring, who found him frustrating and disagreeable. Mrs Goodring tried all the usual strategies, such as engaging Alistair in his learning, setting short-term targets, offering incentives, and so forth, but to no avail. Alistair continued in much the same way as he had always done, other than becoming slightly more mischievous when receiving close adult attention. Then something remarkable happened to transform the whole situation.

As part of a project based on the local environment, Mrs Goodring spent time with her class examining the variety of flora and fauna in the extensive school grounds, which included a copse, games field and uncultivated area. At some point during this experience, Alistair's interest was aroused by the range of birdlife he observed in and around the grounds. Something must have triggered a positive response, for he began to take a keen interest in ornithology. Within a short time, Alistair was asking his teacher to accompany him around the school grounds, so that he could point out the different species of birds. He also asked permission to draw them, tabulate sightings, make notes about their behaviour and investigate through the Internet, all of which he did with great fervour. Mrs Goodring was initially sceptical but came to realise that not only had Alistair acquired a thirst for learning but his behaviour and attitude to school was also improving. The resentful indifference was being replaced by an eagerness to learn that took Mrs Goodring aback. The more she allowed him flexibility to pursue his passion for birds, the better he responded to aspects of the curriculum that he had formerly resisted.

It wasn't all plain sailing. Mrs Goodring still found him to be rather irritating and inwardly wished that he had never been in her class! On the other hand, the transformation in Alistair's attitude to learning also affected his relationships with his classmates and teachers, which gave rise to a genuine hope that the future was now a lot brighter for him. Mrs Goodring's deepest concern was that the rigid curriculum and formalities of secondary schooling might extinguish the flame of enthusiasm that had burned so brightly during the final months of Alistair's time in her class.

Further reading for Chapter 7

Alloway, T.P. and Gathercole, S.E. (2007) *Memory and Learning*, London: Sage.
Provides a coherent overview of the role played by working memory in learning during the school years.
Isaacs, B. (2011) *Understanding the Montessori Approach*, London: David Fulton.
The book provides information and key principles about the approach with regard to early childhood.
Pound, L. and Hughes, C. (2005) *How Children Learn: From Montessori to Vygotsky – educational theories and approaches made easy*, London: Step Forward Publishing.
Summarises the ideas of Montessori, Piaget, Dewey and Donaldson and examines theories relating to early years education, including Steiner, the Italian pre-school of Reggio Emilia and the New Zealand curriculum.
Pritchard, A. (2008) *Ways of Learning: Learning theories and learning styles in the classroom*, London: David Fulton.
Seeks to provide the detail that teachers can utilise in their planning and teaching in order to provide even better opportunities for effective and lasting learning.
Wilson, A. (ed.) (2009) *Creativity in Primary Education*, second edn, Exeter: Learning Matters.
The book explores creativity in a subject-specific context, together with the broader issues of creativity in spiritual, moral, social and cultural education (SMSC), and in the Foundation Stage.

8

The Learning Context

Introduction

Learning does not follow a pre-determined pattern; it relies on a variety of factors, including intellectual capacity, motivation, determination, quality of teaching, experience in learning, relevance of the subject matter. The circumstances in which people find themselves have a major effect on the quality of learning; for instance, someone anxious about missing a train won't be able to concentrate on the closing minutes of the lecture as well as someone who lives around the corner and has time to spare. The personality of the teacher, the importance of the occasion, the physical conditions of the room, availability of resources, and the extent to which a child feels at ease in the surroundings, all affect the learning experience. This chapter contains information and suggestions about ways in which the learning climate can be enhanced in such a way that pupils can make confident progress in their work.

Situational learning

It is clear to anyone who works in school that learning is powerfully influenced by three main factors: situation, motivation and emotion. If it were not so, we could dispense with schools and teachers and send 'electronic teaching machines' to do the job. Every learning experience is 'situational' and affected by the physical and social context. Thus, within the physical environment, the numerous interactions that take place daily between children and adults, and between different children, impact upon the quality of learning because: (1) we learn from one another; (2) energy is generated through human interaction; and (3) mutual endeavour leads to a sense of teamwork and raises aspirations (increasingly through a mood of competitiveness, as children move through primary school).

The nature of these interactions depends on the power relationships and authority structures that exist in a classroom. If pupils feel relaxed and confident when seeking adult help, they can channel their energies into the task rather than worrying about doing or saying the acceptable thing and avoiding adult wrath. Similarly, if there is an ease of relationship and spirit of tolerance among the children, they can concentrate on their work and not on worrying about friendship patterns or being marginalised. It is the teacher's responsibility to establish a facilitative and co-operative climate such that learning can proceed unhindered by social conflict or emotional insecurity.

There is also the broader social context to consider, not least the fact that technological and social changes have influenced the skills needed for daily living, people's priorities and their expectations. As Turner-Bisset (2003) argues, classrooms must move with the times and consider the teaching and learning needs of primary education in this century rather than those that existed in the last. On the other hand, there are certain teaching and learning needs that remain unchanged across the generations: the need for security, affirmation and respect, set within a framework of fundamental skill acquisition (such as reading and communicating effectively) and mutually beneficial moral boundaries.

Teachers' attitudes to the work also affect learning. The depth of a teacher's motivation and expectations about pupil achievement make a profound difference to the way in which children approach the work. A teacher who is enthusiastic about the tasks that the children are engaged with, clarifies what is expected from them and gives clear guidance about what can be achieved, will not be disappointed with the outcome. Children respond well to adults who display a positive attitude and belief about attainment and celebrate successes rather than highlighting minor errors.

Pupils' attitudes towards themselves also profoundly influence the quality of learning and the impact of this particular factor on the quality of learning and achievement is increasingly viewed as being of crucial importance. Although a degree of anticipatory tension can spur children to success, too much anxiety hinders progress. Investing in a learning climate that is 'relaxed but purposeful' is time and effort well spent. It is a common experience in classrooms that while some children adopt a very positive attitude despite their limitations, others are doubtful about their ability to cope despite their obvious competence and, perhaps, previous successes. By contrast to fearful anxiety, a pupil's enthusiasm pumps oxygen to the brain and stimulates its efficient operation.

Creating an invigorating learning climate

Katz and Chard (2000) remind us that from a child's point of view, school is real life, not contrived or pretend, so children need to make learning an adventure which, like the lives they like to lead in and out of school, is sometimes challenging, sometimes perplexing, sometimes thrilling, sometimes mundane, but always motivating. Although certain parts of the curriculum evoke greater fervour than others, teachers should strive to create a learning environment that offers diverse experiences, excites children's interest and, wherever possible, builds on their enthusiasm. The following four principles for creating such a learning climate apply to every age group and situation: (1) help children to feel that learning is worthwhile; (2) feed and exercise children's imaginations; (3) explain the reason for the lesson; (4) convince children that they can be successful. Thus:

Help children to feel that learning is worthwhile

Learning becomes worthwhile when four factors apply: (1) the content is interesting and relevant; (2) the lesson is presented imaginatively, see also below; (3) the tasks associated with the lesson present an attainable challenge; and (4) the learning climate is lively and encouraging. You have a vital role to play in achieving these goals. Thus:

- Even when the lesson content is mundane, you can explain its usefulness and link it with past learning.
- By the tone of your voice, the passion of your delivery and the incorporation of visual material, story, verbal exchanges and collaborative activity, you can inspire children and engage their minds.
- You can differentiate tasks in such a way that each child can succeed and feel pleased with her or his efforts, which in turn helps to enhance self-image and motivation.

- Your friendly but purposeful approach to teaching, emphasis on positive aspects of learning and patient explanations can transform the climate from one of stale conformity to energetic vibrancy.

In helping children to feel that learning is worthwhile, it is important not to dismiss underachievement by using tired excuses such as 'boys will be boys' or 'that sort of child never makes an effort' or 'well, you can't expect anything more' (see also Chapter 3). High expectations are fed by adult enthusiasm and a positive attitude. You won't convince every pupil that the work is beneficial; some children are resistant to such claims. Over time, however, a combination of your bright personality, optimistic approach and encouragement, plus interesting lesson content, will convince the vast majority of pupils to apply themselves wholeheartedly.

Feed and exercise children's imaginations

Stirring children's imaginations is important in learning and a key feature of creativity. The root of the word imagination is, as we have already noted, 'imagine', which can be thought of as a 'mental picture' or 'seeing in the mind's eye'. Although the methods by which stirring imagination can be achieved vary with age of child, there are a number of common stimuli that can be usefully employed:

- posing questions that cause the children to think deeply;
- offering real-life or fictitious scenarios to highlight key points or offer examples;
- using familiar objects in unfamiliar ways to offer differing perspectives on a subject;
- using unfamiliar objects as a source of awe and wonder;
- using powerful music, expressive poems or stimulating pictures to evoke an emotional response;
- giving children opportunity to share their own life experiences with others in the class.

Stirring children's imaginations may be an end in itself (for sheer joy) but is more often used as either a starting point or an accelerator in the learning process. As Napoleon Bonaparte is supposed to have commented: 'The human race is governed by its imagination.' Further advice about using imagination can be found under 'Creativity' in the previous chapter.

Explain the reason for the lesson

Children will sometimes ask a teacher or assistant, 'What are we doing this for?' Unease about the lesson or the relevance of a particular activity can result in older and bolder pupils asking the question directly, or it might be expressed through a superficial commitment to the task, yawning or other restless behaviour. Pupil misgivings of this kind can be minimised by explaining the purpose to the children beforehand and by being honest with children when they express their doubts. The process of explaining the purpose beforehand should be rooted in the learning intentions for the lesson but more pragmatic explanations are sometimes equally valuable. For example, you might tell the children that they need to spend time practising their sums because you want to move on to a different topic and cannot do so until the job is completed. You might tell them that you want them to finish writing the story because it is parents' evening soon and you want to show Mum what they have achieved. Being honest with children is not the same as being apologetic, though there are occasions when you will need to admit that although the content is not particularly interesting, it is a necessary prerequisite for subsequent, more exciting work. Your responses will vary according to circumstances but should be an explanation and not indicate that the child has a choice (unless, of course, this is the case). You may be faced with an option when dealing with a recalcitrant child about whether to insist or compromise, but dealing with stubborn children is an issue for Chapter 12 and will not be pursued here.

Convince children that they can be successful

The tone of the preceding parts of this chapter should have convinced you that whereas children need to develop self-motivation, such an attitude must be nurtured by teachers. Merely encouraging a child to do well will not, of itself, produce a sudden transformation from uncertainty to optimism. However, a positive approach, coupled with appropriate support and direction will allow a child to persevere in the certain knowledge that there is an adult 'safety net' underneath. Over time the buoyant and cheerful mood you exude will spread throughout the class and, coupled with appropriate external rewards (such as stickers and merit cards), will influence the children's expectations and strengthen their mood of determination. Your positive approach will not affect pupils in the same way and there will always be occasions when, with your very best efforts, a child simply refuses to take an upbeat view of his or her potential and prefers to remain sullenly defeatist. Occasionally, a pupil who is inwardly quite confident will pretend to be downcast because it invites the teacher's close attention, in which case you need to be patient but firm. Despite the complications and challenges, it is nevertheless true that a 'we can' approach to learning leads to an overall increase in self-esteem, work of higher quality and better levels of co-operation. But don't expect such a transformation to happen overnight.

Good practice

Read how one trainee teacher was able to enthuse all the children in the class. This sparkling description shows how an ordinary lesson can be transformed when children are liberated within a secure framework of adult support:

> We had worked hard listening to Vivaldi's *The Four Seasons*, thinking about what he was trying to say with his music and then, as the piece called 'Summer' built to a crescendo, the children were finding it hard to keep still. Toes were tapping, bottoms wriggling and heads moving. I encouraged them to take on the role of the conductor, using their hands and arms, but also moving with the music. We turned the music up really loud and got completely caught up in it. It was a wonderful sight to see them all enjoying the music so much. Hannah, a little girl with Down's Syndrome, had a huge grin on her face and was dancing around to the rhythm.

Promoting confidence in learning

We have already noted that pupils vary in the level of confidence they experience about the work they are asked to complete. Even the most assured children can have misgivings in particular areas of the curriculum; for example, it is common for a girl who is thriving in literacy to be anxious about mathematics. There are three sets of conditions that assist the promotion of pupil confidence in learning: first, to feel secure; second, to know the rules; third, to be clear about the lesson intentions. Thus:

Children need to feel secure

Security and confidence in the person of the teacher is particularly important when teachers are asking questions or inviting responses from the class. Timid children are unlikely to risk answering if by doing so they are met by the teacher's exasperation or their responses are treated with disdain. Teachers who treat all answers seriously (including incorrect ones) and encourage the children who give them by praising their efforts will soon have the class clamouring to participate. Similarly, if a new skill or concept has to be mastered, your patience and understanding can transform children's tentativeness into feverish enthusiasm. The maxim to 'have a go and enjoy the ride!' if promoted and practised within a safe environment, acts as a springboard for progress and success; and there will never be a dull moment!

Children need to know the rules

Teachers who spend time explaining and clarifying the details of an activity or the procedures for involvement at the start of the session will have to spend less time during the lesson in reminding children of the expected standards, repeatedly answering the same queries and rebuking those who are off-course. Boundaries for behaviour and action allow children to explore with confidence but establishing the boundaries does not mean, of course, that there isn't room for negotiation or that there will never be misunderstandings about what is allowable and what is proscribed. It is simply the fact that learning has more chance to be effective when everyone is clear about the basic rules of the game.

Children need to be clear about the lesson intentions

Some lessons are largely for the purpose of gaining knowledge through information offered directly by the teacher or from a technology source. Other lessons are more concerned with understanding processes; yet others demand skill mastery. Most lessons involve all three dimensions in different proportions. Children should be told about the lesson purpose prior to being informed about what they have to do, though the level of detail will vary, depending on the place of the lesson in the overall scheme of things. For instance, if the lesson is in the middle of a sequence of sessions on the same subject or area of learning, it is normally adequate to remind the children of what was explained to them before the start of the first lesson in the sequence and summarise key points. Again, if you want the session to contain an aura of mystery, such as in a science investigation, you might want to give rather fewer details about specific expectations. Some classrooms have a small whiteboard affixed to the wall on which the teacher writes the lesson purpose prior to commencement; other teachers print out the objective and ask children to affix it to their work, though this practice is unduly laborious and, frankly, scarcely worth the effort. That's a decision you will have to make.

Although sharing the lesson/session intention(s) is important, it is a mistake to place too much emphasis on intended outcomes if it acts to exclude less obvious ones. Pratt and Berry (2007) argue that sharing the learning objectives in too much detail can be counterproductive, as it reduces the joy of discovery. The extent to which you give pupils the learning intentions, and the amount of detail you provide, depends to a large degree on the lesson purpose: if it is dominated by information and factual knowledge that can easily be defined and assessed (such as memorising key events in history) then a fixed learning objective is more relevant than if the purpose is exploratory and involves play or problem solving, in which case the final outcome is likely to be more diverse. Teaching and learning cannot be neatly packaged into a linear process from introduction to conclusion. Nevertheless, the more that you are prepared to involve children in their learning and make its purpose and usefulness explicit, the more the learning climate is likely to be vibrant and motivating. See also the previous chapter for a discussion about objectives-led learning.

Reinforcing learning

It is essential for teachers to seize every opportunity to reinforce learning. For example, during question-and-answer sessions it is useful to repeat a good or thoughtful answer for the benefit of all the children, some of whom might not have heard the original response. In some cases, an answer can spark ideas and open possibilities that may not have occurred to the other children or even to you. At key moments during the task ('activity') phase a brief comment to the whole group or class about a specific learning point can focus the children's attention on improving their work in particular ways. For example, you might comment out loud how pleased you are that Kolby has set out his ideas so carefully and, perhaps, hold up the piece of work to show and explain to the rest of the class precisely what you mean. And of course the final few minutes of a lesson or session is normally a good time to summarise key points and emphasise their significance or provide further examples or extend pupils' thinking by asking a challenging question about 'where next?' or 'what if?' You can also promote learning by highlighting impressive aspects of children's work, commending the individual and disseminating the information. For example:

'Yes, Toby, well done. Did you hear what Toby said, everyone? He said that...'

'What a lovely idea, Georgia, I hadn't thought of counting them in that way. I think we could all have a go at...'

'Now that's a brilliant suggestion, Raj. I love the way you used the things we've been doing and added your own ideas. I hope that everyone heard when Raj explained how we could...'

'Alice, what a clever technique! Come and stand by me and show everyone else in the class what you did, please...'

In addition make positive comments about children's attitudes and willingness to persevere; for example:

'I'm pleased with the way you have kept trying, Mustafa. Well done!'

'Thank you for helping the others in your group, Sara; I'm very impressed.'

'You haven't quite finished, Alan, but you are a star for working so hard.'

The well-known expression, the 3 Rs, normally refers to the fundamental abilities of reading (R), writing (R) and arithmetic (R). However, there are other forms of 3R, not least the essential teaching skill expressed by the mantra: *Reinforce, Reinforce, Reinforce.* Good teachers recognise that deep, secure learning comes through the process of 'gradual assimilation' rather than 'single exposure'. Thus, teachers use a variety of means to reinforce learning, such as repetition, chanting, question-and-answer, discussion, written exercises, drama and quizzes. Reinforcing is not the same as doing the same thing repeatedly to 'hammer' the idea into a pupil's mind; it is helping children to develop a variety of perspectives on the same concept, problem or issue by use of different teaching and learning approaches, including verbal, visual, written and kinaesthetic ('handling').

Good practice

Use expressions that invite pupils to adopt a slightly different perspective on learning by commencing with expressions such as: 'In other words...' and 'Take a situation where...' and 'So that is the same as saying...' and 'If we look at it in another way...' and 'Imagine that...'

Retention in learning

Suffice it to say at this point that the teaching methods employed by teachers strongly influence the effectiveness with which children are able to learn. For instance, Koshy (2000) refers to the fact that different teaching approaches in mathematics have markedly different outcomes in terms of retention rate. Thus, whereas only about 5 per cent of the information presented in a formal lecture is retained, the figure increases with other strategies:

10 per cent retention when the same words are read
20 per cent retention when audio-visual aids are used
30 per cent retention for a demonstration
50 per cent retention for a discussion group
75 per cent retention for practising by doing
90 per cent retention when teaching others the immediate use of the learning.

Although retaining facts is only one dimension of learning and the above figures are only approximations, they suggest that direct transmission of information to children is unlikely to be effective if it is the sole means to present knowledge. The opportunity to read relevant text, listen to sounds or see images, watch an adult showing how something is done, discuss the lesson content with others, engage in practical activities and make use of peer tuition, can all enhance the quality of learning.

In addition, children learn best in different ways. Some children find it easy to understand written information, others prefer to hear it explained verbally, others like pictorial representations and yet others benefit from diagrams. Most children benefit from a combination of approaches, so it pays to bear this fact in mind when planning lessons. For instance, you may want to read an extract of text (with or without involving the children), explain the concepts/ issues/key points, provide visual aids and use the board to demonstrate stages of progression. Claims that children can be neatly divided into (for instance) 'visual learners' or 'tactile learners', and so forth is at best naïve and at worst positively harmful, because it can lead to an artificial and fragmented teaching style. See Chapter 9 for fuller details about visual, auditory and kinaesthetic learning styles (VAK).

It is also helpful to allow children some degree of choice when it comes to presenting their answers. While you should be cautious about giving too much latitude to a child who dislikes writing and wants to use pictures instead, a little flexibility on your part to encourage some of both types of recording is worth considering. While some boys (in particular) are averse to writing things down and need to be cajoled into doing so, the value of employing alternative means of recording is always worth considering.

Using homework to extend and reinforce learning

Teachers provide relevant forms of homework and other out-of-class tasks both to consolidate and extend the work that has been carried out during the school day, promoting independence in learning and, ideally, the active involvement of parents. In setting homework tasks, bear in mind that it has to be as appropriate to the age and ability of the pupil as the work in school is intended to be. Homework also has to be realistic and manageable as there is little point in having grandiose schemes that are impossible for the children to complete, even with adult support, or that require sophisticated equipment or expensive resources (Kidwell 2004). For instance, tasks should not assume that ICT equipment is available in the home. See also Chapter 4 for suggestions about parental involvement with homework.

The most straightforward type of homework is when a task is given to children such that (1) they are all able to engage with it at their own intellectual level, and (2) the end product can be marked easily. Suitable homework might include giving the children an observation activity (such as mapping the pattern formation on wallpaper and carpets); consulting with an adult about living history (such as life in the 1950s); or paper-and-pencil activities (such as learning key vocabulary or completing as many sums as possible in a given time). For younger children, additional reading is frequently used, with a parent signing in a 'reading record book' to confirm that it has been done.

Homework is most useful if it builds on previous school-based work or begins to open up new avenues of learning. Some homework consists of 'finishing off' incomplete work from the day; however, this penalises slower workers and does little to extend the more able. Other than familiar paper-and-pencil types, the best type of homework is of the 'project' kind, where children are given a number of activities that have to be completed over a period of time (a half-term, say). Homework can provide a starting point for discussion and sharing experiences, the very heart blood of learning, and a useful spur in promoting dialogue in learning ('dialogic learning'; see next chapter for further information on this topic and details of dialogic reading).

It is wise to remember that homework has to be monitored and assessed if it is to be truly useful, so the more elaborate you make it, the more time and effort has to be expended in dealing with the results. It might be appropriate use of a teaching assistant (TA) to check that homework has been completed and offer advice about difficulties.

Homework tasks need to be organised in such a way that children can cope unaided if necessary and, ideally, be directly linked to the learning objectives that you have established in class work. The tasks, therefore, provide consolidation and extension opportunities that would have been available in school had time permitted it. Formative feedback on homework tasks is not always possible, owing to time constraints and the many other demands upon a teacher. However, pupils can be inducted into sharing their work with a classmate, though this apparently simple procedure is more difficult than it sounds, as evaluation is demanding enough for adults, let alone for children. One way or another, comments must be made about the overall quality of homework tasks with indicators about improvements or implications.

Good practice

For one week's homework ask the children to prepare a three-minute talk about 'my favourite toy/hobby/day out'. Younger children can base their talk on pictures; older ones can use more sophisticated means if they choose. Shy children can be asked gentle questions by an adult about their topic in front of their classmates. Make sure that the process is fun and non-competitive. You might be surprised at the depth of knowledge that some children possess.

Dialogue for learning

The benefits of talk

Many experts have argued that pupils learn more effectively when they are given the opportunity to talk about their work, express their feelings and offer comment on issues. Killick (2006) even argues that young children 'can be observed to display a high degree of skill in organising groups, negotiating solutions and to have a high degree of insight into others' feelings, motives and worries' (p. 51). Myhill and Jones (2009) argue that although the method of talking about a subject before writing about it ('oral rehearsal') is becoming more common in schools, the process by which the talk translates to text is less clear. The authors suggest that oral rehearsal might provide the 'ideal bridge' between the creative, spontaneous, content-forming talk that is used to generate ideas, and the more ordered, scripted nature of writing.

The term 'oracy' is a shorthand for the speaking and listening that takes place during collaborative sessions. A lot of emphasis is placed upon the potential for learning when children are given properly constructed opportunities to explore dilemmas, make decisions, experiment with ideas and draw conclusions through working together rather than singly. Oracy as a learning tool is predicated on a belief that by allowing children the space and time to talk together about a common interest their combined contributions, knowledge, skills, understanding and wisdom lead to a more satisfactory learning outcome than one person working alone.

Allowing children opportunities to talk to others enables them to move outside their familiar world and explore different avenues of thinking, recognise life's complexities through the eyes and mind of another person, visualise possibilities and occasionally fantasise. The opportunity to hear their own voices and opinions taken seriously allows insecure children to gain confidence and can enhance their self-belief. Not only does dialogue help children to learn through sharing ideas with others but, with guidance from a sensitive adult, helps them to learn to evaluate different opinions and, where appropriate, to offer their support in helping others to search for solutions.

There are many forms of talk that help children to master cerebral and social skills. They can recount an interesting experience, tell a joke, comment on what is said by others, wonder out loud and express concerns about a situation. Children can be taught how to debate, offer advice and disagree. They can provide information, explain how something is done and suggest alternatives. In other words, children's insights and present sources of knowledge are a rich resource waiting to be unearthed. However, it cannot be assumed that children will be able to handle all these elements of talk unaided, so you need to offer them wise guidance about doing so.

Promoting dialogue

Learning through dialogue does not and will not happen automatically simply because children are split into groups and given something to talk about. It needs to be developed in the same way as any other learning technique such as scientific enquiry, manipulating figures or shaping a clay pot. Dialogue is, perhaps, an inadequate word to explain the complexity of multiple interactions between a selected group of children and the learning that ensues. A more satisfactory expression might be 'critical dialogue' to indicate the interrogative nature of the happening or 'focused dialogue' to indicate its purposeful nature. As noted in the previous chapter, *dialogic* learning involves a dialogue in which different pupils provide valid arguments based on facts and not on feelings or the individual's strength of personality. Some children are naturally talkative and dominate conversations to the detriment of more passive types. Other children find it difficult to express their thoughts and ideas, so prefer to remain silent rather than expose their inadequacy. Teachers need to take these factors into account when planning strategies for teaching and learning. See Littleton and Howe (2009) for an in-depth analysis of issues.

If learning through dialogue is to be effective, three things need to be in place. First, a suitably positive classroom learning climate must have been created such that teacher and children are mutually supportive and encouraging. If, as a trainee teacher, you find that such conditions are not ideal, this does not preclude collaborative enterprises but means that you will have to work even harder to establish and maintain the right atmosphere by your accessible approach, approving manner and clear instructions.

Second, children must be inculcated into thinking about their learning rather than passively receiving it from an adult. This process takes perseverance because a lot of teaching in the core subjects especially is dominated by a philosophy of 'teacher gives, pupil receives'. By posing interesting and speculative questions, encouraging children to think aloud and providing alternative explanations for events and phenomena, you can gradually foster a more inquisitive attitude and thirst for knowledge.

Third, children must be given strategies for taking turns and offering an opinion. Even adults struggle to conform to the conversational 'rules of engagement', especially when the topic is controversial, so little wonder that some children blurt out what they are thinking at the first opportunity. Last, and importantly, children must be taught how to listen to one another. This apparently 'natural' ability is anything but natural for a lot of children; however, the skill can be improved and refined in three ways:

1. The teacher models the importance of careful listening by repeating or summarising for the benefit of the whole class what a child has said.
2. Children are given opportunity to summarise what another child has said after being selected by the teacher to do so.
3. Play a 'repeat after me' game based on the US Marines' strategy of the group echoing the leader's statements. The activity is also great fun.

Preparing the children

A variety of practical considerations have to be taken into account in making the most effective use of time spent on dialogue. First, it is better to put children into homogeneous groups initially (capable pupils together, less capable pupils together) rather than mixed ones. In mixed groups the dominant children tend to do all the talking and, although you can monitor the situation to some extent, less confident children often merely sit and listen rather than participating. In homogeneous groups, a group consisting of assertive children is invariably loud and bold as the personalities compete for dominance. A group consisting of quieter children usually struggles to make headway but the under-confident children are more likely to have opportunity to say something.

Second, it is worth giving pupils something to talk about in the early stages by providing them with a subject for debate. As pupils grow more experienced and confident, you can allow them to raise their own topics, but probably within certain boundaries (e.g. relating to the present cross-curricular theme or topic). Sometimes the issue arises naturally from the curriculum work that you are covering with the children. On other occasions, a national or international event will trigger considerable interest and you decide to 'catch the moment' (a necessary part of teaching at all times). However, you may decide that as a means of promoting dialogue and stimulating discussion you are going to set up a contrived situation and maintain close control over what happens, at least in the early stages. The close control approach allows you to teach or reinforce the necessary skills for effective speaking and listening before exploiting other learning opportunities.

Third, children should be encouraged to think and organise their thoughts before speaking. There is a fine balance to be achieved between verbal spontaneity and talking nonsense. Saying the first thing that comes into their heads can lead to children being ridiculed. On the other hand, too much time spent deliberating can result in missed opportunities. It takes some children a lot of courage to make a verbal contribution, so it might on occasions be necessary to employ a strategy to facilitate it without causing embarrassment. For example, children can be taught to jot down a few ideas on paper prior to the main discussion or work in pairs/with an adult to compile a short list of key points.

Finally, it is helpful to encourage children to speak aloud what they want to say in their heads before opening their mouths. This is also a useful strategy for trainee teachers. Telling children to 'hear it in your head first' is particularly useful for diffident pupils and an alternative to writing ideas down.

Time considerations

Despite the growth in interactive teaching involving teacher–pupil exchanges, the incidence of extended dialogue has become less evident in primary teaching because teachers have been encouraged to inject 'pace' into the lessons and plan sessions under specific time constraints, most notably in literacy sessions. As a result, some teachers do not feel comfortable in allowing children room to pursue an argument, explore an issue or express an opinion unless it can be done succinctly and strictly within the constraints of the stated learning target. In addition, some younger children speak slowly and others need opportunity to deliberate, pause and retrace their steps. If time is taken up by a child's extended verbal contribution, the squeeze on the remaining lesson phases (e.g. group activity, recording, plenary) becomes a serious factor in managing the lesson. There is a balance to be struck between encouraging dialogue and completing what you have planned for the lesson.

In being aware of time factors, it is also worth remembering that the partitioning of lessons into units of equivalent length, usually about an hour per session, is for convenience rather than necessarily being based on children's learning needs. Trainee teachers are sometimes fearful (with some justification) that they may invite criticism from the tutor or observer if they do not adhere to the familiar lesson structure. Nevertheless, if you are in a position where you want to develop children's verbal skills but are sensitive to time constraints, there are a number of ways in which the problem can be addressed:

- First, discuss the issue with the host teacher and find out whether there is any flexibility allowable in the length of session. To extend a discussion, for instance, it might be necessary to straddle a session before and after a break time.
- Introduce the strategy of 'tell a friend what you think before you tell the teacher' during interactive and 'on the carpet' sessions.
- Make stronger use of teamwork, whereby a number of children work in pairs or groups to discuss and solve problems.
- Allocate specific slots in the timetable for the purpose of talking about issues. It is sensible to start with a familiar issue and introduce more challenging ones when the children become familiar with the process.

A scan of the above factors shows the difficulty and complexity of trying to promote learning through dialogue. As teacher, you have to model the attributes and carefully guide children's attitudes so that they gradually learn to speak and listen effectively. It is far from easy to involve all the children in a whole-class discussion, so if the children are inexperienced in verbalising their thoughts and ideas or tend to be excitable, it is best to begin with discussion in small groups. Once the children become more confident and understand the system, you can consider having a reporting-back time and wider debate.

Group work and dialogue

The concept of learning through dialogue has been resurrected to an extent through the emphasis on adult–pupil verbal interaction that forms such a crucial part of formal literacy and mathematics sessions. More recently, attention has been focused on the significance of pupil–pupil interaction through the establishment of collaborative learning that can take a number of forms. First, the teacher establishes a practical problem-solving situation related to the existing curriculum work for the children to resolve by discussing approaches and then acting upon the agreed procedure. For example, children may be offered three possible ways to improve the tidiness of the playground, such as: (1) to erect a larger number of bins; (2) for each class to take a turn in being playground monitors; and (3) for the establishment of regular playground 'guardians'.

Second, the teacher establishes a theoretical problem-solving situation based on present curriculum work in which the members of the group have to discuss the options and arrive at an agreed solution or position on the matter. The teacher outlines the issues, invites preliminary comments from the children and presents them with the problem to be discussed in groups of (say) four or five children. For example, in the area of citizenship the issue may relate to an issue of *fair distribution*. Younger pupils might be asked to talk about ways to ensure that every child has an equal chance to use the classroom-based computers. Older pupils might be asked to discuss ways in which money raised for good causes overseas will not be squandered through bureaucracy or the actions of corrupt leaders.

Third, the children raise an issue about which they feel strongly with the teacher during the teacher–class interactive session. The teacher then helps the children to shape their ideas into a proposition, which each group discusses. For example, children have firm opinions about friendship patterns, school rules, homework, children's television programmes, playground behaviour and associated topics, all of which may provide fertile ground for exploring important principles.

In each of the three circumstances noted above, the groups combine after a suitable time to contribute their ideas and, after further discussion, arrive at a consensus or the teacher summarises the conflicting positions. Children need to be shown that having different views about issues is perfectly acceptable, providing there is evidence to support their assertions. If a child has to disagree with a classmate, it should not be done disagreeably!

Although it is tempting to set children to work in groups and stand back, thereby not interacting with them until work is finished or a child asks a question, your role in stimulating children's verbal contributions is significant. While you will not want to swamp the children so that they are unable to express their own ideas, it is overly optimistic to imagine that you have no part to play in the proceedings once the children are talking. However, it has been known for trainee teachers to become so engrossed in one group that they forget what the remainder of the class is up to, so stay alert and make sure that you scan the room regularly or walk around and note what is happening, intervening as necessary.

Activate your thinking!

During the collaborative activity, which children were the thinkers and which children were the followers? What evidence informed your conclusions?

Good practice

Think of a 'discussion topic for the week' and introduce it each Monday morning. Allow brief opportunities throughout the week for discussion and on Friday afternoon gather thoughts and ideas in a forum.

Cross-reference: Guided Reader Extract 3

The teacher's role in dialogue

In promoting the concept of learning through dialogue, it is important to keep your eye on the central purposes of the exercise, namely, to learn from one another by pooling ideas and expertise, and to enhance social cohesion through shared experiences. The teacher has an essential role to play in the proceedings, expressed in one of three ways: (1) acting as expert; (2) acting as facilitator; (3) acting as a participant.

Acting as an expert

That is, you provide knowledge, information and advice, as and when you consider necessary. Being an expert may militate against free discussion and expressions of opinions if the children perceive that there is a 'right' answer and that you are the final arbiter of what is acceptable, but consider yourself a resource to be used as much as any other. There is a place for pupils to act as expert if the area of discussion is in their own field of interest (e.g. a hobby or pastime).

Acting as a facilitator

That is, you ensure that the conditions are right for children to learn through talking. The conditions must include mutual respect and an agreed method of proceeding, but also the provision of adequate time to delve into the area of interest and a pleasant working environment: airy, light and uncluttered. You keep a low profile in respect of what is being said but monitor the way in which contributions are made and pupil involvement.

Acting as a participant

That is, you take part as a 'temporary' member of a group or the class. In this role, you take your turn in the same way as everyone else. In such a case, there is no hierarchy and no imposed authority, other than to keep things orderly and moving forward. You can only occupy this 'neutral' role when you have complete confidence in the children concerned; you might be fortunate to inherit such a situation but probably need to view it as a longer-term goal.

Classroom management considerations include the need to structure opportunities for one-to-one listening and group-to-group listening, to teach children to rephrase what others have said and ask them sensible questions and to enthuse about other children's verbal contributions as a means of encouraging them. In working with young children, skills can be enhanced through games and fun activities that foster listening. For example, well-known games such as 'Simon Says' and 'Chinese Whispers' require children to concentrate on what is being said by others. There are also opportunities through circle time to facilitate taking turns and hearing what other children say.

Activate your thinking!

Write down some responses that a 4-, 7- or 10-year-old might give to each of the following questions:

What do you like to talk about with your friends?
When do you talk to your teacher?
When does the teacher talk to you?
What do you mainly talk about during class lessons/sessions?
Who does most talking in class?

Good practice

Other organisational considerations for learning through dialogue include:

Deciding how much (if anything) should be written down
Having paper, pencils, computers or other recording instruments available and accessible
Seating arrangements for the groups
Roles for different group members
Specific targets for achievement in the time available
The way that ideas will be shared between groups
The activities that follow the dialogue.

Talk and pedagogy

Teachers commonly interact with pupils by inviting spoken contributions to subjects that the teacher raises and to which the children respond. The teacher then approves the response and comments further (or perhaps asks a question). The children respond again and the teacher confirms or queries the responses. The pattern is set: teacher speaks, children respond, teacher praises or redirects. Superficially, there is an active dialogue, especially if the teacher invites the children to provide alternatives, give examples or offer suggestions. Yet even this apparently rich learning environment may be less efficacious than it appears. For instance, it is the teacher who raises all the issues and asks all the questions. It is the teacher who determines the quality of the children's responses. It is the teacher who decides when to move on to the next point or lesson phase. In the practicalities of teaching lessons within a given time frame these practices are difficult to avoid if the session is ever to finish; after all, the lesson content has to be covered and there is not an endless amount of time available for child-initiated talk and questions.

On the other hand, such a strongly adult-led approach assumes that all ideas must come from the teacher and that children cannot learn without being led through the process, step by step. Dialogue for learning places more emphasis on the pupil contribution, while not losing sight of the crucial teacher role. In this respect it differs from collaborative group work in which the children talk among themselves within the confine of the group.

Talk for learning

Using pupils' talk for learning (see, for example, Luxford and Smart 2009) can be described by identifying the nature of the talk and the conditions for its use. Three opportunities for talk are commonly used in classrooms, namely, through:

1. discussion
2. debate
3. decision-making.

Although there is a degree of overlap in the three forms, we will deal with each one separately, with particular emphasis on discussion.

Discussion

Components of discussion

Discussion involves verbal contributions that approach a theme or topic from a variety of directions and requires that pupils have sufficient knowledge of the subject to offer an opinion, state beliefs, suggest alternatives or summarise a position. To ensure effective discussion, participants must first develop a variety of skills, such that they can:

- communicate clearly;
- listen carefully to each other;
- express their own views carefully;
- respond constructively to what others say;
- acknowledge that a variety of views exist;
- show a determination to develop their knowledge, understanding or judgement.

As with all spoken language, discussion necessitates careful listening as well as marshalling and articulation of ideas. Such qualities are not easily acquired by children but can be shaped and steered by a teacher who is willing to give them the time and opportunity to express their thoughts. One of the challenges for teachers is to help children to understand that discussion is an opportunity not merely to put a point of view but to acknowledge and receive another person's perspective. Even adults find it hard to be disciplined in discussions, so little wonder that children also find it hard. Dillon (1994) provides a helpful description:

> Discussion is a form of group interaction, people talking back-and-forth with one another. What they talk about is an issue, some topic that is in question for them. Their talk consists of advancing and examining different proposals over the issue.
>
> (p. 7)

Fisher (2005: 49) suggests that the word 'discussion' has two common uses: (1) a general term to cover a wide range of informal situations where talk occurs between people; and (2) a specific meaning involving a particular form of group interaction where members join together to address an issue of common concern, during which they exchange different points of view in an attempt to reach a better understanding. Fisher refers to this second usage as a 'community of enquiry' and stresses that seven moral principles need to operate to facilitate the discussion: orderliness; reasonableness; truthfulness; freedom of expression; equality of opportunity; respect for others; and open-mindedness.

Use of talking points

It is evident that pupils can only discuss a topic if there is something that merits being discussed. For instance, the worthiness of a cause, the correctness of a decision and the ethics of a controversial issue all provide fertile ground for talking to one another. Dawes (2011) contends that resources for 'talking points' are a means of stimulating and supporting extended talk about a topic in different curriculum areas in which children are encouraged to confront their own ideas and those of others. Consequently, creative cross-curricular learning can be fostered as children share experiences and knowledge and listen to one another's opinions. The talking points can start, continue or end a lesson or topic and also facilitate whole-class dialogue. Thus, younger children might discuss how best to take care of their 'snacks', ways to share toys or whether it is right to speak to strangers in the street. Older pupils may discuss issues of 'fairness', equality and classroom sanctions. Children of all ages can contribute to a discussion about local issues (such as a proposed road scheme), national issues (such as how to care for the elderly) and world issues (such as conservation). Opportunities also exist through personal, social and health education and citizenship.

Classroom practice

Teachers who wish to promote discussion should take account of four factors, namely (1) physical environment; (2) size of group; (3) range of ideas; (4) teacher's role. Thus:

Physical environment

The context should be stress-free and settled but also purposeful, as additional noise and distractions detract from the concentrated attention that discussions deserve. Children should, if possible, work in natural light and the room temperature should be appropriate for the task.

Size of group

With older pupils it is sometimes better to split into smaller units of (say) four children to discuss the issues, with a subsequent report-back and plenary in which summary comments can be made by a representative from each group. Younger children are usually better off working within a whole-class situation (such as 'circle time') where the teacher can exercise a more immediate influence upon the proceedings and ensure that timid children are included.

Range of ideas

While it is important that issues do not lie beyond children's experience or imagination, the best discussions deal with matters that are of direct concern to the children but allow them to think beyond the immediacy of present circumstances. There is a place for drawing upon children's interest in the mystery of the 'unseen', providing the discussion does not degenerate into silliness and trivia. Reading aloud an unusual poem, humorous story or intriguing extract can trigger excitement and stimulate talk.

The teacher's role

The teacher's role depends upon the nature of the discussion as to how intimately the teacher is involved. If the teacher intervenes too much, discussion will be stifled; if too little, discussion may move too far from the intended topic or dissolve into a series of unconnected comments. There are occasions when the conversation strays from the topic and you may be tempted to 'pull it back' by a sharp reminder about the main purpose of the task. However, it pays to be less hasty, for children need short bursts of relaxed talk before returning to the central issue.

Debate

Debate follows more closely prescribed rules than discussion and is more carefully structured. It therefore requires formal organisation and tends to be restricted to work with older children. Class debates and those attached to school projects help children to develop critical-thinking skills, learn tolerance for opposing viewpoints and build skills of personal expression and self-esteem. Debates can also help pupils to understand that friends who do not share their opinion are not stupid; they simply have a different point of view.

Prior to the debate, pupils need time to research the given topic, talk informally to one another and, perhaps, record some of their findings in a form that can be later shared. The search for information can also be extended into homework tasks. During the debate, children who have volunteered to speak are given a period of time (say two minutes) in which to do so without interruption. The rest of the class have to sit patiently until the contribution has been concluded before being given about one minute to think about a helpful question or speculative comment. When the opportunity comes for questions and comments, no one is allowed to preface their comment with the words 'Yes, but...' or similar negative overtones. Once the questions and comments are exhausted, another speaker is permitted the same amount of time to present information and ideas. Ideally, speakers should offer contrasting views so that when the process of contributing, questioning and commenting is complete, a more interactive plenary is able to take place.

During the debate, the teacher needs to ensure that time is carefully monitored, issues are noted and contributions of all types are considered fairly by pupils. At the end of the lesson, teachers also have an important function in drawing together the different threads of the arguments, thanking the main participants and, most importantly, reminding the class about the significance of the debate in terms of the overall learning intentions. Although debate is of itself a valuable means of stimulating interest and inculcating children into mature thinking and a tolerant consideration of differing (or similar) viewpoints, it is doubly worthwhile if it can be seen as directly contributing towards longer-term curriculum subject goals. If you have established a relaxed and respectful relationship with the children, it is useful to ask the participants how they felt before, during and after the session.

Good practice

Topics for debate might include societal issues such as whether wealthier countries should send more aid to poorer nations, but also those of more immediate interest to pupils, such as the amount of PE and games on the curriculum; whether pupils should be allowed to bring iPods to school; the pros and cons of separating boys and girls for activities; and other ideas suggested by the children.

Joint decision-making

Decision-making is a strategy used principally in collaborative problem solving and investigations in areas of science and mathematics, and in resolving ethical dilemmas. It is most effective for groups of about four children working towards a shared aim. Teachers sometimes give specific roles to individual members of the group (such as chair, secretary, scribe, timekeeper), though it is normally more successful to allow children to sort themselves out or take turns in the different roles. Decision-making processes require a lot of teacher preparation in setting the scene, explaining the parameters of the task and organising groups. As with discussion and debate, teachers have a responsibility to encourage all children to participate, to discourage some pupils from dominating the talk and to generate sufficient enthusiasm for children to feel that their efforts are worthwhile. Time must be allowed for feedback from selected children from each group and, where appropriate, questions and comments. If necessary, some 'overspill' time must be allowed to save rushing the concluding phase, which can reveal some powerful themes. Decision-making can be used to resolve genuine problems (such as the citing of waste bins), gain a consensus prior to a school council meeting (about, say, how to supervise children who come to school early) or interrogate a fictional scenario (such as what action should be taken in the event of everything that is touched by fingers turning to gold).

Public speaking and debating helps children to extend their vocabulary, structure their thoughts and think on their feet but it takes time to train children in making the most effective use of their opportunities for talk, and many teachers find that it is several weeks before the strategy is working smoothly. Your role is crucial in planning and organising, managing the lesson and maintaining a sense of purpose and direction without crushing pupils' enthusiasm or causing them to feel that they can only express opinions of which you approve.

Thinking and learning

From the moment they arrive in primary school, children can be introduced to complex methods of thinking if ideas and concepts are introduced in clear and imaginative ways. It is vital for children to possess and develop their thinking, as the application of practical skills that involve only a small amount of thought – colloquially known as being on autopilot – leads to inertia and passivity, limiting children's capacity to think more widely and imaginatively. Simister (2004) studied the effects of teaching a 'thinking skills' syllabus of twenty-five lessons to a group of 10-year-old pupils and suggested that pupils' curiosity, inventiveness, willingness to discuss issues, ability to think laterally about given situations and understanding of the decision-making process can all be enhanced through specific skills teaching.

Educators tend to agree that the approaches and techniques associated with thinking skills need to be integrated or 'infused' into lessons rather than taught as discrete skills or lessons dedicated to the purpose; others argue that both approaches are necessary. Circle time – an approach by which children have an opportunity to express considered views openly and without censure – is one occasion when thinking skills can be specifically developed within a non-threatening and familiar setting. Robson (2006) identifies five thinking skills as important in assisting children to know 'why', as well as knowing 'what':

1. Information-processing
2. Reasoning
3. Enquiry
4. Creative thinking
5. Evaluation skills.

Information-processing skills enable pupils to locate and collect relevant information, to sort, classify, sequence, compare and contrast, and to analyse part/whole relationships. *Reasoning* skills enable pupils to give reasons for opinions and actions; to draw inferences and make deductions; to use precise language to explain what they think; and to make judgements and decisions informed by reasons or evidence. *Enquiry* skills enable pupils to ask questions; to pose and define problems; to plan what to do and how to research the problem; to predict outcomes and anticipate consequences; and to test conclusions and improve ideas. *Creative* thinking skills enable pupils to generate and extend ideas; to suggest hypotheses; to apply imagination; and to look for alternative outcomes. *Evaluation* skills enable pupils to assess information, to judge the value of what they read, hear and do, to develop criteria for judging the value of their own and others' work or ideas, and to have confidence in their judgements.

Activate your thinking!

Consider the following questions:

1. How might you promote a 'think first, speak later' tendency in children?
2. What is meant by 'getting your brain in gear' before you speak?
3. Is thinking the same as talking to yourself?
4. Can you think without words?
5. When do people talk to themselves?

> **Good practice**
>
> From an early years perspective, Call and Featherstone (2010) stress the need to maintain a balance between child-initiated and adult-led activities, and to make the most of existing resources. The authors also stress the importance of collaborative working, outdoor learning and managing ICT to promote thinking skills in younger children, though they advise teachers to be alert to the dangers of information overload.
>
> Call, N. and Featherstone, S. (2010) *The Thinking Child*, second edn, London: Continuum.

Learning through play

Teachers need to be clear about a number of principles before they incorporate play into their repertoire of enquiry-based strategies. These principles relate to ways in which children learn, how they understand the world and their need to express themselves imaginatively. If teachers believe that children learn by engaging with issues and life situations through play, there needs to be evidence to support that view. If teachers are disparaging about play and see it as a holding activity to keep children happy while the real work goes on around them, then it is difficult to justify play as an essential element of a teaching and learning strategy. However, it is worth noting that reducing the time made available for children's spontaneous ('free') play could be denying them the chance to learn valuable social behaviour, develop their vocabulary and perfect fundamental motor skills, such as balance and co-ordination, all of which are refined through the medium of play.

Defining play

We noted in Chapter 3 that all children love to play and that a lack of desire to do so is viewed with anxiety by parents and teachers. Bruce (2001) maintains that play helps children to learn in at least five powerful ways (see p. 8, amended):

1. to become symbol-makers by making one item stand for another (such as a stick becoming a wand);
2. to think in abstract ways that take them beyond the here and now;
3. to develop theory of mind, an understanding of the way others think and feel, and relate to people;
4. to make changes, transforming their lives and events, using imagination and creating alternative possibilities;
5. to be flexible thinkers, so that intelligence continues to develop throughout life.

O'Hara (2004) suggests that there are four types of play: structured, free, exploratory and social. *Structured* play is planned and initiated by the adult. *Free* play is spontaneous. *Exploratory* play is when children experiment with tools, equipment and materials (including sand and water). *Social* play provides 'opportunities to learn about and practise the rules, rituals and norms of society' (p. 79). Play as an essential part of the educative process and a powerful learning agent (see, for example, Griffiths 1998). Orr (2003) presents a compelling argument for play as a vital agent in the development of children suffering from disabilities. Garrick (2004) argues the importance of outdoor play (see also a discussion of outdoor education in Chapter 3).

There are numerous texts that provide an in-depth analysis of the arguments supporting the educational value of play; for example, Manning-Morton and Thorp 2003; Kalliala 2004; Brock *et al.* 2009; Macintyre 2011. Arguments propounded by Cohen (2006a), with reference to work by Apter and Kerr (1991) consider all play (adults as well as children) as being a *state of mind* rather than a series of behaviours. The author distinguishes between a 'playful' state of mind, in which the individual is able to explore and elaborate a variety of skills and test them to the limits in a free and imaginative way, and a 'serious' state of mind, which is goal-orientated. Cohen further suggests that if deep learning is to occur, it is necessary for play to translate from the 'pretend' (or 'playful') state to what he refers to as a 'serious' one. When in the 'serious' state, a child selects from the playful agenda and begins to articulate his or her ideas. In other words, it is not enough for you to simply let pupils play freely, but to do so in the expectation that the repertoire of skills and insights that they gain will be transformed into a better understanding of the world, increase self-confidence, develop new ideas, reduce anxiety and reinforce social relationships.

Activate your thinking!

What strategies and checks might you employ to try and ensure that 'pretend' play is being transformed into 'serious' learning?

Organising play

Most teachers of young children use play as a means of enquiry-based learning; teachers of junior-age pupils tend to encourage play only within the confines of a controlled learning environment (notably in drama). For younger children who are familiar with school routines and able to cope with more structure, play may be timetabled or used informally as an incentive to complete formal tasks. For older children, play can be a vehicle to explore issues and confront life choices through improvisation, and to be introduced to the demands and responsibilities of team membership. A teacher's planned intentions for a child of any age will always be limited by the child's enthusiasm for and ownership of the task. This principle applies to play as much as any other form of learning.

Johnston (2002) stresses the importance of adult–child and child–child interaction as the basis for effective early learning. She suggests that adults affect children's learning through interacting with them in two principal ways. First, the adult provides a role model for the children and shows them by example (such as showing enthusiasm). Second, adults focus the children's attention and raise issues by asking open-ended questions. Johnston underlines that, by interacting with children, adults can learn alongside them, as 'It is important that children do not see adults as having a complete set of knowledge, understandings and skills' (p. 29).

Teachers take account of the different forms of play when organising and monitoring activities. For instance, *parallel play* describes a situation where pupils play side by side but with little or no interaction. A desire for isolation during play is normal, providing it does not become an obsession, as children require a balance of social and solitary play. Pupils benefit from the social learning that is gained through sharing and co-operating with other children during group play and it might signal a problem (e.g. mild autism) if children insist on playing on their own for most or all of the time (see Casey 2005 for suggestions about inclusive play). Elements of *imaginary play* are also significant for older primary pupils engaged in producing spontaneous drama sequences and acting out contrived scenes. Experienced teachers learn to judge when to become involved in children's play and when to observe and allow children to take the initiative.

For further information about organising and managing learning, see Chapter 10.

Teaching gifted and talented children

Definitions

A lot of attention is rightly given to the needs of less able children: however, rather less has been paid to the needs of the more able (sometimes referred to as 'gifted'). There are numerous definitions of the terms 'gifted' and 'talented' though it is often employed in a single phrase: 'gifted and talented' (GAT). However, a commonly held view is that 'gifted' describes an exceptional ability in literacy, mathematics, science, history, geography, design and technology, and religious education. The word 'talented', on the other hand, tends to be reserved for children who display exceptional ability in other curriculum areas where there is more of a public performance element: art and design, music, PE, dance, drama. Bates and Munday (2005) define gifted children as 'those who exhibit high ability across one or more academic subject areas', and talented children as 'those who excel in a specific subject area; either socially – in terms of leadership – or in sport, the performing arts or design and technology' (p. 4). However, Knowles (2006, referring to Sternberg and Davidson 2005) offers a different perspective, claiming that giftedness is the potential a child may possess in a particular subject or area of human activity, characterised by the child's ability to learn in that area faster than his or her peer group. By way of contrast, talent is seen by Knowles as 'the *realisation* of that giftedness; in effect, the performance of that giftedness' (2006: 150, original emphasis). Whatever definition we adopt, it is likely that gifted and talented pupils will typically comprise between 5 and 10 per cent of the class. In other words, in a class of thirty children there are likely to be two or three children in the gifted and talented category.

The prominence of gifted or talented ability should not be considered as being either innate or absent; that is, either a child 'has it' or does not 'have it'. Macintyre (2008) deals with neurological development and addresses issues such as what it is that enables children to do well and whether there is a gene for genius. Although it is normally quite easy to distinguish the very able children (i.e. those possessing exceptional innate abilities) from the majority, the learning environment can also have an impact on the *emergence* of the gift or talent (see Hymer and Michel 2002 for practical ideas and suggestions). Bates and Munday (2005) warn that 'children develop at different rates according to their home and school influences, and their potential for achievement may well remain undiscovered and untapped well into their teenage years' (p. 8). Furthermore, it is possible to be so insistent that gifted and talented children conform to the pre-determined lesson format and learning target that they become dispirited and begin to underperform.

Implications for teaching

After identifying the factors that separate outstanding ability from the good and very good, one of your tasks is to be sensitive and flexible in the extent to which you prescribe learning outcomes. A characteristic of GAT children is that they learn things that were unanticipated and may be unimpressed with teachers' priorities for learning; indeed, being too rigid can restrict their progress. It helps to remember that many pioneers and entrepreneurs were headstrong in their determination to pursue their own ideas and dismiss more conventional pathways. For instance, Einstein rebelled when his tutors insisted on promoting old-style scientific theories. The great inventor Edison was so single-minded that he drove his teachers to distraction and had to be educated at home. Effective teaching promotes independent learning skills (Wilson and Murdock 2009) and fosters creativity in very able pupils, and schools are becoming more adept in early intervention and shaping an education suitable for the needs of the gifted and talented. Nonetheless, it is important to realise that there is no single curriculum and teaching approach suitable for all gifted children: each case has to be dealt with on its individual merits. Sometimes, this fact means that you have to adjust your approach by reducing the amount of didactic ('direct') teaching and providing greater scope for pupils to show initiative through problem-solving activities and investigations. Ruf (2005) reminds us that gifted children can get 'left behind' because their uniqueness 'renders them particularly vulnerable and requires modifications in parenting, teaching and counselling in order for them to develop optimally' (p. 31). There is no single curriculum or teaching approach suitable for all gifted children: each pupil has to be dealt with on an individual basis.

Modes of behaviour and attitudes

When a task is challenging and interesting, gifted and talented pupils are distinguished by their high level of enthusiasm and wholehearted responses. Typically, these pupils will be characterised by some or all of the following behaviour:

- Intensely focused on the task
- Asking insightful questions to probe and clarify concepts
- Seeing possibilities beyond the obvious solution
- Thriving on the challenges and complexity of the problem
- Making abstract connections between pieces of information
- Offering original and unusual solutions
- Posing questions beyond the immediate remit of the task.

Part of the challenge for teachers lies in the fact that as some gifted and talented children are unconventional, their behaviour might be interpreted as antisocial because they push the boundaries, ask probing questions and insist on being innovative rather than compliant. Some *talented* children (in the field of sport or arts, say) might not shine at mathematics and literacy; as a result they are obliged to spend additional time on these subjects, which reduces the opportunity for them to display their creative abilities in areas where their natural abilities lie. Yet other children have latent talent that requires a stimulus before it is released. Unfortunately, children from poorer homes are less likely to attend (say) out-of-school ballet, dance, craft or sporting sessions, at which they might have excelled. Again, the heavy demands made by planning, teaching, assessing, meetings, marking, reporting, extra-curricular activities, and so forth sometimes mean that a teacher is already stretched to the limit and has little time to identify individual talents; consequently, the child with potential is not offered the support and encouragement to fulfil his or her potential. Despite these challenges, you owe it to children to make every effort to help them exploit their potential and every school is now required to have a policy covering such matters (see Eyre and McClure 2001).

Helping *gifted* children in core subjects is easier for teachers in that there is a considerable amount of time spent on them, so it is easier to identify exceptional ability and differentiate the work accordingly, particularly in English and mathematics. Recognising giftedness in science is more complex and may not become evident until secondary school when pupils engage with scientific concepts, wrestle with specialist terminology and bring their insights to bear on completing formal experiments.

Learning climate and giftedness

Gifted and talented children may be emotionally sensitive and need time and opportunity to develop their knowledge within a secure classroom environment, though this advice applies to all children at every level. However, to promote giftedness, the learning culture should ideally take account of:

- learners' interest in the topic, theme or subject;
- learners' preferred style of learning, without becoming obsessive about it (see the section on VAK in Chapter 9);
- opportunities for learners to be increasingly independent and autonomous, with appropriate training in necessary skills;
- the need for openly sharing ideas and initiatives with others through formally designed discussions and spontaneously;
- identifying cross-curricular links;
- opportunities for wider application of knowledge (preferably in genuine rather than contrived situations);
- the use of a variety of resources, ideas, methods of approach and tasks;
- encouraging a reflective and probing attitude to learning.

To make optimum progress, a learning climate has to be created in which mistakes are used constructively, children are encouraged to discuss their learning with adults and other pupils, and opportunities are afforded for them to explore challenging ideas. While it is unlikely that anyone would disagree with such sound advice, there are practical reasons why such an approach can be easier to say than to do. First, studies of more able pupils in larger classes indicate that teachers tend to leave them alone to get on by themselves or simply give them additional work to keep them busy rather than to stretch their minds. The highest levels of performance are achieved when teachers interact with pupils in a way that encourages them to grapple with more demanding concepts and levels of understanding than other children. By contrast, the imposition of artificial ceilings in tasks result in pupil frustration. Dickinson (1996) found that able pupils wanted to be challenged and find fulfilment through active dialogue with the teacher. They wanted to be 'challenged within the curriculum rather than by special provision outside it' (p. 8); that is, able pupils did not want to be isolated from the regular tasks and activities, but rather to be given the opportunity to extend their thinking and be innovative within the same areas of learning. More able pupils were more motivated by teachers' comments than by grades and wanted to receive truthful, realistic and challenging feedback. See Fleetham (2008) about ways to identify GAT pupils and provide exciting and challenging tasks for them in the classroom.

Limiting pupils' potential

Able pupils of whatever type are not always easily identifiable because teachers sometime struggle to disentangle pupils' *potential* from their visible performance. Gifted and talented pupils can underachieve in the same way as other children, especially if they lack motivation or if, owing to their quizzical attitude, teachers diagnose them as uncooperative instead of intelligent. Denton and Postlethwaite (1985) offer a useful list of characteristics that help teachers to identify very able (gifted) pupils (see Table 8.1).

The majority of able pupils take their work seriously and want to do well. Their attainment can be suppressed by teacher insensitivity, mundane tasks and being treated 'differently' from everyone else, thereby gaining a reputation as a 'swot' or 'weird'. The challenge of presenting academic success as desirable is most acute among a small percentage of older primary-age boys, who may view sporting prowess and gang membership as more significant than gaining high grades in academic work. Disillusionment with schooling is an attitude that can easily be carried with them into secondary education and lead to underachievement, so you have an important task to persuade them otherwise. As part of this process you may need to offer these underachievers some 'earned autonomy', whereby they are allowed greater choice as a reward for satisfactory task completion.

Teachers also need to be aware that able pupils do not necessarily possess the full range of fundamental skills that may be assumed of them. For instance, Dean (2008) notes that boys, in particular, struggle to keep pace with the demands of writing and sometimes underachieve, and offers suggestions about helping able pupils to reach their full potential in reading and writing. Some very able pupils exhibit odd characteristics that mark them out as being atypical and invite teasing from other children. Others will excel in every curriculum area (including sports) and thereby attract huge admiration from their peers. Howe (1990) warns that although able children may not react in expected ways, close parental involvement, coupled with high expectations, yields rewards. Teachers need, therefore, to be alert to the possibilities and challenges that such children present. Few children are naturally good at everything but, with perseverance and determination, many are capable of achieving a higher level of success than was initially evident.

Different ways of being intelligent

We noted in Chapter 4 that in recent years there has been an increase in interest in the principle of 'multiple intelligences' popularised by Howard Gardner (1983, 1999). This awkward phrase reminds teachers of two important principles. First, children can be successful in a variety of ways and not only in the more obviously measurable ones. Thus, Gardner suggests

TABLE 8.1 Characteristics of gifted pupils (based on Denton and Postlethwaite 1985)

superior powers of reasoning	intellectual curiosity
alertness and quick responses to new ideas	quick memorising
ease of learning	interest in the nature of humanity
wide range of interests	unusual imagination
broad attention span	able to follow complex directions
superior vocabulary	rapid readers
independence in working	enjoy a range of hobbies
advanced reading skills	wide-ranging reading habits
keen powers of observation	effective users of the library
initiative and originality	superior in maths problem solving

that we each have different intelligences for expressing ourselves and for solving problems. Because we experience life in different ways and have different emotional responses to the same stimuli, it is appropriate for us to express those responses in a variety of ways; for example, emotions may be expressed through language or the employment of visual images or movement. The second principle is that intelligence is not fixed and can be enhanced, developed and matured through appropriate teaching, high levels of motivation and determination. The stereotypical comment made by children that 'I am rubbish at such-and-such a subject' betrays a belief that they are either good at something or not good at it, and that this situation is irretrievable. However, the evidence does not support this gloomy outlook. Skilled teachers try hard to develop in the children a different attitude towards themselves and wean them off adopting such a negative viewpoint. Your enthusiasm, teaching skills, ability to motivate and close relationship with pupils may expose gifts and talents of which you were unaware; such a positive attitude on your part will certainly help all the children to fulfil their potential, whatever their innate abilities.

Garnett (2006: 44–6) offers fuller descriptions and examples for each of the Gardner 'intelligences', a selection from which include:

> *Verbal/Linguistic* – reading, writing, listening and speaking ... creating stories, using metaphors and similes, symbolism and conceptual patterning ... humour, jokes, puns, play on words and the ability to quickly acquire other languages.
>
> *Musical/Rhythmic* – tapping out intricate rhythms ... [Pupils] might like to have soft music in the background to help them concentrate.
>
> *Logical/Mathematical* – Pupils with a strong leaning to this intelligence may like to develop strategies, perform experiments, reason things out, work with numbers, and explore patterns and relationships.
>
> *Visual/Spatial* – [Pupils] tend to have active imaginations and are good at expressing their ideas and thoughts through drawings, paintings, sculpture, patterns and colour schemes.
>
> *Body/Kinaesthetic* – [Pupils] like to learn through touching, physical movement, manipulating concrete objects, interacting with their environment and 'making and doing'.
>
> *Interpersonal* – [Pupils] like organising, collaborating and solving problems between people. They notice and react well to the moods of their friends.
>
> *Intrapersonal* – [Pupils] are good at taking responsibility for their own learning. They typically enjoy working alone and are more uncomfortable in groups and will not usually volunteer to make whole-class contributions.

With respect to the additional two categories, Fisher (2005) reasons that the eighth intelligence (naturalistic) can be defined as our capacity to investigate the physical world, which enables us to find out more about the outside world in a systematic way. Fisher refers to the ninth intelligence, which Gardner calls 'existential intelligence', as 'philosophical', stating that: 'It expresses itself in the ability to ask deep questions about human existence, such as the meaning of life and why we die' (p. 12). Fisher agrees that the concept of multiple intelligences is a contested one but that it seems to fit how humans respond to the world. He also makes the point that there may be other forms of intelligence, such as spiritual intelligence (a concept rejected by Garner but accepted by some other psychologists), that have not yet been defined. Furthermore, intelligences do not have to stand alone but can and do combine in different ways.

Benefits and drawbacks of multiple intelligences

Gardner's work has value if it encourages us to identify special capability and build on natural strengths. There is, however, a danger attached to holding a rigid adherence to the principal of multiple intelligences. It is easy to envisage that in attempting to move away from the concept of a single intelligence (the intelligence quotient, IQ) towards multiple intelligence, the Gardner categorisation could become equally unhelpful if it is used as an alternative labelling system for children – which is quite contrary to Gardner's intentions. Thus, certain pupils might be deemed to possess only specific types of 'intelligence', with the net effect that expectations are raised in these areas but suppressed in the areas where children are not judged to have such 'inclinations'. Indeed, it is quite possible to predict a scenario in which a child will simply refuse to try in the mistaken belief that 'I don't have such and such an intelligence, so it's pointless.' There is the world of difference between identifying natural strengths and ignoring the fact that weaker areas can become stronger with perseverance and whole-hearted application. An awareness of the fact that children have different learning preferences and potential that can be exploited and enhanced is obviously a positive approach to education. Ignoring the fact that every child is capable of improvement and even excelling in areas (intelligences) that do not appear to be naturally evident, is not.

Activate your thinking!

All children are gifted. Some just open their presents later than others.

(Anon)

Good practice

Many teachers, especially of younger children, argue for more 'hands-on' learning opportunities across the curriculum, not confining them to dedicated practical subjects such as design and technology (Glynn 2001). For instance, the lesson introduction might involve an action game or physical responses from pupils, so that in addition to the usual 'raise a hand', children may be asked to touch their noses if they know the answer or tap their foreheads gently to indicate that they are thinking. The tasks that pupils undertake can be orientated towards more discovery learning ('finding out') and investigation, as opposed to systematic paper-and-pencil exercises or discussion. See Chapter 7 for an in-depth analysis of discovery methods.

Glynn, C. (2001) *Learning on Their Feet: A sourcebook for kinaesthetic learning across the curriculum*, Shoreham, VT: Discover Writing Press.

Understanding the brain

Brain development

People do not learn and gain knowledge in a vacuum. Brain patterns form at an early stage of a child's development in the womb, as a necessary condition for intellectual development (Fox *et al.* 2010) and continues after birth; consequently, the process of shaping a child's understanding of the world is a continuous process, not a fixed position. In other words, the idea that some children are, so to speak, 'naturally bright' or 'naturally dull' is misleading. In fact, the neurological ('nerve system') influences that orientate a person's thinking, reasoning and insights from conception, birth and into early infancy are stimulated and modified by the *social* situation: influence of adults, physical environment, quality of spoken language opportunities, love, care, compassion, range of enlightening experiences, and so forth. Put simply, the development of an intellect does not rely solely on immutable and pre-ordained brain quality but also on the many and varied influences in daily life, including school as an educational setting, the adults that work there and the children that attend.

Emotions and relationships

As the area of the brain that regulates emotion is shaped early on through life experiences and fashioned inside and outside school by regular interaction with others, so-called 'emotional intelligence' – the ability to be at ease with oneself and relate to others appropriately – is critical to life success (Gardner 1983). If children are deprived of an intimate relationship with adults and their peers during the years preceding formal schooling, they will probably struggle later on to form suitable human attachments and might have difficulty in making friends or being part of a group. Ideal learning environments are those that reduce a child's stress level to the absolute minimum, while maintaining high levels of motivation. Derrington and Goddard (2008) argue that teachers need to employ a 'whole brain' approach to teaching and learning, involving a process of self-evaluation to explore and interpret their preferred ways of thinking, acting and relating to pupils to better understand the impact of these on children.

Left and right sides of the brain

Studies also indicate that each side of the brain performs different functions, with one side dominating. If the *left* side of the brain dominates, a person is likely to be analytical, whereas if the *right* side dominates a person is more holistic or global. Thus, a left-brain-orientated pupil prefers to learn in a step-by-step sequential format, initially concentrating on the fine details and working towards a broad understanding, a function that is described as *inductive*, i.e. evidence is gathered from a lot of detail to create a general principle. By contrast, dominance of the right side of the brain means that the pupil prefers to learn by starting with the general principle and then working out the specific details, a function described as *deductive*, i.e. knowledge in different contexts is 'deduced' from the key principle. Specifically, a person with a right-sided inclination tends to be more random, intuitive and subjective than the left-sided person, preferring to look at the whole picture rather than the individual parts.

An implication of the dominance of the left or right side of the brain and its effect on a person's learning preferences is that children tend to think and learn in different ways – some will tend to be more inductive and others more deductive. Consequently, in any group or class of children there will be evidence of a variety of learning characteristics, as pupils develop and cultivate ways of responding to their experiences and the information presented to them.

Although the model of left- and right-side brain dominance summarised above is contestable, awareness of the implications can assist teachers in at least two ways: (1) to take account of pupils' different forms of reasoning when presenting information, explaining procedures and setting tasks; (2) to recognise that pupils who struggle (say) to understand and engage with an activity might benefit from being encouraged to approach learning from a different perspective. The second of these implications involves a degree of flexibility on your part, as you accommodate a pupil's predilections towards what might be unconventional methods of solving problems.

Activate your thinking!

As children's brains are naturally predisposed to learn, it is not so much a case of asking *how* children learn but explaining why they are reluctant or fail to do so.

Case study

The children in Year 4 were learning their five times table and every member of the class or group was able to chant the table without a mistake and give correct and immediate answers to individual computation questions asked by the teacher. Initially the teacher was very pleased, but he quickly recognised that although superficially every child had 'learned' their tables, their conceptual grasp varied considerably:

- Shena could respond correctly when asked a straight question, such as the answer to four times five, but had little understanding beyond the immediate answer. For instance, she did not realise that twenty is composed of two tens.
- Gareth could work out the answer by adding five and five and five and five very rapidly. He was a little slow in finding the answer but at least he understood that multiplication is equivalent to multiple adding.
- Nicu knew the answer, too, but had grasped that five times four is also twenty. He also realised that the total bill for four items costing £5 each totalled £20.
- Skye not only knew the answer but could also tell the teacher what forty times five equals.

Although the teacher was initially satisfied that each child was equally competent in their grasp of the computation, the reality was more complex. Once he spent time talking to the children about the work and setting them a variety of tasks to test their grasp of the concepts, he was able to structure future lessons in a more informed manner. Although all the children were able to respond at a functional level and get the correct answer to the computation problem, some had a sound conceptual grasp of the mathematical principles and a small number were able to apply their learning to other situations. The bare test result was insufficiently rigorous to expose the true position.

Further reading for Chapter 8

Harnett, P. (2007) *Supporting Children's Learning in the Primary and Early Years*, Abingdon: Routledge.
Helps trainee teachers and newly qualified teachers reflect on the professional decisions they need to make, including making children agents of their own learning.

Jones, D. and Hodson, P. (2011) *Unlocking Speaking and Listening*, second edn, Abingdon: Routledge.
The authors explore the need for teachers to develop and encourage children's talk and use it as a means of learning central to effective primary practice.

Medwell, J. and Wray, D. (2012) *Speaking and Listening in Primary Schools*, Exeter: Learning Matters.
The book addresses the development, learning and teaching of speaking and listening, covering key subject knowledge and offering suggestions for teaching activities and assessment.

Reid, G. (2007) *Effective Learning Strategies for the Classroom*, London: Sage.
Focuses on recognising and meeting the individual needs of different kinds of learners and providing strategies for helping pupils develop their own successful approach to learning.
Simister, C.J. (2007) *How to Teach Thinking and Learning Skills*, London: Sage.
A series of ready-to-use lessons, using games, activities and group with a CD-ROM.

9

Planning and Teaching Skills

Introduction

In this chapter we focus on the range of teaching skills and strategies needed to develop effective classroom practice and enhance children's learning. Of the many teaching skills that teachers have to master, it is planning and the production of lesson plans that are among those of greatest importance yet, in some respects, hardest to master. Issues relating to differentiation, individual learning needs, body language and adult–pupil interaction, notably the use of questions, are also considered in depth. The various practices for teaching reading and spelling are presented as key issues for every primary teacher, especially those who work with younger pupils.

Lesson planning

The process of planning

When trainee teachers begin teaching, they go into their first session clutching a lesson plan like a lifesaver, fearful that it may slip from their grasp and they will sink and drown. As they become more confident, they are able to set the plan aside and concentrate on improving their lesson presentation, interaction with pupils and exercising control. Over time, they think less of merely surviving to the end of the session and more about what the children are learning. They realise that the best-laid plans can prove to be unsatisfactory unless they are clear about three things: (1) what the children already know; (2) the most effective way to organise for learning; and (3) how to make an accurate assessment of what is presently being learned to inform future planning (also referred to as assessment for learning, AFL; see Chapter 11 for details).

Trainees gradually become aware that children take differing amounts of time to grasp concepts and remember facts, and that most children do not learn in a smooth, uninterrupted way but are like the tide moving up the beach in a series of waves: sometimes gaining ground, sometimes slipping back, occasionally surging forward. Lesson plans become more comprehensive as they make allowance for faster and slower workers, less able and more able pupils, and the vagaries of classroom life. Trainees realise that a short lesson at the end of the day following an exciting PE session requires a different approach from one of normal length during the early part of the day. As the trainee becomes familiar with the class situation, lesson plans are developed with closer respect to pupils' previous learning and anticipated future progress. Both immediate and cumulative learning outcomes are taken into account in determining the structure and content of future sessions. Spontaneous opportunities are seized and 'milked' for all they are worth, even if they do not conform exactly to the anticipated lesson direction.

Lesson *planning* is an active process, requiring some knowledge of the school's existing plans and schemes of work (see, for instance, Butt 2006). Schemes of work set out the organisation and content for each subject of the curriculum across a full year and each Key Stage. The scheme for individual subject areas consists of curriculum units and supporting information about planning and teaching the subject. Each scheme indicates the likely progression that children will make in their learning, ways to include pupils with special learning needs and links with other subjects and areas of the curriculum. In drawing up successful lesson plans, it is important for trainee teachers to do so in accordance with the school's medium-term school curriculum plan (often spanning half a term) and to collaborate with other teachers who have responsibility for the same age group or subject (often formally done weekly or fortnightly, though regular informal liaison is essential).

Continuity in planning

At the start of a school experience, it is likely that you will teach 'one-off' lessons and there will be little chance of experiencing continuity from session to session. You may initially have little grasp of the overall curriculum direction for the class and feel slightly bewildered about priorities and longer-term goals. If so, do not be overly anxious, as most teachers concentrate the majority of their efforts into the immediate lesson patterns and the week or two that lie ahead rather than peering too far forward. Over time, you will become more knowledgeable about the full curriculum and the selection of material from the extensive amount of information now available through online and paper-based resources.

As more teaching responsibility is allocated to you, you begin to perceive teaching and learning as a continuous unfolding of related knowledge, skills and understanding across days and weeks, rather than within a single session. When you start teaching a series of lessons rather than individual and stand-alone ones, each session should begin by rehearsing some of the key points from the previous one and linking the present one with them. Assessment of one lesson enables the next one to be planned more accurately by using evidence about the way that the children responded to the tasks, answered questions and completed the activities. The planning process supports progression in learning through continuity from one session to the next as the threads of learning are woven together and teaching is targeted using information from previous lessons. *Continuity* refers to the close relationship required between the learning objectives/intentions from lesson to lesson. It is achieved when there is a discernible thread of knowledge, skills and understanding running through a series of lessons. *Progression* refers to the need for children to build upon their existing knowledge, skills and understanding in a systematic fashion so that they achieve higher levels of attainment (though, as we noted earlier, this process is often rugged rather than sleek).

Effective planning

To be effective, every lesson plan should contain a number of key elements, as follows, notably:

- Lesson purpose(s)
- Lesson content
- What pupils need to know

- What pupils need to understand
- Skills that pupils need to apply
- Links with previous lessons
- Resources (including human resources)
- Vocabulary
- Special needs provision
- Questions
- Assessment criteria.

Lesson purpose(s)

These are often referred to in the form of 'learning objectives', though 'learning intentions' is a more appropriate term, as it is not always possible to predict precisely what children will learn. Lesson objectives should be clear and specific. Vague ideas about purpose and broadly based aims are inadequate, especially in mathematics and literacy. Sometimes the same learning objectives apply to several consecutive sessions, requiring only minor adjustment over the period of teaching them. Although the objectives apply to every child in general terms, the specific needs of particular children must be taken into account through differentiating the tasks or, if giving the same task, modifying your expectations to take account of differing pupil abilities (see later in this chapter).

Lesson content

Normally, the lesson content is set within a National Curriculum Programme of Study (PoS) or relates to a literacy and numeracy strategy or agreed scheme of work. Schools follow a variety of subtly different programmes, and frequently use units of work or guidance material from (say) the Qualifications and Curriculum Authority (QCA). Many schools have incorporated the precise wording of the particular document source into their planning and even provided details of suitable tasks and activities to support learning in that area. There is, however, a growing recognition that if content is linked too tightly to tasks, creativity and innovation might be sacrificed for 'correctness'.

What pupils need to know

It is essential to note what pupils are expected to know, both factually (i.e. commonly agreed knowledge) and implicitly (i.e. knowledge that is shaped from individual thought and reflection) as a result of the lesson or, in many cases, series of lessons. This is often closely related to programmes of study ('knowing what') but may include less immediate but equally important forms of knowledge, such as 'knowing how' and 'knowing why'. In considering what knowledge children should acquire, it is important not to confuse it with 'information'. There is a plethora of information available through numerous sources. Children need careful guidance about ways to access information (through the Internet, for instance) and how to be discriminating about the facts that are presented. For example, it is relatively simple to accumulate information about Queen Victoria and inventions of that era (a popular theme in schools) but more challenging to consider Victoria as a person and why inventiveness was such a characteristic of the nineteenth century. It is even harder to evaluate the merits of prevailing social conditions during that period when measured against industrial development. The enhancement of pupil knowledge that you hope they gain during the lesson(s) must, of course, be built on their existing knowledge. Sometimes, the opening phase of the lesson in which you link the present session with the previous one takes longer than you imagine, as you have to spend time reminding the children of what you thought they knew but seem to have forgotten.

What pupils need to understand

This is composed of the main ideas and principles that are significant in the lesson, often referred to as 'understanding'. The concepts from previous teaching should be identified that require reinforcing or revising, together with those that you intend to introduce or develop in the present lesson. Conceptual development is more difficult to pinpoint in a lesson plan than knowledge or skills, as it encapsulates a large number of variables and ways of seeing things. Understanding rarely emerges quickly, though it might appear so when 'the light comes on' in children's heads. It requires careful and persistent explanation, engagement with practical tasks, talking about the issues, trying things out, making errors, adjustments, revision, rehearsal and repetition. Every teacher has experienced the frustration that comes when children appear to understand one day only to have forgotten by the next, or seem to grasp an idea during the teacher–pupil interactive phase but are unable to apply these insights when presented with a problem to solve. One can only assume that the simplistic notion of 'plan–teach–task–assess' as a linear process was dreamed up by someone for whom learning comes easily; most of us are not as gifted. Indeed, it is fair to say that certain forms of understanding take years to mature, especially those with a 'values' dimension that require discernment and judgement. As a teacher, you can assist the process of understanding, but you must be realistic about what can be achieved in a single session.

Skills that pupils need to apply

Most learning requires the application of particular skills. These may be of a practical kind (such as knowing how to use equipment) or cerebral kind (such as knowing how to orientate a map or manipulate data) or social kind (such as working as a team member). In your plan, skills should be listed under: (1) those which pupils have already mastered that are needed to complete the tasks and activities; and (2) those that are being introduced, developed or revised through the activities. If a skill or skills – say, the skills required for composing and writing a letter to a friend – are highly under-developed, much of the lesson would focus on demonstrating and explaining their use. If pupils have a tentative grasp of the skills but little experience of using them, the introductory lesson phase might be brief and the task/activity phase longer, as children grapple with the process of (in this instance) letter-writing. It might also be appropriate to utilise some form of 'writing frame' (see Chapter 6) to facilitate the procedure. If children are already quite skilled in composing a letter, the lesson is likely to take a different form as they utilise these skills in a real-life context, such as writing to a child in another country/culture.

Links with previous lessons

As mentioned earlier, very few lessons happen in isolation. Mentioning to pupils the links with previous sessions enhances the sense of continuity in learning and helps them to see the relevance of the present activities. Children are obviously not concerned with the details of lesson planning that you have spent so much time agonising over, but explaining the purpose of the present session and, where possible, offering them a glimpse of what lies ahead ensures that pupils enjoy greater ownership of the process.

Resources

Resources can consist of practical items or human assistance, so the lesson plan details should include: (1) a list of the equipment needed by you to teach and by the children to aid their task completion; and (2) information about the role of the adult helper (TA or parent). If equipment requires special training or there are health and safety factors to consider, these must, of course, be taken into account when planning the lesson, as even commonly used resources can pose dangers if procedures are not correctly followed. Resources should always be appropriate for the task; for instance, paints should be mixed in a container or on a palate that has been created for the purpose, and not in a plastic cup. It is also unwise to 'make do' if such action increases the risk attached to it. For example, using faulty PE equipment that could result in injury. Classroom resources should be correctly labelled and accessible, i.e. stored at an appropriate height for the children to reach comfortably; heavier items should be dealt with by an adult; procedures for accessing and returning items must be established; working areas should be of appropriate size for the activity.

Vocabulary

Significant words and expressions, especially subject-related ones, should be noted on your plan. In some lessons it is useful to write down examples of sentences containing the key words to use as part of the teaching because this strategy reinforces pupil learning; for example, the meaning and use of a word such as 'docile' is explained far more clearly by a sentence such as, 'The grumpy dog became more docile once he had gobbled down a bowl of food.' If vocabulary is needed for written work and pupils' anxiety about spelling is likely to detract them from the main lesson purpose, it is worth writing a list of the words in bold pen on a large sheet of paper and putting the list in a prominent position for children to use, or producing cards for groups of children on tables or making them available on the computer. Children should, ideally, try to spell words for themselves first, but it is counter-productive if a session is dominated by literacy concerns instead of mastering (say) scientific concepts or locational mapwork. In science, particularly, there is a regrettable tendency to focus on presentation rather than experimentation. It is also worth being aware that subject-related terms can be a mystery to children unless explained in context. For example, it is by no means certain that children understand commonly used words such as 'monarchy' in history, 'landscape' in geography, 'religion' in RE, 'pitch' in music, and so forth. Take nothing for granted.

Special needs provision

Less able and more able children, as well as all those that lie between, must be catered for in every lesson. To do so is likely to entail them doing separate tasks or modifying the lesson so that the less able are able to find success in the elementary component tasks and the more able can extend their learning through open-ended activities that require higher-level thinking skills, such as speculating, drawing comparisons and evaluating. Pupils with special learning needs have to be catered for in the early stages of the lesson, too, using techniques such as: (1) speaking more slowly and deliberately to children for whom English is not their first language; (2) allowing the children more thinking time in answering your questions; (3)

encouraging a group or whole-class response (e.g. 'thumbs up, thumbs down' to agree or disagree), which allows under-confident pupils to remain anonymous, rather than a relentless focus on individuals, which tends to highlight the inadequacies of slower learners. If less able children are extracted from the lesson for tuition purposes, you need to take account of the way in which they will be incorporated back into the lesson on their return. In addition, it has become increasingly important to be sensitive to the individual needs of each child, which may, for instance, involve 'booster' sessions (one-to-one using a TA) or intensive 'coaching' through after-school classes and computer-assisted learning. Your lesson plan cannot incorporate all these variables but it is important to be aware of them in creating it.

Questions

Questions that you will use with pupils, particularly in the opening lesson phase, should be listed under two broad headings:

1. Those to assess pupils' knowledge ('closed' types)
2. Those to make pupils think and reflect ('open' types).

Listing questions might appear to be an additional and unnecessary burden but for inexperienced teachers, especially, it is important to know what you are likely to ask and to ensure that some open questions are included. More details about questioning can be found later in this chapter.

Assessment criteria

In determining the assessment criteria, it helps to remember that assessments fall broadly into two forms: (1) assessment *for* learning (AFL) in which the teacher is making rapid evaluations of pupil progress and feeding back information to the children to help shape their learning and focus on achieving the intended learning outcomes; and (2) assessment *of* learning (AOL) which takes the form of a spoken or written test of pupil knowledge and understanding, frequently through the expedient of a mark, grade or visual indicator (e.g. a sticker). Assessment of learning should always relate closely to the original lesson objectives, for the simple reason that AOL is a means by which you ascertain how successfully the children have attained the hoped-for outcomes. Although it is not possible to employ all types of AFL during a lesson (see 'Good practice' below), careful observation of children's progress and purposeful use of the plenary will provide a lot of information about their understanding and progress. You should make it your aim to initially categorise the children under one of three broad headings in respect of the tasks they do:

- Coped comfortably
- Struggled to cope
- Required more challenge.

The use of the three categories is a starting point for more sophisticated analysis. For example, a child deemed to 'cope comfortably' might have done so because the work was appropriate or because he or she was capable of tackling more challenging tasks but was unmotivated to do so. Again, a child struggling to cope might have found the work too difficult or might have been confused, feeling unwell or lacking confidence rather than being short of ability.

It is, of course, your responsibility to monitor progress throughout the session and in the final work product to identify pupil misunderstandings with a view to correcting them during a future lesson. See Chapter 11 for further details about assessment, recording and reporting.

Good practice

Assessment for learning can take one or more of the following forms:

- asking pertinent questions to see if a child has grasped the point;
- asking a child to explain something to another child;
- clarifying a misconception that is evident from what a child says;
- noting correct and incorrect written answers and exploring the misconceptions;
- asking a child to repeat a process (e.g. on the computer or with equipment) with an adult present.

Cross-reference: Guided Reader Extract 27

Lesson review

The process of review is an important part of the learning process, as it allows the teacher to draw together some of the various task and activity strands that have characterised the lesson. The word 'plenary' is sometimes used to denote the fact that the whole class/group are present and involved in this review procedure. Children normally love the opportunity to talk about their work and show off their models, charts, pictures and drawings. Teachers have a vital role to play in the process of gathering the class together and enthusing about pupils' achievements. Sometimes a review requires the teacher to spend just a minute or two summarising outcomes. Sometimes it involves the teacher selecting children at random to tell the rest of the class what they have found out or done. Occasionally it involves one child speaking on behalf of the collaborating group to explain what they have found out together. Other strategies include children:

- showing or reading aloud their work to everybody;
- saying what surprised or pleased them about their work;
- voting on which idea or approach they preferred;
- telling someone other than their immediate partner about what they did.

Whichever method (or combination of methods) is used to involve pupils, it is important to ensure that you receive every contribution enthusiastically. Even comments from children that are self-evident or replicating what has already been said should receive praise and commendation. Very young or shy children also need to feel that they have contributed towards this phase of the lesson, even if they have not said anything, achieved by asking for a joint show of hands about different aspects of the lesson and praising everyone. One way or another, a plenary session, however brief, should reinforce learning and provide encouragement and a sense of fulfilment for the children, who have, after all, just devoted a lot of time and effort in achieving the result. There are many occasions when the last moments of a lesson can be used to remind the children of what is coming after the break or during the next lesson in that subject. One way or another you should make a conscious effort to conclude the lesson on a positive note, even if things have not been as smooth and satisfying as you hoped.

Activate your thinking!

Lesson plans should be your guide and not your master.

Good practice

If your lesson plan proved to be unsatisfactory, reflect upon the following possible causes:

- The plan was too rigid or too random.
- You failed to make small modifications during the lesson in response to the classroom circumstances.
- The work was not pitched at an appropriate level, with resulting confusion.
- You tried to follow the plan as if it were a set of instructions rather than a summary of points.

Evaluation of planning

It is worth noting that the most effective lessons are those in which teachers have high expectations, offer their pupils clear instructions, help them to identify their own learning targets and encourage an active, purposeful dialogue about the lesson content. By contrast, weaker lessons are vague, teacher-dominated, routine or repetitive and badly paced. The best lessons are those in which the teacher uses an appropriate range of teaching strategies, monitors and intervenes progress, and sets appropriate challenges with respect to the ability range of children.

We noted above that it is useful for teachers to share with pupils the learning intentions and, perhaps, provide a visual reminder of it, which often takes the form of a written notice on display written in child-friendly language. Children need to reach the point where they understand that the tasks and activities are not an end in themselves but part of a wider learning intention. Planning for learning involves much more than finding appropriate activities for pupils to do, though they are usually much more interested in *what* they are doing than *why*. Contrast the following exchanges between a visitor and two children engaged in the same activity:

VISITOR TO CLASSROOM: What are you doing?
CHILD 1: I'm cutting out words and sticking them in the gaps in the sentences.
VISITOR TO CLASSROOM: What are you doing?
CHILD 2: I'm finding a way to use more interesting adjectives in my poem.

The first child was concerned solely with the activity in which she was engaged. The second child saw that the activity served a larger purpose. It is similar to the story of two men cutting stone for a building. On being asked what they were doing, the first replied that he was cutting bricks, the second that he was helping to build a cathedral. It is clear which of the two responses conveys the more positive message.

In evaluating the success of your planning, bear in mind that lesson purpose will vary according to the class circumstances, as even tried and tested formats have to be modified for different groups of children depending upon pupils' previous experiences, the level of their knowledge and their grasp of the concepts. The lesson format that succeeded with one group may prove inadequate with another unless you take account of individual needs, current rate of progress and time factors. As Hart (2000) rightly reminds us, 'Classroom dynamics are so complex that it is impossible to predict or fully control what will happen when decisions made at the point of planning are translated into practice' (p. 7). Nevertheless, careful and detailed thought about the practicalities of lesson implementation prior to the commencement of the session, as well as during it, increases the likelihood of success. On the other hand, if some lessons do not turn out as expected it might be that they have taken a turn for the better, not for the worse.

Activate your thinking!

There's a difference between lesson objectives (your overall purpose), learning intentions (what you hope children will learn) and learning outcomes (what they *do* learn).

Lessons that span several sessions

Unless there is a specific and easily measured lesson outcome (such as whether the children can add in twos or spell certain words) it is usually not possible or desirable to try and 'achieve' learning objectives through individual and isolated sessions, though in some subjects the limited curriculum time makes it unavoidable. The unsuitability of trying to match closely a single task or activity with a single objective fails to reflect the fact that deep learning is best achieved in stages by being initiated during one lesson, developed in a subsequent lesson or lessons and concluded at a later stage after a lot of rehearsal, practice, discussion, problem-solving and investigation.

Although the process of introducing the lesson, allocating tasks and evaluating outcomes during each teaching session is a useful method of managing the session, it is also important to take a longer-term view of the teaching and learning process. Lessons do not always fit neatly into a one-hour slot and the learning intentions normally require more time to fulfil than a single timetabled session allows, other than at a superficial level. Three factors have to be taken into account when planning lessons that span several sessions. First, short-term lesson objectives (per single session) have to be subsumed within the overall lesson purpose. Second, the sessions should be reasonably close together to facilitate continuity. Third, children who have been absent will need opportunity to catch up.

To give an example, the main purpose of the 'learning episode' might be to inculcate in children the skills of discernment about the value of primary sources as historical evidence. To accomplish this purpose, the teacher might wish to spend a whole lesson introducing the significance of historical evidence to the class through demonstration and transmission teaching, plus (say) the visit of an expert to the classroom, the use of video material, and so forth. In this example, the opening lesson in the sequence would not necessarily involve any practical pupil activity to consolidate learning, though it is to be hoped that questions and comments would be generated. A second session might consist of sub-dividing the class into collaborative groups for the purpose of examining archival items. In this case, pupils would be involved in a lot of practical experience but, perhaps, record only tentative findings. A third session might involve drawing together the threads of the two previous sessions, sharing findings, raising issues, drawing conclusions and recording results. In such a situation, the overall structure of the 'lesson' would be spread across three sessions, as no single session would be sufficiently long to incorporate all the features needed to achieve the stated learning intentions. Consequently, the principal learning objectives would be achieved in stages; for instance:

Phase 1: Introduction to historical evidence (teacher-led).

Phase 2: Hearing from, and putting questions to, an eyewitness (guest speaker).

Phase 3: Collaborative tasks: to begin writing up findings and incorporate further information.

Phase 4: Complete writing up findings.

Phase 5: Publicly sharing results (initially in class, then more widely).

Of course, the above example is itself contrived; in reality, the time needed for each phase might prove to be longer or shorter than anticipated. The introduction of tightly defined teaching sessions and the strong advice from school inspection reports about the importance of systematic lesson structures can deter new and trainee teachers in particular from thinking imaginatively about ways that learning can be organised across a number of sessions. However, lessons that straddle sessions provide the opportunity to explore ideas within a more natural and less rigid framework than attempting to cram every element of the learning episode into a single, artificially designated period of time. Although the principal learning objectives will require a longer period of time to be achieved than in a single session, the short-term objectives attached to each session combine to contribute to the final outcome.

The spiral curriculum

All learning intentions must take careful account of pupils' existing abilities, experience and knowledge. It is important to recognise that there is often a need to rehearse, reinforce and restate ideas before a child's grasp of the concepts involved is secure. The term 'spiral' or 'cyclic' curriculum is sometimes used to describe the process of returning to an area of learning in order to remind children of what they are meant to know and enhance their understanding by reflecting on previous knowledge.

Reinforcement of previous learning is facilitated if you use the introduction to each lesson as an opportunity to remind children of what has gone before, ask some suitable questions to stimulate thinking, point out the implications of previous learning and so forth. Similarly, the end of some sessions is not only useful to rehearse the key points of the lesson but to draw together the threads from across a series of lessons and consolidate the outcomes.

Although lessons are usually planned within an overall framework in which the learning outcomes are identified with reference to statutory documentation, it is essential to gradually allow opportunities for reinforcement and the development of new ideas through more demanding work and challenges. More able pupils can use these opportunities to forge ahead by using their initiative to explore fresh avenues of thought and build upon their existing knowledge in innovative ways. Less able pupils can gain confidence and raise their self-esteem by dealing with familiar concepts in novel ways, such as using diagrams instead of extended writing. Reinforcement is most effective when children are offered the chance to engage with a variety of stimulating tasks through which they can develop, practise and rehearse their ideas. Tedious repetition is not a substitute for imaginative teaching approaches.

Although the 'spiralling' process is most commonly used from session to session across a short time span, depth of understanding can take years to mature. For example, imagine trying to explain to a class of 6-year-old children about the change of state from a tadpole to a frog. Now consider doing the same thing with a class of 11-year-olds. Although the learning objective would be similar ('understanding the process of change') the level of detail and complexity would differ greatly. In such cases, the spiralling involves a revisiting of the topic not only during the period of time allocated to its study (two weeks, say) but also across a much wider period of time, in which case the children's increased general knowledge and experience of the subject area (in this example, science) can be used as a vehicle for enhancing pupil learning. This process underlines the importance of ascertaining the children's level of understanding at the commencement of a new topic, as it is easy to underestimate or overestimate it and inappropriately pitch the learning requirements.

Differentiation

Grouping children

All classes and groups of children are of mixed ability. They contain slower and faster workers, less and more intelligent, keen and apathetic, confident and insecure. No matter how carefully pupils are divided on the basis of ability, each group will contain a range of different types of children whose learning and academic requirements have to be taken into account during lesson preparation and teaching. In fact, it is a child's legal right to have a curriculum that is differentiated to meet his or her needs (O'Brien and Guiney 2001). Medwell (2006) argues that differentiation affects a variety of aspects of planning and teaching, including the following elements (amended):

- *Presentation:* using a variety of media to present ideas, vocabulary and visual representations, including use of ICT.
- *Content:* ensuring there is content that suits all children and additional content for more capable pupils.
- *Resources:* making use of writing frames ('a blueprint' structure), word banks, alternative and simpler vocabulary for children for whom English is an additional language.
- *Grouping:* putting children of similar ability together or pairing a less capable child with a more able child or adult.
- *Task:* matching tasks to pupils' abilities (as far as possible).
- *Support:* offering adult support where needed and appropriate.
- *Time:* giving more or less time for completion of tasks.

The concept of differentiation is based on the premise that pupils differ in the extent to which they can absorb information, grasp ideas and apply themselves to a task, thereby necessitating variations in the work demands and teacher expectations. The advantages and disadvantages attached to mixed and 'homogeneous' ability grouping (also referred to as 'setting' or 'streaming') have been debated at length. While it seems sensible to put pupils of similar academic development in a particular subject together and adjust the teaching appropriate to their needs, it is also the case that even within a single ability group there is often considerable diversity in terms of speed of work, persistence, grasp of concepts and skill development. Gifted and talented pupils are believed to make more progress when placed in their own separate ability group but, by contrast, putting slow learning children together in a 'low-ability' group can result in focusing on a narrower curriculum (notably the so-called 'basics'), with the danger of reduced pupil motivation, lower teacher expectations, associated discipline problems and lacklustre learning.

Types of differentiation

In the light of this diversity, teachers are faced with a choice about the way they organise children's learning (see also Chapter 10). The first type is differentiation by *outcome* in which all pupils are engaging with similar curriculum material at a variety of conceptual levels. For example, differentiation by outcome is appropriate when children are working independently or in matching pairs, when they will progress at varying rates, depending on their abilities. However, in this situation, the teacher's expectations for pupils differ according to their academic competence. Such an approach is not to accept low standards from less capable children and demand high standards from brighter pupils, but to acknowledge that the key factor is children making *optimum* progress according to their competence. Strugglers may make a supreme effort to do their best yet produce work of lower quality than a gifted child who is coasting; in such a scenario, it is the struggler and not the bright child who should receive your commendation.

Second, differentiation by *task*, in which case pupils of different ability work on related but different activities: more able pupils are given the most challenging tasks, children of lesser ability are given easier tasks appropriate to their needs. For example, different groups (or 'sets') in mathematics will attend to tasks that are geared specifically to their capability, sometimes designated A, B, C, etc. or given names, such as 'Lions, Tigers and Bears' to try and disguise the hierarchy, though in fact the children are not fooled in the slightest by such connivances. In differentiation by task, therefore, the children in a single group are dealing with work that is broadly within their conceptual grasp and therefore have a good chance of keeping pace with all the other pupils in the same group. For older primary children this 'task' system of organising for learning is commonly used, so that pupils of similar ability across several classes can be taught together; for instance, children from three parallel classes are allocated to groups with some children from their own class and the remainder from the other two classes. This system of grouping allows teachers to plan more specifically for the narrower range of academic needs of the pupils in the group and requires less differentiation.

Time factors

It is soon apparent that slow learning children normally require more time to reach the same point in their learning than more capable ones. However, a small number of *capable* children are slow and methodical in their work, not because they lack the ability but because they are highly conscientious and anxious to avoid making mistakes. Paradoxically, some *less able* children complete work quickly because they can only engage with the concepts at a relatively superficial level and skate across the activities without properly engaging with the learning; you have the difficult job of commending their application to the task in hand while encouraging them to be more conscientious and thoughtful in their work. More able children need opportunities to extend their thinking, rather than merely repeating 'more of the same' type of work, which, though it guarantees a high success rate, ultimately leads to stagnation. It is important to ensure that planning allows for every child to gain initial success relatively easily before moving on to more interesting tasks that require determination and perseverance to complete. There is general agreement that early success builds a firm foundation of confidence and understanding on which more advanced concepts can be built, so time spent in the early stages pays dividends in the long term.

Some able children struggle to complete their work on time because they want to divert from the standard approaches advocated by an adult and try out their own methods; other children simply like to spend time pondering issues and are reluctant to conform to adult-imposed time pressures. Your introduction to the lesson must clarify the amount of flexibility you are prepared to allow, taking account of the fact that many children are stimulated and motivated by opportunities to consolidate their learning through open-ended activities (without any clear end-point), problem solving (finding answers to a specified problem by various means) and investigations (identifying the problem before seeking a solution). See Figure 9.1.

Every teacher has to take account of the resource and time implications of trying to develop too many tasks and activities for children in an attempt to cater for everybody's individual needs. Such a personalised curriculum is impractical other than for classes numbered in single figures. Planning must rely on a satisfactory grouping of children so that each group can cope with the demands of the work, and individuals can develop and enhance their own understanding, knowledge and skills in the subject. The allocation of teaching assistants to offer a child-specific training or coaching in an area of difficulty (e.g. Reading Recovery) is usually determined by the head teacher or member of staff with responsibility for standards of attainment in that curriculum area (e.g. the literacy leader).

Activate your thinking!

Towards the end of the time allocated to group work, the children are still engrossed in their activities. What factors would you take account of in deciding whether to allow them additional time or to move to the next phase of the lesson?

Personalised learning

Definitions

The concept of a 'personalised education' and 'personalised learning' has entered the lexicon in recent years. Definitions are far from universally agreed, though Bird (2006) helpfully suggests that models of a personalised education can be compared with assembling a motor vehicle. The first model is a version in which every pupil has an *identical* main chassis, frame, engine, body and wheels; however, each pupil has a *stylised* section, unique to each child, and special. The second model is a version in which the basic composition of chassis, frame, engine, body and wheels is present in every vehicle, but the composition of the vehicle is slightly different. In this case each pupil's education is individualised, while superficially similar. Bird goes on to explain that personalised learning is not the individualised learning of the past, characterised by each child engaged on solitary learning paths – often dominated by worksheets – or letting children choose what they want to do, which runs the risk of them

1   Open-ended activities without specified end-points

2   Problem solving by use of various means

3   Investigating an identified problem

FIGURE 9.1 Three motivating strategies for consolidating children's learning

selecting easy tasks that fail to stretch their minds. Rather, it is encouraging pupils to be involved in establishing their own targets for learning and monitoring their progress.

Sebba *et al.* (2007) describe how schools use personalised learning to target specific interventions, which are then developed more widely. Thus, literacy interventions, programmes and support, initially aimed at pupils with identified special educational needs and provision for gifted and talented pupils, can be targeted at one particular group of pupils and gradually extended across the school. See Chapter 13 for information about children's special needs.

Personalisation and learning styles

There is a tension between personalised learning, pupil choice, curriculum coverage and national expectations. Teachers have to find ways to accommodate pupils' aspirations, while ensuring that test results don't suffer, notably for pupils in Key Stage 2. In addition, teachers have to be cognisant of how 'learning styles' impinge upon the way in which teaching and learning are organised and managed. If, as claimed by some educationists, children have different styles of learning, teachers have to: (1) discern the nature of this preferred style; and (2) adjust their approach to take account of the different styles. There are conceptual and practical difficulties facing teachers when they attempt to accommodate pupils' learning styles into classroom practice. Bird (see above) cites five different ways in which learning styles are categorised:

1. Visual, auditory, kinaesthetic/tactile (note that the first three of these 'styles' are often referred to by the acronym VAK)
2. Reflectors, activists, theorists and pragmatists
3. Innovative, analytic, common sense and dynamic
4. Field-dependent and field-independent
5. Sequential/global; visual/verbal; sensory/intuitive; active/reflective.

The VAK model of learning types (visual, auditory, kinaesthetic) is based on the premise that every person learns best when exposed to one of three approaches, or a particular combination of them:

- Visual approach (in which pupils learn best by seeing)
- Auditory approach (in which pupils learn best by hearing)
- Kinaesthetic (in which pupils learn best by doing).

Visual learners are often characterised by rapid speech and making remarks such as 'it looks fine to me'; they enjoy writing, seeing and drawing diagrams and imagining possibilities. In this regard, spatial-temporal reasoning is the ability to visualise spatial patterns and mentally manipulate them over a time-ordered sequence. Spatial means pertaining to, involving or having the nature of space. Temporal means of, relating to or limited by time. In practice, spatial-temporary means an ability to envision and rotate images in the mind.

Auditory learners tend to prefer to have information presented to them and enjoy explaining something to someone else; they might have a tendency to sit upright and look directly ahead; they may also make comments such as 'I hear what you are saying.' However, it is worth noting Cullingford's comment that 'babies in the womb are constantly interacting with their surroundings which, in those conditions, consist of sound and sensation' (Cullingford 2007: 136). The unborn child has no choice but to rely on auditory learning, notably the mother's voice, though there are claims that certain types of music can also have a soothing or a stimulating effect.

Kinaesthetic (tactile) learners often exhibit a restless temperament, with short concentration spans; they like to make things and 'fiddle' around with items; they also tend to avoid eye contact and get inspired by colour, movement and practical task completion. There is a strong argument to be made for a distinction between 'kinaesthetic', which is characterised by experiential activities, such as playing board games, construction modelling with large items and outdoor activities (e.g. making shelters using natural materials), and 'tactile', which involves more delicate, hands-on experiences, such as clay modelling or tending plants.

Some authors add a further category: *read/write* (R) – indicating a preference for information displayed in word form – to create the acronym VARK. In a systematic study of primary-aged children using the work of well-known picture-book artists, Arizpe and Styles (2002) investigated how children from a variety of backgrounds and ages read visual texts. The authors found that children are surprisingly sophisticated readers of visual texts, and able to make sense of complex images on a variety of levels. They are able to understand different viewpoints, analyse moods, messages and emotions, and articulate personal responses to picture-books, even when they struggle with the written word.

Personalisation and pupil needs

A moment's thought will reveal the impossibility of organising your teaching in such a way that different groups of children are divided on the basis of an alleged preferred learning style (Franklin 2006). In practice, a more realistic approach is to enrich all the pupils' learning experiences through rehearsal and reinforcement by taking account of the categories listed above but not being slavishly driven by them. In other words, use every weapon in your teaching armoury and don't rely on a single approach to promote learning.

In practice, children learn best when you use a combination of learning approaches and organise teaching in such a way that it takes account of, but does not try to match in every respect, an individual's learning tendencies. In fact, it is wrong to try and artificially allocate each child to just one of the VAK categories, as labelling of this kind can limit pupils' potential for learning by lowering expectations that they might learn effectively through one or more of the other approaches.

Experience shows that a child's learning preference does not always correspond with the way that he or she learns best; for instance, a child may *prefer* learning through visual means but *in reality* make most advancement through (say) reading or listening to the teacher. Good teachers take account of learning styles by employing a variety of strategies, including explanations, visual illustrations and opportunities for pupils to touch and feel, but they are aware that the prime intention is to help children gain knowledge and shape their understanding. The means of achieving this singularly vital goal will depend on the individual pupil concerned and the subject matter in hand and cannot be reduced to a formula or prescription.

Body language

To effectively implement lesson planning, every teacher needs to have a repertoire of teaching skills to promote learning, including the effective use of body language, widely defined as the gestures, postures and facial expressions by which a person manifests physical, mental and/or emotional states, and communicates non-verbally with others. Thus, head movements, eye contact, hand gestures, body position and tone of voice are used to express an individual's emotions, feelings, and attitudes.

Body language is significant because communication takes place non-verbally on the part of one person to another, which can have a considerable impact on his or her reaction, behaviour and conduct. Teachers are performers, not in the same way as a stage artist who aims to receive public acclaim, but rather as a means of improving the quality of interacting effectively with the children. Although it is important for teachers to avoid artificial behaviour and react spontaneously in the classroom, there are techniques that can be useful in gaining and maintaining children's attention, particularly during interactive phases of a lesson and especially during whole-class questioning. These techniques are based on the premise that a teacher's body language (stance, voice tone, gesticulation, eye contact, etc.) has the potential to generate and maintain interest among the children, convey important non-verbal messages about appropriate behaviour, enhance pupil response rate to questions, create enthusiasm and excite a powerful learning environment. There are five principal types of body language that are significant:

1. Speech patterns
2. Head position
3. Eye movement
4. Pauses
5. Stance.

Speech patterns

In life generally, listeners use the quality of speech as an indicator of a speaker's competence and sincerity; the same rule applies in the classroom. Some inexperienced teachers make the mistake of thinking that they will endear themselves to the children by using casual or slang expressions. In fact, the opposite is true. If teachers want to establish and maintain their authority, they should speak plainly at all times and (other than with children who have specialised language needs) never attempt to modify it for the sake of effect. Some teachers gradually slip into using an unnatural tone of voice when addressing children (and sometimes, parents), which can sound patronising and false. Good speech comes through correct breathing and posture, and as the voice is of prime importance in teaching it is worth taking care of it (Hayes 1998; Kovacic 2005; see also 'Care of the voice' in Chapter 4). A simple strategy such as relaxing the shoulders and breathing through the nose deeply into the lungs to a count of five, then exhaling slowly through the mouth to a count of five, then ten, then fifteen, has a remarkably beneficial effect if practised regularly.

Some teachers have mellifluous, natural voices that sound like a mountain stream: clear, cool and smooth. Other teachers sound more like an old steam engine whistle: shrill, scratchy and hard on the ears. Pity the poor children who have to listen to them day after day. Most teachers' voices lie somewhere between these extremes, but all practitioners need to improve their voice quality and technique by learning to relax when they speak, breathe naturally and stand or sit comfortably.

It is not necessary to have a very loud voice to deliver your lines effectively, though those teachers with quiet voices have to work hard on diction to ensure that all the children can hear what is said. Quiet speech can carry to the far corners of the room if it is well articulated, whereas muffled loud speech is difficult to absorb, especially if it 'bombards' the children with a torrent of words and few pauses. If you have a strong dialect, you might need to improve the roundness of your vowels and the crispness of your consonants. In addition, it is worthwhile varying your speech pattern by occasionally slowing, accelerating or changing pitch as a means of emphasising key words, heightening interest in a phrase or adding character to the voice tone. The impact of changes in speech pattern can be increased by the use of strong but kindly eye contact and, where appropriate, adopting a fresh physical stance. Variation in speech pattern is particularly important during the opening phase of a lesson when seeking to maintain the children's attention and engage their enthusiasm. It requires considerable skill to keep every child on board and actively participating, so it is essential to develop a repertoire of verbal delivery modes when explaining, reading aloud, questioning and responding to the children.

Having clear speech necessitates having relaxed face muscles and jaw, which can be achieved through regular use of a few simple exercises, such as: (1) making wide chewing motions while humming gently; and (2) carefully opening your mouth as wide as possible (as if about to yawn), while gently moving your jaw in circles and from side to side. Clarity of speech can be improved by practising tongue twisters (of the 'She sells sea-shells on the sea shore' type). Begin by repeating the words slowly and gradually building up speed until you are saying the sentence at normal conversation speed. It can also help to exaggerate the words, thereby forcing your tongue, jaw and lips to work hard. If you are an inexperienced speaker you can hone your speaking skills in front of a mirror, being careful to stay relaxed (avoid hunching your shoulders or tensing your hands). Take note of any strange faces that you pull or involuntary twitches, all of which indicate muscle tension and interfere with the quality of communication. As a rule, never use 'speed talk' except to make a special point or gain children's attention; after doing so, revert to a normal or slightly reduced speed immediately afterwards.

In Chapter 14 of her book, Cowley (2003) suggests that caring for the voice requires that you attend to a range of issues, as follows (added comments are in the square brackets):

- Control the volume. [Avoid getting progressively louder.]
- Learn to hear yourself. [The acid test is whether you would want to listen to yourself all day.]
- Never shout. [Speaking strongly is a different matter.]
- Be quiet but deadly. [Leave no doubt in pupils' minds that you mean business.]
- Control the tone. [Don't let it control you.]
- Get their attention first. [This is a basic classroom technique and reduces the likelihood that you will have to raise your voice.]
- Have a calm and quiet classroom. [See Chapter 12 for detailed information about behaviour issues.]
- You be teacher [as well as being the class leader].

The author also advocates minimising the need to raise the voice by getting physically closer to pupils when addressing them; this technique works well but you should be careful not to appear threatening. Cowley adds that you should make it your aim to use your voice less – by employing hand signals, for instance – drink plenty of water and, if possible, receive voice training. All good advice.

Good practice

Practise varying your voice tone by:

- injecting expression during storytelling;
- speaking slowly, firmly and deliberately to emphasise points;
- showing enthusiasm when introducing a topic;
- explaining things with precise and accurate phrasing.

Head position

When addressing a group of children, it is important to keep the eyes level and speak directly ahead of you as much as possible, for three reasons: (1) it gives you an air of authority; (2) it helps the voice to carry further; (3) it allows air to pass freely from your lungs to your larynx and tongue. However, moving the position of the head slightly can be used to good effect. For example, staring down momentarily (especially with arms folded) carries the message that you are deep in thought, and may serve to increase the children's curiosity. Staring straight ahead with a serious face for a few seconds without looking at anyone in particular can be used to convey the fact that you are waiting for the children's close attention. A gentle nodding of the head, with soft eye contact and affirmative sounds, indicates that you are very interested in what children are saying and happy to be patient until the child has finished speaking. By contrast, staring up at the ceiling denotes a degree of impatience and unwilling-ness to tolerate the situation any longer. Of course, head position alone is not going to provide an automatic solution to the vagaries of classroom life or convince the children of your mood, but in conjunction with words and eye movement can be positively effective. It is also important to stress that the less often you have to turn your back on the class, the more direct eye contact with them is made possible and the less chance you have of injuring neck muscles as you swivel back and forth. There are three possibilities to reduce the amount of 'back-turning':

1. Have resources available; for example, cards or a sheet or computer monitor with key words prominently displayed. If you use a series of individual cards, display them in advance of the lesson.
2. Invite children to come forward and write the words, draw the diagram or list the numbers. However, be aware that the involvement of children in this way tends to slow the pace of the lesson and may be practically difficult.
3. Use electronic means (such as an overhead projector, interactive whiteboard or Power-Point). The employment of any electrical equipment involves space management and attention to health and safety factors.

A simple exercise to improve neck muscles and head movement is to stand still with feet apart, looking directly forward before turning the head over a count of three (say) to the left, holding for a further count of three, before returning slowly to the starting position. Repeat the exercise by moving the head to the right using the same procedure. You can also gently and slowly tip your head backwards until you are looking at the ceiling and forwards until you are staring at your toes. It is essential not to hurry or exert any strain on your body. If in doubt, take professional advice beforehand.

Eye movement

The eyes are probably the most expressive part of the body and often reveal a great deal about what someone is thinking. Chaplain (2003) suggests that eyes transmit two types of information. First, they indicate that the adult is prepared to receive information by showing that the lines of communication are open. Second, they demonstrate an interest in the other person or persons. Eyes betray the truth about us, and disclose whether we are sad, mad, glad or bad. Teachers in a variety of teaching situations use their eyes a great deal to bond with the children, transmit unspoken meaning and influence actions, so it is worth being aware of how you might use them. For instance, wide eyes convey your enthusiasm, amazement or incredulity, whereas narrowed eyes suggest to children that you are concentrating or mentally interrogating the facts. Many teachers develop what is often known as the 'hard stare' with fixed eyes as a method of discouraging children from unwise behaviour without having to say a word to them. On the other hand, teachers also find that a twinkling eye, a flashed smile and a simple nod of approval can transform a child's attitude and enthusiasm for learning by conveying approval, amusement and affirmation. During interactive sessions it is important to maintain good eye contact to convey approval, amusement and affirmation.

Similarly, children should be encouraged to look into your eyes when you are speaking and when they wish to offer a comment or answer a question. If you are very inexperienced, this process of 'eyeballing' can be rather embarrassing, as you become aware that every child is looking straight at you. Over time it becomes a vital part of your teaching armoury. Since approval by touch has become more problematic in school, affirmation through the use of the eyes has assumed even greater significance and must be fully exploited if you want to communicate effectively with the class.

Pauses

Ollin (2008) suggests that many different types of silence may be used productively in pedagogical practice. Based on her study of twenty-five teachers, she concluded that some teachers make conscious decisions to abstain from intervening to assist their continuous reading of what is happening in the classroom. Although it is generally wise to maintain a steady flow of words, delivered in an interesting way (see 'Speech patterns', earlier in this chapter) there are numerous occasions when intentional pauses are useful. For instance, in the midst of speaking, you may gaze thoughtfully at the children or make a brief diversionary movement (such as stroking the chin or tapping a pencil on paper) before continuing. This technique has three benefits. First, it allows you to gain some thinking time. Second, it offers a moment of respite from talking so that the children can re-focus on the lesson. Third, the silence causes the children to gain a sense of anticipation about what follows. The impact of interrupted action is enhanced if the first few words after the pause are spoken deliberately and slowly. If the pause is part of a discipline strategy, it is often worth adding a soft but firm 'Sit up and look at me, please' at the same time. Although it is important not to use this strategy too often or impose an extended silence, using the opportunity to scan the class and make numerous eye contacts often provides a psychological 'cohesion'. Remember, too, that what seems to be a lengthy pause to you (five seconds, say) feels much shorter to the children. It conveys a strong sense to pupils of an adult being in command of the situation.

Stance

Maintaining a set position from which you speak to the children is useful in that it gives them a single focal point on which to concentrate and does not cause any distractions that constant movement back and forth tends to invite (the 'tennis match' syndrome, looking from one side to the other and back again). At the other extreme, a rigid pose does little to transmit a message to the children that the lesson is going to be exciting or worthy of close attention. By deliberately changing your physical position and occasionally adopting a fresh stance, however, you are encouraging the children to follow your movements closely and, if used in conjunction with some of the other strategies described in this section, will help to keep them on their toes. Thus, to sit for a short time when you have been standing, turning your back momentarily on the class before gently spinning back to face them, putting hands on hips, and even folding and unfolding your arms, can all recapture children's attention. If the change of position is accompanied by a slight adjustment to another feature of the physical environment (such as straightening a chair), the impact is even more pronounced. It is important to limit the number of occasions that you adopt these fresh stances but with concomitant changes in voice tone it can have a surprisingly powerful impact on children's concentration level.

The strategies described above should be viewed as teaching skills that can be used to enhance effectiveness, and not as clever gimmicks to cover inadequacies in planning and knowledge of the subject or as showmanship. Whatever decisions you make about your use of speech, head, eye, pause and stance, it is important to constantly review and evaluate your classroom presence and the way that you engage with the children, especially when you are leading and they are listening. Exaggerated body language can lead to discipline problems if children perceive the way that you behave as whimsical. Equally, a lifeless presentation results in a lack of stimulation and a dreary learning environment. Your lessons should not be like a circus act, but neither should they resemble a funeral service.

Having focused upon the significance of body language, we now consider a variety of other teaching skills commonly used in teaching, starting with possibly the single most important one: interacting with pupils.

Interactive teaching skills

Principles

The concept and practice of 'interactive teaching' has become embedded within every teacher's vocabulary, not least because of its use in government advice about literacy teaching (see Moyles *et al.* 2003). However, defining the term is less straightforward. Merry and Moyles (2003) distinguish between interactive teaching that is concerned with 'surface features' of classroom techniques (e.g. asking questions) and 'deep' strategies and interactions. Thus, deep interactive teaching 'appears to be a reciprocal process, genuinely taking on board the pupils' thinking as well as the teachers' objectives, and trying to encourage the children to reflect on and develop their own ideas' (p. 29). Teachers are called upon to make dozens of small decisions every day and to cope with a large number of demands, not only with respect to the activity of teaching but also ways to respond to individual children and colleagues.

It has to be acknowledged that even with the most orderly class and well-mannered children, high levels of interaction place a strain on maintaining an orderly environment. You have to strike a balance between keeping pupils engaged, eliciting responses and ensuring that the situation does not become frenetic. Although you might be keen to exploit the benefits gained through interactive teaching, it is normally advisable in the early encounters with a class to use a more didactic approach and gradually invite active pupil participation, as and when you have established full authority.

Cross-reference: Guided Reader Extract 40

Addressing the whole class

In recent years the ability to address the whole class and hold their attention has assumed increasing importance. Successful whole-class teaching requires a combination of seven inter-related qualities. First, a firm grasp of the subject material so that you don't have to keep referring to notes. Second, familiarity with the lesson structure, assisted, perhaps, by having a summary written in bold letters in a convenient place. Third, use of a calm and clear voice, aided by careful articulation and a rich tone. Fourth, developing a lively (but not frenzied) manner to engage children's interest using strong eye contact and varied facial expression. Fifth, having access to relevant resources, including basic items such as board pens. Sixth, using questions effectively. Seventh, thinking on your feet. Each of these seven qualities can be improved through practice. Thus:

Grasp of the material

This ability requires dedicated study and, importantly, translating the content so that it can be presented to the children by using vocabulary and concepts that are appropriate for them. If you only have a partial grasp of the material, this insufficiency will be reflected in the quality of your explanations, which are likely to be overly complex and convoluted. It is not difficult to make something simple sound complicated. However, it takes a great deal of careful thought and study to create something straightforward and understandable out of complex material.

Clarity about lesson structure

This quality is not merely a case of knowing the sequence of events, though this is clearly a fundamental requirement. It involves weaving together the lesson elements so that the total experience makes sense to the children who are on the receiving end. Each part of the lesson is referred to as a 'phase' and the move from one phase to the next is often the time when a lesson can lose momentum, so your ability to link the phases is crucial to successful learning.

Articulation

Use of a calm and clear voice is, as noted earlier, an essential attribute. You do not need to possess a loud voice to be effective but you must be able to speak distinctly in such a way that the children enjoy the sound of your voice. The single most important factor in maintaining good articulation is having a regular supply of breath to 'feed' your speaking, so being relaxed and disciplining yourself to take a regular intake of air is essential. Anxiety can cause inexperienced teachers to speak too quickly or slur their words or 'drop' their consonants. It can also lead to a colourless or monotonous tone. Away from prying eyes, you can improve suppleness in your facial muscles by gently rubbing your cheeks, moving your lips around in a circular motion, sticking out your tongue and opening your eyes wide for a few seconds, repeating the process several times. Momentarily slowing your speed of speech and occasional bursts of speed to punctuate the regular delivery can help to add colour to your talking.

Lively manner

Some teachers can make even the dullest lesson material sound interesting by effective use of the voice (see earlier in this chapter), raising rhetorical questions, reminding the children of what they already know, rehearsing ideas and summarising viewpoints. The use of illustrations, stories and occasional humour help to oil the wheels of an exposition, though it is important to restrict the number of these assisting strategies lest the lesson loses its direction or becomes trivialised. Some teachers have been known to use a sing-song tone or sing little ditties to reinforce a point.

Use of resources

Resources should be not only available but accessible. You should give plenty of thought to the practicalities of handling them while speaking to the children and interacting with them. For instance, you should take account of factors such as the time taken to distribute items, collect them in, check their condition, and so forth. Health and safety considerations are also important: ensuring that larger items are stable; avoiding the need to stretch excessively; wearing protective clothing where necessary; washing hands, and so forth.

Use of questions

This skill is so important in teaching that it merits a full section to itself later in the chapter. You can begin to hone your questioning skills by clarifying in your own mind the purpose of the question, and whether it is to assess what the children already know, expand their thinking, raise issues or generate interest in a topic. The best types of questions may raise issues that require in-depth exploration through dialogue. Once you know the purpose for asking the question it is easier to frame it meaningfully. By mentally putting yourself in the children's place you can anticipate the sorts of responses they might provide. However, as Hargreaves *et al.* (2003) noted in their study of interactive teaching, children were rarely given 'time and space to offer extended responses, to enter into a genuine dialogue with their teachers or to ask exploratory or higher order questions of their teachers' (p. 123). See later in this chapter for detailed information about asking different types of questions.

Thinking on your feet

Perhaps the most difficult aspect of whole-class teaching is developing an ability to think quickly and involve the children in the lesson through verbal contributions, responses to questions, feedback and practical actions (such as writing on a whiteboard). For inexperienced trainees it is better to maintain close control over the proceedings rather than be too ambitious. Thus, to use pre-determined questions, give instructions and limit pupil choice. Over time, you can gradually introduce greater spontaneity to the proceedings. As with all teaching skills it is sensible to practise the session in your mind and 'hear' yourself speaking to the children. In the pressure of handling the whole class it is possible to allow the lesson to 'accelerate' and find yourself carried along much faster than you intended, with the result that what was meant to be an interactive phase deteriorates into a monologue. One way to reduce the likelihood of this happening is to 'write in' deliberate pauses to your lesson plan and discipline yourself to count to five in your head from time to time.

Good practice

Begin whole-class teaching in a straightforward way, such as reading or telling a story, giving a single piece of information or instruction. As you gain confidence, gradually increase the tempo and complexity.

Working with children seated

The intimacy of group interaction, especially 'on the carpet', raises class management issues that are different from those when the class are seated on chairs. Some younger children in particular are inclined to call out, move around the floor and sit where they cannot see or be seen. Other children seem to have an irresistible desire to sneak up on to the nearest available chair. You have to decide whether or not to be very firm about such behaviour or acknowledge that it is an acceptable price to pay for the increased involvement that close physical proximity allows. As you invite and encourage verbal participation, watch out for less able children who do not think for themselves but take their cue from more able or confident children around them. It is difficult to spot that a child is feeding off his or her more illustrious classmates but there are a number of indicators:

- They raise their hands/whiteboards/number fans a second or two after the majority.
- They sit towards the back so that they can be concealed from the teacher while having a view of other children.
- They shoot their hands in the air before anyone else and feign enthusiasm for answering the question, but if selected to answer offer a lame response, suddenly 'forget' or repeat a whispered answer from a more able child.

Such forms of behaviour have their origins in low confidence, an inability to cope with the conceptual demands of the questioning or (in a very few cases) unwillingness to make the necessary effort to think. To remedy such behaviour, consider whether your teaching is sufficiently targeted and differentiated. If not, it is likely that you will have to introduce some simpler questions or explain concepts using more straightforward terms. Second, decide whether you are placing more emphasis on speed of response than thoughtful replies. Some children need a little longer than their classmates for their brains to process the information and become despondent if quick thinkers constantly upstage them. Third, determine whether some children are cloaking their unwillingness to make a genuine effort by going through the motions of eagerness, not expending any mental energy to solve the problems that have been posed. One positive way of combating such pretence is to ask a question and insist that children work in pairs to produce a response before asking for feedback. Such a strategy does not work immediately; it requires perseverance, and the reluctant learner might still try to sit back and let his or her classmates do all the thinking.

Working with children seated is particularly apt when reading or telling a story, reciting a poem, showing an item of interest and allowing children to share experiences or hobbies. It can seal the adult–child relationship and be a time of fun, reinforcing learning and intimacy. Make sure that the time is well spent.

Activate your thinking!

How can you involve children who think a lot but rarely volunteer answers?

Good practice

Establish procedures for coming to, and exiting from, the carpet; for example, tiptoe-ing, allocating specific places, chanting softly, no shoes, no touching, etc. In the case of top juniors, consider whether the physical constraints of size (large bodies, large feet) make 'the carpet' an appropriate learning zone.

TEACHING READING AND SPELLING

Learning to read

Reading ability as a continuum

The ability to read is essential for children growing up in the twenty-first century, as the printed word dominates the way that society operates. About 5 per cent of pupils learn to read effortlessly and one quarter learn to read without any great difficulty when they are given systematic and regular instruction. Reading is a multi-faceted process involving word recognition, comprehension and fluency and is the foundational skill for all school-based learning. In many ways there is no such thing as 'having learned to read' because reading cannot properly be defined in terms of a 'can do' or 'cannot do' skill; there is a continuum that stretches from people who read fluently and with understanding to people who struggle to say the words or extract meaning from the text.

Early years development

The most important period for literacy development is during the early childhood years from birth to 8 years, where regular exposure to books and stories is a crucial factor in learning to read. Parents can prepare their children to read by spending time with them, talking to them about interesting things in the world, telling and reading stories, and asking and answering their questions. By the time most children start the reception year in school at age 5 years they will have learned a lot about spoken and written forms of language; played, explored and made discoveries at home and in other settings; and watched, listened to and interacted with adults and other children.

Different techniques

Many people in middle to later life probably learned to read through the medium of phonics (see later in this section), together with a whole-word recognition look-and-say approach; that is, to memorise words from their distinctive 'shapes' and through recognising letters and their sounds from the alphabet. However, use of word recognition disadvantages children with poor visual memory and recall. A 'whole-language' approach to reading was popular during the later years of the twentieth century – incorporating reading, writing, speaking and listening ('oracy'), and focusing on 'real books' rather than using a reading scheme – an approach sometimes associated with a child-centred philosophy of education. However, neglect of phonics in the whole-language approach was found to be a problem in deciphering longer words with multiple syllables.

Shared reading

Holdaway (1979) is credited with developing the 'shared reading' model, in which teacher and pupils simultaneously read aloud from a large-format text. Wyse *et al.* (2007: 88–9) suggest that the key features of such a shared reading experience include:

- a text pitched at or above average attainment level;
- a shared text, such as a 'big book' or other enlarged print or multiple copies of the text in normal size;
- high quality teacher interaction;
- discussions about the text, focusing on meanings and on words and sentences;
- the modelling of the reading process;
- teaching that is informed by lesson (learning) objectives;
- preparation for main activities.

The model builds from research indicating that storybook reading is a critically important factor in young children's reading development. Oversized books (often referred to as 'big books') are frequently used, with enlarged print and imposing illustrations to ensure that children can actively participate 'on the carpet'. As the teacher reads the book aloud, the children can see and enjoy the print and illustrations, occasionally reading in unison. The texts need to be those that appeal to the children; chant and song can also be employed to heighten the level of involvement. This interactive approach to reading can be used when revisiting favourite poems, jingles, songs and stories or giving close attention to specific words, letters and sounds. A new story can be introduced as a means of explaining how to work out unfamiliar words, such that shared reading provides a springboard for independent and group reading.

Whatever method or strategy you favour, there is agreement among educators that for young children to learn to read effectively, they need access to books containing common words that are interesting to them and capable of being sounded out. Sometimes, children are so busy concentrating on sounding the words and blending the sounds that they don't think about the meaning, so you have to remind children about the significance of words, relate them to the accompanying pictures and use example sentences that include the word or words. Reading becomes more meaningful as children master the connection between different sounds and become familiar with the written words through stories, rhymes and songs.

Activate your thinking!

National reading tests have been introduced as part of a more comprehensive overhaul of the school system in Wales. Failure to achieve the standard can mean that the school concerned faces closure. A national literacy plan, including reading tests, has been designed to make sure fewer pupils fall behind their reading age. The plan will focus on 7- to 11-year-olds and involve catch-up reading programmes and elements to stretch the more able pupils.

Reading in unison

When reading a passage in unison with children (notably, during a literacy lesson), it is important to read much more slowly than you imagine to be necessary, or the middle-range and weaker readers will soon get left behind. It is common experience that while the whole class reads the text initially, numbers gradually drop off as the pace quickens, with the result that by the end of the passage only the teacher and the best readers (usually sitting near the front) are still reading. The other children are merely 'mouthing' the words or will have stopped trying to keep up. There are a number of strategies that you can use to maintain full involvement. For example:

- You stop reading and allow the children to continue reading on their own for a short time.
- You stress certain words (such as adjectives) and encourage the children to do the same during a second reading of the passage.
- You ask the children to speak specified words in a different way (such as whispering the first word in a sentence or emphasising the last one).
- You and the children read alternate lines or sentences.

Depending upon the length of the passage, there is much to be gained from a second reading or repeating key phrases to reinforce understanding, allowing children another opportunity to grapple with difficult words and spellings, and helping slower learners catch up. Although extracts of text are valuable as starting points for exploring aspects of language, their particular vocabulary and syntax should not restrict the breadth of your questions and explanations. Thus, by asking the children if they can, for instance, suggest alternative words, provide a variation in the sentence construction, think of rhyming words, and so forth, you extend the range of their thinking beyond the immediacy of the passage and begin to expand pupils' creativity.

Most children, regardless of age, benefit from being invited to evaluate aspects of the text, such as whether it conveys meaning clearly and whether the writing excites interest. Depending on the lesson purpose and time available, more able/older children can be asked to speculate about what the author was trying to achieve and to what extent she or he succeeded, or even what mood the author was in when the piece was written. Explorations of this sort that move children beyond the immediacy of print and get them to think hard about deeper meanings serve to enhance interest and excite a mood of reflection and questioning. They also make teaching more enjoyable and satisfying for you.

Using phonics

Analytic and synthetic approaches

Even though children benefit from being read to in school and at home, and pick up familiar words and phrases from daily life (e.g. advertisements), a programme of targeted tuition in reading is still necessary, of which phonics forms an integral part (e.g. Starrett 2007). Teachers use two broad approaches. In *analytic* phonics the teacher builds up the sounds to make a word, which is shown to the child at the same time; for example, a teacher might sound out the letters of 'f-l-a-g' and then ask the child to repeat the word. In *synthetic* phonics the children learn forty-four sounds of letters or groups of letters while being encouraged to look at books containing the words. Both analytic and synthetic approaches require the learner to have some phonological awareness (the ability to hear and discriminate sounds in spoken words) and can contribute to furthering children's development. Although most teachers use a balanced combination of analytic and synthetic approaches, the use of synthetic phonics is becoming a popular method in the UK (Johnston and Watson 2007).

Procedures

The phonics method requires knowledge of the sounds of letters and the effect of the position of the letter upon its sound as an essential means of mastering the mechanics of reading (L. Williams 2008). The method relies on children first being taught the alphabet and learning the names of the letters and the sounds they make. Once they have learnt the letter sounds, they begin to blend two letters together to make simple words, then three letters, then four, and so on. Eventually the words combine to create simple sentences. Phonics is generally seen to be more suitable for younger pupils in the early stages of learning, though it can also be valuable in teaching an older primary child who is experiencing learning difficulties. The teaching should be embedded within meaningful and purposeful texts and a variety of reading activities.

Later, children begin to: link sounds to letters; name and sound the letters of the alphabet; recognise letter shapes; and know what each one sounds like. They learn to hear and say sounds in the order in which they occur in the word and sound out and blend the *phonemes* – the smallest unit in the word that is capable of conveying a distinction in meaning, such as the 'c' of cat and the 'p' of pin, always in order from left to right. (Note that older children who learned to speak a different first language might be used to reading from right to left and will take some time to adjust their technique.)

Progression

Over time, pupils begin to recognise common *digraphs* – a pair of letters representing a single speech sound, such as the 'ph' in 'phone' or the 'ea' in 'seal' – and read some high-frequency words spontaneously. Children start to identify the constituent parts of two-syllable (e.g. arm-chair, 'arm' and 'chair') and three-syllable words (e.g. computer), increase their skill in reading and spelling and create a capacity to concentrate on meaning. Children eventually learn to apply their phonic skills and knowledge to recognise and spell an increasing number of complex words (see, for example, Pinnell and Fountas 1998), such that they can read a larger range of high- and medium-frequency words.

The aim of systematic phonics work is that children progress as quickly as possible to independent reading and writing. The priority gradually shifts from 'learning to read' to 'reading to learn' as pupils secure the alphabetic code, become confident in decoding and recognising words, and begin to read for purpose and pleasure. By the age of about 7 years, the majority of children should be well on the way to becoming fluent readers by decoding words on the page automatically.

Activate your thinking!

Some reading specialists argue that the spelling-to-sound correspondences of English are so confusing that blending and sounding out is likely to lead to confusion rather than enlightenment; nevertheless, the majority of educationists believe that phonics has an important role to play in learning to read.

Good practice

In being taught phonics, children should first learn that words are constructed from *phonemes*. Pupils must also: (1) grasp the fundamental fact that phonemes can be represented by different *graphemes* – all the letters and letter combinations that represent a phoneme; for example, that f, ph and gh all apply to the phoneme /f/ as in 'fun', 'phone', 'laugh'; (2) become familiar with a small selection of common consonants – that is, all alphabet letters except a, e, i, o, u – and vowels (a, e, i, o, u, and sometimes y, as in the word 'hymn') such that they are able to blend them together in reading simple consonant–vowel–consonant (cvc) words and segment them to support spelling.

Dialogic reading

When teachers share a book with pupils, it is normal for the adult to read and the children to listen. By contrast, *dialogic reading* is posited on the assumption that children learn most from books when they are actively involved. Dialogic reading therefore involves reading *with* the child rather than reading *to* the child, in the belief that the way in which we read to children is as important as how frequently we read to them. Dialogic reading utilises three techniques: (1) asking the children 'what?' questions; (2) asking the children open-ended questions; (3) expanding upon the comments that pupils offer during the dialogic session. These three techniques are intended to encourage children to engage with the contents, talk freely about the things they hear and offer descriptions and comments about the things they see in books (e.g. using illustrations). Consequently, in dialogic reading, the adult encourages the child to become the storyteller and the adult becomes the listener, the questioner and the audience for the child. Dialogic reading therefore takes place when children and adults are having a conversation about a book.

Dialogic reading is not intended to replace reading to the class but to supplement it by implementing some of the above techniques. In your enthusiasm for dialogic reading, it pays to remember that children benefit from being read to in at least three ways: (1) they grow to love and value books; (2) they use their imaginations to envisage the situations that are being described; (3) they generate their own questions without being prompted by an adult.

Activate your thinking!

While dialogic reading is educationally defensible, it is possible for stories to be so blighted by constant analysis and adult-generated questions that they lose their ability to charm and enthral children.

Teaching spelling

There are three basic approaches to teaching spelling: (1) whole-word; (2) phonemic; (3) morphemic. The *whole-word* approach requires pupils to memorise the spelling of individual words, with the names of letters spoken out loud in order. There are no rules involved; children just receive rote information such as being told that, for example, the word 'rabbit' is spelled with the letters r-a-b-b-i-t. The advantage of whole-word spelling is for teaching words that cannot be spelled by applying simple spelling rules, for example 'tomb' or 'suit'. The disadvantage of whole-word spelling is that each word or small set of similar words (e.g. ride, side, hide) has to be taught separately, so it is quite time-consuming, and for busy teachers and assistants tends to be a rather inefficient, if generally thorough, method.

The *phonemic* approach to spelling is based on sound-symbol relationships. It involves teaching children the letters for various sounds, e.g. the sound /p/ is spelled 'p'. The main advantage of the phonemic method is that it offers generalisations for spelling many words and word parts. The phonemic approach is less appropriate when it is applied to words of more than one syllable; this is particularly true for words containing an unstressed vowel that sounds like 'uh' and could be spelled with any vowel letter. For example, the 'uh' in the word 'relative' (rel-uh-tiv) could, in theory, be spelled with any of the five vowels.

The *morphemic* approach to spelling teaches children to spell morphemes (the smallest unit of meaning) and put the units together to form words. The main advantage of using morphemes (also known as 'morphographs') is that a small number of them can be combined to form a large number of words, so the approach is most efficient for multi-syllabic words (e.g. con/tent/ed). The disadvantage of a morphemic approach is that learning to spell morphemes may depend on tricky sound-symbol and whole-word analyses.

Jones (2002) advises that there are five basic rules to help improve spelling: (1) practice makes perfect; (2) avoid trying to learn all the words at once; (3) review repeatedly; (4) practise spelling as if you expect to spell the words correctly; (5) use the words you have practised. To practise spelling a word, children can trace, copy and recall the word, or speak it out loud and then write it down, saying each letter expressively. The word is then written a second time but the last letter is omitted; then the last two letters; then the last three letters and so on. For longer words (e.g. 'understanding'), the same procedure can be followed except that the syllables (under/stand/ing) are omitted one by one.

Young (2008) suggests that collated research studies provide a broad consensus that children pass through stages of understanding in spelling, though there is disagreement about the precise nature of the stages:

1. Random symbols to represent words
2. Some sounds in words represented
3. All sounds in words represented
4. Awareness of orthographic patterns
5. Application of syllable rules
6. Application of derivational/meaning knowledge
7. Generally accurate spellings (see p. 128).

When drawing attention to a significant key word, phrase or idea, use it in a sentence and encourage the children to do the same. This process of contextualising reinforces the meaning and aids children's understanding. The strategy is particularly useful in a number of instances. First, with words that are spelt the same but pronounced differently (heteronyms) – e.g. to *wind* a clock or to feel the *wind* in your face. Second, for words that sound the same but have different meanings (homophones) – e.g. their, they're, there. Third, for words that are spelled and sounded the same but have different meanings in different contexts – e.g. to tie the *bow* on your shoe; to bend the *bow* and shoot the arrow. Finally, for unfamiliar words and phrases.

Teaching poetry

Poetry provokes a variety of reactions in children and in adults, which is probably due to the trend towards analysing and interrogating text instead of merely enjoying and relishing it for its own sake. As a result, the teaching of poetry has suffered in recent years. Pagett (2007) warns that teachers are sometimes nervous about using the poetry medium because of fears about their own ability to teach it; however, she is dismissive of such attitudes and argues that:

> Poetry can be powerful – not if it is locked in the pages of an unopened book but if it is read and engaged with. It can enable us to look afresh at fairly mundane things, affect our emotions and make us think.
>
> (p. 89)

Pagett offers a variety of practical suggestions about promoting poetry, including: (1) learning a favourite poem by heart; (2) placing poetry posters around the school with sections of poems for children to read; (3) reading poems aloud and imaginatively to children; (4) using existing models of poems to write one of the same style; (5) incorporating musical instruments into a performance; (6) supporting children's engagement through drama and art. See also Foale and Pagett (2008) for creative ideas for the use of poetry, including links with other subject areas.

Reinforcing concepts

Continuity in learning is at the heart of lesson planning and teaching. To ensure that children learn thoroughly, it is important to revise and rehearse learning episodes in such a way that pupils engage with the subject matter at a variety of levels, notably through listening to the teacher, engaging in dialogue, reading, writing, representing ideas through diagrams and drawings, acting out scenes, problem solving, and so on. For example, a common way to reinforce a concept after receiving a correct answer from a child is to repeat the answer, several times if necessary, to ensure that all the children have heard. Thus:

TEACHER:	If I have five sweets and Jenny gives me five more sweets, put your hand up if you know how many sweets I will have altogether.
CHILD (selected to answer):	Ten.
TEACHER:	That's right, Sam, well done. I'll have ten … but ten what?
CHILD:	Ten sweets.
TEACHER:	Yes, ten sweets, because five and five is ten, so five sweets and five sweets mean that I will end up with ten sweets. Let's look at some pictures to prove that Sam is correct when she says that adding five sweets to five sweets gives us ten sweets.

Notice that the teacher in the example is reinforcing the concept both verbally and diagrammatically to accommodate the children's different learning preferences. Some children can grasp a concept simply by listening, other children by speaking to another and yet others by seeing it presented visually. Less able children may need some tactile (touching) experience, so if time permits, one such child can come to the front and help the teacher while she or he counts (say) two lots of five cubes into the child's hand. Most children benefit from a combination of learning modes.

The time spent in reinforcing concepts in this way is certainly not wasted. On the contrary, coverage of the lesson content without ensuring that all the children grasp the principles leads to a flurry of questions from anxious children and disappointing outcomes when they tackle any associated tasks you put in front of them. A tentative grasp of a concept might result in children answering your questions correctly and even completing the task/activity attached to the learning; however, their understanding and grasp of the subject matter will soon evaporate unless the points are driven home, using whatever means necessary.

Responding to changing circumstances

The longer that a lesson phase continues, the less likely that the children with limited concentration will attend to what is being said. (See Chapter 12 for more information about pupils with attention deficit problems.) There is a fine line to be drawn between persevering with a lesson — refusing to be deterred by daydreamers and restless children and insisting on full attention — and curtailing what you are doing because the children's flagging attention indicates that they are bored or 'saturated' with content. To guide your decision bear in mind four points:

1.   Boredom comes because the work is irrelevant or too hard/easy to understand or you have talked too long without involving the children in something meaningful for them.
2.   There is a difference between deliberately disruptive action and restless behaviour. A danger sign is when restlessness begins to affect normally compliant children as well as the usual characters.
3.   While it is sensible to try and keep to your intended lesson timings, they should be viewed as flexible rather than inviolable.
4.   Your awareness of the class's general mood rather than the inappropriate behaviour of a few children should drive changes in lesson direction.

The lesson plan obviously has to be sufficiently flexible to accommodate a variety of different circumstances that arise during the session, though if you are inexperienced it is wise to conform as closely as possible to your plan and allocate the time accordingly. However, as you grow more confident you will find opportunity to make a larger number of on-the-spot modifications. For example, if the children take longer over tasks than anticipated or are immersed in fruitful collaboration, you may opt to extend this phase of the lesson and reduce the end phase. Similarly, one part of the lesson nearly always involves a phase of teacher questions and pupil answers, but the introduction of a small number of speculative questions (as opposed to ones requiring a correct answer) can stimulate bursts of ideas and the generation of children's own questions. Speculative questions also encourage children to make informed guesses and allow them to employ their imaginations (see Hayes 2009b: Chapter 4). To make best use of this creative energy and maximise the learning that results, you might decide to let the discussion run for a few more minutes than you planned. This approach is good educational practice and should not be confused with slackness. If your lesson is being observed it is sensible to state clearly in your plan that 'spontaneous opportunities will be followed through as appropriate' so that the evaluator does not think that you have lost your way.

Activate your thinking!

If you don't explain to the observer the reasons for your subtle changes of direction during the lesson, it might be concluded that you were being wayward rather than responsive.

Good practice

Children cannot be expected to maintain a high level of concentration throughout every moment of a lesson, especially during the middle part of the session, so try to offer some variety in teaching and learning, utilising the VAK principle: visual, auditory and kinaesthetic (hands-on).

Using whiteboards and fans

It has become common practice to make use of child-sized plastic 'whiteboards' and marker pens to promote a higher level of participation, principally during maths lessons. In principle, this method has much to commend it; unfortunately, practical considerations (mess from pens, wiping boards, pens that run dry, etc.) detract from their effective use. If children are using individual whiteboards and markers, suggest from time to time that they show what they have written to a friend before showing it to you. This strategy has three advantages. First, it breaks the monotony of 'write it down and show me'. Second, it helps less able children to gain confidence from working co-operatively. Third, it gives you space to look around more carefully than is normally possible to see if any children are uncertain or mistaken. If you note that a child or some children have made an error, it might be appropriate to say something to the effect: 'Well done everyone for being so sensible. I noticed that one or two people got a bit muddled about...' rather than drawing attention to specific individuals. A teaching assistant, suitably positioned, can send non-verbal messages to you about what is happening.

Response boards (whiteboards) and number 'fans' are used during interactive sessions to elicit a whole-class response to a question, rather than merely selecting a single child whose hand is up in the air. There are practical points to consider when using whiteboards (see also later in this chapter):

- It is essential to have a supply and reserve supply of pens.
- Forbid children to elaborate what they write by drawing fancy patterns on the board.
- The boards need to be properly and regularly cleaned.
- Watch for less confident children that conceal their answers from you by keeping the board out of view.
- Be aware that less confident children will sit so that they can see what a more able child writes, then hurriedly copy before raising the board.

There are also a number of practical points to bear in mind with use of fans:

- Small fingers may struggle to manipulate the fan.
- It is difficult to scan all of the children to see how many answers are correct and if there are errors.

- Younger children may reverse numbers.
- The fans need to be put to one side when finished with or they may be used as . . . fans.

The advantage of whiteboards and fans is that they have the potential to stimulate a higher degree of participation from a larger number of children. However, as they can generally be used only for 'closed answers' (where there is only one correct response) they encourage teachers to use fewer speculative or 'let us imagine' or propositional questions. Consequently, the session becomes dominated by questions asked by the teacher and correct/incorrect answers given by the children. This scenario can lead to an extreme situation in which the teacher is using question-and-answer to extract responses, when it would be much easier to tell the children directly. Another factor that can intrude into the dynamics of questioning is that whereas it is important to praise good responses, offering equally effusive praise to unexceptional replies demeans the commendation given for outstanding ones.

Activate your thinking!

Do you ever ask a question when you should be giving information? Do you ever provide information when you should be asking a question?

Organisational skills

Organising and managing for learning is dealt with more fully in Chapter 10. Suffice it to say at this point that clarification of task, specificity about expectations, appropriate intervention, support for writing tasks and knowing how to end a session successfully are basic skills that every teacher must acquire.

Specificity about your expectations

It is important to distinguish between instructional and invitational comments. The instructional comment anticipates compliance. The invitational comment is a recommendation rather than a command. Inexperienced teachers sometimes confuse the two and find that they have to revert to an instruction after initially using an invitation. It is possible for what is intended as a *command* to end up sounding like a *choice* or an *aspiration*. For example, consider the difference between:

'Can you keep your fingers away from the equipment, please?' (choice)
'I'd like it if you did not touch the equipment' (aspiration)
'Do not touch the equipment and keep your hands under the table' (command).

It is important to be clear in your own mind which of these three types of statements (choice, aspiration, command) you are employing and make it equally clear to the children what you want. Basically, if you intend something to happen, use the command preference; if you want children to think about their actions, use an aspirational statement; if you want them to make the final decision, offer a choice of options.

Clarifying tasks

Inexperienced teachers can be tempted to reduce the length of the introductory phase and get children working on the set tasks quickly in the hope that lesson management will be more straightforward. However, curtailing the instructional element is often counter-productive, as the lesson lacks a strong foundation; time is then wasted later in answering children's queries and rectifying misunderstandings. When children say that they 'don't get it' or sit staring miserably at the page, you have to determine whether they are bored, confused or out of their depth. More often than not the child does not have the confidence or the knowledge/understanding to tackle the work, in which case you have to decide which of the two reasons (low confidence or weak knowledge) is relevant, a job made much easier when you get to know the class. Some children are academically capable but very tentative when faced with a task to complete. This category of children are doubly disadvantaged because they feel (probably correctly) that they ought to be able to do the work and hesitate to ask an adult for fear of being told so. By contrast, a less able child may feel more comfortable asking for adult support. It is best to engage the timid academic child (regardless of ability) in a cheerful manner, using a question-and-answer approach to reveal the nature of the learning blockage. In doing so, you should avoid giving the impression that you are surprised or disappointed with the child. Simply direct them, check that they understand and say, 'Well done!'

Intervening appropriately

Decisions about how much to intervene when children are working require considerable discernment (see also Chapter 11 regarding assessment issues). Sometimes children do not understand the concepts involved. Sometimes they have not grasped the nature of the task. Over-eagerness on your part to assist a child can mean that the child does not have sufficient opportunity to flex his or her intellectual muscle and engage with the challenge.

On the other hand, reluctance to offer help to pupils can mean that the child is left floundering and becomes demoralised or demotivated as a result. As a rule, if you have explained the task carefully, clarified procedural issues and provided appropriate resources, there is every reason to assume that all the children will be able to make a reasonable effort to tackle the work that you have set them to do. Their failure or inability to engage with the tasks and activities should not be taken as a signal that they cannot or that they will not try. It might be that children lack the confidence to proceed, in which case your intervention (explaining, directing, posing questions, prescribing solutions, etc.) offers the necessary reassurance for them to move ahead assuredly. Once children are busy addressing the challenges before them, your role changes from one of manager to assessor. That is, you cease offering advice and support about how to go about doing the work and begin to make a judgement about the understanding that a child demonstrates or skill level attained.

Offering support for writing tasks

After enjoying a stimulating interactive session, children are often asked to record their ideas on paper. More able and confident children can usually make a 'running start' at such a task, but other children may spend some time in applying themselves, either because they are unsure what to write or because they are aware of their shortcomings as writers and hesitant to commit themselves in print. Teachers differ in the extent to which they believe it appropriate to 'pump prime' the children so that they can make a more positive beginning. Some teachers feel that it is important to give the children time to mentally grapple with their ideas and learn significant lessons about 'learning to learn' as a result. Other teachers foster peer support, whereby children work in pairs to share ideas before recording anything. Yet other teachers provide structured guidance in the belief that leaving less confident children to struggle on unaided invites restless behaviour and little being achieved during the lesson. All three approaches are appropriate on different occasions and rely on professional judgement as to the best course of action.

The most effective teachers discern when it is best to leave children alone to grapple with their ideas, when to promote peer support and when to intervene directly and give specific guidance. You might decide that it is sensible to offer the children some 'starters' in the way of (say) opening phrases or an outline consisting of subheadings as a means of avoiding the 'blank page' syndrome that sometimes has a paralysing effect on children. For younger children, the same principles obtain, though there may be several adults to provide ideas and encourage children to think for themselves. A lot depends on what you are trying to achieve in the lesson or sessions. If you want a tailored piece of writing using a specific writing 'frame' then it is probably appropriate to offer closely structured support and guidance, such as supplying key vocabulary (written on cards, say), suggesting phrases that will enhance the quality of the writing and insisting on correct presentation. If the work is being used for formal assessment purposes, then you will need to spend much longer in explaining the task so that subsequent adult intervention is kept to the absolute minimum and the children are left to cope in the best way they can (see Table 9.1). Preparation for national tests is one such example of when the non–intervention approach is used. See QCA (2009) for information about writing assessment guidelines ('assessment of writing'). See also in this volume, 'Encouraging children to write', Chapter 4 and 'Writing frames', Chapter 6.

Lesson ending

Most lessons incorporate a plenary (also known as 'lesson review', see earlier in this chapter) as a matter of course, but it is important to be clear about its purpose. For example, the following are common possibilities (with nominal times attached to each):

- a brief time to celebrate achievement and give a few morale-boosting comments (two or three minutes);
- a time to share a few examples of good practice; for example, reading aloud samples of written work, holding up pictures/diagrams and pinpointing their qualities (five–ten minutes);
- a longer time to 'report back' findings randomly from (say) a science investigation (ten–twelve minutes);
- an extended time for representatives from groups to report back and demonstrate outcomes to the other groups (twelve–fifteen minutes).

TABLE 9.1 Support for tasks

TYPE OF TASK	PREPARATION	ADULT INVOLVEMENT	OUTCOME
Formally assessed	Exact instructions	Overseeing completion	Marks and grades
Specified	Task allocation	Intervention and support	Criteria-evaluated
Creative	Discussing options	Advisory role	Collaborative endeavour

After the above and before clearing away, invoke a twenty-second 'freeze' (no-one moves) while you explain that nobody leaves before the room is spick and span. You will need to ensure, however, that in their haste the children don't cut corners and cram items into trays and containers. It is also right to insist that the children put items not only in the proper place but also correctly orientated. For example, that books have the main title showing, book spines are upright, uncompleted work is face up with the child's name clearly visible, and so on. These procedural niceties are not being fussy but contribute to an orderly well-run classroom that benefits you and the children.

Activate your thinking!

It is worth inculcating basic, clean working habits into your lessons from the outset. Attention to small but important details makes a large difference to classroom efficiency, such as insisting that aprons are folded before being carefully placed into a box or hooked properly on to pegs and not allowed to slide on to the cloakroom floor. Naturally, if food is involved the strictest hygiene must be observed.

Good practice

Use a 'pat yourself on the knee' as an alternative to 'pat yourself on the back' when the class has done well. If you ask the children to clap for any reason, teach them how to do it using their middle three fingers on a flat palm. This technique gives a clearer, sharper tone to the clap and minimises the chances of a cacophony.

Instruction

The importance of establishing learning objectives and the need to clarify learning intentions for the children in guiding lesson planning was emphasised earlier in this chapter, together with a caution that it was possible for children to spend time engaged in activities without actually learning very much. One of the direct teaching strategies that aims to combat this unsatisfactory state of affairs is through *instruction*. Despite the rather dated sound to the word, instruction is an essential part of effective teaching and a necessary skill for every teacher. Instruction takes a variety of forms but is associated with one or more of three interrelated approaches: namely, explanation, exposition and demonstration. Thus:

Explanation

Explanation is a method by which a teacher offers information, explores situations and justifies decisions or positions in a rational, structured manner. It is a technique often used in response to the question 'why?' and frequently employs examples to illustrate key points. Explanations must pay careful attention to the age of the children by using appropriate language and terminology. As explanations rely solely on the spoken word, the information must be presented in such a way that children are given time to absorb what is said, think about the implications and ask questions of clarification. Like all good teaching, explanations should build on the children's existing knowledge and understanding.

Exposition

Exposition is a step up from explanation, involving graphic illustrations, critique or commentary on an activity or a set of principles. Exposition is literally an 'exposing' or 'opening up' of a position, as viewed from a variety of perspectives. During exposition, teachers use persuasion, project their personalities into the verbal element and exhibit a little flamboyance or indulge their enthusiasms. For instance, an exposition could focus upon the harmful exploitation of indigenous populations by foreign explorers. In this case, illustrations might include statistical details of economies before and after foreign intervention, a critique of the benefits and losses which result and encouragement for the children to raise their own questions after carefully considering the issues. With younger children, an exposition may deal with issues of road safety, healthy eating or moral qualities such as kindness. It is worth noting that the main feature of *expositional writing* is its explanatory purpose.

Activate your thinking!

Part of a teacher's skill of exposition lies in knowing when to stop talking because the pupils have stopped listening (Haydn 2006: 126).

Haydn, T. (2006) *Managing Pupil Behaviour*, Abingdon: Routledge.

Demonstration

Demonstration includes elements of exposition but makes use of more varied resources and equipment, together with presentations of the techniques, skills or procedures associated with the activity. For instance, a teacher may demonstrate the correct handling and techniques associated with a variety of percussion instruments or the way to access an index or think strategically in a games session. Demonstration depends on the teacher having a firm grasp of the processes and able to show them to an audience at the same time as talking them through the stages, so it requires that the teacher possesses a firm grasp of content. A summary of the three types of instruction is shown in Table 9.2.

Ways to enhance instruction

Like any other approach used obsessively, direct instructional teaching can lose its freshness and become another tiresome teaching method so, as with other teaching skills, the guiding principle should be 'appropriateness for purpose'. Instruction can be enhanced in many different ways, as follows.

Keep the monologue succinct. Avoid droning on and on until the children lose interest. Children sometimes appear to be listening, when they have 'switched off 'and are daydreaming. Making

TABLE 9.2 Forms of instruction

TYPE	VERBAL ELEMENT	PRACTICAL ELEMENT	VISUAL ELEMENT
Explanation	Major	Minor	Minor
Exposition	Major	Minor	Major
Demonstration	Minor	Major	Major

a provisional decision in your lesson planning about the amount of time you intend to spend on the instruction will act as a constraint on your excessive use of monologue.

Concentrate on gaining good eye contact with as wide a range of children as possible. It is tempting to select the dependable children to answer questions, respond to your points and to offer the contributors positive non-verbal reinforcement (such as nods, smiles and sitting erect) while avoiding the same level of interaction with the others. In an interactive lesson phase you should make it your aim to catch the eye of every child as often as possible. You can increase the quality of the interaction by widening your own eyes and brightening your face when you look at a child and momentarily holding their eyes with your own without making them feel uncomfortable.

Pause from time to time to recap, allow questions, and encourage pupils to discuss with their partners. In doing so, it is important to guide children into what precisely they should be discussing and how to go about it. You will also need to set a time limit, but don't be surprised if it is difficult to restore order. The use of a small tinkling bell or similar device to indicate a thirty-second warning before they need to attend to what you are saying works surprisingly well.

Distinguish between children exchanging comments during an exposition (due to boredom or uncertainty) and the excited buzz of chatter that may occur due to their enthusiasm about the ideas being presented. Inexperienced teachers become unsettled if children start to exchange comments during the presentation, assuming it to be the start of misbehaviour. It is not worth getting annoyed with the children concerned unless it is obviously a wilful action. Instead, try to catch their eyes while continuing with the exposition and give a little shake of the head to indicate your displeasure. If normally sensible children start talking it is often the case that they are excited about an aspect of the lesson rather than bored. A simple 'Hold on, girls, please, you will get your chance to say something in a moment' (or similar) is normally sufficient to restore order.

Deal as calmly as possible with any inappropriate comments from pupils without losing the flow of ideas. Children sometimes call out because they cannot contain themselves, sometimes because they forget that they should remain silent and occasionally because they are being mischievous. You have to make a rapid decision about the reason for the comments and respond appropriately. For instance, holding your arm outstretched, palm facing the transgressor, will usually curtail them speaking. Meanwhile, you can continue with the instruction.

Ensure that resources are close at hand before the session begins. Their availability is an important factor in successful exposition and, especially, in demonstration. It pays to think through resource issues carefully beforehand. Efficient use of resources not only facilitates a smooth passage for your teaching but also promotes a strong sense of security among the children as they see that you are coping confidently. Make sure that they are easily available and you have a flat surface to place them on.

Use children's excitement positively. For instance you can say something like: 'I'm glad that my idea appeals to you. From your reaction, I shall expect you to come up with plenty of useful suggestions.' Although a small number of children get carried away with enthusiasm, especially when they observe a stimulating practical demonstration, console yourself with the thought that it is better for them to be excited than to be bored.

Avoid following a stimulating period of instruction with a mundane activity. For instance, children quickly lose enthusiasm when a stimulating visual demonstration is followed by a dull writing task. There is a time for simply savouring the moment, which generates interest among the children and stimulates constructive talk (Coultas 2007).

Keep pupils engaged with the topic. Morgan and Saxton (1991) stress that all effective teaching depends upon recognising that effective learning takes place when pupils are active participants in what is going on. In this respect, lively exchanges and use of interesting questions from teachers and pupils have the power 'to generate ideas, spur the imagination and incite both teacher and (pupils) into a shared creative learning experience' (p. 7). Unlike adult-driven learning that relies on extrinsic motivation (sometimes referred to by the awkward word 'behaviourism'), an approach involving significant restructuring of existing cognitive structures through a major personal investment on the part of the learner that uses strategies that help learners actively to assimilate and accommodate new material is known as 'constructivism' (see also Wray 2006).

Consolidation

Instruction is often followed by consolidation of children's learning using strategies such as *imitation*, whereby the children copy the teacher's technique. For instance, 5-year-olds may copy particular letter shapes; 10-year-olds may replicate a specific catching technique in PE. Imitation is then followed by *practice*, in which children perfect the technique. For instance, 5-year-olds use the letters in a variety of interesting contexts; 10-year-olds spend time catching the ball when it is thrown to them from different positions. Other reinforcement activities include *experimentation*, where children are given the opportunity to plan and execute their own ideas. For instance, 5-year-olds make patterns with the letter shapes; 10-year-olds make up their own game incorporating the catching technique. It may also be appropriate to encourage children to become even more innovative, where children use the ideas for a variety of purposes and outcomes. For instance, 5-year-olds produce paintings based on the letter shapes; 10-year-olds develop variants on the basic catching technique by formulating rules and organising a simple competition.

Questioning

Types of questions

Teachers ask dozens of questions each day in their teaching, broadly categorised into two types. *Closed* questions have a single correct answer. *Open* questions require children to speculate and evaluate alternatives. Both open and closed forms of questioning are widely used in teaching, though there is a tendency for teachers to use far more closed than open ones.

Teachers normally ask closed questions when they want to stir children's memories about previous work or to assess their knowledge and understanding of a specified content. Teachers use *open* questions as a means of stimulating interest and discussion, and extending children's thinking by making them consider possibilities that lie beyond those that are immediately obvious. Both types of question have their place in teaching, though the overuse of closed questioning can make children unsettled if they know that the teacher is looking for a specific response. The best teachers do not become irritated by wrong answers but try to probe the reasons for the incorrect responses.

Medwell (2007) argues that there are two types of wrong answers, 'those due to carelessness or lack of effort, and those due to a lack of understanding or knowledge'. She suggests that an appropriate strategy for dealing with the first category of response (carelessness or lack of effort) is to move on to the next child as quickly as possible. In the second category of response she advises, 'prompt the child by simplifying the question [perhaps breaking it into a series of small steps] or hinting' (p. 65, author's brackets). Of course, you still have to make a judgement about which of the two categories applies before taking appropriate action; such judgement is a skill that matures with time and experience, and inevitably you will occasionally reach incorrect conclusions. Sometimes, in the pressure of an intensive interactive session or in a trainee's desire to ensure that the lesson maintains pace, the opportunity to follow up children's errors during 'closed' questioning' is missed.

By contrast, *open* questions invite children to be more adventurous in their responses, though open/speculative questions require more time for answers, so fewer of them can be posed. Sotto (1994) reminds us that it is useful to follow a factual question with a more probing one:

> Teachers might first ask a question, which requires the recall of information, but good teachers follow that with a question which requires a reasoned reply. No job in the world can be done by (only) remembering facts.

> (p. 175)

To take a simple example of this, the closed question might be 'Which city in America is known as The Big Apple?' After receiving the correct answer (New York), follow-up questions might include: 'Where do you think the name might have come from?' or 'Why isn't New York the capital city of America?' or 'If New York changed its name, what would you call it, and why?'

Questions can also be classified as *productive* or *unproductive* with respect to pupil learning. Productive questions include: (1) those where children answer thoughtfully; (2) those that scrutinise issues closely; (3) those where further information or clarification is sought; and (4) those in which the children have to consider and evaluate propositions. There is also a value in posing more hypothetical questions for older children in particular, by which they are encouraged to consider situations and convey opinions, values and perceptions.

Unproductive questions, on the other hand, are poorly focused, require a right or wrong answer (unless they are being used as an assessment tool) and oblige the children to guess what the adult is thinking, in which case the teacher spends a sizeable amount of time selecting from raised hands until a correct answer is (eventually) given. The productive/unproductive polarisation is not absolute, as your ability to put across the question, make it relevant to the children and interact with the class also contributes to the value of the question and its usefulness in learning. Your personality, zest and commitment can sometimes transform even the dullest situation into a stimulating one.

Questioning techniques

As in so many teaching situations, careful listening and affirming comments are prerequisites for successful interaction and creating a positive climate of 'yes, have a go', as opposed to 'dare not even try'. Research on the curriculum at the University of Southampton (2002) concluded that the questioning technique falls into five broad headings. First, it provides increasing attainment through developing wider skills associated with literacy and communication, discussion and enabling pupils to examine/question their own learning. Second, it enhances retention, such as reinforcement that can happen during the plenary. Third, it encourages participation. Fourth, it aids classroom management, such as keeping pupils actively involved in lessons. Fifth, it supports personal and social education, such as encouraging self-assessment, team-building, developing enquiring attitudes and expressing personal opinions.

Improving your questioning technique

Questioning skills do not come naturally for most teachers: they have to be practised and developed in the same way as any other teaching ability. Younger children also have to be inculcated into the process of question-and-answer, as some of them may be used only to answering straightforward questions spontaneously. As a result, they find rhetorical questions difficult to handle and may, in their excitement, call out answers randomly. As children get older, their attitude towards teachers' questions depends not only upon their knowledge of the area under scrutiny but also whether they feel confident to answer the particular questions. This reluctance is particularly evident if the children are anxious about the adult response that an incorrect answer might induce. Children will understandably prefer to say nothing if they feel that their responses will be trivialised or if they fear humiliation in front of their classmates.

Inexperienced teachers do not always take full advantage of the opportunities that questioning offers. Poor practice includes failing to acknowledge correct responses by pupils, not waiting for their attention before asking the questions and not encouraging pupils to ask their own questions. Less experienced teachers also tend to be impatient in waiting for answers from pupils, ask questions in a monotone, allow the pace of the lesson to falter and forget to praise genuine efforts as well as correct answers. Fisher (2005) claims that a common response to why teachers use questions is that they motivate, test knowledge and promote reflection, analysis and enquiry. However, the practice, he argues, differs markedly from the theory. Thus:

> Questions are supposed to offer intellectual challenge, to encourage children to think. In practice, many of the questions teachers use inhibit intellectual activity and save pupils from the effort of having to think.

(p. 17)

Fisher's stern warning is worth heeding.

It is part of your role as teacher to encourage every child to participate in question-and-answer sessions and to acknowledge every opinion that is offered. Importantly, implement a code of conduct from the start in which mockery and sneering at someone's answer is strictly forbidden. Kerry (1998) insists that the children must be convinced that the aim of questioning is to share knowledge and ideas within a supportive framework where each serious comment is valued. The creation of a learning environment in which children are encouraged to respond to open questions and teachers display a genuine interest in their answers is therefore essential. Harlen (2000) claims that this supportive style of teaching motivates children to answer questions without fear attached to being wrong. In this way, misunderstandings can be used constructively as a basis for formative assessment and future learning.

Open-ended provocative questions are less easy for trainee teachers to employ because they are difficult to think of and children's responses are harder to manage. The teacher not only has to select a child to give his or her response but also has to *evaluate* the quality and appropriateness of the reply. This process requires alertness, careful listening to what children say and sensitivity when trying to encourage responses from children.

Time factors

The length of time that teachers are prepared to wait for answers to questions is a key factor governing the success of the interactions. Some children think slowly and deeply, while others are more spontaneous and willing to risk making mistakes for the pleasure of being chosen by the teacher to give the answer. Owing to the emphasis on maintaining pace in lessons, a lot of teachers are nervous about silence and giving children time to consider their replies. Nevertheless, allowing children to cogitate for longer improves the quality of their answers, whereas peppering questions at them in the expectation of immediate responses tends to lead to superficiality – though there is a place for rapid questioning, especially with older primary pupils. Waiting for a little longer for an answer is likely to result in answers of a higher cognitive value and to produce deep, rather than shallow, forms of learning. It is, therefore, essential to be clear in your mind about the purpose that the questions are serving and adjust them accordingly. See, for example, advice in Baumfield and Mroz (2004) and Walsh and Sattes (2005). You have the difficult task of trying to balance the benefits gained from giving additional time for answers against the danger that a drop in tempo might result in restless behaviour.

Activate your thinking!

How many questions do you ask in each lesson? How many are necessary? How many are productive?

Good practice

To avoid marginalising the less able and less confident children, employ the following strategies occasionally:

> Offer an either/or pair of answers and ask children to wink at you with one eye if they agree with the first and both eyes if they agree with the second.
> Ask a question but only allow responses from a defined group of children (such as those with birthdays in months ending with 'ber').
> Ask a question, give the children ten seconds to whisper what they think in their neighbour's ear then reveal the answer before asking them to raise their hands if their neighbours were correct.

Use of the board

Despite the availability of overhead projectors, interactive whiteboards, computers and other sophisticated teaching aids, many teachers still rely on some form of wall–mounted or free-standing board, normally a 'whiteboard'. There are many different ways of using (and mis-using) the whiteboard; this section provides some suggestions for more effective use. The following basic principles should be adhered to carefully.

Ensure that the surface is kept in good condition

There is little point in trying to write on a greasy or scratched surface; it sets a poor example, ruins the marker and makes accurate writing or drawing a problem. A few minutes spent preparing the board each week pays dividends.

Have the proper markers available

Some boards require special markers and will be damaged by others. It is essential to replace tops firmly to prolong the life of the pen. (This practice also applies to children when they use miniature whiteboards.)

Check that the board is at an appropriate height

It is easy for children to strain their eyes or adopt an uncomfortable position in order to see clearly, so be aware of this fact when organising seating in the room. Glare on the board also reduces visibility and might make it unreadable.

Avoid damage

Although a fixed board is a tempting target for special displays, the damage inflicted by staples, pins and adhesive can be irreparable. Fitness for purpose must be the mantra.

Help with copying from the board

Many children find it difficult to copy from a board or screen owing to the need to look up and down while transferring information to paper. If asked to write quickly, less able pupils are likely to make spelling, punctuation and letter formation errors. Furthermore, teachers' handwriting varies in quality. If children need to read something off the board, teachers must ensure that their writing is large and clear. In particular, children seated at the sides of the classroom can find it difficult to read certain words if the light creates a glare. It pays to sit with the children for a time to understand the problems they may be experiencing.

Use the board as a memory aid

In direct teaching to a group or the whole class, the teacher can use a board as a memory aid by writing a list and referring to each point in turn. Sometimes the board is useful to demonstrate the correct way to set out a piece of work (in maths, say) or the heading for a letter. Similarly, it is useful to write up spellings or list words suggested by children in advance of free writing sessions. Some teachers encourage the children to use the whiteboard during a lesson for noting ideas or recording findings.

Finally, the above uses are valid and can facilitate learning, but there are times when board work can lead to bored work. For instance, it is not sensible to expect a class of thirty children to strain their necks or have to keep coming up to the board to read something because it cannot be seen from the back of the room. Similarly, too much copying can dull the mind and create an intellectual malaise.

Activate your thinking!

If copying from the board presents so many problems, is it really worth incorporating the technique into your lesson?

Good practice

To check that all children can see adequately it is worth positioning yourself before the lesson begins at different points around the room (preferably at chair height) to see whether you can see without squinting.

Using worksheets

'Worksheets' (also known as activity sheets) is a general term used to describe written material that has been produced by a teacher, downloaded from one of the many websites or taken from one of the activity books that allow multiple copying. (*Note:* replication of copyright material without permission is an offence.) To a certain extent, information technology (especially computers) has reduced the need for worksheets and some schools have a policy that discourages or even prohibits them. Nevertheless, worksheets can be extremely useful in teaching and tend to fall into one or more of four broad categories:

Information sheets that children can use as a starting point for thematic or topic work. Typically, the sheets will give some background information and children will be encouraged to research further (from a book, the library or the Internet) to gain fresh insights or enlarge their knowledge base.

Practice sheets that give examples for children to work through to reinforce previous learning. Computation, phonics and English grammar are commonly practised in this way. Practice sheets sometimes require a series of correct answers – for example, to correctly insert an appropriate word or phrase.

Investigation sheets that set out starting points and problems for children to solve using their own ideas and ingenuity. Investigative sheets are normally used by groups of children engaged on a collaborative project.

Task sheets contain the requirements for completion of a project, areas to investigate, problems to solve or questions that serve a variety of different functions. Task sheets are used in situations in which pupils are expected to demonstrate a high level of autonomy in organising their work. For instance, a task sheet might set out what the teacher expects each child to complete over the course of a day or have space for agreed pupil targets.

Worksheets provide a useful tool in the teaching and learning programme. They ensure that teachers plan ahead, think through the work and, if the teacher creates the sheet, relate closely to the work in hand. Unfortunately, there is sometimes a tendency to use worksheets obsessively and neglect other important teaching strategies. In particular, practice sheets can be downloaded electronically and used as a means of keeping children occupied or as a substitute for proper teaching strategies such as instruction, exploration and collaborative learning. Although the first few minutes of using worksheets are normally orderly, the lesson sometimes degenerates into a situation in which restless and frustrated children lose heart and regularly call upon (increasingly overworked) adults for assistance. There is also a challenge in ensuring that the sheet is appropriate for the pupils using it; differentiation is a key issue to consider when deciding whether or not to use a worksheet.

If used sparingly and imaginatively, worksheets can provide children with a ready source of information, opportunities to practise work examples, a starting point for more innovative work or a reminder about key aspects of the work. However, a number of safeguards are needed:

- They should not be seen as a substitute for other teaching methods but rather as a supplement.
- A limited amount of information should be placed on a single sheet.
- The purpose of the sheet should be clearly explained to the children.
- Practice sheets must allow for variations in ability, beginning with easier examples and gradually increasing the level of difficulty or using separate sheets, each one slightly more demanding than the previous one.
- The teacher should try to review the key points following their completion rather than just collecting them in for marking.
- Opportunities for collaboration should be exploited.

Worksheets can be very useful for a busy teacher but there are hidden time costs: preparation, reproduction and assessment. There are large numbers of worksheets available from different sources but they must always be contextualised to serve the particular learning needs of the class. Too often, worksheets end up half-completed, languishing in children's trays until the next time they clear them out, when they are discarded without exploiting their value. Although worksheets provide a tempting option as a 'holding task' for a group while dealing with other children who require direct teaching or supervision, these occasions should be kept to a minimum.

Case study

When he commenced the placement, Bart found that the class teacher made handling 5- and 6-year-olds look simple. Perhaps teaching young children wouldn't be so bad after all. From the moment Bart was first introduced to the children, he was amazed at how small they were. In turn, they stared up at his six-foot frame with wide-eyed astonishment. One little girl asked him if he was the new head teacher. A diminutive little boy called Devon (who was to be the bane of Bart's life in school) pointed at him and screeched out that he was a giant! The class teacher, Mrs Williams, introduced him to the class as a 'new teacher who has come to help us', which made Bart feel much better. He hated being referred to as a student. The first few days came and went, and as he settled into the situation Bart realised that there was a lot more to teaching young children than he had imagined. For a start, they were much more dependent on adults than he had been used to with older primary children. Their concentration span was shorter and they lacked some of the most basic skills that he had taken for granted with 10-year-olds. Procedural matters had to be explained carefully and some children still got into a muddle. On the other hand, Bart found himself enjoying the attention he received as the only male teacher in the school and quite liked the spontaneity that characterised certain parts of the day. He also noticed, and was a bit surprised by, the formality of some teaching. Bart had in his mind that little children just played. Mrs Williams explained that although she would not choose to teach so formally, it was important that the children did well in tests or the school could be marked out as a 'failing school'. Bart shuddered at the prospect.

After a few days getting to know the children by working with small groups, Bart began to teach his first whole-class lessons. He used a modified version of the plans that had been successful with older children and decided to demonstrate his interactive abilities as early as possible to impress the class teacher and establish his authority. The topic was 'Colour' and Bart had a large poster of a rainbow to use as a visual aid. He sat the children on the carpet and they waited with anticipation. Mrs Williams sat behind them, smiling encouragingly. Bart began briskly, asking the children to tell him about their favourite colours. He had not anticipated the flurry of answers that came flying at him. Some children shouted out their preferences, one little girl began telling him that her bedroom had been painted yellow, and Devon, the diminutive boy, started laughing and shaking his head from side to side. Bart was stunned and held up his hand for them to stop, urging them to sit still and be sensible. The noise subsided, but Amy stood up and tapped him on the shoulder to tell him that her bedroom was also painted yellow. Bart did not want to know. Mrs Williams uttered a few 'shush' sounds and spoke directly to Devon, who immediately sat bolt upright before shrinking and burying his face in his lap.

Bart continued and got out the picture of the rainbow from behind the table, pinning it to the board. Several children called out what it was and several claimed loudly to have seen a rainbow yesterday. One boy said that his uncle had flown through a rainbow, another pointed out that the corner of the picture was creased. Bart smiled and pretended to be pleased that the children were responding so enthusiastically. Inwardly he felt vulnerable and wanted to be stern but feared that it might be inappropriate with young children, so he commended them instead: 'Well done; well done, everybody.' He then read the class a short poem about a rainbow in a slightly breathless and exaggerated way to keep their attention, a strategy that was only partially successful.

Bart decided to take a direct approach to impose some order and began talking rapidly, telling the children about features of the rainbow and how it was created. He did not venture further questions and talked 'over' the children when they tried to interrupt him. After about ten more minutes, Bart told them to sit up and listen, which to his relief they did almost immediately. He explained that they were going to draw a picture of the rainbow and complete a worksheet (a scaled-down version of one that he had originally prepared himself for older children) in which they had to match words and provide the correct 'describing' words for blanks in sentences. The children moved to their tables and got down to work very quickly. Bart was pleased at first but soon became alarmed to see that a number of children were using the wrong colours for the rainbow; others were pressing the pastel crayons too heavily and a few were colouring the words that they were supposed to use for sentences. The TA asked him gently whether he wanted the children to work alone or together (he said he didn't mind). He heard Mrs Williams tell her group that they should try on spare paper before attempting the proper drawing. Two children told Bart that they didn't know how to draw a rainbow. A steady drift of children wandered from their seats to look more closely at the picture on the board before skipping back, adding some detail, then returning to the board again. Bart had simply not expected that such an apparently simple task would become so involved.

To Bart's credit, and with the patient assistance of the class teacher and assistant, he managed to hold the lesson together and was even able to bring the children together at the end for a useful sharing time. After the lesson he was extremely relieved to see the children leave for playtime and felt quite exhausted. Mrs Williams gave him a reassuring smile and steered him towards the staffroom for a cup of tea.

After school that night, Bart and Mrs Williams sat down and talked about the lesson. 'I know it was a disaster,' Bart began, but the teacher shook her head. 'It wasn't a disaster at all. It's not at all easy working with young children, and very tiring.' Bart had begun to realise the truth of what she said, and when he went home that evening and was asked how the day had gone he admitted ruefully that it had been a challenge. 'I told you it wasn't easy with younger ones,' sympathised one of the female students. Bart agreed and realised that he would need to think very hard about his teaching approach and attitude if he were to do better next time.

Evaluation of Bart's lesson

- Planning for younger children needed to take account of their experience and existing knowledge; modifying an old plan from Key Stage 2 was unsatisfactory.
- It was a good idea to use a question to invite interest, but also important to clarify the ground rules for children's responses.
- The use of an interesting story involving a rainbow was a useful alternative strategy for gaining interest and raising questions.
- The direct transmission of information (keeping on talking so that the children do not) was useful as a temporary control strategy but hopeless in terms of children's learning.
- Young children need more time to absorb, reflect and explore concepts, so it was important for him to speak quite slowly and deliberately, to pause between statements and use appropriate vocabulary.
- Clarification of task demands and expectations needed to be reinforced to prevent a tide of queries from children.
- It was important to be aware of children with special learning and emotional needs, such as those who lacked confidence and needed a lot of reassurance.
- It takes time to settle down with a new class; young children have an insatiable curiosity, particularly about a new grown-up in the class.

Footnote
After qualifying, Bart was appointed as a teacher for a Year 1 class.

Further reading for Chapter 9

Butt, G. (2006) *Lesson Planning*, London: Continuum.
Contains a lot of advice, schedules and suggestions for effective planning.
Davies, A. (2007) *Storytelling in the Classroom*, London: Sage.
Helps primary teachers to develop their storytelling, including how to create the plot and characters, enhance presentation techniques and use voice and expression effectively.
Lewis, M. and Ellis, S. (2006) *Phonics*, London: Sage.
Offers advice on how to understand the various theories about phonics and applying the knowledge in practical teaching.
Morgan, N. and Saxton, J. (1994) *Asking Better Questions*, Markham, Ontario: Pembroke Publishers.
The authors list and describe an extensive typology of question types as a means of encouraging teachers to consider the varied ways in which they use questioning techniques.
Overall, L. and Sangster, M. (2003) *Primary Teacher's Handbook*, London: Continuum.
This book is an A to Z of guidance that includes suggestions about teaching skills that primary teachers use regularly.
Watkin, N. and Ahrenfelt, J. (2006) *100 Ideas for Essential Teaching Skills*, London: Continuum.
Ideas include designing challenging lessons, keeping pupils interested and on task, and organising the teaching to control challenging behaviour.

Organising and Managing Learning

Introduction

We noted in Chapters 8 and 9 that learning is neither a random process nor something that can be reduced to a simple formula. Teachers need to be clear about the conditions that contribute to a vibrant learning environment, including knowledge and insights about the best way to organise and manage lessons. Broadly speaking, organisation is the structure that facilitates effective teaching and learning; management is the means by which it is achieved. The chapter explores the many facets of high quality organising and the different forms of managing to facilitate teaching opportunities and promote sound learning and discipline. The content includes advice and suggestions about the use of time, the special needs of younger pupils, frameworks for teaching literacy and mathematics, and the use of ICT. The final section introduces the concept of managing oneself and surviving in the job.

Effective teaching

We noted in earlier chapters that successful lessons do not happen by chance; they result from a combination of careful planning, sensible organisation, skilful lesson management and enthusiastic teaching that also allows for spontaneous opportunities, creativity and the needs of pupils of all abilities. Paying attention to three factors enhances the likelihood that your teaching will be effective:

1. The ability to think ahead
2. Purposeful reflection about ways to improve teaching and learning
3. The significance of interpersonal relationships.

Thinking ahead

The ability to think and plan ahead is vital if you are to succeed as a teacher. Effective teaching is not only about coping with the immediate classroom situation but relies on advance thought about resource provision and activities appropriate to the age and ability of the class, and likely pupil reactions and needs. Inexperienced teachers tend to stare fixedly at the path beneath their feet; they must learn to look up and see the road stretching ahead. Although your priority is bound to be the very next lesson, try to step back and see its place in terms of the wider picture.

Purposeful reflection

Purposeful reflection to improve practice lies at the heart of improvement (see, for instance, Larrivee 2008; Marcos *et al.* 2011). Teachers are professionals for many reasons: their length of training, the significance of their job to society, the extent of their responsibilities, their level of expertise and, above all, in their capacity to critically evaluate their teaching (Silcock and Brundrett 2002). The need to carry on learning applies as much to seasoned professionals as to novices. Over recent years, there has been an increased emphasis upon establishing continuity between initial and in-service training, underlining the need for all teachers to enhance and update their professional skills, and understanding the significance of new initiatives, surveys and research findings. Standards of attainment no longer apply solely to newly qualified teachers but also to those in the induction year and beyond. Consequently, it is important that all teachers learn to evaluate their own teaching through discussion with colleagues, engagement with scholarly activities such as reading professional journals and gaining advanced professional qualifications. Opportunities for gaining Master's Degree qualifications have become increasingly important in recent years, in some cases commencing during pre-service training (see Hayes 2011, *The Guided Reader to Teaching and Learning*, and the cross-references to it throughout this book). All of this endeavour must be grounded in regular reflection on the best teaching approaches and strategies and, increasingly, keeping sources of evidence to support claims about professional attainment.

Interpersonal relationships

Professional progress is not rooted solely in issues regarding the mechanics of teaching but also in understanding the significance of human interaction, emotions and behaviour. Constant interrogation of the role of relationships in learning is not only important for the general classroom ethos and children's wellbeing, it also has implications for effective organisation and classroom management. For instance, it is not sufficient merely to inform the children about standards of behaviour or expected procedures; you must also explain why they are necessary, thereby involving pupils in decisions that influence their lives. Children are more likely to develop an affinity with a teacher who takes the time and trouble to include them in the decision-making process – if only to inform them about why something has already been decided – than with one who treats them like passive recipients. The teacher is, of course, ultimately responsible for what happens in the classroom, but in the meantime the children will increase in self-confidence and awareness of the issues if they develop a sense of ownership over events that directly impinge upon their lives. For very young children the decisions might involve something as simple as determining a sensible way to store wet paintings. For top infants, involvement might be at the level of discussing ways to organise the fiction books. For junior-age children the issue might relate to collaborative groups and seating arrangements. Whatever the issue, the process of teaching and learning is enhanced when children's views are taken into account and valued. All children are attracted to teachers who take the time and trouble to engage with the class and treat them civilly.

Activate your thinking!

Every adult working in primary education needs to possess strong interpersonal and communication skills exercised within a climate of patience, flexibility and dependability. Effective communicators are characterised by being able to make decisions with confidence, demonstrate a willingness to ask for help when needed and be open to suggestions and ideas.

Cross-reference: Guided Reader Extract 42

Organising learning

The classroom environment

Most primary teachers spend the majority of their teaching time in the same room and need to feel comfortable in their surroundings (see Hastings and Wood 2002 for advice about classroom layout). Despite the increase in subject specialists, advanced skills teachers, TAs and curriculum subject co-ordinators, the familiar pattern of one teacher taking responsibility for the learning, welfare and motivation of around thirty youngsters remains commonplace in schools. It was noted in earlier chapters that teachers' job satisfaction depends principally on the success they make in shaping the lives of 'their' children. The conditions they create for learning are one factor that contributes to the extent to which this aim is achieved. One sign of a teacher's commitment to children is the appearance of the classroom, including its cleanliness, order and purposefulness (sometimes referred to as the classroom 'climate'). Despite the increasing demands made on teachers to achieve ever-higher standards in English (literacy) and mathematics, primary teachers and their assistants show a determination to give sufficient time to the look of the room, especially enlivening it with artwork and children's creations.

Classrooms vary in size and shape; few are ideal for every purpose. Some will suit a particular teaching approach; others will be a source of frustration to the teacher because of the room's odd shape, lack of access to resources or location (such as being at the far end of the main school building). Whatever the conditions, however, visitors will use classroom appearance as one of the measures to assess the teacher's professionalism and, perhaps, the quality of the school. Head teachers frequently show prospective parents around and make a habit of delaying in some classrooms and passing hastily through others. The reason for this behaviour is obvious.

It is important to examine a classroom from the pupils' perspective. What do the children see when they first enter the room? Does it look inviting, tidy, thoughtfully arranged? Is there an air of disarray and confusion, or of dowdiness? Are tables and chairs of suitable size? Are trays, books and resources clearly marked and accessible? A useful exercise is to kneel down in various parts of the room to take a 'pupil's eye' view, including the doorway, and scan it for a few moments to see how things might be improved with a small amount of effort. The room can also be examined from an adult's perspective. Is there an air of efficiency due to the arrangement of furniture, tidiness and the obvious care that has been given to the overall layout? Does the classroom look cared for and the sort of place where everyone can work safely and efficiently? Is there a feeling of purpose, enriched by interactive displays, examples of good quality children's work on the walls, and well-marshalled resources? A classroom like this can bring prestige and attention from the people who matter: children, parents, governors and other members of staff.

Activate your thinking!

An orderly classroom should be bright, purposeful and inspiring – not dull, clinical and unduly formal.

Seating arrangements

In making decisions about seating, it is important to be clear about the basis on which decisions are made. A few teachers give the children complete freedom about where they sit; others allow children to sit where they prefer for a week or two until the children's academic ability, self-discipline and inclination to work become apparent, when changes are made accordingly. In most cases, children are allocated a place for the majority of lessons and remain there unless they are moved for a specific purpose (e.g. a collaborative task or art and craft activity).

Most teachers take account of friendship patterns in making decisions. In doing so, there are a number of factors to consider. First, if children sit with their friends it can result in them chattering and disrupting proceedings; on the other hand, they are more likely to co-operate with someone they know and like. Second, if friends are separated they can be tempted to wander across the room to make contact, send hand signal messages or (worse) call out to each other. Third, although a seating arrangement made on the grounds of friendship is popular with children, it might create problems when pupils of similar academic ability need to work together. Finally, less capable children can be tempted to copy from their more able partners, though this tendency should not be confused with genuine co-operation, when children are encouraged to provide peer support for one another.

Teachers who dictate the seating pattern will reduce some of these potential problems but generate others. For instance, many children feel more secure when sitting next to a friend and are unhappy if separated. Teachers may inadvertently place children together who dislike each other, with the inevitable disruptive consequences. Most teachers try to strike a balance between keeping friends together in situations where grouping does not rely principally on academic ability, and separating them where this is necessary because of the differentiated requirements of tasks and activities (e.g. in mathematics).

Many teachers group the pupils based on ability in reading and writing other than for timetabled maths sessions. During work outside the core subjects, pupils' expertise in areas as diverse as ball skills (in PE), computer skills (in ICT), communication skills (in discussions and collaborative problem solving) and organisational skills (in teamwork activities) need to be taken into account when deciding on where they should sit or stand. In making decisions about seating arrangements, therefore, you need to be clear about what you mean by the phrase 'academic ability', as it can be defined in a number of different ways. In addition, three other factors have to be considered: the children's ages, your teaching style and prevailing circumstances. Thus:

The age of the children

Nursery-age children are usually given a great deal of freedom of choice, depending upon the availability of adults to supervise their activities. By contrast, younger school-age children are likely to need guidance about where to sit but are unlikely to be choosy about who sits next to them. Older children are much clearer about their friendship preferences and more assertive as a result. On the other hand, older primary children tend to be academically grouped and there are higher expectations about formal work outcomes; choice of partner is as likely to be influenced by the perceived usefulness of the classmate in helping to complete work, or the given activity, as it is by friendship.

J. Clarke (2008) advises that in the case of younger children, each area of the classroom should have a purpose, so that children know where to go when they want to plan, discover, answer questions or gather information. These areas might be play-based – such as role play, small world, creative workshop, investigate, malleable play – or they might be curriculum-based; for example, writing, science, mathematics, book corner, art and craft.

Your teaching style

If the class is taught as a whole rather than in groups, single tables with two pupils per table is normally considered to be the best format. If collaborative tasks predominate, groups of about four sitting around two adjoining tables is often appropriate. The structured patterns of lessons in mathematics and literacy do not leave much room for manoeuvre, as pupils are normally together at the start and conclusion of the lesson and separated into ability groups for the activity section of the lesson. If teachers use a board or screen to illustrate what they are teaching, children must be seated in such a way that they can see clearly without getting a stiff neck or having to strain their eyes.

Prevailing circumstances

Most teachers have a basic pattern of organisation but vary the set-up according to the circumstances. For instance, tables might be placed together for the purpose of sharing resources for a large-scale project. Children sometimes need to move around the room if there is a 'circus' of various tasks to be completed in a given time (in science, say), where each task is located in a different area of the room. There are also practical factors to be taken into account if children have special learning needs and, for example, require more space for wheelchair access or specially adapted working surfaces for children with limited upper-body mobility. The cardinal rule is simple: whether you spend most time on direct interactive teaching, or on group work, or on promoting individual learning, the room layout needs to facilitate rather than to hinder learning.

Health and safety

Whether a classroom is brand new or an ageing Victorian relic, the children need to be able to move around easily and use equipment safely. Every lesson should be planned with 'risk factors' in mind. If the risk factor is high, more adult supervision, discipline measures and training about the correct use of equipment is needed (see also Chapter 4). Practical and outdoor activities require particular care.

Teaching approach

Your teaching approach also has an impact upon the level of safety required, especially in respect of children's movements around the room. Generally, less pupil mobility reduces the likelihood of accidents; greater mobility necessitates more stringent safety measures. Pupils have less need to move when all the resources required for the task are readily accessible and where the teacher moves about the room to see pupils, rather than the pupils leaving their places to see the teacher. Some teachers favour inviting children who are seated on the carpet to use the interactive whiteboard or to explain what they have been doing or to offer an opinion; while such a strategy maintains interest and cultivates a climate of shared endeavour, it is time-consuming and can lead to accidentally crushed fingers as a child weaves through the group.

Learning climate

The learning climate also plays a part in health and safety. Some classrooms have a settled feel to them as pupils move about purposefully and get on with their work without undue fuss. Other classrooms seem like a disaster waiting to happen, as pupils mill about aimlessly, apparently lacking motivation and arguing about resources with other pupils. Many classrooms vary between a settled feel during teacher-led phases and an increase in noise and bustle when pupils are engaged in tasks that require independent thinking and initiative. Genuinely collaborative activities are especially prone to more noise – it is difficult, for instance, to imagine a time when design and technology experiments with 8-year-olds can or should be carried out in sterile, near silent conditions. There is, however, a big difference between enthusiastic application to the job by keen young minds and irresponsible behaviour from pupils who are determined to take advantage of their liberty. You have to strike a balance between allowing children the liberty to exercise initiative and being insistent on proper codes of conduct. Nevertheless, there are at least ten health and safety rules of which to be acutely and constantly aware:

1. Pathways should be clear so that pupils can walk unhindered. Tables and chairs should be set out so that children do not have to squeeze past or risk tripping over obstacles such as bags and trailing straps.
2. Pupils carrying out activities that require large areas should be given the appropriate spaces in which to work.
3. Equipment and resources should be stored so that they can be reached without stretching or pulling items down from the shelf, especially heavy items.
4. Wet activities should be kept to a designated area away from main walkways, and sink areas should be kept free from furniture.
5. Pupils must be taught how and when to wash their hands thoroughly, especially before meals.
6. Pupils' view of the board and other visual aids should be unhindered.
7. Pupils should not have to sit next to a draughty window, a hot radiator or a tall piece of furniture with objects resting on top.
8. Pupils should only use specialist equipment with adult supervision and after proper training.
9. Pupils must not be allowed to put small objects in their mouths.
10. Pupils should walk and not run in the classroom.

Vulnerable children

Health and safety issues are particularly relevant for vulnerable pupils: for example, the very young, those with disabilities and children with allergies. However, all children should know how to use equipment correctly and should never be 'let loose' without training. In a situation where a number of different activities are taking place in the room simultaneously, you must ensure that sufficient adult help and supervision is available. In 'large space' activities involving heavy or hazardous equipment, all possible safety checks should be made beforehand and limits imposed upon access. It is better to use a limited range of equipment safely than to attempt too much at one time, lose control of events and create unsafe working conditions. Even young children will, with encouragement, offer their own suggestions about improvements in safety procedures. If your instincts alert you to possible danger or hazards, take additional precautions and seek advice.

Large space activities also invite other potential hazards, such as children bumping into each other when running about, injuries from bats and sticks, and over-zealous physical exertion. Some children simply get carried away and don't hear your commands, so it is essential to rehearse your expectations with them and insist on immediate compliance. Although some teachers and head teachers dislike the use of a whistle, it penetrates noise far better than (say) a tambourine, bell or shaker.

Resources

The level of resources can make a considerable difference to the quality of teaching and learning, and contribute towards higher standards. Teachers are wonderfully inventive and make a little go a long way, but there is a limit to what can be accomplished. A good supply of resources, accessible and clearly labelled, makes life easier for everyone and smartens the appearance of the classroom. Pupils need to be taught how to use equipment, care for materials and, essentially, return items to their correct place after use.

Nature of the task

The type of resources will, of course, vary according to the nature of the task. A messy, creative activity (such as clay work) necessitates the availability of raw materials, tools, protective clothing and suitable working conditions such as a cleanable, flat surface located some distance from other activities. By contrast, a deskwork activity involving a single, self-contained worksheet requiring only writing implements is relatively easy to organise, which is one of the reasons that teachers favour such paper-based tasks. Teachers need to be sensitive to the way that a shortage of resources (such as a lack of aprons) and insufficient time spent on training children to use things (such as a measuring scale) can result in arguments, unsatisfactory quality of work and avoidable accidents.

Preserving the resources

There are also financial and practical implications if resources are abused. For instance, lined paper is expensive and if used inappropriately can result in it ending up in the bin with just a few misspelled scrawled words at the top of the page. Meanwhile the child finds another fresh piece and is busy making the same mistakes. In recent years there has been a move back towards the use of exercise books, which can be collected and stored with minimum effort. Even so, there are many occasions when drafts of work on single sheets need to be kept safely for future use. While the use of digital cameras and computer technology has reduced problems of safe storage to some extent, procedures for use of consumable resources are still an important element of efficient classroom practice. Similarly, incorrect use of tools can lead to expensive breakages. The rule is simple: use the correct equipment for the job and monitor use of consumables to minimise waste.

Use of ICT

As inferred above, all schools now have a range of computers and other ICT resources to support learning. Sometimes they are held in a central area, sometimes they are allocated to different classrooms; frequently both options are available. Each situation creates different organisational challenges. If there is a computer suite away from the classroom, both the supervision of children and careful timetabling are essential considerations. If computers are located in classrooms, managing access is a priority. The use of a trained TA makes a considerable difference to the ease with which computer access is managed, but you still need to ensure that you have briefed the assistant and clarified what you want pupils to achieve through its use.

Time factors

Preparing resources for a lesson can be time-consuming. Ideally, most of it should be completed during the previous evening and, where possible, left in place for easy and immediate access, especially for the first session of the day. However, it is sometimes better to wait until the morning before distributing your precious wares. For instance, if the equipment is delicate or expensive, it is preferable to wait until the last moment before setting it out immediately before the session. If an equipment cupboard key is required, allowance must be made for the time it will take to collect and return it. Some resources for the afternoon session have to be organised during the lunch break. Again, logistical considerations are important, such as whether the room is being used for (say) a lunchtime activity, or whether a sudden downpour of rain will bring the class back inside to descend on the carefully prepared items that you so lovingly placed on tables when the room was empty.

Thinking ahead

As part of the art and design curriculum, children need to be taught how to plan, make and evaluate artefacts and experience projects in textiles, food, wood and recycled materials, which are often linked to other subjects: for example, making lighthouses as part of the science curriculum about sources of energy and electricity. Such large space activities inevitably carry resource implications: collections of items for use have to be gathered; sticky tape and adhesive pots have to be distributed in advance; clay has to be accessible; tables have to be reorganised, and so on. Similarly, equipment has to be checked in advance of PE lessons; drama 'props' have to be put in position to facilitate the acting sequence; the floor space has to be cleared before a dance session; computers have to be switched on, programs set up and paper trays filled for printing. If arrangements are not in hand, the lesson gets off to a bad start as organising resources absorbs the time and effort that ought to have gone into active teaching, the exception being when the involvement of the children in the organisation forms an important part of the lesson. As in many complex organisational situations the support of a TA is hugely beneficial; so much so, in fact, that it is often more sensible to adopt a less complex approach when adult assistance is unavailable.

Activate your thinking!

Well-organised lessons lead to settled children and improved learning. A summary of questions helps to point up ways of increasing the likelihood that your lessons will run smoothly, as follows:

1. Is there sufficient time during one lesson to achieve all that you planned or are you being too ambitious?
2. Have you sorted out in advance the activities that different children will be involved in doing?
3. Does the TA know what is required of her?
4. Are interruptions likely to take place during the lesson (for example, children leaving the room for special tuition)?
5. Are lessons immediately before or after any events (such as assembly, singing practice or play rehearsals) that might affect the time available or pupils' concentration?

Attention to the details of organisation and daily priorities pays rich dividends. Spending a few minutes reflecting systematically upon the working day is amply rewarded by the improved efficiency. It is worth developing the habit of sketching out each day's predicted pattern and needs during the previous evening, as having a well-considered framework allows unanticipated events and disruptions to the programme to be more easily accommodated.

Good practice

Before the start of each day and each session, take a moment to rehearse the programme in your mind in the form of a 'storyboard' to foresee possible hindrances and opportunities. Many teachers write down an outline of the day for pupils; it also acts as a reminder for the adults.

Displays

Many primary school classrooms are enlivened by displays of children's work, paintings, models and exhibits. Despite the objectives-driven nature of modern primary school life, many teachers extol the virtues of colourful and well-displayed classrooms and invest a lot of energy into ensuring that pupils' work is visible.

Some corridors are festooned with colourful motifs and stimulating pictures, all of which take a lot of time and energy to produce (see Jackson 1993; Cooper *et al.* 1996; Beasley and Moberley 2000). In recent years, the increased emphasis upon the core subjects has been matched by a similar reduction in time spent on the creative subjects; as a result, many teachers find that preparation, planning, marking and target setting consumes some of the time they might formerly have used for displaying work. Although TAs can take responsibility for organising the displays, they are often used to support the teaching of literacy and numeracy and offering specialist, targeted help to children deemed 'behind' in their academic work; as a consequence, they are in a similar position to teachers in having less opportunity to be involved in other tasks. An additional factor to consider is that some assistants do not possess display skills or may not produce the sort of display that the teacher had in mind, so active liaison between teacher and assistant is essential.

If displays are going to serve a useful purpose, consideration must be given to the following four factors, namely, selection of work for display; what displays achieve; changing the displays; and discarding old displays. Thus:

Selecting work for display

Criteria are needed for selection. For instance, you might want to display a single piece of work from every child, in which case some poor work will be on general view; or alternatively select the best examples, in which cases the less able children will never see their work on display. Gathering large amounts of completed work into a simply produced homemade book is sometimes preferable to pinning up the work on a board. Digital photographs of work can be permanently on show by means of a suitable electronic display unit.

What displays achieve

While displaying work has the benefits mentioned earlier, the quest to cover walls with work can become wasteful unless the purpose for doing so is clear. Displayed work should act as an incentive for pupils to complete work of similar quality, assist learning by offering interesting ideas, and stimulate children's imagination. You can use work on display to point out high standards of attainment, commend the children who have produced it, and praise the unity of a whole-class endeavour.

Changing the displays

The fresh colours of a newly finished painting, the visual impact of a recently completed model and the charming eloquence of a poem about autumn leaves can quickly fade into an untidy collection of curled edges, cracked paint and out-of-season writing. Teachers are sometimes embarrassed to discover that the display of tessellations is more than a term old or the winter frieze is gathering dust in a revealing stream of summer sunshine. Time passes rapidly in the bustle of classroom life and displays soon become dated. A simple plan of action for changing wall displays will help to avoid the discomfiture of snowmen in June.

Discarding old displays

Wall-mounted displays are often in a poor condition by the time they have completed their useful life and it is sometimes best to quietly dispose of them. On other occasions, the children want to take their work home, in which case it is essential that teachers have checked first that they are happy for parents to examine the work close up. Sometimes a piece of work is required for a pupil's Record of Achievement folder (see Chapter 11); if so, details of the child's name, the date of completion and a brief note about the circumstances under which it was produced are needed.

Good practice

Discuss your plan of action for changing displays with the TA and draw up a schedule. Check discreetly that the assistant has the necessary skills to make a good job of it. If not, suggest that you and the teaching assistant work co-operatively to create the display. Assistants are often enthusiastic about using a camera to capture images.

Managing learning

Forms of management

It is unrealistic to think that because the classroom organisation has been carried out efficiently in advance of the lesson, everything will proceed without a hitch. The best teachers not only organise but also ensure that they manage classroom affairs (presenting content, explaining, answering pupil queries, monitoring activities, intervening, guiding, assessing, encouraging) so as to ensure the most favourable conditions for learning. The concept of effective management is now strongly rooted in classroom practice, such that poor management is likely to result in weaker teaching and pupil underachievement.

Management is derived from the root 'manage', a word we use in a variety of expressions that emphasise successful practice or a successful outcome. Examples of how the word is used include:

'I managed to get it in on time.' That is, I succeeded in meeting the deadline.
'She managed the final question.' That is, that she had sufficient knowledge to tackle the problem.
'He managed to control the class.' That is, he had the ability to handle the situation.

The use of such expressions points to three different aspects of management that you need to take into account: (1) time management; (2) information management; and (3) human management. For example, in the expressions noted above, there are underlying assumptions about each of the three forms of management:

1. that the person has taken responsibility to meet the deadline (time management);
2. that the person was sufficiently well informed to meet a requirement (information management);
3. that the person coped with the challenges presented by the children (human management).

The significance of these three elements for teachers, who need to meet deadlines (such as finishing lessons on time), to be well informed (in particular, to have good subject knowledge) and cope with pupils (establishing and maintaining order) is considerable. A summary of the practical implications helps to underline these points.

Time management

Good time management establishes a framework for working, both within individual lessons and across a whole day. It allows for the quirks of classroom life, accommodates the unexpected and ensures that time is used appropriately. This does not mean that every moment is accounted for in the planning process or that pupils have to keep their 'noses to the grindstone' but rather that time is utilised purposefully and effectively. More information about time management can be found in this chapter.

Information management

Good information management ensures that the teacher has a good grasp of the subject and knows how to access additional sources as required. Teachers who are good at managing information will have the confidence to share ideas with pupils, show interest in their discoveries, monitor their understanding and encourage them to find out more by using their initiative. They are often skilled in explaining tricky concepts using child-friendly vocabulary.

Human management

This aspect involves finding ways of relating effectively to pupils and assistants, and engaging them in the teaching and learning process. Human management is facilitated by clarifying boundaries of behaviour for pupils, using stimulating teaching approaches and presenting ideas in a comprehensible form. Good human managers respect and take seriously genuine concerns and make allowances for pupils' failings. The learning environment is characterised by a sense of wellbeing, mutual respect, high expectation and undisguised celebration of progress. A motto for such classroom situations might be 'all for one and one for all'.

Organisation and management are mutually dependent for successful teaching and learning. Someone who is a good organiser but a poor manager promises much and delivers little. Someone who is a poor organiser but a good manager makes the most of the situation despite the low level of preparation. Someone who is both a good organiser and a good manager not only promises much in advance but makes the fullest use of teaching opportunities for the benefit of every pupil.

Managing time effectively

We have seen that a characteristic of successful teachers is their ability to organise and manage their time effectively. The best teachers are normally skilful in making the best use of available opportunities to press home teaching points; they seem to achieve more than their colleagues and produce work of a higher standard. Brown and Ralph (1994) argue that although time itself cannot be managed, our *use* of it can. In other words, we manage the way that we manage our time. They suggest that a well-ordered routine not only leads to greater achievement but also reduces stress levels. Brown and Ralph summarise the position as follows:

> Time is irreplaceable and has no substitute. You can't borrow or steal time or change it in any way; all you can do is to make the optimum use of the time you've got.
>
> (p. 58)

Every teacher finds that, unless priorities are established, the hours slip past and essential things remain untouched while trivial issues or those that emerge unexpectedly take precedence. For example, imagine putting up a display during the break when the resources for the literacy session that followed were still not in place. Imagine chatting casually to a parent at the start of the day while the nursery nurse was anxiously waiting for you to discuss a particular child's needs. Imagine arriving late for the lesson because you had been doing some photocopying that could and should have been done the night before. Imagine spending the first ten minutes of a lesson in sorting children into groups because you had not bothered beforehand. Imagine arriving in the hall for a movement session with children, only to discover that because you had been late going to bed the previous night you had overslept and, in your haste, had left the music CD at home.

The above examples merely serve to confirm the principle that poor time management is detrimental to your work as a teacher, so it is essential to learn to 'think ahead' by deciding in advance what is *essential*, what is *necessary* and what is *non-essential*. You then decide what is *pressing* and what can wait. To avoid being overwhelmed it is useful to make a determined effort to categorise tasks under one of the following four headings:

NOT PRESSING and TRIVIAL
PRESSING but TRIVIAL
PRESSING and SIGNIFICANT
NOT PRESSING but SIGNIFICANT

It is not worth wasting time on things that are neither pressing nor significant, even if they interest you, and pressing tasks that are relatively unimportant should be dealt with as quickly as possible without trying to be a perfectionist. On the other hand, if something is pressing and significant it obviously has to be done as soon as possible. The fact that you have a hundred other things to do cannot be used as an excuse. You simply have to spend less time on existing tasks and respond to the new priority. As a trainee teacher, lesson preparation will nearly always take prime position. Seek advice from your mentor if you are suddenly faced with an unexpected, urgent task and feel overwhelmed, or fear that you might neglect the priorities because someone is insisting on an immediate response. As much of a teacher's work is regular and ongoing, use of a *daily planner* with interim targets is essential if you are to avoid last-minute panic.

It takes trainee teachers time to recognise that completing forms, filling in lists and other mundane tasks often have a greater significance than they realise. Experienced colleagues will advise you about priorities and the categorisation listed above will help you to negotiate them. Papworth (2003) in his 'secrets of time' suggests that effective time management relies on four factors:

1.   Have an excellent reason
2.   Have an excellent plan
3.   Do the right thing
4.   Do the thing right.

Despite Papworth's useful guidance, there are always unexpected demands being made of teachers, and you need to ensure that a sudden influx of essential tasks through a lack of forward planning, or allowing minor tasks to metamorphose into major ones because of time pressures, doesn't submerge you. Obviously a job that is pressing and significant has to be tackled first; everything else can wait. However, if too many tasks fall into this category, it should act as a warning to you that you are failing to plan far enough in advance of the dead-line. The majority of essential tasks should be non-urgent because you have left sufficient time for them to be dealt with. In the hurry and scurry of school life, there are occasions when unexpected events conspire to upset your carefully laid plans, but make it a rule not to be caught out too often.

It is not sufficient to leave space for things to be done; you should also identify the right time and place for accomplishing them. For example, while it is essential to have your resources marshalled in advance of the lesson, a telephone call about arrangements for an educational visit can only be made during break times. It is also important to balance the time it will take (say) to consult with a colleague with what needs to be organised for the lesson that follows. Quite simply, there may not be time to do both. Again, information might be needed from pupils at the start of the day about numbers who wish to participate in a particular event or you might have to transmit information to them about changes in the timetable pattern or a coming event, all of which absorbs precious moments. Similarly, if a parent has requested a brief informal discussion after school, the meeting needs to be made a priority over putting up a wall display or marking books. The balance of each day is likely to be different and unexpected events can disrupt the best-laid plans; nevertheless, the importance of looking and planning ahead is crucial to success. It is not only during lessons that you need to keep a close eye on the clock, but during every part of the day, until it becomes instinctive. Failure to manage your time means that events control you when you should be controlling the events.

Effective management of time is a necessary skill for the smooth flow of lessons, administration and decision-making, but it also has more profound implications for your peace of mind and enjoyment of the job. In their longitudinal study of stress among teachers in school, Carlyle and Woods (2002) found that poor time management was one of a number of factors that contributed to exhaustion and demoralisation. The intensification of work practices and increasing societal expectations of educators placed further time pressures on practitioners and exacerbated feelings of helplessness and being unable to cope. Similarly, Day *et al.* (2007) warn how work intensification 'leads to reduced time for relaxation and re-skilling, can cause chronic and persistent work overload [and] can reduce quality of service' (p. 26). The message for all teachers is, quite simply, to ensure that they don't allow themselves to work so hard that their effectiveness is adversely affected. It is possible to *feel* that you are doing a good job because of the effort that you are making when in fact the belief is illusory because you are 'running on empty'.

Good practice

A useful strategy to protect against damaging time stress is to compile each evening a list of things that need to be done before school begins, during the lunch break and after school.

Managing individuals, groups and the whole class

The successful management of lessons relies heavily on selecting the most suitable teaching strategy to accomplish the intended outcome. In the following section, we focus upon teaching children in three different settings and evaluate the different demands that each of them makes upon the teacher's skill and expertise, namely: one-to-one contact, in groups and with a whole class.

One-to-one contact

Benefits and risks

One-to-one opportunities exist both in the regular monitoring of progress during a lesson and in giving specific attention to a child's particular learning needs. Owing to large class sizes, there are few chances to give one pupil exclusive attention for any length of time, but when you do so they prove to be extremely worthwhile, as a breakthrough in learning often takes place when a child has an adult's exclusive attention. There are at least four reasons for this acceleration in learning:

1. The child can receive individual help that targets specific problems.
2. The child can ask the teacher questions without publicly exposing his or her ignorance.
3. Work can be closely and accurately monitored.
4. A closer relationship develops between teacher and child.

However, there are possible disadvantages if the individual attention is prolonged:

- The child may become over-dependent on adult help.
- The child might have less opportunity for collaboration with other children.
- The child has less opportunity to reflect and develop solutions.
- The child may miss other important teaching and learning opportunities from which classmates are benefiting during the personalised period.

One-to-one interaction is intensive and demanding, and can make surprisingly heavy demands upon the adult. In addition, during regular teaching sessions, too much attention given to one child can lead to a suspicion of favouritism among pupils who don't benefit from such exclusive service. Although it is often necessary to offer a struggling child extra support through coaching, the danger of teachers neglecting their responsibility to the rest of the class while concentrating on an individual is always present; this factor is one of the reasons that TAs are often so employed. Younger and more timid children especially need to be helped to bridge the gap that exists between what they can manage to do alone with guidance and encouragement, and what they can do with active and focused support. Shy children tend to participate less in class, hesitate to respond to questions and often give shorter and less elaborate answers. The shy child's hesitation may have more to do with anxiety about being wrong than about lack of ability, so you have to weigh up the pros and cons of offering one-to-one support. See also Chapter 11 for further details about appropriate intervention.

Time considerations

If teachers have a teaching assistant available, they may be able to manage priorities in such a way that one or other of them has the opportunity to spend additional time with the needy child. A large number of schools offer additional support for children who might benefit from extra tuition, though these tend to be related to those who have the potential to achieve a higher level in the national tests. Otherwise, space has to be found during assembly time, break time, quiet reading sessions, shared class times and the like to give extra support. None of these options is ideal as they place an additional burden upon the teacher; nevertheless, certain one-to-one tasks are unavoidable and have to be accommodated somehow in the teaching programme, including:

- hearing children read, though this process may be as part of small-group work;
- conferencing (discussing the child's work in depth on a one-to-one basis, see below);
- discussing homework tasks, especially where the child has struggled or been tardy (see Chapter 8).

HEARING CHILDREN READ

Even experienced practitioners find that hearing children read is particularly challenging and they use various means to cope with the problem of fitting them in during each week.

Teachers of younger primary children utilise parents, TAs and odd occasions when the majority of the class are engaged in self-sustained play activities in order to hear readers. Teachers at Key Stage 2 find that although good readers enjoy reading to an adult, it becomes less and less useful as the children can read silently much more quickly than aloud, with the consequence that reading aloud may reduce their fluency. In recent years there has been a move away from hearing a child read on a one-to-one basis for at least three reasons. First, it is time-consuming; hearing each child read for only two minutes requires an absolute minimum of one hour. Second, it 'ties up' the adult concerned. Third, it prevents the teacher from employing the time to promote reading in other ways.

A balance has to be struck between hearing readers to monitor their grasp of concepts, pronunciation and intonation, and wasting valuable time working one-to-one with a child who is an independent reader and does not need to practise aloud. Many teachers accept that one-to-one engagement is unrealistic, so they utilise whole-class reading, group reading (where a number of children have the same book in front of them) or paired reading (where a more capable child assists a less capable one) as a means of coping with or enhancing the quality of reading. None of these methods are free from problems and, despite the cost in time and effort, individual attention is sometimes the best option. Children who have severe problems with reading will normally receive targeted attention and a specially designed programme, though care must be taken that time spent on providing additional support does not deprive them of other learning opportunities or make them feel an oddity. It is noteworthy that while strenuous efforts are made to find time for individual reading, the same determination is much less evident in mathematics or other curriculum subjects.

CONFERENCING

Conferencing normally takes place about once each term and is a means of reviewing work and setting longer-term learning targets with (rather than for) the child. The teacher spends a few minutes exclusively with one child, discussing his or her work, considering the progress made and, perhaps, selecting pieces of work for a Record of Achievement folder that will accompany the child through the school. These occasions need to be planned carefully and consideration has to be given to issues of privacy, confidentiality and the means of sustaining uninterrupted contact, which is organisationally far from easy. Some schools have a policy of using a substitute teacher during the 'conferencing season' to supervise the rest of the class. Other situations are less ideal and require the sort of imaginative strategies demanded for hearing readers (see above). Experienced and trained TAs, especially higher-level assistants, are sometimes available to undertake such a task. Some schools utilise a 'target review sheet' (TRS) to help children and teachers reflect upon the work that has taken place and potentially what lies ahead. Typically, a TRS will contain such information as the following (child perspectives are shown in brackets):

- Name of child and the date of completion
- Past achievements (in child-speak: 'what I have achieved so far')
- Analysis of previous success ('the reasons I have done well')
- Future plans ('things I still need to persevere with to achieve')
- Analysis of struggles ('reasons I have found things hard')
- Aspirations ('new goals I set for myself')
- Strategies to achieve future success ('how I can do better at my work')
- Celebrating success ('things I can feel proud about').

The format can, of course, vary according to the age group of children and specific purpose for which the TRS is used. With young pupils it is helpful if each child shares with an adult, who writes down what is said and agreed. In many ways, the exact nature of the written evidence is less important than the conversation itself and the opportunity to reflect on progress. In practice, there are so many different things that could be written down that some selection is inevitable. If the child is 'driving' the agenda, then the adult has to accept that the priorities may differ from what have been anticipated or desired. Encouraging children to establish their own short-term targets for learning on a more regular basis can be assimilated into the warp and weave of regular teaching. Longer-term targets (half-termly, say) are, of course, more general in character and may be so broad that they hardly warrant special attention. Nevertheless, the principle of involving children in thinking about their learning and, to an extent, monitoring their progress is now embedded in varying degrees in the practice of nearly all schools. The ongoing assessment of individual children is addressed further in Chapter 11.

Activate your thinking!

Consider the truth of this principle: groups can be taught but only individuals can learn.

Groups

We have already seen that the dividing of the class into groups is an important part of organising for learning. Division into groups is most often based upon the academic ability of the children for core areas (maths, science, English), friendship groups for creative activities (notably PE and art) and a mixture of friendship and ability for collaborative work in other non-core subjects. For instance, there might be three ability sets for mathematics, friendship groups for drama, and a mixture of children for project, thematic or topic work in the humanities.

In determining the pattern of group work, the demands made of teachers grow in proportion to the number and complexity of groups operating, so handling several groups engaged in similar tasks is easier to cope with than groups working in different areas. Dividing the class into groups must be considered alongside the challenging process of monitoring, recording of children's progress, and bringing the session to a satisfactory conclusion: the larger the number of groups, the more complex these processes become.

Many teachers are agreed that the importance attached to formal testing and national strategies for literacy and numeracy have resulted in less opportunity and time for spontaneity, thereby obliging them to become highly specific in their direction of group work. This specificity of learning objectives has sometimes resulted in less time for exploratory, enquiry-based learning.

The teacher's role

As a rule, teacher input is normally required before children can purposefully engage with tasks and open-ended problem-solving activities. Thus, explanation about the computer program system precedes pupils exploring its full potential; similarly, the creativity in drama emerges from a close study of the original example provided by the teacher or coach.

In addition to direct teaching, teachers have a responsibility to provide the necessary structure and circumstances within which the children can subsequently explore ideas and investigate processes, a function sometimes referred to as 'scaffolding'. This procedure does not imply that children do not possess original ideas of their own; on the contrary, a well-structured approach to experiential teaching and learning will facilitate children's contributions by providing a knowledge base or equipping them with the necessary concepts or skills. The assumption is that children will find out many things for themselves and learn more thoroughly providing they are given appropriate knowledge, guidance and resources as a foundation on which to build their ideas and innovate. You create the secure learning environment and resources and establish the boundaries; the children explore the space.

Children working together

As children work together they experience a range of emotions and challenges which have as much to do with learning to get along with one another as with solving problems or exploring concepts. Biott and Easen (1994) comment on the significance of friendship groups in particular:

> Friendship groups offer opportunities for children to learn social competences in situations where they feel they can act upon shared understandings of how to be both cooperative and assertive.

> (p. 65)

While there is always a danger of friends spending too much time talking about out-of-school affairs when they should be concentrating on the work in hand, the risks should be weighed against the advantages to be gained through close social interaction and mutual support in the pursuit of common aims (Street 2004). See Figure 10.1 and the 'Promoting dialogue' section in Chapter 8.

Teachers also have to decide whether group work is intended to enhance collaboration or is used as an organisational tool: that is, whether children sit together in groups to achieve a

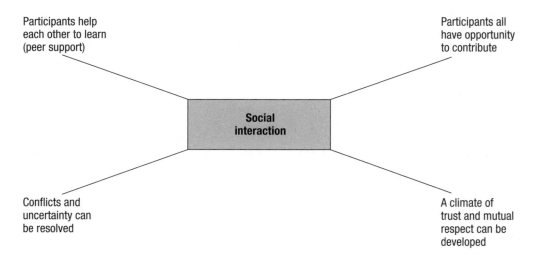

FIGURE 10.1 Social factors in collaboration

common learning objective (collaboration) or whether they sit together and are generally co-operative while working to keep things orderly. The desirable aim to foster collaboration has to be approached wisely, for experience teaches us that although children sit together they do not necessarily work together. There are three reasons for this reluctance: (1) they have a deep-rooted concern that the interaction is a form of 'cheating'; (2) they lack the necessary skills to relate to others in a group; and (3) they prefer to work separately and resent being obliged to take account of other views and preferences. If you want foster collaboration, you need to explain the process, teach the skills and clarify the boundaries. It is important to stress that assisting a classmate is admirable and to insist that everyone has a responsibility to contribute, not merely the assertive pupils. Collaboration is typically associated with investigative, enquiry-based tasks, whereas co-operation is associated with children working independently or in pairs but being mutually supportive while they do so. The relationship between these elements can be shown as follows:

Investigative task → collaborative grouping → joint outcome

Independent tasks → co-operative grouping → separate outcomes

Fisher (2005: 92) suggests that collaborative work gives children the opportunity to benefit in five ways: (1) they learn from each other; (2) they engage in exploratory talk to broaden understanding; (3) they develop problem-solving strategies; (4) they learn to take turns, negotiate with others, see other points of view and argue for their own point of view; (5) they are able to build relationships with a wider circle of people. He adds that it is to be expected that children working together will achieve more than working singly, but that for collaborative groups to be successful they have to be planned, monitored and supported. Collaborative tasks require the active involvement of every child to achieve the objective. Between them, pupils in a group need to offer a range of skills, principally the ability to speculate, predict, justify, evaluate and generalise (see Figure 10.2).

Even collaborative grouping can result in the exclusion of individual children from the process due to their insecurity, lack of experience as a group member or dominance by the

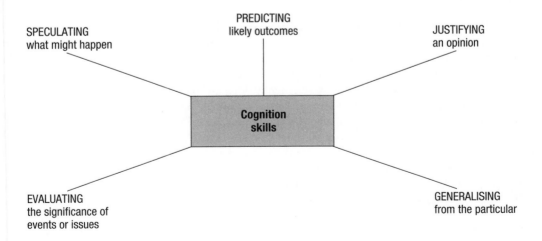

FIGURE 10.2 Cognition skills needed for collaboration

stronger characters. Collaborative group work needs crew members; there is no room for passengers. The joint activities do not detract from the principle that each child has a personal responsibility for learning, as no one can learn for somebody else; however, collaborative activities have the potential to be mutually beneficial.

Good practice

Evaluate the way in which pupil groupings facilitate: (1) co-operative learning and (2) collaborative learning. Reorganise the tables or seating arrangements to minimise unhelpful conversations and maximise learning.

Monitoring single groups

Close attention to a single group of children is difficult when the whole class has to be managed. Inexperienced teachers can find themselves involved with one table of children, attempting to give them full attention, while the remainder of the class drift along restlessly, wave their hands aloft seeking help or form queues while they wait for attention. You have to decide how much to permit random questions to you 'across the room' from the children at other tables and how much to insist that they persevere until you are available to come and assist them. Even with a TA to support you, overall class management is your responsibility and control issues can soon emerge if the children are unclear about the work or cannot proceed for lack of resources and direction. Consequently, in designing tasks for groups, a number of considerations have to be taken into account, especially with enquiry-based tasks (both practical or paper-based), of which the following are significant:

- Ensure that the children understand what is required of them.
- Try to create the conditions such that pupils are offered some ownership of ideas and, where possible, given permission and encouragement to interpret the task rather than follow instructions slavishly.
- Provide the resources and clarify the extent to which children can be autonomous in their use.
- Clarify who handles the resources; who takes responsibility for recording results; who reports back; and how each child is to be involved in the venture.
- Match task to ability or create a series of linked activities, each one more challenging than the preceding one. See varieties of whole-class management, later in this chapter.
- Make sure that the activity lasts sufficiently long to allow children to become fully involved but not so long that they suffer from discouragement or task fatigue.
- Keep noise levels suitably restrained (but avoid insisting on quiet or the whole purpose of dialogue in collaboration is stymied).
- Be explicit about how much needs to be recorded and how it should be done (formally written or lists or diagrams or pictures, etc.).
- Regulate the children's movement around the room.
- Give regular guidance about time factors.

Group work makes heavy demands upon teachers who need to find the opportunity to review their classroom management, intervene where necessary and maintain a whole-class perspective. The involvement of a TA is important as a means of spreading the responsibility for advising, monitoring progress and maintaining order. Opportunity for groups to share findings with the members of other groups helps to strengthen and extend learning. Make sure that you leave sufficient time towards the end of the session for this vital lesson component ('the plenary') or as soon after as practically possible.

Good practice

Never assume that a so-called 'independent' group can be fully independent. Spend extra time explaining the task to them so as to avoid a situation in which the children are struggling to cope without direct adult intervention or simply unable to proceed. Always include a straightforward open-ended element to engage their interest, should they conclude the main activity sooner than anticipated. For instance, 'Think of how many ways you can...' or 'Now make up some similar sums for a friend to try' or 'Draw a picture of how you might have looked as a Victorian.'

Cross-reference: Guided Reader Extract 4

Whole-class teaching

Public performance

Dealing with the class as an undifferentiated whole requires additional and different skills from one-to-one and group work. Kutnick (1994) describes whole-class teaching as 'an efficient means of transmitting information to a large number of children simultaneously' but alerts teachers to the extent of their 'didactic control of knowledge and socialisation in the classroom' (p. 25) as they do so. Whole-class teaching therefore demands a high level of skill and application to keep pupils attending and interested for the given period of time. There is some evidence that more frequent and regular use of whole-class teaching might help to raise standards in literacy and numeracy, though there are limitations attached to this approach, too, especially in the light of an emphasis on what is fashionably called individualised learning.

Many teachers find that their public performance in front of the whole class is central to successful teaching, as well as establishing their reputation, and for inexperienced teachers it is essential that they undertake thorough practice of performance prior to the teaching session. There are few experienced teachers who can stand up and offer accurate information, demonstrate ideas and control a question-and-answer session without spending a lot of time in preparation, so you won't be any different. Some teachers write out a memory aid on a sheet of paper, which they place in a strategic spot or on a large card that they pin to the back wall and glance at occasionally as a reminder of key points. As a trainee teacher, there is no shame in referring to your lesson plan, though the more that you can operate without having to stop and look down at your notes, the more in control of events you will look, feel and sound. The ideal is to have the lesson 'storyboard' clear in your mind and only refer to plans for the details (see Chapter 9).

In gauging the quality of pupils' responses during interaction, you need to take account of the fact that working closely with the whole class raises different issues from working with a single group of children (see Baines *et al.* 2008). Group work is more intimate and intensive and tends to invite spontaneity, so teachers must make it clear to what extent they welcome such behaviour. In whole-class teaching, however, there are numerous practical issues, such as sweeping your gaze around the room, speaking loudly and clearly enough so that everyone can hear, using visual aids and technology, selecting children to answer questions from a wide range of volunteers and ensuring that children don't have their hands up for too long. Experienced practitioners look for ways of eliciting a response other than an individual pupil answering, such as 'whisper what you think to a friend' or giving an either/or option and asking children to select one of them by using a simple voting technique (e.g. thumbs up/thumbs down).

Good practice

If you lack confidence in front of the whole class, practise and record yourself before-hand and write down the questions that you are going to use with them. Listen to the clarity with which you are expressing yourself. Give some thought to the types of responses your words and questions might elicit from the children and how you will use their answers to enhance learning.

Whole-class lesson procedures

Instructing is an essential element of whole-class management and if it is linked with the variety of organisation discussed earlier in this chapter, it is possible to represent this diagram-matically (see Figure 10.3). In broad terms, Phase 1 links the lesson with previous work,

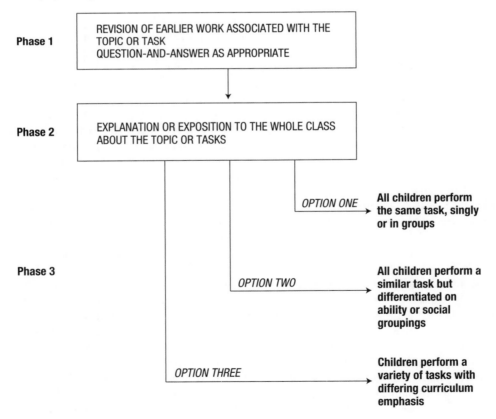

FIGURE 10.3 Lessons which commence with a whole-class briefing

reminding children of what went before and explaining the relevance of previous learning. In your haste to get the present lesson moving, it is essential not to overlook the importance of this phase. Without linking present knowledge to existing knowledge the process of learning becomes a detached exercise for children and is unlikely to produce the best outcome. One way in which pupils' memories can be stirred and the new lesson introduced is by the use of question-and-answer. The opening phase is followed by a second phase consisting of direct instruction, which is then followed by a whole-class briefing. In the third phase, the class is divided up for activities using one of the options selected by the teacher. Most often, therefore, the introduction is followed by a question-and-answer period for the purpose of task clarification or raising ideas, which in turn leads to one of the teaching and learning types indicated in Figure 10.4, referring to teaching and learning types based on a whole-class introduction.

Time spent on the introductory part of the lesson should be seen as an investment, ensuring that you do not have to repeat the same information and explanations to different children, who remain confused about what to do and how to go about it. Although some children require an adult's close direction during the lesson, the greater the independence they ultimately achieve, the greater the freedom for the teacher to monitor class progress and to engage in one-to-one or group interactions.

Teaching the class together for part or all of a session is an opportunity for teachers to perfect their ability to articulate clearly, assert their authority and pace their delivery in a

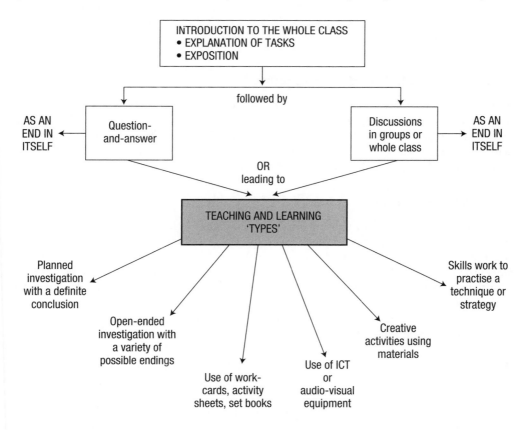

FIGURE 10.4 Teaching and learning types based on whole-class introduction

stimulating way that engages the children's interest. The teacher's personality is a critical factor in the prevailing mood: dictatorial or responsive, warm or aloof, humorous or sullen, encouraging or demoralising, harsh or sympathetic. There are issues of class control and discipline to consider but these should not detract from the value and sense of achievement that come about as a result of dealing with the class as a whole. Whatever the lesson structure adopted when working with the whole class, a number of issues are central to success:

- Children need to sense the teacher's enthusiasm for the subject matter in the way that the task is introduced, expectations are explained and questions are invited.
- Children learn more if they are informed about the lesson purpose and why the tasks and activities are necessary to enhance learning.
- The activity phase must allow for the fact that children work at different rates and there is often wide variance in concentration level and commitment.

With greater experience, many of the above procedures and practices will be spontaneous; as a beginner teacher, however, it is essential to master the basics by identifying them, practising them, addressing weaknesses and learning from accomplished colleagues. Don't be discouraged if you stumble and feel vulnerable in the early stages of handling the whole class; it is an extremely difficult skill to acquire and in a very real sense you will never stop learning about the most effective approach to employ. You also have to face the fact that strategies and techniques that suit one class are not necessarily appropriate for the next. That's part of the challenge and the joy of teaching!

Varieties of whole-class management

Whole-class sessions are often associated with the formal structure of literacy or numeracy lessons; however, there are a number of other variations in organising lessons, of which six approaches are seen in primary schools. For ease of reference, these forms of task management will be referred to as 'linear', 'circular', 'staged', 'spoked', 'single' and 'stepped'. Each approach has advantages and limitations, as follows.

Linear task management

This approach consists of a single whole-class introduction followed by tasks that gradually increase in difficulty as groups of pupils work their way through them. All children attempt task one, some will proceed to task two, fewer still to task three and so on. The teacher monitors progress by checking that a particular task has been completed successfully before permitting children to proceed to further tasks (see Figure 10.5). Only the more able or those who work harder or faster are likely to reach the later tasks. Consequently, linear management lends itself to a straightforward form of differentiation in which a single task, progressively more difficult, is used as the lesson spine. There are a number of implications:

- The later tasks must be a little more challenging than the earlier ones.
- There is a danger that the more able and less motivated children will linger unduly on the less demanding tasks.
- If children work in mixed ability groups on a task organised within the linear approach, the more able may be slowed down or the less able may be carried along without gaining proper understanding.

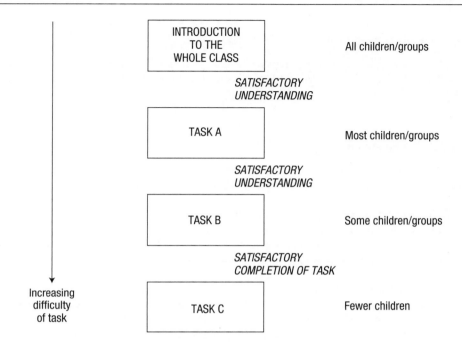

FIGURE 10.5 The linear approach

Another challenge for teachers is how best to pick up the threads of learning next time the class meets for that particular subject or topic, as different groups and individuals will have reached a variety of end-points during the previous session, thus placing heavy demands on the quality and quantity of assessment required to ascertain progress. A good introduction in the next lesson becomes essential for the purpose of reviewing the preceding one, clarifying understanding and setting fresh targets based on progress to date. The same issue applies to the children who were, for whatever reason, absent in earlier sessions.

Linear task management is sometimes used with worksheets in subjects like mathematics, in which sequential learning is more easily planned, or in topic areas where there are a number of different experiences and skills to be covered sequentially over a period of time. However, there are a number of challenges for teachers adopting this approach:

■ Some children view the process as a competition and tend to rush ahead.
■ Teachers can become overwhelmed by monitoring during the lesson, as they keep track of children completing different tasks at various times throughout a session.
■ Children can be demoralised as they compare themselves unfavourably with their more capable classmates.
■ Subsequent lessons can deteriorate into 'Carry on with the work you left off last time' and lack any direct teacher input.
■ The progress gap between the less and more able, or between the faster and ponderous workers, becomes more pronounced.

Activate your thinking!

All five groups in the class have completed task A, three have completed task B, one is part way through task C and one group is ready to begin the final task. How will you begin the next session?

Circular task management

Following a whole-class introduction, a second type of task management is to organise learning using a circular approach. It differs from the linear in two important respects:

1. Whereas with a linear approach children can work individually, in pairs or in groups, the circular approach relies on group work.
2. Whereas children can proceed through the range of linear tasks at varying rates, the circular approach requires synchronised completion.

The circular approach can be used where groups are involved in working on different tasks from the same curriculum area (say, history) or tasks from different subject areas within a common theme (e.g. festivals). It is most commonly used in science or other enquiry-based sessions. Following the introduction, each group is allocated a specific task and given a time limit within which to complete it. To ensure that groups finish at about the same time requires meticulous planning and is usually not possible within the confines of (say) a typical fifty-five-minute session without undue haste and prematurely concluding tasks. Teachers need to form pupil groups so that they are of comparable size and ability, and provide sufficient resources so that each group engages with the full range of tasks in the given time.

Holding activities made available for quicker workers should serve a purpose rather than merely keeping children busy for a while, though occasionally it is necessary to utilise an unrelated activity (such as choosing a book to read quietly). Groups that take longer than expected to finish often require additional support or be encouraged to modify the original task to make it more manageable. However, it is inevitable that some slower workers will struggle to complete the task fully in the given time and accelerate in the final few minutes as they try to finish it, with the inevitable adverse impact on quality.

Circular tasks must be of broadly equivalent length if the system is to have any chance of operating successfully; however, despite organising the activities in such a way that they require the same time to complete, some tasks inevitably require longer than others and groups work at different speeds. This fact sometimes leads to an excessive reliance on 'holding tasks' for some groups if they finish early and undue pressure on others to hurry and finish if they take too long to complete. Time is therefore a key factor in managing the circular approach, as to maximise resource usage and maintain control all groups must change task simultaneously (see Figure 10.6).

The tasks can be designed to vary the nature of the challenge; thus, children involved in the open-ended task might move on to a creative task; the group practising skills might tackle a planned investigation, and so on. The circular approach aims to give every child the opportunity to be involved in many different types of work over a given period, which sometimes extends across several sessions or a day set aside for the purpose. For example, a mathematics problem-solving 'circus' requires considerable flexibility and is unlikely to fit snugly into the timetabled sessions.

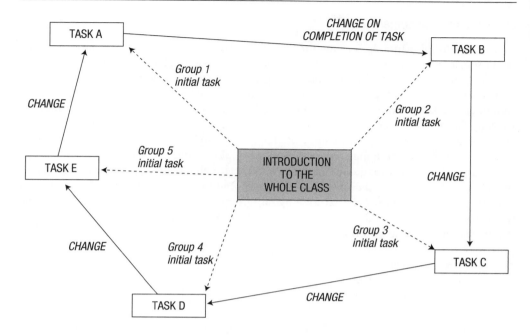

FIGURE 10.6 The circular approach

Managing resources is particularly important to the smooth flow of sessions. For instance, a lot of disruption can be caused if a group finds that some of the batteries are dead and the bulbs fade when it is their turn to try the circuit experiments.

Many teachers discover that although the circular approach is challenging and difficult to organise, it is also motivating and stimulating when it works well. It is not advisable to attempt the circular approach unless you are convinced of its benefits over and above other approaches or in specialised situations with well-established resources and prescribed activities (such as the whole class working on a series of designated science experiments). Trainee teachers should only attempt such complex organisation of learning with the co-operation of the host teacher and at least one other adult.

Activate your thinking!

Halfway through a set of activities based on a circular form of organisation, Angie returns from a music lesson, having missed a considerable amount of her group's previous two tasks. How might Angie be helped to catch up? (1) Join other groups on a random basis to experience each activity superficially; or (2) find out from other group members what has happened so far; or (3) talk to the teacher about the missed tasks; or (4) wait until the review phase to hear from classmates about what they did and found.

Staged task management

Another means of managing learning for the whole class is when children are engaged in different subject activities (or at least different aspects of the same subject area) at the same time within the same general topic. This form of organisation is rarely used owing to the introduction of structured teaching in literacy and mathematics, but offers an exciting alternative for ambitious teachers. Groups are normally based on academic ability. One group may be working on an aspect of mathematics, another group employing written English, a third group on artwork. If the groups consist of children of varying academic ability, then within each of these broad groupings differentiation takes place *within* a single group rather than across groups. For instance, group 1, consisting of twelve children, might be sub-divided into two ability sub-groups for their maths work; group 2 in two sub-groups working in pairs on different aspects of reported speech for English; group 3 could be working together but be found at different stages in developing a composite picture in art. Thus, the following organisation exists in the same classroom:

> *Maths group:* two ability sub-groups
> *English group:* work in pairs
> *Art group:* collaborative activities.

Sometimes the broad curriculum groupings are within the same topic or subject area. Thus, for the history unit about explorers, group 1 might be finding out about the lives of individual explorers, group 2 plotting their courses on outline maps, and group 3 writing about the realities and hardships of travel:

> *Group 1:* Researching the lives of explorers (cross–curricular)
> *Group 2:* Plotting journeys on a map (geography)
> *Group 3:* Writing about the hazards of travel (literacy).

In the subject area of music, a class of Year 1 children could be developing ideas about performing and composing, as follows:

> *Group 1:* Creating simple musical patterns using resonators
> *Group 2:* Experimenting with low notes using different shapes
> *Group 3:* Making plucking instruments.

A high level of organisation and planning is necessary where a number of groups of this type are involved, not only to ensure that they are clear about the tasks but also to manage their progress. As a rule, a teaching assistant is needed to support learning and monitor progress.

Sometimes a modified version of the staged approach is used if a whole-class enterprise is intended, whereby the briefings all take place before any of the groups begin work on their specific activity. For instance, in a large space session where groups of children are working in the hall on a theme (different dance forms, say), the teacher speaks to the assembled class about each activity first, so that when the groups are later drawn together all the children are aware of what the others have been doing. If groups change activity at some point, the whole-class briefing enables the transition to take place without further lengthy explanations. This approach demands that the children listen attentively throughout the teacher's explanations and understand the purpose of the final combined enterprise. This approach requires that your account of the tasks is precise, concise and clear, or when the children change activity they will need reminding of what they have to do. In this modified version of the staged task approach:

> *Stage 1:* All the children listen while each group is briefed.
> *Stage 2:* Separate groups are involved with their activities.
> *Stage 3:* Groups are brought together to discuss and share ideas.
> *Stage 4:* Activities are reassigned and the process continues.

The staged approach makes a number of demands of teachers:

- Instructions must be explicit.
- Resources must be in place before the children are briefed.
- The last group to be briefed should not be kept waiting too long.
- The opening and closing minutes of a session are likely to be quite intensive.

In common with the linear and circular methods, the staged approach requires careful planning, attention to learning objectives and close monitoring of children's progress. Many teachers of younger children use a form of staged approach but only when there is a TA or another reliable adult available, as this makes this approach more manageable and places fewer demands on the teacher. In common with the circular approach, if groups swap activities at some mid-point in the session, the staged approach requires that tasks are of similar duration, that there is account taken of more and less able children, and that early finishers are not left without a purposeful activity.

Spoked task management

Probably the most common form of managing learning is to organise children into ability groups and provide a separate but related task for each of the groups. The introductory phase of the lesson brings all the children together for the purpose of explaining and exploring the topic, raising issues, asking questions and so forth, before sending the children to their activities. The number of groups will vary according to the pupils' ability and experience. Group size is typically around eight to ten children. Thus, in a class of thirty, three or four different and suitable tasks have to be provided for the session, usually in the same subject area. At the end of the task phase, children complete their work and, where relevant, reconvene as a whole class to evaluate the learning, share findings and clarify points.

The spoked approach places a heavy burden of preparation on teachers, as it requires them to design a variety of activities, monitor progress across the range of tasks and evaluate separate outcomes. It has the advantage of targeting learning and facilitating differentiation. Although you may want to concentrate on guiding one group in particular while the others work independently, in reality all children require some support and advice from an adult to make optimum progress. Without such help, pupils 'tread water' until assistance arrives, even if you encourage peer support. Ideally, the system works most effectively when the teacher is liberated from the constraints of monitoring a group and can move freely about the room, offering support as necessary.

Single task management

We have already been alerted to the importance of matching the demands of tasks to the capability and learning experiences of the children. Poor matching leads to underachievement (if the task is too easy) or frustration and low esteem (if the task is too hard). This principle is not to argue for some sort of precision engineering in the ability–task link but rather that structuring the lesson with a keen awareness of pupils' existing knowledge, understanding and potential for advancement is an essential prerequisite for success learning. Alternative ways of differentiating are discussed more fully in Chapter 9.

The single task approach is used when every group or individual is engaged on a similar task in a specific curriculum subject or area but *the teacher has different expectations* for each group/child, depending upon their ability and previous experience of the work. Following the introduction and explanation of the task to the whole class, each group is allocated the same resources and given a similar length of time to complete the problem, investigation, experiment or research. As part of this process, children write up the work in different ways. For instance, a less capable group might be encouraged to use more diagrammatic representations than the extended written forms used by a more able group. Towards the end of the session time, the groups report their progress and compare findings. The teacher is able to draw the various strands together, acknowledge the diversity of outcomes and weave them into a comprehensible set of conclusions (see Figure 10.7).

The single task approach offers a number of advantages:

- A single set of learning objectives can be established that apply to all pupils.
- The process is relatively easily managed.
- All the children are involved throughout the lesson.
- Groups of children do not have to wait around to receive specific instructions before commencing their task.

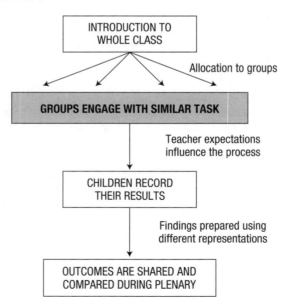

FIGURE 10.7 Single task approach

■ The teacher is able to make reference during the lesson to the progress of other groups working on the same or similar task.

There are also disadvantages, as follows:

■ The single task has to be carefully planned and appropriate to every child.
■ There have to be sufficient resources for everyone to do the same task/activity at the same time.
■ As in all collaborative ventures, the group composition has to be appropriate to avoid children becoming marginalised (unless the children are working individually).
■ The teacher requires a high level of skill to draw out all the learning points in a way that can be understood by all the children and allow slower learners to feel satisfied that their contribution is valued.

The single task approach, like any other teaching method, is better under certain circumstances than others. In particular, it has value in investigative, open-ended tasks in which collaboration and whole-class sharing are significant. However, the principles can be applied to literacy and numeracy sessions in which lesson objectives are common for the whole class and the children tend to be allocated similar group tasks to reinforce and extend their learning. Owing to the fact that the single task approach is relatively easy to manage compared with others referred to above, it dominates much of formal primary education practice.

Stepped task management

The stepped approach is most commonly used in organising and managing large space lessons (PE, gymnastics, games and drama) and requires specific and detailed explanations/demonstrations by the teacher, followed by more independent activities undertaken by pupils. In the stepped approach, all the children are introduced to an elementary task, which they then explore or practise for a given length of time, followed by introductions to increasingly complex tasks, each of which the children engage with as individuals, pairs or small groups. Thus:

TASK ONE (elementary) leads on to TASK TWO (more involved) leads on to TASK THREE (most complex).

It is often the case that the teacher encourages children to try a form of the activity on their own initially, then (say) in pairs, then as a small group. Depending on the theme and subject, it might be appropriate to bring the whole class together to demonstrate progress, asking each group to report in turn. The overall whole-class management for each task will look something like this, beginning with the elementary task:

1. The teacher introduces the activity and explains/demonstrates what the children have to do.
2. The children practise the skills individually or in pairs.
3. Individuals or pairs combine to create small groups, who work together.
4. Each group takes a turn to show what it has done to the rest of the class.

Once you are happy that the first task is successfully completed, the class is brought together and the second task is explained or demonstrated. Depending on the nature of the task, children repeat the sequence noted above or work in small groups immediately. The pattern is repeated for the third task, and so on.

One advantage of the stepped approach is that it enables you to explore each step fully until you are satisfied with the product. If the children are not progressing as you hoped they would, you can spend longer on enhancing the skills or techniques required, rehearse the ideas and repeat the activities. If they make more rapid progress, it is relatively simple to move on to the next task with minimum delay or offer the children the opportunity to explore the theme to promote initiative and creativity.

In practice, the lesson sometimes does not progress as smoothly as the above description implies, but the stepped principle of exploring thoroughly a relatively easily controlled task before moving on to a slightly more complex one offers great scope for pupils learning new skills while having ample opportunities to interpret the task creatively and develop their own ideas.

Managing the learning of young children

Principles and framework

There are numerous basic and essential teaching strategies for the effective management of young children: clarity of explanation, use of repetition, employment of visual aids, setting a number of short-term goals, active use of TAs and the development of reading skills. The Foundation Stage was the name given to the first part of the National Curriculum (NC), focusing on children from the age of 3 years to the end of reception year (aged 5 years), though use of the term 'foundation' in government documentation is a controversial one (Fisher 2002), implying as it does that early learning merely provides the necessary bedrock for further learning and is not valuable in its own right. The philosophy underpinning the Foundation Stage was that learning should be planned and structured with an emphasis on fun and relevant activities that motivate young children. From 2008 the Birth to Three Matters framework and the Foundation Stage merged to form a single Early Years Foundation Stage (EYFS) covering care, learning and development in all early years settings from birth to the August after their fifth birthday. In effect, the EYFS is separate from the NC, though there is meant to be a synergy between the two. The EYFS welfare requirements are intended to safeguard and promote children's welfare in four key areas:

1. The suitability of the adults that look after them
2. Safe and suitable premises, environment and equipment
3. Every child receiving an enjoyable and challenging learning experience
4. The records, policies and procedures for the safe and efficient management of settings and meeting the needs of the children.

The principle underpinning the EYFS is that every child is an individual with unique needs and entitled to have the opportunity to learn at his or her own pace and preference; consequently, all children should be able to work and play in a safe and secure environment to explore and investigate the world. Personal, social and emotional development involving children's emotional wellbeing, developing respect for others, and building social skills and a positive disposition to learn is viewed as being of central importance. It is important to remember that young children have already had a number of years of education in the care of parents and family, so continued partnership and discussion with parents is essential when formulating policy and practice (Feinstein et al. 2008).

Implementation

Implementing the EYFS curriculum requires thorough preparation but also sufficient flexibility to allow children to initiate some activities themselves. However, a vital aspect of the adult role is to intervene and assist children when they are frustrated with their inability to complete a task or are thwarted in their enthusiasm to perform an activity, where possible offering them alternative activities and the support to complete them successfully. As in all areas of school life, reinforcement of positive behaviour, acknowledgement of effort and praise for achievements should form an integral part of daily practice. Regular monitoring and evaluation can take place using observation checklists, child development profiles and, crucially, regular meetings between groups of staff.

The EYFS guidance promotes the importance of outdoor opportunities as being crucial to a child's growth and development, and the expectation that, wherever possible, there should be access to an outdoor play area for every child (see Chapter 3 for more information about play). In practice, this facility may not be immediately accessible in every case, but it is hoped that other arrangements can be safely made so that children have some opportunity for playing outdoors. Many schools have developed their facilities to provide under-cover play areas, which nevertheless require regular adult supervision and monitoring.

In teaching children to read and spell, there is a lot of emphasis on the use of systematic and discrete phonics, as the prime approach to help children recognise key words. The phonics teaching should use familiar and well-known stories, characters and situations to engage the children's interest; it should also be multi-sensory: visual, aural and tactile. All four interdependent strands of language, speaking, listening, reading and writing, are significant but it is particularly important to foster speaking and listening skills, as these lay the foundation for later reading and writing and help to develop the full range of children's communication skills. Further information about learning to read can be found in Chapter 9. Use of phonics is also addressed later in this chapter.

Good practice

The emphasis on speaking and listening ('oracy') that is fostered in early years education should be continued into Key Stages 1 and 2 through structured opportunities in literacy sessions and collaborative activities, and through creating a learning environment in which children's questions, views and opinions, properly expressed, are invited and valued. See Dawes (2010) for techniques about the direct teaching of speaking and listening and ways in which children can use one another as a rich resource.

Dawes, L. (2010) *Creating a Speaking and Listening Classroom*, London: David Fulton.

A revised version of the EYFS Statutory Framework and Practice Guidance document was published in May 2008 with changes intended to clarify areas where feedback indicated it would be helpful (QCA 2008). Four areas were highlighted:

1. *A unique child:* Every child is a competent learner from birth who can be resilient, capable, confident and self-assured.
2. *Positive relationships:* Children learn to be strong and independent from a base of loving and secure relationships with parents and/or a key person.

3. *Enabling environments:* The environment plays a key role in supporting and extending children's development and learning.

4. *Learning and development:* Children develop and learn in different ways and at different rates and all areas of learning and development are equally important and interconnected.

Early learning goals

The early learning goals include six areas of learning and (non-statutory) 'stepping stones' of progress towards the goals. The guidance clarifies strategies by which teachers and other adults working in educational settings (not only schools) can help children to make optimum progress. The six areas of learning are organised as follows:

1. Personal, social and emotional development
2. Communication, language and literacy
3. Mathematical development
4. Knowledge and understanding of the world
5. Physical development
6. Creative development.

Curriculum guidance contains examples to help teachers and support staffs identify the progress that children are making and suggest how the practitioner can use this information to support and consolidate learning and help children to make progress. The guidance is intended to help practitioners ensure that each child is given the opportunity to make good progress towards the early learning goals and in a few cases to exceed them. The sections entitled 'communication, language and literacy' (see, for instance, Bradford 2009) and 'mathematical development' cover the stage for children aged 3 to the end of the reception year. In theory, the early learning goals synchronise with the objectives in the frameworks for teaching literacy and mathematics throughout the reception year, facilitating ease of planning. See, for example, Smidt and Green (2009) for advice about planning. Reception teachers have a choice about whether to cover daily literacy and mathematics lessons across the day or in a single unit of time. In order to ensure a smooth transition to more formal lessons during Year 1 (children aged 5 to 6 years), daily literacy and mathematics lessons are both intended to be in place by the end of the reception year.

The curriculum guidance stresses that the six areas of learning are intended to help practitioners plan the learning environment, activities and experiences for children, and provide a framework for the early years curriculum. However, this does not mean that young children's learning needs to be divided into separate and distinct areas, but rather that the document assists teachers in organising the curriculum. Thus, one 'unit' of experience may provide a child with opportunities to develop a number of competencies, skills and concepts across several areas of knowledge. For instance, creating a 'shop' area may help children to develop social skills, communicate their ideas to others, handle elementary money exchanges and use their experiences from shopping as a guide to appropriate behaviour when dealing with people. Thus, children can develop language, mathematical, physical, personal and social skills through a single activity, though it is far from easy for a teacher to monitor progress and development in each area for every child when using this 'mixed economy' approach.

The EYFS uses practitioners' observational assessment of children's progress in everyday activities on an ongoing basis to inform how they can best plan further learning and development activities appropriate to the stage that each child has reached. Assessment results also allow the staff to provide parents and other professionals with more accurate information about the children's progress.

Thus, the early learning goals establish expectations that most children are likely to reach by the end of the stage but are not intended to provide a rigid curriculum but rather provide a structure for planning to be built on for future learning. By the end of the stage, it is likely that some children will have exceeded the goals, whereas other children will be working towards some or all of them. Those who are still 'working towards' normally include younger children (summer born), those without much or any previous early years experience (nursery education), those with special educational needs and those learning English as an additional language (EAL).

Activate your thinking!

Many teachers complain that the assessment detail required about 4- and 5-year-old children is excessively complex and unnecessarily time-consuming to record; others argue that more accurate and detailed assessments help teachers to identify learning needs and adjust their teaching accordingly. See the next chapter for more information about assessing pupils' progress.

Stepping stones

The curriculum guidance identifies 'stepping stones' of progress towards the early learning goals intended to help practitioners understand and interpret what the goals mean for young children throughout this stage. The stepping stones identify the sorts of knowledge, skills, understanding and attitudes that children need if they are to 'achieve' these early learning goals by the end of the stage. Progression is shown by the use of yellow, then blue and then green bands that are not intended to be age-related goals, and the number of steps varies between and within areas of learning. In some cases the stepping stones relate to an individual aspect of an early learning goal, while in others a group of closely linked aspects are brought together.

Although the stepping stones are not age-related, it is anticipated that most 3-year-old children will be better described by the steps described through the yellow band, while the green band will usually reflect the attainment of 5-year-old children. The stepping stones tend to be presented in a hierarchical order but not all children conform to this sequence of learning. Inevitably, some stepping stones will be achieved quickly, whereas others will take considerably longer to achieve. Thus, some children will attain confidence in some of the later stepping stones but struggle with some of the earlier ones. Ideally, as children move from one stone to another, they should take with them what they have already learned and continue to practise, refine and use their previous learning. In truth, many things have to be revised, updated and reinforced for, as we noted in Chapters 7 and 8, learning is not a smooth, predictable process.

Once children reach the reception class, the teacher in charge has a major responsibility to monitor and assess children's competence and progress. Completion of the full schedule is onerous and many versions of this 'baseline assessment' have been suggested and used. The final observational assessment – or Early Years Foundation Stage profile – is recorded at the end of the reception year.

Activate your thinking!

Teachers are required to ensure that children make good progress to 'meet' the early learning goals or, if possible, 'exceed' them. How, if at all, can teachers ensure that these goals are met? How might children be moved from 'meeting' to 'exceeding'? How does such a view of learning square with a child's natural maturation and development?

Good practice

Careful sequencing of points, appropriately presented, is essential, especially for less able pupils and younger children, as it offers them a framework within which they can build their understanding. There is also a limit to the amount of information that children can hold in their minds at one time, so visual aids such as a picture, chart or summary sheet should be used as memory aids and reinforcing points.

Primary Framework for literacy and mathematics

Changes in the framework

The changes contained in the renewed Primary Framework for literacy and mathematics (DfES 2006a) compared with the original national strategies for literacy and numeracy (mathematics) are said to build upon research and evaluation undertaken since the introduction of the strategies at the end of the 1990s. The structured approaches to literacy and mathematics lessons as promoted in the original frameworks continue to be recommended as a useful model for lesson planning; the new guidance, however, promotes greater flexibility. In particular, links between mathematics, literacy and other subjects are promoted, along with a range of different lesson structures and mini plenary sessions (as opposed to a single slot at the end of the lesson). The framework is organised into 'strands' (twelve for literacy and seven for mathematics) relating directly to the early learning goals and to English and mathematics at Key Stage 1 and Key Stage 2. The construction of the frameworks around strands helps teachers to highlight some of the specific aspects of literacy and mathematics that some children find difficult to learn.

The slimmed-down learning objectives from Foundation Stage to Year 6 are presented in two ways: (1) by year or stage; and (2) by learning objectives presented across the strands showing the specific progression in learning through each strand. Foundation Stage elements mirror the relevant sections in the EYFS (see earlier) and the objectives are referenced to the early learning goals. Objectives also show Year 6 progression into Year 7. The main changes relevant to the primary phase of education include:

- creating a clearer set of outcomes to support teachers and practitioners in planning for progression in literacy and mathematics;
- helping raise the attainment of all children, personalise learning and secure intervention for those children who need it;
- bringing an increased sense of drive and momentum to literacy and mathematics through the primary phase, involving some scaling up of expectations and a greater focus upon planning for progression;

- supporting schools and settings in implementing high quality teaching of phonics and early reading;
- introducing a new, electronic format that allows for customised planning, teaching and assessment, linking to a wide range of teaching and learning resources.

Literacy

Background

The original National Literacy Strategy (NLS) was launched in 1998 as part of the government's attempts to raise standards in schools. Basic literacy involves the ability to read and write, and to speak and listen; however, fuller details were included in the framework document. Teachers were only given a small amount of flexibility in the way they planned and taught literacy, as the structure of the literacy hour itself was tightly defined. The literacy hour framework was meant to introduce common practices and routines across the school in order that the quality of teaching and its impact upon pupils' achievements could be easily monitored. It did, however, require a considerable amount of effort on the part of teachers and pupils to maintain the approach from day to day. As such, it was essential to avoid any sense of 'here we go again' but rather to use the time as a stimulating opportunity to interact with children and establish a sound basis for other curriculum work. Three 'strands' to literacy work were identified for all children:

Word level: emphasising phonics, spelling and vocabulary
Sentence level: emphasising grammar and punctuation
Text level: emphasising comprehension and composition.

For details about the literacy curriculum, see Chapter 6.

Primary National Strategy framework

The Primary National Strategy framework (PNS) for literacy was introduced in 2006 and incorporates recommendations from a review about effective strategies for the teaching of reading, and replaced the NLS. The PNS places much stronger emphasis on drama and speaking and listening and on assessment for learning (AFL). Four seminal principles were applied in developing the framework:

1. To ensure the best teaching of early reading
2. To build on high quality speaking and listening
3. Systematic high quality phonics teaching as main first strategy
4. The use of so-called synthetic phonics in building words; for example, c-a-t = cat (see Chapter 9).

In addition, children should experience a rich literacy experience, including drama, stories, speaking and listening around this. Communication skills depend on children being competent in a number of key skills, together with having the confidence, opportunity, encouragement, support and disposition to use them. There is a greater focus upon teachers and practitioners using their assessment to personalise learning than in the NLS. The PNS framework for literacy has twelve strands, with learning objectives listed as follows:

1. Speaking
2. Listening and responding
3. Group discussion/interaction
4. Drama
5. Word recognition
6. Word structure and spelling
7. Understanding and interpreting texts
8. Engaging with and responding to texts
9. Creating and shaping texts
10. Text structure and organisation
11. Sentence structure and punctuation
12. Presentation.

Objectives from each strand are united within coherent units of work that may last three to five weeks. Through these units, speaking and listening, reading and writing are developed. The objectives are presented by year group from Foundation Year (reception) to Year 6. They are not split into terms as in the NLS. They are not under headings of word, sentence and text. Objectives are also presented by strand, e.g. strand 1 (speaking) contains objectives from Foundation to Year 6, so that a model of progression is included. Online resources on the PNS literacy site exemplify how to plan and include units for teachers to work from. The EYFS (see earlier) is intended to feed seamlessly into the PNS framework for literacy.

Attention to children with English as an additional language and to the progress of boys in general remains high. The introduction of more screen-based texts is evident through the objectives and there is an emphasis on creating cross-curricular links where possible, a practice not promoted in the original strategy. The original 'searchlights' model of reading has been subsumed into 'the simple view of reading' based on the idea that children need to develop word recognition and language comprehension skills. These are presented as two complementary processes.

Hardman *et al.* (2003) noted that, during literacy lessons, even teachers who used a strongly interactive style tended to focus on question-and-answer that required low cognition and asked only a small number of genuinely challenging questions that caused pupils to think hard. Teachers were also inclined to accept brief answers from children instead of probing what they had said and encouraging them to think more deeply. The teachers who were willing to dwell on a topic of interest for a little longer generally elicited more thoughtful and extensive responses. Teachers of younger children were especially prone to accepting superficial answers, and opportunities for sustained and extended dialogue were rare. Westwood (2004) refers to the importance of 'metacognition' in promoting pupil thinking and addressing learning difficulties, which 'often involves inner verbal self-instruction and self-questioning – talking to one's self in order to focus, reflect, control or review' (p. 29). Studies suggest that these objectives are not pursued with sufficient rigour by many teachers. For further information about questioning, see the appropriate section in the previous chapter.

Mathematics

Numeracy teaching

The first National Numeracy Strategy (NNS) was implemented in September 1999 in an attempt to raise teachers' expectations and improve standards in mathematics. For further details about the numeracy curriculum, see Chapter 6. Numeracy was broadly defined as knowing about numbers and number operations and required an ability and inclination to solve numerical problems, including those involving money or measures. It also demanded that pupils became familiar with the ways in which numerical information is gathered by counting and measuring, and presented in the form of graphs, charts and tables. Every teacher had to teach maths daily for between forty-five minutes and an hour, and lessons incorporating the following elements:

- Regular oral and mental work
- Good quality questioning to the whole class
- A variety of whole-class teaching and group work
- Instruction, demonstration and explanation
- Formal and informal assessment of pupils' progress
- Identifying and correcting pupils' misconceptions.

The original strategy encouraged teaching approaches that gave more emphasis to oral and mental work before written methods were introduced. As calculation skills require that pupils must learn some things by heart, daily practice to reinforce their grasp of the facts was (and still is) seen as essential, supported by the use of correct vocabulary and notation. Numeracy was to be used in subject areas outside the immediate maths lesson.

Effective teaching that involved using whole-class teaching was at the core of lessons, supposedly as a vehicle for pupils to respond to questions, ask their own questions, learn from one another and explain where they are unsure about mathematical concepts or techniques. Teachers had to be ready to listen closely to what children are saying and offer comment which helps them think 'beyond' the immediate problem and consider the way that maths influences real-life situations. Naturally, such responsive and interactive teaching methods are to be applauded and invite wholehearted approval. The strengths and limitations of whole-class teaching were explored earlier in this chapter.

The NNS fostered a view that group work had to be differentiated with respect to pupils' attainment, though teachers found that creating too many groups could be counter-productive as classroom management becomes difficult due to the spread of demands upon the teacher's time. In one sense, there can be as many 'groups' as pupils in the class because every child has particular and exclusive needs. Paired work is a helpful strategy, using activities such as number games where pupils can probe one another's thinking and interact purposefully. Although individual work has its place in teaching maths, used excessively it can lead to teachers spending too much time 'troubleshooting' when pupils are 'stuck' and insufficient time on teaching the strategies needed by every child in the class for solving mathematical problems.

The renewed framework

The renewed framework (introduced in 2006) is different from the 1999 framework in that it refers specifically to 'mathematics' and not to the unsatisfactory overarching term 'numeracy'. It also differs in three other ways:

1. It is an electronic version linked to a range of teaching and learning resources, intended to help teachers to plan, teach and assess more easily with regard to their own pupils.

2. Only seven strands of learning in mathematics are identified to give a broad overview of the mathematics curriculum in the primary phase.

3. Objectives have been slimmed down to sharpen attention on the important aspects of mathematics that need to be taught.

The seven strands of learning are as follows:

1. Using and applying mathematics
2. Counting and understanding number
3. Knowing and using number facts
4. Calculating
5. Understanding shape
6. Measuring
7. Handling data.

Of particular interest in the new framework is the place of problem solving, reasoning and the newly defined numeracy, which is located within processes such as seeking patterns, making connections, recognising relationships, working with numbers, shapes, space and measures, and counting, sorting and matching. Children are encouraged to use their knowledge and skills in these areas to solve problems, generate new questions and make connections across other areas.

For younger pupils in particular, mathematical understanding should be developed and enhanced through teaching strategies that incorporate stories, songs, games and imaginative play. In practice, this diversity of options allows you to be creative in your approach and not to feel locked into narrowly focused and formal teaching, but to be more adventurous in allowing children to explore ways in which mathematics has relevance to many different contexts. Thus, you can promote an understanding of maths indoors (such as studying wallpaper patterns) and outdoors (such as commercial product use), in everyday activities (such as volume of water used for washing) and financial transactions (such as making regular monthly payments).

Parental attitudes to mathematics

Parents are important in promoting positive attitudes towards maths and supporting their children's learning. As such, regular homework and close liaison between parents and schools is essential to consolidate learning in school. Street et al. (2009) focus on numeracy ('numbers') as a social practice and report on their investigations into the meanings and uses of numeracy in school and home and community contexts. The authors note considerable variation in what they refer to as the 'cultural resources' available in different homes and the way it appears to impact on children's achievements in numeracy, such that the closer the 'match' between home and school resources, the more likely that the child will do well in the subject.

While acknowledging the truth in Street et al.'s assertions, we also have to bear in mind that some parents have a negative attitude to maths and others do not possess more than a basic level of understanding of the subject. Children from weak academic backgrounds may be further disadvantaged if parents respond negatively to a school's request for their help. Similarly, account needs to be taken of children with special educational needs and English as an additional language in determining the most effective teaching approaches and extended learning requirements.

Activate your thinking!

How much mental agility do the children require to respond to your questions? How much opportunity do you give them to ponder problems at length?

The use of ICT

Over recent years, there has been a significant change in the status of Information and Communications Technology (ICT) in primary schools, leading to a situation in which it is now considered to be one of the 'core' areas of the curriculum, alongside English, mathematics and science. Governments have also shown themselves to be committed to supporting the development of ICT in education. Computers are such an integral part of modern-day life that it would be perverse if schools did not reflect the use of this technology in their teaching and learning programmes. A lot of money has been allocated to promote and fund the purchase of computers and every primary school in the United Kingdom has numerous machines and associated gadgetry, with at least one person with special expertise to advise about their classroom use – either a teacher or a teaching assistant. Most schools have a contract with a suitably qualified person to maintain and repair faulty computers.

Using ICT in teaching

The standards for the award of Qualified Teacher Status (QTS) state that ICT has an important role to play in most aspects of teachers' work in schools: in the act of teaching itself and also promoting learning for individuals, small groups and whole classes. ICT has become increasingly influential in the processes of planning, assessment, evaluation, administration and management. ICT has become especially significant in compiling statistics of children's test performances and producing detailed facts for parents about their children's progress. Two of the Q-Standards for QTS in England and Wales state that trainee teachers should: (1) know how to use skills in literacy, numeracy and ICT to support their teaching and wider professional activities; and (2) be able to design opportunities for learners to develop their literacy, numeracy and ICT skills. Not only should you be able to use ICT in your teaching but you should also be able to complete pupils' records of progress, prepare resources for pupils and reduce the time you spend on administrative tasks. See Ferrigan (2011) for useful advice about passing the ICT skills test.

In supporting good practice in teaching, ICT can, for example, enable a teacher to respond to a pupil's piece of writing at different stages of the process through the fact that the text can be saved and progressively modified over a period of time. Within the context of mathematics, a child can be encouraged to develop logical thinking from an activity that involves instructing a programmable robot to follow a particular path, and then modifying these instructions in the light of the robot's movement.

A further point is associated with teachers' ability to use ICT in a way that supports their own professional role. Commonly, teachers download the latest guidance for aspects of teaching such as 'support for early years' from a website, or using a word-processor to prepare a standardised template for lesson planning, and to find the desired teaching post. However, it is worth noting the warning from Allen *et al.* (2007) who suggest that, 'Even in areas where there is rich provision of equipment and/or Internet connections, it is possible to find evidence that the computer is not always fully or usefully integrated into the curriculum' (p. 14). Indeed, you could discover that your knowledge and expertise exceeds that of the host teacher.

The National Curriculum for ICT

The statutory statement on the use of information and communication technology across the curriculum within the National Curriculum states that pupils should be given opportunities to apply and develop their ICT capability through the use of ICT tools to support their learning in all subjects with the exception of physical education throughout Key Stages 1 and 2. Pupils should be able to use ICT tools appropriately to help them to find, explore, analyse, exchange and present information clearly and creatively after considered thought and selection. You can teach pupils how to employ ICT for rapid access to ideas and experiences from a wide range of people, communities and cultures. For instance, you may be able to 'twin' with a school in another part of the world to exchange ideas and learn about one another's cultures. Increased capability in the use of ICT promotes initiative and independent learning, with pupils being sufficiently knowledgeable to make informed judgements about when and where to use technology to best effect. In other words, random use of ICT, however skilful, is unsatisfactory; discrimination over its use is as important as the technical abilities that children employ. See D. Hall (2009) for advice about assessing whether ICT is preferable to other approaches for enhancing learning.

Organisation of ICT resources

Schools will organise their ICT resources in different ways, according to the number of computers for use and the space that is available to house them. Decisions about organisation may also be influenced by a teacher's preferences with regard to teaching and learning style (see above). Many schools will have at least one computer suite that is used to accommodate large groups or even a whole class of children such that they can all work at the computers at the same time. The suite will normally consist of a room that can either be booked in advance by the teacher or will be timetabled for each class throughout the week. Most teachers like to have several computers in or very close to their own classroom, enabling the children to make use of them throughout the day to access the Internet or print out completed work. Some schools have invested large amounts of capital and expertise in providing sophisticated technology and laptops for every pupil.

Over recent years nearly all schools have purchased interactive whiteboards (IWB) for use in the classroom and it is not uncommon for an IWB to be seen in every room. These resources have proved to be particularly effective in whole-class teaching situations: for example, as part of a literacy or numeracy lesson. Another way that schools have chosen to deploy their ICT resources is by setting up clusters of computers in, for example, the library or other open-access areas around the building so that groups can work with (say) a TA to explore or revise an area of learning. A much more flexible solution to the problem of providing access to ICT for the pupils is to employ portable computers that can be moved to wherever the children happen to be working, which may be outside the classroom (or even at home). However, cost constraints, monitoring of use and concerns about damage to the machines generally restrict such ambition. A few schools have created electronic links between school and home to facilitate (for instance) homework submission.

Activate your thinking!

It is estimated that about one million children do not have access to a computer at home. In what ways might such pupils in your class be so disadvantaged? How will you ensure that homework does not rely on the availability of a home computer? See Selwyn *et al.* (2010) for children's perceptions and insights into the use of ICT.

Selwyn, N., Potter, J. and Cranmer, S. (2010) *Primary Schools and ICT: Learning from pupil perspectives*, London: Continuum.

Management of self

Keeping things in perspective

Enthusiasm in teaching is important and can sometimes compensate for other shortcomings. However, even the greatest enthusiasm fades in the fierce glare of regular classroom commitments and other school responsibilities, which can exhaust even the fittest teacher. All too easily, the early gush of commitment to the job can be replaced by the heaviness of fatigue, so it is important to keep things in perspective and take note of the fact that:

■ teachers are only one of the children's educators;
■ children suffer if teachers work so hard that they become exhausted;
■ every teacher has poor lessons from time to time;
■ mistakes are inevitable and should be viewed constructively rather than as a cause for despair.

Teaching is both exhilarating and tiring: exhilarating because of the engagement in an exciting and stimulating process; tiring because of the constant expenditure of effort to ensure that the children are learning and on-task. The personal satisfaction gained as a result of a good lesson can keep a teacher fresh and in good spirits long after it is finished. Tiredness, on the other hand, can lead to listlessness and a distorted sense of priorities. Minor problems expand and fill the horizon. A tutor's constructive advice feels like a major reprimand. A lively group of children comes across as an untamed rabble.

Pacing yourself

In addition, sensible pacing of your efforts throughout each lesson and pausing from time to time to enable body and mind to relax are essential for combating the danger of exhaustion, which tends to creep up on you unawares. However, it is possible to retain a relaxed yet purposeful approach during lessons if you:

1. feel in control of the situation;
2. provide appropriate learning opportunities for the children so that they are happily occupied;
3. do not attempt to achieve too much in a single lesson;
4. ensure that the children work as hard as you do.

The third point is often overlooked. Inexperienced teachers tend to squeeze as much as they can into a session in the mistaken belief that it somehow demonstrates their commitment and determination to promote learning. In fact, when you have a class of your own you will soon discover that although you achieve curriculum coverage, there is little deep learning involved. It is far better to *cover a little* of the curriculum and *uncover a lot* of learning, than attempt to cover a lot and understand a little.

Safeguarding strategies

If every lesson is spent hauling the class along, like a mule pulling a cart through a swamp, then it is little wonder that teachers tire quickly. If you flit from one child to another in an effort to respond to everyone's questions, behaviour and demands, you will soon feel exhausted and dispirited. If you spend most of the lesson on direct teaching, leaving yourself little time to recover between sessions, your energy level will drop rapidly. Good teachers do not exhibit manic behaviour but pace themselves in such a way that over the weeks and months of the term they can maintain the consistency necessary for effectiveness. This stable state is not easily attained and you must make sure that you don't confuse thoroughness with saturation. You should not, therefore:

- spend too much time talking during a session;
- rush around doing things for the children that they can do for themselves;
- feel guilty that you are not 'actively on task' for every moment of a session.

You should make sure, however, that you:

- leave opportunity for moving around the class to monitor and praise the children in their work;
- encourage children to be independent and to try to resolve their own problems, with peer support as appropriate;
- step back from the flurry of activity, review the success of your classroom management and calmly assess pupil progress.

Activate your thinking!

It is generally agreed that an on-task work rate of about 75 per cent is reasonable. How do the children and you compare with this figure?

Good practice

O'Flynn and Kennedy (2003: 140–5) suggest a number of strategies for surviving in the job, including: (1) build regular physical activity into your routine; (2) plan some quiet relaxation time each day; (3) seek support and help others who need it; (4) conserve energy during the day by remaining calm and pacing yourself; and (5) aim for good enough, not perfect.

O'Flynn, S. and Kennedy, H. (2003) *Get Their Attention*, London: David Fulton.

Survival strategies

Management of self can be compared to an aeroplane pilot who sometimes has to grip the controls and steer the plane in a pre-determined flightpath, sometimes has to manoeuvre and change course if the conditions demand it and sometimes puts the plane on automatic pilot to chat with crew and passengers. For the pilot, different amounts of concentration are required at different stages of the journey. The take-off and landing present the most hazardous and stressful stages, whereas the main part of the journey allows for moments of relaxation and flexibility. There would be a sharp decrease in air travel if passengers believed that the pilot was continuously under pressure. Similarly, those teachers who never use the 'autopilot' during a session have either failed to plan their lessons appropriately or fear that if they take their hands off the controls for two minutes the enterprise will crash.

Unless teachers find some time for stepping back and gaining an overall impression of the children's progress and the direction of the lesson, they will be swept along from start to finish and feel more tired than the children by the end of it. Unfortunately, some teachers feel guilty about separating themselves from the main action for a time, either because they think that they will be failing in their job or because they fear disruptive behaviour. Such emotions are particularly acute among trainees, who also fear being 'marked down' by a tutor if they draw breath for an instant. These concerns are understandable but unnecessary for two principal reasons:

1. The well-organised lesson does not require constant teacher intervention and interaction with pupils. It should be possible to stand still for a few moments and scan the class without the lesson falling apart.
2. Stepping back actually enhances the teacher's ability to monitor and assess the situation and take appropriate action or make suitable responses.

Activate your thinking!

Who is more tired at the end of the session, you or the children?

Good practice

Find a way to isolate yourself from the class for a minute or two each lesson whenever possible by standing at a particular spot in the room with your arms folded to observe what is happening without being disturbed. If you let the children know what you are doing they will soon stop bothering you because they know this is your 'time-out'.

Case study

A group of six Year 2 children, mixed ability and academically weak, were working with a trainee teacher, Mia, in an art area adjacent to the main classroom. The area had two tables, a sink, a workbench and various science and technology resources. Mia planned to introduce the lesson by reference to previous work and to explain what the children were to do. She was going to instruct them to pour lukewarm water into glass bottles and wrap them in different materials (secured with elastic bands) to insulate them. The children's task would then be to measure the temperature both immediately and after a ten-minute interval. Mia hoped that in doing so they would come to realise that the temperature loss was different depending on the material used, thereby reinforcing the concept of insulation.

During the ten-minute 'cooling time' interval, Mia decided to engage the children in a series of questions and answers so that they would not become restless. After that time she would let them measure the water temperature a second time, feel the outside of the bottle and make statements about the insulation properties of the materials. Finally, she thought that it would be a good idea for the children to share their experiences in a plenary, in which she would record their answers on a large sheet of paper under three main headings: *What we did/What happened/What this means*.

The problems

The lesson idea was sound and the practical work had the potential to take learning forward and engage the children's enthusiastic participation. However, by the end of the session Mia was weary, frustrated and a bit depressed about the children's fractious behaviour and way the lesson had deteriorated. The reasons for this disappointing outcome can be explained as follows.

First, Mia did not clarify the significance of the current work for the children or explain what she hoped they would learn. Consequently, it seemed to the children as if they were being taken on a 'mystery tour' rather than having a reasonably clear idea about their ultimate destination. Second, there were a variety of organisational and management problems that Mia had failed to foresee:

- The bottles were made of glass, and potentially hazardous.
- Water spilled over the table and soaked some of the photocopied sheets.
- The scissors were not sharp enough to cut the material properly, which meant that the children became reliant on adult help and the process was slowed.
- The thermometers were too closely calibrated and difficult for children to read.
- Children held the thermometers in the water so that they touched the bottom of the bottle, thereby giving a false reading.
- The slowness of the wrapping meant that considerable temperature losses occurred before the insulation material could be placed around the bottle.
- Children fiddled with the bottles and fabrics during the question-and-answer time, annoying the trainee and souring the atmosphere.
- The process of writing down children's responses on to the sheet of paper was ponderous for the teacher and difficult for them to read owing to her hurried scrawl.

Most worryingly, Mia had not grasped the basic scientific principle for herself. When the children felt the warmth coming through to the outside of the bottles, they ignored the data from the temperature measurements (though in fact they were generally inaccurate) and assumed that the warmest bottle was the best insulated, when in fact it was the other way around. Far from explaining the true situation, Mia brightly confirmed their comments and commended them for getting things correct.

Further reading for Chapter 10

Barber, D., Cooper, L. and Meeson, G. (2007) *Learning and Teaching with Interactive Whiteboards: Primary and early years*, Exeter: Learning Matters.

Takes a thematic approach, examining key issues required to gain greatest benefit from this technology.

Brunton, P. and Thornton, L. (2009) *Healthy Living in the Early Years Foundation Stage*, London: Optimus Education.

The authors offer advice to Foundation Stage practitioners about exercise, healthy eating, staying safe and emotional wellbeing.

Drake, J. (2003) *Organising Play in the Early Years*, London: David Fulton.

Full of interesting ideas and activities that provide plenty of useful material for teachers of younger children.

Haynes, J. (2008) *Children as Philosophers: Learning through enquiry and dialogue in the primary classroom*, Abingdon: Routledge.

The author suggests ways in which primary teachers can introduce philosophical enquiry to personal, social and health education, and to citizenship teaching, across the curriculum.

Joliffe, W. (2007) *Cooperative Learning in the Classroom*, London: Sage.

Promotes structuring lesson activities to encourage pupils to work collaboratively in pairs or small groups to support each other's learning.

Packard, N. and Higgins, S. (2007) *The Really Useful ICT Book*, Abingdon: Routledge.

Helps teachers and assistants understand how and why ICT can enhance their teaching and open up learning opportunities for pupils.

Smith, J. (2010) *Talk, Thinking and Philosophy in the Primary Classroom*, Exeter: Learning Matters.

The author emphasises the importance of talk, thinking and philosophy, and ways in which teachers might help pupils to develop and use these skills most effectively.

CHAPTER

 # Assessment, Recording and Reporting

Introduction

In this chapter we explore the many facets of the assessment process, ways in which information about children's academic, physical and social progress can be recorded, and some techniques for reporting to parents and colleagues. The balance of the chapter deals with an exploration of assessment for learning (AFL, formative assessment) and assessment of learning (AOL, summative assessment), the importance of monitoring and intervention, and the factors influencing a teacher's judgements about a child's attainment.

ASSESSMENT

Forms of assessment

The close relationship between effective planning, monitoring of progress and assessment that informs further planning has been a theme throughout this book. The importance of clarifying learning objectives and appropriately differentiating work to take account of children of varying abilities has been placed firmly at the heart of the teaching and learning process, though, as we have often noted, it is important to avoid making pupil learning intentions so rigid that spontaneous opportunities are neglected. In particular, any assessment of children's progress has to be considered within the teaching programme as a whole, for pupil progress is not only an indicator of children's ability but also of the appropriateness of the curriculum provision and the skill of the teacher to motivate and inspire.

MARRA

All those seeking qualified teacher status need to demonstrate competence in monitoring, assessment, recording, reporting and accountability to pupils, colleagues and parents, compositely referred to by the acronym MARRA (Headington 2000). Perceptive monitoring of pupil progress is an essential component of teaching, as there is a close correlation between how well it is carried out and the quality of children's learning. Some teachers tend to associate pupil observation with the formal procedures attached to inspections, in which particular behaviours and decisions are deemed to be good, bad or indifferent (Hargreaves and Wolfe 2007).

Assessment and learning

Assessment should not be viewed in isolation but as part of a broader picture that is built up over time by teachers' evaluation of pupils' progress and, where appropriate, results from formal tests. The teacher's role in the process is crucial as children are observed daily and a picture of their understanding and attainment is acquired through regular verbal and social interaction in the classroom setting. As Stierer *et al.* (1993) rightly comment:

> the assessment of young children can only be valid and authentic when it is achieved through the gradual building up of a picture of the child based upon evidence collected over time in a range of everyday contexts.
>
> (p. 9)

Lloyd and Beard (1995) argue that assessment opportunities exist whenever children are working alone, in a group, on problem–solving activities, in fantasy play and in the play-ground, as well as in the structured classroom environment. Drummond (2003) similarly argues that assessment involves far more than pragmatic procedural conformity or a means of social control. Rather, assessment makes 'moral and philosophical demands on our thinking ... The practice of effective assessment requires a thorough understanding and acceptance of the concept of rights, responsibility and power, lying at the heart of our work as teachers' (p. 11). Drummond offers numerous examples from classroom practice to unravel the com-plexity of children's learning. She insists that whatever the external requirements of product-focused assessment, teachers must be aware of the sense of personal failure that assessments can engender. Drummond suggests that all educators are alert to three fundamental questions in respect of learning: (1) What is there to see? (2) How best can we understand what we see? (3) How can we put our understanding to good use?

As explored in Chapters 7 and 8, however, it is often a challenge for teachers to know what children know. Indeed, the notion that a teacher can look into the head of each and every child to ascertain precisely what the child understands about every aspect of every subject is clearly impossible. And even if it *were* possible to do so, devising a programme of work and teaching approach to fully respond to all the vagaries of children's knowledge and understanding would make equally impossible demands of practitioners. In reality, assessment helps teachers to understand better where children are placed with regard to key concepts and the acquisition of facts. It is only the children who can make sense of things and establish meaning for themselves. Assessment, therefore, is a process to assist teachers in facilitating learning but not a guarantee of it.

Assessment, teaching and learning

Assessment takes many different forms, some of which are carried out formally in response to specific criteria and others that are rooted in regular classroom interactions. However, with regard to assessment criteria, it is important to focus on concepts and skills and not on super-ficial knowledge. For instance, in a design and technology experiment that involves children creating a wheeled vehicle to ascertain (say) factors influencing movement down a slope, assessment criteria should relate to the conceptual principles underpinning the lesson rather than just the ability to handle materials. Thus, criteria might include: (1) understanding that there is a causal relationship between incline and speed; (2) the ability to make comparisons between the performances of varied types of moving object, and so forth. The criteria that focus on learning are different in kind, and more important, than those of a functional nature, such as being able to construct a moving object or use materials appropriately. Assessment has three implications for teaching: (1) all assessment should help teachers to plan more effectively; (2) assessments can have important consequences for a child's future; (3) assessments have implications for the school and staff. Thus:

All assessment should help teachers to plan more effectively

Assessment is of little value in its own right unless teachers use the results to modify their practice, teaching approach and curriculum content. The collation of formal test results is an important element of publicly demonstrating pupil progress but is an end result and not the core of a teacher's work. The quality of children's learning, their ability to co-operate and collaborate, and the continuity of experience all contribute to the evidence upon which teachers can base amendments to the teaching programme.

Assessments can have important consequences for a child's future

If assessments are used as a basis for decisions about pupil competence, allocation to groups and (when they transfer to secondary education) future school placements, there needs to be confirmatory evidence which can be used for verification. Some schools maintain records that consist of photocopied samples of children's work taken (say) once per term to illustrate the sort of progress that they are making over time. However, results in national tests (so-called SATs) and end-of-year tests have become increasingly significant.

Assessments have implications for the school and staff

The results of national assessments are used as a measure of a school's effectiveness and have funding, as well as professional, implications. A lot of time is spent by teachers of Year 2 and Year 6 children (in particular) in preparing them for the end-of-Key-Stage tests. The results of the Key Stage 2 tests are collated and published. League tables of school performance have now become an annual event, and the figures are pored over by parents and politicians.

Assessment data

For all teachers, assessment involves a great deal of informal data gathered throughout the day as pupils work with set tasks. This informal assessment is carried out by listening to what children say, watching the mistakes they make, reflecting on the reasons for errors and misconceptions and asking questions to clarify the extent of their understanding. Interestingly, in their study of effective primary teaching Gipps et al. (1999) found that 'Over half the teachers explained that they used listening as an assessment technique' (p. 81). Similarly, Broadhead (2006) emphasises the importance of careful observation, interaction and reflection about the work and progress of younger children in particular. In doing so, teachers have to recognise that children's mistakes can be due to misunderstanding about what is required rather than the inability to grasp the concept. A poorly produced piece of work may say more about motivation, misunderstanding or uncertainty about the task than about a lack of conceptual understanding.

Teachers often find it helpful to use *elicitation* techniques to gain a clearer picture about the things that children know, understand and have experienced. In addition to information gleaned through discussion and question-and-answer, three elicitation methods are helpful:

1. Divide the children into pairs or small groups with a blank sheet of paper and ask them to write down as many words associated with the topic as they can think of. Groups of younger children require direct adult assistance with the task.
2. As in point 1 above, but give the children a number of key words or phrases (five, say) to use as starting points for a 'bike wheel' diagram, with spokes from the centre and other associated words written at the end of each spoke.
3. As in point 2 above, but incorporating pictures, diagrams and other visual representations.

Following this opportunity to record their ideas, the information on the sheets can be shared with the rest of the class and, perhaps, placed around the room on temporary display. Discussion with pupils about the content of the sheets will not only assist in clarifying children's familiarity with the curriculum area but also, crucially, the depth of understanding they possess.

Assessment in the Foundation Stage

Assessment based on the Early Years Foundation Stage (EYFS) curriculum helps teachers to develop a richer and more diverse perspective on the attributes that children should be encouraged to develop, using the following ten headings:

1. Personal, social and emotional wellbeing of children
2. Attitude and disposition to learning
3. Social skills
4. Attention skills and persistence
5. Language and communication skills
6. Reading and writing skills
7. Mathematical ability
8. Knowledge and understanding of the world
9. Physical development
10. Creative development.

The *Foundation Stage Profile* is a way of summing up a child's progress and learning across the six areas of learning at the end of the Foundation Stage (see also Chapter 10). Thus: personal, social and emotional development; communication, language and literacy; mathematical development; knowledge and understanding of the world; physical development; creative development.

The Foundation Stage Profile is made up of thirteen scales based on the early learning goals and stepping stones set out in curriculum guidance for the Foundation Stage. See Chapter 10 for information about stepping stones. The Department for Children, Schools and Families (DCSF) has published a Foundation Stage Profile handbook and advice about observing children as guidance for practitioners on how to make assessments on the basis of their observations and knowledge of the whole child. See also Riddell-Leech (2008) for information about observing children within the Early Years Foundation Stage and links to the National Primary Strategy.

When considering the development of 'the whole child' these assessment points remind us that while academic prowess is important, educational progress involves the heart and mind, as well as the head. There are some key qualities (such as creativity), which, though they defy quantitative measurement, are nevertheless prized attributes if children are to attain their potential and eventually become thinking, responsible adults. See Doddington and Hilton (2007: Chapter 4) for an exploration of the concept of child-centred education and the 'whole child' as a person.

Assessing Pupil Progress (APP)

APP stands for *Assessing Pupil Progress*. It consists of a series of tick sheets that the teacher uses to assess the level of attainment that a child has reached in areas that include writing, mathematics, reading and speaking and listening. Depending on future policy, it is possible that APP might be used to assess science, too. In some schools only a random number of children (six, say) are assessed closely; for instance, using two high, two middle and two lower achievers. Pupils with special learning needs or weak command of English are not normally included in the sample. The teacher 'levels' several pieces of work towards the end of the half-term as a way to reveal the gaps that the children have in their learning, make plans to remedy the weaknesses and thereby move them forward during the next half-term. At its best it is an effective tool but at its worst it deteriorates into an onerous paper exercise. In schools where teachers are obliged to use APP for every child rather than for selected pupils, the accompanying workload is extremely heavy. Despite the diagnostic value of APP, there seems to be consensus among teachers that the system's usefulness scarcely justifies the time and effort it demands.

Making effective assessments

Carrying out effective assessment for every child in the class is a demanding and difficult skill and requires teachers and their assistants to be alert and closely engaged with children's understanding of the work. Wragg (1997) reminds us that in the classroom environment, where so much is happening so quickly, 'teachers have to think on their feet and are denied the luxury of hours of reflection over each of their pedagogical choices' so that 'assessment has to be carried out on the move' (p. 5). Accurate assessments therefore require a combination of these rapid skills during lessons (for immediate purposes) and creating a composite picture over the longer term. Every decision about the quality of children's work also needs to be made with reference to a number of factors, including:

1. The child's age
2. The child's work habits
3. The child's past accomplishments
4. The learning climate
5. The quality of the teaching.

The child's age

Assessment approaches will vary according to the age of the child. Older primary school pupils tend to produce a great deal of written and other 'visual' forms of work that can be used for formative assessment purposes and designated a numerical figure as measured against standardised attainment-level descriptions. However, since younger pupils produce relatively little written output, teachers have to rely more on their observations of children and listen attentively to the things that they say about their work that reveal the depth of knowledge and understanding. The younger the child, the less the evidence of learning is tangible and the more the teacher has to rely on observation and discussion with the child about the work.

The child's work habits

Children may be slow workers or deep thinkers or both. They may struggle with particular aspects of the work but excel in other, related parts. There will be gaps in their knowledge due to a failure to grasp ideas initially through a lack of motivation, immaturity or poor teaching. Some children hesitate to tackle unfamiliar or demanding tasks; others relish the challenge. Many children operate more effectively when working with a partner. These factors should be taken into account when work is assessed if you are to gain a true picture of the child's progress.

A slow worker may produce a high quality final product if allowed extra time. A faster worker may be capable of a better end product if the first attempt is treated as a draft. Children working in pairs may accomplish more if together or (perhaps) separated or placed with someone different. The flexibility introduced through the Primary National Strategy framework (PNS) for literacy and mathematics (formerly 'numeracy') and emphasis on individual learning offers opportunity to be more imaginative about ways of organising for learning (see Chapter 10). You are constantly faced with challenges about determining the quality of attainment that might have been possible for a child under different circumstances. Although you can only use 'hard' evidence to assess progress, an awareness of pupils' work habits will assist you in evaluating what they are capable of achieving, raising expectations and establishing realistic learning targets.

The child's past accomplishments

The longer teachers spend with a group of children, the more effective they are in assessing their achievements and potential. A child may have made considerable strides to accomplish something, which, for other more capable children, would be unacceptably poor. Over time, it becomes evident whether children are progressing satisfactorily with reference to past achievements or whether their present work rate and performance indicate that they are being lazy, indifferent or unmotivated. In fact, a lot of a teacher's work is taken up with rehearsing knowledge and reinforcing understanding that has been introduced at an earlier stage. Although formal assessments such as national tests and tasks provide a grade or figure, they do not take account of these distinctive factors. It is part of your responsibility to help children to develop less secure areas of their knowledge and understanding; it is also essential that your expectations are reasonable and informed by earlier achievements or gaps in knowledge.

The learning climate

Lesson management takes place under varying circumstances: some teachers and children enjoy undisturbed tranquillity; others endure the loud noises from local building work. Some lessons take place within the regular rhythm of daily lessons; others are wedged between getting changed after swimming and going home at the end of the day. Some lessons are uninterrupted; others stop and start as children go out for music lessons, extra tuition and so forth, or children come with messages and requests. The quality of resources can also affect achievement, particularly when children are engaging with experiential tasks in which practical investigations form the heart of the lesson. Similarly, the behaviour of peers and numbers of pupils in the room can all have an effect on learning outcomes, notably in the personal attention that an adult can give a child. Teachers need to be wise when selecting work that is 'typical' of a child's ability to ensure that adverse contextual factors did not appreciably influence the outcome. As a trainee teacher, you have probably been asked to collect samples of work to inform your assessments; in all cases, take note of the circumstances that pertained to the task completion, as the 'raw' evidence doesn't tell the whole story.

Activate your thinking!

Children are sometimes blamed for underachieving or producing a poor piece of work when in fact the teacher must bear some of the responsibility. If an explanation of the task is poor, expectations are not clarified or organisation is clumsy, it should be no surprise if the results are disappointing.

Good practice

Resist using a single piece of work, taken at random, to draw significant conclusions about a child's attainment and ability. Always use a range of evidence unless you are using a standardised test (and even then be aware that some children underperform in formal settings).

Cross-reference: Guided Reader Extract 5

Formative assessment (assessment for learning, AFL)

The type of assessment that is ongoing and helps children to improve the quality of their work is referred to as *formative assessment* and is found in the warp and weave of classroom life (e.g. Torrance and Pryor 1998; Drummond 2003; Lord and Slinn 2007). In recent years the process of formative assessment has been re-branded as 'assessment for learning' (AFL), with an emphasis on the word 'for'. Bates and Munday (2005: based on pp. 58–9) suggest that the key features of AFL include:

- Learning objectives are made clear to pupils and success criteria are established.
- Learning (as opposed to task outcome) is reviewed at the end of the lesson or lessons.
- Oral and written feedback enables pupils to understand what they have achieved and how to move forward in their learning.
- Pupils are involved through peer- and self-assessment.
- Pupils are encouraged (with adult support) to set achievable personal targets.
- Teachers and pupils work together to create a climate of success in the classroom.

Facilitating formative assessment

Good relationships and a relaxed atmosphere allow the assessment process to take place constructively and unthreateningly. The use of question-and-answer sessions, child–teacher dialogue and the teacher's professional judgements are all important elements of formative assessment. The teacher's informal records (both written and remembered) will be full of perceptive observations about individuals:

'Emma benefited from the extra help in spelling.'

'John still struggles to grasp the concept of area.'

'Ranjit is showing a talent for expressive painting.'

'Briony works well with a partner but seems lost when asked to work alone.'

'Ziad is a good reader but struggles at number work.'

'Yin seems to be tone deaf.'

And a thousand other insights that help to build up a picture of an individual child and guide future planning and appropriate work. These perceptions are not gained, of course, through detached observation and evaluation of children's work, but rather through active involvement in their learning by observing, asking questions and simply talking to children about what they are doing and what they understand. An integral element of this involvement is *monitoring* (close awareness of what children are doing and thinking) and *intervening* (offering direct and indirect support to children while they are engaged in work). Direct support might come through an instruction, firm advice about decisions or giving a piece of information. Indirect support might take the form of a commending comment, clarifying the options without offering a preference or asking another pupil to share ideas.

Zone of proximal development

Unless you sit with your eyes and ears closed during a lesson, it is impossible to avoid monitoring progress; however, to become proficient and enhance your professional skills requires more than a casual acquaintance with such complex judgements. Children will normally let a teacher know if they have concerns or questions about tasks, but it is also important to develop the skill of scanning the class to pick up clues about the level of adult support that is needed by a child. The relationship between monitoring and intervening is not an exact science. Sometimes you may be aware that a child is struggling but decide to delay your intervention to allow opportunity for the child to think and engage with the problem. On other occasions you may decide to be highly specific and tell the child precisely what must be done.

The influential Russian psychologist, Lev Vygotsky (1896–1934) famously referred to the difference between what children can achieve with help from a more knowledgeable teacher (adult or child) and what they can do without guidance as the 'zone of proximal development' (ZPD). The active intervention and support of adults in children's learning as they try to narrow the ZPD is equivalent to scaffold placed around a house as it is constructed. As a child grasps the concept and gains the necessary understanding, the amount of 'scaffolding' (i.e. adult support) is reduced. Once the child is in a position to progress independently the support is removed completely, though further scaffolding might be required as the child engages with more advanced challenges.

Formative assessment and learning

The formative assessment of children's progress provides insights into at least five aspects of a lesson:

1. The clarity of the task (your responsibility), because unless the clarity of the task is explicit, it is highly likely that pupils will be confused or produce unsatisfactory work.
2. The child's conceptual grasp of the task: if the child lacks understanding, it is likely that you have assumed too much previous knowledge or made the work too difficult.
3. The child's willingness to persevere with the task, which might signal lack of interest, fatigue, confusion, a poor attitude or a weak aptitude for learning.
4. The level of a child's self-confidence, because low self-confidence usually results in underachievement and means that the child needs your help to build self-belief.
5. The extent of the child's ultimate success in accomplishing the task, in light of which points (1) to (4) above may need to be reviewed and appropriate remedies put in place.

If the end result is disappointing, you should adjust your teaching in one or more of the following ways:

1. Spend more time explaining what the children have to do, where it fits with previous learning and how to go about it.
2. Revise basic knowledge, offer explanations in a different way from those used originally; invite the children to repeat and rehearse ideas; use story, examples taken from familiar scenarios and explanatory diagrams.
3. Set short-term targets (making the target time as low as a few minutes initially and gradually increasing the time) and offer close support and encouragement.
4. Praise effort as much as result; offer reassurance; quietly celebrate small amounts of progress.

As you become more familiar with the class and the evidence accumulates, the general observations noted earlier can be sharpened:

'Emma can now learn a list of words and get them correct in a spelling test but cannot use them successfully in a piece of open written work.'

'John understands that units of measurement are needed to measure area but cannot understand why using smaller units produces a larger total.'

'Ranjit has an excellent sense of perspective in drawing but lacks imagination.'

'Briony has a good brain and grasps ideas quickly but is afraid of making a mistake.'

'Ziad can read aloud accurately but without any great understanding.'

'Yin copes with the lower ranges but gets lost as the notes rise.'

It is not difficult to see that formative assessments are of little value unless action is taken to remedy a situation or encourage greater achievement. The process may be considered as comprising five stages:

Stage 1: Gaining a general impression from the children's work and verbal comments.

Stage 2: Making a more precise judgement over time about the child's aptitude and ability.

Stage 3: Taking action to improve, remediate or adjust the situation.

Stage 4: Making a more detailed assessment of pupil progress on the basis of the revised work programme.

Stage 5: Making further modifications to the work schedule on the basis of identified individual needs.

Two important points need to be understood. First, the best formative assessments are also *diagnostic*: that is, not merely descriptive but providing evidence to assist in the formulation of appropriate teaching and learning strategies. Second, there is a limit to the amount of informal formative assessment that a teacher can record or remember. A system has to be established whereby the evidence from children's work and their responses to questions and so forth can be confirmed and, in some cases, quantified. Thus:

By how much has Emma's spelling improved and in which areas?

Does John have similar difficulty with other aspects of measurement?

Can Ranjit transfer his skills to planning in DT?

What is Briony capable of achieving when given plenty of reassurance?

Would Ziad benefit from focusing on specific aspects of textual interpretation?

Is Yin's problem one of confidence or competence or due to physical problems (e.g. hearing loss)?

Answers to the above questions allow you to modify work for an individual child or for a group of children, in order to improve their chances of grasping the skills and concepts in the area of weakness or enhancing their experience in areas of strength.

Despite the helpful information accrued through assessment, it is important to be reminded that the simplistic notion of a procedure whereby teachers introduce a topic, set tasks, assess pupil progress and adjust their teaching accordingly is an idealised version of the reality. Ultimately, children must make sense of learning for themselves, aided by knowledgeable adults and peers. In this regard, it is worth bearing in mind that some pupils fail to learn because their home circumstances and background limit their motivation or have an adverse impact on achievement.

Activate your thinking!

Novice teachers tend to hurry their explanation about what they expect pupils to do and the standard they require. Asking children if they understand what needs to be done will normally elicit an affirmative reply, whether or not they really do! Poor application to the task and the disappointing final results merely serve to illustrate the confusion.

Monitoring

As referred to in the previous section, monitoring progress is an essential skill for every teacher to develop and is concerned with two aspects of classroom life: effective learning and effective discipline. The two elements are often closely related; well-behaved and motivated children have a much better chance of doing well than restless, bored ones. The following five factors need to be considered as part of the ongoing process of assessing pupils' progress through monitoring.

The clarity of the task

Whether there are specific areas of the work causing concern to one or more pupils that need your attention. If the number of pupils is greater than two or three, it is likely that you have not explained what you expect sufficiently clearly.

The task demands

Whether the demands made by the task are enthusing and motivating pupils. It soon becomes clear whether the children are keen to complete the task or activity because they are engaged with it or because they want to finish and move on.

The availability and distribution of resources

Whether every pupil is receiving a fair share of resources and gaining access to the equipment. Squabbling over equipment is one of the most disrupting influences during practical lessons.

The level of co-operation/collaboration

Whether children are working together responsibly. Co-operation is a key factor, but one of the more difficult parts of monitoring progress, as more dominant pupils can easily overwhelm the more timid children, who simply acquiesce to their classmates' demands.

The standard of work

Whether pupils' achievements align with their capability and potential. Again, this skill is far from easy to master and requires that you have spent plenty of time with the children. Some clever children choose to conceal their ability; some children engage superficially with the work or lean heavily on others to avoid having to apply themselves to the task. Disentangling these complex threads requires discernment.

Teacher assessment of pupil attainment relies largely upon monitoring their progress during the lesson and examining the results of their endeavours by looking at their written and recorded work. Monitoring progress during the lesson involves three stages:

1. Seeing what needs to be seen
2. Drawing the correct conclusions
3. Deciding on appropriate action.

Seeing what needs to be seen

Monitoring demands focused and deliberate observation of a given situation. It isn't simply a matter of looking but of looking with a purpose. For instance, in a typical 'play' situation, you might be interested in children's language development, ability to sequence events, problem solving, social interaction, imaginative use of resources or friendship patterns.

Drawing the correct conclusions

It is one thing to observe carefully, it is quite another to reach a valid conclusion: for instance, whether particular forms of pupil behaviour contribute to or detract from effective learning or whether the work is inappropriate or the child is demoralised.

Deciding on appropriate action

That is, determining the appropriate form of intervention based on decisions above. For example, whether to stand back or to give precise information or to ask a question or to suggest a course of action. See below.

Intervention

Factors influencing intervention

Considering that the monitoring process has to take place spontaneously on numerous occasions during each session, it is hardly surprising that inexperienced teachers sometimes find it difficult to be aware of what is happening throughout the classroom. Before you can make decisions about suitable intervention strategies, you have to synthesise factors that arise from the monitoring process and make a number of judgements as a consequence: (1) general class order; (2) the behaviour of individuals; (3) health and safety factors.

- *General class order* Are pupils concentrating satisfactorily on their work? Is the noise level appropriate? Are groups collaborating or chattering? Is the movement around the room purposeful?
- *The behaviour of individuals* Is the child sufficiently compliant, bearing in mind his or her previous history? How many minor infringements should be ignored (if any)? How often should verbal reprimands be used? See also Chapter 12.
- *Health and safety factors* Are the pupils' actions potentially dangerous? Is the situation one of 'reasonable risk'? How long should the situation be left? Will pupils' common sense prevail?

During monitoring of pupils' work, teachers confirm the acceptability of children's effort and progress by the nature of their responses. Every time you tick a page, express pleasure about a pupil's efforts or commend what is done, you are providing a confirmation of their validity. Of course, the opposite is true, in that every time you express doubt or suggest alternatives or offer guarded praise, the children become less secure unless you make it clear that there is a way to remedy the position, such as to work harder, be more careful, use a different technique, concentrate on a particular aspect of the task, and so forth. Indeed, offering immediate endorsement of a child's work provides valuable incentive and is preferable to the familiar and rather uninspiring process of: work is set/children do the work/the work is handed in/the teacher assesses the work/the work is handed back. As a rule, the more feedback you can give 'on the spot', the more the child benefits. See also below under 'Feedback'.

Impact on learning

We noted above that monitoring and intervening are closely allied and, in a very real way, two sides of the same coin to aid learning and guide pupil progress. Children need adult and peer support in their endeavour to master new skills and concepts and the idea of 'scaffolding' learning by providing advice and guidance to steer children towards deeper understanding and extending their knowledge is well established (see earlier in this chapter). Teacher intervention is a vital component of the scaffolding process and can be required for any one of at least five reasons:

1. The teacher's poor initial lesson introduction, resourcing or organisation means that further explanation about completing the task or activity is required.
2. Poor ability-matching between child/group and task such that the work is too conceptually demanding.
3. The child's lack of confidence (as opposed to ability) leading to tentativeness in tackling the work.
4. The child's lack of the necessary skills, leading to poor quality or low standards of achievement.
5. The child's lack of concentration, leading to the need for regular reminders.

Knowing when to intervene

Regardless of the subject matter or area of learning, every teaching and learning situation requires a variety of intervention skills and adult judgements that can make the difference between an active, progressive atmosphere and an oppressive, anxious one. The following factors are significant.

Standing back

The relationship between monitoring and intervening is fluid. Sometimes a teacher is aware that a child is struggling but decides to delay intervening such that the child/group has more opportunity to think and engage with the problem. On other occasions the teacher may decide to be specific and tell the child precisely what has to be done. Awareness of children's progress through observation of their behaviour and information gleaned from their work provide insights into their grasp of the task, confidence in tackling the work and understanding of the teacher's expectations. To ensure the best outcome, all primary teachers need to become skilled observers of children and keen judges of how much support to offer.

Experienced teachers seem to develop an aptitude for spotting the events, comments and behaviours that require immediate attention, those that can be left for a time and those which are best ignored. It is important to weigh up the situation, remain calm and avoid saying too much before the child has had time to speak and the facts become clear. Once the position has been clarified, appropriate action can follow, though its precise nature has to be determined immediately. In practice, it takes time and hard-won experience to make correct decisions of this nature.

Allowing time for pupils' self-correction

As noted above, it is sometimes useful to allow time for the pupil to self-correct or take advice from a friend rather than rushing in straight away, particularly if the lesson purpose is principally about allowing pupils to grapple with difficulties rather than providing immediate solutions (e.g. in enquiry-based/problem-solving activities). Children need to be taught self-sufficiency rather than unintentionally promoting their over-reliance on a teacher, but there is little point in leaving a child to flounder for too long without offering help. See later in this section about appropriate intervention.

Knowing how to say what needs to be said

Two teachers monitor children's work and offer suggestions for improvement: the first teacher depresses the pupil by being heavily critical and failing to offer guidance other than saying the child must try harder; the second brings about the desired change by the use of carefully chosen words, precise guidance and suitable target setting. It is obvious which of the two approaches is going to bring about enhanced learning. Ask the child for his or her opinion of the work or ask a question such as, 'If you were the teacher, what would you say about your work?' though some care has to be exercised, as bolder pupils will sometimes reply that it is 'fine'. In such instances, simply respond by saying, 'Then I'm afraid that you would not make a very good teacher' and proceed to point out where improvements should be made.

Good practice

Never be afraid to insist that work is repeated and done properly if you are convinced that the child has made little or no effort to do well. Disregard the child's protests. Once it becomes clear to the class that you will not tolerate sloppy work, you'll be amazed at the transformation. If the low standard is for other reasons then, of course, respond by advising and offering targeted guidance.

Taking account of task ownership

Unless the occasion is a formal test, in which adult assistance is not permitted, every teacher has to balance the importance of offering encouragement and guidance to children against intervening to such an extent that the child loses ownership of the task. Many children are happy to be told instead of putting their minds to the problem, and as most pupils want to please the teacher there is always the danger that your suggestions will be accepted uncritically. Consequently, a pattern of behaviour emerges:

1. Child engages with task.
2. Child encounters difficulty.
3. Child asks for assistance and advice.
4. Teacher obliges by helping and giving specific guidance.
5. Child re-engages with task, implementing the teacher's suggestions as if they were commands. And so the cycle repeats.

It is useful to introduce a 'delayed intervention' by employing phrases such as 'Have a try for yourself first and I'll come back in a moment if you are still stuck' or 'Ask a friend first before you ask me again.' You can also use a three-step procedure that children must always follow, namely: (1) think for yourself; (2) ask a classmate; and (3) ask an adult. Consequently, the behaviour pattern is gradually changed, as follows:

1. Child engages with task.
2. Child encounters difficulty.
3. Child thinks about solutions for one minute.
4. Child seeks advice from a friend.
5. Child seeks advice from an adult.
6. Child decides on the best course of action and re-engages with the task.

A lot depends on the nature of the lesson as to how flexibly the steps need to be followed; for instance, you may want the children to work independently and not liaise with classmates. Nevertheless, the principle of encouraging children to think for themselves before seeking help allows you to evaluate children's ability to solve problems and persevere, rather than their ability to prise information from an adult. Much formative assessment is based upon this interplay between intervention and giving children time and freedom to explore, evaluate, experiment, argue and so forth.

Assessments must, therefore, take into account the extent of teacher intervention and the level of peer involvement, in evaluating work quality and alerting you to possible pupil misconceptions or misunderstandings. You have to weigh the benefits of co-operation and shared learning experiences with the possible disadvantage that one child may do most of the thinking and planning, while the other has minimal involvement.

Good practice

Make it clear at the start of the session or activity the extent to which you want the children to: (1) work unaided; (2) actively collaborate with classmates; and (3) actively seek advice from an adult.

Taking account of circumstances

Teachers also have to make allowances for particular times of the day and circumstances in judging how and when to intervene. Experienced teachers allow children time to settle after a 'wet' playtime rather than raise tension by being unduly assertive; they are likely be more lenient with the work standards of a pupil who has come to school burdened with emotional cares than with one who is being careless or surly. Over time, all teachers tend to fall into particular patterns of monitoring and intervention that have consequences in promoting sound learning and discipline, or not. As a result, it is essential to think carefully whether your intervention strategies are the most effective ones in the circumstances or whether different actions might result in more successful learning outcomes in the longer term. Making such judgements comes as a result of time spent engaged in active classroom teaching, reflection on children's responses and evaluation of work quality. Your teaching assistant will also be a valuable source of advice, so don't be afraid to seek it.

Activate your thinking!

Consider the truth of the following statement: every intervention is preceded by an assessment based on careful monitoring of a child's progress.

Good practice

Categorise the types of active intervention you commonly use under the following headings: (1) those that result from a child's question; (2) those that result from your awareness of a problem; and (3) those that enhance work that is already of good quality.

Summative assessment

Terminology

By contrast with ongoing formative assessments, those that take place at the end of a definable period of time such as the end of a day or half-term or year or at the conclusion of a Key Stage are referred to as summative assessments. Whereas *summative assessment* tends to be applied to assessments that relate to pupil attainment over a period of time, the associated phrase, 'assessment of learning' (AOL) is normally used with respect to assessments attached to particular lessons. AOL occurs when a teacher makes an evaluation of pupils' work based on criteria appropriate to the task being assessed. For instance, a set of arithmetic problems is likely to receive a mark, whereas a written task might receive a grade, a written comment or another indicator of the teacher's assessment, such as a sticker. The AOL process also alerts teachers to specific problems, misconceptions and misunderstandings that can be addressed in future lessons (Hansen 2011).

The purpose of summative assessment

The outcomes from summative assessments are intended to confirm the teacher's opinion of what children have learned and what progress has been made since the previous comparable activity or test. Summative assessment is rather more systematic in character than formative assessment and can take the form of a written or verbal test carried out under specified conditions or a series of small tasks with which children have to engage in order to show their level of competence. The most significant type of summative assessment is through the national tasks and tests that relate to the core subjects of the National Curriculum, the results of which must be made available to the parents of each child. Some schools provide parents with the teacher's own assessment of the child's progress in all curriculum subjects once a year. Reports on art, music and PE only refer to end of Key Stage descriptions rather than the level descriptions used for the other non-core subjects (see Chapter 6). A summative assessment is not required for religious education. The use of ICT is now firmly established in schools, and pupils' ability needs to be monitored closely and their progress noted in reports to parents. ICT is sometimes referred to as the 'fourth core subject' to highlight its significance.

Some pupils (notably those with special educational needs) struggle with regular work to such an extent that they are not even able to reach the first level of the National Curriculum, in which case there exist a set of indicators known as the P scales to record their achievement. The P scales are divided into eight levels from P1 (the lowest) to P8 (the highest), though the first three levels (P1, P2 and P3) are not subject-specific. In extreme cases, children may only have a tentative grasp of people, events and objects and rely heavily on their senses (e.g. through touching) to elicit a response, in which case P1 would be an appropriate level.

Summative assessment and target setting

Summative assessments also have to take account of short-term target setting (see later in this chapter) whereby pupils are given specific learning targets to achieve by a given time. Although the targets do not form part of the formal assessment process, they help teachers to keep close track of certain (measurable) aspects of pupil achievement. Enthusiasts argue that through target setting, the summative and formative assessments merge: the formative element influences children's progress that is ultimately identified through the summative assessment. In turn, the summative element provides information for teachers to become more alert to the suitability of their formative assessment, and so on. The process of assessment and recording and reporting children's progress is a crucial element of the teacher's work. The reality of classroom teaching is that formative and summative assessments are not as distinctive as might be thought from reading some of the literature produced on the subject. Like most aspects of education, dealing with children and their learning is far more complex than a simple model of assessment suggests.

Benefits and limitations of summative assessment

Although summative assessment forms an integral part of every teacher's agenda, there are some important considerations of which to take account. For instance, studies suggest that summative assessment has an adverse effect on low-achieving pupils' self-esteem compared with the impact it has on higher achievers and the frequent use of practice tests in advance of 'the real thing' reinforces less able pupils' negative self-image. Similarly, major test events can cause considerable anxiety, especially among vulnerable pupils generally and girls in particular. On the other hand, some children thrive on tests, notably academically and confident pupils who view them as an opportunity to demonstrate their prowess and compete against children of similar ability. The overall effect is therefore to increase the gap between the motivation levels of high and low achievers. Some teachers also argue that summative assessment relies too heavily on extrinsic forms of motivation, whereby pupils respond to the promise of some kind of reward (high marks, accolades, merits, adult pleasure), rather than intrinsic motivation in which they perform because they are interested in the subject area and want to do the work for their own satisfaction.

There is also ample evidence that 'teaching to the test' unhelpfully narrows the curriculum, by placing an undue emphasis on literacy and mathematics at the expense of the non-core subjects. One result of curriculum 'narrowing' is a distortion of teaching approaches, such that teachers adopt a more didactic (transmission) style of teaching and stop employing more exploratory, enquiry-based methods.

In practice, teachers can spend a lot of time on preparing for and conducting assessments of pupils' learning, which may reduce their motivation and create restless behaviour, especially if 'practice' tests and 'cramming' (now referred to more eloquently as 'coaching') dominate curriculum time and pupils feel constrained and/or deprived of other, more enjoyable experiences. If you are placed with a Year 6 class in the spring term these challenges will be particularly acute, but an increasing number of schools have non-statutory end-of-year tests for years other than Year 2 and Year 6, so the issues are widespread.

Testing does not only take place as end-of-year events; there are numerous occasions when a formal, measurable assessment of ability is used to indicate pupil progress. It might be argued that summative assessment is being carried out every time (say) a child reads to an adult and a record is made of progress, or a spelling test is given to the whole class. Teachers have a responsibility to ensure that children (especially in Key Stage 2) approach tests seriously, while reassuring anxious pupils that they can only do their best and that weak results do not reflect badly on their characters unless, of course, they have been lazy or indifferent.

Activate your thinking!

Consider the validity of this statement: 'It is impossible to carry out an assessment *for* learning without also doing an assessment *of* learning.'

Cross-reference: Guided Reader Extract 6

Feedback to children

Effective feedback

One of the principal ways in which a positive learning environment can be achieved is through effective and sensitive feedback to children about the quality of their work (S. Clarke 2008). It is essential to ensure that the process of marking/grading work provides information not only for the teacher but also for pupils by offering useful data to them about the quality of their endeavours and their overall progress. Sometimes the feedback will be verbal and sometimes in the form of a grade, mark, smiley face or another symbol, remembering that the child who has persevered to achieve something worthwhile deserves the same level of commendation as the more capable pupil who finds the work relatively straightforward.

It is also important for teachers to avoid falling into the 'yes, but' habit, whereby children never receive unconditional praise because the imperfections of the work are highlighted at the same time as the approval. Although it is part of your role to help children improve their work, this should not be done at the expense of them feeling that absolutely nothing will ever satisfy their finicky teacher. In addition, take account of circumstances in making judgements. For example:

- the difficulty of the work and its suitability for the children concerned;
- the time available for task completion, especially in the case of slow workers (who may or may not be academically capable);
- whether the child was trying to be innovative – sometimes the wholly compliant pupil finishes the task and receives deserved praise, whereas the creative pupil does not and receives undeserved criticism;
- whether the task was individual, in pairs or group.

Avoid the impression that the *only* reason the children are doing the work is to please you. In reality, most children rely on adults for affirmation, encouragement and close guidance, but ultimately they should be self-motivating and independent learners, such that they use a teacher as a safety net rather than being constrained by a harness.

In striving to help pupils become more self-sufficient, keep your eye on the long-term goals for children's attitude to their own learning, sometimes referred to as 'meta-learning'. Thus, children should become enthusiastic and motivated, self-sufficient and independent, and each confident at his or her own level of ability. A positive sign your pupils are moving in this direction is when they spontaneously assist and advise their classmates about the work.

Activate your thinking!

Part of the teacher's role is to raise children's self-esteem by promoting a culture of success and encouraging children to tackle problems without fearing the consequences of failure. How do you rate yourself in this regard?

Good practice

1. Mark as much as possible with the child present and celebrate achievement spontaneously.
2. Consider the *effort* made as well as the outcome, being careful not to foster excessive competitiveness.

Terminology in feedback

The need for accurate formative assessment also places a responsibility upon teachers to ensure that they use the most appropriate descriptors. For instance, when describing a child's work, teachers frequently make use of a general term such as 'good'. In doing so, they can be making a number of different statements:

It is good compared with the last piece of similar work the child completed.

It is good compared with other children's work in the group or class.

It is good because the child has made a considerable effort to do well, despite the relatively poor quality of the end final product.

It is good compared with other children of the same age generally (in a parallel class, say).

A similar list can be made about why you might describe the work as 'poor'. And even if a piece of work is judged as poor, you have then to determine what should be done about it. Simply telling children that their work is poor or giving them a low mark/grade is probably only confirming what they already know, so you need to employ strategies to assist children to do better next time or to improve the current piece of work. Such strategies could involve spending time with an individual privately, asking for the attention of the group and making a general statement about the issue, or providing direct teaching to the whole class in the form of explanations, demonstrations or exposition as a means of revising or reinforcing the concept, skill or procedure.

If one child is struggling, it is almost certain that a number of pupils will not have grasped the same point and will need a few minutes of intensive tuition before they can proceed. It is pointless explaining the same thing to four or five individuals when you could explain it once to all of them. Of course, it is always possible that the task is too intellectually demanding for the children or requires the employment of skills that they do not possess. There will be occasions when you need to redress the mismatch between task and ability, provide more straightforward remedial work or modify your expectations. There is little purpose served by trying to coerce pupils into doing something that is simply beyond their capability. Take a pace back, reinforce their previous learning then move ahead with renewed vigour.

Diagnostic feedback

Positive remarks about a child's progress may be useful as a means of encouragement but unhelpful in diagnosis. A 'Good, well done' indicates a teacher's pleasure but may have limited value for ensuring that the child has thoroughly grasped the intended concept, skill or knowledge. A 'Good, well done, I can see that you have really tried hard' indicates that the teacher is pleased with the effort made despite the outcome. However, a 'Good, well done in (these particular ways)' is better still. The distinction between the different expressions is significant for children who may subconsciously perceive that the only way to earn favour with the teacher is to 'do good work'.

More open relationships result in a fuller discourse between you and the child and pave the way for more focused attention on specific areas of work that need attention. Most children try hard for most of the time, but it is worth reminding yourself that everyone, including adults, has off-days, so don't get tense about pupils' underachievement; they may just be bored or feeling unwell or distracted. Simply tell them what you expect and what you believe they are capable of achieving. Try to avoid being submerged in the moment-by-moment intensity of classroom life; instead, step back occasionally and take a longer-term perspective of pupil progress.

Activate your thinking!

Whatever forms assessment takes, three factors are always relevant:

1. Knowing where a child 'started from' before trying to assess progress
2. Ensuring the form of measurement of ability is valid (i.e. it measures what it is supposed to measure)
3. Establishing a close link between assessment, planning and record-keeping.

Good practice

As you give feedback, put yourself in the children's place and imagine the impact of your words upon their determination to do better and on their self-esteem.

Assessment and learning objectives

It is important in assessing children's progress to bear in mind the learning objectives and continuity, expressed through building conceptual understanding in a systematic (though not inflexible) way. Many tasks and activities involve several stages before completion. For example, a full painting will probably require time to be spent on colour mixing, painting a backwash, use of different paint textures and addition of fine detail that may not be achievable in the space of a single session owing to practical factors of paint drying, available space and maintaining children's concentration levels. In English, draft versions of a piece of writing usually contain misspellings and grammatical errors that may need to be corrected before the final version is produced. It would be unreasonable to treat these early stages as if they were the completed task and base judgements upon them, though teachers pick up many clues by observing how a child approaches the work and the kinds of errors made.

The establishment of clear learning objectives and sufficient time spent explaining the nature of the tasks to the children is essential if they are to make efficient use of their opportunities. Children sometimes rush to complete a piece of work for fear that time constraints make such haste necessary, when a more considered and thorough job would have been possible had you made the position clearer and, perhaps, tried to achieve less coverage of the curriculum and greater depth of understanding. For instance, consider how planning a number of maths lessons on naming and using common coinage with reception-age children might link with assessment criteria. Thus, you might design a series of sessions consisting of four broad phases:

Phase 1: Understanding the use of pennies to pay for goods up to the value of 5p.
Phase 2: Understanding the use of pennies to pay for goods up to the value of 10p.
Phase 3: Establishing the exchange relationship between 1p, 2p and 10p coins.
Phase 4: Establishing the exchange relationship between 1p, 2p, 5p and 10p coins.

Of course, each phase will not necessarily correspond to a single lesson and will need to be broken down into sub-units. In addition, the concepts associated with each phase will almost certainly have to be revised and rehearsed a number of times before learning is secure. The problem for every teacher is to determine when such certainty has been accomplished; using assessment criteria provides a means by which teachers can confirm pupils' understanding about the concepts. Thus, in the above example, each set of objectives is accompanied by a corresponding set of criteria that are used to assess the children's progress. Thus, Phase 1 assessment criteria might be that the children can:

- identify and name pennies;
- count out the coins up to 5p;
- exchange the coins for items costing up to 5p.

Similarly, Phase 2 assessment criteria might be that the children can:

- count out the pennies up to 10p;
- count the cost of buying more than one item up to 10p.

Phase 3 assessment criteria might be that the children can:

- identify and name the 2p coin;
- exchange pennies for 2p coins;
- count the amounts of money using 1p and 2p coins up to a maximum of 10p.

Finally, Phase 4 assessment criteria might be that the children can:

- identify and name 5p coins;
- exchange 1p and 2p coins for 5p coins;
- exchange 1p, 2p and 5p coins for one or more items costing up to 10p.

There may be disagreement among teachers about the precise ordering of the criteria and the way that they are arranged, but the principle of linking lesson objectives and the assessment of pupil attainment across a period of time is one which underpins planning. Although children do not learn in the smooth, uninterrupted fashion that the above criteria might suggest, the concept of employing assessments that are closely linked to learning objectives is valid for all subject areas.

The above comments and insights should have convinced you that keeping track of children's progress requires careful judgement about the evidence to use in forming an opinion. It is one of the key skills for teachers and well worth persevering to master. The issue of recording pupil attainment is addressed later in the chapter.

Target setting

Principles and practice

In recent years, the need to identify and reach targets has become rooted in work at every level of society and schools are no exception. Willick (2006) argues: 'Developing and setting clear goals is a critical aspect of motivation and this involves being able to conceptualise the gains involved in reaching that goal' (p. 46).

The principles of target setting are that targets should be at three levels: school, class and child. The targets must be realistic, manageable and challenging and based on an analysis of data from children's achievements, including regular summative assessments. Targets should be expressed in appropriate language that children can understand, and shared with children (in the short term) and with parents (in the long term). Children should participate in establishing and meeting targets, which should be regularly reviewed. It is important that targets are supported and met by effective teaching, learning and assessment, and not allowed to become free-standing entities, detached from the regular classwork and homework. Target setting has, therefore, become significant for every teacher and is important at three levels:

1. Immediate targets for individual children in different subject areas
2. Longer-term targets for children over (say) half a term
3. Targets for year groups of children in national tests (Year 2 and, especially, Year 6).

Short-term targets

These targets are based upon children's ongoing classroom work. As teachers evaluate pupils' progress, particular aspects of their work are identified as needing special attention and improvement. Recognition of pupils' achievements inevitably involves seeing how the present work can be improved or built upon, and responding accordingly. The process of 'recognition and response' has, of course, been at the heart of teaching for generations; however, today such issues are very much at the forefront of education debate and political priority. Older pupils can take more responsibility for monitoring their own progress and establishing realistic targets; younger ones will need the strong support of teachers to identify specific ways in which improvements can be identified and addressed. Regardless of specific circumstances, target setting for individual children needs to take place with respect to a number of key factors: (1) they must be specific; (2) they must be realistic; (3) they must take account of time; (4) they must be manageable.

First, *target setting must be specific*. Broad targets such as 'I must get better at reading' are inadequate. Instead, a target such as 'I must learn to pause at full stops when reading out loud' or 'I must select non-fiction books for personal reading' should be identified. Similarly, in maths there is little point in setting a target such as 'I must learn my multiplication tables' but rather (say), 'I must learn to do multiplications other than through multiple addition.' Target setting can also include specific aspects of improving presentation of work, learning to work as a member of a group and mastering skills and techniques.

Second, *target setting must be realistic*. Learning does not follow clearly defined pathways. It is gradual and, in some cases, rather serendipitous. If targets are too ambitious, children will lose heart. If they are undemanding, children will not take them seriously. Learning will not necessarily come more quickly simply because targets have been set. Nevertheless, a sensible target can act as a prompt or encouragement for children to focus their energies constructively.

Third, *target setting must take account of time factors*. Most concepts and skills are not mastered overnight; it takes a lot of trial and error, perseverance and determination before understanding comes and abilities are honed. Although it is easy to monitor the setting of (say) a few spellings to be learned at home, targets which involve a lot of library or Internet research (for instance) will take longer to achieve than those which can be done more or less instantly.

Finally, *target setting must be manageable*. There is little point in having a system that is so unwieldy that it demands an unreasonable amount of effort to keep it on track. Sophisticated systems are fine in theory but usually crumble on the sharp edge of reality. Manageable strategies include giving children small 'Targets' notebooks to write down their targets or, where appropriate, have them written by the teacher. Again, some teachers use a system of marking work in different coloured pens or markers to indicate that the area of work requires improvement or needs to be more thoroughly learned. Whatever system is adopted, it is important to minimise your workload and not distract from the main purpose of promoting successful learning by creating a lot of additional and unnecessary paperwork for yourself. There's more than enough already!

Longer-term targets

Most schools encourage the children to 'look ahead' and discuss with the teacher and/or their classmates the things that they are keen to improve and attain over (say) the next half-term. It is impossible and undesirable for children to become submerged in minutiae, such that they become obsessed by the need to 'hit' a large number of disparate targets, but a sensible discussion about key learning needs can help to focus attention on desirable outcomes. For instance, a child might be struggling in changing from printing letters to a cursive script and require guidance, constant practice and opportunities to use the skill in extended writing. Again, a child may be perplexed by the concept of division of whole numbers in mathematics, necessitating a considerable amount of concentration and wrestling with the principles that support the operation, perhaps supported by a teaching assistant. These major learning needs, suitably modified for individuals, are appropriate to use for medium-term targets.

By contrast to the more immediate targets that can be achieved through pupils' self-motivation and resoluteness, longer-term targets necessitate a need for expert advice and support from an informed adult, notably the teacher, who has a wider perspective of learning needs and can see further along the pupil learning curve. In other words, the mere agreement about a target serves limited purpose unless there is a strategy to help the child achieve it and some way of monitoring it. A great deal of the guidance will emerge by way of regular teaching; however, aspects of learning that are specific to individual pupils can be enriched through targeted classwork and homework, together with one-to-one coaching where such opportunities exist.

Identifying when a target has been 'achieved' or 'met' can prove to be problematic, as even the most carefully defined outcomes are subject to personal opinion and interpretation. For example, it is difficult to determine (say) whether a child is writing more creatively or is able to participate more constructively in a discussion than was previously the case, as progress is usually slow and changes in competence are not immediately obvious. Nevertheless, it is important to review targets periodically and help children to take some ownership of their learning instead of relying wholly on an adult's direction and approval.

Targets for year groups

National tests have become increasingly important for all schools as a failure to improve year upon year can bring about additional inspections or intervention by the local authority. The establishment of targets has created a considerable amount of activity in schools as they have responded to the considerable challenge in raising standards of literacy and mathematics in the national tests (popularly known as SATs, originally standard assessment *tasks*, later to become standard assessment *tests*). Part of the process of reaching and maintaining these standards involves a process known as Agreement Trialling, in which teachers responsible for children of the same age in a district (or, in the case of large schools, within the school) meet to consider their assessments of work to ensure that there is a degree of comparability.

On the other hand, it is possible that pupils may be burdened with the weight of teacher expectations, especially if they fail to achieve at least level 2 by the end of Key Stage 1 or at least level 4 by the end of Key Stage 2 in the tests. Many schools give 'booster classes' to underachieving pupils at Key Stage 2, which, though they may have a positive impact upon formal attainment, can be deleterious to children's self-esteem and confidence if they perceive themselves to be recipients of the additional support because they are failures. It is therefore essential for teachers to keep target setting in proportion and not allow it to completely dominate the educational agenda.

Many schools use end-of-year (non-statutory) tests to monitor pupil progress and identify weaknesses. A few schools test children every half-term. With the advent of 'value-added' league tables that rely on the *progress* that children have made from the previously established benchmark, even schools with a large number of children attaining level 4 in the end-of-Key-Stage tests are being obliged to aim for an increase in the number attaining level 5. Schools compile impressive sets of statistics to demonstrate results in national tests for literacy, mathematics and science at the end of Key Stages 1 and 2; predicted results for children currently in Years 4 and 5; and a Foundation Stage Profile.

While it is reasonable to expect teachers to deliver on standards, there is an increasing understanding on the part of policy-makers that the one-size-fits-all philosophy pervading the education system has to be more sensitive to local factors. The group of children in front of you will never be identical to another group, yet the same expectations apply to all. A degree of recognition has been accorded to the fact that every school has specific needs and is set in a unique situation by allowing a degree of flexibility in curriculum content and emphasis, notably schools given 'academy' status and 'free schools' (established and run by parents and members of the local community).

Limitations of targets

Setting targets depends on teachers being clear about what children know and planning lessons accordingly. However, there are strict limits on how detailed these insights can be. While it is relatively simple to ascertain whether children possess certain forms of knowledge, such as being able to recite the alphabet, count to twenty or know historical dates, it is almost impossible to discern precisely what every child understands about (say) human behaviour or the morality of historical events. These limitations have two consequences. First, it is tempting to concentrate your attention exclusively on aspects of knowledge that are measurable. Second, the concept of matching teaching to 'gaps in children's knowledge' is something of a fallacy. Setting targets is a useful strategy for maintaining a well-controlled teaching system but to be truly effective it must also acknowledge that not everything worth knowing falls neatly into the teach/assess/amend teaching formula. Teachers are understandably reluctant to improve test results for the sole purpose of complying with political ambitions or advancing their own career prospects, but in the prevailing climate it is difficult to resist making it a priority.

Activate your thinking!

What do you understand by the expression 'raising standards'? Does it only mean 'raising test scores'?

Assessing collaborative activities

Assessment of individual children is more difficult when they are involved in collaborative work. Although enhancing pupil skills in collaborating is a valuable dimension of learning, it can also mask the progress made by individuals in the group. Most teachers rightly view the sight of children explaining to and assisting one another to complete tasks as worthwhile; however, this is different from one child acting as a surrogate teacher and continually intervening in another child's work or detrimentally dominating proceedings. If, say, four groups of children are engaged in doing the same task, there will be four different levels of task interpretation and outcome depending upon the ability and expertise within the group. To make any sort of meaningful assessment, you will need to be aware of the group's academic condition and previous learning when determining what constitutes a satisfactory learning outcome, as demonstrated by the group's decisions, task completion, recording of findings or presentations to other pupils.

From Figure 11.1 we can see that the least able group (A) is likely follow the procedures without deviating from the teacher's instructions. Group B might follow the procedures but

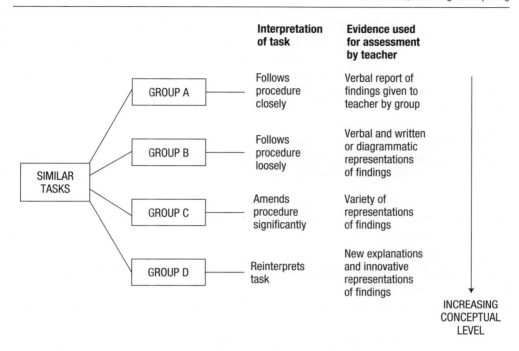

FIGURE 11.1 Assessment of groups through outcomes

interpret them more imaginatively. It can be anticipated that Group C will amend the procedures significantly and introduce their own ideas and modifications, while Group D (the most able) will reinterpret the task and develop a wholly innovative approach that answers slightly different questions and involves other learning 'pathways' from those envisaged by the teacher. Although teachers will expect all children to use their intellects and make the best contribution possible in finding solutions or strategies to complete the activity, they will also take into account the potential and limitations of each group. Thus, Group A will be commended for accurately following the set procedure while Group D's accomplishments will be assessed using a different and possibly stricter set of criteria based perhaps on the effectiveness of their solutions. If, on the other hand, Group C operated only at the level expected from Group A the teacher might reasonably conclude that the task was too tedious, the group was underperforming or the teacher's original expectations of the group's capability were unrealistic.

Differentiating in this way by a consideration of *outcome* provides the teacher with a means of acknowledging a group's particular contribution and effort without directly comparing group with group. Pupils in the less able group might achieve a lot within the limits of their capability and the teacher's expectations, while pupils in the other groups might complete what is required of them but without flair or being innovative, in which case they would be judged as underachieving.

Confirmation of pupil progress in learning (as opposed to immediate assessments) will therefore rely upon the individual's contribution to the group effort as perceived by the teacher, subsequent work in the same area of learning, ability to explain things coherently and the quality of the write-up or other representation of the work such as diagrams, maps, pictures or models. Sometimes a teacher's assessment will be based on factors other than the final work outcome. For instance, you might want to evaluate pupils' willingness to co-operate, their power of creative thought, enthusiasm or commitment to completing the task; these 'non-measurables' are important assessments which relate more closely to social behaviour, personal growth and attitude than to quantifiable academic performance but make a vital contribution to producing a fully educated person.

Activate your thinking!

Sometimes the best you can do is to assess the effectiveness of the group as a whole rather than the individuals that compose it.

Good practice

Select a 'key' child from each group each week for careful observation and assessment. Choose a new target child from each group every week until you have worked your way through them all.

Assessing children for whom English is an additional language

In 2007 the standards for qualified teacher status in England – those for Wales and Scotland are very similar but are described and presented differently – were produced by the Training and Development Agency (TDA) include the requirement that newly qualified teachers should:

> Know how to make effective personalised provision for those they teach, including those for whom English is an additional language [EAL] or who have special educational needs or disabilities, and how to take practical account of diversity and promote equality and inclusion in their teaching.

In particular, there is a need to assess pupils' competence in English through their ability to comprehend through listening, speaking, reading and writing. Policy with regard to bilingual children (those who speak two or more languages, though not necessarily fluently) has developed considerably in recent years due to the sharp increase in immigration. The Primary National Strategy document *Learning and Teaching for Bilingual Children in the Primary Years* (DCSF 2006) was introduced into schools during 2007–8 and provides guidance on EAL pedagogy, planning and assessment, as well as containing practical materials and examples that cover most aspects of teaching bilingual pupils in mainstream primary classrooms.

Pupils' responsiveness when hearing English spoken can be assessed with reference to the 'extended scale for listening' (QCA 2000) and their ability to speak and use spoken English can be assessed with reference to the 'extended scale for speaking'. Similarly, their familiarity with the conventions of print and understanding written English can be assessed with reference to the 'extended scale for reading' and their ability to write for different purposes can be assessed with reference to the 'extended scale for writing'. Broadly, it should be possible to make judgements for listening, speaking, reading and writing using the descriptions below. Thus:

Listening

You can distinguish between children who respond to spoken English in specific circumstances (e.g. a regular instruction such as 'please sit down'), those who can understand what is said but do not respond, and those children who can talk to others as a result of their understanding.

Speaking

You can distinguish between children who are able to say a few words, those who can sustain a conversation, and those who can modify their speech according to context and circumstances.

Reading

You can distinguish between children who are able to grasp basic written conventions, those who can read with support, and those who can read with a large degree of independence.

Writing

You can distinguish between children who are able to write English letters and their name, those who can use letter patterns, and those who can write recognisable letters, words and phrases.

Formal assessment of English as an additional language is described with reference to a scale consisting of four stages for those who have yet to reach NC Attainment Target 1, namely:

- Step 1: for the least competent users
- Step 2: for more competent users
- Level 1: 'threshold'
- Level 2: 'secure'.

Characteristics of each stage are described closely in QCA (2000: 12–15). The scale for speaking and listening is separately listed for the four stages but is combined for level 2 and above. There are separate scales for reading and for writing. As with all assessments, however, the purpose of placing a child at a particular stage is not for the sake of completing a record sheet and satisfying external requirements, but to assist you and the teaching assistants or language specialists in determining how best to support the child's learning. Subsequent planning of an appropriate curriculum programme for children with EAL will depend upon a variety of factors, not least whether there are other children in the class with the same first language and the availability of a TA. It is also important to take account of the disorientation that a child experiences when suddenly thrust into a confusing new situation, with unfamiliar language, cultural norms and procedures. Every new child takes time to adjust to the pattern of working, and this problem is magnified for a child who speaks little or no English.

Your assessment record might consist of a summary paragraph about the child's abilities in speaking and listening, samples of written work as evidence for writing, and regular reading records for progress in reading. Assessment profiles of this kind should allow you to trace the child's curriculum experience in school and provide diagnostic information that allows you to discuss the child's progress with other staff and parents. As a trainee teacher you will need to take advice from experienced colleagues and, in particular, from the teacher in the school charged with such matters (e.g. SENCO, leader for literacy).

Activate your thinking!

Put yourself in the place of a child newly arrived from overseas with little knowledge of the English language, indigenous customs or school procedures. Scary, isn't it?

Good practice

Use assessment as a forum for celebrating success, not highlighting failure.

Recording and reporting

Keeping records

The emphasis throughout this book has been upon the interrelationship between planning, assessment, record-keeping and reporting children's progress to parents, both informally and formally. Few practitioners enjoy keeping records, but they are a necessary part of professional responsibility. They can provide information about curriculum coverage, pupil progress and issues that arise from teaching and learning. Following any block of teaching and learning, teachers are confronted with a number of questions with respect to pupils' attainment:

How much did the children learn from the lesson or lessons?
What evidence is there of individual progress?
What evidence is there of group (collaborative) progress?
How will this information affect future lesson planning?
How will the evidence be recorded?

Although teachers hold a lot of information about children in their heads, there is a need to keep written records that assist with the twin requirements of assisting with future lesson plans and reporting to parents. One of the principal difficulties for teachers is deciding what to record and what to omit. It is no exaggeration to claim that teachers could spend more time recording than they do in teaching if they attempted to write down everything. In addition to influencing their planning, both trainee teachers and qualified ones have to ensure that their records are up to date, though for rather different reasons.

The best reporting systems provide up-to-date and accurate information about school attainment so that parents also have a clearer idea about the assistance they can offer at home. Teachers have to strike a balance between providing sufficient information to satisfy the curiosity and 'need to know' of parents and overloading them with detail. Some reports are many pages long and saturated with facts about curriculum coverage, raising suspicions that such actions are an exercise in vanity on the part of the school rather than providing what most parents have any interest in seeing. In addition to their children's academic progress, most parents are also interested in knowing about their social development, friendship patterns and attitudes towards learning across the board.

Forms of records

Trainee teachers need to show to their tutors that they are engaging with the process of evaluating pupils' work, assessing their progress and noting outcomes (summative in character). Qualified teachers need to provide evidence for their teacher assessments; to have forms of evidence to support their decisions; and to supply information required in respect of performance management (salary increases and promotion to senior posts). Consequently, the precise forms of records that are maintained depend upon their particular purpose. Records take a variety of forms and are kept for a number of different purposes, including the following.

- *Organisational planning* This type of record is based on curriculum coverage. For example, noting which group has covered which topic and modifying the content of future lessons as a result.
- *Strategy for managing* This type of record is purely organisational and acts as a reminder for teachers and assistants about the children's level of engagement with work. For example, checking who has read to the teacher during the week, noting who has used the computer, and so on.
- *National Curriculum demands* This type of record offers evidence of children's progress that helps to inform formal teacher assessments: in particular, evidence for end-of-Key-Stage assessments.
- *Information for parents* This type of record is a summary of key facts for easy transmission to a third party: for example, informal notes in preparation for parents' evening.
- *Recognition of children's efforts* This type of record consists of representative samples of children's work for inclusion in a Record of Achievement folder, class books, wall displays, etc.

The most immediate records for teachers to maintain are those that show areas of work covered (curriculum coverage) and those that show children's progress (individual records). It is important to distinguish between the two types of records for, as noted earlier, mere completion of a task or activity does not necessarily show the extent of understanding or mastery.

Activate your thinking!

Why are you spending so much time keeping records? Who are they for? What do they achieve? Can the process be simplified? Do they enhance your teaching?

Good practice

Some teachers keep minimal records and only complete the formal ones under sufferance; other teachers seem to make a virtue of maintaining detailed and meticulous records. Aim for a mid-way point between these two extremes.

Curriculum coverage

Records of curriculum coverage take many forms. The best are straightforward to use and easy to modify. A rigid, over-detailed format is time-consuming, rarely justifies the effort and should not be confused with the detail required for end-of-Key-Stage national tests and tasks. Many schools plan in half-termly blocks in which the main topic, theme or subject is identified and NC links established, particularly with literacy and mathematics, but more loosely in the case of other subject areas. A weekly or fortnightly overview is then drawn up by staff teams that teach the same age group or by individual teachers if there is a single class in the year; lesson planning emerges from this common structure. The subsequent records of curriculum coverage reflect the nature of the planning and are likely to take one of two forms: (1) records that state curriculum coverage based primarily on programmes of study (PoS); and (2) records based primarily on concepts, skills and knowledge.

Much depends on the way in which a particular school organises its learning programme: the more subject-centred the programme, the more likely that PoS predominates. The more process-centred or thematic the programme, the more likely that concepts and skills are emphasised. Two simple examples of *pro formas* are shown in Figures 11.2 and 11.3.

Record of activities for the whole class

Figure 11.2 can be used when the activities (or tasks) are appropriate to the whole class. For example, the children might all be doing some observational drawing. The record sheet will help the teacher to see who has completed the task and who has not. The names of the children are written in the left-hand column. The activity is written in the skewed box near the top of the page. The appropriate box is ticked or shaded when the child has completed the activity or task. A simpler version with fewer names can be adopted to record the work of a single group. If several groups are involved with different curriculum areas, the need for maintaining careful records is even greater and several copies of the *pro forma* will be needed.

A curriculum continuity planning sheet

Figure 11.3 indicates the sort of straightforward record that can be made of coverage in core subjects that provides an overview of the planning process. The numbers on the left-hand side refer to the weeks of the topic, theme or project. A note of the specific teaching area covered or the NC reference can be made in the subject columns. The sheet can be modified in imaginative and useful ways; a similar format can, of course, be used for other subjects.

Records of individual pupil progress

Keeping specific records for each child is probably of most interest and concern to new teachers. Since it is not possible to assess a child's thought processes directly, teachers have to collect *evidence* relating to the product of those thought processes. The most usual product is a piece of written work, but observations help the teacher by providing information from ongoing interactions while the child is working (see, for instance, Nilsen 2004; Fawcett 2009).

Records of activities covered with a group or class are important but do not tell you anything about the assessment relating to an individual pupil. Use of National Curriculum documents assists in planning and monitoring curriculum coverage but is less helpful for charting individual progress. Ideally, it is desirable to plan every intended learning outcome for each child, monitor progress, assess the extent of the learning and record it in a manageable form. In practice, this is impossible unless the class is exceptionally small.

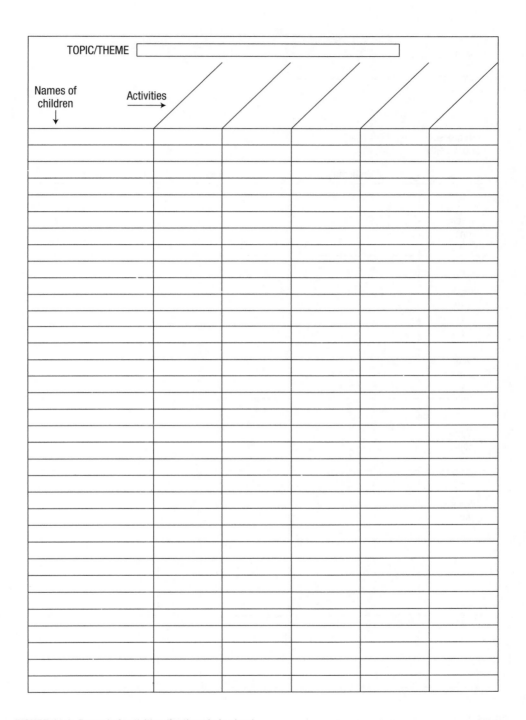

FIGURE 11.2 Record of activities (for the whole class)

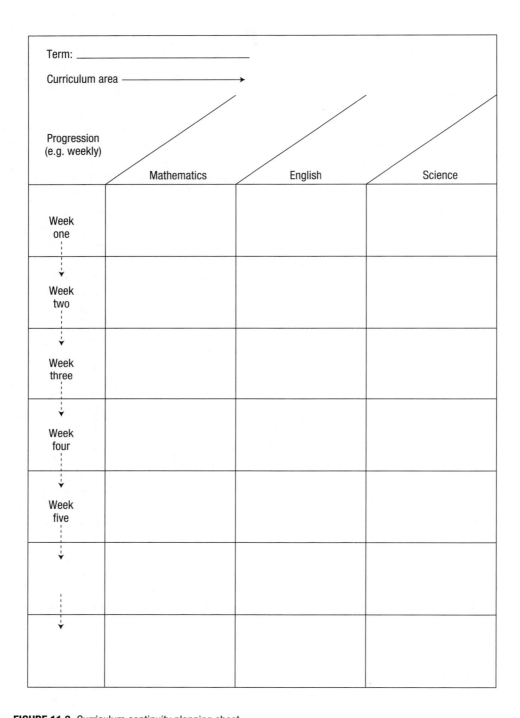

FIGURE 11.3 Curriculum continuity planning sheet

Teachers can suffer agonies of conscience over the fact that their files are not full of pages of information plotting the progress of every child in every aspect of learning in every subject area, but such self-recrimination is unnecessary. As noted in earlier chapters, learning is rarely smooth and uninterrupted, but it is in the ongoing process of formative assessment where children are deemed to have gained a broad grasp of the intended outcome if they complete the set work to the teacher's satisfaction. Careful monitoring of the ongoing work, together with individual notes made about each child's perceived difficulties, is preferable to endlessly listing the things that the child knows and understands. Put simply: spend more time noting the things that a child does *not* know rather than the things the child *does* know; in other words, spend a much smaller amount of time recording the things they do know than the things with which they are still struggling. The information in records can then be used diagnostically to improve future teaching and learning rather than as a list of content coverage. This practice of focusing on the problems is not being negative or dismissive of a child's achievements; it is an approach to keeping records, which is for the most part carried out away from the classroom.

Whether to record

The most careful and detailed records have to be kept for literacy (English) and mathematics. Information can be gained from in-class tests, completed exercises as part of the regular class work and pupils' verbal contributions. However, it is not necessary, sensible or realistic to maintain detailed records for all children of every step they take in their learning. If you are uncertain about whether or not to record an aspect of children's progress, use the following three criteria in helping to make a decision: (1) Will you need to share the information with the child or another adult (e.g. a special needs teacher or a parent)? (2) Will details be required to support a judgement about grade allocation (e.g. for the purpose of allocation to a maths or English 'set' or teacher assessment at the end of a Key Stage)? (3) Will the information help you to plan future lessons to accommodate individual pupil learning requirements? Unless you have a very small class, several assistants or exceptionally fast handwriting, there is little point in recording too much information, other than that which might be requested by your training provider. On the other hand, too little recorded information can be interpreted as poor practice.

Activate your thinking!

The more information children are given about what they are meant to achieve, the more they can be involved in monitoring their own progress.

Good practice

In maintaining records, assume that if children complete the tasks and activities without excessive adult support, they have at least a reasonable grasp of content and understand the associated concepts.

Manageable record-keeping

As a first step in assessing and recording individuals' progress during tasks and activities that you have allocated for children to complete as part of the regular lesson structure, it is helpful to use a 'Goldilocks and the Three Bears' approach in monitoring the way that children progress and cope with the work. A small number of children may struggle because the content of lessons is 'too hot'. A small number may sail through because the content is 'too cold'. The majority will cope comfortably because the content is just the right temperature. By informally placing children in one of the three categories, it soon becomes obvious where the problems lie and what sort of help is needed. For example:

Too hot: Malichaba, Esmie, Tallis.
Too cold: Damien, Chris, Becks, Amanda.
Just right: The rest of the class.

Consequently, pupils in the 'too hot' category require less demanding challenges, whereas those in the 'too cold' category need to have their intellects extended. While focusing on pupils at the ends of the spectrum, be careful not to ignore the potential of middle-of-the-road children, who may not excel or struggle but still deserve as much attention as those at the extremes. The process is more manageable and representative of true ability if records show the extent of individual progress across a *series* of lessons rather than a single one. Although this unsophisticated approach cannot be used for formal records, it is useful as a memory aid for busy teachers and a surprisingly effective working tool.

In an attempt to balance reality with aspiration, some schools have more sophisticated records relating to the core subjects only, one sheet per child. These usually contain details about the content and learning relating to particular attainment targets in a subject; the categories are ticked or blocked according to an agreed system and kept with the child's records, sometimes together with a sample of work for evidence. Schools will often have an agreed marking policy to support the monitoring process so that there is consistency across and within year groups. As a trainee teacher, you might have to use an existing school record system or complete sample records on *pro formas* supplied by the faculty/college.

Typically, inexperienced trainees are asked to identify a small number of children and track their progress closely; more experienced trainees, especially those in their final placement, should be looking ahead to the time when they will have responsibility for a full class of children and thinking in terms of tracking each child – though this goal is far from easy to achieve and most teachers end up 'blocking' groups of children who are of similar competence, and allocating the same or similar comment, grade or mark to each of them.

Activate your thinking!

After three weeks with your class, a parent comes into the room and approaches you.
   'Hello,' she smiles, 'I'm Molly's mum. I wondered how she was getting on in her work.'
   Where would you begin? What would you say?

Good practice

Consider how you would explain the way in which you record children's progress to an interested friend who does not work in education.

Reports and reporting

Earlier in this chapter, it was emphasised that records of children's progress and attainment serve two principal purposes. First, so that you have access to data that can influence lesson planning; second, to provide information in formal records for other audiences, notably colleagues and parents. The report set out below is genuine, though some details have been altered to ensure anonymity. As a trainee teacher, it is very unlikely that you will be required to write such a report, but as soon as you qualify and take responsibility for your own class, you will have to do so. In studying the example, bear in mind that parts of the text are generated by computer software, but that the teacher still needs to know individual children well enough to provide specific insights into their progress. No report can say everything about a child, so a selection of key issues and learning outcomes is inevitable. Making this selection provides one of the key challenges for a teacher, who may be writing up to thirty reports for infants and even more for juniors. In addition, the new responsibilities of teaching assistants can include the administration (but not the writing) of reports, though how this works in practice will depend upon school circumstances.

Case study: sample report for parents

Marshall, Year 3

VISITS
Autumn term: museum, local priory, woodland walk.
Spring term: cathedral.
Summer term: local mosque, local Christian centre.

ENGLISH
Reading curriculum
- Range of fiction genre, including play scripts and poetry
- Library skills and use of the Dewey system
- Research skills, scanning, skimming, note-taking
- Phonics and spelling.

Writing curriculum
- Writing for a variety of purposes (creative, narrative, persuasive, research, expressive, instructional)
- Sentence grammar and punctuation.

Reading: Marshall has made good overall progress. His expression is developing well and he is noticing punctuation in the text. He is able to talk about his reading and make inferences from the text. Marshall receives extra literacy support and is able to apply skills learnt to his own reading. He has begun to scan text to find information.

Writing: Marshall has made steady progress. He has lovely ideas for story-writing and is remembering to use adjectives to create a picture for the reader. Sometimes his

---

enthusiasm to write means that Marshall misses out words and forgets to use punctuation, making it difficult to follow the story plot. He can use a simple dictionary but does not always check his spellings. In handwriting, Marshall still needs to make tall and short letters more clearly distinguishable. He can join up his letters but does not always do so.

Speaking and listening: Marshall is able to listen and ask questions to help his understanding. He has an intermittent stammer that can cause him difficulty in expressing himself.

Next steps in English: Marshall needs to make inferences from the text when reading. In writing, he needs to check his work more carefully to make sure that sentences make sense. He needs to think more carefully before speaking during discussions.

MATHEMATICS
Mini-topic curriculum
- 2D and 3D shape
- Symmetry
- Weight and length as forms of measurement
- Data-handling
- Angles and movement
- Volume and capacity
- Time.

Marshall has worked hard and made steady progress. At the start of the year he found mental/oral subtraction problems difficult but is now much more confident. He is able to find the inverse for addition and subtraction sentences and is being encouraged to use more than one strategy to solve problems.

Next steps in mathematics: Marshall needs to look carefully at a number sequence to find pattern and use this to predict the next number.

SCIENCE
Curriculum
- Shadows and reflections
- Earth in Space
- Materials and their uses
- Changing materials
- Teeth and healthy eating
- Living things and their environment
- Green plants as organisms.

Marshall is able to talk about the properties of materials and sort them into groups according to their properties. He can describe differences between living and non-living things and has begun to think about factors that cause change.

Next steps in science: to plan a fair investigation where only one factor will change, other factors remaining constant.

HISTORY
Curriculum
- Romans as an in-depth study
- Anglo-Saxons (outline study)
- Vikings (outline study).

Marshall thoroughly enjoyed the visit to see the Roman exhibits at the museum and the old Roman wall. His hands-on experience brought history to life for him. He has developed a growing awareness of chronology and can give some reasons why people leave their homelands and settle in another country.

GEOGRAPHY
Curriculum
- Locality studies: the local woodland walk
- Settlements: the country of Zambia
- Mapping skills and co-ordinates.

Marshall can compare different localities, noticing similarities and differences in land use and physical features such as valleys and wooded areas. He is aware of how some land use has changed and can make suggestions as to how it might be improved.

ART
Curriculum
- Colour-mixing and combinations
- Powder paints portraits
- Observational drawings of plants and flowers
- Batik flowers and weavings.

Marshall has worked hard to create texture in his artwork with paints, drawings and textiles. Following the educational visit, he produced a weaving that reflects the colours and feelings of the landscape. He includes a lot of fine detail in all his drawings.

MUSIC
Curriculum
- Structure and pitch
- Duration and dynamics
- Timbre and texture
- Listening and appraising
- Composing own music.

Marshall is now able to recognise notes of differing pitch (high, low, the same). He has created repeated sound patterns and has begun to work with others to fit patterns together. He has also started to understand that layering sounds creates musical texture.

PHYSICAL EDUCATION
Curriculum
- Games – sending and receiving ball-skills, racket-skills, team games
- Gym – pathways and levels using floor and apparatus
- Dance – linking movements, responding to narratives, rhythm and tempo.

Marshall shows good control when planning a sequence of actions, both on the floor and on benches. In games he has learned the skills of attack and defence, as well as developing accurate overarm and underarm throws.

RELIGIOUS EDUCATION
Curriculum
- Exploring what is meant by faith and the difference it can make to people's lives
- The place of worship and prayer

- Signs and symbols
- The significance of Christmas and Easter
- Basics of Christianity and Islam.

Marshall is able to think about his own experiences, commitments and values, and contrast them with those of other people. He can explain how some aspects of religious belief are practised. He can retell the Easter story in his own words.

DESIGN TECHNOLOGY
Curriculum
- Making permanent joins
- Investigating different temporary joins
- Making picture frames
- Moving toys
- Linkages and levers
- Problem-solving 3D-construction challenges.

Marshall knows how to join a range of different materials to create permanent and temporary fixtures. He can talk about the uses for different joins. He has used his skills to create a picture frame.

INFORMATION TECHNOLOGY
Curriculum
- Word-processing and text handling
- Textease
- Graphics
- Data-handling
- Control and programming using Roamer
- Creating and sending emails.

Marshall has used computer software to recreate part of an artist's picture and used the full range of tools to create texture. He has used a simulation program, involving mathematical problems and logical thinking. He has input data for data-handling and used word-processing. Marshall has a reasonable grasp of the function and purpose of emails.

PERSONAL, SOCIAL, CITIZENSHIP AND HEALTH EDUCATION
Curriculum
- Friends and relationships
- Healthy living
- Keeping safe.

Marshall is now able to express his opinions and give reasons for doing so. With adult support, he is able to contribute towards setting termly targets for his development. He is also able to identify things he has achieved. Marshall understands why rules are needed and has begun to exercise a level of responsibility in the classroom.

SUMMARY
Marshall has been a lovely member of the class. He has grown up a lot during the year and is taking more responsibility for his own learning. He still struggles to concentrate for any length of time and is sometimes easily distracted. Marshall tends to be careless with his work and needs to check more carefully before being satisfied. He loves to play with other children but does not have a close or special friend.

Attendance
- Number of sessions attended since last September 292
- Total possible sessions since last September 308
- Percentage attendance 95 per cent
- Number of unauthorised absences 0.

Further reading for Chapter 11

Briggs, M., Woodfield, A., Martin, C. and Swatton, P. (2008) *Assessment for Learning and Teaching in Primary Schools*, second edn, Exeter: Learning Matters.
The text is written for trainee teachers and newly qualified teachers teaching in Key Stages 1 and 2 who wish to develop their understanding and practice of assessment; it emphasises peer assessment and target setting linked to personalised learning.
Drummond, M. J. (2003) *Assessing Children's Learning*, London: David Fulton.
The author provides a balance of theoretical perspective and practical examples, written by an author with considerable experience in this field.
Johnson, S. (2011) *Assessing Learning in the Primary Classroom*, Abingdon: Routledge.
An examination of concepts critical to a professional understanding of aspects of a teacher's role in assessing learning, the principles underpinning effective assessment, the different forms it can take and the different purposes it serves.
Lord, L. and Slinn, K. (2007) *Curriculum Planning and Assessment for the Foundation Stage*, London: Sage.
The book offers guidance about assessing learning and how to help children in an early years setting achieve high standards. Includes a CD-ROM.
Trodd, L. and Goodliff, G. (2007) *Achieving EYPS: Success in your assessment*, Exeter: Learning Matters.
Structured around the three skills areas of communication, decision-making and leadership, with reference to the early years standards.

Part 4

Challenging Pupils

12 Behaviour Management and Classroom Discipline

Introduction

Trainee teachers whose greatest concern is exercising class discipline should be reassured that most children enjoy school, behave sensibly for the majority of the time and want to have a positive relationship with adults and other pupils. This chapter explores a range of issues associated with children's behaviour and the strategies available for ensuring that the teaching and learning process is not hindered by the struggle to maintain order. A variety of discipline strategies are offered for consideration but these are underpinned by an acknowledgement that behind every settled classroom is a lot of hard work by the teacher in establishing and maintaining positive relationships, generating work that motivates the children and enforcing an agreed behaviour policy.

A positive learning environment

It takes a visitor only a few minutes in a classroom to detect whether or not a teacher has managed to establish and maintain a positive learning environment. In the best-run classrooms, the children are lively but not silly, speak naturally to adults, treat one another kindly and do their best to succeed. Teachers use a positive tone, employ humour without appearing foolish and rarely raise their voices. The children respond to instructions, and even to being chastened, without rancour or discord. The prevailing mood is 'all for one and one for all', rather than 'first to the top gets the prize'. Trainee teachers often say of such situations: 'That is how I want my own classroom to be one day.'

Terminology

Terminology is important when considering issues of control and discipline. Bad behaviour involves making a judgement about someone's actions and intent. In school, the person evaluating the behaviour is usually the teacher and the one being judged, the pupil. Bad behaviour may be wilful (deliberate) or unintended. Similarly, all children (and adults, for that matter) are capable of *irresponsible* behaviour when, for a short period of time, common sense and rational thought seem to disappear. Such moments are different from the concept of indiscipline which occurs when children know what they should do but choose not to do it.

Although the terminology used for class control issues varies, the word 'behaviour' tends to refer to the child's actions whereas 'control' and 'discipline' are more likely to be applied to the teacher's actions. That is, the teacher attempts to influence the child's behaviour through effective discipline in the belief that this is the most effective way of exercising control. However, the imposition of external constraints has limited value in as much as children ultimately need to exercise self-control rather than have it imposed on them. As Wright (2006) reminds us, a situation can arise in which a teacher 'seems to be naturally popular or charismatic' with the result that pupils want to please her or him; in doing so, however, the children may 'not assume responsibility for their own behaviour' (p. 53). Consequently, when a different teacher is in charge, pupils who were well behaved with the first teacher fail to be for the next. This phenomenon has many facets, not least the bond that develops between the majority of teachers and their classes over a period of time, which the new or substitute teacher cannot possibly establish overnight.

Norms of behaviour

It is important to remember that the term 'behaviour' does not simply encompass a child being good or naughty; it also includes other manifestations such as exhibiting shyness, withdrawal from mainstream activities and idleness. These, too, are behaviours seen in classrooms with which teachers have to cope and, hopefully, change for the better. As in all aspects of work with children, there are no absolutes in respect of creating a purposeful learning climate, as the content of this chapter acknowledges. There are, none the less, principles and strategies that assist rather than obstruct the process.

Teachers quickly discover that children's willingness to comply and conform to established norms of behaviour varies considerably. Some children do not have the maturity, willpower or awareness of conventions to fully grasp what 'behaving' means or the self-control to change their responses. As a result, the unacceptable behaviour continues and inexperienced teachers in particular become increasingly exasperated, berating the child by fruitlessly repeating the demand to 'behave' (or a similar command). In addition, a small number of pupils understand the conventions but choose to wilfully disregard them. Children therefore need to be provided with an enforceable rule framework, sensibly but consistently applied, within which they can gradually strengthen their own self-control. Dreikurs et al. (1998) stress the importance of helping children to take responsibility for their own actions. They cite an example of a boy who kept calling out in class. The teacher despaired of finding a solution until she asked the boy himself for his suggestions. He imposed a sanction on himself (loss of two minutes' free time for each transgression) and the problem was cured within a week. Alas, not all situations are so easily remedied, but the principle of involving children in suggesting solutions to their problems can be a valuable one, providing it is clear that you are the final arbiter in any dispute about the method.

Modelling behaviour

Newell and Jeffery (2002: 43–8) emphasise that teachers should model good behaviour to children. Strategies include being prepared to say sorry, explaining that teachers as well as children have rights (e.g. to be listened to politely), taking a keen interest in learning, demonstrating a strong sense of purpose in teaching and showing that the challenge of arresting difficult behaviour is not insurmountable. Teachers have to take into account the age and experience of the children, as well as school behaviour policies, but the twin principles of consistency and fairness must apply whatever the circumstances. As Chaplain (2006) notes, 'Rules alone do not guarantee good behaviour. They need to be linked to consequences – which means *consistently* rewarding pupils who follow the rules and applying sanctions as a deterrent to those who do not' (p. 110, author's emphasis). The issue of rewards, punishments and sanctions is addressed later in this chapter.

However much the children may resist responding to your instructions, you must continue to insist until they do so, however unwillingly. In the process of doing so, make sure of at least three things. First, do not lose your temper or make vulnerable, compliant children suffer for the sins of the few; aim to be pleasantly firm. Second, expect to be unpopular for a time; it's a price worth paying. Third, you can ease up after a while but revert to a formal approach at the first sign of nonsense.

Good practice

Seize the initiative early on. Don't allow yourself to be quizzed by the children, however sincerely interested in you they may appear to be. Just be politely friendly and firmly insistent during the early encounters. Don't court popularity; let it emerge naturally.

Unacceptable behaviour

Unacceptable behaviour takes many forms. A minority of children constantly push the boundaries set by adults and their names are upon every teacher's lips. Some children cause trouble for certain teachers but act sensibly for others. While children who actively resist conforming and behave unreasonably may require specialist help and formal intervention techniques, the majority can be dealt with using basic classroom rules and procedures. McPhillimy (1996) issues a warning about the need for teachers to examine the *cause* of problems rather than their symptoms:

> Misbehaviour in itself is therefore mainly a symptom of a problem rather than the problem itself. If the underlying problems are dealt with, then the symptom is likely to disappear.
>
> (p. 61)

While McPhillimy's assertion is somewhat optimistic, learning to cope with the vagaries of children's behaviour is helped when teachers admit that unacceptable behaviour is sometimes due to an uncertainty in children's minds about where the boundaries lie.

It is also important for teachers to recognise the difference between two types of inappropriate behaviour – namely, children who misbehave and children who fail to conform. Children who *misbehave* often do so out of choice. They understand the rules but make a decision to disregard them; they are also aware of the likely consequences but hope that they won't get caught or are insufficiently impressed by the sanction to worry if it is applied. Younger children are more likely to misbehave through a lack of understanding of how the rules and school conventions operate, exacerbated by confusion about adult expectations or even an inbuilt naughtiness (not a popular word but very apt in some cases). See Chapter 3 for further insights into misbehaviour.

Non-conformist children

Some children *fail to conform*, either because they genuinely do not see the need to do so or because they lack the maturity to comply. In most cases, the situation can be remedied by patient, persistent explanation and use of peer pressure to make them fall in line. Pupils who are new to school may be unaware of what is required; older ones may be egocentric or come from a family/cultural background that fosters single-mindedness. Typically, the behaviour of non-conformist children varies little inside and outside school. Such children seem puzzled when confronted by an insistent teacher who explains to them that a particular action is not acceptable. Parents, when asked about their non-conformist children, will often sigh and admit that they cannot do anything much with them either. Children who fail to conform may be highly motivated or sluggish, popular or aloof, pleasant or miserable, but they have in common their persistent refusal or inability to act in a conventional manner. Non-conformists wander when they are meant to be seated, approach their work differently from others, insist on working alone instead of collaboratively and show an attitude towards the teacher which varies from disdain to wild enthusiasm. Repeated day after day, the irregular behaviour can, understandably, cause teachers to become irritated and frustrated with the child.

It is desirable but far from easy to channel the energies of non-conformist children into productive activities. Teachers are keen to curb the unacceptable behaviour but also fear that if they are too insistent the child concerned may suffer a loss of confidence or start to rebel and turn into a persistent offender. Regular calm explanations about what is acceptable and proscribed, and consistent teacher direction, can help to regulate the situation, but the children's inability to grasp conventions normally makes the process protracted. It is also a sobering truth that inappropriate behaviour of all types does not necessarily arise through pupils' inability to understand what is expected of them but rather from a teacher's failure to gain pupils' respect. Children are especially disdainful of teachers with a timid personality, a mundane teaching approach or lessons that have little purpose or relevance to them. In such cases, efforts to gain control are likely to falter, however hard you try.

Activate your thinking!

Consider the children in your class who exhibit inappropriate behaviour. Try to categorise as follows:

Those who are regularly mischievous but generally harmless.
Those who misbehave wilfully.
Those who are non-conformists.
Consider how you might react to the same sort of inappropriate behaviour from a child in each of the categories.

Order and orderliness

When teachers have to deal with unsatisfactory behaviour, it is a signal that something has already gone wrong, so it is important to give serious thought as to why it has happened and whether it can be prevented in the future. If a framework of rules is established early on, discussed with the children and frequently reviewed, it provides a yardstick against which to judge behaviour and determine sanctions (where appropriate). However, it is important to distinguish between 'order' in the classroom and an 'orderly' classroom. Order can be achieved by insisting that the children adhere to a rigid set of requirements of the 'do this but do not do that' type, reminiscent of military commands. Children have only to step slightly out of line to invoke a sanction, placing a considerable strain on the harmonious classroom environment that you are trying to achieve. Orderliness, on the other hand, stresses the fact that the classroom functions smoothly because everyone is clear about the boundaries, involved in reviewing them and invited to talk sensibly about infringements. Transgressions are best dealt with through a calm response and desire to resolve a situation rather than a frenzied one with threats and reprisals.

In an orderly classroom, teachers are uncompromising about dealing firmly with deliberate improper behaviour, but are genuinely more concerned with achieving satisfactory outcomes than inflexibly applying sanctions like a judge in a courtroom. Indeed, Willick (2006) warns against the 'over-reliance on sanctions that can create an atmosphere of distrust, fear and resentment, as well as having a negative effect on relationships' (p. 72). Punishments should be reserved for deliberate offending against the rules. Unintended infringements and silliness can normally be resolved through dialogue with the child and establishing a strategy for rectifying the situation. Roache and Lewis (2011) support the judicious use of a combination of strategies involving the use of hinting, involvement, discussion, recognition and rewards. They suggest that there are considerable benefits to be achieved through a regulated process of positive discipline strategies, by means of which teachers and students can develop mutual respect and trust.

Adult–child relationships

As noted in Chapters 1 and 3, the majority of pupils of all ages want to do well and please their teacher. Effective working relationships develop gradually through regular interaction between adult and child, relevant work and interesting lessons. Teachers who are harsh, unreasonable, condescending or insincere are inviting problems of indiscipline as children react negatively towards such attitudes or lose confidence and thereby underachieve. A positive classroom climate is assisted by being firm, fair and tolerant of genuine mistakes. Teachers who have a natural manner and develop a sincere approach to their teaching, aided by a cheerful disposition, are unlikely to suffer unduly from misbehaving pupils. Good relationships are not built overnight, however; they require perseverance, application and a genuine desire to help children succeed. The challenge for teachers is to be caring without being cosy.

Children react adversely against autocratic teachers, those who try to lord it over them and those who demand too much, too soon, without offering patient help and advice in the completion of tasks. It is essential for teachers to win pupils' co-operation and show that they like them, but in such a way that the separate adult and child identities are maintained. To win co-operation necessitates teachers taking a real interest in the children, listening to their comments and requests, and responding with positive suggestions, praise, encouragement and trust. With reference to what he refers to as 'adult attachment theory', Riley (2010) argues that teachers who are able to accurately interpret the underlying relationship processes that are taking place can learn to influence the dynamics of any class *proactively* ('in advance') rather than *reactively*. Even so, all teachers have times when they struggle to make headway with their class; the bank of goodwill that is stored up during the 'plentiful' times needs to be there to draw on in the hard times.

Developing a philosophy

Establishing and maintaining high standards of behaviour depend, in part, upon a teacher's philosophy of education (see Bailey 2010). As noted elsewhere in this book, qualified teachers will use teaching strategies and approaches that reflect their own beliefs about the ways that children learn best. Teachers who are willing to persevere in order to achieve their educational aims, yet who are ready to accept advice and modify their practices accordingly, are usually at ease with themselves about their work, and transmit this confidence to their pupils. Teachers who have no clear idea about the direction of their teaching, and meander from one extreme to another, are almost certain to produce an unstable learning environment and create a strained atmosphere. Trainee teachers are, to a large extent, bound by the host teacher's preferences and ideals. However, over the period of the school placement you should be able to gently influence the situation, such that your developing beliefs about teaching and learning can be tested, refined and implemented during your interaction with the pupils.

True freedom for pupils

Some inexperienced teachers seem to imagine that if wrong behaviours are ignored they will fade away naturally. However, offering pupils 'freedom to explore' is not the same as giving them 'freedom to behave in any way they choose'. Children need to know what is judged to be acceptable and appropriate behaviour, including the way they address one another and the teacher, their application to the task in hand and the extent of their co-operation. The occasional unsettling incident, in which children say, in effect, that they are free to do what they want in any way they want, provides a stark reminder that selfish behaviour leads to unhappiness and insecurity. While you will doubtless be striving to involve children in decisions about their lives in school, your position as the experienced adult entitles you to be the final arbiter.

Being positive

Most unsatisfactory behaviour can be resolved without causing humiliation or loss of face to either child or adult. This is not the same as saying that children should get away with things, as they need to realise that every action has a consequence. Some children are unaware of the impact their behaviour has on others and it needs to be pointed out to them that they have responsibilities as well as rights. The majority of children respond positively to genuine praise and encouragement, and even the most mischievous tyke prefers specific guidance and the opportunity to master skills and to learn something new to aimlessly causing disruption. Kohn (2004) warns, however, that teachers need to be careful not to create what he describes as 'praise junkies', as a calculated tactic to control children's behaviour rather than as a genuine expression of admiration. Although class control and discipline require the application of appropriate techniques and strategies to curb inappropriate behaviour and ensure that potential troublemakers are kept in check, the most effective learning environment grows in the soil of high motivation and a desire to learn. Children will not want to misbehave if, in doing so, they reduce the thrill and adventure that happy learning experiences bring.

Good practice

Without being naïve, try to expect the best rather than the worst from pupils. If you expect problems, you won't be disappointed! Begin each day with a positive attitude and do not allow the harmonious classroom climate you've worked so hard to achieve to be hijacked by an individual's erratic behaviour.

Cross-reference: Guided Reader Extract 47

The teacher's role

Self-awareness

Although it is not popular to say so, teachers can sometimes contribute to the causes of bad behaviour. Unfairness, impatience and poor lesson preparation can create the conditions for resentment and discontent to occur. The end result is a deterioration of the atmosphere, control problems and a negative impact on learning. Nevertheless, if children are regularly proving to be a headache, it is important to take a step back and consider reasons other than placing the blame wholly on them.

There are a number of ways in which poor behaviour might be, at least in part, a reflection of the teacher's failings; for example, it might come about through a lack of dialogue with the children that leads to misunderstandings, intolerance, inappropriate lessons, harsh sanctions or petty fault-finding. However, as Haydn (2012) notes, most pupils behave better when the teacher comes into the session equipped with a well-prepared lesson. Haydn cannily points out that pupils as well as teachers differentiate, but while teachers focus on the tasks, pupils focus on the teachers. Be warned!

Conflict in the classroom is not inevitable and can usually be avoided by following the advice offered elsewhere in this chapter and implementing appropriate strategies. In addition, by using the strategies listed below, your classroom has a good chance of becoming the positive and industrious working environment you want it to be, and your lessons will be a joy instead of a chore.

Sincere care

Although teachers care about their pupils, it probably does not occur to most pupils that this is so. Teachers have, therefore, to demonstrate a caring attitude through the way they address children, the interest they show in their welfare and the action they take to ensure that justice is done and that no child is disadvantaged. Caring is also shown by insisting that rules are followed and by giving vulnerable children a secure framework within which to develop good patterns of behaviour. A useful strategy is to tell gripping stories and explore folklore that promotes positive values, or talk about heroes who were compassionate in their dealings with others.

Staying calm and alert

Teachers have little chance of improving a situation of potential conflict if they lose their self-control. When problems appear to be developing, it is important to reassure pupils (as well as yourself) that things are in hand. You will be better equipped to cope by breathing deeply, speaking a little more slowly than usual, smiling gently when speaking and keeping wide-open eyes. Potentially difficult situations can often be defused if teachers simply refuse to be rattled by them. Even if an unwanted incident occurs, make sure that you are decisive but not explosive. Avoid staring at the ceiling, making tough-sounding (but largely ineffective) comments to no one in particular, and continuing with the lesson but speaking louder and louder in an attempt to counteract the growing noise level. A crisp command to 'sit up straight, look this way and keep your hands folded' (or similar) is preferable to melodramatics.

Delaying judgement

Taking time to discover the facts before making a judgement or accusation and issuing sanctions is essential in settling disputes. It is better to spend a little time sorting out a *real* problem than acting decisively in dealing with an imagined one. Pupils become exasperated and annoyed when teachers blunder in and make matters worse by jumping to unwarranted conclusions. On the other hand, when the position is clearer, do not hesitate to make tough decisions in cases of serious misconduct. It is quite normal for the injured party to make protestations and accusations about the alleged perpetrator; after restoring a sense of order allow each person to speak in turn. Do not over-react to any of the things that are said, however alarming they sound. Look into the child's eyes and you will get a good idea about whether he or she is telling the truth. Words can deceive; the eyes cannot lie.

Concentrating on what children are saying

The only way for adults to discover the truth is to listen carefully to what children have to say. Some teachers try to listen but owing to the pressure of the moment do not properly hear what is being said. Wise (2000) argues that the most effective teacher–pupil relationships are built by teachers listening attentively to their pupils and hearing their voices. This principle is highly relevant to situations of conflict, especially when a child is feeling unfairly treated. The opportunity to tell a receptive adult about the problem is often sufficient, particularly for a younger child, who will skip away happily and join her friends. When faced with contradictory statements, it is a general rule that the testimony of sulky children, however persuasive, needs to be treated with a degree of scepticism.

Entering a constructive dialogue

Although children normally begin by defending their actions, accusing others or reacting angrily, it is important to introduce a positive element to the conversation as soon as possible. Skilled teachers ask distracting questions which focus attention away from the problem. For example: 'Whose class are you in?' or 'Have you told Mrs Osman about your concerns yet?' rather than 'Who started hitting first?' When you know the children better, you might be able to introduce a 'say these words back to me' strategy, whereby you ask each child in turn to echo something like, 'I want to be happy in school' and 'I want to be friends with everyone', or use an expression that has become a favourite with the class from (say) a story or poem or TV programme. It doesn't resolve the problem but facilitates a more rational discussion about doing so. Once the children become less animated and begin to speak in a natural tone, the main issues can usually be discussed without undue rancour.

Avoiding banal questions

Some questions that teachers ask are not really questions at all, but rather a poor attempt to exercise control. For example:

> *The unanswerable question:* For goodness sake, what's the matter with you today?
> *The threatening question:* Are you going to finish that work or do you want to stay in at playtime?

The self-evident question: Do you mean to say that you weren't listening when I told everyone what I wanted you all to do?

The banal question: Would you behave like that at home?

Such pointless questions are likely to irritate children and may invite ridicule and sarcasm from older pupils. Far better to say something like this:

'You seem very unsettled today. Is there any reason for the fact that you are saying silly things? (Pause) Well, please keep quiet and don't talk to anyone for the next five minutes.'

'Do you know how to do your work? (Pause) Well, we only have ten minutes until we clear up before playtime, so you'll have to work extra hard to finish.'

'Graham, please whisper to Jack what I said to everyone a few moments ago about what I wanted you to do. (Pause) Jack, please tell Graham what he just said. Thank you.'

'Sara, we don't allow rude words in school. Please do not say it again.' (But don't be surprised if Sara innocently asks you why it is rude.) Rude words are initially a source of amusement for children but if not kept in check can be used as insults.

Facilitating agreement

In situations of potential conflict, it is possible for teachers to deal with the immediate circumstances but fail to offer pupils a strategy for the future. Once a satisfactory dialogue has been established, children must be given clearly defined steps to follow so that improvements can be monitored and approved, by both the teacher and the child. If you don't offer such strategies, you will probably be dealing repeatedly with the same issue.

Cross-reference: Guided Reader Extract 21

Silly behaviour

Disruption

It is important to be reminded of the basic truth that children are just that, children. Most of them enjoy life and have fun; they want to do well at school and be happy with their friends. In the average class, the vast majority are likeable and a pleasure to teach. Very few children are deviant, though some are regular rule-breakers and persistent offenders (see later in this chapter). It is likely that such children have poor parenting or suffer from a negative attitude that creates in them a tendency to defy authority or to be self-centred rather than compliant. However, most unacceptable behaviour is due to silliness rather than deviance and takes a variety of forms:

Uncontrolled behaviour: shouting out an answer to a question without permission. More often than not, this response is attributable to enthusiasm more than naughtiness.

Arrogant: calling out a 'clever' remark.

Distractive: showing off by doing something daring.

Detached: deliberately working very slowly.

Spiteful: teasing another child.

Insolent: asking pointless questions or making crude remarks.

Deceptive: pretending not to understand.

These instances are common only in a very small number of classrooms and are associated with inappropriate work, boredom or general lack of respect for adults. Silly behaviour can signal that it is time to change content, terminate a teaching approach or re-evaluate lesson management. On such occasions it is important that teachers try to *understand* the behaviour and respond constructively rather than unthinkingly. Thus, with respect to the above seven categories:

Uncontrolled behaviour: children who call out without permission lack self-discipline or do not understand the rules. The most appropriate response is to ask the child to tell you the rule; if an answer is not forthcoming, ask another child to state it then check that the offender understands.

Arrogant behaviour: children who call out a silly remark may be signalling a lack of respect for the teacher or simply showing off to impress friends. You can ask the child to stand up and, after getting the other children quiet, insists that he or she repeats the comment. This action may well trigger raucous laughter, but ignore it, remain stony-faced and insist that the child repeats the comment once again. After three or four repeats the humour will dry up and it will be obvious to everyone that arrogant remarks are simply not worth making. After the lesson talk to the child individually and sternly, in sight of another adult. Note, however, that the 'stand up and repeat what you said' technique is a fairly high-risk strategy because if it fails to quell the amusement, you might be embarrassed. An alternative is to ignore the perpetrator and say sternly to the rest of the class, 'Sit up and fold your arms if you think that Osborn would do what he did if (name of the head teacher or most admired teacher) were teaching you. Exactly! Then please don't do it with me, either, Osborn!'

Distractive behaviour: children who show off are probably doing so because it is more enjoyable than concentrating on tedious or demanding work. Apart from making the work more interesting or, perhaps, adjusting the nature of the task to make it more manageable, the most effective strategy is to set short time-related targets and monitor them closely.

Detached behaviour: children who work very slowly may be showing that they are not prepared to engage with uninteresting or unduly demanding activities. Some children suffer from diagnosable attention-deficit, which may require specialist advice; on the other hand the child may be lazy or indifferent. Such problems usually take a considerable amount of time to resolve, so trainee teachers can only keep the class teacher informed of developments and persevere.

Spiteful behaviour: children who deliberately tease another child are enjoying the power that accompanies ridicule. Immediate action is required. Follow the school's guidelines and keep a record of incidents. The principle of 'showing respect' has been somewhat over-exposed in recent years but is still a necessary one.

Insolent behaviour: children who ask pointless questions are wasting time but skilfully avoiding confrontation with the teacher by giving the appearance of interest. Refuse to play this game. One useful strategy is to be dismissive of the question and turn your attention immediately to another matter. If the child persists, ask him or her to write the question down and sign it. Insolent children thrive on the oxygen of publicity, so make sure you deprive them of it.

Deceptive behaviour: children who pretend not to understand may be trying to undermine the teacher's authority and create a distraction from the main point of the lesson. As you become aware of deceptive behaviour it is a relatively simply matter to tell the child to see you during the break to discuss the matter. The chances are that he or she will be first out of the door.

These instances of disruption are used by the very small number of children who have decided that messing about is preferable to concentrating on the work; their actions are deliberate but not necessarily serious if attended to appropriately from an early stage. Although teachers rightly feel annoyed by the disruptions, they can also act as a warning signal about the need to review the lesson's effectiveness and relevance. It is difficult to make every lesson stimulating and enthralling for all children – nor should you attempt to do so – but persistent boredom not only affects the quality of the children's work but also influences their attitudes towards you (see Figure 12.1).

Holding measures

It can take time to diagnose and remedy underlying causes of poor behaviour, so teachers sometimes have to resort to *holding measures* as a temporary means of counteracting the behaviour until the position is clearer. Examples of holding methods for each of the above categories of silly behaviour (see previous section) might include the following set of reactions:

Uncontrolled behaviour: 'Olive, you forgot our count to three before you speak rule. Please remember in future.' (The response is merely a statement of fact and avoids attributing blame.)

Arrogant behaviour: 'John, remember to put your hand up first and take your turn if you've anything to say.' (The response strengthens the teacher's authority, reminds everyone of the rules and avoids confrontation with John.)

Distractive behaviour: 'Please sit still on your chair, Rhoda, we don't want anyone injured, thank you.' (The response focuses upon Rhoda's welfare rather than her inappropriate behaviour.)

Detached behaviour: 'Are you finding this difficult, Ellie? Perhaps I can help you along a bit.' (The response allows the teacher to set short-term targets for Ellie.)

Spiteful behaviour: 'If you've got anything to say, Ben, say something kind; otherwise keep quiet. Let's see how helpful you can be for the remainder of the lesson; I might ask you about it after everyone has gone out.' (The response indicates the teacher's displeasure, sets boundaries upon Ben's behaviour and offers him the chance to redeem himself.)

Insolent behaviour: 'Put your hand up if you think you know the answer to Gordon's question.' (The response focuses upon Gordon's 'ignorance' and allows other children to gain satisfaction from offering the correct answer. An ironic afterthought is also useful: 'It

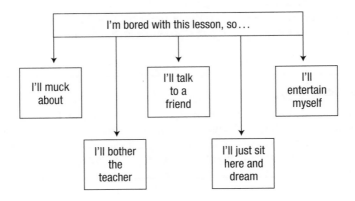

FIGURE 12.1 The consequences of boredom

looks as if everybody knew the answer except you, Gordon. You will need to concentrate harder if you want to keep up with the others.')

Deceptive behaviour: 'If you don't understand by now, Julie, you'd better stay behind after the lesson and I'll explain it to you then.' (The response calls Julie's bluff and puts the onus upon her to complete the work.)

These holding responses do not solve the underlying problem but allow you to continue the lesson without undue disruption, losing face or causing damage to relationships. If the behaviour is repeated or is serious, you will certainly want to see the child after the session and express disapproval in an uncharged atmosphere or in the presence of a senior teacher. Note that teachers who rely on the holding strategy without looking more deeply into the situation are likely to experience a recurrence of the unwanted behaviour and further struggles to maintain order.

Activate your thinking!

Poor behaviour will never improve unless the conditions change.

Good practice

Don't just remind the children of the agreed procedure; rehearse it with them.

Follow-up

Whenever possible, speak to a child directly after the session about the unacceptable behaviour. Make sure that other children nearby do not interrupt you. Tell the child how you feel. Express your disappointment. Ask for an explanation. Listen carefully to the reply. Don't patronise or ridicule. Stay calm and serious but speak naturally. Look the child in the eye and try to show that you are interested in what she or he has to say. If appropriate, ask the child what he or she suggests can be done to improve the situation. End the conversation positively and indicate that you are expecting something better in future. Over the next few sessions, do not pay the child unnatural attention but if possible find opportunity to commend work without fuss. Don't expect miracles. Keep things in proportion. React but don't over-react to silly behaviour.

Good practice

Try treating silly pupils with a greater level of seriousness than their behaviour deserves. Pretend that they are sensible children and trust them with some responsibility. Speak to them in a more 'grown-up' way. Evaluate over a period of a few days whether the way you treat them affects the way they behave.

Deviant behaviour

Characteristics of deviancy

In contrast to silliness, deviant forms of behaviour can be intimidating to the teacher and threaten the wellbeing of the other children. Deviant behaviour is typified by one or more of the following: belligerent answering back, fierce anger, agitated protest and shouting, and refusal to do any work. Every school has a policy for dealing with this rare form of indiscipline and the agreed procedures have to be consistently followed if progress is to be made. If the child exhibits worrying traits of the sort described, it is certain that the head teacher is already well aware of the problem and parents have been contacted; however, you must still ensure that you keep senior staff informed about developments. In situations where there are repeated instances of wilful behaviour, write a brief note of each incident (what happened and when) for future reference.

Deviant behaviour in which pupils are wilfully disobedient or defiant is thankfully rare but can be unnerving for teachers, who then agonise over ways in which they might contain a situation that will certainly not correct itself without intervention. While action is being taken with the assistance of more experienced colleagues, you will have to be sternly insistent and openly state to the child the things that will not be tolerated. Setting realistic and enforceable short-term goals is essential, but in reality you might have to accommodate minor points of poor behaviour when addressing the central misdemeanour. For example, if a boy is behaving wildly in a games' session, the fact that he is using bad language is not of prime importance and can be dealt with when the situation is calm. Similarly, a young girl throwing a tantrum can tie her flapping shoelaces later when she is more reasonable. These 'secondary' matters *should* eventually be dealt with but not in the heat of battle, unless they provide a useful distraction from the problem.

Strategies for resolution

Inducements to more acceptable behaviour have to be used within a strictly defined code, explained to the child and, if possible, agreed verbally by him or her. More serious situations will involve the SENCO and, perhaps, a school–home agreement involving parents. Progress with pupils showing deviant tendencies is likely to be slow and in a tiny minority of cases a trainee teacher on placement may only see marginal improvement during his or her time in school. If the indiscipline becomes very serious and other children's learning is deemed to be suffering, the head teacher may decide to remove the transgressor from the classroom or, in the most extreme cases, exclude the child from school. Unfortunately, children who exhibit deviant behaviour often come from homes in which such behaviour is condoned or parents are grappling with similar challenges themselves. Inexperienced teachers should never be, and rarely are, left to struggle unassisted with devious children. When the behaviour is deemed to be sufficiently serious, a learning support assistant may be allocated to work with the child for part of the day. Despite every commendable intention on the part of school staff, there will undoubtedly be bad days in the midst of more normal ones.

Attention deficit and hyperactivity disorder (ADHD)

Distinctiveness of ADHD

ADHD is a developmental disorder that affects approximately one pupil in every class. It often emerges during early childhood and is characterised by a persistent pattern of either (1) inattention and/or (2) hyperactivity, 'excessively active', as well as forgetfulness, poor impulse control and a tendency to be easily distracted. Note that a child can be hyperactive and have weak concentration; or have weak concentration yet not suffer from hyperactivity. In other words, use of the all-encompassing label can be unhelpful. It is important to distinguish children who are deliberately behaving in a deviant manner (but do not suffer from ADHD) from those who are struggling with a diagnosable condition such as ADHD (see, for example, Kewley 2001; Lougy *et al.* 2007). Boys are about three times more likely than girls to be diagnosed with ADHD, though it's not yet clear about the reasons. Children with the condition act without thinking; they are excessively lively and have trouble focusing on a task. They might understand what's expected of them but have trouble following it through because they can't sit still, pay attention or attend to detail for sufficiently long.

Causes and consequences

Although there is still active debate about the concept of ADHD, the principle for every teacher should be to deal with the causes of the behaviour as well as the consequences. In doing so, it is generally accepted that the disorder takes one of three forms: (1) inattentiveness; (2) hyperactive-impulsiveness; and (3) a combination of types 1 and 2. It is obvious that the most challenging behaviour occurs in type 3. The condition of *inattentiveness* is characterised by some or all of the following:

- Lack of attention to detail; a tendency to make careless errors
- Short concentration span (for example, when playing)
- Poor organisational skills; messy; random
- Inconsistent listening skills
- Avoidance of tasks or activities that require prolonged mental effort
- Easily distracted
- Forgetful
- Tendency to mislay or lose items.

Type 2, *hyperactivity-impulsiveness*, is characterised by:

- Difficulty in sitting still; fidgeting, squirming in the seat
- Unpredictable tendency to run, sprint or dash about
- Excessively talking and moving about
- Calling out random answers to questions
- Reluctance to take turns or queue up
- Constantly interrupting, imposing on and annoying classmates.

It is important to remember that children genuinely suffering from ADHD are not 'being naughty' in the commonly accepted sense of the word; they may be suffering from an undetectable brain disorder or have been affected by (say) difficulties during the mother's pregnancy or environmental factors (e.g. a chaotic lifestyle at home or even too much exposure to TV/video games).

Effect on children's achievements

Compared to their peers, children who are battling with acute forms of ADHD are more likely to have poorer marks and grades, lower scores on standardised tests and greater incidence of special needs support, and to make heavy use of 'specialist' services (e.g. counselling). Pupils are also more likely to have a higher absenteeism rate and to fall seriously behind in most aspects of their primary schoolwork. In future years, these children are unlikely to reach their potential or even complete their schooling. Children with ADHD have a higher chance of being rejected socially by their peers and to experience greater difficulties in forming relationships. In addition, teachers are very likely to perceive these pupils negatively – owing principally to the disruption and extra work they create – and thereby label them adversely with respect to intelligence, personality and behaviour.

Strategies to assist pupils

Teachers can assist these children – indeed, *all* children – by using a variety of strategies, including:

- ensuring a regular routine, e.g. using a specific peg to hang coats; sitting on the same chair in the same place; always occupying the same position in a line of children;
- providing specific assistance in organising belongings, trays, books, and so forth;
- minimising the chances of distraction by careful positioning of the child's seating, insisting that other children do not become bothersome and allowing extra time to complete an absorbing task;
- using brief and clear instructions;
- limiting choices to two or three rather than having many choices;
- employing an easily comprehended reward system, with smaller, short-term rewards (e.g. having first choice of toys; being allowed to use the computer during a wet playtime) as well as major long-term ones (such as a certificate or special mention in assembly);
- using loss of privilege as the main discipline tactic;
- finding and promoting any interest or talent that the child possesses.

As a trainee teacher, you will find it hard to distinguish between pupils who deliberately 'play you up' because they choose to do so, and pupils who suffer from a disorder that creates inattentiveness (e.g. 'daydreaming') or impulsive behaviour. Seek advice from more experienced colleagues (including TAs) and avoid becoming unduly frustrated with the child. Look for redeeming features, such as simplicity of character, enthusiasm and spontaneity, rather than dwelling endlessly on the flaws.

As acutely active children appear unable to 'switch off' their minds, they might need a familiar source of comfort: for example, hugging a soft toy (younger children) or holding a mascot or prized possession (for older children). Additional classroom assistant support is essential under such extreme circumstances – a mature, unflappable assistant who genuinely enjoys the challenge of working with such children is particularly valuable.

> **Activate your thinking!**
>
> Children might have low attention levels ('attention deficit') or might be excessively active ('hyperactivity') or suffer from both types. Labelling children as 'having ADHD' is not necessarily in their best interests.

Responding to unacceptable behaviour

Achieving the right balance

Taking suitable action when faced with poor behaviour is one of the challenges that teachers face as they seek to establish a well-controlled yet inspiring classroom environment. Tolerance of minor instances of unacceptable behaviour will be counter-productive if it leads to a worsening situation in the long run. On the other hand, early intervention can also be unhelpful if it disrupts the flow of a lesson, sours the atmosphere or creates unease among more timid children. Some trainee teachers regret that they were 'too soft' early on in their teaching and insufficiently firm in the opening encounters with a new class. Others employ unnecessarily heavy-handed tactics when a lighter touch would be enough, thereby causing ill-feeling and dismay among the children. There is always a danger of developing an impulsive response to every slight breach of the rules that result in stress for both teacher and children, so-called 'zero tolerance'.

Circumstances need to be taken into account when deciding how to respond to misbehaviour. For instance, the child who is normally sensible but on one occasion excitedly throws screwed-up paper at a friend is unlikely to repeat the action if chastened; it would be foolish to over-react by using fierce remarks or invoking a sanction. On the other hand, a persistently troublesome child is unlikely to respond to a gentle approach or to sanctions that have been used repeatedly without effect. In this case, a much firmer response is required (in accordance with school policy). Similarly, common sense suggests that end-of-term bravado or wet playtime excitement induces unnatural behaviour and should be treated understandingly. At the other extreme, a single act of bullying needs to be dealt with firmly, regardless of the circumstances (see Chapter 3).

Action–reaction process

If a teacher shows agitation every time a child is perceived as behaving unacceptably, it is the child who is controlling the situation and not the teacher. Unless the boundaries of acceptable behaviour are clear, the action–reaction process continues, both teacher and child become edgy, and nothing is improved. During succeeding days, the pattern is repeated:

Step 1: Child behaves unacceptably → Teacher responds agitatedly.
Step 2: Child repeats the behaviour → Teacher responds sternly.
Step 3: Child repeats the behaviour once again → Teacher imposes sanction. And so on.

The problem with this action–reaction process is not only that the child is dictating the pattern of teacher response but also that the causes of the unacceptable behaviour are not being addressed. In particular, a characteristic of effective behaviour management is that it *acts* to *prevent*, deter or reduce the undesirable actions, rather than remedying them once they have occurred.

Understanding the distinction between 'prevention' and 'cure' is important for every practitioner. Put bluntly, poor behaviour can be an indication of failure in behaviour management. Whether unacceptable behaviour is an occasional wilful act or a persistent trend, teachers understandably interpret it as a challenge or threat to their authority and a reflection on their ability to cope. However, if these feelings result in a series of instinctive, defensive reactions, little is gained and the situation will probably worsen. Teachers rightly argue that 'something has to be done', but it is not merely a case of 'doing something' but of doing the right thing. In deciding upon the most appropriate strategy to use, three factors need to be considered:

1. A teacher might not recognise the message the behaviour carries.
2. There might be differences between the teacher's and the children's perceptions.
3. Children might be experiencing hardship outside school.

Not recognising the message

As noted earlier, poor behaviour sometimes indicates that there is something wrong with the lesson, the teacher's attitude or the teaching approach. It is easy to blame the children or refer to a class as 'difficult' without examining teaching factors that might be contributing to the problem. Inappropriate work, over-reliance on a single teaching method or poor organisation can create or foster a restless climate. On the other hand, the children might be in 'one of those moods' that day, the causes of which are indeterminable.

Differences in perceptions

Although there are obvious instances of unacceptable behaviour, adults can find themselves attaching far more significance to an act than was intended by the pupil. Even wilful behaviour is not necessarily directed at the teacher but is sometimes a consequence of youthful exuberance or high spirits. Learning to distinguish between silliness and wilfulness is a skill that every practitioner needs to sharpen. Deciding on the motive makes a considerable difference to the way you respond.

Hardship outside school

Uncertainty or anguish about personal circumstances can make it almost impossible for a pupil to behave rationally. Children, like all of us, react differently when home life or relationships are unsteady. Allowance needs to be made for irrational behaviour from a normally compliant child. Although you cannot allow children to behave badly persistently without taking action, it is often sufficient to have a quiet word after the session to ascertain the source of the problem.

Challenges for trainees

Responding to unacceptable behaviour is a challenge for every teacher. It requires patient, determined application, particularly in new situations. Strategies that appear to work with one group of pupils may be less successful with a different set of pupils, even in an almost identical situation. The challenges are particularly acute when starting to teach in a new school, where codes of conduct and accepted procedures are taken for granted by the existing staff and pupils but have yet to be learned by the new teacher. Trainee teachers on placement are, of course, regularly experiencing this impediment, but Neill and Caswell (1993) describe how this situation faces all new teachers, even experienced ones:

> Experienced teachers who move to a new school are sometimes surprised by the sudden need to put effort into controlling their classes. They are not always aware how much they previously relied on their thorough, but subliminal, knowledge of the formal and informal procedures of their old school and their reputation among the children.
>
> (p. 4)

Consequently, if you are a trainee teacher on school experience, it is hardly surprising if the first few weeks with a new class prove to be challenging. In every placement there is a 'tipping point', after which the situation settles and the conditions improve, or they remain as unsatisfactory but you manage to survive, howbeit miserably. The trainees whose circumstances improve are those who resolve early behavioural challenges and strive to create a relaxed but purposeful learning climate, where mutual respect and the desire to succeed are normal. Trainees who merely survive are those who never manage to resolve the challenges; instead, they adjust their teaching approach – usually becoming more formal and austere – to contain the worst of the behaviour. It is obvious which of the two situations is preferable. Killick (2006) reminds us that being relaxed is important for thinking in a more creative way, and adds that if people are feeling as if they are being evaluated this is likely to lead to increased arousal. He summarises his argument with reference to Stallard (2002) in a simple sub-heading: 'Think good – feel good; feel good – learn good'.

One way or another it is essential that you do not exacerbate control and discipline problems by your ignorance of the way things are done in the school/classroom or pupils' expectations about what is required of them. If children sense that you are allowing them liberties that their other teachers forbid, they are likely to take advantage of you. The obvious remedy is to spend time discussing existing policies and strategies with the resident teachers on a regular basis. One way and another, you have to learn fast!

Activate your thinking!

Consider the extent to which pupils' behaviour patterns have been determined by: (1) their uncertainty about the rules; (2) their wilfulness; and (3) your own lack of dynamism and resourcefulness.

Key strategies for classroom harmony

There is no such thing as 'the answer' to establishing and maintaining classroom order. Some teachers appear to create a wonderful working atmosphere with minimum effort; others never succeed in doing so. The majority of teachers do a good job and are constantly trying to improve their techniques and approach. Despite these realities, there are generally agreed principles to assist rather than hinder matters; the following offers a summary of key strategies that will help to promote harmonious teaching and learning.

Speak naturally

Shouting rarely works and creates unpleasantness, as well as injuring your voice. Developing a strong voice takes practice but is more effective than a shrill or strained one. Ideally, the way you speak should be natural and carry authority for, as Rogers (1998) puts it, 'the adult tongue is a powerful weapon' (p. 223). See also Rogers (2006).

Distinguish between enthusiasm and disobedience

Some children get so absorbed in their work that they are reluctant to stop. Avoid being irritated; instead say something like, 'I'm pleased that you are so keen on your work, Jack, but everyone is waiting for you.' Younger children's voices become high-pitched if they get carried away with enthusiasm for what they are doing. Persevere with gentle, personal (rather than public) reminders to individual children to keep their voices down. A request to 'speak in a whisper, please' or similar will normally restore order, at least for a time. It is worth modelling the different voices to a younger child and encouraging him or her to practise using an appropriate tone along with you.

Make your instructions direct and specific

A comment like: 'Douglas, please concentrate on what Rachel is saying' is preferable to 'Douglas, stop messing about with Wayne.' Again, it is better to say, 'Put your pencils down after finishing the next sentence and look this way' than to say, 'Everybody pay attention to me.' Many teachers give out too many general statements such as 'Settle down' or 'Get on with your work quietly' or the ubiquitous 'Sh-hh' rather than giving specific commands.

Relax your voice when asking for children's attention

If possible, lower the pitch of your voice rather than raising it. Give pupils time to respond. If they are slow in doing what you have asked, use a technique such as 'fingers on lips' (or the agreed signal to pay attention) or say, 'If the person next to you is not yet paying attention, please whisper in his ear that we are waiting.' Do not, of course, simply stand and do nothing as if you were powerless, but avoid getting frantic and, crucially, do not allow other children to say 'shh' or rebuke classmates on your behalf, which undermines your authority. Once the situation is calm, explain what pleased and displeased you and emphasise firmly how you want the children to respond in future.

Decide when it is right to get angry

Some trainee teachers feel awkward about expressing anger. Instead, they hold their feelings in and pretend to be sweet and sugary with the children. In fact, anger is neither right nor wrong. It depends on the way in which it is used. In the general run of classroom life, a teacher who frequently got angry would be either a nervous wreck or terrorising the children. Anger should be expressed calmly but assertively through voice tone and body language. The best teachers do not have to shout but have the ability to speak with such precision that even the worst offender is chastened. Be serious when you need to be without being grumpy.

Avoid losing your temper

Most adults can, if they wish, frighten children by their rage and outbursts. This form of conduct is professionally unacceptable and might even be interpreted as bullying. If you feel yourself 'coming to the boil' it is better to stop the lesson and stare through the window for a few seconds, hands loosely at your side and breathing deeply. Speaking more slowly and deliberately, deepening the tone and moving a little closer to the children will convey your feelings and could save you from saying something in the heat of the moment that you later regret. It is particularly galling when you sense that the children are being wilfully mischievous to 'wind you up', but focus on the basic advice given in this chapter and don't be a helpless victim of your own emotions.

Commend appropriate behaviour

When pupils respond appropriately to your commands, rebukes or warnings, thank them briefly and continue with the lesson *immediately*. Do not begin a speech to the effect that you are not prepared to be kept waiting like this in future or similar tirades. When a class is settling or coming to order, commend the children who are doing well rather than spending all your time criticising the uncooperative types. When the class is settled you can spend a moment saying 'Well done. I was very pleased that so many of you tidied up so quickly. Thank you. A few of you were leaving it to the others. I've made a note of who you are and next time I shall expect you to make a special effort.' Even in your commendations, be fairly brisk and sound as if you expected good behaviour rather than giving the impression that you are meekly grateful for their co-operation (even if you feel that way).

Use humour appropriately

Hobday-Kutsch and McVittie (2002) note that adults and older children use humour as a negotiating tool to determine where power resides in the classroom. They claim on the basis of observations and interviews that most children and adults new to the school realise quite quickly that certain forms of spoken language and discourse are appropriate and others are proscribed. You can gain a lot of credibility by being lighthearted and seeing the amusing side of life, providing you avoid the trap of thinking that such behaviour will automatically endear you to children. If the rest of your work as a teacher is poor, no amount of joking will compensate. In addition, a minority of pupils 'feed off' humour to elicit a response from their peers and, after a time, their classmates begin to look to them to make funny comments that are likely to become increasingly cheeky. Pupils who find much of what they do at school to be irrelevant and tedious use humour as a means of relieving tension and getting through the day, despite the sanctions that such fooling around might incur. It is essential for you to distinguish between a pleasantry and rudeness, and to have sufficient authority to restore order when needed.

Cross-reference: Guided Reader Extract 20

Motivate pupils to secure best results

It is important to remind yourself of the cardinal truth that motivated children rarely misbehave. If pupils are under-stimulated, unclear about standards of work and get away with a final product of mediocre quality, then it is little wonder that their behaviour deteriorates and their respect for you diminishes. Make your classroom buzz with interest and become a place where children can learn about the world, themselves and one another. Reassure them that getting something wrong or misunderstanding an idea is an integral part of the learning process; celebrate achievements cheerfully; share humorous moments; be serious when necessary; have fun; be the sort of teacher they will one day tell their grandchildren about. Learn together for the sheer joy of it.

Learning to cope with every eventuality

First encounters

Throughout student life, trainee teachers dream of the time when they will have their own classes, free from the constraints of fitting in with someone else's routines and preferences, and liberated from being assessed by class teachers, mentors and college tutors. In reality, to have your own class is both delightful and daunting: delightful because it is the culmination of years of study and provides the opportunity to exercise your own judgement; daunting because you quickly become aware of the enormous responsibility lying before you. To paraphrase comments from many newly qualified teachers as they reflect upon their first day with a class: 'When you walk into that classroom, shut the door and look at the class of children in front of you, you suddenly realise that you are on your own. You don't know whether to cry from fear or elation.' This mixture of emotions that wells up when newly qualified teachers first face their class is a powerful one. Trainee teachers, standing in front of a new class for the first time, experience similar feelings. See Chapter 14 for details about the first year as a qualified teacher.

Over the coming days and weeks, nervous new teachers discover that they are not alone, that education is a joint endeavour involving colleagues, parents and numerous unseen members of the community. Nevertheless, those first few days are important in respect of maintaining and establishing order. More experienced teachers have the advantage of knowing the ropes and having had opportunities to establish their relationships and school-wide reputation; new teachers have not. Teachers are described by the children in various ways:

'Miss Chapman's really nice and reads us funny poems.'

'Mr Howard plays his guitar and does singing with you.'

'Mrs Ballam brings in animals from home.'

'Mr Fielding'll *do* you if you muck about.'

And so on. After teaching for a year or so, the reputation of teachers (for better or worse) goes before them and provides a platform for establishing a satisfactory learning environment. The new teacher and the trainee teacher, entering the classroom for the first time, do not have this advantage, and need to work hard to ensure that things run smoothly. In doing so, a number of assumptions can be made:

- The children will be as excited and expectant as you are.
- Many children will test the boundaries of behaviour and note your reactions.

- No matter how much planning is done, it will take time before lessons and sessions settle into a routine.
- There will be some misunderstandings as the settling process takes place.
- Regardless of everything else, relationships lie at the heart of successful teaching and learning.

Even experienced teachers find that it can take several weeks before the classroom rhythm becomes established. In particular, the first few days are crucial. Younger children require specific guidance about basic procedures; older ones need to know how the new person's expectations and ideas differ from those of previous teachers. Even if you feel insecure and uncertain about what to expect, you need to give a strong impression of decisiveness and confidence to convince the class that you are in control and intend to be taken seriously. As part of the settling procedures, certain times of the day and certain events provide opportunities for unacceptable behaviour. Teachers sometimes refer to these occasions as the 'sticky spots' and the following are most common.

The start of a session

This is an important phase of every lesson. Simple strategies such as counting down from five to one, encouraging children to chant a simple rhyme as they settle or subtracting the time you are kept waiting from their playtime assists a smooth start. Eventually you will want the children to settle without direction, though very young children might still need guidance about where to sit. If the children have been in assembly just beforehand, it is sensible to use a few physical stretching exercises or give them a minor desk-task for a few minutes (such as copying some spellings or drawing a diagram) before commencing the formal session.

After a wet playtime

A wet playtime means that the children will have been inside with little chance to expend their energy. The classroom may be hot and airless and the children restless. Consequently, except in the worst weather, it is worth opening the windows for a few minutes and (again) spending a short time in a simple but orderly whole-class activity: for example, using a 'do this, do that' game or write–draw five creatures that wriggle to move (or a similar straightforward task that helps them to concentrate). Although the settling activity absorbs a few minutes of the lesson, it is preferable to making an attempt to begin the main session with a class full of unsettled children who have little inclination to learn and possibly having to use ultra-stern discipline to achieve order.

Moving out of the classroom

Children who tend to misbehave usually find some opportunity to do so when moving to a new location. Consistent routines and clearly rehearsed expectations will reduce the likelihood of silliness, but the prankster or mischief-maker will sometimes take delight in disrupting proceedings by showing off, making strange noises, stepping out of line and squabbling over who should be first/last in the queue. Until the situation is under control, you need to be firmly insistent and rigorous in approach, involving TAs for support (but not doing your job for you) wherever possible. Later on, when things have become settled, a more relaxed approach will be possible. Strategies such as standing at the front of the queue, facing the children, asking them to stand upright and still, and choosing who should go first and last (with a promise that it will be someone different next time) all help to maintain an orderly atmosphere. Hopefully, by the time the children are approaching the top end of the junior phase, they will have sufficient self-control to be allowed greater autonomy; but you might be shocked how uncooperative pupils of all ages are capable of being when they think they can get away with it.

Special occasions

Children would not be children if they did not get excited during special occasions. Changes of routine, greater freedom of movement around the school, a flurry of teacher activity and the arrival of visitors, all combine to create an atmosphere in which conventional procedures fluctuate from normal. Even sensible children can exhibit a mischievous side to their natures; passive children become active and active children become hyperactive. At such times, you need to remain exceptionally calm and highly directive, rather than offering alternatives and making requests. It is possible for adults to get caught up in the frenzy and worsen the situation by over-reacting and becoming as feverish as some of the children. A cool, purposeful attitude and firmness mixed with understanding can help to keep matters under control, but don't expect life to be normal until the event is over.

As with all aspects of school life, there is no substitute for thinking ahead. Most problems can be avoided through sensible preparation and recognising that there will always be situations in which some children try to take advantage and others simply get carried away with the elation of the moment. Nevertheless, a failure to come to grips with the sticky moments can jeopardise the rest of the teaching programme, as bad habits spread to other areas of classroom life. So don't be caught out.

Strategies for improving classroom behaviour

Working atmosphere

Every teacher wants to have a well-ordered classroom in which children are learning, teaching is taking place effectively and there is a sense of purpose and endeavour. No teacher wants to waste time in dealing with squabbles, confrontation or pettiness that result in an unsatisfactory lesson and a reduction in pupils' appetite for learning, even those with a positive attitude. Chapman (1995) summarises the position succinctly:

> If I cannot manage a class sufficiently well, the most invigorating and original lesson will fail. If I cannot control children using positive means wherever possible, then their self-esteem and motivation will be damaged.
>
> (p. 36)

Dockrell and Shield (2006) concluded from their research that general 'babble' in the classroom was particularly disadvantageous to pupils with special educational needs.

Cross-reference: Guided Reader Extract 49

The folly of simple solutions

It was noted earlier in the chapter that there is no substitute for having effective working relationships with children, interesting and relevant work for them to do, and clarity of purpose. We have also seen that the key to dealing successfully with misbehaviour is to try and prevent it from happening in the first place. Most experienced teachers seem to handle incidents as they occur but this instinctive response is due to years of coping with similar circumstances and having an armoury of available strategies. The correct action comes so naturally that they rarely reflect on why they act as they do. However, it is worth remembering that every experienced teacher has worked hard to reach this point of competence and works almost as hard to maintain it by wisely implementing proven techniques and reflecting on potential improvements. New teachers soon find out there are no quick-fix solutions to gaining and maintaining control in the classroom.

Some trainees could be deceived into thinking that if they could only discover the right strategy to use with children, then all their discipline problems would be solved. They imagine that if they look hard enough, they will discover a method to combat all ills. Consequently, slogans are employed to reassure anxious students. For instance:

'Begin by being fierce and ease off later.'

'Let them know who is the boss.'

'Don't smile for quite a while.'

'Keep their heads down and don't give them a moment to breathe.'

While there may be some truth in each of these and similar statements, they offer a distorted view of the centrality of adult–child relationships in maintaining a healthy learning environment and the need to balance the need to establish authority with the benefits that accrue from engaging in a positive and motivating way with pupils. In fact, as noted earlier, the best teachers rarely need to employ such stern, and ultimately unsustainable, tactics.

Helpful and unhelpful strategies

Bearing in mind the cardinal rule that a strategy is only as useful as the wisdom with which the teacher employs it, helpful strategies include the following:

- Gazing hard at the transgressor and acknowledging the pupil's appropriate response
- Going across and speaking quietly but firmly to the individual concerned
- Signalling the child to come across to you and explaining your dissatisfaction
- Chivvying and gently chiding ('Come on Andrew, more work and less chatter please')
- Giving a specific command to clarify work expectations ('Sam, I want you to have finished that page by ten o'clock please').

Whereas unhelpful strategies include the following:

- Shouting (other than in cases of health and safety)
- Calling out an individual's name across the room in a fierce voice (as it distracts everyone else and draws attention to the transgressor)

- Using a pseudo-question as part of a generalised command to no one in particular such as 'Can everybody get on quietly, please' (as this is often ignored by those concerned)
- Using the same child's name in a non-specific rebuke such as 'Daniel, get on with your work' (Daniel needs to be given an unambiguously definite instruction).

It takes time and experience to know which approach to use on which occasion and with which child. Sometimes it is difficult to achieve a satisfactory approach and there is bound to be a time of adjustment with a new class. Grossman (2003) reminds us that different children respond differently when adults speak to them, especially regarding their inappropriate behaviour. For instance, it is normal to expect a child to look at the adult when being spoken to; however, Grossman explains how children from certain cultures are taught that it is discourteous to look at an adult when being addressed, and consequently some pupils may appear to be insolent by refusing to look the teacher in the eye when in fact they are displaying good manners. Other children come from backgrounds where a more formal adult–child relationship is normal and struggle to cope with a more casual relationship. Pupils who appear to resist your friendly overtones might simply be reflecting a cultural norm by maintaining a suitable 'distance' from you, which can be interpreted by you as aloofness rather than respect. With such a multiplicity of combinations, even after some weeks of regular contact, it is not possible to get your reaction right every time; this is a fact that you will have to live with.

Whatever strategies you use to improve pupils' behaviour, it is important to resist lapsing into an artificial pattern of responses in the hope of gaining popularity or creating a false climate of enthusiasm for learning. McPhillimy (1996) views the matter like this: 'Mechanical, calculated smiles and praise, as well as being morally repellent, are very unlikely to be effective as a reward' (p. 80). We also noted in Chapter 4 a warning by Wright (2006) about the danger of becoming a 'passive' teacher and trying to become popular as a mask for an inability to act decisively and show classroom leadership. Do not allow yourself to lapse into such a defensive state of mind and action.

Pandering to the few

To avoid the risk of confrontation, it is tempting to take the easy route and pander to the small number of disruptive children at the expense of the others. For instance, a teacher might decide not to tackle an adventurous lesson for fear that the unusual circumstances or increased opportunities for naughtiness will prove irresistible to the disrupters and the whole lesson purpose will be undermined. Instead, they opt for a heads-down, individual paper-and-pencil approach, resulting in a far less engaging teaching and learning environment. While a heads-down approach has advantages in reducing noise level and leaving the teacher available to monitor the classroom more easily, it is difficult to maintain such an approach without stagnation and alienating the children who wish to benefit from exciting opportunities. As we noted earlier in this chapter, any containing strategy must, like most control techniques, be used sparingly, for in the longer term the innovative and interesting lesson will provide the foundation for strengthening the bonds between teacher and children and enhancing the learning environment. A small number of ill-mannered children can wholly occupy your thoughts, both during and outside the school day. They are the ones that can make you orientate much of what you plan, and most of your decisions and actions, towards keeping them out of mischief.

Activate your thinking!

There always have been and always will be naughty children. It's a fact of life! The crucial thing is the way that you respond to the situation, both practically *and* emotionally.

The significance of body language

Body language has been described as the gestures, postures and facial expressions by which a person manifests physical, mental and/or emotional states, and communicates non-verbally (without speech) with others. Thus, head and hand movements, eye contact, body position and tone of voice express an individual's emotions, feelings, and attitudes (Bolton 1979). For further details, see Chapter 9. Cook and Goldin-Meadow (2006) found that when teachers gave instructions using gesture, the children were likely to employ that problem-solving strategy using their own gestures. The authors concluded that using *gesture* during instruction encourages children to produce gestures of their own, which, in turn, leads to more effective learning. They also tentatively claim that children are able to use gesturing with their hands as a means of changing their minds and the direction of their thinking.

Body language can be a significant factor in maintaining effective discipline. Neill and Caswell (1993) claim that teachers' verbal communication strategies can account for up to 80 per cent of the impression they convey to pupils and have at least four important functions:

1. Gaining pupils' attention
2. Conveying the teacher's enthusiasm to the class
3. Dealing with confrontations and other control issues
4. Relating to individuals during lessons.

Neill and Caswell argue that non-verbal signals send messages to pupils that identify teachers' feelings (both positive and negative) and support their spoken word. Thus, as well as teachers preparing lessons thoroughly and developing effective speech, they also need to cultivate appropriate body language.

Positive body language

Positive body language should include the following:

- Good eye contact with children
- Affirmative nods (expressing interest and approval of child)
- Expressive and reassuring facial tones
- Open body position (indicating trust)
- Facing a child directly when speaking one-to-one
- Squatting or sitting at children's eye level when speaking one-to-one
- Smiling and laughing at genuinely humorous situations.

Less helpful body language

Less helpful body language includes the following:

- Minimal eye contact
- Sighs and distracted facial movements, suggesting boredom or limited interest
- Stony-faced responses, indicating a lack of warmth
- Compressed body position (arms crossed or elbows squeezed into the ribs), conveying unease
- Side-on position when speaking to individuals, indicating adult superiority
- Scowling, accompanying loud verbal rebukes
- Maintaining a rigid stance when speaking one-to-one
- 'Never smile until Christmas' attitude.

However, 'less helpful' body language, if used occasionally, can be a powerful device for showing disapproval. If teachers are respected and liked by the children, such action can reinforce their authority. On the other hand, without children's respect the use of negative body language can lead to a further breakdown in relationships.

Cross-reference: Guided Reader Extract 41

Dealing with rude behaviour

It is unusual to encounter insolent behaviour in primary schools, though it would be foolish to imagine that it can never happen, even under the most settled circumstances. Despite following the strategies suggested earlier in the chapter, you might discover that you are faced with some difficult and unsettling conflicts from time to time, especially if you are a trainee teacher working with a demanding group of older children.

Pupils ignore you

If you are addressing a large group or class and some pupils ignore what you are saying, it is reasonable to stop, wait and make a comment such as 'Please look this way and watch my lips.' It may be, of course, that the very children you are concerned about will not respond because they are not listening in the first place. In such a situation, it is helpful to put the person's name in front of the statement; thus: 'Patty, please look this way and watch my lips. Thank you,' though avoid attaching the same child's name to a reprimand too often or the name itself gains a 'naughty' connotation. If you are speaking to a small group of pupils and one or more begin to look around at their friends or stare away while you are speaking, it may be that you have not yet established your authority in the class, or that the children are nervous about the close encounter with you, or that they do not acknowledge your status. It is essential to remain unruffled, ask for their attention, and to say what needs to be said clearly and unambiguously (without threats). Whenever possible, end the conversation on a positive note, even if it's only: 'Do you understand what I have said to you?' and if they affirm it: 'Well done. Off you go.' If you feel that there are deeper issues at stake it is not worth trying to resolve them through a single conversation. However, you can begin the process of establishing your presence as a teacher by being clear, definite and showing that you won't stand any nonsense.

Pupils talk when you are talking

It is irritating when you are addressing the class and a few children start to giggle among themselves or exchange whispers. On such occasions it is perfectly in order to stop what you are saying abruptly and coldly stare at the miscreants until they come to order. When you recommence, keep your eyes fixed on them for the next few seconds and then, as you relax into your theme, make a deliberate point of looking at them from time to time. If the behaviour continues, stop again and, using hand signals only (not speaking) indicate that one of the children should sit elsewhere out of direct eye line with the others. The next time you reach a suitable point, praise the children for their attention and also remind them about the courtesy rule that it is rude to interrupt when someone else is speaking. If you feel strongly enough, you can ask the perpetrators to see you at the end of the session. Note that it is unwise and counter-productive to create a fuss during the lesson if avoidable; but don't let the matter rest.

Activate your thinking!

Try hard not to feel personally slighted by children who fail to keep quiet when you are speaking. It is likely that they would happily behave the same way with the regular teachers but fear the consequences if they do. Take note of that fact!

Good practice

If you are uncertain about tackling calling out, consider asking the main perpetrators for their ideas about resolving the matter. You might be surprised how effective their suggestions are. At the very least, it will put it at the top of the agenda.

Pupils answer back

Children answer back for a variety of reasons. They may find what you say unsatisfactory or unhelpful or confusing. They may just want to show off in front of their friends. A small number of children answer back because they do not have the social skills to cope with the situation. You have to determine which of these reasons is the most likely. It is usually fairly plain when a child is trying to attract attention and a simple response such as: 'Please don't show off, Eric,' before continuing immediately with what you were saying is surprisingly effective. If the behaviour continues, you must exert your authority quickly and calmly to prevent the situation getting out of hand. There are a number of possible approaches:

Use an indirect strategy such as: 'Stephen, please sit up straight, keep your hands and tongue still and look at me.' This approach has the advantage of diverting attention from the original behaviour but needs to be followed up at a later stage (perhaps after the class has gone out) when you can warn the child that you will not tolerate such rudeness.

Respond with a sense of mock outrage, such as saying quietly (in a cold tone of amazed incredulity): 'What did you say?' If the child refuses to respond, then add: 'Don't let me hear you calling out in class like that again. If you want to say something put your hand up like everybody else,' before continuing.

Align yourself with another teacher, such as saying: 'Alexis, you would not speak to Mrs Archer like that, so please don't do it with me.' If the child persists or argues back then say to the rest of the children, 'Please put your hand up if you know what Alexis should have done,' wait for correct response, then remind Alexis that, as everybody else seems to know the rule, you would be grateful if she would kindly do the same.

Use an abrupt approach, such as 'Stop. No. You know the rule, Chang, so please don't interrupt me or call out.' A palm held out towards the child adds weight to your comments. If possible (but not threateningly) take a pace or two forward and lean forward while speaking to emphasise the fact that the child is not going to 'hide' behind the space between you.

Whatever response seems appropriate, keep the lesson flowing but do not ignore rude or 'smart' remarks that other children have obviously heard, as if they had never been made. It also goes without saying that you should make quite sure that the child really *was* answering back and not merely struggling to find the right form of words to add a useful comment. Clearly stated rules for classroom talk, understood by all the children, make your task of maintaining order much simpler. Obviously, calling out is more prevalent during adult–pupil interactive sessions, especially when a variety of viewpoints are being sought; in the light of this fact, it is better to use less interactive methods until you are more confident about maintaining order.

Pupils treat your commands as optional

Very young children do not always realise that what an adult says, an adult means. They set their minds on doing something and the fact that you have told them to do something else seems to have little impact. In such cases, a lot of patient perseverance is required, taking into account that some of the children may have come from a home, nursery or play-school situation where they could make many more of their own decisions and therefore perceive a teacher's insistence as unreasonable. With the majority of children, loving firmness and persuasion (such as mentioning the exciting things that are possible *when* they have completed the task you have set them) usually does the trick.

Older pupils can be more mischievous and pretend that they do not understand in the hope that you will give up trying to explain. A group of children may decide not to obey what you have said, either because they do not want to do it or because they genuinely think that there is a better option. When children ignore your request, it is normally best to ask them what they are doing and why they are doing it. If they give a reasonable response, you might allow them to carry on (at least for a time) while reminding them that in future they should consult you first before making decisions. If you are not happy that they should continue, ask them what they *ought* to be doing and do not let them off the hook until they tell you. You can then insist that they do what they are told and offer full support while they do so, including approximate time allocation, such as: 'You should manage to finish this part by half past eleven.'

Pupils treat a teacher's instructions as optional for many reasons, not least that they have misunderstood what has been said to them; your clarity of speech and careful lesson management is therefore essential in minimising the risk. Deliberate avoidance is an entirely different matter.

Pupils respond with ribald comments

This behaviour normally applies to a tiny minority of older primary pupils and happens for one of four reasons:

1. The children are over-excited and need to calm down before lesson progress can be made.
2. They have got away with it before and are trying their luck again.

3. They are bored and distracted by the lesson content or the teacher's lacklustre delivery.
4. They lack motivation generally and have become disaffected with school.

Your response depends upon the reason for the behaviour, as follows:

If the children are over-excited and calling out silly things you have a choice over whether to change course for a few minutes and give the whole class a straightforward task until they are more composed (during which time you can quietly single out the culprits and speak sternly to them).

If they are trying their luck, use one of the tactics suggested earlier for when children call out.

If they are bored, you need to increase the lesson's tempo, ask some interesting questions or get the class working on group activities fairly quickly. Your low expectations can also trigger restlessness as it induces a 'why bother?' or 'this is too easy' attitude.

Disaffection has deeper roots and you cannot hope to solve the situation by yourself. It is worth noting, however, that Kinder *et al.* (1996) claim that disaffection is normally the result of boredom, anger or even fear. They suggest that improvement will come gradually as lessons are made more relevant, teachers are perceived as fair, pupils are treated with respect rather than disdain and (in some cases) parents are involved in working out solutions (see also Crozier and Reay 2005). Such improvement does not take place overnight.

Flickers of such behaviour need not spell disaster if the warning signs are heeded and appropriate action is taken quickly. Such action involves teachers in making the correct responses but also, more importantly, examining their lesson content, delivery, organisation and management to see if negative pupil behaviour results from one or more weaknesses in these areas. Rude behaviour is always unsettling, sometimes worrying and occasionally frightening for teachers. If handled badly it can result in confrontations and angry scenes. If handled correctly it is an opportunity to learn about effective classroom strategies for dealing with disruptive youngsters. Trainee teachers should never hesitate to seek advice and assistance from a tutor or host teacher. Don't be tempted to imagine that matters will somehow resolve themselves if you keep quiet and hope for the best. They won't.

Activate your thinking!

Barnes (2006: 3) argues that a small number of disaffected older pupils simply dislike being told what to do by *anyone*. 'They bring with them a negative pattern from childhood that persists whenever they are asked to do something. These are the opportunists looking for ways to torpedo sessions and opt out of making the effort to learn.'

Barnes, R. (2006) *The Practical Guide to Primary Classroom Management*, London: Sage.

Good practice

Aim to be friendly towards children but not 'chummy' with them.

Special cases

Every child is special

All children are special to their parents, friends and family. Somebody treasures even the children who cause a teacher anguish and frustration. Trainee teachers who imagine that the mother or father of the class troublemaker feels the same resentment towards the child as they do have a nasty shock in store. Although parents may acknowledge their son's disobedience or daughter's shortcomings, such an admission does not diminish their love and they will quickly defend their offspring if they think that the teacher is unfairly critical. A few parents will defend their children even when it is blatantly obvious to everyone else where the blame lies.

All teachers experience children who cause particular problems through being uncooperative, unwilling or unsettled. A minority of uncooperative children will resist offers of help, disturb others in the class and generally upset the classroom atmosphere. Particularly difficult children act as a distressing reminder that sometimes, despite a teacher's best efforts, there appears to be little that can be done in the short term to remedy the situation. A child who struggles with academic work may react to his or her difficulties by behaving erratically. A disturbed child may be academically capable but fall behind through having a poor attitude or personality defect. The reverse is also true: a child who succeeds will behave in a more settled manner; the child whose circumstances become more secure will begin to gain success in schoolwork. It is important to be aware of these links as the special needs of children are evaluated (see Chapter 13). By adopting a positive attitude, taking an interest in the children's out-of-school interests and enthusing about their achievements, you have more chance of eliciting the very best from every child, but occasional reversals of fortune are inevitable.

Emerging problems

Children at every stage present their own challenges and joys; as such, there is no 'easy' age group. Different teachers like working with different year groups and it is interesting to reflect upon the similarities and variations in emphasis between the responsibilities and challenges facing teachers of nursery, Key Stage 1 and Key Stage 2. In previous chapters, we saw how difficult some young children find the adjustment to school routines to be. Teachers of Key Stage 1 children spend a lot of time and effort encouraging good learning habits, independence and basic skills. Teachers of 7- to 9-year-olds cope with classes of very mixed ability (socially and academically), in which some children still display immature behaviour, while others display surprising sophistication and make heavy demands upon the teacher's resourcefulness. During the transition between Key Stages 1 and 2, children with dominant personalities emerge and children with learning difficulties are more easily identified than they were in previous years, where maturity factors, such as limited communication skills, made evaluations of need more problematic. Some groups of older children provide particular challenges to a teacher's ability to maintain control and ingenuity, requiring courage and tenacity mixed with imaginative teaching.

Older primary boys

Although all children exhibit inappropriate behaviour at times, it is often with the oldest boys that control issues become most sharply focused. Such pupils can be simultaneously a delight and infuriatingly troublesome. In recent years, more emphasis has been placed on early diagnosis of emotional and learning shortcomings, in the sensible belief that early identification is far preferable to later attempts to rescue lost causes. Teachers of younger and older pupils are therefore all working towards the same end goal, namely well-adjusted young people and future citizens. See Chapter 4 for introductory comments about gender factors.

Older boys are nearly always enthused by sport (especially football), swapping collected cards, playing electronic games, displaying their latest fashion fads and, in some cases, showing off to or studiously avoiding contact with, the girls. These characteristics are not true of every older boy, of course, but even the most enthusiastic teacher can feel exhausted after handling their loud demands, excited responses, intensity of feelings and the rapid movement from protective comradeship to antagonistic dispute. The expression that 'boys will be boys' may invite criticisms of stereotyping but does indicate the impact that groups of older boys, who have often been together in school since they were very small, can prove a handful (as well as a source of fulfilment) for any teacher.

It is important to recognise that high spirits rather than wilfulness are at the heart of much banter and conceited behaviour exhibited by older boys. Things matter deeply to them and often lead to expressions of indignation and highly charged reactions as they attempt to justify their behaviour or criticise others. Although not every older boy behaves in this manner, many do so, and with this in mind teachers must ensure they adhere to the following three principles.

Be firm but not unreasonable

For instance, to punish an older boy who loves to play a sport by denying him the chance to do so because of his overzealous behaviour in a lesson can be counter-productive, resulting in grievance, frustration and resentment (though such a course of action might be necessary if the noncooperation persists). Usually the mild threat of such a sanction will cause a sporty boy to try to mend his ways, so give credit for effort, even if the behaviour remains less than perfect. There is a fine line between being resolute, even strict, and using your adult authority like a battering ram to combat bad behaviour. Make it a rule that, in the words of Gilbert and Sullivan, the punishment should fit the crime.

Do not allow assertive boys to dominate

It is quite common to observe boys with commanding personalities suppressing, excluding or even tyrannising more passive and vulnerable children, who tend to avoid them and play among themselves. You must not allow this so-called 'macho' behaviour by a small number of characters to frighten other children or undermine their self-esteem. The non-sporty boys sometimes have a difficult job to compete and find their place in the social hierarchy; it is your responsibility to ensure that they have opportunities to succeed and gain status in other ways, such as encouraging them to share their skills gained in activities out of school. In doing so, make sure that the items of interest are not perceived as 'babyish' by the other children, or more harm than good will be done. Your sensitivity and wisdom in monitoring the situation is essential.

Insist on consistency of effort

Make it clear that the high standards the boys set themselves in sporting activities are equally necessary in academic work. Some boys who throw themselves into outdoor activities are loath to apply the same rigour to their class work. It is useful to face this inconsistency openly with them and attempt to feed their enthusiasm into the academic rather than suppress their love of physical activities.

Making learning relevant

It is easy to be sceptical about difficult boys' specific needs by arguing that teachers should not 'pander' to them but insist that they do what they are told, just as sensible children are expected to do. While there is much to commend in this tough-minded approach, teachers have to live with the reality of managing challenging behaviour every day, while doing their best to ensure that such pupils learn and progress. Garnett (2006) argues that school is too content-driven for many boys and has little relevance for them. He notes that boys tend to be characterised by eight tendencies:

1. More competitive
2. Rush to finish their written work
3. Unconcerned about presentation
4. Inconsistent spelling and grammar
5. Sometimes make inaccurate verbal comments
6. Indulge in aggressive or physical 'horseplay'
7. More outgoing and friendly
8. Show off and take centre-stage.

Whereas girls tend to show seven characteristics:

1. Willingly collaborate
2. Willing to persevere with tasks
3. Take care over presentation of work
4. More accurate with spelling, grammar and content
5. Quieter than boys and happy with a small group of friends
6. Rarely indulge in 'horseplay'
7. More self-conscious. (Adapted from Garnett 2006: 80.)

These characteristics are, of course, only generalisations. There are plenty of exceptions. However, his summary of typical behaviours may assist you to keep matters in perspective when boys behave unhelpfully. Garnett recommends that improving attainment among boys require that teachers pay attention to nine factors: (1) promoting active learning; (2) developing high-order skills; (3) creating effective learning zones (emphasising boys' need to feel comfortable in their immediate learning environment); (4) promoting success; (5) providing effective feedback, with an emphasis on skills and content rather than on presentation; (6) recognising and creating learning windows, when pupils are at their most attentive; (7) developing good relationships; (8) developing productive pedagogy, with a high degree of pupil involvement; and (9) incorporating their perspectives.

There is a sense in which the above advice applies to all children, girls as well as boys, but the recommended practices particularly resonate with the needs of some older boys, who might appear confident and a little cocky, but are inwardly insecure and anxious. There is little point in trying to win children's co-operation by being rigid, criticising the appearance of work, emphasising the end-product at the expense of the process and even humiliating them; in the case of many boys, such an approach will only increase antagonism and inflame resentment. Boys are always hoping that their teacher will be a hero or heroine, so use your talents and skills to fascinate them and engineer such an accolade.

Older boys are an exhausting but exciting group to work with. If teachers can win their hearts by exuding energy, fairness and enthusiasm they will secure undying loyalty and receive commitment and wholehearted zest for learning.

Older primary girls

Maturity and growth

Most girls are enthusiastic about schoolwork and determined to do well. Every survey shows that the majority of girls make more rapid progress, both academically and socially, than boys of the same age. You must bear this fact in mind in addressing the needs of the class, though resist making it an excuse for low achievement on the boys' part. After all, nurture (upbringing) also plays a part in determining behaviour, as do 'natural' tendencies and character traits – so gender is only one of many influences on attainment. A small number of mature older girls find it hard to feel part of a primary school culture and express this by psychologically (and sometimes literally) separating themselves from other children or showing disdain for academic work and sport. Girls normally mature earlier than boys and precocious older children may find that they are emotionally and physically advanced compared with their classmates. They have to cope with adolescence and rapid growth at a time when they are still in the primary school environment. This process can be difficult for them to accept and result in phases of intensity, exaggerated behaviour and an explosion of boy-related imagery, conversation and action. It is important to remember that these girls are grappling with a rapid series of changes in their lives and bodies and need to be treated with courtesy and consistency, while insisting on basic standards of behaviour from them.

Dominant girls

It is sensible to avoid heavy-handed approaches that threaten to humiliate older girls or, at the other extreme, being patronising to them. Younger male teachers, in particular, need to be discreet: thus, although gentle teasing and pleasantries are part of the interactive process and can lead to a healthy relationship, men should think carefully about words and body language which might be misconstrued by older girls. Dominant older girls can also be bossy and unkind to their less mature peers and, in some cases, may try to lure passive girls into a closely knit group whose membership is open only to those who will espouse their particular, strictly defined attitudes. In dealing with older dominant girls, a number of factors need to be considered, as follows.

Those who mature early do not do so out of choice

It is easy for a teacher to resent these hormonal intrusions into the otherwise child-like environment. A tolerant understanding of the emotions at work is essential.

Mature older girls are still primary school pupils

They therefore come under the same general rules of conduct as everyone else. Although sensible discretion needs to be exercised, it would be a mistake for teachers to allow any non-conformist behaviour to dominate classroom or school life to the detriment of other children and the quality of their teaching.

Unkind words and vindictive attitudes towards weaker children are serious

Such behaviour should be dealt with according to the school's agreed policy. For trainee teachers, unsure about how to cope with regular minor instances of gossip or unkindness, the best course of action is to seek advice from senior colleagues. It is helpful for you to introduce an easily remembered rule of the kind, 'If you must say something about someone, say something helpful.' The same rule applies to all children, of course.

Girl–boy relationships must be monitored

Firm control needs to be exercised over mature girls who might endeavour to draw less mature, wide-eyed boys into silly or disruptive behaviour. Most boys are, in truth, thankful to be extracted from such situations. Renold (2005) conducted extensive group interviews and observation of older primary-aged pupils in school and found that children's sexuality is embedded in school-based cultures and associated gender identities.

Helping girls to succeed

The vast majority of girls enjoy doing well in school as much as, and in most cases more than, most boys do. Owing to the fact that slow learners and troublesome pupils are more likely to be boys than girls, and therefore require more attention, support and managing, it is possible for girls' education to suffer; this danger is most acute for quiet girls who don't make a fuss and get on with their work without being prompted. In fact, girls need to be encouraged to build on their natural strengths and employ them across the curriculum, especially in areas where they may have been traditionally less successful (e.g. problem solving in mathematics). In particular, girls can use their verbal communication skills to good effect in collaborating with other pupils. Girls sometimes have to be offered additional support in technological activities to ensure that they do not allow themselves to be overshadowed by dominant boys.

Although a minority of older girls can be irritating owing to their casual approach and restless behaviour, they usually respond well to teachers who offer them the opportunity to behave maturely within clearly defined limits. Despite the unpredictable behaviour of the few, they often prove to be among the most loyal and supportive class members during times of crisis. Maturity cuts both ways. On the one hand it may serve to upset and unsettle. On the other hand, it can produce remarkable examples of loyalty, sensitivity and enthusiasm to delight and encourage weary teachers. As with every age group, your own positive attitude, high expectations and good humour will combat most unsavoury elements of behaviour and, coupled with a lively approach in the classroom, bring out the best in every child (see, for example, Burgess *et al.* 2000; Loomans and Kolberg 2002).

Good practice

While boys have to be taught how to resolve situations of potential conflict and listen carefully to other people's points of view, some girls have to be made aware of the powerful and potentially damaging effect of their words on others.

Cross-reference: Guided Reader Extract 19

Demoralised children

Occasionally, teachers come across children who, for various reasons, seem to have given up on school (Makins 1997; Ravet 2007). They might not be persistent troublemakers and may even plod along with the work, albeit unenthusiastically, but it is evident that they have lost heart and are simply passing the time as comfortably as possible before leaving the school and moving on to secondary education. Typically, such children will be found at the upper end of the school, though younger children can show signs of a similar attitude. Although the reasons for such negativity (such as home circumstances) lie outside the teacher's immediate control, there are a number of positive strategies worth considering that help children regain their zest for school and learning in general, notably:

Find regular opportunities to interact on a one-to-one basis

In the busyness of the day it is difficult to find opportunities to interact with every pupil other than during the formal teaching programme, when the adult–child relationship is influenced by academic considerations rather than social ones. However, a deliberate attempt to exchange a private word with key individuals each day helps to build understanding and convince the children that your interest in them goes beyond merely improving academic results. Such worthy intentions are not easily achievable because (1) the children resist your advances and (2) they are usually more intent on talking to their friends in the playground than to their teacher. Nevertheless, it is worth trying to establish a more informal relationship with any child who seems to be demoralised. Although TAs play a significant role in pursuit of this goal, your involvement is crucial, though you should approach things casually and with a light touch for fear of alarming the child and making matters worse.

Avoid making a big fuss

Unless they are displaying their disillusionment by wilful misbehaviour, demoralised children often shun the limelight and do not want to be the public centre of a teacher's attention. Attempts to grant them a form of 'celebrity status' by making an undue fuss of their endeavours or behaviour can backfire and cause them to become even more inhibited or withdrawn. By giving individuals deliberate, regular and low-key attention, you can gradually enhance their feelings of self-worth and raise their self-esteem. Giving them small but necessary tasks to do is a useful way of helping them to feel more involved in classroom life.

Take an interest in their out-of-school activities

Children who lack academic motivation will sometimes spark into life when a teacher shows an interest in their hobbies or pastimes. The occasional enquiry about how they are getting on in a sports tournament or competition or in collecting items of interest can sometimes initiate a trust in the teacher, which in turn increases the child's determination to succeed in schoolwork, too. Note, by contrast, that while enthusiasm and encouragement are usually beneficial, coercive methods to achievement can have damaging effects on pupils (McMahon 2007).

Enthuse gently about their successes

Depressed or unmotivated children not only believe that they have failed in the past but convince themselves that they are incapable of improving their situation. You can contribute to the confidence-building process by making specific comments about positive achievements and highlighting genuine areas of improvement, while avoiding contrived praise. Although it takes time to convince demoralised children that they can succeed, they need help in being able to recognise where progress has been made and (like every other pupil) how to improve their existing achievements. Your initial attempts to praise their good work may be rebuffed, but perseverance brings its own reward (see below).

Request their assistance

Asking children who seem to have given up to assist another child or to take responsibility for a small but important task is a useful means of building self-confidence. Pupils who have become used to a cycle of failure and defeatism might take some persuading that they have the capability to undertake the task, but small victories accumulate and create an archive of success to which you can refer as a sign of what the child can achieve.

Persevere

Confidence and self-belief in a demoralised child are not developed overnight. However, if you are willing to persevere and establish an open, positive approach with pupils, celebrate modest achievements and offer specific support when progress is slow, they have more chance to rediscover a zest for learning. When you are tempted to be discouraged because nothing positive appears to be happening, remind yourself of how much that child will benefit from your caring approach, which Liston and Garrison (2004) courageously and correctly refer to as 'loving'. One of the principal reasons that many people become teachers is because they enjoy working with and supporting children. Helping those who are finding life difficult to cope with or have lost hope is an excellent opportunity to gain that kind of fulfilment.

Activate your thinking!

Children are asking one question above all others: 'How much are you interested in me as a person?'

Good practice

Use the above strategies over a period of two weeks to evaluate the improvement in the attitude towards and aptitude for work of any disaffected children. In so doing, ensure that you make a clear distinction between disaffected children, lazy children and mischievous children.

Confidence and judgement

Establishing and maintaining class discipline is a difficult and demanding task for every teacher, especially for trainee teachers and inexperienced practitioners. However, we have noted the axiom that all teachers can improve the situation by ensuring that lessons are interesting and relevant, instructions are clear and specific and responses to unacceptable behaviour are appropriate. In fact, all teachers who successfully maintain order possess two essential qualities: *confidence* and *wise judgement*.

Expressing your confidence

Your *confidence* emerges gradually. It grows when you know what you are doing and why. It is a delicate flower and can easily be crushed by a poor lesson, an unthinking comment from a colleague or a seemingly intractable situation involving a recalcitrant pupil. A positive attitude, firm but natural speech, strong enthusiastic personality and appropriate body language all contribute towards building your confidence. It is helpful to remember that you are a capable adult who possesses the knowledge and skills to teach effectively. Consequently, nothing (and certainly not a naughty child or unthinking adult) is going to deter you from achieving your goals. In addition, however, it is equally important to recognise that some problems (including discipline) will be the result of your own inexperience; be encouraged to know, however, that acting upon advice from others and your own thoughtful deliberations will combine to improve the situation gradually over time. It takes courage to step over the threshold of a classroom and handle large numbers of immature little people, so don't imagine that your tentativeness is an indication of your incompetence. Far from it!

Exercising wise judgement

The ability to make *wise judgements* and to recognise when you have made them is difficult to define, as so many things happen before, during and after lessons that there is rarely much opportunity to reflect-in-action (Schön 1983). Some teachers seem to possess an instinct for handling situations well; most of us have to learn the hard way. However, the following strategies will help you to improve your success rate and give you the necessary confidence to be decisive yet able to accept and remedy your shortcomings:

- Have a big 'presence' around the room by moving around, engaging with pupils, smiling a lot, using expressive body language and maintaining good eye contact.
- Practise your diction and speak at a speed that allows pupils time to absorb what you are saying, using a lively tone and maintaining an attractive 'ring' in your voice (not shrill).
- Maintain a steady pace to the lesson with occasional bursts of speed (perhaps through asking a few snappy questions) and periods of reflection (where pupils have to think deeply).
- Communicate your enthusiasm through firm statements of approval and praise for genuine achievement.
- Avoid confrontation wherever possible, but if this is not possible try to ensure that the outcome leaves both your authority and the pupil's dignity intact.
- Avoid shouting but cultivate a strong voice through regular breathing exercises, standing erect and 'bringing your voice forward' from the throat to the front of the mouth.
- Use a variety of good quality questions (closed and open) and show a keen interest in pupils' replies, both correct and incorrect.

- Organise thoroughly and anticipate sticky spots (see earlier in this chapter).
- Do not introduce activities or interactive forms of teaching that might excite too much fervour until you are sure that you have sufficient class control.
- When unacceptable behaviour occurs, concentrate on the act rather than the perpetrator.
- Think positive. Be positive.
- Convince yourself and your children that they have got a teacher in a million – which, of course, they have!

Activate your thinking!

How would you act wisely in the following circumstances?

1. The more assertive children are dominating the use of equipment during collaborative activities.
2. Freda, aged 9, tells you that she does not have to do what you say because you are 'only a student'.
3. The same two children are always last to be chosen for games' activities.
4. You are told a racist joke by a child in the class.
5. You are asked to make sure that the books on the classroom shelves are suitable for children.
6. Meena, aged 8, comes to you in tears because no one wants to play with her.
7. A child confides in you that his parents are separating.
8. Some children in your class complain that a girl who is new to the school has been swearing openly at other children. [Note: Would it make a difference if you knew that the girl was from a very unsettled background?]
9. A parent tells you that she did not want her 5-year-old sitting next to a particular child because the child smells.
10. A parent tells you that she does not want her able 10-year-old sitting by a less able child because the child is always asking questions about the work.

Case study

It is Wednesday morning in a Year 4 class. Tim and Ali, firm friends, sit together pondering the work in front of them. The trainee teacher is still finding her feet and determined to clamp down on inappropriate behaviour.

Trainee: Okay, get on with your work.

Tim: (speaking to Ali) What are we meant to be doing?

Ali: I dunno. (Tim gazes around hoping to gain a clue from what the other children are doing.)

Tim: We're supposed to write something down about the things we saw on our walk, I think.

Ali: I dunno. I'm just gonna write something. It doesn't matter. (Ali begins to write studiously, bent over his paper, hoping that the trainee doesn't look too closely.)

Tim: I'll ask Angie. (He gets up and wanders over to Angie.)

Trainee: (crossly) Sit down, Tim, and get on with your work.

Tim: I was just asking Angie something.

Angie: (a conscientious girl, anxious that she might be getting in trouble, glances nervously at the trainee) Go away, Tim. You're bothering me.

Trainee: (assuming that Tim is being troublesome) Sit ... down ... and ... get on.

Tim: (slumps back into his seat, chin on hand) This is useless.

Fifteen minutes later Ali has written half a page of low-level work but in bold handwriting. Tim has scrawled a few indecipherable words on the sheet and sits staring vacantly into space. The trainee is praising Angie and others for their efforts. She walks across to Ali and Tim.

Ali: (glancing up) Look, Miss, what I done.

Trainee: (without reading it closely but noticing the tidiness and length and relieved that he has made an effort) Well done, Ali, that's excellent. (Turns to Tim, looks at his paper and scowls.) What on earth do you call that? (Tim says nothing.) Right. You can stay in at playtime and finish it off.

Tim: (urgently) But Miss, I've got to see Mr Ward about playing in the team and ...

Trainee: You can forget about that. I'm sick of you messing about and not doing your work and if you say another word you can come with me and see Mr Pretiman. (Tim visibly shrinks; Ali glances across sympathetically; a few children in the corner snigger quietly.)

The trainee's perception of the boys' behaviour was affected by her initial belief that Tim was causing trouble. From this point, the relationship between adult and child became tense. Dialogue was limited through the trainee's unwillingness to ensure that Tim was clear about the task and to offer some ongoing 'scaffolding' to his learning through appropriate monitoring and intervention. Her failure to explain the task adequately and her apparent reluctance to attend to Tim's individual learning needs meant that at the end of the allotted time his progress was minimal and she felt obliged to invoke sanctions. The end result was an unhappy child and a strained trainee. Tim was far from being a model pupil and his unwillingness to consult the trainee teacher may have been a contributing factor, but the trainee made the situation worse by her ill-judged comments and hasty reactions.

Activate your thinking!

- What steps might have been taken to ensure that the boys were clear about the task?
- What are the prospects for settled relationships and effective teaching and learning if these conditions persist?
- What is the trainee likely to say to Ali's and Tim's parents during the parent interviews?

Good practice

Examine your class list and sub-divide the children into three broad categories:

1. The majority who endeavour to work hard and do their best
2. The number who will get away with doing the bare minimum
3. The minority who cause regular problems.

Reflect upon appropriate strategies for moving children from group 2 to group 1, and from group 3 to group 2. Now celebrate that there are so many names in the first group.

Further reading for Chapter 12

Adams, K. (2009) *Behaviour for Learning in the Primary School*, Exeter: Learning Matters.

The book explores the concept of behaviour for learning with reference to the Every Child Matters agenda: relationship with self, relationships with others and relationships with the curriculum.

Bentham, S. and Hutchins, R. (2012) *Improving Pupil Motivation Together: Teachers and teaching assistants working collaboratively*, Abingdon: Routledge.

Teaching assistants are often asked to work with pupils who are difficult to motivate and who find learning challenging. The authors demonstrate how pupil motivation can be enhanced if teachers and teaching assistants work together.

Chaplain, R. (2011) *Managing Behaviour in the Primary Classroom*, Abingdon: Routledge.

The author explores the organisational and structural aspects of schools, and the interpersonal relationships between teachers and pupils in establishing and maintaining classroom order.

Haydn, T. (2012) *Managing Pupil Behaviour: Improving the classroom atmosphere*, Abingdon: Routledge.

The book draws on the views of over 100 teachers and 700 pupils to determine what factors help teachers to manage learning effectively in their classrooms.

Lopez, N. (2011) *Hopeful Girls, Troubled Boys*, second edn, Abingdon: Routledge.

The author explains why teenage girls of colour are succeeding at higher rates than their male counterparts; the girls maintain optimistic outlooks on their lives, while boys are ambivalent about the promises of education.

O'Regan, F. (2002) *How to Teach and Manage Children with ADHD*, Whitstone, NY: LDA Publishers.

Attention deficit and hyperactivity disorder is a condition normally associated with boys; however, a section of O'Regan's book deals with the specific needs of girls.

Rogers, B. (2006) *Classroom Behaviour*, London: Paul Chapman.

Offers a wide repertoire of relational management skills and guidance for putting professional integrity and emotional literacy into practice from an early stage.

13 Inclusion and Special Educational Needs

Introduction

Over the past twenty-five years or so the education of children with special educational needs (SEN) has assumed an increasingly high profile in schools. Once seen as a specialist area, it is now the responsibility of every teacher. This chapter starts by reviewing background information about relevant legislation and giving a historical perspective on the subject. An understanding of the terms 'special educational needs' and 'inclusion' is then explored, with reference to the Code of Practice. Finally, advice is offered about successfully dealing with SEN in the classroom, including writing an individual education plan (IEP) and working with other professionals.

A brief history

Barton and Tomlinson (1984) trace the changes in statutory categories for special provision in Britain. Thus, in 1886 there was statutory provision for those diagnosed as Idiots and Imbeciles. These seemingly insulting terms were at the time clearly defined clinical categories, comprising those that we would now describe as having profound or severe learning difficulties. By the end of the century categories of schools for the blind and deaf had also been established. Schools were founded for the indigent blind, the word 'indigent' meaning needy or impoverished; stereotyping expressions such as 'the blind beggar' is one such example. These institutions taught crafts and trades that would facilitate some sort of financial independence for pupils when they had completed the course (e.g. as piano tuners for the blind and partially sighted), and were seen as a philanthropic act of kindness and charity. Separate institutions were set up for the 'physically defective', again focusing on learning a trade that would offer future employment and security. After the First World War came the development of separate schools and classes for the 'feeble minded', who were judged incapable of following the normal curriculum. The growth of educational psychology under Cyril Burt saw the widespread use of intelligence quotient (IQ) tests to identify those in need of special education (an IQ of 70 or below being the cut-off point).

When the 1944 Act secured universal free education, including secondary education, it was deemed necessary to extend this right to all 'educable handicapped children'. Consequently, until the 1981 Act, special educational provision was premised on categories of handicap (e.g. malfunctioning limbs), rather than educational need and access to a common school experience and curriculum. Numerous problems emerged as educationists attempted to make a success of the system which tended to take account of the 'handicap' as the prime consideration and educational need as the subordinate one; naturally, this approach resulted in many academically capable young people with physical handicaps becoming frustrated and marginalised, with accompanying low status and few opportunities to acquire employment appropriate to their abilities. These and many other related issues led to the questioning of the then existing forms of provision and the categories and labels that were in use, and a switch to focusing instead on the actual educational needs of children. This bold move engendered the current debate, including the use of language in labelling (see below) and issues about segregation, integration and inclusion.

Until 1971 about 1 per cent of the population was deemed uneducable, and did not attend conventional school at all. When this population became the responsibility of the then Department of Education and Science, a committee was set up under Baroness Warnock to report on the education of 'handicapped' children (the Warnock Report). The committee widened its brief, abandoning the notion of handicaps and establishing instead the notion of special educational needs or SEN; it moved beyond the pupils who were at that time educated in special schools to an estimated 20 per cent of children who were likely to experience some form of special needs at some time in their school careers. This larger group had formerly been referred to as 'remedial' or slow learners.

The report *Children with Special Educational Needs* was published in 1978 and paved the way for the far-reaching legislation of the Education Act 1981. The Act stated that where possible: (1) children with SEN should be educated alongside their non-disabled peers, and (2) their resource needs should be safeguarded by a 'statement of need' that would be binding on the local authority. The pre-existing categories of handicap were abolished and replaced with a single notion of special educational need. However, a set of descriptive categories was still deemed necessary, such as moderate learning difficulties, hearing impaired, etc. The Act came into force on 1 April 1983 and the period since then has been characterised by the teaching profession moving from a *segregated* form of provision (where pupils with identifiable needs are separately educated) to an *inclusive* one (where pupils are educated together).

Owing to the fact that Britain had an entrenched system of segregation during the early 1980s, changing attitudes and practices has proved to be a challenging task. British teachers in mainstream schools were used to a system that spared them from having to deal directly with needy pupils, as the children were in other specialist institutions. Furthermore, there were specialist schools and a variety of qualified and experienced professionals who rightly prided themselves on their ability to deal with the children's needs in separate accommodation, and it was difficult for them to forego the status of being experts in a certain field (e.g. educating visually impaired children). In recent years there has been a tacit acknowledgement by government that the abolition of all specialist schools on moral or educational grounds is unwise, and debate still rages over the acceptability and desirability of retaining some unique specialist provision, howbeit located on the site of a mainstream school. As Phtiaka (1997) pointedly asks: how special do you need to be to find yourself in a special school?

Activate your thinking!

What do you 'see' first, the person of the child or the child's disability?

The language of special education

Children's needs and statementing

Prior to the 1981 Act labels were used to describe the features that led to educational difficulty, e.g. an educationally sub-normal child, a blind child. The Warnock Report sought to move away from this and focus on the needs of the children in the particular context of provision in which they found themselves. As early as 1984, Lady Warnock herself admitted regret about coining the term 'special educational needs' and wondered how long it would be before the word 'special' accrued pejorative connotations. We can now see that in the intervening period the term has indeed come to function as a label for children, rather than focusing on their needs. In every staffroom it is possible to hear talk of 'SEN children' or 'statemented children', neither of which term is accurate, as a statement of special educational needs is supposed to refer to the provision, and not to the child. In 2011, concerns were raised at government level about the ponderous process of statementing and the increasingly large numbers of children that were being absorbed into the special needs system of referral, with the resulting cost implications, especially the high staffing requirements. The debate continues.

There is a considerable variability in the use of statements across the country. Possession of a statement often says as much about the *situation* the child is in than anything intrinsic to the child, yet labels that focus on the child are still in common use. As more and more money is devolved to schools there are signs that the use of the statement will decline; indeed, the use of the terms 'learning needs' and 'learning difficulties' is now in vogue. Additionally, the universal acceptance that all children have strengths and weaknesses in specific subject areas – as opposed to being viewed as either 'generally able' or 'generally not able' – has paved the way for a re-evaluation of individual learning needs ('individualisation') and ways in which weaker areas can be addressed, and stronger areas enhanced (so-called 'personalisation'). These various terms may, in turn, become labels rather than educational principles, but the concept of meeting each child at the point of his or her need across the curriculum has become accepted practice (though in reality, the vast majority of resources are directed towards literacy and mathematics). It is important to see children as individuals with different needs that change over time rather than members of a group, all assumed to have the same characteristics requiring identical treatment.

Use of vocabulary

Using language accurately and appropriately is something to which every teacher should aspire, and it is important to avoid unintentionally giving offence or being insulting by the inaccurate use of terms. This issue is given a thorough airing in Corbett's thought-provoking book, provocatively entitled *Bad-Mouthing: The language of special needs* (Corbett 1995). Basically, the situation can be greatly improved if teachers abide by three simple precepts:

- Avoid language that is clearly insulting or inaccurate, e.g. 'mongol', 'spastic', 'cripple'.
- Avoid patronising euphemisms, e.g. 'vertically challenged', 'differently enabled', etc.
- Use the preferred terminology of the group in question, e.g. 'Down (or Down's) Syndrome', 'deaf', and so on.

It is inevitable that vocabulary will change over time; it is, however, a sign of respect when talking to children and their families that you have made the effort to adopt non-offensive terminology or, if uncertain, have taken the trouble to ask them about their preference.

Most of the categories of learning difficulties listed earlier are typically of low incidence. For instance, you might never teach a child with Down (or Down's) Syndrome or with autistic spectrum disorder ('autism', see below). However, it is important for you to develop an inclusive philosophy that extends to all pupils, being willing to support a range of learning difficulties where necessary, and knowing where to go for additional knowledge and support at the appropriate time. The special educational needs Code of Practice gives useful outlines, there is a plethora of practical guides and texts available, and the Internet provides a valuable source of information, though the sheer volume of material on each topic can be daunting.

Autism

Autism spectrum disorder

Autism is a disorder that includes a broad range of symptoms and is therefore often referred to as a spectrum disorder: hence 'autism spectrum disorder' or ASD. It is a lifelong developmental disability that affects the way a person relates to and interacts with other people. The most striking symptom of ASD is difficulty with social communication, such as maintaining eye contact, conducting a normal conversation and viewing events and issues from another person's perspective. The prevalence of autism in school-age children is difficult to specify, but approximately one person in every 100 is affected by the disorder to some degree; in other words, it is likely that out of three parallel classes in a year group, one pupil will suffer from the condition. Statistics suggest that the number of pupils diagnosed with some form of autism is growing, including a worrying increase in confirmed cases among pre-school children.

Triad of impairment

To be diagnosed as 'being autistic', children must have persistent difficulty in three areas of their development: (1) with language and communication; (2) in social understanding and interactions; (3) with flexibility of thought and imagination. These three elements are sometimes referred to as the 'triad of impairment'. A child with autism can exhibit these difficulties to varying degrees and the condition can encompass a wide spectrum (Wing 2003).

Asperger syndrome

Asperger syndrome (AS) is a form of autism and considered a part of the autism spectrum. The significant difference between AS and extreme autism is that people with AS usually develop speech at a normal age while people with autism normally have speech delays. Children with AS are generally very bright and verbally adept, but also suffer from significant social deficits; they are often limited in their imaginations and capacity for creative play. The pain and anguish felt by parents of children with AS can only be imagined, and their anxiety about the absence of an agreed strategy, treatment or intervention that can help to transform the behaviour and future lives of their children. Our responsibility as teachers is first and foremost located in the wellbeing of children but the implications go much wider.

Classroom behaviour

Children with the kind of symptoms described above do not readily respond to humour, irony or sarcasm and tend to interpret instructions literally, rather than understanding the subtleties attached to words. As a result, it is easy for an adult to interpret their behaviour as misbehaviour rather than a spontaneous 'autistic' response. Such children are also likely to have trouble grasping rules that require thoughtful interpretation, so require a lot of adult guidance to know what kind of behaviour is appropriate and acceptable, together with regular reminders about the correct course of action (Notbohm 2007).

During lessons, children with autism can develop their own agendas and take a different direction from the one initiated by the teacher, causing a degree of exasperation for the teacher, especially when the child's actions are potentially hazardous. Pupils exhibit a form of obsessive behaviour and become completely engrossed in a certain topic or line of enquiry to the exclusion of all else, which is a major concern for teachers trying to follow a prescribed curriculum.

Dyslexia

Characteristics

The majority of people who suffer from dyslexia have difficulty with writing, reading and spelling; the condition is viewed by most educators as a learning disability. Children who read very slowly and hesitantly, without fluency and word by word, or who constantly lose their place in the text, have reading problems associated with dyslexia. Pavey and Harper-Jones (2007) note that dyslexia is evident when accurate and fluent word reading and/or spelling develops very incompletely or with great difficulty. About 4 per cent of the population has severe dyslexia, while a further 6 per cent experience mild to moderate problems; consequently, in a class of thirty children, about three pupils are likely to struggle from the disorder to some extent.

Learning issues

Dyslexia is sometimes used to refer to a child who has an average or above average intelligence with a reading grade some one or more years below the expected level, though it has been diagnosed in pupils possessing all levels of intelligence, including those who are exceptionally able. A common problem for readers is reversing letters like *b* and *d*, either when reading or when writing. Sometimes a child will read (or write) words like 'tar' instead of 'rat' and 'won' instead of 'now'; they can become easily disorientated and struggle to discriminate left and right, east and west – important to remember this fact during map-reading and physical activities that require correct orientation (e.g. country dancing).

Another frequent sign of dyslexia is elisions (omissions) from words: for example, when a child reads or writes 'car' when the word is actually 'care'. A child may try to sound out the letters of the word (i.e. phonetically) but then be unable to say the correct word; for example, sounding the letters 't-a-p' but then being unable to say 'tap'. The child may read or write the letters of a word in the wrong order, such as 'left' for 'felt', or the syllables in the wrong order, such as 'emeny' for 'enemy', or *words* in the wrong order, such as 'is he' for 'he is'. As a result, children suffering from dyslexia read with limited understanding of the meaning or remember little of what they have read. Typically, such children spell words as they sound: for example, 'rite' instead of 'right'; as a result, poor and/or slow handwriting becomes a further hindrance to progress.

Teaching approaches

Compensating for dyslexia depends on the severity of difficulty. In cases linked to visual differences, some teachers believe that a coloured overlay across the page and tinted lenses lead to improvement because they can stop the letters from 'dancing on the page' – a common complaint by children with dyslexia. Frost and Emery (2000) suggest that teachers can intervene in a number of ways, a modified version of which appears below:

1. Teach children similarities and differences between how something is said and how it is written.
2. Provide direct instruction in language analysis and the alphabetic code.
3. Give explicit instruction in segmenting and blending speech sounds, helping children to process progressively larger chunks of words.
4. Use techniques that make phonemes (the smallest units of meaningful sounds) more concrete: for example, phonemes and syllables can be represented by blocks where children can be taught how to add, omit, substitute and rearrange them.
5. Model skills in various reading contexts; review previous reading lessons and relate to current lessons.
6. Discuss the specific purposes and goals of each reading lesson.
7. Provide regular practice with reading materials where the content is located in familiar contexts and include many words that children can decode (to build confidence).
8. As a core sight vocabulary is acquired, expose children to more irregular words to increase reading accuracy.
9. Teach for comprehension by introducing conceptually important vocabulary prior to initial reading and asking children to retell the story and answer questions regarding explicit ('blatant') and implicit ('hidden') content.
10. Teach children the main components of most stories (i.e. character, setting, etc.) and how to identify and use these components to help them remember the story.
11. Teach reading and spelling in conjunction, and how to correctly spell the words they read.
12. Provide positive, explicit and corrective feedback. Praise effort as well as success.

Activate your thinking!

The British Dyslexia Association, BDA (www.bdadyslexia.org.uk) promotes early identification and support in schools to ensure opportunity to learn for dyslexic learners. Reid (2005, 2007b) offers suggestions about practical approaches that can be used for assessment, teaching and learning.

Reid, G. (2005) *Dyslexia and Inclusion: Classroom approaches for assessment, teaching and learning*, London: David Fulton/NASEN.
Reid, G. (2007b) *100 Ideas for Supporting Pupils with Dyslexia*, London: Continuum.

Good practice

Reading Recovery (www.readingrecovery.ioe.ac.uk) is an early literacy intervention programme designed for children who have literacy difficulties at the end of their first year at primary school. It involves reading and writing in a daily one-to-one lesson with a trained teacher for a period of between fifteen and twenty weeks. It is claimed that at the end of the time, most children have caught up with their classmates and can read and write at a level appropriate for their age.

Dyspraxia

In the past dyspraxia has been referred to as 'clumsy child syndrome' but the reality is considerably more complex. Dyspraxia is a developmental difficulty that can overlap with other conditions such as dyslexia, attention deficit hyperactivity disorder (ADHD) and social and communication difficulties, including Asperger syndrome. It affects about 6 per cent of the population and is three times more likely to affect boys than girls. There is no cure but early diagnosis is essential if steps are to be taken to assist a child with the condition. In school or when playing with other children, a child with dyspraxia can experience anxiety, lack concentration and struggle to understand the rules. The child is also likely to have more difficulty than most in passing a ball and can easily trip up when trying to control it with feet. *The Good Schools Guide* (2008) suggests that typical problems in school include:

- difficulties following long instructions, and in planning and organising work and themselves;
- difficulty copying text from book or whiteboard;
- variable ability – better some days than others and may get tired more easily;
- low self-esteem and frustration, which will sometimes result in disruptive behaviour;
- difficulty in ball sports;
- difficulty writing at speed or drawing neatly;
- slower getting changed for games lessons.

Coping with other children's ridicule is an important issue of which parents and adults in school must be aware, as it not only damages the child's confidence but can also result in bullying and being ostracised. For example, the child may be among the last to be 'chosen' by classmates for the team in a competitive situation. However, it is perfectly possible for children struggling with dyspraxia to succeed in other areas of life, such as swimming or board games or IT (see Macintyre 2008 for other practical suggestions). The Dyspraxia Association (www.bdadyslexia.org.uk) provides classroom guidelines for schools and teachers, aimed at helping teachers to make classroom life more comfortable and productive for the affected pupils. Your role is to be well informed and practical as you quietly encourage and help the children. After all, they didn't choose to be uncoordinated, did they?

Hearing loss

Not all disabilities are chronic (persistent) ones; for instance, teachers need to be aware of the common condition known as 'glue ear', which adversely affects many children's hearing, howbeit temporarily. Many young children experience heavy catarrh, which leads to an intermittent hearing loss that can have an adverse effect on language development. The condition eases as the child grows older but the gaps in learning can remain, and the effects on further development are cumulative and need to be addressed by remedial work and offering one-to-one coaching where possible. Decongestants and the fitting of grommets (by means of a small operation) can alleviate the symptoms created by being 'blocked up' and allow the child full access to language, especially at the vital early stages when sound symbol correspondence is being cemented. Nevertheless, you should be on the lookout for children suffering intermittent hearing loss, urge parents to take medical action and ensure that the child, who might appear distant or confused, is able to understand the teaching that he or she is experiencing, especially in speaking and listening. It is tempting to label a child as a 'day-dreamer' or even as having symptoms of 'attention deficit' when the problem has a more straightforward explanation. No one expects you to be an amateur paramedic; it is simply a case of being alert to the possibility of hearing loss being a factor in a child's learning and behaviour.

Activate your thinking!

What labels have you heard used to describe children with SEN? Consider whether labels tell us more about the people using them, rather than those they purport to describe.

Segregation, integration or inclusive education?

Segregation

A key determinant of our success in educating children with special educational needs is our view about what should be done to enhance their learning, and whereabouts particular forms of intervention should be placed in the schooling process. The ideology behind segregation is that we are only responsible for children of 'normal' abilities, as defined by their intellectual capacity and physical capability, and that specialist teachers should take the residue (i.e. children deemed 'not normal') elsewhere, so that (the argument goes) teachers don't need to change their regular classroom practice to accommodate the 'misfits'. The flaws in this argument hardly require exploring, not least because defining the concept of 'normal' is highly problematic, but there are also both moral and legal obligations on schools to offer all pupils the best available education.

It can be argued that the concept of 'segregation' applies not only to separate schools designated as 'special', but also to a form of educational partitioning that can take place *within* mainstream schools by, for instance, the creation of special classes for the least able, groups permanently composed on ability lines and (notably) withdrawal from class for extra help on an ongoing basis through 'coaching' – often from a teaching assistant. However, there is a less visible form of segregation that occurs when an assistant is allocated to one pupil who is considered to need close tuition and sits with him or her, thereby accentuating the pupil's unique problems and possibly disempowering the child from becoming an independent learner.

All children have varying abilities in different areas, so even if they benefit from individual instruction in one area it does not mean that they should be excluded from the other wider class and social activities. Even where children value and benefit from separate treatment, there can be stigmas attached to being seen as different by other members of the class, many of which are subliminal. The practice of removal may give unhelpful messages to the children about their perceived low standing, with the resulting damage to their self-esteem and confidence. Of course, the opposite can also be true: the children feel special and privileged to be given exclusive attention. No doubt, some children are only too happy to leave the confines of the classroom for a time. Nevertheless, due to the factors outlined above and the staffing costs involved, there has been a move towards more integrative and inclusive practices, as described below.

Activate your thinking!

Try to imagine what it must feel like to be treated differently from most other children and lose touch with aspects of mainstream classroom life.

Now imagine what it feels like to have special and exclusive attention from an adult, whose sole aim is to help you improve academically.

Integration

Integration is the name originally given to the process whereby pupils who had been separated from mainstream education owing to their behaviour or physical disabilities were brought back into regular schooling, either moving from special to mainstream schooling, or by adopting class or group-based activities rather than individual 'remediation' in isolation. As a consequence, children with special needs were to be integrated or re-integrated into the heart of regular school life, but the nature of the school system remained largely unchanged. In other words, the basic assumptions about the distinctive curriculum, assessment methods and teaching for such pupils remained unaltered. The underlying purpose was seen as 'fitting' the child to the existing provision, not adjusting the provision according to the needs of the child.

As the school system had not been designed on the principles of inclusive assumptions, the practices it had developed over the period of segregation were not based on the particular needs of individuals. For instance, the buildings were often inaccessible to anyone who had mobility problems; the curriculum was inflexible; and the practices of grading made it inevitable that a certain percentage of children would experience stigmatising failure. It was probably optimistic to believe that the deleterious consequences of segregation could be alleviated by easing a few more disabled people into a system that was not designed with their special requirements in mind. From this point, however, educational policy started to move towards the principle of an *inclusive* system to meet all needs, though initially the practices that were used for integration continued, the concept merely being referred to as inclusion (see below).

Inclusive education

Inclusive education is best understood as an aim, aspiration or even a philosophy, rather than as a set of techniques that can be applied to a situation (such as in school). The school community is charged with offering education to all members of the community that it serves by modifying the way that all those involved work so that all needs are considered, such that practices that tended to exclude pupils are replaced by more inclusive practices (Hayward 2006). Moving in an inclusive direction entails a problem-solving exercise on behalf of all those involved. Jacklin, Griffiths and Robinson (2006) stress that the entitlement for all children to receive a rich and relevant education involves

> differentiated teaching, supporting and extending the least and most able pupils, and above all, setting high expectations and standards for all, irrespective of gender, ethnicity, race, disability or social background, are all part of the day to day role of a primary teacher.

(p. 78)

They admit that such demands are likely to overwhelm beginner teachers and recommend six strategies (see pp. 89–90 for the full details):

1. Remember the needs of all pupils, rather than a few individuals or groups.
2. Be aware of your own bias and preconceptions and do not allow them to interfere with your professional responsibilities.
3. Talk to and observe experienced teachers.
4. Draw on the expertise of specialist units or teachers in the school, as well as outside experts.
5. Work alongside TAs to help support learning.
6. Use your ongoing evaluations and assessment of children's learning to support your planning and teaching. (Modified list)

Activate your thinking!

What are the advantages and disadvantages attached to an inclusive system of education: (1) from the pupils' perspective; (2) from the teacher's perspective; (3) from the whole-class perspective?

The role of the teacher in addressing special educational needs

Principles

Three principles underpin the provision of effective learning opportunities for all children in school. The first is that teachers are required to set suitable challenges for all pupils, including less able and more able ones. The second is for teachers to respond to pupils' diverse needs by creating a productive learning environment ('climate'), offer all children an equal opportunity to access resources and participate in activities, assess their progress and set them suitable challenges. The third is for teachers, in conjunction with other colleagues where necessary, to combat potential barriers to learning for individuals and groups of pupils with disabilities and those for whom English is an additional language (EAL). Pupils for whom English is not a first language may learn to speak and write but not possess the cultural insights that make learning meaningful (Gregory 2008). Some children who struggle with English (including language-impoverished indigenous pupils for whom English is the first language) may excel in an area that does not depend as heavily on the written or spoken word, such as arithmetic ('numeracy'), drama or physical activity. Other children are not used to listening or simply cannot absorb what an adult says because of communication difficulties.

Code of Practice

The duties of schools and teachers are clearly laid out in the Code of Practice and the Special Needs and Disability Act. All schools should have copies of relevant documents, as well as a set of practical pamphlets on implementing the Code of Practice. The Code outlines the framework for identifying, assessing and making provision for children's special educational needs, though the actual assessment and teaching measures used are left for individual teachers and schools to develop. Whenever and wherever you work in a school it is essential to be aware of the identity and role of the special educational needs co-ordinator (SENCO), though note that school governors have statutory roles in constructing policy for special educational needs.

Hodkinson and Vickerman (2009) acknowledge that there are no 'hard and fast' categories of special educational needs, and that the wide spectrum of need is frequently interrelated. They point out, however, that the Code indicates that a child's needs and requirements are likely to fall into one or more of four areas, namely: (1) communication and interaction; (2) cognition and learning; (3) behaviour, emotional and social development; and (4) sensory and/or physical.

The SEN Code sets out a graduated approach to the identification and assessment of special needs and also the provision of suitable resources (including personnel). It makes clear that the Code is only concerned with interventions that are additional to or different from those provided as part of the school's usual differentiated curriculum and strategies. In other words, it should normally be possible to accommodate the range of pupil learning needs within the format of the regular lesson structure without triggering a request for additional intervention via the Code. Specifically focused and planned teaching, together with consistent discipline, should help to avoid unmanageable difficulties in learning from arising. Despite teachers' best efforts, however, it is likely that some children will experience difficulties that require extra or different kinds of support for learning. The Code describes two stages at which this more focused assessment and provision operate; these have been referred to as *School Action* and *School Action Plus*.

At the level of *School Action*, the teacher decides that the child appears to need additional support to help his or her progress (statistically, the child is likely to be a boy), following consultation with parents. The SENCO is then involved, and short-term support from outside agencies may be involved (see the section 'Every Child Matters', later in this chapter). Information about the child's academic progress is gathered, together with evidence collected about the interventions that have been previously tried. The information is recorded on the child's individual record, and an individual education plan (IEP) is produced laying out the plans for the next stage of the pupil's education.

School Action Plus involves a request for help from external services, and will normally follow a decision made by the SENCO and colleagues, in consultation with parents, after the evidence from a review of the IEP indicates that there is a need to consult specialists. A range of specialists might be approached, depending on the nature of the need, and a new IEP produced on the basis of their advice. As the IEP is reviewed and monitored, the school can request a statutory assessment from the local authority if the pupil is a significant cause for concern. This assessment process may lead to a formal statement of special educational needs that will specify the additional support required or, in some cases, a move to specialist provision from outside the school. At this stage it is necessary to define more specifically the nature of the child's special need. Note that, unlike previous forms of labelling (see earlier), the categories below focus on learning needs or a description of the physical limitation, and not an implied 'deficiency' in the person of the child. The suggested categories are as follows:

Cognition and learning needs

- Specific learning difficulty (SpLD)
- Moderate learning difficulty (MLD)
- Severe learning difficulty (SLD)

- Profound and multiple learning difficulty (PMLD)
- Behaviour, emotional and social difficulty (BESD).

Behaviour, emotional and social development needs

(A single category)

Communication and interaction needs

- Speech, language and communication needs (SLCN)
- Autistic spectrum disorder (ASD).

Sensory and/or physical needs

- Visual impairment (VI)
- Hearing impairment (HI)
- Multi-sensory impairment (MSI)
- Physical disability (PD).

Other (OTH)

Note that Chapter 7 of the Code of Practice goes into more detail about these categories and the resultant needs of the children.

Activate your thinking!

In early 2011, the government put forward proposals to scrap the two categories that cover the majority of children with special needs – *School Action* and *School Action Plus* – and replace them with a school-based scheme, aimed at raising pupil attainment. This policy change reflects concerns that the label of special educational needs can be applied too broadly, losing focus on those children with the greatest need. The system aims to address children's needs in a more integrated way, bringing together schools, health and social care.

Good practice

The SENCO's role has become one of the most important in the school but it is far from easy and involves a considerable amount of hard work and responsibility (see Edwards 2010; Cheminais 2010). Every colleague in such a position expects and deserves your full support and co-operation.

Edwards, S. (2010) *The SENCO Survival Guide*, London: David Fulton/NASEN.
Cheminais, R. (2010) *Rita Cheminais' Handbook for New SENCOs*, London: Sage.

Special educational needs and assessment

Appropriate assessment

There was a time when specialist teachers were equipped with a battery of tests and associated remedial programmes that were designed to identify and 'remediate' weaknesses in child's abilities through a diagnostic approach. The emphasis has now changed to looking at all children in terms of access to the curriculum, which is already assumed to be differentiated for a range of needs, and thereby open to a school's normal assessment procedures. Importantly, teachers look for strengths as well as weaknesses in pupils' work and attitude. They pay close attention to different ways in which learning can be enhanced, and monitor and celebrate progress at all levels. Importantly, teachers search for alternative learning strategies that are appropriate for the individual, rather than trying to remedy the child's perceived shortcomings by a 'quick-fix' solution. For instance, they might incorporate more visual and kinaesthetic ('hands-on') experiences into a lesson and reduce the number of words that the children have to read (see Chapter 9 under 'Personalised learning' for further details about VAK and VARK).

If the general assessment policy for all children can be used or adapted for every member of the class, the regular pattern of teaching and learning will provide the information that teachers require to assess the pupil's specific needs, rather than employing a formal test. Whichever method of assessment is employed, it can be used to inform the establishment of targets for groups of children of similar ability. This broad process provides a platform for the more fine-grained assessment that is needed to support the range of specific needs (see Figure 13.1). It is worth reflecting on the fact that assessments can only ever give an indication of a child's competence; tailor-made lessons that are intended to 'match' precisely the content, style and task with each pupil's ability and capability are unrealistic and result in untold complication.

Assessment and teaching approach

For children with special needs, therefore, trainees should monitor closely any strategies that have been tried by the host teachers and assistants, learning from them and giving careful consideration to the implications for your own practice. As a picture of the pupil's favoured learning styles and areas of particular difficulty is slowly constructed, you will begin to understand better what works for each child. Many children learn best through a visual or a kinaesthetic mode; others benefit from diagrams; yet others enjoy the medium of stories; of course,

1   REGULAR TEACHING provides *assessment information.*

2   ASSESSMENT INFORMATION generates *learning targets.*

3   LEARNING TARGETS are *monitored* by the teacher.

4   MONITORING provides *finer-grained assessment* information.

5   FINER-GRAINED ASSESSMENTS facilitate individualised support for pupils' learning needs.

FIGURE 13.1 Teaching assessment targets and individual needs

most pupils learn best from a combination of approaches. All teachers need first to take account of the preferred learning style or styles of the pupil, then to devise strategies that capitalise on his or her strengths. However, despite the apparent simplicity of this explanation, the reality is rarely as straightforward, not least because a proportion of children with learning needs also struggle with emotional disquiet, expressed as poor behaviour, inability to concentrate or low self-concept. Academic considerations are extremely important but form only part of the total picture.

Good practice

As far as possible, assessment should form part of the normal classroom experience.

Learning needs

The challenge of writing down

Some children become disenchanted with school, not because they find the curriculum uninteresting but because they are daunted by the demand to write everything down, when writing for them is a slow, exacting process. Of course, teachers must help every child to be more literate, but not at the expense of loss of motivation. There are many ways to evidence learning other than by individual children recording outcomes in written form without adult support. For example, evidence of children's learning can be provided through oral presentations, drawing, singing, drama, by contributing to group posters or presentations, or by having another child doing the writing task. (See also the use of story explored by Leicester and Johnson 2004.)

Writing is activated in the mind, so the process of physically writing things down, or scribing, is a separate (though closely related) activity. Thus, many famous authors have exciting ideas in their heads and choose to use audio technology and secretarial services, rather than writing manually to express what they want to say. Similarly, pupils with special educational needs can be encouraged to be writers if someone else (e.g. learning support assistant or classmate) assists with the act of writing. Drafting and editing discussions, where an adult or more capable pupil discusses with the individual ways to improve and enhance what has been accomplished so far, can be used to help the child shape and refine the writing. The process also gradually gives him or her more responsibility for the surface features of the work – such as punctuation and sentence construction – as well as content.

Stimulating interest

We noted earlier that it is depressing to witness children with SEN effectively being excluded from more stimulating elements of the work by being given repetitive, low-level tasks that do not engage the mind in the distinctive processes of the subject. For instance, investigative science is an area of the curriculum that fascinates children, where they enjoy the chance to observe, categorise, hypothesise and experiment. None of these processes necessarily involve writing, though recording in some form (e.g. a *pro forma*) is an important element of the process. Unfortunately, it is sometimes the case that children with SEN are denied involvement in these exciting opportunities, and are offered instead simplified worksheets, filling in gaps so that vocabulary can be learnt, and similar mundane tasks. In such cases, they are really only receiving extra English tuition, with the main subject providing the backdrop.

The same issue can be applied to other subjects such as history and geography, where the pupil needs first to be engaged with the processes and vocabulary of the subject. Only then should close attention be given to refining their recording skills. Crucially, it is vital to avoid subjecting children to a plethora of worksheets or exercises before they are offered the opportunity to do anything interesting; neither should they be sent off just to 'draw a picture of it' while their peers are engaged in genuine problem-solving activities.

Activate your thinking!

Children with special educational needs require stimulation, not stagnation.

Good practice

Always ensure that children with special learning needs have access to as many exciting opportunities to learn as every other member of the class.

Targets and the individual education plan

Establishing targets

We noted earlier that the individual education plan (IEP) is an important tool in meeting a child's learning needs. The precise content of the plan varies somewhat, but contains the following information:

- The short-term targets established for the child
- The most appropriate teaching strategies to be used
- The provision to be put in place (level of adult support, additional resources, etc.)
- When the plan is to be reviewed
- Success and/or exit criteria (i.e. ways in which the project is evaluated)
- Outcomes recorded when the IEP is reviewed.

The IEP should only record that which is additional to or different from the school's differentiated curriculum plan for all children. It should be crisply written and focus on three or four individual targets, chosen from those relating to the key areas of communication, literacy, mathematics and behaviour/social skills that match the child's needs. Crucially, the IEP must be discussed with the child and (ideally) the parents. There are three other factors associated with effective target setting of which teachers have to take account. First, targets that are too general are difficult to monitor because it is hard to know when they have been achieved. Second, targets that are too specific tend to narrow children's perspectives and lead to rote learning. Third, some targets focus on improved understanding, whereas others have more to do with mastery of specific knowledge. As with all learning, the more that children are involved in understanding and monitoring their own targets, the more likely it is that they will be attained.

It is important to realise that while the targets are individual in that they relate to a child's specific needs, this fact does not imply that they involve only individual, solitary tasks. Many effective targets outline strategies for including the pupil in collaborative or whole-class activities, especially where this has been a problem in the past.

Workable targets will be as precise as possible, such that the particular elements that the child has to concentrate on are capable of being defined, monitored and assessed. For example, if concentrating on spelling is identified as a target, there is little point in giving spellings for a test without offering advice about strategies for mastering them or using the words in sentences. When vague descriptors are used to define targets, such as 'improve spelling' or 'behave appropriately', there is little clue as to what the child should do specifically and it is extremely difficult to show that progress is being made. Under such conditions, target setting becomes a pointless ritual and makes little contribution to learning.

Targets for success

The number of targets should never exceed three or four and be achievable with reasonable effort. It is disheartening for a child to have a page of work returned with only suggestions for improvement written on it, and no positive feedback. Children are tempted to give up if they perceive that the task of meeting an adult's aspirations is beyond their capability. If, however, their attention is directed to specific, achievable targets, they can, with your support and assistance, find success and become more optimistic about their future chances of doing well. Too many children expend great energy and no little ingenuity in avoiding tasks because the fear of failure is too great. The secret is for you to engage them in progressively demanding experiences that facilitate success, while offering appropriate support, and creating a history of achievement, rather than compounding failure. At the same time it is essential to encourage a risk-taking climate and engender a belief in pupils that it is better to have made the effort and fallen short than never to have made the effort at all.

Teaching approaches and special needs

Starting points

Teaching children with special educational needs should be seen as a subset of good teaching for all pupils, not as a different kind of practice. It is helpful to remember that everyone finds difficulty in learning certain things at some level, but we can all make progress when the conditions are favourable and supportive. By the time children start school they have already shown themselves to be expert at learning, having absorbed more in their first five years than they will ever learn again. A typical school beginner has a vocabulary of more than 2,000 words and the speech of almost all 5-year-olds is intelligible, consisting of well-structured sentences and correct use of verb tense. However, between 10 and 20 per cent of children at this stage will have a speech or language difficulty (e.g. lisping) that may necessitate specialist support. The majority of 5-year-olds can write most or all of the letters of the alphabet and identify the sounds that correspond with many of them. Naturally, children will continue to learn things that are important and useful to them outside their school education. It is therefore more positive to view the child as a teaching challenge or potential success, rather than as someone with a 'learning difficulty'.

Flexibility in approach

Flexibility is a key factor in every form of teaching. If a child is finding difficulty in learning then it is wise to try a different approach, rather than repeating the same teaching more slowly (like a tourist attempting to order food in a foreign restaurant). Keys to flexibility include:

- A concentration on oral work
- Sustained meaningful talk through discussion
- Use of group and peer support (collaborative exercises)
- Use of a range of sources in providing evidence of learning (not merely written)
- A concentration on the processes of learning as they vary across subjects.

Most importantly it is always necessary to try to discern what meaning children are trying to make or express, rather than discounting their efforts as misunderstanding. Pupils' miscues can be very revealing and provide a starting point for building on their ideas rather than demolishing them and starting again. For instance, when setting out subtraction sums such as 45–27, then some children always subtract the smaller from the larger digit and will come up with the answer as 22 (4–2 = 2 and 7–5 = 2). The children concerned are clearly capable of subtracting but have either misunderstood the algorithm or have not developed a sense of place value. The perceptive teacher sees the incorrect answer as providing an opportunity to explore the child's lack of full understanding and not simply as something wrong that must be repeated. Some seemingly bizarre answers or contributions in class discussion often make perfect sense if you are willing to explore the meaning that the child is intending and identify gaps in knowledge or concepts that can be used as a basis for the next stage in the pupil's learning. Too often, however, a teacher already has the correct response in mind and quickly moves on to a child who can give the approved answer, thereby overlooking the opportunity that the original misconception has provided to deepen learning. The need for flexibility, either through providing different explanations using alternative means or exploring errors to pinpoint the problem, is particularly relevant in the case where a child has learning difficulties.

Activate your thinking!

Some children give inaccurate responses as a method of deflecting attention, as the teacher often dismisses the inadequate answer and moves quickly on to another pupil. How will you deal with such a situation?

Exploiting pupil expertise

The importance of oral work for children with special educational needs in a group or paired context cannot be overstated. McNamara and Moreton (2001) offer a very useful rationale and many examples of good practice in arguing that the best way to learn something is to have to teach it. Whenever possible, you should provide the children with the experience of being 'the expert' in at least one small area of the curriculum, as this is a powerfully affirming experience for a child used to being labelled a 'slow learner'. The most appropriate place to begin is with an area that interests the individual and to allow him or her to share informally with the group. For example, a child might have a hobby or interest, collect unusual items, have visited a strange place or met a celebrity. Some children are remarkably good at mimicking famous personalities, performing 'magic' tricks or acting out a scene. Yet others can share photographs from an event or holiday, bring in a mysterious object or talk about a favourite film, and so on. Make sure that classmates greet every contribution, however modest it might be, with enthusiasm.

Every Child Matters

Networking

A 'joined up' provision for children and young people up to the age of 19 years has its roots in the initiative *Every Child Matters: Change for Children* (ECM; DfES 2005), the aim of which is for all children, regardless of their background or circumstances, to be supported in staying healthy and safe, achieving success, making a positive contribution to society and given skills to understand and handle money as a step towards achieving economic wellbeing. As a result, the organisations involved in providing services to children (hospitals, schools, police, voluntary groups and so on) are, at least in principle, networked to share information and work together to protect and empower children and young people. The first Children's Commissioner for England was appointed in March 2005 to pay particular attention to gathering and promoting the views of those children and young people considered to be most vulnerable. Thus, *Every Child Matters* establishes five outcomes that matter most to children and young people:

1. Being healthy: enjoying good physical and mental health and living a healthy lifestyle.
2. Staying safe: being protected from harm and neglect.
3. Enjoying and achieving: getting the most out of life and developing the skills for adulthood.
4. Making a positive contribution: being involved with the community and not engaging in antisocial or offending behaviour.
5. Economic wellbeing: not being prevented by economic disadvantage from achieving their full potential in life.

While the vast majority of practitioners will view these aspirations as unexceptional and a reflection of what arises naturally in teaching, the ECM agenda is making the implicit ('instinctive beliefs') more explicit (demonstrated in practice). All teachers need to show that they are taking these issues seriously in at least three ways:

- Through the formal curriculum (what is taught)
- How they relate to pupils and encourage them to relate to others
- Their active engagement with non-education services.

The third bullet point is especially significant, in that in supporting children, and particularly those with special educational needs, you will inevitably have some contact with a range of other professionals. Learning to work co-operatively and take and give direction appropriately are essential skills that need to be developed. The key colleague is almost certain to be the SENCO, so it is vital that you liaise about the additional help for children and practitioners (Cheminais 2005). Some schools have appointed a person with special responsibility for implementing the ECM requirements.

Support services

Most local authorities have a range of advisory teachers that are available for help and advice. These include specialists in teaching the hearing impaired, visually impaired and other areas of learning difficulty, behaviour support teams, a range of para-professionals such as speech therapists and physiotherapists, social workers, educational welfare officers and medical services. As more multi-agency work is being encouraged, teachers have to be aware of the range of available services in the area. Trainee teachers are unlikely to have direct dealings with these service providers, but it is your responsibility to be alert to their existence and identify ways in which they are able to help you.

Outside the immediate professional domain you might need to liaise with parents and members of the community who volunteer their services. If you are new to the school it is essential to find out how the system operates and to be clear about what specific support you would like parents to give. Parents' evenings are a useful occasion to make suggestions about helpful and unhelpful methods of supporting a child, during which it is better to concentrate on strategies to support learning (such as the value of reading aloud to the child) than suggestions about discipline strategies. Nevertheless, as Knowles (2006) rightly argues:

> If ECM is going to have a positive impact on children's lives, the key to its success is the realisation of the duty on children's services' agents to co-operate and work constructively with families ... [and] ... acknowledge the importance of seeing the child and his/her family in a holistic manner and work within a framework of joint understanding.
>
> (p. 45)

See Chapter 5 for more information about working with other adults.

Cross-reference: Guided Reader Extract 30

In conclusion, it is possible and desirable for all teachers to develop their teaching to be more accessible and inclusive. Perhaps the pupils who find the greatest difficulty in learning can also be teachers' best critics, indicating the areas in which they need to be clearer or more flexible in approach. If you make learning easier for those experiencing the greatest difficulty, there is a strong likelihood that you will improve it for every child in your class.

Further reading for Chapter 13

Cheminais, R. (2001) *Developing Inclusive School Practice: A practical guide*, London: David Fulton.
An easy-to-follow guide, clearly presented and imaginatively structured.
Cheminais, R. (2010) *Rita Cheminais' Handbook for New SENCOs*, London: Sage.
The book is targeted at SENCOs who are new to their role and participating in the National SEN Coordination Award programme supported by the TDA.
Crosse, K. (2008) *Introducing English as an Additional Language to Young Children*, London: Sage.
Helps teachers to develop the confidence in meeting the individual needs of young children with English as an additional language.
Glazzard, J., Hughes, A., Netherwood, A., Neve, L. and Stokoe, J. (2010) *Teaching Primary Special Educational Needs*, Exeter: Learning Matters.
The authors explain the SEN Code of Conduct and provide detailed guidance on individual education plans (IEPs).
Hall, W. (2009) *Dyslexia in the Primary Classroom*, Exeter: Learning Matters.
Hall's book contains numerous suggestions for teachers about implementing strategies in the classroom and school.

Hannell, G. (2004) *Dyslexia Action Plans for Successful Learning*, Minnetonka, MN: Peytral Publications.

The author covers a wide range of areas, including learning letters and sounds; reading, recognising commonly used words; phonics; reading comprehension; visual tracking; language skills; spelling; written language; proofreading; handwriting; letter and number reversal; spatial awareness and mathematics.

Spooner, W. (2010) *The SEN Handbook for Trainee Teachers, NQTs and Teaching Assistants*, second edition, London: David Fulton/Nasen.

Spooner grapples with a variety of key issues through the use of vignettes and case studies to illuminate appropriate strategies when working with children struggling with special learning needs.

Part 5

Qualified Status

14

The Induction Year

Introduction

You've made it! Congratulations! All the hard work has paid off and now you are a qualified teacher, ready to take charge of your own class. All newly qualified teachers are required to serve an induction year, which was introduced to provide a solid basis for professional and career development. At its best, induction helps new teachers to show their potential, make steady progress in becoming effective practitioners and make a positive impact on the school's overall development and, in particular, the education of the children for whom you have responsibility. This chapter contains advice about achieving these goals.

Getting the job

Making the application

You saw the job advertised and made your application. When the governors received your form, they probably knew nothing about you unless you taught there during a school experience placement, so the form was initially their only source of evidence. They were persuaded that you were someone worth considering further, so they followed up one or more of your referees. Eventually they decided to put you on a 'short list' and invite you for a more formal interview (though the degree of formality varies considerably from school to school). In doing so, the head teacher and governors were asking five basic questions about the candidates:

1. Can this person handle a class competently? (That is, can this person not only teach well but also maintain class order?)
2. Will this person fit into our staff team? (Is she or he reasonable, pleasant, honest, sympathetic?)
3. How will parents react to this person? (Is she or he approachable, a good communicator, understanding of parental concerns?)
4. Will this person help to raise standards of academic achievement, especially in core subjects? (Will she or he ensure that pupils make good quantifiable progress?)
5. Has this person got a creative and innovative streak to inspire children, encourage colleagues and enliven the school environment?

They saw from your initial application that you were someone who might fit the bill, especially with regard to the first four points noted above. You were invited to look around the school and sensibly kept a low profile, while staying alert and picking up clues about the school's priorities. Before the formal interview, you will have written down some likely questions that the panel might ask you and recorded your answers. See Figure 14.1 for examples of questions. You were horrified how hesitant you sounded (everyone has a similar reaction to the sound of their own voice) but it gave you time to think through and clarify your beliefs prior to the interview, such that you had your answers reasonably well formulated.

The interview

During interview the panel expected you to be passionate about your desire to teach in *their* school (not just any old school). Your letter of application was further scrutinised, your references studied closely, and your response to a series of probing questions satisfied them that you were the person for the job. Perhaps you were asked questions such as:

- How will you organise for learning in literacy to differentiate for the ability range?
- What do you understand by personalising learning and its application to teaching?
- How will you organise your room and what will it tell us about your teaching?
- What sort of things will you do to promote children's thinking skills?
- How will you ensure that gifted and talented children achieve their potential?
- Can you give us some examples of how you use assessment for learning?
- Can you describe for us the sorts of contributions that you can make to the school's work in your specialist curriculum area?
- What skills and qualities can you bring to the existing staff team?
- What sort of things will you do to promote an effective working relationship with parents?
- How will you know that you are succeeding in raising standards?

Of course, you might have been asked a completely different set of questions or they might have been phrased differently – that it why it is so important to do plenty of research beforehand and talk to anyone who has recently been interviewed as to the nature of the questions. During your interview, you were probably not confident with every answer and did not try to pretend that you knew something if you were uncertain. However, you did your best to be honest, upbeat, cheerful but not unnatural, relaxed but alert. You listened carefully to the questions and thought briefly before you responded. You were positive but tempered it by stressing that you wanted to continue learning throughout your career and do well for the children. You did not raise dilemmas or problematic issues or admit to misgivings about aspects of the job that you secretly held. You were aware of the school's hope to appoint someone with expertise in a named subject area, so had thought long and hard about ways in which you would enthuse colleagues and bring them on board, rather than burdening or patronising them. Finally, despite your nerves and uncertainty about some of the tougher questions put to you, a combination of your bright personality and confident responses reassured the head and governors that you were an excellent prospect and convinced them that you were the best person for the job. Well done! Now the fun begins!

How would you respond to the following interview questions? Consider possible follow-up questions that the panel might ask you.

Professional requirements
What makes a good teacher and how do you know you are one?
What sort of classroom learning climate will you try to promote and how will you go about doing so?

Teaching and learning
How do you motivate children to learn, especially reluctant ones?
How do you go about setting high expectations for the full range of ability while taking account of individual differences?

Adult relationships
How will you lead and assist colleagues who are unsure about your specialist subject area? (Note! It is fairly common for the panel to ask specifically how you, as a younger person, will work with older colleagues, some of whom might be resistant to change.)
What practical steps will you take to involve parents in their children's learning?

Self-development
How will you know if you are succeeding as a teacher?
What sort of professional training will help you to progress as a teacher?

Preparation and planning
How do you plan and organise your literacy lessons?
How do you go about linking learning objectives with assessment criteria?

Purposeful teaching
How do you keep your teaching fresh and full of vitality?
Give us some examples from your time in school of your creative teaching.

Special needs
How do you envisage an 'inclusion' policy operating in your classroom?
How do you differentiate lessons to accommodate faster and slower learners?

Organising and managing
Teachers are busy people. How do you prioritise your time and workload?
Tell us about your work with teaching assistants. What have you found to be the most important factors in establishing an effective relationship?

Behaviour and discipline
Describe the way that you ensure that children are well disciplined without being crushed in spirit.
What sorts of rewards do you believe are appropriate for this age group?

Extended professionalism
Tell us something about the duties of a teacher other than teaching. What activities have you been involved in outside the classroom?
Apart from the formal parents' evening, how will you ensure that parents are kept informed about their children's progress?

Assessment
How do you implement 'assessment for learning' in your regular teaching?
How will you use pupil assessment to improve teaching and learning?

Equal opportunities
What steps will you take to ensure that all children have a fair chance to succeed?
What practical steps will you take to ensure that children with English as another language are clear about your expectations for behaviour and the quality of their work?

FIGURE 14.1 Possible interview questions

Activate your thinking!

Kizlik (2008) offers a range of advice about the sorts of things that new teachers should pay heed to when they are interviewed, including:

- dressing appropriately to make a good first impression, as choice of clothing tells a lot about the person;
- pronouncing words correctly, speaking at a sensible rate (not too fast) and avoiding the ubiquitous '*like*' as a form of punctuation;
- bringing a well-organised portfolio that documents classroom work, having carefully checked all spelling and grammar;
- being sure of what they believe about education and why they believe it;
- having appropriate samples of technology skills, such as graphic designs, presentation software and word-processing available for scrutiny if requested by the panel;
- conveying a sense of mastery of subject content and its place in the curriculum;
- having a discipline/classroom management system and being ready to justify it;
- speaking clearly and directly, looking panel members in the eyes, asking relevant questions to clarify points (if necessary) and thanking them for the opportunity to be interviewed.

Kizlik, B. (2008) *Things to Say and Do at that First Teaching Interview*, ADPRIMA, online at www.adprima.com/interview.htm.

Good practice

Ask some friends or a tutor or a helpful teacher to conduct a mock interview with you. Take it as seriously as possible. Ask them to press you fairly hard about a range of classroom issues. Perhaps they can use some of the suggested interview questions in this section as a guide.

Making the transition

Becoming a real teacher

It takes time to change from being a student to being a 'real' teacher. Newcomers have to adjust quickly to the community, get to know people, routines and procedures, appreciate the ethos of the school and understand protocol. Breaking into the professional circle can be forbidding and requires a blend of tact and assertion. You have been a trainee teacher but suddenly, like a chrysalis turning into a butterfly, you grow your wings and become a fully fledged teacher 'overnight'. If you don't feel like one and wonder if it can really be true, don't be alarmed. Most newly qualified teachers (NQTs) wonder how they are ever going to survive and whether they have got what it takes to make a success of the job. It is not uncommon to experience a sharp decline in confidence following the end of your training course and, though you wonder at yourself for feeling this way, to half-wish that you could be a student again with all the protection it afforded. When you were training, the children in your teaching experience schools asked you the same question at the start of every new placement: 'Are you a real teacher?' You hardly knew how to reply but probably ended up by sounding a little indignant and replying that *of course* you were a real teacher (but not feeling like one at all). You longed for the day when you could answer the question honestly, but now that the day has arrived you still find yourself wondering if it is really true. Excitement and terror circulate your mind and heart like an unholy alliance of boiling hot oil and freezing cold water.

Anxieties felt by new teachers

Other anxieties may begin to emerge. What if a parent asks if this is your first class? What if colleagues begin to probe your subject knowledge, classroom management expertise and understanding of assessment and reporting procedures? In fact, what if someone begins to expose all the sorts of things that troubled you as a student, but that you successfully concealed from the tutor? In short, what if you are found out! Mild panic might set in as you realise that you know absolutely *nothing* about teaching, you don't know why on earth it ever occurred to you to do the job, and you wonder why you didn't take your friend's advice and backpack around the globe instead. 'Too late now!' you lament. Bubb (2007) notes that the confidence of new teachers is initially high but gradually reduces, as the realities of the job hit home and energy levels dip. She suggests that by the end of the first term, confidence reaches its lowest point but then begins to move up sharply during the remainder of the year. Jacklin *et al.* (2006) refer to the study they conducted, in which newly qualified teachers all admitted to the swing of emotions they experienced during the first term in particular. Thus:

> At times they felt confident, excited, enthusiastic and part of a team within the school. At other times they felt anxious, isolated and worried about their own and their pupils' progress ... They told us that often they felt as if they should know the answers and were concerned that others would see their questions as trivial.
>
> (p. 29)

It is worth noting from the above research that the swinging emotions were present in beginner teachers regardless of the level of support they were receiving in the school; so you are not alone. If you are feeling this way, you can be reassured that the anxieties will gradually subside. Although some parents may ask if this is your first class, and colleagues will chat about aspects of school life and how to cope with it, they rarely do so with ill intent. In fact, parents often like their children to have new teachers in the belief that they will introduce fresh ideas and sparkle to the teaching and learning environment. Many colleagues are hoping to get some useful suggestions from you to use in their own lessons. The arrival of this talented young star (you) is eagerly awaited, so make sure you don't do or say too much at the start that reveals your insecurities and damages your image. On the other hand, it is instructive that research by Day *et al.* (2007) suggests that 'teachers do not necessarily become more effective as they grow older ... teachers in their early professional life phases ... are more likely to be effective than their counterparts in the middle and later professional life phases' (p. 256). Although these conclusions must be treated with a degree of caution, they should provide reassurance that 'inexperience' does not necessarily equate to 'ineffective'.

Gaining confidence

To a certain extent, the nervous tension that rises from the pit of your stomach towards the end of the holiday period will be a feature throughout your career. If you ask experienced teachers about the few days leading up to the start of a new term, they will confess that it is a miserable time as doubts about their own ability to cope with the demands of the job surface and uncertainty hangs over them like a damp fog. Once they are back in school and the new term begins, the tension evaporates in the fever pitch of meeting the children, organising lessons, relating to colleagues and parents, re-establishing their credentials as a teacher to be reckoned with and reminding themselves that they have not, after all, lost their ability to thrive and prosper in teaching. So don't be surprised if you have similar sorts of worries before the start of every term and equally powerful feelings of reassurance once it begins.

New challenges

Being a qualified teacher carries many advantages over being a trainee teacher. For a start, you will not have a tutor observing your lessons, though you will not be spared this ordeal entirely as there will be occasions when a senior colleague comes to watch you teach (probably once or twice per term; peer observation is also common in schools). However, you will be able to discuss issues on an equal footing rather than feeling at the mercy of the university assessment system. Second, in the earlier stages of the school year there are far fewer forms to complete, though as the year unfolds there will be a lot of recording and report-writing to do. Third, there will not be any need to write screeds of self-analysis about how you might have improved your lesson or what went wrong during the session (although it is worth keeping a diary about important issues that emerge throughout the year).

The most notable advantage about leaving student days behind is being able to relish the freedom you gain from knowing that you are no longer dealing with somebody else's class and will not, after a period of some weeks, have to hand the children over to the regular teacher again and trudge wearily back to college for more lectures. Now you have an opportunity to show what you are made of. Gradually, however, other aspects of the job will emerge that you might or might not be expecting. The rest of this chapter is designed to help you anticipate some of those challenges, deal with them effectively and play your part in providing the sort of education that you would want for your own children, were they in your class.

Requirements during the first year of teaching

Developing expertise

As part of teachers' continued professional development, each is allocated a fellow staff member to be a mentor (induction tutor) who will help the NQT to negotiate his or her first year. The induction tutor offers advice about many aspects of school life, such as time management, handling paperwork, dealing with troublesome children, relating to parents and maintaining a reasonable work/leisure balance. By the end of their induction year, all new teachers must have demonstrated their mastery of the qualified teacher status (QTS) standards on a consistent and sustained basis, while teaching continuously in a school, with the direct and personal responsibility and accountability for pupil performance that accompanies it. They must also have shown that they have built on, and progressed beyond, the QTS standards in key areas such as managing pupil behaviour and contributing to pupils' learning, and to the planning and achievement of their school's performance targets.

Induction standards

The induction standards for newly qualified teachers consist of six categories that are intended to build on the standards for QTS and must be 'achieved' by the end of your induction, with the emphasis on 'end'. Thus:

> *Induction standard (a) Professional values and practice* Seek and use opportunities to work collaboratively with colleagues to raise standards by sharing effective practice in the school.
>
> *Induction standard (b) Knowledge and understanding* Show a commitment to their professional development by identifying areas in which they need to improve their professional knowledge, understanding and practice in order to teach more effectively in their current post and taking steps to address these needs (with support).
>
> *Induction standard (c) Teaching: special educational needs* Plan effectively to meet the needs of pupils in their classes with special educational needs, with or without statements, and in consultation with the SENCO contribute to the preparation, implementation, monitoring and review of individual education plans (IEPs) or the equivalent.
>
> *Induction standard (d) Teaching: liaising with parents and carers* Liaise effectively with parents or carers on pupils' progress and achievements.
>
> *Induction standard (e) Teaching: working as part of a team* Work effectively as part of a team and, as appropriate to the post in which they are completing induction, liaise with, deploy and guide the work of other adults who support pupils' learning.
>
> *Induction standard (f) Teaching: securing appropriate behaviour* Secure a standard of behaviour that enables pupils to learn, and act to pre-empt and deal with inappropriate behaviour in the context of the behaviour policy of the school.

Schools are expected to provide new teachers with the support they need in order to demonstrate that they are meeting the standards. NQTs need to take account of the induction standards when they meet with their induction tutors as they establish objectives and plan professional development opportunities. NQTs should not simply 'tick off' standards as achieved too early in the induction year but rather see each standard or part of a standard well established over a period of time before recording it as being 'achieved'. In fact, a careful look at the induction standards (above) shows that it is far more difficult to fail to reach them than to succeed. In practice, the vast majority of new teachers are successful; in the extremely rare case where there are problems (unless it is inappropriate professional conduct) there is normally opportunity to redeem the situation. It is, of course, important to view the induction year as an exciting opportunity to build upon your existing professional expertise with the help and support of more experienced colleagues, and not a depressing re-run of the fearsome pressures that you felt during your training. Jacklin *et al.* (2006) offer wise advice in this regard. Thus:

> Remember that the purpose of engaging in professional development is to improve your understanding, knowledge and skills, to develop your practice and its impact on pupil learning. Think small, be focused, work with colleagues and enjoy it.
>
> (p. 167)

Over time, the precise wording of the standards changes but the principles embodies within them remain unaltered and can be summarised as follows: (1) be professional; (2) know your stuff; (3) cater for every child's needs; (4) liaise with other adults; (5) work as part of a team;

(6) maintain classroom discipline. These attributes take only seconds to write down but months and years of perseverance to get right. Gear up for the long haul, but in the meantime, try to enjoy the journey.

Activate your thinking!

You are not expected to be teacher of the year within the first twelve months but it's good to show that one day you could be!

Completing the induction year

The induction ('probationary') year can be served in any maintained school that has been granted the right to do so. Naturally, if the school is unusual for any reason (e.g. an overseas establishment) you should first check with the national regulating authority before proceeding. There are a number of specified exceptions, where it is not permitted for a newly qualified teacher hoping to gain full professional accreditation to serve all or part of the year, including:

- Pupil referral units
- Secure training centres
- Schools requiring special measures, unless one of Her Majesty's Inspectors certifies in writing that the school is suitable for providing induction
- Independent schools that do not meet specified criteria
- Further education colleges, unless it is a sixth-form college
- Independent nursery schools and other early years settings that do not meet the criteria described in the section on independent schools above
- British schools abroad, though there are a number of exceptions.

In particular, if you are interested in working in an independent school (including those abroad), it is essential to check that the school is approved to run an induction programme. Normally, NQTs will start their induction year as soon as they leave training college and commence their first permanent teaching post. Those who only manage to acquire a temporary post lasting less than one year can build up to a total of one year in different schools. For instance, an NQT might find employment in three separate schools, each lasting one term, or work for two terms in one school and a term in a second school. In unusual circumstances such as lengthy sick leave or maternity leave, the induction process can be extended beyond the one year until the equivalent amount of time has been served.

If an NQT has been absent from work for thirty school days or more during the induction period, the induction period is extended by the aggregate total of absences. For example, if they are absent for a total of thirty-five days, the extension will be for that length of time. If a female NQT has a break in the induction which includes statutory maternity leave, she may choose whether or not to have the induction extended by the equivalent of the part of her absence which was statutory maternity leave. A final decision is normally made by the NQT when she returns to work and has given the matter careful thought, but any such request has to be considered by school governors. However, if an NQT chooses not to extend her induction period following an absence of maternity leave she is still assessed on the same basis as any other NQT. Note that conditions vary slightly between England and other parts of the UK.

Receiving support during the year

NQTs are entitled to receive support from the head teacher, induction tutor and colleagues, and must reach clearly defined standards in their classroom practice and wider professional conduct as staff members (Cole 2002, see also above). The induction tutor might be a senior teacher (in a larger school) and the deputy head or experienced teacher (in a smaller school). In addition to providing regular advice about aspects of the teacher role, the tutor will encourage you to contribute to curriculum working parties, act as a guide in visiting other local schools (including a special school) to enhance your knowledge and experience of education, and facilitate your initial liaison with the SENCO. In the unlikely event that you are offered any choice in selecting the tutor, note that Jonson (2008) emphasises that a tutor must possess high quality mentoring skills, such as demonstration teaching, positive observation and feedback, informal communication, role modelling and providing direct assistance.

Conditions of service

The school's responsibility

The induction year is intended to provide NQTs with a bridge from initial teacher training to effective professional practice. Conditions of service include the provision of well-targeted monitoring and support, a reduced timetable (even taking account of planning, preparation and assessment time), and help nurturing an ethos of continuing professional development (CPD) and career development. NQTs will not normally be expected to cope with excessive demands by (say) having responsibility for a very large class or a group of particularly difficult pupils. They should teach for only about 90 per cent of the time to give them opportunity to gain wider experience by working alongside a colleague, visiting other classes and local schools, and attending in-service courses. The school normally accedes to these conditions, though there are occasions when you might find slight deviations from the norm; for instance, a class could contain more than thirty pupils, or children with serious behaviour problems and/or learning difficulties. These rare circumstances can also occur in smaller schools where there is little flexibility over class rotation.

Liaison with colleagues

Establishing and maintaining contact with other new teachers in the area is also essential, as it is easy for NQTs to become isolated in their first post and imagine that they are the only teacher in the world struggling with discipline and keeping pace with the relentless demands that teaching sometimes imposes. As Cockburn (1996) realistically acknowledges:

> Whether you are an experienced teacher or new to the profession, starting a new job is often an exhilarating, challenging and daunting experience rolled into one.
>
> (p. 27)

Part of your development as a teacher is learning to work closely with and alongside colleagues, accept majority decisions and strive to operate within the agreed guidelines and policies. You will not be comfortable with everything that is taking place when you arrive at the school or all the subsequent decisions. Some aspects of school life will irritate you. Some colleagues will disappoint you. Some procedures will appear unnecessary or irksome.

Although you are entitled to ask for explanations about why things are done in certain ways, it is important to understand that every new teacher has to learn to fit into the school situation as it exists and accommodate its vagaries. A willingness to accept the existing norms is not to say that with the help of your influence certain aspects might change or be modified over time, but the best forms of change come slowly and, however convinced you may be that you know best, it is wise to listen, watch and wait before passing judgement. Your contributions to debate will be valued and respected if you express them with humility and a genuine willingness to learn. As the old saying goes, fools rush in where angels fear to tread.

As a qualified teacher you are expected to contribute towards the whole school endeavour. As a newly qualified person, you might not believe that you have much to offer your colleagues, but this is untrue. Other teachers and ancillary staff, while anxious that you settle in quickly and do well in your job, also hope that you will play your part in being an effective team member. Head teachers want teachers that help to raise morale, work well with colleagues and parents, and provide a positive role model.

Succeeding in your induction year

Be positive

You will have worked very hard to gain QTS and been looking forward with eager anticipation to the day when you have responsibility for your own class. In the light of all the effort you have made to reach this point, the induction year can give the appearance of being yet another hurdle to surmount. However, it is important to view the year as part of the support mechanism available to new teachers, without which you would be less equipped to deal with the rigours of teaching. As you may have noted above, the induction year standards are not dissimilar to those for qualified teacher status. Basically, you need to be able to demonstrate your competence in planning, teaching, class management, monitoring, assessing, recording and reporting, though there is greater emphasis for you to take account of the needs of individual children and ensure that every child is catered for (see Chapter 13). There are also expectations with respect to deploying and working with other adults (including parents), implementing school policies (such as dealing with bullying and racial harassment) and taking responsibility for your professional development.

Success in the induction year is much less a case of whether or not you will pass (as almost everyone does) but of how much progress you make as a teacher during that time. If you end the year feeling more confident about the job and your ability to thrive, then the year has been a success. Remember that the induction year is only the first of many years that you will spend as a teacher, so see your progress in the longer term, rather than 'surviving' to the end of next term (Holmes 2004; Bubb 2009).

Work well with others

Active and enthusiastic collaboration is at the heart of effective schools, so make it your aim to get on well with everyone, including non-teaching staff, and maintain a positive attitude towards life. You do not have to go around the school with a permanent grin on your face, of course. A pleasant smile and responsive manner is quite sufficient to convince those around you that you are worth all the effort they expend on your behalf. Similarly, the respect that you display towards other adults working in the school will help to seal your reputation as a person of integrity. As we noted earlier in this book, positive attitudes are contagious; they not only affect the quality of interpersonal relationships with colleagues but also have an impact upon the teaching and learning environment.

Effective schools are also places where teamwork and staff loyalty are embedded into the fabric. Being a teacher, like most other jobs, is as much about corporate endeavour and teamwork as the technical ability to teach. Once you enter a school, you have a responsibility to a range of different groups: children, parents, governors, members of the community and your colleagues. Even if you are a novice teacher, you must still demonstrate a willingness to support other teachers and trainee teachers in their efforts to improve their practice and contribute to the children's education. Genuine comments to members of staff expressing your appreciation for their help and the way that you value their guidance will greatly encourage them. Similarly, the caring way in which you react to colleagues, especially when they need someone to talk to about important issues, will create enormous goodwill and strong feelings of camaraderie that are essential for effective teamwork. Commitment to fellow workers goes beyond sitting and listening while they sound off their complaints; it involves being willing to act for your colleagues in practical and active ways whenever possible. Strive to become the sort of teacher that *you* would hope to see in a colleague.

Safeguard reflective practice

As a trainee teacher, you were almost certainly encouraged by your tutors to become a 'reflective practitioner', by which they meant to think deeply and carefully about the rationale underpinning aspects of your teaching. One of the earliest proponents of the concept of reflection was John Dewey (1859–1952), later followed by Donald Schön and, more recently, Andrew Pollard (e.g. Pollard 2008). Reflection is not to be confused with fantasising or daydreaming – though there may be a small place for both if they serve to expand your thinking and relieve the tension. Some educationists prefer the concept of 'professional learning', which indicates that the reflecting is not carried out as a form of mental gymnastics but, rather, a means of understanding the work of the teacher and its implications for your own and your pupils' understanding. In short, it is to give serious consideration to the advice offered by others and evaluate its validity and appropriateness, rather than accepting it uncritically.

Despite the fact that 'reflection' is normally used as a noun (the reflection) it can also be viewed in the form of an adverbial clause (i.e. behaving reflectively). That is, an intelligent consideration of existing practice should be a continuous process (reflecting *during* practice) as well as a later event (reflecting *on* practice). The principal benefit attached to reflecting during and on practice is that it is a contributing factor towards teaching effectiveness. It is also an antidote to an instrumental (clinical/technicist) view of improvement. Pollard (2005) asserts that 'novice teachers such as those in initial teacher training may use reflection to improve on specific and immediate practical skills' (p. 12).

A study by Chetkuti *et al.* (2011) appears to confirm the view that for novice teachers, the purpose of reflection remains an individualistic objective to solve classroom dilemmas, rather than as a contribution to wider professional knowledge. All the teachers interviewed in the study asserted that they continued to reflect during their first year of teaching, howbeit in most cases in an informal rather than systematic manner. Nevertheless, their reflection was limited to their immediate environment rather than encompassing the social and cultural environment in which they were teaching.

Cross-reference: Guided Reader Extract 39

Peer coaching

Peer coaching is a system in which colleagues of similar professional status work together supportively to develop personally and professionally as a means of strengthening less well-developed areas of knowledge and expertise, and enhancing stronger ones. Typically, two teachers meet together regularly to share ideas, discuss current issues and refine identified aspects of their practice. The relationship between participants is built on confidentiality and trust within a relaxed and secure environment; consequently, peer coaching should not form part of any appraisal scheme or evaluation of competence.

Areas of classroom practice under scrutiny are likely to include the following: organisation and management of learning; teaching effectiveness; control and discipline; and assessment of pupil achievement. Peer coaching helps colleagues to develop a shared vocabulary and gain insights into issues that might otherwise be kept private. Peer *review* differs from peer coaching in that it involves a more experienced or knowledgeable teacher (in a specified subject or technique) being linked with a less experienced colleague or one who will benefit from the colleague's expertise. Commonly, issues, principles and strategies that emerge from the detailed analysis and sharing of information between two or three members of staff are, subsequently, more widely disseminated within the school.

Your willingness to be involved in self- and peer-evaluation of practice forms the foundation upon which you can play an important role in promoting reflection in your pupils by using a variety of open-ended and speculative questions (see Chapter 9) that cause children to think, analyse, reflect, make suggestions and offer alternative perspectives. A regulated curriculum and objectives-driven lessons, policed through national testing, have the potential to create a generation of children that feel disengaged from learning as they fail to see its relevance for their lives. By contrast, an open-minded attitude towards learning from every available source is more likely to result in deep and committed learning.

Activate your thinking!

Donald Schön introduced innovative ideas about concepts such as 'the learning society', 'double-loop learning', 'reflection-in-action' and 'reflection-on-action', much of which has significantly influenced education practice.

Getting on well with the head teacher

You will probably have quite a lot of contact with the head teacher during your early days in school as a qualified teacher. Many head teachers make a special point of nursing new members of staff through their first few weeks in the job rather than leaving it all to the induction tutor. Others believe that it is better to stay at a distance and allow new teachers to make their mistakes in private. Although head teachers tend to be extremely busy at the start of term and may seem a bit distracted, you should not misinterpret this as unfriendliness. Over time, you will discover that heads are under a lot of pressure to achieve high standards of education in the school, though many of their struggles take place behind closed doors as they liaise and meet with a variety of interested parties and fight to ensure that the school receives its proper share of resources. It might appear to you that a head is a free agent, who can make autonomous decisions without regard to what others think; in fact, heads are obliged to seek the views of parents and discuss with governors any significant changes they are hoping to make in the school.

Head teachers have normally spent many years in school and cannot be fooled by a jaunty remark and artificial smile, but they appreciate those who have the courtesy and maturity to make good eye contact and speak out clearly. If at some point in the future you apply for a post in another school, you will need to put the head teacher as one of your referees; as heads talk to one another regularly, there is a strong chance that your reputation will reach the ears of other local head teachers. You can be sure that whether the head is highly personable or somewhat aloof, you are rarely off his or her mind when you first arrive in school.

The head might decide to observe you teaching once or twice during the year, and although the prospect of this event might cause you to tremble, remember that heads are obliged to monitor staff progress and they are keen for you to succeed, not to flounder. In turn, head teachers also need encouragement, too, so don't be slow in conveying your thanks for their support.

Activate your thinking!

How true are the following? (1) I am displaying a willing, enthusiastic approach to the job; (2) I am doing my best to value those around me; and (3) I am making the best of those things that irritate me.

Good practice

When speaking to the head, always remember that she or he is committing an immense amount of time and energy to making the school successful, so be sensitive about making unguarded remarks that might be interpreted as criticism.

Contributing expertise

School-wide influence

Every teacher has some special skill or ability that may be useful for the common good and benefit colleagues and children. Learning to learn from one another is something that every school has recognised as important and taking responsibility for your own professional development is an important element of your role (see Chapter 16). NQTs are sometimes appointed on the understanding that they will try to contribute curriculum strengths as a co-ordinator, leader or even as a curriculum manager throughout the school. However, this additional responsibility can be difficult for even the most experienced teachers and places heavy demands upon an already busy person (Farmery 2004). There is always so much to do and think about in school life that finding the time and opportunity to work as a subject specialist alongside colleagues, advise them about possibilities for developing a curriculum area or occasionally take their class for the subject, is far from easy.

All schools have a development programme in which subjects and topics are examined systematically, which gives teachers responsible for that area the opportunity to share and to exercise leadership during the discussions. You might be asked to provide a draft policy statement, guidelines or a review of the existing situation. The extra responsibility for curriculum development or an aspect of learning (such as assessment and recording) has to be fitted alongside your other teaching duties. Few schools have the resources to give teachers much time to pursue these responsibilities during the school day, though with the restructuring of the workforce it can be possible to free some time through use of experienced TAs to oversee the class while you are absent on these other subject-related duties.

Contributing at staff meetings

As part of team membership, all teachers have to attend staff meetings. Full meetings are normally held once a week, though additional team planning meetings and age-phase meetings commonly occur on a fortnightly basis. Attendance at meetings can become burdensome and all teachers have to make allowance for the time and energy they consume. It can be a bit galling to attend a meeting when you are desperate to mark books, organise equipment or complete some records, but you simply have to accept the fact and organise your day accordingly.

When decisions have to be made, some schools make them on a strictly democratic basis in which a vote is taken; more commonly, curriculum leaders and senior staff draw up papers for discussion and present suggestions about future programme modifications. These are subsequently discussed and revised until a suitable format is agreed across the staff.

As a new staff member, you probably feel a bit reluctant to speak out and it is certainly wise to orientate and find out what has been discussed previously before bursting forth with your ideas, only to discover that similar ones have been considered prior to your arrival and, for a variety of reasons, rejected. After a few weeks, it is worth offering some uncontentious comments or simply stating that you agree with a particular proposition. Avoid referring to something marvellous from a previous school, especially if it is fairly local; such enthusiastic endorsement of another establishment does not tend to go down well. If you want to make a more substantive contribution, think out beforehand precisely what you are going to say; preface your statement to convey tentativeness and professional humility, using phrases such as: 'I wonder if it is worth?' and 'Is there any value in?' You can expect to be questioned about your ideas; simply state what you are thinking about and studiously avoid giving your colleagues an education lecture.

Full staff membership

Despite a degree of scepticism that sometimes characterises staffroom discussions, the large majority of teachers welcome clearly presented ideas that will help their teaching and supervisory responsibilities but are suspicious of innovations which they perceive as reducing their autonomy. Local authorities (LAs) also put pressure on to schools to adjust what are perceived as weaker areas as indicated through test results; they are generally less concerned about non-core subjects. A coming inspection sends shivers down the spine of every practitioner and school governor, and numerous preparation meetings are held beforehand, though schools deemed successful in a full inspection may then receive a 'short' inspection with only a few days' notice. Make sure you do everything you can to contribute to the team effort: get records up to date, talk to the children about their work, liaise with colleagues, complete necessary assessments and give your classroom a facelift. You are now a full member of staff and inexperience is not a valid excuse for inadequate preparation.

Informal leadership

Although certain teachers have formal responsibilities for areas of school life, there are a number of teachers in every school who, by dint of personality, length of service at the school or experience are the 'unofficial leaders' of the staffroom. To the newcomer, unofficial leaders may not appear initially to be influential but behind the scenes they are affecting the course of staff opinion and attitudes towards options and decisions. You might find yourself benefiting greatly from their informal advice and counsel, though exercise caution if they seem to be anti-establishment or bitter about a specific issue.

Older, experienced teachers can offer leadership through their calm presence during turbulent times. Younger staff can lead through their infectious enthusiasm, willingness to embrace change and introduction of new ideas. The secret of effective informal leadership is to support the official leadership wholeheartedly, while using every opportunity to encourage others, empathise with the downhearted, sympathise with the broken-hearted and provide practical support and advice to colleagues in need. The best informal leaders do not seek adulation or power for its own sake; instead, they gain satisfaction from being positively influential and genuinely admired by staff and parents. Despite being a new teacher, you can soon become a significant voice on the staff if you demonstrate these qualities.

Extra allowances

From time to time, the school governors decide that the school's budget allows them to give teachers an extra allowance for their contribution as curriculum leaders. Additional increments are offered to the teacher directly or, more usually, the post is advertised internally and any member of staff can apply. The requirements of the post may vary: 'language co-ordinator' or 'assessment at Key Stage 1' or 'curriculum leader in science'. Some teachers may have passed through the 'threshold' and be on an upper pay scale; others are designated 'excellent teachers' (ETs) and yet others, 'advanced skills teachers' (AST), a position gained after passing a national assessment. ETs have a distinctive role in helping other teachers improve their effectiveness and are intended to have a major impact on improving pupil attainment across the whole school. ASTs are given additional payment and increased non-contact time in order to share their skills and experience with other teachers, within their own school and from other schools. The salary scale for teachers consists of six annual increase points followed by a three-point pay scale for teachers above the threshold. Teachers with additional responsibilities are placed on one of the two levels of Teaching and Learning Responsibility (TLR) payments. All teachers after the induction year have the opportunity to apply for promoted posts, but with budget constraints the opportunities to move beyond the main pay spine are fewer than was the case in the recent past.

Activate your thinking!

What percentage of your time should be spent throughout a week on classroom teaching, other supervisory duties, attendance at meetings and general preparation and maintenance tasks? How might this balance of activities vary at certain times of the year?

> **Good practice**
>
> Make a firm decision that you will gain a reputation as a positive and caring person.

Growth as a teacher

Basic requirements

However well you performed as a trainee teacher, there will always be areas of your teaching requiring attention. Even some of the most fundamental skills, such as maintaining class control, can initially prove difficult during your first post. It takes time to settle in and find your feet, so you will have to persevere and use every strategy at your disposal to avoid feeling overwhelmed. Focus on key areas of teaching and learning, relating to pupils, colleagues, parents and other professionals, enhancing your professional development, and fostering collegiality and equal opportunities. There is also an expectation that you make yourself familiar with, and take account of, the legal framework affecting all those who work in schools. On top of all these demands, try hard to cultivate relationships and uphold your professional integrity by being reliable and trustworthy (Arthur *et al.* 2005). As you increase in confidence and find your way through the initial challenges, allow the following six principles to act as a guide:

1. Learn to trust your own judgement but make sure it is well informed.
2. Share your concerns and joys with colleagues and friends but avoid pouring out your heart publicly.
3. Pace yourself so that you don't attempt too much, too soon.
4. Use every possible resource available, including published material such as textbooks and electronic sources.
5. Listen to and observe more experienced colleagues.
6. Take regular rest and holidays.

Career entry and development profile

Your career entry and development profile (CEDP) provides a useful starting point for future career development and should be used alongside the issues arising from the regular review meetings with your tutor to shape and refine your skills. For instance, your CEDP may show that you have had little opportunity to master aspects of ICT or gained limited experience of teaching PE while you were a trainee teacher. Whatever the specific area for enhancement, you will be encouraged to learn from other colleagues with more expertise and attend appropriate courses to extend your knowledge. Do not be embarrassed to admit that you have areas that require further development, as even qualified teachers need to update and refine their knowledge and understanding, regardless of the years they have been teaching.

Monitoring your progress

Whatever your subject expertise, you need to concentrate on the following aspects of your role during the induction year, and persevere with those aspects that you find difficult. All of the areas listed below have been addressed in earlier chapters (see Part 3) but the following list, which is based on guidelines for the induction of new teachers, offers a useful checklist to monitor your progress:

Classroom climate

Every teacher is instrumental in helping to create socially responsible attitudes among pupils by encouraging co-operation and collaboration rather than animosity and selfish forms of competition. Your teaching will be sensitive to the ethnic and cultural diversity in your class and valuing every child as a unique and special individual.

Classroom order

Securing good classroom order by establishing effective relationships with pupils and clarifying with your pupils what you are, and are not, prepared to tolerate resides at the heart of successful teaching and learning. Frankly, if you cannot maintain good order and establish a positive ethos, you are not going to enjoy other aspects of your role. In this regard, Dixie (2007) offers a stark warning about the significance of what he calls 'the establishment phase' by stressing that it is important for teachers of all ages and experience to be clear about exactly who they are, what they believe in and what they expect from their pupils. Moran *et al.* (2009) stress the importance of establishing clear classroom procedures, particularly as a means of building a foundation for a successful first year with new entrants. In other words, start as you mean to go on by insisting on basic courtesies and procedures, but accept that you will gradually adjust your discipline strategies as you gain confidence and experience.

Lesson planning

Planning lessons thoroughly is essential, but with awareness that teaching is not a precise science: that is, to be willing to deviate from the plan if, during teaching, it becomes clear that a different approach or change of emphasis is necessary. One of the differences between your time as a trainee and a qualified teacher is that you are responsible for continuous sessions, day after day, so planning tends to be with blocks of lessons in mind, rather than individual and discrete ones. In other words, your focus becomes much longer term than was likely the case prior to qualifying.

Individual differences

In conjunction with assessment (see below) your role in identifying and supporting low achievers, either through appropriate tasks, support from peers through collaborative activities or help from a TA forms an integral element of your teaching. You must liaise with the SENCO or senior teacher for pupils who provide exceptional challenges and try to involve parents from an early stage. At the same time, ensure that more capable pupils are given suitably challenging tasks that oblige them to use their ingenuity and creative spark, notably by setting problem-solving activities.

Assessment

Assessing pupils against tests and targets has dominated educational practice over the past decade. This practice involves taking account of pupils' previous achievements from reports, notes and conversations with other teachers and (in some cases) parents, and talking to the children themselves. It is also monitoring daily progress, identifying children who might be underachieving in literacy and mathematics, and providing additional resources to remedy perceived pupil shortcomings. In your rush to complete seemingly endless assessment forms, remember that it is the effectiveness of your regular feedback to children that makes the crucial difference in their learning, not the amount you write down (see Chapter 11).

Target setting

Monitoring pupils' progress and setting appropriate learning targets for groups of children and individuals have become key features of teaching in recent times. For instance, a group of children may need more opportunity to work co-operatively; an individual might need to be set specific time limits to complete work or given a longer-term goal, such as mastering a family of spellings or learning how to access information sources. It is important to discuss targets with children and help them to monitor their own progress wherever realistic to do so. In doing so, keep the process simple and maintain a 'light touch'.

Home–school liaison

You need to take every opportunity through formal and informal liaison with parents to express your enthusiasm for their children's progress and communicate your pleasure (and occasional concerns) by word of mouth and letter. This contact is particularly important for new school entrants in the Foundation Stage of their education; parents of older children are just as interested in their children's progress and happiness, but may be less available for regular informal discussions. See Chapter 5 for details about liaising with parents.

Working with TAs

Ensuring that teaching assistants are clear about their role and your expectations of them has become increasingly significant in recent years. It is worth remembering that assistants now have the opportunity to gain formal qualifications and regularly update their skills, and there is a possibility that the TA is a qualified teacher who, for a variety of possible reasons, decided to become an assistant. Experienced TAs or higher level teaching assistants (HLTAs) may be capable of supervising a group or even the whole class during your absence from the room, which makes it doubly important that you have fully briefed them. Good TAs are worth their weight in gold, so never take them for granted.

Staff membership

As noted on a number of occasions throughout this book (including earlier in this chapter), playing your part as a team member by offering support and encouragement to those with whom you work is vitally important. You also have a professional responsibility to implement school policies as fully as possible and to inform senior staff where you experience difficulties in so doing. As part of your wider role you should contribute to extra-curricular activities where appropriate, though not at the expense of your regular teaching. Helping to maintain and enhance the school's reputation in the community by your positive attitude, creative teaching and personable manner also forms part of being a staff member. News travels fast in a school community and your actions will quickly become known and talked about by colleagues, pupils and parents.

If the above list looks daunting, remember that you have already demonstrated your capability during pre-service training and have a whole year to improve weaker areas. Some requirements will naturally fall into place; others will need perseverance over a period of time. Mistakes and occasional instances of poor judgement are inevitable; try to take it in your stride and not become dispirited if things don't quite go to plan. The induction year will almost certainly prove to be the most demanding, exhausting, worthwhile and exciting time of your life thus far.

Cross-reference: Guided Reader Extract 35

Doing your best

Keep things in perspective

You want to do well in your new job, of course, but beware of trying to do everything at once. It is true that you are to some extent under scrutiny, but most teachers are too busy with their own affairs to worry overly about what you are getting up to. It is important to recognise that you will tire very quickly during the first term, so it is essential to pace yourself and not to develop a whirlwind mentality, flitting from one thing to another like a performer keeping plates spinning on the end of a dozen canes. You will want to be determined but not frantic; conscientious but not a perfectionist; idealistic but also keeping your feet firmly anchored to the ground. Contrary to how it might be expressed in the media and by some politicians, the future educational success of the kingdom does not rely wholly on you! You are neither responsible for every bit of learning that children experience nor the only contributor to the aspirations of every parent. It is true, of course, that you have an important role in ensuring that your class makes good progress in learning, and there would be something strange about teachers who were not interested in making sure that their pupils attained the highest standards, but you are not the only interested party or influential factor. Some children are motivated by caring and thoughtful parents; others are not. Some children have material advantages that benefit their progress; others are impoverished. Some children are emotionally secure; others are vulnerable or even frightened. As the teacher, you have to provide the best education for them that it is reasonable to expect, but you are not a miracle worker and should not attempt to be so.

Don't be heroic

The truth about being a teacher is that even if you worked twenty-four hours every day and performed heroic deeds, it would not satisfy all the demands that are made of you. Regardless of the time you arrive at school and leave for home; despite the countless hours you commit to preparation, marking and dealing with individual needs and parental concerns, and no matter how far you sacrifice your life to the education movement, it will never be enough. It may sound trite, but the old adage that you can only do your best applies to teaching as much as to any other job. Some teachers allow the job to dominate their lives and seem to spend every waking hour in tasks associated with it. Although it can be difficult to stop yourself from becoming obsessed with your new role, it is important to resist the relentless demands that are made of you by the many different people associated with the school. Like the waves of the sea, additional work and commitments will keep rolling up to your feet, and though you may sometimes feel like King Canute in trying to repel the tide, it is worth persevering to develop a lifestyle that allows for recreation and separation from the job's requirements.

This will not be easy. Most NQTs acknowledge that the first year is difficult, demanding, stimulating and a bit scary; yours will not be any different. The advice contained within this book should help you to keep things under control but one thing is for sure: if you don't look after yourself, nobody else will. Healthy fatigue is one thing; exhaustion from over-commitment is quite another.

Don't try to be admired

Although you are new and feel vulnerable, the children and parents see you as 'the teacher' (albeit youthful-looking, perhaps) and do not distinguish you from any other teacher in the school. So you do not have to prove yourself in the same way as when you were a trainee. You can move into the realms of super-teacher and being the focus for hero-worship when you have got a few years of teaching under your belt. Concentrate on your classroom work, make an effort to be a supportive colleague and a good team member, and don't use your inexperience as an excuse for poor performance. Although you will hope to impress the people around you (colleagues, pupils, parents) by being conscientious and persevering, it is a mistake to try and invoke their admiration. In truth, you will never really know what people think of you, so beyond being sensibly hardworking, pleasant and reliable, it is better to relax, enjoy your work as much as possible, and let your actions do the talking.

> ### Activate your thinking!
>
> Bubb (2007) makes the point that there is a huge difference between novice teachers and experienced ones. She writes: 'Like any skill or craft, learning to teach is a developmental process characterised by devastating disasters and spectacular successes. Teaching is a job that can never be done perfectly – one can always improve' (p. 4).
>
> Bubb, S. (2007) *Successful Induction*, London: Paul Chapman.

Cross-reference: Guided Reader Extract 26

Health issues

Be realistic

Illness is an unfortunate fact of life, and everyone is prone to succumb to it at some time or another. As a student teacher, it was possible to miss a couple of lectures if you felt ill or, if it was during a teaching experience, to grit your teeth and struggle on for a few weeks until the end of the placement. As a qualified teacher the battle to retain good health is complicated by two facts. First, the daily contact with children increases the likelihood that you will pick up infections. Second, as you are now the responsible person for your class, you will be reluctant to take time off and – so it feels – disadvantage the children. You might also be anxious lest your colleagues or the head teacher interpret your absence as a sign of weakness. Worries about comments such as 'They don't make them like they used to' and 'The slightest little thing and these new teachers take a day off' can unduly influence your decisions and tempt you to struggle into work when you should have stayed at home. While such determination is commendable at one level, it is almost certain to prove counter-productive. As O'Flynn and Kennedy (2003) state emphatically, should teachers fall ill and need time off, they are likely to be horrified by how easily they have been replaced and by how little the system cares for them.

Safeguarding your health

It is important that you protect your health to minimise the possibility of picking up every nasty bug that is floating around the school, so it is essential to do regular exercise and maintain a balanced lifestyle. On the other hand, even the fittest person suffers from ill health occasionally, so you should not view time off work as a crime. In fact, if you go into school when you are unwell, you can cause one of four unpleasant effects:

1. You are unable to teach properly, so the children's learning is impaired.
2. The illness tends to make you less tolerant and more grumpy than usual, adversely affecting your relationship with the class.
3. Others on the staff catch your germs, causing more staff and pupil absences.
4. You further damage your health by working when you should be resting.

In short, if you are unfit for work you should not agonise about it, but accept the fact and let the school know as soon as possible. If you feel unwell during the previous evening, inform the appropriate person straight away; say that you are coming down with something and will probably need to take time off. If, by the following morning, you have made a miraculous recovery, inform the contact person immediately to prevent any unnecessary arrangements being made to cover your class. The chances are that if you feel really unwell in the evening, you will not have recovered sufficiently by the next day.

Keep the school informed

If possible, try to indicate how long you expect to be off work. This information helps the head teacher or the person responsible for finding a replacement to plan whether there is a need for substitute teachers or, if necessary, whether to farm out groups of children from your class to other teachers. If it is not possible to say how long you expect to be off school, keep the secretary/administrator or head teacher informed of your progress. One of the least glamorous tasks in a school is finding cover for absent staff, so do what you can to ease the burden.

No going back!

When you return to work, it will be assumed that you are fit and well. Do not expect too much sympathy or any allowance for the fact that you are still struggling with the aftermath of an illness. This attitude is not callousness, but simply a reflection of the fact that it is not practical to nurse along a half-fit colleague; either you are well enough to do the job or you are not. If you go into school when you should still be off sick, you can antagonise other staff who perceive your courage as foolhardiness. Once you step over the threshold, you are back!

Activate your thinking!

Teachers who take care of themselves are in a better condition to take care of the children.

> **Good practice**
>
> Studies indicate that physical fatigue has a negative effect on the voice. Some voice specialists recommend a diet that includes whole grain, fruit and vegetables, as these foods contain important vitamins A, E and C, which help to keep the mucus membranes that line the throat healthy. See also Chapter 9 for details of caring for the voice.

Dealing with your emotions

Coping with strain

One of the unexpected elements of being a teacher is the emotional strain it creates. All NQTs know that the job will be demanding and consume a lot of time and energy. They may be less prepared for the inner turmoil that can sometimes threaten to undermine the good work they are doing. You know from your student days that concerns about whether you were good enough to reach the standard and cope with the numerous demands that were placed on you, while working as a guest in someone else's classroom, threatened to overwhelm you on occasions. You know how a single wretched lesson could undermine your confidence; and why was it that the tutor was always there to observe you teaching when things went wrong and never present when you had a wonderful session? But even when you are qualified there are questions that can disturb and unsettle you, including:

- Am I coping with my responsibilities or are people secretly saying that I'm not up to the job?
- Am I placing my efforts where they are most needed?
- How do the support staff feel about me?
- Did I do/say the right thing when I dealt with the incidence of misbehaviour?
- Will the child be encouraged or upset after I spoke to him about his ability to improve with more effort?
- How will parents react when they hear that I kept their daughter in during break time to finish her work?
- Is the child all right after sustaining that small bump on the head during PE?
- Did I speak out of turn during the staff meeting when I expressed my frustration with the present break time arrangement?
- Can I ever hope to motivate that difficult child?

And so forth. There are no easy ways to deal with emotional pressures, but it is important to remind yourself regularly that you have been appointed on merit. Other candidates applied for the job, but only you were successful. Nevertheless, you have to accept that in the rush and tumble of school life you will make minor errors of judgement. These occasions do not, however, spell the end of your teaching career.

In trying to maintain a sensible perspective on events, it is helpful to remember that every NQT has had to tread the same path as you have. Some new teachers have a fairly smooth passage; others struggle to accommodate the demands of the job or work with colleagues who have a different view of life and education from their own. However, it might be the case that those who have fewer problems are the less ambitious teachers, preferring to 'play safe' and maintain a strictly controlled environment based on closely regulated lessons and rigidly enforced behaviour management.

More ambitious new teachers may encounter more problems initially because they want to 'light a fire' and passion for learning in children through creative teaching and innovative activities. As a result, children become more animated, noisier and self-confident, with the discipline challenges that such behaviour evokes and the inevitable sidelong looks from colleagues. On the other hand, the ambitious teacher might become more accomplished than his or her cautious peer and ultimately gain greater rewards from the job.

Good practice

Make good use of your induction tutor and cultivate a few confidantes from your acquaintances outside school with whom you can share your concerns. Under no circumstances should you suffer in silence.

Hazards of being a perfectionist

O'Flynn and Kennedy (2003) describe an occupational hazard of teaching as being 'stuck in a correcting, improving, self-righteous mode of being, which is too narrow to allow for human frailties'. The authors explain that some teachers 'work themselves to the bone, even to the extent that they break themselves physically or mentally' owing to the fact that 'their need to prove themselves takes precedence over everything else' (pp. 142–3). You can avoid falling into this trap by resisting the tendency to link your inexperience with incompetence. The former condition (inexperience) is true of every new teacher, whereas the latter condition (incompetence) is rarely true of *any* teacher. Try to focus your attention on your positive attributes and successes and, if problems begin to emerge, seek advice earlier rather than later. In addition to the induction tutor, it can also be useful to confide in a friendly older colleague who understands what you are going through and will help you to be more objective in your view of your progress. See also the checklist below.

Most teachers encourage children to keep a profile of their achievements but fail to do the same for themselves. Your emotional stability is likely to ebb and flow throughout the term. Fatigue, over-commitment and a defensive attitude all conspire to drain your energy, reduce your confidence and open you to fears and doubts which would not normally bother you. Give your emotions as much attention as you do to every other part of your mind and body; and look forward to Friday evening.

Checklist

At the end of your first half-term as an NQT, divide the following list into three groups: (a) those things you are doing well; (b) those you are doing satisfactorily; and (c) those you are doing badly. It is likely that nearly all will fall into the first two categories. Thus:

1. I am taking an interest in the welfare of individual pupils.
2. I am preparing my lessons thoroughly.
3. I am taking account of differences in pupils' ability.

4. I am teaching consistently.
5. I am maintaining an industrious classroom climate.
6. I am getting on with my colleagues.
7. I am making contact with parents.
8. I am keeping up with my marking.
9. I am setting suitable homework tasks.
10. I am keeping my room in reasonable order.
11. I am attending the required staff and team meetings.
12. I am motivating and inspiring the children.

Good practice

Prepare as much in advance of the first day as possible, such as drawing up class and group lists, blank sticker charts, sets of high and medium frequency words (and assessment charts), a multiplication square and name tags. You might also want to produce flashcards, merit cards, wall posters for display and templates for handouts. Some teachers like to label key items and resources, produce an attractive 'roll of honour' for birthdays, and make pupil self-evaluation slips with phrases that a child can complete after the activity, such as 'I did well at...' and 'I struggled with...' and 'I would like to know more about...'

Case study

When Carmen was appointed to a post in a large infant school as a teacher for reception-aged children, a male teacher who was just completing his induction year gave her the following advice. First, he suggested that it was useful to sort out certain details before the term began, even though in the normal way a TA might do some of the tasks:

- The names, ages, dates of birth and any major details of children's ability and aptitude.
- Reports and records, school policies, schemes of work, long-term plans.
- Special needs children and their support.
- Samples of children's previous work.
- The names of other teachers, assistants, administrative staff, caretaker and cleaners.
- The school prospectus.
- Staff handouts on health and safety (including fire alarm procedures).
- The person you can contact out of school hours for help/advice.
- Timetables, school starting and finishing times, breaks, lunch times.
- Procedures for attendance registers and dinner registers.
- Times of assemblies and if/when your class may be involved (though don't volunteer too quickly).
- Regular weekly meetings and events, such as staff meetings, team meetings.
- Important dates during the first term that you need to know in advance, such as parents' evenings, staff training days.
- The system for setting and monitoring homework.
- The school's dress code, including expectations for PE and games.

- How tea and coffee are provided; how to pay for it; whether you need your own cup.
- Whether you will be required to do any additional duties, such as bus duty.

He also recommended:

- Put names on drawers and pegs, and make sure resources are clearly labelled.
- Plan the furniture layout, including where to site computers to suit your way of working (you're in charge now).
- Check that you have sufficient stock for the first couple of weeks, including paper of various kinds, exercise books, paper, pencils, markers, scissors...
- Set up a book display and have some tried and tested storybooks for reading to the class.
- Ensure that you are familiar with the IT provision, including software.
- Make a simple, bold but interesting display, perhaps including some artefacts with a few questions.
- Check the whereabouts of the equipment for PE and games. If possible, make an inventory.
- Have paper cut to a variety of sizes, ready at hand.
- Have a good supply of easy-to-do worksheets and handouts to give you a breathing space during the first few intensive days.

Within the first week:

- Establish your ground rules immediately but don't expect miracles. Learn to persevere.
- Explain to the children your expectations about behaviour and standards of work and regularly remind them.
- Be firm about the need to share, your dislike of bullying and your insistence on a harmonious working environment.
- Establish a clear system for leaving and entering the classroom.
- Make sure that you have informal contact with parents at the start and end of the day.
- Ensure that all your children achieve success in some aspect of their work as early as possible.
- Praise and commend genuine effort at every opportunity.

Be realistic:

- Do not to try to 'make a big impression'. Be yourself. Don't get exhausted. Work steadily.
- You may get the feeling that you are being watched. You are. Use it to show what you are made of.
- Parents will be asking what you are like. Consider what the children might be saying about you at home but don't agonise.
- Fabulous lessons can wait for a while until you have settled and established your routines.
- Don't be too upset when you make mistakes; learn from them quickly and move on. Children have short memories.
- However successful you were on final teaching practice, the first half-term of your first post is likely to be quite demanding. Try to stay cheerful but don't be afraid to seek advice if you are struggling.

The common experience of new teachers is that sorting out the classroom often takes much longer than they expected. Although colleagues are as helpful as possible, everyone is so busy at the start of the term that they cannot spare much time to help you. Even if you are not able to fulfil all of the above action points, things fall into place very quickly once the term begins. The more that has been dealt with beforehand, however, the easier the start to the new term becomes.

Further reading for Chapter 14

Bubb, S. (2007) *Successful Induction*, London: Paul Chapman.

A guide to surviving the tricky bits of the first year of teaching, offering information, practical tips, anecdotes, handy checklists and examples from genuine situations.

Ghaye, A. and Ghaye, K. (2004) *Teaching and Learning Through Critical Reflective Practice*, London: David Fulton.

The authors provide a model of the teacher as a reflective learner.

Jacklin, A., Griffiths, V. and Robinson, C. (2006) *Beginning Primary Teaching*, Maidenhead: Open University Press.

Draws on the experiences of new teachers and provides authentic accounts of their early encounters, challenges and achievements.

Lush, V. (2009) *Get Ready to Teach*, London: Longman.

An easy-to-read book with lots of practical advice and tips covering issues relevant to primary and secondary teaching.

Rogers, B. (2012) *The Essential Guide to Managing Teacher Stress*, Harlow: Pearson.

This book deals with issues of challenging children, concerns about discipline in today's classrooms, and the stress they create for teachers

Wallace, W. (2005) *Oranges and Lemons: Life in an inner-city primary school*, Abingdon: Routledge.

Focuses on the progress of individual children from their time as new entrants and illuminates contemporary urban school life, including the way that teachers and support staff cope with the demands and pressures.

15

Issues Teachers Face

Introduction

This short chapter consists of eight *Discussion Points*, in which a typical situation from school life is described for each point and alternatives offered to assist you in reaching conclusions about the most appropriate strategy and action. The issues raised and suggestions proposed can be used to stimulate your thinking or as a basis for discussion or as starting points for more advanced study.

Discussion Points

Teachers are constantly faced with situations that require a combination of professional wisdom, keen judgement and pragmatism. Here are eight typical circumstances with which teachers are confronted.

1 Parents come in to talk to me when I'm most busy

It is not uncommon for parents of younger pupils, in particular, to visit the classroom first thing in the morning just as you are busily welcoming the children, making final checks and mentally preparing for the opening session. Parents normally only want a quick word and won't detain you for long; occasionally, a parent who has time on her hands will take up too much of yours. Five guiding principles will help you to deal with the situation.

First, don't view the parent as 'a nuisance' but as someone interested enough to make the effort to come into school.

Second, listen carefully to what is communicated and, if necessary, make a quick note of the details; it's surprisingly easy to listen and yet not connect with what is being said!

Third, be polite and helpful, regardless of your inner feelings.

Fourth, don't hesitate to apologise and turn your attention to a child in need of assistance, even if the parent is in full flow.

Fifth, if you have an assistant, make good use of her or him to answer factual questions.

2 My senior colleague in the parallel class strongly advocates a teaching approach with which I'm uneasy and I feel under pressure to conform

No one teaches like you. No one can make you teach like she does or he does. You are, however, placed in something of a dilemma when your partner teacher has strong views about *fundamental* approaches that differ from your own. For instance, your colleague might favour less/more opportunities for children to play and explore than you do; he or she might be an advocate of individual tasks when you are dedicated to more collaborative activities; there might be disagreement about acceptable noise levels, the amount of computer use, etc. There are five points of which to take account.

First, if you are new to the school, it is worth taking careful notice of what your colleague says, which is doubtless based on hard-won experience.

Second, try to open up a relaxed dialogue instead of retreating into a sullen defensiveness; in the long run it is better to be transparent and honest.

Third, unless you team-teach, there is no reason why you should slavishly follow your colleague's advice; over time, you will settle to a rhythm of teaching with which you feel more comfortable.

Fourth, seek advice from your induction tutor (if you are a newly qualified teacher) or ask for a confidential chat with the head teacher or a relevant staff member if you are feeling unhappy; in doing so, avoid any criticism of your colleague whatsoever.

Finally, try hard not to be upset and grim about the difficulty; instead of complaining behind the person's back, seek a solution.

3 One child is taking up too much of my time and mental energy

It is difficult for someone who has never worked in a school to understand how easy it is for a child to dominate a teacher's time and drain the emotions. The expression 'get under my skin' is most apt when you have a pupil who is so demanding, so obstinate and so reluctant to conform that you realise you are adjusting your teaching to try and ensure that he (occasionally, she) is less likely to cause problems, rather than for the best educational and social interests – an approach often referred to as 'keeping their heads down'. If the child is outrageously behaved, there are mechanisms in place to help and support you. If the child is struggling academically, there are procedures to address the learning needs. However, although these latter two categories of pupils (badly behaved/slow learners) absorb a lot of your time and energy, they don't necessarily get under your skin in the way that certain other children are capable of doing. The circumstances vary so widely that it is almost impossible to provide you with a foolproof plan of action to combat being irritated and even distressed by such pupils; nevertheless, it is worth bearing in mind the following five points.

First, children that unsettle you are probably unsettled children. In other words, your instinctive unease is probably justified, so examine the underlying causes as well as the outward behaviour.

Second, the child will probably have a history of 'odd' behaviour and previous teachers can be an important source of advice and reassurance.

Third, when the child begins to inhabit your every waking moment, seek help urgently. Your emotional stability is a vitally significant factor in being an effective teacher; don't allow it to be undermined by one child's odd temperament.

Fourth, try to take a positive perspective; think of commendable features – for instance, the child's punctuality, neatness and tidiness, skill at sport, or whatever.

Finally, if you allow a child to soak up too much of your attention, it means that you could be neglecting the other twenty-nine pupils. Don't allow the situation to become so fraught that you suddenly 'explode' and trigger a serious incident. Take action now!

4 I cope reasonably well on most days but find myself under great pressure when I have extra duties to perform

When the majority of trainee teachers qualify, they rightly believe that the job of a teacher is principally about teaching. In practice, however, a lot of time is spent on other duties and on certain days there can be additional supervisory tasks plus (say) running a lunchtime club, thereby disrupting your regular routine. You can find yourself hurrying into the classroom feeling less prepared and orientated towards teaching than would otherwise be the case. It is not possible to wholly offset the impact of extra duties, but consideration of the following four aspects should help to reduce it.

First, on days where there are time constraints, keep your lesson plans and organisation uncomplicated. These are not the occasions to experiment with that energy-sapping scientific investigation, or to take children on a tour of the school grounds looking for different kinds of seeds, or to employ that fantastic but complex IT resource. Instead, make full use of book resources, paper-and-pencil exercises and easily managed tasks.

Second, set up resources as far in advance as possible. For instance, duplicate the activity sheets the previous evening; write up the list of words on the board for use after the break; ask the assistant to check the PE equipment for you; photocopy a series of blank *pro forma* cartoon strip boxes for pupils to fill in.

Third, make sure that you have sufficient to eat and drink during the breaks, preferably when seated and not 'on the run'. It is surprisingly easy to become so absorbed in the busy-ness of the day that you neglect your basic needs.

Finally, encourage the children to be self-sufficient; appoint sensible pupils to be monitors; give the class scope to be inventive rather than spoonfeed them; allow yourself opportunities to 'step back' during the session.

5 The teaching assistant is rather aloof and unreceptive to my suggestions about classroom procedures and her role during lessons

Assistants are normally a teacher's greatest ally and an immense source of help and support. Occasionally the opposite is true and the assistant is domineering or seemingly immune to your overtures of goodwill and friendship. It is highly likely that unless you have a child with special needs, who requires the close attention of a TA throughout the day, or work with very young children, you will share the assistant with another class. Owing to the work pressures on teachers, some assistants complain that they have been given too much responsibility for supervising the class while the teacher is busy with other duties. Others feel under-used and long to employ their expertise more fully. An assistant can be aloof for a number of reasons: (1) it is an element of her personality; (2) she is bored with the job; (3) she is resentful towards you; (4) she is resentful towards teachers in general; (5) she is shy rather than unfriendly; (6) she is struggling with personal issues outside school that are affecting her attitude inside school. It is worth making an effort to discover which of these reasons (or combination of them) lies at the root of the behaviour.

If the reason seems to be (1) above, you can only do your best to be bright and cheerful and, perhaps, agree with her a list of things you would like her to do on a regular basis. If you suspect (2), you can offer her more interesting jobs, which require her to use initiative and skills she possesses. If you suspect (3) or (4), it might be worth airing a question such as: 'Have you ever thought of becoming a teacher?' The answer will tell you a lot! If you suspect (5), your gentle coaxing and warmth will soon reveal the truth. If you suspect (6), wait until you have eliminated (1) to (5) and draw alongside her until she is ready to confide in you – though it might require considerable patience.

In addition to these strategies, it is worth asking advice from your tutor/colleague about the best way to handle the situation. In doing so, make sure you express your concerns in terms of your *own* possible shortcomings in the relationship, rather than drawing attention to the assistant's perceived failings. Nothing stays secret for long in a primary school, so exercise great discretion when talking about your assistant, as it can rebound on you and permanently sour relationships. For further information and advice about teaching assistants, see Chapter 5.

6 I have a number of intelligent but very slow workers in the class and I'm worried that they will fall behind

There are three common misconceptions about the link between intelligence, speed of work and achievement. The first is that intelligent children are invariably hard-working and determined. The second is that faster workers achieve more than slower ones. The third is that slow workers are less able. In fact, the relationship between the three characteristics is far more complex. Children work slowly for four principal reasons: (1) they don't properly understand what is required; (2) they struggle with the concepts; (3) they lack motivation; (4) they do everything slowly; it is part of their makeup.

To combat their *lack of understanding*, you need to check that your explanation about what you want pupils to do is clear and explicit.

To address *struggles with concepts* necessitates more thorough assessment of the pupil's understanding and adjustment to lesson planning.

If a pupil *lacks motivation*, decide whether it is the individual child or a more widespread problem in the class; if the latter, adjust your teaching approach so that it becomes more interactive.

To help children who *do everything slowly*, it is worth discussing the matter with the school SENCO and, subsequently, with parents. The sluggishness could be 'one of those things' or a health and welfare issue or pure lack of motivation. If the class as a whole appear to be unwilling or unable to complete work in good time, set specific time constraints, including (if necessary) keeping children in at break time to complete the work. However, be careful not to penalise children who are genuinely slower workers or create a learning climate where accuracy is sacrificed for speed. For more information about these issues, see Chapter 3 (about children) and Chapters 7 and 8 (about learning).

7 A child in my class does not have any close friends and seems rather miserable

As noted in Chapter 4 and elsewhere in this book, friendship is extremely important to children. The need to belong and be accepted is significant for all of us, but is most keenly felt by the young. If a child seems devoid of intimate (as opposed to casual) friends, it is for one of four reasons: (1) extreme shyness; (2) being 'different' in a way that other children view negatively; (3) communication barriers; (4) unpleasant personality. Each of the causes requires different responses from you.

Shyness is closely associated with confidence level; it takes time to get alongside the child, offer gentle encouragement, applaud effort and, perhaps, pair the child for part of the time with a more confident and caring classmate. Although you are unlikely to see rapid results, your careful, deliberate approach will eventually pay dividends as the child starts to relate more easily to others.

Being different comes in many guises. In addition to the familiar ones, some children are unpopular for reasons that adults find hard to comprehend, such as particular hair colour; tone of voice; unusual gait; small eyes; or similar, seemingly inconsequential characteristics. These children are often last to be chosen and left as the 'odd one out' after others pair up. Primarily, you must persevere to create an inclusive classroom with a positive outlook and an emphasis on mutual support and acceptance. Perhaps the unfavoured child is good at, or has a great knowledge of, something that does not figure in the conventional curriculum (e.g. a hobby, a musical instrument, singing or a sport) that he or she can share with the rest of the class or demonstrate. You might also consider coaching the child in a skill such as public speaking for use in drama or assembly or giving a recitation or mime, in fact anything that raises the child's self-esteem and impresses classmates.

Communication barriers take many forms, including autism; ear, nose and throat problems; persistent anxiety; and poor spoken language skills. For information about autism, see Chapter 13. Facial abnormalities can occur owing to Down Syndrome or poor teeth or a minor disfigurement; some children do not suffer from any of these conditions but lisp badly or have other speech impediments. It is almost certain that, in serious cases, the child will be receiving specialist help. Children with minor problems grow more conscious of being different as they grow older, but your own positive and patient attitude towards the child will greatly influence the other pupils' behaviour. It is probably unwise to attempt any form of 'speech-training' but singing as a class is a great 'leveller' and, rather perversely, a child struggling with normal speech can sometimes sing quite clearly. Poor language skills can be addressed through regular opportunities for speaking and listening, extending children's vocabulary, recitations in unison, drama and collaborative discussions.

Finally, if others exclude a classmate owing to an *unpleasant personality*, you will need to convince the child that there is more to be gained by being kind and co-operative than by being selfish and mean-spirited. Such children are often deeply unhappy and, despite their disagreeable manner, need to be treated more as 'victims' than perpetrators. Adopting a firm but compassionate approach is far from easy, especially if you find the child hard to like, but it is the only way ahead if things are to change. Be aware in doing so that ill-natured pupils have the potential to bully others as a means of gaining status and receiving a grisly form of admiration from their peers. It is commendable to be patient with such children but unkind behaviour cannot and must not be permitted.

8 I'm uneasy that the use of technology is dominating school life to the exclusion of other teaching approaches

The past few decades have seen tremendous advancements in the use of technology. While most of the progress has benefited learning and, to an extent, simplified paperwork (e.g. writing reports), an over-reliance on technology has also been the subject of considerable debate and controversy. There has been much greater emphasis in recent years on visual forms of communication, which has tended to reduce a reliance on the auditory element (i.e. teacher monologue). Paradoxically, however, the use of computer images sometimes acts to stimulate even more direct transmission teaching, which has undergone something of a renaissance in recent years.

Computers have allowed pupils access to a large amount of information; and the new generation of software exposes children to a variety of exercises in every conceivable area of knowledge at different levels of difficulty. It challenges their thinking by use of animated 'decision-making' scenarios; it assesses their knowledge through graded tests; and it provides fun activities with an educational content. Pupils can also use computers for a variety of innovative practices, such as creating diagrams, charts, spreadsheets and the like, as well as producing artistic creations and innovative ideas in the area of art and design. In other words, information technology has altered the style of teaching and learning dramatically, and spawned a generation of pupils who are sometimes more at ease with a keyboard than with pencil-and-paper activities and messy 'hands-on' approaches.

The shift from a 'discovery' form of active participation to a 'desk-bound' form has not been popular with every teacher, notably early years practitioners, some of whom are uneasy about what they see as the adverse effects of IT on spontaneous play and enquiry-based learning. In your deliberations, it is worth taking account of five points. First, technology is here to stay; it is unlikely to be superseded during your career, though doubtless it will grow more sophisticated. Second, some of your colleagues use IT effectively; learn from them. Third, it is a requirement that schools teach ICT, so it forms part of your responsibilities. Fourth, children have been brought up in a technologically sophisticated age, so are generally relaxed, even a little blasé, about computers and related gadgetry. Finally, educationists have come to realise that technology must be the slave and not master of learning – the key question to ask is whether its use will enhance or detract from the quality of the children's education; if it is the former, use it well; if the latter, find a better way.

Further reading for Chapter 15

Arthur, J. and Cremin, T. (eds) (2010) *Learning to Teach in the Primary School*, second edn, Abingdon: Routledge.
Different authors contribute a wide range of perspectives on numerous practical issues relating to the work of the teacher, including aspects of research and gaining further qualifications (e.g. at Master's level).
Bentley-Davies, C. (2010) *How to be an Amazing Teacher*, Carmarthen: Crown House.
A book with a secondary orientation, but the author openly confronts the joys and sorrows of teaching, including (in the final section) some of the specific issues that challenge every teacher.
Hansen, A. (2011) *Primary Professional Studies: Transforming primary QTS*, Exeter: Learning Matters.
The book covers aspects of teaching and learning through the curriculum, the developing child, the developing teacher and teaching skills.
Jesson, J. and Peacock, G. (2011) *The Really Useful ICT Book*, London: David Fulton.
A book for primary teachers who want to improve their expertise and confidence in ICT, including advice about using technology to enhance cross-curricular work.

16

Progressing as a Teacher

Introduction

There is a great deal of truth in the oft-quoted axiom that you either progress or retrogress as a teacher but can never stand still. In this final chapter, we examine some of the issues and practicalities associated with keeping your work as a teacher vibrant and fresh, including the concept of belonging to a professional community and, despite the many challenges and occasional setbacks, relishing the joys of the job.

Professional learning

Although you are rightly concerned with the successful completion of your training course and acquisition of QTS, your development does not stop there, as there is always more professional learning to do. The induction year means that you will have to continue extending your expertise throughout the first year of teaching, but beyond that point your future progress will depend upon your enthusiasm, commitment and ambition. After the initial settling period is over, it is surprisingly easy to lapse into a self-satisfied mode and imagine that somehow you have 'arrived' in teaching. Moore (2001) makes the point that reflecting on practice can sometimes lead to self-recrimination and not to the intended improvement in practice. The author advocates that a more reflexive approach (looking at cause and effect) is the way for teachers to resist an agonising introspective about their shortcomings and instead recognise the ways in which our lives and experiences shape the way we act. Once these factors are recognised, action can be taken to correct and adjust present behaviour without unnecessary loss of self-confidence. In fact, the best teachers are those who are never fully satisfied with their performance and consider themselves to be life-long achievers (Chappell 2003).

Cross-reference: Guided Reader Extract 54

Growth or stagnation

Teachers who grow complacent are in danger of atrophying, depending too heavily on past experiences and growing stale without realising it. Despite all the emphasis on standards for going through the 'threshold', and becoming an expert or advanced skills teacher, it is actually possible to get worse at teaching as well as better at it because you learn how to give the right appearances without actually being different; you effectively 'tread water'.

Once qualified, you will find that most of your attention is focused on your classroom teaching and also on learning to prosper as a member of the staff team. There are publications to consult that summarise recent education research findings, but many teachers admit that they never read a journal unless they are taking an advanced course or degree. This tendency is understandable but regrettable. There are a number of publications specifically designed to help busy teachers keep abreast of key findings and it is worth consulting one with summaries of findings from a broad range of education interests – rather than those issued by the government, which are sometimes self-congratulatory and non-specific.

Cross-reference: Guided Reader Extract 23

Stay positive

There are a number of factors influencing a teacher's self-worth and positive attitude: (1) general competence and skills; (2) gaining approval from significant others, such as parents; (3) receiving support from colleagues; (4) being convinced that teaching makes a positive difference to children's lives; (5) strong moral convictions, including religious faith. A mysterious contradiction exists in that teachers often seem to be complaining about the unreasonable demands placed on them yet they continue to love the job, which suggests that altruism and motivation to work with and help children outweigh self-doubt.

In addition to ensuring that their staff have good teaching skills and knowledge of the curriculum and enjoy a good working relationship with children, head teachers and governors value particular characteristics in their teachers. See how you shape up as someone who is willing to:

1. continue learning and persevering;
2. assume a fair share of the responsibilities;
3. take a positive approach to the job;
4. relate well to colleagues, ancillary staff and parents;
5. see the funny side of life;
6. contribute positively to the full breadth of school life;
7. encourage others whenever a suitable opportunity arises.

Heads and governors are not well disposed towards teachers who think they know it all, constantly complain, put minimal effort into their work and walk around with a glum face as if the world owed them a living. By contrast, they will celebrate the positive difference that you make to the atmosphere of the staffroom and school by your presence. Regardless of things that cause you concern, trying hard to look and sound positive about the job and life in general pays dividends for both you and your colleagues.

Learning communities

As a new member of staff, you join the school's *learning community*, which consists largely of staff and pupils but can also include parents, governors and others with a specific interest in the school. Influenced by the work of Lave and Wenger (1991), the expressions 'learning community' and 'learning society' have entered the United Kingdom education vocabulary in more recent years, loosely defined as a group of people who share common values and beliefs that are actively engaged in learning together by sharing knowledge, experiences and insights with each other. Communities try to promote attitudes of tolerance and the rights of all individuals. If your school is federated with other schools, the community extends well beyond the boundaries of the immediate catchment area.

In the late 1990s and beyond, the Scottish Executive started to promote the notion of community *education* as opposed to community learning, with the emphasis on a dynamic learning society. Thus, from the executive summary (Scottish Executive 1999):

> A democratic and socially just society should enable all of its citizens, in particular those who are socially excluded, to develop their potential to the full and to have the capacity, individually and collectively, to meet the challenge of change. The learning society will provide an active and informed citizenship.

Typically, the school staff will address a specific curriculum issue by sub-dividing into year groups and reporting back to the whole staff for discussion about the implications for implementation.

Cross-reference: Guided Reader Extract 37

Relish the joys of teaching

Be courageous

As a teacher, you require a particular kind of courage, which incorporates four character strengths – bravery, persistence, integrity and vitality. *Bravery* is the ability to do what you think is right even if it involves personal sacrifice. Every day you can be brave by living your life in a consistent manner that reflects your values, character and aspirations. *Persistence* is the ability to get back up after being knocked down. You can display persistence by a dogged refusal to allow setbacks to deter you from doing what is right. *Integrity* is earned by ensuring that the things you say and do are in harmony with your beliefs and values. People with integrity take personal responsibility for their lives and don't blame others for disappointments or obstacles. *Vitality* brings enthusiasm and energy to whatever task you are doing, however trivial, while exuding positive expectations (Schmidt 2007).

Be happy

Regardless of the difficulties and challenges that your first year of teaching brings, it is good to remind yourself that this is the way that you want to spend your working life. It is true to say that with the exception of parents, teachers are some of the most influential figures in children's lives, and the effect of their teaching will far outlive the whims of governments, policy-makers and educationists. Eaude (2006) reflects on the role as follows: 'As a teacher, you are important. Part of the excitement of teaching is to create a world of opportunities, with power to transform and create' (p. 110).

You will not always do well and go home with a spring in your step. Some days you will feel, and perhaps will be, uninspiring and less effective than normal. On other days your most carefully laid plans will fall apart at the seams. Despite the occasional setback, however, there are many privileges attached to being in the job, not least the thought that the impact of your words, actions and reactions will play a significant part in shaping and developing young lives. Nothing can take that entitlement and responsibility away from you.

When next you are shopping locally and you see a child pointing in your direction and hear a small voice proudly declaring to anyone who cares to listen, 'That's my teacher,' your heart will glow with pride until it could burst.

Activate your thinking!

Think of ways to bring joy into the classroom. Smile and laugh at children's innocent antics and remarks. Be willing to dance, sing, cheer, celebrate, empathise and love. Look for ways to make even mundane learning interesting. Think of the thousands of children you will influence as a teacher. Never lose sight of your calling.

Good practice

Write down this list of statements. Pin them up somewhere. Read and inwardly digest them each day:

I contribute to the development of good relationships in the school.
I have a reputation for being a pleasant, warm and caring person.
Children in my class are making good progress with me.
I keep events in proportion and do not become too anxious or too indifferent.
The school would be a poorer place without me.

Now start believing them!

Cross-reference: Guided Reader Extract 38

Further reading for Chapter 16

Brighouse, T. and Woods, D. (2006) *The Joy of Teaching*, Abingdon: RoutledgeFalmer.
The book celebrates the importance of teachers, reminds current teachers why they joined the profession, encourages others to join and reflects on the craft and artistry of teaching.
Dunn, D. (2011) *How to be an Outstanding Primary School Teacher*, London: Continuum.
This book contains activities and techniques for improving teaching using numerous lesson starters, plenaries and websites.
Field, K. (2006) 'Continuing your professional development', in J. Arthur, T. Grainger, and D. Wray (eds) *Learning to Teach in the Primary School*, Abingdon: Routledge. See Unit 9.3.
Although some information is a little dated, Field explains the thinking behind CPD and the way in which the system works locally and nationally.
Hayes, D. (2009) *Primary Teaching Today*, Abingdon: Routledge.
Takes the reader behind the scenes and alerts them to the fundamental attitudes and practices that every new primary teacher must acquire to be successful and contented in the job.

References

About.com (2011) *Homeschooling*, on-line at http://homeschooling.about.com.

Acker, S. (1999) *The Realities of Teachers' Work*, London: Cassell.

Adams, J.C. (2002) *Local Delivery of a National Agenda: Citizenship, rights and the changing role of school governors in England and Wales*, Hertfordshire: University of Hertfordshire.

Adamson, S. (2007) *Start Here: What new school governors need to know*, Norwich: Adamson Publishing.

Alderson, P. (1999) *Young Children's Rights: Beliefs, principles and practice*, London: Save the Children/Jessica Kingsley.

Alexander, R.J. (2009) *Children, Their World, Their Education: Final report and recommendations of the Cambridge Primary Review*, Abingdon: Routledge.

Allen, J., Potter, J., Sharp, J. and Turvey, K. (2007) *Primary ICT: Knowledge, understanding and practice*, Exeter: Learning Matters.

Alloway, T.P. and Gathercole, S.E. (2007) *Memory and Learning*, London: Sage.

Apter, M. and Kerr, J.H. (1991) *Adult Play*, Amsterdam: Swets and Zeitlinger.

Arizpe, E. and Styles, M. (2002) *Children Reading Pictures: Interpreting visual texts*, Abingdon: Routledge.

Arnall, J. (2007) *Discipline without Distress*, Berkeley, CA: Discipline Without Distress Publishing.

Arthur, J., Davison, J. and Lewis, M. (2005) *Professional Values and Practice: Achieving the standards for QTS*, Abingdon: RoutledgeFalmer.

Arthur, J., Grainger, T. and Wray, D. (eds) (2006) *Learning to Teach in the Primary School*, Abingdon: Routledge.

Atherton, J.S. (2005) *Learning and Teaching: Bloom's taxonomy*, on-line at www.learningandteaching.info/learning/bloomtax.htm.

Bailey, R. (ed.) (2010) *The Philosophy of Education*, London: Continuum.

Baines, E., Blatchford, P. and Kutnick, P. (2008) *Promoting Effective Group Work in the Classroom*, London: David Fulton.

Balding, J. (1996) *Bully Off: Young people that fear going to school*, Exeter: Schools Health Education Unit, Exeter University.

Balshaw, M.H. (1999) *Help in the Classroom*, second edn, London: David Fulton.

Barber, D., Cooper, L. and Meeson, G. (2007) *Learning and Teaching with Interactive Whiteboards: Primary and early years*, Exeter: Learning Matters.

Barnes, R. (2006) *The Practical Guide to Primary Classroom Management*, London: Sage.

Barton, E.A. (2006) *Bully Prevention*, second edn, London: Corwin Press.

Barton, L. and Tomlinson, S. (1984) 'The politics of integration in England', in L. Barton and S. Tomlinson (eds) *Special Education and Social Interests*, London: Crook Helm.

Bates, J. and Munday, S. (2005) *Able, Gifted and Talented*, London: Continuum.

Baumfield, V. and Mroz, M. (2004) 'Investigating pupils' questions in the primary school', in E.C. Wragg (ed.) *Teaching and Learning*, Abingdon: Routledge.

Beach, N., Evans, J. and Spruce, G. (2010) *Making Music in the Primary School*, London: David Fulton.

Beam, A. (2009) *Assisting Numeracy: A handbook for teaching assistants*, London: Beam Education (Nelson Thornes).

Beaudoin, M.N. and Taylor, M. (2004) *Creating a Positive School Climate*, London: Sage.

Beasley, G. and Moberley, A. (2000) *Seasonal Displays*, Pittsburgh, PA: Scholastic.

Bell, L. (2009) *Peer Support in the Primary Playground*, London: Optimus Education.

Bentham, S. (2005) *Teaching Assistants' Guide to Managing Classroom Behaviour*, Abingdon: Routledge.

Bentham, S. and Hutchins, R. (2008) *A Teaching Assistant's Guide to Completing NVQ Level 3: Understanding knowledge and meeting performance indicators*, Abingdon: Routledge.

Bentham, S. and Hutchins, R. (2012) *Improving Pupil Motivation Together: Teachers and teaching assistants working collaboratively*, Abingdon: Routledge.

Best, B. and Thomas, W. (2007) *The Creative Teaching and Learning Toolkit*, London: Continuum.

Beveridge, S. (2004) *Children, Families and Schools: Developing partnerships for inclusive education*, London: RoutledgeFalmer.

Beverton, S. (2006) 'Collaborating with parents', in J. Arthur, T. Grainger and D. Wray (eds) *Learning to Teach in the Primary School*, Abingdon: Routledge.

Bilton, H. (2002) *Outdoor Play in the Early Years: Management and innovation*, second edn, London: David Fulton.

Biott, C. and Easen, P. (1994) *Collaborative Learning in Staffrooms and Classrooms*, London: David Fulton.

Bird, R. (2006) 'Personalisation: what does it mean?' *Secondary Headship*, 49 (November), pp. 4–5.

Blythe, S.G. (2009) *Attention, Balance and Coordination: The ABC of learning success*, London: Wiley-Blackwell.

Bolton, R. (1979) *People Skills*, New York: Simon & Schuster.

Bradford, H. (2009) *Communication, Language and Literacy in the EYFS*, London: David Fulton.

Brandling, R. (1982) *A Year in the Primary School*, London: Ward Lock.

Briggs, M., Woodfield, A., Martin, C. and Swatton, P. (2003) *Assessment for Learning and Teaching in Primary Schools*, Exeter: Learning Matters.

Brighouse, T. and Woods, D. (2006) *The Joy of Teaching*, Abingdon: RoutledgeFalmer.

Broadhead, P. (2006) 'Developing an understanding of young children's learning through play', *British Educational Research Journal*, 32 (2), pp. 191–207.

Broadhead, P. and Burt, A. (2012) *Understanding Young Children's Learning Through Play*, Abingdon: Routledge.

Brock, A., Dodds, S., Jarvis, P. and Olusoga, Y. (2009) *Perspectives on Play*, London: Pearson/Longman.

Brooker, L. (2002) *Starting School: Young children learning cultures*, Maidenhead: Open University Press.

Brown, B. (1998) *Unlearning Discrimination in the Early Years*, Stoke-on-Trent: Trentham Books.

Brown, M. and Ralph, S. (1994) *Managing Stress in Schools*, Plymouth: Northcote House.

Bruce, T. (2001) *Learning through Play*, London: Hodder & Stoughton.

Bubb, S. (2007) *Successful Induction*, London: Paul Chapman.

Bubb, S. (2009) *The Insider's Guide for New Teachers*, second edn, Abingdon: RoutledgeFalmer.

Bubb, S. and Earley, P. (2004) *Managing Teacher Workload: Work–life balance and wellbeing*, London: Paul Chapman.

Bubb, S., Heilbron, R., Jones, C., Totterdell, M. and Bailey, M. (2002) *Improving Induction*, Abingdon: RoutledgeFalmer.

Burgess, R., Nelson, C. and Dreyer, D. (2000) *Laughing Lessons*, Minneapolis, MN: Free Spirit Publishing.

Burnett, G. and Jarvis, K. (2004) *Parents First*, Carmarthen: Crown House.

Burnham, L. (2006) *101 Essential Lists for Teaching Assistants*, London: Continuum.

Butt, G. (2006) *Lesson Planning*, London: Continuum.

Byre, B. (1993) *Coping with Bullying at School*, London: Cassell.

Cairns, J., Gardner, R. and Lawton, D. (2005) *Faith Schools: Consensus or conflict?* London: Routledge.

Call, N.J. (1999) Brain-based Learning in Practice: About the brain, on-line at www.acceleratedlearning.co.uk.

Call, N.J. and Featherstone, S. (2010) *The Thinking Child*, second edn, London: Continuum.

Campbell, A. and Fairbairn, G. (eds) (2005) *Working with Support in the Classroom*, London: Paul Chapman.

Carlyle, D. and Woods, P. (2002) *Emotions of Teacher Stress*, Stoke-on-Trent: Trentham Books.

Carpenter, B., Ashdown, R. and Bovair, K. (eds) (1996) *Enabling access: Effective teaching and learning for pupils with learning difficulties*, London: David Fulton.

Carr, D. (2003) *Making Sense of Education*, Abingdon: Routledge.

Carroll, M. and Hannay, J. (2010) *Developing Physical Health and Well-Being through Gymnastic Activity (5–7)*, London: David Fulton.

Carroll, M. and Hannay, J. (2011) *Developing Physical Health and Well-Being through Gymnastic Activity (7–14)*, London: David Fulton.

Carter, J. (2002) *Just Imagine: Creative ideas for creative writing*, London: David Fulton.

Casey, T. (2005) *Inclusive Play*, London: Paul Chapman.

Casey, T. (2007) *Environments for Outdoor Play*, London: Sage.

Catling, S. and Willy, T. (2009) *Teaching Primary Geography*, Exeter: Learning Matters.

Chaplain, R. (2003) *Teaching without Disruption in the Primary School*, Abingdon: RoutledgeFalmer.

Chaplain, R. (2006) 'Managing classroom behaviour', in J. Arthur, T. Grainger and D. Wray (eds) *Learning to Teach in the Primary School*, Abingdon: Routledge.

Chapman, R. (1995) 'New to teaching', in J. Bell (ed.) *Teachers Talk About Teaching*, Maidenhead: Open University Press.

Chappell, C. (2003) *Reconstructing the Lifelong Learner*, Abingdon: Routledge.

Charlton, T., Jones, K. and Flores-Hole, H. (1996) 'The effects of teacher behaviour upon pupil behaviour', in T. Charlton, K. Jones and M. Cummings (eds) *Pupil Needs and Classroom Practices*, Cheltenham: Park Published Papers.

Cheminais, R. (2005) *Every Child Matters: A new role for SENCOS*, London: David Fulton.

Cheminais, R. (2008) *Every Child Matters: A practical guide for teaching assistants*, London: David Fulton.

Cheminais, R. (2009) *Effective Multi-agency Partnerships: Putting Every Child Matters into practice*, London: Sage.

Cheminais, R. (2010) *Rita Cheminais' Handbook for New SENCOs*, London: Sage.

Chetkuti, D., Buhagiar, M.A. and Cardona, A. (2011) 'The professional development portfolio: learning through reflection in the first year of teaching', *Reflective Practice*, 12 (1), pp. 61–72.

Children's Society (2007) *Good Childhood Inquiry: Happiness*, London: Church of England Children's Society.

Cipani, E. (2007) *Class Management for All Teachers*, New York: Prentice Hall.

Clark, A., Kjorholt, A.T. and Moss, P. (2005) *Beyond Listening: Children's perspectives on early childhood services*, Bristol: Policy Press.

Clark, C.M. (1995) *Thoughtful Teaching*, London: Cassell.

Clarke, J. (2008) 'Learning and thinking', *Early Years Update* (April), on-line via www.teachingexpertise.com.

Clarke, S. (2001) *Unlocking Formative Assessment*, London: Hodder & Stoughton.

Clarke, S. (2008) *Active Learning Through Formative Assessment*, London: Hodder Education.

Claxton, G. (2004) *Teaching Children to Learn: Beyond flatpacks and fine words, Burning Issues in Primary Education Teaching No. 11*, Birmingham: National Primary Trust.

Clipson-Boyles, S. (2011) *Teaching the Primary Curriculum through Drama*, Abingdon: Routledge.

Cockburn, A.D. (1996) *Teaching Under Pressure*, London: Falmer Press.

Cohen, D. (2006a) *The Development of Play*, third edn, Abingdon: Routledge.

Cohen, D. (2006b) *Social Skills for Primary Pupils*, Birmingham: Questions Publishing.

Cole, M. (ed.) (2002) *Professional Issues for Teachers and Student Teachers*, second edn, London: David Fulton.

Coles, R. (1990) *The Spiritual Life of Children*, Boston: Houghton Mifflin.

Collins, M. (2001) *Because We're Worth It: Enhancing self-esteem in young children*, Bristol: Lucky Duck Publishing.

Collins, M. (2007) *Circle Time for the Very Young*, second edn, London: Sage.

Connolly, P. (2004) *Boys and Schooling in the Early Years*, Abingdon: Routledge.

Cook, S.W. and Goldin-Meadow, S. (2006) 'The role of gesturing: do children use their hands to change their minds?' *Journal of Cognition and Development*, 7 (2), pp. 211–32.

Cooper, H. and Hyland, R. (2000) *Children's Perceptions of Learning with Trainee Teachers*, Abingdon: Routledge.

Cooper, H., Hegarty, P. and Simco, N. (1996) *Display in the Classroom: Principles, practice and learning theory*, London: David Fulton.

Corbett J. (1995) *Bad-mouthing: The language of special needs*, London: Falmer Press.

Corrie, C. (2003) *Becoming Emotionally Intelligent*, Stafford: Network Educational Press.

Cotton, T. (1998) *Thinking about Teaching*, London: Hodder & Stoughton.

Coultas, V. (2007) *Constructive Talking in Challenging Classrooms*, Abingdon: Routledge.

Cousins, L., Higgs, M. and Leader, J. (2004) *Making the Most of Your Teaching Assistants*, London: PfP.

Cowie, H. and Colliety, P. (2010) 'Cyberbullying: sanctions or sensitivity', *Pastoral Care in Education*, 28 (4), pp. 261–8.

Cowley, S. (2003) *Teaching Clinic*, London: Continuum.

Cox, S. and Heames, R. (1999) *Managing the Pressures in Teaching*, London: Hodder & Stoughton.

Craft, A. (2005) *Creativity in our Schools: Tensions and dilemmas*, Abingdon: Routledge.

Craft, A. and Jeffrey, B. (2008) 'Creativity and performativity in teaching and learning: tensions, dilemmas, constraints, accommodations and synthesis', *British Journal of Educational Research*, 34 (5), pp. 577–84.

Cramp, A. (2008) 'Knowing me, knowing you: building valuable relationships outside the classroom', *Education 3–13*, 36 (2), pp. 171–82.

Cremin, T., Burnard, P. and Craft, A. (2006) 'Pedagogy and possibility thinking in the early years', *Thinking Skills and Creativity*, 1 (2), pp. 108–19.

Crosse, K. (2008) *Introducing English as an Additional Language to Young Children*, London: Sage.

Crozier, G. and Reay, D. (2005) *Activating Participation*, Stoke-on-Trent: Trentham.

Cullingford, C. (1997) 'Assessment, evaluation and the effective school', in C. Cullingford (ed.) *Assessment Versus Evaluation*, London: Cassell.

Cullingford, C. (2002) *The Best Years of their Lives? Pupils' experience of school*, London: Kogan Page.

Cullingford, C. (2007) 'Creativity and pupils' experience of school', *Education 3–13*, 35 (2), pp. 133–42.

Cullingford-Agnew, S. (2006) *Becoming a Higher Level Teaching Assistant: Primary SEN*, Exeter: Learning Matters.

Cushman, P. and Cowan, J. (2010) 'Enhancing student self-worth in the primary school learning environment: teachers' views and students' views', *Pastoral Care in Education*, 28 (2), pp. 81–95.

Dalton, J. and Fairchild, L. (2004) *The Compassionate Classroom: Lessons that nurture wisdom and empathy*, Chicago, IL: Zephyr Press.

Davies, A. (2007) *Storytelling in the Classroom*, London: Sage.

Dawes, L. (2010) *Creating a Speaking and Listening Classroom*, London: David Fulton.

Dawes, L. (2011) *Talking Points: Discussion activities in the primary classroom*, Abingdon: Routledge.

Day, A. (2011) *Drama Sessions for Primary Schools and Drama Clubs*, Abingdon: Routledge.

Day, C. (2004) *A Passion for Teaching*, Abingdon: RoutledgeFalmer.

Day, C., Sammons, P., Stobart, G., Kington, A. and Gu, Q. (2007) *Teachers Matter*, Maidenhead: Open University Press.

Dean, G. (1998) *Challenging the More Able Language User*, London: NACE/David Fulton.

Dean, J. (2001) *The Effective School Governor*, Abingdon: RoutledgeFalmer.

Dean, J. (2008) *Organising Learning in the Primary School*, Abingdon: Routledge.

Deed, C., Bellhouse, B. and Johnston, G. (2007) *Using Circle Time to Learn about Stories*, London: Sage.

Denton, C. and Postlethwaite, K. (1985) *Able Children: Identifying them in the classroom*, Windsor: NFER-Nelson.

Department for Children, Schools and Families (DSCF) (2006) *Learning and Teaching for Bilingual Children in the Primary Years*, London: DCSF Publications.

Department for Children, Schools and Families (DCSF) (2009) *Supporting Parents with Their Children's 'At Home' Learning and Development*, Research Report RR138, London: DCSF Publications.

Department for Education and Employment (DfEE) (1998) *Health and Safety of Pupils on Educational Visits*, London: DfEE Publications.

Department for Education and Skills (DfES) (2002) *Special Educational Needs Code of Practice*, Annesley: DfES Publications.

Department for Education and Skills (DfES) (2005) *Every Child Matters*, London: DfES Publications Centre.

Department for Education and Skills (DfES) (2006a) *Primary National Strategy*, London: DfES Publications Centre.

Department for Education and Skills (DfES) (2006b) *Learning and Teaching for Bilingual Children in the Primary Years*, London: DfES Publications Centre.

Department for Education and Skills (DfES) (2007) *Social and Emotional Aspects of Learning*, London: DfES Publications Centre.

Derrington, C. and Goddard, H. (2008) *Whole-brain Behaviour Management in the Classroom*, Abingdon: Routledge.

Desforges, C. (1995) 'Teaching for order and control', in C. Desforges (ed.) *An Introduction to Teaching*, Oxford: Blackwell.

Desforges, C. and Abouchaar, A. (2003) *The Impact of Parental Involvement, Parental Support and Family Education on Pupil Achievement and Adjustment: A literature review*, Research Report 433 for the DfES, London: Queen's Printer.

Dewey, J. (1910/1997) *How We Think*, New York: Dover Publications.

Dickinson, C. (1996) *Effective Learning Activities*, Stafford: Network Educational Press.

Dillon, J.T. (1994) *Using Discussion in Classrooms*, Maidenhead: Open University Press.

Dixie, G. (2007) *Managing Your Classroom*, London: Continuum.

Dockrell, J.E and Shield, B.M. (2006) 'Acoustical barriers in classrooms: the impact of noise on performance in the classroom', *British Educational Research Journal*, 32 (3), pp. 509–25.

Doddington, C. and Hilton, M. (2007) *Child-centred Education*, London: Sage.

Doona, J. (2011) *Shakespeare for the Primary School: 50 lesson plans using drama*, Abingdon: Routledge.

Doust, S. and Doust, R. (2001) *Governor's Handbook: A comprehensive guide to the duties and responsibilities of school governors in England and Wales*, London: Advisory Centre for Education.

Drake, J. (2003) *Organising Play in the Early Years*, London: David Fulton.

Drake, J. (2009) *Planning for Children's Play and Learning*, third edn, London: David Fulton.

Dreikurs, R., Grunwald, B.B. and Pepper, F.C. (1998) *Maintaining Sanity in the Classroom*, Abingdon: Routledge.

Drummond, M.J. (2003) *Assessing Children's Learning*, second edn, London: David Fulton.

Duffy, B. (1998) *Supporting Creativity and Imagination in the Early Years*, Maidenhead: Open University Press.

Dweck, C.S. (2000) *Self-Theories: Their role in motivation, personality and development*, Hove: Psychology Press.

Eaude, T. (2006) *Children's Spiritual, Moral, Social and Cultural Development*, Exeter: Learning Matters.

Edwards, S. (2010) *The SENCO Survival Guide*, London: David Fulton/NASEN.

Eisner, E. (2002) *The Arts and the Creation of Mind*, New York: Yale University Press.

Eke, R. and Lee, J. (2008) *Using Talk Effectively in the Primary School*, London: David Fulton.

Ephgrave, A. (2011) *The Reception Year in Action*, Abingdon: Routledge.

Epstein, D., Elwood, J., Hey, V. and Maw, J. (1998) *Failing Boys? Issues in gender and achievement*, Maidenhead: Open University Press.

Erricker, C., Ota, C. and Erricker, J. (2001) *Spiritual Education: Religious, cultural and social differences*, Abingdon: Routledge.

Eyre, D. and McClure, L. (eds) (2001) *Curriculum Provision for the Gifted and Talented in the Primary School*, London: David Fulton/NACE.

Eysenck, H. (2000) *Intelligence: A new look*, Edison, NJ: Transaction Publishers.

Farmery, C. (2004) *Successful Subject Co-ordination*, London: Continuum.

Fawcett, M. (2009) *Learning Through Child Observation*, second edn, London: Jessica Kingsley.

Featherstone, S. (2001) *The Little Book of Outdoor Play*, London: Featherstone Education.

Feinstein, L., Duckworth, K. and Sabates, R. (2008) *Education and the Family*, Abingdon: Routledge.

Ferrigan, C. (2011) *Passing the ICT Skills Test*, fourth edn, Exeter: Learning Matters.

Filer, J. (2011) *Setting Up Parental Support in Schools and Early Years Settings*, London: David Fulton.

Fisher, J. (2002) *The Foundations of Learning*, Maidenhead: Open University Press.

Fisher, R. (2004) 'What is creativity?' in R. Fisher and M. Williams (eds) *Unlocking Creativity*, London: David Fulton.

Fisher, R. (2005) *Teaching Children to Learn*, Cheltenham: Stanley Thornes.

Fisher, R. (2009) *Creative Dialogue: Talk for thinking in the classroom*, London: David Fulton.

Fitzgerald, D. (2004) *Parent Partnerships in the Early Years*, London: Continuum.

Fleetham, M. (2008) *Including Gifted, Talented and Able Children in the Primary Classroom*, Abingdon: Routledge.

Florian, L., Rouse, M. and Hawkins, K.B. (2007) *Achievement and Inclusion in Schools*, Abingdon: Routledge.

Foale, J. and Pagett, L. (2007) *Creative Approaches to Poetry for the Primary Framework for Literacy*, London: David Fulton.

Fox, S. and Surtees, L. (2010) *Mathematics across the Curriculum: Problem-solving, reasoning and numeracy in primary schools*, London: Continuum.

Fox, S.E., Levitt, P. and Nelson, C.A. (2010) 'How the timing and quality of early experiences influence the development of brain architecture', *Child Development*, 81 (1), pp. 28–40.

Francis, B. and Skelton, C. (2005) *Gender and Achievement*, Abingdon: Routledge.

Franklin, S. (2006) 'VAKing out learning styles', *Education 3–13*, 34 (1), pp. 81–7.

Fried, R. (1995) *The Passionate Teacher: A practical guide*, Boston, MA: Beacon Press.

Frost, J.A. and Emery, M.J. (2000) *Academic Interventions for Children with Dyslexia who have Phonological Core Deficits*, on-line at www.kidsource.com/kidsource/content2/dyslexia.html.

Galton, M. (2007) *Learning and Teaching in the Primary Classroom*, London: Sage.

Gardner, H. (1983) *Frames of Mind: The theory of multiple intelligences*, New York: Basic Books.

Gardner, H. (1999) *Intelligence Reframed*, New York: Basic Books.

Gardner, J. (2006) 'Children who have English as an additional language', in G. Knowles (ed.) *Supporting Inclusive Practice*, Exeter: Learning Matters.

Garnett, S. (2006) *Using Brainpower in the Classroom*, Abingdon: Routledge.

Garrick, R. (2004) *Outdoor Play in the Early Years*, London: Continuum.

Gill, V. (1998) *The Ten Commandments of Good Teaching*, Thousand Oaks, CA: Corwin Press/Sage Publications.

Gipps, C., McCallum, B. and Hargreaves, E. (1999) *What Makes a Good Primary School Teacher?* Abingdon: RoutledgeFalmer.

Glynn, C. (2001) *Learning on Their Feet: A sourcebook for kinaesthetic learning across the curriculum*, Shoreham, VT: Discover Writing Press.

Goleman, D. (1995) *Emotional Intelligence*, New York: Bantam.

Goleman, D. (1999) *Working with Emotional Intelligence*, London: Bloomsbury.

Goleman, D. (2005) *Emotional Intelligence*, second edn, New York: Bantam Books.

Good Schools Guide (2008) *Dyspraxia*, Liverpool: Lucas Publications.

Grant-Williams, R. (2002) *Voice Power*, New York: AMACOM.

Greenwood, C. (2004) *Understanding the Needs of Parents: Guidelines for effective collaboration with parents of children with SEN*, London: David Fulton.

Gregory, E. (2008) *Learning to Read in a New Language: Making sense of words and worlds*, London: Paul Chapman.

Griffiths, N. (1998) *A Corner to Learn*, Cheltenham: Stanley Thornes.

Grossman, H. (2003) *Classroom Behaviour Management for Diverse and Inclusive Schools*, Lanham, MD: Rowman and Littlefield.

Hall, D. (2009) *The ICT Handbook for Primary Teachers*, Abingdon: Routledge.

Hall, W. (2009) *Dyslexia in the Primary Classroom*, Exeter: Learning Matters.

Hallgarten, J. (2000) *Parents Exist, OK? Issues and visions for parent–school relationships*, London: IPPR.

Hancock, R. and Collins, J. (eds) (2005) *Primary Teaching Assistants*, London: David Fulton.

Hansen, A. (2011) *Children's Errors in Mathematics*, Exeter: Learning Matters.

Hardman, F., Smith, F. and Wall, K. (2003) 'Interactive whole class teaching in the National Literacy Strategy', *Cambridge Journal of Education*, 33 (2), pp. 197–215.

Hargreaves, L. and Wolfe, S. (2007) 'Observing closely to see more clearly: observation in the primary classroom', in J. Moyles (ed.) *Beginning Teaching, Beginning Learning in Primary Education*, Maidenhead: Open University.

Hargreaves, L., Pell, A. and Merry, R. (2003) 'Teacher–pupil interaction and interactive teaching', in J. Moyles, L. Hargreaves, R. Merry, F. Paterson and V. Esarte-Sarries, *Interactive Teaching in the Primary School*, Maidenhead: Open University Press.

Harlen, W. (2000) *The Teaching of Science in Primary Schools*, third edn, London: David Fulton.

Harnett, P. (2007) *Supporting Children's Learning in the Primary and Early Years*, Abingdon: Routledge.

Harriman, H. (2008) *The Outdoor Classroom: A place to learn*, Swindon: Red Robin Books.

Harrop, A. and Williams, T. (1992) 'Rewards and punishments in the primary school: pupils' perceptions and teachers' usage', *Educational Psychology*, 7 (4), pp. 211–15.

Hart, S. (2000) *Thinking Through Teaching*, London: David Fulton.

Hart, T. (2003) *The Secret Spiritual World of Children*, San Francisco: New World Library.

Hastings, N. and Wood, K.C. (2002) *Reorganising Primary Classroom Learning*, Maidenhead: Open University Press.

Hawkes, N. (2000) 'The role of the school assembly', *Living Values Education*, on-line at www.livingvalues.net/reference/assembly.html.

Haydn, T. (2006) *Managing Pupil Behaviour*, Abingdon: Routledge.

Haydn, T. (2012) *Managing Pupil Behaviour: Improving the classroom atmosphere*, Abingdon: Routledge.

Hayes, C. (2006) *Stress Relief for Teachers*, Abingdon: Routledge.

Hayes, D. (1998) *Effective Verbal Communication*, London: Hodder & Stoughton.

Hayes, D. (2002) 'Prospering on school placement', *Primary Practice*, 32 (Autumn), pp. 32–4.

Hayes, D. (2006) *Inspiring Primary Teaching*, Exeter: Learning Matters.

Hayes, D. (ed.) (2007) *Joyful Teaching and Learning in the Primary School*, Exeter: Learning Matters.

Hayes, D. (2009a) *Learning and Teaching in Primary Schools: Achieving QTS (2009)*, Exeter: Learning Matters.

Hayes, D. (2009b) *Primary Teaching Today*, Abingdon: Routledge.

Hayes, D. (2011) *The Guided Reader to Teaching and Learning*, London: David Fulton.

Haynes, J. (2007) 'Thinking together: enjoying dialogue with children', in D. Hayes (ed.) *Joyful Teaching and Learning in the Primary School*, Exeter: Learning Matters.

Hayward, A. (2006) *Making Inclusion Happen*, London: Paul Chapman.

Headington, R. (2000) *Monitoring, Assessment, Recording, Reporting and Accountability*, London: David Fulton.

Hewitt, S. (2007) *Bullying*, London: Franklin Watts.

Heyda, P.A. (2002) *The Primary Teacher's Survival Guide*, Portsmouth, NH: Heinemann.

Hicks, D. (2001) *Citizenship for the Future: A practical classroom guide*, Godalming: World Wildlife Fund.

Hislam, J. and Lall, R. (2007) 'How oral story can develop creative thinking', in J. Moyles (ed.) *Beginning Teaching, Beginning Learning in Primary Education*, Maidenhead: Open University Press.

HM Inspectorate of Education (2001) *Improving Physical Education in Primary Schools*, Edinburgh: The Stationery Office.

Hobday-Kutsch, J. and McVittie, J. (2002) 'Just clowning around: classroom perspectives on children's humour', *Canadian Journal of Education*, 27 (2/3), pp. 195–210.

Hodkinson, A. and Vickerman, P. (2009) *Key Issues in Special Educational Needs*, London: Sage.

Holdaway, D. (1979) *The Foundations of Literacy*, Sydney: Ashton Scholastic.

Holmes, E. (2003) *The Newly Qualified Teacher's Handbook*, London: Kogan Page.

Holmes, E. (2004) *Teacher Wellbeing: Looking after yourself and your career in the classroom*, London: RoutledgeFalmer.

Hood, P. (2008) 'What do we teachers need to know to enhance our creativity?' *Education 3–13*, 36 (2), pp. 139–51.

Hooks, B. (2009) *Teaching Critical Thinking*, Abingdon: Routledge.

Houghton, D. and McColgan, M. (1995) *Working with Children*, London: Collins Educational.

Howe, M.J.A. (1990) *Sense and Nonsense about Hothouse Children*, Leicester: BPS Books.

Hughes, P. (2009) *Breaking Barriers to Learning*, Abingdon: Routledge.

Hughes, M., Wikeley, F. and Nash, T. (1994) *Parents and Their Children's Schools*, London: Blackwell.

Hutchinson, N. and Smith, H. (2003) *Changing Behaviour in the Early Years*, London: David Fulton.

Huxtable, M., Hurford, R. and Mounter, J. (2009) *Creative and Philosophical Thinking in Primary Schools*, London: Optimus.

Hymer, B. and Michel, D. (2002) *Gifted and Talented Learners*, London: NACE/David Fulton.

Ivatts, A. (2006) *The Situation Regarding Current Policy, Provision and Practice in Elective Home Education for Gypsy, Roma and Traveller Children*, Annersley: DfES Publications.

Jacklin, A., Griffiths, V. and Robinson, C. (2006) *Beginning Primary Teaching*, Maidenhead: Open University Press.

Jackson, M. (1987) 'Making sense of school', in A. Pollard (ed.) *Children and Their Primary Schools: A new perspective*, Lewes: Falmer Press.

Jackson, M. (1993) *Creative Display and Environment*, London: Hodder & Stoughton.

Jaksec, C.M. (2005) *Difficult Parent, Thousand Oaks*, CA: Corwin Press.

James, F. and Brownsword, K. (1994) *A Positive Approach*, Twickenham: Belair Publications.

Jeffrey, B. and Woods, P. (2003) *The Creative School*, Abingdon: RoutledgeFalmer.

Jeffrey, B. and Woods, P. (2009) *Creative Learning in the Primary School*, Abingdon: Routledge.

Jelly, M. (2000) *Involving Pupils in Practice*, London: David Fulton.

Johnson, C. (2004) 'Creative drama: thinking from within', in R. Fisher and M. Williams (eds) *Unlocking Creativity*, London: David Fulton.

Johnston, J. (2002) 'Teaching and learning in the early years', in J. Johnston, D. Chater and D. Bell (eds) *Teaching the Primary Curriculum*, Maidenhead: Open University.

Johnston, R.S. and Watson, J.E. (2007) *Teaching Synthetic Phonics*, Exeter: Learning Matters.

Joliffe, W. (2007) *Cooperative Learning in the Classroom*, London: Sage.

Jonasson, C. (2011) 'The dynamics of absence behaviour: interrelations between absence from class and absence in class', *Educational Research*, 53 (1), pp. 17–32.

Jones, P. and Robson, C. (2008) *Teaching Music in Primary Schools*, Exeter: Learning Matters.

Jones, R. and Wyse, D. (2004) *Creativity in the Primary Curriculum*, London: David Fulton.

Jones, S. (2002) Five Guidelines for Learning Spelling and Six Ways for Practicing Spelling, on-line at www.ldonline.org/article/6192.

Jonson, K.F. (2008) *Being an Effective Mentor: How to help beginning teachers succeed*, London: Corwin Press.

Kaldi, S., Filippatou, D. and Govaris, C. (2011) 'Project-based learning in primary schools: its effects on pupils' learning and attitudes', *Education 3–13*, 39 (1), pp. 35–47.

Kalliala, M. (2004) *Play Culture in the Changing World*, Maidenhead: Open University Press.

Katz, L.G. (1995) *How Can We Strengthen Children's Self-Esteem?* Illinois: ERIC Clearinghouse on Elementary and Early Childhood Education; on-line via www.kidsource.com.

Katz, L.G. and Chard, S.C. (2000) *Engaging Children's Minds: The project approach*, second edn, Stamford, CT: Alex Publishers.

Kay, J. (2003) *Teaching Assistants' Handbook*, London: Continuum.

Kelly, P. (2007) 'The joy of enhancing children's learning', in D. Hayes (ed.) *Joyful Teaching and Learning in the Primary School*, Exeter: Learning Matters.

Kendall-Seatter, S. (2005) *Primary Professional Studies*, Exeter: Learning Matters.

Kerry, T. (1998) *Questioning and Explaining in Classrooms*, London: Hodder & Stoughton.

Kewley, G.D. (2001) *Attention Deficit Hyperactivity Disorder*, London: David Fulton.

Key, P. and Stillman, J. (2009) *Teaching Primary Art and Design*, Exeter: Learning Matters.

Kidwell, V. (2004) *Homework*, London: Continuum.

Killick, S. (2006) *Emotional Literacy at the Heart of the School Ethos*, London: Paul Chapman.

Kinder, K., Wakefield, A. and Wilkin, A. (1996) *Talking Back: Pupils' views on disaffection*, Slough: NFER.

Kizlik, B. (2008) *Things to Say and Do at that First Teaching Interview*, ADPRIMA, on-line at www.adprima.com/interview.htm.

Knight, S. (2009) *Forest Schools and Outdoor Learning in the Early Years*, London: Sage.

Knowles, G. (2006) 'Gifted and talented', in G. Knowles (ed.) *Supporting Inclusive Practice*, Exeter: Learning Matters.

Knowles, G. (2009) *Ensuring Every Child Matters*, London: Sage.

Kohn, A. (2004) *What Does It Mean to be Well Educated?* Boston, MA: Beacon Press.

Koshy, V. (2000) *Mathematics for Primary Teachers*, Abingdon: Routledge.

Kovacic, G. (2005) 'Voice education in teacher training', *Journal of Education for Teaching*, 31 (2), pp. 87–97.

Kreider, H. (2000) *The National Network of Partnership Schools: A model for family–school–community partnerships*, Cambridge, MA: University of Harvard, Harvard Family Research Project.

Kutnick, P. (1994) 'Use and effectiveness of groups in classrooms: towards a pedagogy', in P. Kutnick and C. Rogers (eds) *Groups in Schools*, London: Cassell.

Kyriacou, C. (2003) *Helping Troubled Pupils*, London: Nelson Thornes.

Kyriacou, C. (2009) 'The five dimensions of social pedagogy within schools', *Pastoral Care in Education*, 27 (2), pp. 101–8.

Larrivee, B. (2008) 'Meeting the challenge of preparing reflective practitioners', *The New Educator*, 4 (2), pp. 87–106.

Lave, J. and Wenger, E. (1991) *Situated Learning: Legitimate peripheral participation*, Cambridge: Cambridge University Press.

Lawrence, D. (2006) *Enhancing Self-Esteem in the Classroom*, third edn, London: Paul Chapman.

Lawson, S. (1994) *Helping Children Cope with Bullying*, London: Sheldon Press.

Layard, R. and Dunn, J. (2009) *A Good Childhood: Searching for values in a competitive age*, London: Penguin.

Learning Theories Knowledgebase (2011) 'Discovery learning (Bruner)', Learning-Theories.com, online at HYPERLINK "http://www.learning-theories.com/discovery-learning-bruner.html" www.learning-theories.com/discovery-learning-bruner.html.

Lee, C. (2004) *Preventing Bullying in School*, London: Sage.

Leedham, W. and Murphy, M. (2007) 'Joyful history', in D. Hayes (ed.) *Joyful Teaching and Learning in the Primary School*, Exeter: Learning Matters.

Leeson, C. (2007) 'My life in care: experiences of non-participation in decision making processes', *Child and Family Social Work*, 12 (3), pp. 268–77.

Leicester, M. and Johnson, G. (2004) *Stories for Inclusive Schools: Developing young pupils' skills in assembly and in the classroom*, Abingdon: RoutledgeFalmer.

Lerner, M. (2000) *Spirit Matters*, Charlottesville, VA: Hampton Roads Publishing.

Lewis, M. and Ellis, S. (2006) *Phonics*, London: Sage.

Lickona, T. (1999) *Educating for Character*, New York: Bantam Press.

Liston, D. and Garrison, J. (2004) 'Love revived and examined', in D. Liston and J. Garrison (eds) *Teaching, Learning and Loving*, Abingdon: RoutledgeFalmer.

Littleton, K. and Howe, C. (2009) *Educational Dialogues*, Abingdon: Routledge.

Lloyd, C. and Beard, J. (1995) *Managing Classroom Collaboration*, London: Cassell.

Lloyd, G. (ed.) (2004) *Problem Girls*, Abingdon: RoutledgeFalmer.

Loomans, D. and Kolberg, K. (2002) *The Laughing Classroom*, Novato, CA: H.J. Kramer.

Lord, L. and Slinn, K. (2007) *Curriculum Planning and Assessment for the Foundation Stage*, London: Sage.

Lougy, R.A., DeRuvo, S.L. and Rosenthal, D.K. (2007) *Teaching Young Children with ADHD*, Thousand Oaks, CA: Corwin Press.

Loveless, A. (2009) *ICT in the Primary School*, Maidenhead: Open University Press.

Lowe, V. (2006) *Stories, Pictures and Reality*, Abingdon: Routledge.

Lucas, A.J. and Dyment, J.E. (2010) 'Where do children choose to play on the school ground? The influence of green design', *Education 3–13*, 38 (2), pp. 177–89.

Luxford, H. and Smart, L. (2009) *Learning Through Talk*, London: David Fulton.

McDermott, D. (2008) *Developing Caring Relationships Among Parents, Children, Schools, and Communities*, London: Sage.

McEwan, E.K. (1998) *How to Deal with Parents who are Angry, Troubled, Afraid or Just Plain Crazy*, Thousand Oaks, CA: Corwin Press.

McGlaughlin, A., Weekes, D. and Wright, C. (2000) *Race, Class and Gender in Exclusion from School*, London: Falmer Press (Routledge).

MacGrath, M. (2000) *The Art of Peaceful Teaching*, London: David Fulton.

McGuinness, C. (1999) *From Thinking Skills to Thinking Classrooms: A review and evaluation of approaches for developing pupils' thinking*, Nottingham: DfEE Publications.

Macintyre, C. (2008) *Dyspraxia 5–14*, London: David Fulton/NASEN.

Macintyre, C. (2011) *Enhancing Learning Through Play: A developmental perspective for early years settings*, second edn, Abingdon: Routledge.

McIntyre-Bhatty, K. (2007) 'Interventions and interrogations: an analysis of recent policy imperatives and their rationales in the case of home education', *Education, Knowledge and Economy*, 1 (3), pp. 241–59.

Mackintosh, M. (2007) 'The joy of teaching and learning geography', in D. Hayes (ed.) *Joyful Teaching and Learning in the Primary School*, Exeter: Learning Matters.

Maclure, M. and Elliott, J. (1993) 'Packaging the primary curriculum: textbooks and the English national curriculum', *Curriculum Journal*, 4 (1), pp. 91–113.

McMahon, R. (2007) *Revolution in the Bleachers*, New York: Gotham Books.

McNamara, S. (1997) 'Children with special educational needs', in N. Kitson and R. Merry (eds) *Teaching in the Primary School*, Abingdon: Routledge.

McNamara, S. and Moreton, G. (2001) *Changing Behaviour*, London: David Fulton.

McNess, E., Broadfoot, P. and Osborn, M. (2003) 'Is the effective compromising the affective?' *British Educational Research Journal*, 29 (2), pp. 243–57.

McPhillimy, B. (1996) *Controlling Your Class*, Chichester: John Wiley.

Makins, V. (1997) *The Invisible Children: Nipping failure in the bud*, London: David Fulton.

Manning-Morton, J. and Thorp, M. (2003) *Times for Play*, Maidenhead: Open University Press.

Manuel, J. and Hughes, J. (2006) 'It has always been my dream: exploring pre service teachers' motivations for choosing teaching', *Teacher Development*, 10 (1), pp. 5–24.

Marcos, J.M., Sanchez, E. and Tilema, H.H. (2011) 'Promoting teacher reflection', *Journal of Education for Teaching*, 37 (1), pp. 21–36.

Martin, F. (2006) *Teaching Geography in Primary Schools*, Cambridge: Chris Kington Publishing.

Maynard, S. (2011) *Teaching Foreign Languages in the Primary School*, Abingdon: Routledge.

Maynard, T. (2001) 'The trainee teacher and the school community of practice', *Cambridge Journal of Education*, 31 (1), pp. 39–52.

Medwell, J. (2006) 'Approaching short-term planning', in J. Arthur, T. Grainger and D. Wray (eds) *Learning to Teach in the Primary School*, Abingdon: Routledge.

Medwell, J. (2007) *Successful Teaching Placement*, Exeter: Learning Matters.

Merry, R. and Moyles, J. (2003) 'Scuppering discussion: interaction in theory and practice', in J. Moyles, L. Hargreaves, R. Merry, F. Paterson and V. Esarte-Sarries, *Interactive Teaching in the Primary School*, Maidenhead: Open University Press.

Mills, J. and Mills, R.W. (1995) *Primary School People: Getting to know your colleagues*, Abingdon: Routledge.

Millum, T. (2011) *Improving Literacy with ICT: Ideas and resources for teaching ages 7–12*, London: Continuum.

Moore, A. (2001) *Teaching and Learning: Pedagogy, curriculum, and culture*, Abingdon: Routledge.

Moran, C., Stobbe, J., Baron, W., Miller, J. and Moir, E. (2009) *Keys to the Elementary Classroom*, Thousand Oaks, CA: Corwin Press.

Morgan, N. and Saxton, J. (1991) *Teaching Questioning and Learning*, Abingdon: Routledge.

Morgan, N. and Saxton, J. (1994) *Asking Better Questions*, Markham, Ontario: Pembroke Publishers.

Morreale, S., Backlud, P., Hay, E. and Moore, M. (2011) 'Assessment of oral communication: a major review of the historical development and trends in the movement from 1975 to 2009', *Communication Education*, 60 (2), pp. 255–78.

Morrison, K. (2001) 'Jurgen Habermas', in J.A. Palmer (ed.) *Fifty Modern Thinkers from Piaget to the Present*, Abingdon: RoutledgeFalmer.

Mosley, J. and Grogan, R. (2002) 'Quality circle time for teachers', *Primary Practice*, 32 (Autumn), pp. 4–8.

Mosley, J. and Sonnet, H. (2006) *Helping Children Deal with Bullying*, Cambridge: LDA.

Moyles, J. (2007) *Beginning Teaching, Beginning Learning in Primary Education*, Maidenhead: Open University Press.

Moyles, J., Hargreaves, L., Merry, R., Paterson, F. and Esarte-Sarries, V. (2003) *Interactive Teaching in the Primary School*, Maidenhead: Open University Press.

Murphy, E. and Lewers, R. (2000) *The Hidden Hurt: How to beat bullying in schools*, Thriplow: Wizard Books.

Music, G. (2010) *Nurturing Natures*, Abingdon: Routledge.

Myhill, D. and Jones, S. (2009) 'How talk becomes text: investigating the concept of oral rehearsal', *British Journal of Educational Studies*, 57 (3), pp. 265–84.

Nambiar, S. (2008) *Teaching is a Passion*, on-line at www.razz-ma-tazz.net/2008/04/09/teaching-is-a-passion.

Napoli, M. (2012) *Selling the Perfect Girl: Girls as consumers, girls as commodities*, Abingdon: Routledge.

Neill, S. and Caswell, C. (1993) *Body Language for Competent Teachers*, Abingdon: Routledge.

Nelson-Jones, R. (2007) *Basic Counselling Skills*, London: Sage.

Newell, S. and Jeffery, D. (2002) *Behaviour Management in the Classroom: A transactional analysis approach*, London: David Fulton.

Newton, L.D. (2012) *Creative Thinking and Problem Solving in the Primary Curriculum*, Abingdon: Routledge.

Nias, D.J. (1997) 'Would schools improve if teachers cared less?' *Education 3–13*, 25 (3), pp. 11–22.

Nias, D.J., Southworth, G.W. and Yeomans, R. (1989) *Staff Relationships in the Primary School: A study of school cultures*, London: Cassell.

Nilsen, B.A. (2004) *Week by Week: Documenting the development of young children*, New York: Thomas Delmar Learning.

Nixon, J. (2007) 'Teachers' legal liabilities and responsibilities', in M. Cole (ed.) *Professional Attributes and Practice*, London: David Fulton.

Notbohm, E. (2007) *Ten Things Every Child with Autism Wishes You Knew*, Arlington, TX: Future Horizons.

O'Brien, L. (2009) 'Learning outdoors: the forest school approach', *Education 3–13*, 37 (1), pp. 45–60.

O'Brien, T. and Guiney, D. (2001) *Differentiation in Teaching and Learning*, London: Continuum.

O'Connor, A. (2011) *Understanding Transition in the Early Years*, London: David Fulton.

O'Flynn, S. and Kennedy, H. (2003) *Get Their Attention*, London: David Fulton.

OFSTED (2009) *Drawing Together: Art, craft and design in schools*, London: Crown Copyright.

O'Hara, M. (2004) *Teaching 3–8*, second edn, London: Continuum.

Ollin, R. (2008) 'Silent pedagogy and rethinking classroom practice: structuring teaching through silence rather than talk', *Cambridge Journal of Education*, 38 (2), pp. 265–80.

O'Quinn, E.J. and Garrison, J. (2004) 'Creating loving relations in the classroom', in D. Liston and J. Garrison (eds) *Teaching, Learning and Loving*, Abingdon: RoutledgeFalmer.

Orr, R. (2003) *My Right to Play*, Maidenhead: Open University Press.

Osguthorpe, R.D. (2008) 'On the reasons we want teachers of good disposition and moral character', *Journal of Teacher Education*, 59 (4), pp. 288–99.

Otterton, M. (2004) *Teaching Techniques*, London: Continuum.

Overall, L. and Sangster, M. (2003) *Primary Teacher's Handbook*, London: Continuum.

Packard, N. and Higgins, S. (2007) *The Really Useful ICT Book*, Abingdon: Routledge.

Pagett, L. (2007) 'The joy of learning poetry off by heart', in D. Hayes (ed.) *Joyful Teaching and Learning in the Primary School*, Exeter: Learning Matters.

Paley, V.G. (2000) *The Kindness of Children*, Harvard: Harvard University Press.

Palmer, S. (2011) *How to Teach Talk for Writing: Ages 8–10 (Speaking Frames)*, Abingdon: Routledge.

Papworth, M. (2003) *Every Minute Counts*, London: Continuum.

Parkinson, R. (2010) *Storytelling and Imagination*, London: David Fulton.

Pavey, B. and Harper-Jones, G. (2007) *The Dyslexia-friendly Primary School: A practical guide for teachers*, London: Sage.

Penn, H. (2005) *Understanding Early Childhood*, Maidenhead: Open University Press.

Pepperell, S., Hopkins, C., Gifford, S. and Tallant, P. (2009) *Mathematics in the Primary School*, second edn, London: David Fulton.

Perkins, D.N. (1992) *Smart Schools*, New York: Free Press.

Phtiaka, H. (1997) *Special Kinds for Special Treatment*, Abingdon: Routledge.

Pinnell, G.S. and Fountas, I.C. (1998) *Word Matters: Teaching phonics and spelling in the reading/writing classroom*, New York: Heinemann.

Pollard, A. (2005) *Reflective Teaching*, second edn, London: Continuum.

Pollard, A. (2008) *Reflective Teaching: Evidence-informed professional practice*, London: Continuum.

Pollard, A. and Filer, A. (1996) *The Social World of Children's Learning*, London: Cassell.

Pollard, A. and Tann, S. (1987, 1993, 1997) *The Reflective Practitioner*, London: Continuum.

Pratt, N. and Berry, J. (2007) 'The joy of mathematics', in D. Hayes (ed.) *Joyful Teaching and Learning in the Primary School*, Exeter: Learning Matters.

Prendiville, F. and Toye, N. (2007) *Speaking and Listening Through Drama*, London: Sage.

Pye, J. (1987) *Invisible Children: Who are the Real Losers at School?* Oxford: Oxford University Press.

Qualifications and Curriculum Authority (QCA) (2000) *A Language in Common*, Sudbury: QCA Publications.

Qualifications and Curriculum Authority (QCA) (2008) *The Foundation Stage: Education for children aged 3 to 5*, London: Crown Copyright.

Qualifications and Curriculum Authority (QCA) (2009) *Writing Assessment Guidelines: Levels 1 and 2*, London: Crown Copyright.

Qualifications and Curriculum Authority (QCA)/DfES (2000) *Curriculum Guidance for the Foundation Stage*, Sudbury: QCA Publications.

Quinn, V. (1997) *Critical Thinking in Young Minds*, London: David Fulton.

Ransom, S. (1993) 'From an entitlement to an empowerment curriculum', in M. Barber and D. Graham, *Sense, Nonsense and the National Curriculum*, London: Falmer Press.

Ravet, J. (2007) *Are We Listening?* Stoke-on-Trent: Trentham.

Reid, G. (2005) *Dyslexia and Inclusion: Classroom approaches for assessment, teaching and learning*, London: David Fulton/NASEN.

Reid, G. (2007a) *Effective Learning Strategies for the Classroom*, London: Sage.

Reid, G. (2007b) *100 Ideas for Supporting Pupils with Dyslexia*, London: Continuum.

Renold, E. (2005) *Girls, Boys and Junior Sexualities*, Abingdon: Routledge.

Richards, C. (2006) 'Primary teaching: a personal perspective', in J. Arthur, T. Grainger and D. Wray (eds) *Learning to Teach in the Primary School*, Abingdon: Routledge.

Richards, C. (2009) 'Primary teaching: a personal perspective', in J. Arthur, T. Grainger and D. Wray (eds) *Learning to Teach in the Primary School*, Abingdon: Routledge.

Riddell-Leech, S. (2008) *How to Observe Children*, London: Heinemann.

Rigby, K. (2001) *Stop the Bullying*, London: Jessica Kingsley.

Riley, P. (2010) *Attachment Theory and the Teacher–Student Relationship*, Abingdon: Routledge.

Roache, J.E. and Lewis, R. (2011) 'The carrot, the stick, or the relationship: what are the effective disciplinary strategies?' *European Journal of Teacher Education*, 34 (2), pp. 233–48.

Robinson, K. (2001) *Out of Our Minds: Learning to be creative*, London: John Wiley.

Robson, S. (2006) *Developing Thinking and Understanding in Young Children*, Abingdon: Routledge.

Roffey, S. (2006) *Circle Time for Emotional Literacy*, London: Paul Chapman.

Roffey, S. and O'Reirdan, T. (2003) *Plans for Better Behaviour in the Primary School*, London: David Fulton.

Rogers, B. (1998) *You Know the Fair Rule*, second edn, London: Pitman Publishing.

Rogers, B. (2006) *Classroom Behaviour: A practical guide to effective teaching, behaviour management and colleague support*, London: Paul Chapman.

Rose, J. (for the DCSF) (2009) *Primary Curriculum Review*, London: Crown Copyright.

Rose, R. (2005) *Becoming a Primary Higher Level Teaching Assistant: Meeting the HLTA standards*, Exeter: Learning Matters.

Ross, A. (2001) 'What is the curriculum?' in J. Collins, K. Insley and J. Sole (eds) *Developing Pedagogy: Researching practice*, London: Paul Chapman/Open University.

Rossano, M.J. (2008) 'The moral faculty: does religion promote moral expertise?' *International Journal for the Psychology of Religion*, 18 (3), pp. 169–94.

Ruf, D.L. (2005) *Losing Our Minds: Gifted children left behind*, Scottsdale, AZ: Great Potential Press.

Ryan, W. (2008) *Leadership with a Moral Purpose*, Carmarthen: Crown House.

Salaman, A. and Tutchell, S. (2005) *Planning Educational Visits for the Early Years*, London: Paul Chapman.

Sallis, J. (2007) *Basics for School Governors*, London: Continuum International.

Salo, U. (2002) 'What a teacher! Students write about teachers', BERA Conference, September, Exeter.

Sanders, C.E. (2004) 'What is bullying?' in C.E. Sanders and G.D. Phye (eds), *Bullying: Implications for the classroom*, Amsterdam: Elsevier.

Sarason, S.B. (1999) *Teaching as a Performing Art*, New York: Teachers College Press.

Schmidt, M. (2007) Teaching Courage, Welches, OR: Kids Talk; on-line at www.shininglightreading.com/kidstalknews.

Schön, D. (1983, second edition 1991) *The Reflective Practitioner: How teachers think*, New York: Basic Books.

Sclafani, J.D. (2004) *The Educated Parent: Recent trends in raising children*, Westport, CT: Greenwood Press.

Scott, C. (2008) *Teaching Children English as an Additional Language: A programme for 7–12 year olds*, London: David Fulton.

Scottish Executive (1999) *Communities: Change through learning. Report of a Working Group on the Future of Community Education*, Edinburgh: The Scottish Office.

Sebba, J., Brown, N., Stewart, S., Galton, M. and James, M. (2007) *An Investigation of Personalised Learning Approaches Used by Schools*, DFES Report RR843, Nottingham: DfES Publications.

Sedgwick, F. (1989) *Here Comes the Assembly Man: A year in the life of a primary school*, Lewes: Falmer Press.

Sedgwick, F. (2007) *So You Want to be a School Teacher?* London: Sage.

Sedgwick, F. (2008) *100 Ideas for Developing Thinking in the Primary School*, London: Continuum.

Sedgwick, F. (2012) *Learning Outside the Primary Classroom*, Abingdon: Routledge.

Seldon, A. (2008) 'Teaching happiness', *Ethos*, on-line at www.ethosjournal.com/archive/item/107-teaching-happiness.

Selwyn, N., Potter, J. and Cranmer, S. (2010) *Primary Schools and ICT: Learning from pupil perspectives*, London: Continuum.

Sharman, C., Cross, W. and Vennis, D. (2000) *Observing Children: A practical guide*, London: Cassell.

Sharp, S., Thompson, D. and Arora, T. (2002) *Bullying*, Abingdon: RoutledgeFalmer.

Shreeve, A. (2002) 'Student perceptions of rewards and sanctions', *Pedagogy, Culture and Society*, 10 (2), pp. 239–56.

Silcock, P. and Brundrett, M. (2002) *Achieving Competence, Success and Excellence in Teaching*, Abingdon: RoutledgeFalmer.

Simister, C.J. (2007) *How to Teach Thinking and Learning Skills*, London: Sage.

Simister, J. (2004) 'To think or not to think', *Improving Schools*, 7 (3), pp. 243–54.

Skelton, C. (2001) *Schooling the Boys: Masculinities and primary education*, Maidenhead: Open University Press.

Smart, J. (1995) *Educational Visits*, Leamington Spa: Campion Communications.

Smethern, L. (2007) 'Retention and intention in teaching careers: will the new generation stay?' *Teachers and Teaching*, 13 (5), pp. 465–81.

Smidt, S. (2006) *The Developing Child in the 21st Century*, Abingdon: Routledge.

Smidt, S. and Green, S. (2009) *Planning for the Early Years Foundation Stage*, London: David Fulton.

Smith, A. (2007) 'Fit for play?' Education 3–13, 35 (1), pp. 17–27.

Smith, C. (2006) 'From special needs to inclusive education', in J. Sharp, S. Ward and L. Hankin (eds) *Education Studies: An issues-based approach*, Exeter: Learning Matters.

Smith, J. (2006) 'Every child a singer: techniques for assisting developing singers', *Music Educators Journal*, 93 (2), pp. 28–34.

Smith, J. and Lynch, J. (2005) *The Primary School Year*, Abingdon: RoutledgeFalmer.

Sotto, E. (1994) *When Teaching Becomes Learning*, Abingdon: Routledge.

Spear, M., Gould, K. and Lee, B. (2000) *Who Would Be a Teacher?* Slough: NFER.

Stacey, M. (1991) *Parents and Teachers Together: Partnership in primary and nursery education*, Maidenhead: Open University Press.

Stallard, P. (2002) *Think Good, Feel Good*, London: John Wiley.

Starbuck, D. (2006) *Creative Teaching: Getting it right*, London: Continuum.

Starrett, E.V. (2007) *Teaching Phonics for Balanced Reading*, San Francisco: Corwin Press.

Stern, J. (2003) *Involving Parents*, London: Continuum.

Sternberg, R.J. and Davidson, J.E. (2005) *Conceptions of Giftedness*, Cambridge: Cambridge University Press.

Stierer, B., Devereux, J., Gifford, S., Laycock, E. and Yerbury, J. (1993) *Profiling, Recording and Observing: A resource pack for the early years*, Abingdon: Routledge.

Street, B., Baker, D. and Tomlin, A. (2009) *Navigating Numeracies: Home–school numeracy practices*, New York: Springer.

Street, J. (2004) *Welcome to Friendship*, Bristol: Lucky Duck Publishing.

Suschitzky, W. and Chapman, J. (1998) *Valued Children, Informed Teaching*, Maidenhead: Open University Press.

TDA (2011) *Standards for Qualified Teachers*, London: Crown Copyright.

Thody, A. and Bowden, D. (2004) *Teacher's Guide to Self-Management*, London: Continuum.

Thomas, G. and Vaughan, M. (eds) (2004) *Inclusive Education: Readings and Reflections*, Maidenhead: Open University Press.

Thornberg, R. (2008) 'The lack of professional knowledge in values education', *Teaching and Teacher Education*, 24 (7), pp. 1791–8.

Thornton, L. and Brunton, P. (2009) *Understanding the Reggio Approach*, London: David Fulton.

Tileston, D.W. (2004) *What Every Teacher Should Know about Classroom Management and Discipline*, Thousand Oaks, CA: Corwin Press.

Tirri, K. (1999) 'Teachers' perceptions of moral dilemmas at school', *Journal of Moral Development*, 28 (1), pp. 31–47.

Tizard, B. and Hughes, M. (1984) *Young Children Learning: Talking and thinking at home and at school*, London: Fontana.

Tizard, B., Blatchford, P., Burke, J., Farquhar, C. and Plewis, I. (1988) *Young Children at School in the Inner City*, London: Erlbaum.

Torrance, H. and Pryor, J. (1998) *Investigating Formative Assessment*, Maidenhead: Open University Press.

Trant, J. (2010) *Successful School Trips*, Harlow: Pearson.

Trodd, L. and Goodliff, G. (2007) *Achieving EYPS: Success in your assessment*, Exeter: Learning Matters.

Troman, G. and Raggi, A. (2008) 'Primary teacher commitment and the attractions of teaching', *Pedagogy, Culture and Society*, 16 (1), pp. 85–99.

Turner-Bisset, R. (2003) 'On the carpet: changing primary teacher contexts', *Education 3–13*, 31 (3), pp. 4–10.

Tyrrell, J. (2001) *The Power of Fantasy in Learning*, Abingdon: Routledge.

Varma, V.P. (ed.) (1993) *Coping with Unhappy Children*, London: Cassell.

Varnava, G. (2002) *How to Stop Bullying: Towards a non-violent school*, London: David Fulton.

Vincent, C. (2000) *Including Parents? Education, citizenship and parental agency*, Maidenhead: Open University Press.

Vincett, K., Cremin, H. and Thomas, G. (2005) *Teachers and Assistants Working Together*, Maidenhead: Open University Press.

Waite, S. (2011) 'Teaching and learning outside the classroom', *Education 3–13*, 39 (1), pp. 65–82.

Waite, S. and Rea, T. (2007) 'Enjoying teaching and learning outside the classroom', in D. Hayes (ed.) *Joyful Teaching and Learning in the Primary School*, Exeter: Learning Matters.

Wallace, W. (2005) *Oranges and Lemons: Life in an inner-city primary school*, Abingdon: Routledge.

Walsh, J.A. and Sattes, B.D. (2005) *Quality Questioning: Research-based practice to engage every learner*, Charlestown, WV: Edvantia.

Waters, M. (1996) *Managing Your Primary Classroom*, London: Collins.

Watkins, C. (2005) *Classrooms as Learning Communities*, Abingdon: Routledge.

Watkins, C., Carnell, E. and Lodge, C. (2007) *Effective Learning in Classrooms*, London: Sage.

Watkinson, A. (2003a) *The Essential Guide for Competent Teaching Assistants*, London: David Fulton.

Watkinson, A. (2003b) *The Essential Guide for Experienced Teaching Assistants*, London: David Fulton.

Watts, R. (2010) 'Responding to children's drawings', *Education 3–13*, 38 (2), pp. 137–53.

Weatherhead, Y. (2007) *Creative Circle Time for Early Years*, London: Sage.

Webb, R. and Vulliamy, G. (1997) *A Comparative Analysis of Curriculum Change in Primary Schools in England and Finland: Final report*, York: University of York.

Weil, Z. (2003) *Above All, Be Kind: Raising a humane child in challenging times*, Gariola Island, British Columbia: New Society Publishers.

Welch, S. and Jones, P. (2010) *Rethinking Children's Rights: Attitudes in contemporary society*, London: Continuum.

Wenham, M. (1995) 'Developing thinking and skills in the arts', in J. Moyles (ed.) *Beginning Teaching, Beginning Learning in Primary Education*, Maidenhead: Open University Press.

Westwood, P. (2004) *Learning and Learning Difficulties*, London: David Fulton.

Whalley, M. (2007) *Involving Parents in Their Children's Learning*, London: Sage.

White, J.P. (2011) *Exploring Well-being in Schools*, Abingdon: Routledge.

Willan, J., Parker-Rees, R. and Savage, J. (eds) (2007) *Early Childhood Studies*, second edn, Exeter: Learning Matters.

Williams, J. and Ryan, J. (2000) 'National testing and the improvement of classroom teaching: can they co-exist?' *British Educational Research Journal*, 26 (1), pp. 49–73.

Williams, L.M. (2008 [1916]) *How to Teach Phonics*, on-line at www.gutenberg.org/ebooks/18119.bibrec.html.

Williams, M. (2009) *Support Teaching and Learning: Developing the role of the teaching assistant*, Bristol: Classroom Resources.

Williams, P. (2008) *Review of Mathematics Teaching in Early Years Settings and Primary Schools*: Final report, London: DCSF.

Willick, S. (2006) *Emotional Literacy at the Heart of the School Ethos*, London: Paul Chapman.

Wilson, D.F. (2004) *Supporting Teachers, Supporting Pupils: The emotions of teaching and learning*, London: Routledge.

Wilson, J. and Murdoch, K. (2009) *Learning for Themselves*, London: David Fulton.

Wing, L. (2003) *The Autistic Spectrum: A guide for parents and professionals*, London: Robinson Publishing.

Wise, S. (2000) *Listen to Me! The voices of pupils with emotional and behavioural difficulties*, Bristol: Lucky Duck Publishing.

Wolfendale, S. and Bastiani, J. (eds) (2000) *The Contribution of Parents to School Effectiveness*, London: David Fulton.

Woods, G. (n.d.) '5 relational tools to make you a better teacher', *Ministry-to-Children.com*, on-line at http://ministry-to-children.com/relational-tools-better-teacher/.

Woods, P. (1997) *Restructuring Schools, Reconstructing Teachers: Responding to change in the primary school*, Maidenhead: Open University Press.

Woods, P. and Carlyle, D. (2002) 'Teacher identities under stress: the emotions of separation and renewal', *International Studies in Sociology of Education*, 12 (2), pp. 169–89.

Wragg, E.C. (1997) *Assessment and Learning*, Abingdon: Routledge.

Wragg, E.C. and Brown, G. (1993) *Explaining*, Abingdon: Routledge.

Wray, D. (2006) 'Looking at learning', in J. Arthur, T. Grainger and D. Wray (eds) *Learning to Teach in the Primary School*, Abingdon: Routledge.

Wright, D. (2006) *Classroom Karma*, London: David Fulton.

Wyse, D. (2001) 'Promising yourself to do better? Target setting and literacy', *Education 3–13*, 29 (2), pp. 13–18.

Wyse, D., Jones, R. and Bradford, H. (2007) *Teaching English, Language and Literacy*, Abingdon: Routledge.

Yelland, N. (ed.) (1998) *Gender in Early Childhood*, Abingdon: Routledge.

York Consulting (for the DfES) (2007) *The Prevalence of Home Education in England: A feasibility study*, Research Report 827, Annesley: DfES Publications.

Young, K. (2008) 'Don't just look, listen: uncovering children's cognitive strategies during spelling-related activities', *Education 3–13*, 36 (2), pp. 127–38.

Zucker, J. and Parker, D. (1999) *A Class Act*, London: Sapphire Publishers.

Index

Page numbers in **bold** denote figures.